THE BOOK OF
MAGICAL PSALMS

Part 1

THE BOOK
OF
MAGICAL PSALMS

Part 1

Shadow Tree Series
Volume 5

Jacobus G. Swart

THE SANGREAL SODALITY PRESS
Johannesburg, Gauteng, South Africa

Second edition
First printing

Published by The Sangreal Sodality Press
74 Twelfth Street
Parkmore 2196
Gauteng
South Africa
Email: jacobsang@gmail.com

ISBN 978-0-620-93176-2

Dedicated to Dirk Cloete

"Unbreakable are links of love which faith and friendship forge among all souls discerning one another by the Light within them. Welcome indeed are they that enter with entitlement our closest circles of companionship."

—William G. Gray (*The Sangreal Sacrament*)

Shadow Tree Series

Contents

Illustrations

Hebrew Transliteration

There are transliterations of Hebrew words and phrases throughout this work. In this regard I have employed the following method. The Hebrew vowels are pronounced:

"a" — like "a" in "father";

"e" — like the "e" in "let" or the way the English pronounce the word "Air" without enunciating the "r";

"i" — like the "ee" in "seek";

"o" — like the "o" in "not" or the longer "au" in "naught"; or again like the sound of the word "Awe";

"u" — like the "oo" in "mood";

"ai" — like the letter "y" in "my" or "igh" in "high" or like the sound of the word "eye"; and

"ei" — like the "ay" in "hay."

The remaining consonants are as written, except for:

"ch" which is pronounced like the guttural "ch" in the Scottish "Loch" or the equivalent in the German "Ich," and "tz" which sounds like the "tz" in "Ritz" or like the "ts" in "hearts."

In most cases an apostrophe (') indicates a glottal stop which sounds like the "i" in "bit" or the concluding "er" in "father," otherwise it is a small break to separate sections of a word or create a double syllable. For example, I often hear people speak of Daat (Knowledge), sounding one long "ah" between the "D" and the concluding "T." The correct pronunciation is however Da'at, the apostrophe indicating that the term comprises actually two syllables, "dah" and "aht." In this word a quick glottal stop separates the one syllable from the other. As a vowel it is the same sound made when one struggles to find the right word, and say something like "er.....er......er......"

One further rule is that the accent in Hebrew is, more often than not, placed on the last syllable of the word. Of course there are numerous instances which disprove this rule, but it applies almost throughout Hebrew incantations, e.g. those found in Merkavistic literature, etc.

"In the year 5340 (1580), on the 20ᵗʰ Adar, at four hours after midnight the three of us left for the Moldau River on the outskirts of Prague... ... .

Introduction

The material shared in this volume spans the broad range of "Jewish magic" practised over the past millennium. In this regard, I have accessed once again the amazing reservoir of primary and secondary works on Jewish magical traditions, much of which I have included in the previous volumes of my "Shadow Tree Series" of works on "Practical Kabbalah." These publications have elicited both praise and scorn for sharing what has been deemed "forbidden." I have received praise from those who acknowledge *"Kabbalah Ma'asit"* ("Practical Kabbalah") to be part of our מסורה (*Mesorah*), i.e. Jewish religious tradition and its transmission, and have been met with total rejection, and even belligerence, from those who are doing their damndest to see Judaism rid of what they consider to be the "weeds of superstition."

Unfortunately this dislike of anything "magical" in Judaism, is exacerbated today by a genre of "occult writings" penned by individuals whose predilection it is to pirate esoteric works, literally lifting large segments verbatim from tomes on "Jewish Magic," and reissuing these in a jumble of sensationalist publications. To these one might add the creators of fake Hebrew amulets, whose aim is to bedazzle the gullible with impressive looking squiggly symbols incorporated in *Kameot* (amulets) sold at exorbitant prices. It appears unimportant to these purveyors of expensive "occult trinkets," that at times their fanciful constructs include symbols of "war" sold as items meant to engender "love"! It is no wonder that such actions comprise a major contribution to "Practical Kabbalah" being relegated a "junk" status.

That being said, "Theoretical Kabbalah" and mainstream Judaism have also been "uneasy bedfellows" at times. In this regard, I noted elsewhere that "sometimes they would be more or

i

less comfortable in their relationship and need of each other, but at other times they would burst into open conflict."[1] Furthermore, whilst several traditional Kabbalists were also practitioners of Jewish Magic, Lurianic Kabbalah has in the main a rather dim view of "Practical Kabbalah." In this regard, Rabbi Chaim Vital, the successor of the Holy Ari, noted that "it is forbidden to make use of it [Practical Kabbalah], since evil necessarily attaches itself to the good. One may actually intend to cleanse his soul, but as a result of the evil, he actually defiles it. Even if one does gain some perception, it is truth intermingled with falsehood. This is especially true today, since the ashes of the Red Heifer no longer exist. [Since one cannot purify himself,] the uncleanliness of the Husks [*Klipot*] attaches itself to the individual who attempts to gain enlightenment through Practical Kabbalah."[2]

It should be noted that the saga of the ashes of the "Red Heifer" originally pertained to being cleansed from the impurities of having touched the body of the deceased, i.e. a corpse. As I am sure readers know well enough, when the second Temple in Jerusalem was destroyed, and sacrifices were no longer made in the sacred sanctuary, the ashes of the red heifer disappeared from Jewish religious life, and it has remained so to this day. However, some rabbinical commentary and mystical speculation revolved around the purported power of the ashes of the red heifer, including references to the Hebrew word for "cow" (פָּרָה— "*parah*") being said to indicate five special powers of *Gevurah* (might). Whatever meaning individuals may derive from these writings on the "Red Heifer," it should be noted that the esoteric Tradition termed "Kabbalah" did not exist in the days of the red heifer sacrifices.

It is certainly true that there were definitely Jewish magical practices doing the rounds in those times, but none of them, either singly or collectively, were ever referenced in terms of impurities which required cleansing with the ashes of the red heifer. In fact, it was not until the sixteenth century, after the Ari discovered that Rabbi Chaim Vital, his foremost disciple, had a predilection for "Jewish Magic," that the saga surfaced about one not being allowed to work the techniques of "Practical Kabbalah" because the ashes of the red heifer were no longer available to remove the impurities resulting from those practices. Whilst it is clear that in this regard Chaim Vital took the words of his master quite seriously, the practise of "Jewish Magic" flourished to this day in the hands of many acclaimed Rabbis, amongst others the astute Rabbi Chayim Josef David Azulai, Rabbi Moses Zacutto, Rabbi Avraham Chamui, Rabbi Binjamin Beinish; Rabbi Elijah Ba'al Shem of Chelm, Rabbi Yitzchak Halpern, Rabbi Shalom Sharabi, the saintly Rabbi Yitzchak Kaduri, and many more. In fact, in our own day the illuminating and undaunting efforts of individuals like Rabbi Ariel bar Tzadok, are dispelling much of the "undeserved darkness" surrounding this much maligned Tradition.

Notwithstanding the fact that these individuals never employed the ashes of the "Red Heifer" to rid themselves of some or other purported "demonic force" which followed their regular sojourns into the domain of "Jewish Magic," Rabbi Chaim Vital's ominous "Practical Kabbalah/Red Heifer" proclamation is today popularly employed by detractors of "Jewish Magic." Otherwise, if this does not succeed in scaring people off "Practical Kabbalah," the next action is to try to draw a distinction between "Practical Kabbalah" and "Jewish Magic," whilst such a distinction does not exist. On the other hand, some religionists openly object to "Practical Kabbalah" without any "Red Heifer" references, stating that Hebrew amulets, adjurations, and the practical applications of Divine Names for a variety of life changing purposes, are interfering with the "hand of the Almighty."

Again there are other Jewish religionists, myself being a case in point, who maintain that the Divine One provided us with a great variety of resources of both the physical and the spiritual kind, in order for us to survive physically, mentally, emotionally, and spiritually on this planet. So-called "magical actions" rank amongst these resources, whether they be delineated "Practical Kabbalah" or "Jewish Magic." As one might expect, there are those who say the *Segulot* (unique spiritual actions [treasures]), *R'fu'ot* (healing procedures), *Kame'ot* (Amulets), *Lachashim* (Incantations), *Hashba'ot* (Adjurations), etc., actually do not work! If that be the case, why fuss so much about those who do employ those techniques in order to change their lives for the better? Why not laugh at this, and dismiss those who use such practices as being foolish?

I gladly admit that I am one of those "fools" who have used, and am still using, a great variety of procedures shared in the extensive literature of "Practical Kabbalah." In this regard, the Hebrew Bible is considered the most primary tool for "magical living," since "the entire Torah is composed of the names of God, and in consequence it has the property of saving and protecting man,"[3] and here the biblical "*Book of Psalms*" is reckoned amongst the greatest and most popular tomes of "Practical Kabbalah" ("Jewish Magic").

✳✳✳

Once again I recommend to those who are studying and practicing the material shared in this tome, to consider commencing any study of Kabbalistic material by sitting in a restful, peaceful manner, and then, with eyes shut for a minute or so, to meditate on these words:

> "Open my eyes so that I may perceive the wonders of Your teaching."

Whisper the phrase repeatedly and allow yourself to "feel" the meaning of the words you are uttering within the depths of your Self. It is again important not to attempt any mental deliberation on the meaning of the actual words, but to simply repeat them a number of times. As stated previously,[6] it is a good idea to read a section in its entirety, without trying to perceive any specific meaning, then to pause for a few seconds, and afterwards attempt to understand within yourself the general meaning of what was being said. In this way you begin to fulfil an important teaching of *Kabbalah*, which tells you to unite two "worlds"—the inner and the outer within your own Being. By allowing yourself to "feel" the meaning of what you are reading, you learn to surrender to the words. You open yourself, again fulfilling one of the requirements of Kabbalistic study, which is to surrender the "me," the ego, and to remove arrogance and bias. You simply attempt to sense with your being what is being portrayed in the section you are perusing. This act is a serious step on the path of perfecting one's personality, because it stops the expansion of the ego, and increases chances of obtaining "True Knowledge."

***

This study would not be complete without acknowledging my friends, my Companions in the Sangreal Sodality, as well as my acquaintances who inspire me, participate in the expansion of my consciousness, enrich my life in so many ways, and who are fetching the very best out of me. In this regard, I wish to make special reference to Dirk Cloete to whom I have dedicated this volume. He is not only one of the greatest and most caring friends one could share ones life with, but he is a veritable cornucopia of magical and mystical insight—a true visionary with formidable research skills. This volume could not have been written without his enormous input and incredible support.

I wish to offer my Gloria, the love of my life, my most profound gratitude for her unwavering love, for her total support in all my endeavours, and for being the joy and laughter in my heart. I further wish to acknowledge my late mentor, William G. Gray, who led me along the "Inner Ways of Truth and Goodness," and taught me how to leave good impressions for fresh toeholds on the sides of the "magic mountain." I once again offer my most heartfelt appreciation to my South African friends and Companions: in Johannesburg Norma Cosani, Gidon Fainman, Geraldine Talbot, Francois le Roux, Gerhardus Muller, Ryan Kay, Simon O'Regan; in Pretoria Carlien Steyn, Helene Vogel and Gerrit Viljoen; in Durban Marq and Penny Smith; and Dirk Cloete and Sean Smith in the fairest of Capes.

I offer my most heartfelt thanks to my dear friend Jonti Mayer for his enormous support in reading and checking the transliterations of the numerous prayers and incantations shared in this tome.

I also wish to acknowledge my Sangreal Sodality Companions and friends residing beyond the borders of South Africa: Marcus Claridge in Scotland, Elizabeth Bennet in England; Hamish Gilbert in Poland, Bence Bodnar, Lukács Gábor, and Dániel Szeretõ in Hungary, Roberto Siqueira Rodrigues in Brazil, Taron Plaza in Japan, Yuriy Fyedin in China; and all intimates "whose identities are known unto Omniscience alone."

In conclusion I wish to pay tribute to John Jones, our dear Companion in the Sangreal Sodality, who departed this domain of mortal incarnation. May his memory be a blessing!!!

I now leave this tome in your care, and pray it will be of most meaningful service to you.

Happy Reading!

Jacobus Swart
Johannesburg
April 2021

. ...By its banks we looked for and found an area with loam and clay, from which we made the form of a man, three cubits long, lying on his back, and then shaped a face, arms, and legs. Then all three of us stood at the golem's feet, staring at his face... ... .

Chapter 1
Mizrach — East
Magic & the Book of Psalms

שמר פיו ולשונו שמר מצרות נפשו

(*shomeir piv ul'shono shomeir mitzarot naf'sho*—
"Whoso keepeth his mouth and his tongue
keepeth his soul from troubles")

—*Proverbs 21:23*

מות וחיים ביד לשון ואהביה יאכל פריה

(*mavet v'chayim b'yad lashon v'ohaveha yochal pir'yah*—
"Death and life are in the power of the tongue;
and they that indulge it shall eat the fruit thereof")

—*Proverbs 18:21*

A. Introduction

Many practitioners of the "magical arts" have emphasised the importance of "speech" as a unique power which directly impacts your personal life in a number of ways, i.e. always in accordance with the intention behind the words being uttered. In this regard, there are exhortations pertaining to you having to be careful not to employ words in your daily language, which would bring, as it were, a curse upon yourself or on your loved ones, e.g. swear upon the life of your child, or of your mother, etc., since such statements could engender disastrous consequences.

Our Sages stressed that "words have great power,"[1] and that you "should not regard the curse of an ordinary person as light in your eyes." [*TB Megillah 15a*] In this regard, we are urged to be fully cognizant at all times of the words we speak, since the very utterance of unpleasant possibilities can engender them in reality. In fact, the *Talmud* maintains that the act of verbalising bad predictions regarding any unfortunate situation which might befall

1

anyone or anything, could invite the "predicted" ominous outcome.[2] Furthermore, we are warned that curses are likely to boomerang and injure the one who uttered the curse. [*Sanhedrin 48b-49a*][3] Thus we are enjoined אל תפתח פה לשטן (*al tif'tach pei l'satan*—"do not give satan an opening"), i.e. do not tempt fate [*TB Ketubot 8b and TB Berachot 19a*], which is the likely reason why the proviso חס ושלום (*chas v'shalom*) or חלילה וחס (*chalilah v'chas*), meaning "Heaven forbid," is added when saying something unpleasant.[4] Regarding both "vows and curses," we are informed that "a vow, let us say, sworn by the life of a child, is a serious matter, for at the least sign of backsliding the spirits are delighted to exact the penalty. And a curse is even more fraught with danger; it is a direct invitation, nay, a command to the spirits to do their worst."[5] Hence Jewish tradition maintains that 'the curse of a sage, even when undeserved, comes to pass," and that, as mentioned, "even the curse of an ordinary person should not be treated lightly."[6] We are thus counselled to "not live among people given to cursing," and to know that "the power of the curse" extends "beyond the grave."[7] Yet, whilst we are admonished not to pronounce a curse over anyone, or utter words which might engender misfortune, we are likewise encouraged to offer a complimentary blessing to anyone who pronounced a blessing over us, so that the one who uttered the benediction may equally benefit therefrom [*BT Megilah 27b*].[8]

We are also informed that the exhortation to "never open one's mouth to Satan," is based on the understanding that "evil talk is nothing less than an invitation to the demons." Joshua Trachtenberg noted that this is "a counsel of perfection, which men could do little more than aspire to,"[9] and that since "our speech is richly peppered with words whose connotation is unpleasant; how open our mouths at all without letting slip out such invitations to Satan?" To this query he noted that in Jewish Tradition "the danger is ever-present, but human ingenuity has devised several means of getting around it."[10] In this regard, Trachtenberg shared the example of "the euphemism," e.g. one would say "'my enemies' instead of 'myself,' and people are not addressed directly, but in the third person, when some unpleasant eventuality is mentioned. To lead the demons astray, the true nature of a disease is hidden, as when the ailment '*mal malant*' is known as '*bon malant*'."[11] He also referenced the custom of withholding the announcement of a serious illness for three days "lest the spirits make a premature end of the invalid when they hear people talking about his infirmity," thus "when a person is sick one must not gossip about his sins."[12] In this regard, he referenced the notion that "when women gossip about an invalid in the presence of children, the ailment is promptly visited upon the young ones."[13] Above all, he reminded us that "the one subject of conversation that is most ardently to be shunned, naturally, is death."[14] Of course, as we know well enough, just as "many a true word is spoken in jest," so is many a malevolent word uttered in anger.

Be that as it may, in magical traditions of every kind, all prayers, adjurations, incantations, spells, etc., rest on a desire for "benevolence" (good fortune) or "malevolence" (misfortune), these being the qualities which motivate the behaviour of practitioners of the "magic" everywhere, who are always acting in accordance with a primary intention to either bestow well-being or bring down damnation upon their fellow humankind. Sometimes they might utter prayers and adjurations spontaneously, e.g. in moments of great desperation, whilst at other times a magical procedure necessitates specially prepared prayers or adjurations accompanied by selected magical objects which are believed to enhance the magical action in a sympathetic manner. Of course, as a friend reminded me recently, one has to be careful with "positive statements" as well, since it is well known that even "positive statements can attract their opposite." It brought to mind an incident in which I witnessed an elderly lady exclaiming "what an ugly baby" over and over, and making spitting sounds whilst gushing over a most beautiful infant. I believe her reactions were to avert the Evil Eye, and to forestall a baneful response from the "invisible kingdom of spirits."

Be that as it may, it is worth noting that at times the doctrines and practices of one magical tradition are incorporated into another, and in this regard the magical use of the biblical Psalms offer a prime example. Considering the fact that countless individuals and groups all over the world are chanting the "Psalms of David" every hour of every day, the *Book of Psalms* is certainly the most popular and most "practically applied" text in the Hebrew Bible. One might rightly expect that this popularity would pertain specifically to Jewish and Christian religionists, but it includes some who would not give a second glance at Jewish Sacred Scriptures, and many of whom vociferously rail against what they term the "Abrahamic Religions," this being a popular pastime amongst witches; assorted pagans; ritual magicians, many of whom claiming to be "non-religious"; and practit.oners of hoodoo, voodoo, and other assorteds.[15]

One may well wonder what it is that makes the Psalms so popular. We are told that the "book of Psalms covers a glorious range of traditional Jewish religious thought, from highly emotional turns of the individual to God, to apotropaic magical invocations intended to defend the reciter from evil powers."[16] Yet, to my mind, it is not only the points raised in this appraisal which underpin the popularity of the Psalms, but rather the fact that they conjoin the most sacred with the most mundane. They address the loftiest "realms of spirit," the lowliest aspects of human existence, and everything in between. The biblical Psalms are not only "highly regarded for their potency, as well as for their beauty and religious fervor,"[17] but also because they allow me to be an ordinary human being whose cries and complaints can be expressed to a "Superhuman Intelligence," without having to feel guilty about voicing my most fundamental "human-ess," as well as to raise my frustrations with the vicissitudes of daily existence on this planet. In fact, they offer ready-made prayers, supplications, and incantations for that matter, for all who find it difficult to express what is in their hearts and in their minds. What is more, the Psalms are considered to be divinely inspired, i.e. sacred, and thus comprise a direct link between a "human mouth" and a "Divine Ear"!

The biblical Psalms offer healing not only for the sick, but for those who are broken hearted; support in dealing with personal battles, both physically and spiritually; strength in moments of great vulnerability; and inspiration to reach ever higher into those realms which are beyond the frailty of our flesh. In the Psalms we find "liberation" from all our fears and from all manner of distress, and that is why the "*Book of Psalms*" is so popular with Jews and gentiles alike, with religionists and with those who do not care for anything religious, or are even "spiritual" for that matter. In this regard, we are told that during the "*Yom Kippur* War" in Israel, a

Rabbi serving as a soldier in the infantry tanks, was reciting the Psalms from his Hebrew Bible "for comfort in this terrifying situation." It is said "his words were picked up on the intercom and the other soldiers asked him what he was reading. When he said it was the Psalms, these 'secular' Israelis said: 'Don't keep them to yourself!' and he carried on reading them out loud."[18] We are informed that the "belief in the efficacy of Psalms in times of distress is very deeply embedded in Jewish thought,"[19] to the extent that it lead to a Yiddish expression "Don't wait for a miracle, *zog tillim,* recite Psalms!"[20]

As is to be expected, Jews traditionally recite the Psalms in Hebrew. However there are Jewish religionists, and indeed many others for that matter, who do not comprehend the underlying reasons behind this practice, who do not acknowledge the necessity for this, and who insist that "it works equally well" in any language. Yet traditional practitioners of Jewish Magic ("Practical Kabbalah"), who do recognise and acknowledge the primary "principles" and "powers" underlying the Hebrew alphabet, will continue to use this acknowledged "sacred tongue." They will also continue to encourage all parties interested in the successful practice of this Tradition to do the same. For them to discard those "principles" and "powers," would be to reject one of the most important teachings to be found in both theoretical and practical Kabbalah, i.e. the primordial creative power of the Hebrew alphabet and language.[21]

As mentioned elsewhere, Kabbalistic tradition teaches that "the whole of creation was manifested through a divine language."[22] In this regard, I noted that "the view that Hebrew was the primordial language of creation found expression in texts like the *Sefer Yetzirah*, the *Sefer ha-Bahir*, and the *Sefer ha-Zohar*,"[23] and was expanded upon in the writings of later Kabbalists, who not only considered creation "to be the result of various combinations [permutations] of the glyphs of the Hebrew alphabet, but that all manifestation is actually clothed, as it were, with these letter combinations."[24] This teaching was not understood in a metaphorical or symbolical manner, but quite literally, e.g. the Hebrew glyphs are actually visible as "lights" inside the physical anatomy of every person, and it is said that the great Isaac Luria, "could 'read' a person in accordance with the sacred glyphs 'made flesh' in the being and body of that individual."[25] In this regard, I previously referenced Chaim Vital, the closest disciple of the Holy Ari, who noted that the Hebrew glyphs "are hidden beneath the skin of a wicked person, but in the case of a person who is purifying the different aspects of his or her being, the divine forces and their expression in the power forms of the Hebrew glyphs are openly revealed on the skin, where 'the skilled eye' can observe them."[26] I also noted that he maintained "the letters of the soul are best displayed on the forehead, because the entire Hebrew alphabet corresponds to *Binah*, the sphere of 'understanding' on the Tree of Life, of which the forehead is a symbol." Chaim Vital, in is own words, said "know that in each and every organ of a person's body, there are letters engraved, informing us about that individual's actions. But the primary place is the forehead....."[27]

Keeping in mind the claim that the Hebrew glyphs "are symbols of divine power, the combination of which lead to the creation of the material world,"[28] i.e. that the Hebrew alphabet comprises "primal forces which combined primordially to manifest all 'forms',"[29] it should come as no surprise why traditional Kabbalists insist that when the Hebrew letters are enunciated "with a suitably associated godly stance or intention, the 'spiritual forces' inherent in those letters are invoked and manifested."[30] Hence I noted that "the Hebrew letters are understood to be living 'Intelligences' with bodies and souls. The written glyph and its verbal pronunciation, comprise the physical part of its manifestation, i.e. the body, whereas in its essence the sign belongs to the subtle realm of 'Angelic Messengers'."[31] Furthermore, since every Hebrew glyph is "governed" by a "Spirit Messenger," i.e. a *Maggid*, "the letters forming words, and the words shaping the sentences of invocations and prayers, combined with the intentions of the utterer of these words, powerfully invoke the 'Spirit Intelligences' associated with the letters."[32]

It is worth noting that Kabbalists traditionally employ three methods to facilitate an alignment with the "Spirit Intelligences" in the Hebrew glyphs, i.e. *mivta*—vocalising the letters, Divine Names, prayers, incantations, etc.; *michtav*—writing them, i.e. writing the letters, Divine and Angelic Names, prayers, Psalms, adjurations, Hebrew amulets, etc.; and *mashav*—contemplating the forms of the Hebrew glyphs.[33] It is for this reason that I encourage readers to recite the Psalms, Hebrew prayers, and incantations in Hebrew, whilst at the same time recognising the right of readers to decide whether they wish to align with the doctrines of traditional Kabbalah or not. Besides, I made it very easy for anyone who cannot read or speak Hebrew, by including a transliteration as well as a translation of every Hebrew text (or Aramaic where applicable) included in this tome. There is also a transliteration guide at the very beginning of this book to aid proper pronunciation.

Be that as it may, it should be noted that the concept of the "Divine Name" is central and of primary importance in "Practical Kabbalah" (Jewish Magic). As mentioned elsewhere, "for Kabbalists the strongest source of Divine Energy is the 'Divine Name',"[34] and "the Names of God provide the Kabbalist with vast powers." No wonder this "stirred a lot of uneasiness and disapproval amongst the orthodoxy."[35] That being said, it should be clearly understood that the Hebrew Divine Names reference "Divine Aspects," and does not in any way relate to the, as it were, "Essence" of the Divine One, which I noted "is altogether beyond any naming."[36] Even with this basic understanding, "Kabbalists were in the main very careful when it came to the utterance of Sacred Names, since it became clear to them that indiscriminate handling would inevitably impact most malevolently on the practitioner."[37] It should be kept in mind that some Divine Names may not be enunciated aloud, "but could be subtly 'sounded' in the heart as a meditation, or strongly reflected mentally and emotionally during long, slow exhalations, because it is understood that 'the Name of God creates and destroys worlds'."[38]

In Jewish Magic the Psalms are often employed in conjunction with Divine Names, some of which are well-known like the Ineffable Name (יהוה—*YHVH*); שדי (*Shadai*); אדני (*Adonai*); etc., whilst a major amount are carefully constructed in highly specialised ways from the capitals or concluding letters of the words comprising selected verses, or formulated from letters transposed by means of unique ciphers, i.e. the Kabbalistic method of תמורה (*Temurah*) in which the Hebrew glyphs can be interchanged in accordance with special rules.[39] In this regard, some of the following varieties feature in the procedures shared in this tome:

וזל	בת	גש	וו	הק	וצ	זפ	חע	טס	ינ	כמ
אב	גת	דש	הר	וק	זצ	חפ	טע	יס	כנ	לם
אג	דת	הש	ור	זק	חצ	טפ	יע	כס	לנ	במ
אד	בג	הוג	וש	זר	חק	מצ	יפ	כע	לס	מן
אה	בד	ות	זש	חר	טק	יצ	כפ	לע	מס	גנ
או	בה	גד	זת	חש	טר	יק	לפ	כצ	מע	נס
אז	בו	גה	חת	טש	יר	כק	לצ	מפ	נע	דס
אח	בז	גו	דה	טת	יש	כר	לק	מצ	נפ	סע
אט	בח	גז	דו	ית	כש	לר	מק	נצ	ספ	הע
אי	בט	גח	דז	הו	כת	לש	מר	נק	סצ	עפ
אכ	בי	גט	דח	הז	לת	מש	נר	סק	עצ	ופ
אל	בכ	גי	דט	הח	וז	מת	נש	סר	עק	פצ
אמ	בל	גכ	די	הט	וח	נת	סש	ער	פק	זצ
אנ	במ	גל	דכ	הי	וט	זח	סת	עש	פר	צק
אס	בנ	גמ	דל	הכ	וי	זט	עת	פש	צר	חק
אע	בס	גנ	דמ	הל	וכ	זי	פת	חט	צש	קר
אפ	בע	גס	דנ	המ	ול	זכ	חי	צת	קש	טר
אצ	בפ	גע	דס	הנ	ומ	זל	טי	חכ	קת	רש
אק	בצ	גפ	דע	הס	ון	זמ	חל	טב	רת	יש
אר	בק	גצ	דפ	הע	וס	זנ	חמ	טל	יכ	שת
אש	בר	גק	דצ	הפ	וע	זס	חנ	טמ	יל	כת
את	בש	גר	דק	הצ	ופ	זע	חס	טנ	ים	כל

To use these ciphers you simply exchange the right letter with the adjacent one on the left in each row, or vice versa, and the most popular amongst these is undoubtedly the one titled א״ת ב״ש (*Atbash*), i.e. the cipher at the very bottom of the table. In this instance *Alef* (א), the first letter of the Hebrew alphabet, is exchanged with *Tav* (ת), the last letter, and likewise the letter *Bet*, the second letter, is interchanged with *Shin* (ש), the second last letter, etc. I previously shared an example of the use of this cipher referencing the word *Sheshach* (ששך) in *Jeremiah 25:26*, which nobody seems to be able to give any meaning to, until the *Atbash* cipher is applied, and then it reveals this word to be the same as *Bavel* (בבל —"Babel").[40] Another cipher which is referenced in the magical applications of the Psalms, is the equally well-known א״ל ב״ם (*Albam*) cipher, which is not included in the table. In this instance the glyphs are interchanged in the following order:[41]

כת	יש	טר	חק	זצ	ופ	הע	דס	גנ	במ	אל

Such ciphers are often employed in magical recipes and in the construction of Hebrew amulets.[42] Kabbalists resorted to these ciphers to arrive at a number of remarkable Divine Names, including variations of the Ineffable Name, like מצפץ (*Matz'patz*), constructed by means of the *Atbash* (א״ת ב״ש) cipher, or שעפס formulated with the *Albam* (א״ל ב״ם) code.[43] A further cipher system which features in the magical use of Psalms, is the one termed א״יק בכ״ר (*Ayak Bachar* or *Aik Bekar*). It is represented as a square comprising nine boxes, each of which comprises three letters whose *gematria* can be reduced to the same single digit, e.g. א [1] – י [10] – ק [100] = 1; ב [2] – כ [20] – ר [200] = 2; etc, as shown below:[44]

גלש	בכר	איק
וסם	הנך	דמת
טצץ	חפף	זען

The title of this system, like those of others in this category, was derived directly from the listed sets of Hebrew letters. As you probably noticed, in order to work this specific cipher, one has to include also the five so-called "final letters," i.e. ךְ [500], ם [600], ן [700], ף [800] and ץ [900]. A further, lesser known system titled ע״טב ס״חא (*Achas Betah*) equally features in the formulation of certain Divine Names in the magical use of the biblical Psalms. In this instance the Hebrew glyphs are respectively placed in their exact order in seven boxes, i.e. *Alef* in the first, *Bet* in the second, etc., up to *Zayin* in the seventh. Then the procedure is repeated with the rest of the Hebrew alphabet, continuing with *Chet* in the first box, *Tet* in the second, etc. The final result comprises seven boxes with three letters each, the last remaining letter being placed at the very end on its own, as indicated below:[45]

ת	זנש	ומר	הלק	דכצ	גיפ	בטע	אחס

In summary, I wish to to remind readers that the practitioners of this Tradition accept the entire Hebrew Bible as an enormous Divine Name. Every word within it is believed to be a "Word of Power," the utterance of which invokes extremely potent forces.[46] Those using incantational texts, like the *Sefer Shimmush Tehillim*, understand quite clearly that "Angels" corresponding to the letters are invoked, when the glyphs of the Hebrew Alphabet are spoken with a suitably associated godly stance or intention.[47] The primary understanding here is that every sign of the alphabet is governed by a *Maggid*, a Celestial Messenger. These Messengers or Angels, are beams of the *Or* (the Light) of *Ein Sof* (the Eternal No-Thing), radiations of the boundless beneficence and qualities emanating from the Divine.[48] They abide in both the mundane and subtle spheres, and govern everything existing in physical manifestation. Since every Hebrew glyph is ruled by a *Maggid*, the letters forming words, and the words forming the sentences of invocations and prayers, combined with the intentions of the utterer of these words, invoke the Spirit Intelligences associated with the letters.[49]

As said, Kabbalists maintain this mundane creation to be comprising a combination of the *Otiot* (the Hebrew glyphs [alphabet]), in the shape of names and patterns. Besides their designation and configuration, the signs of the Hebrew Alphabet include "quantity" and "magnitude." Thus a "Kabbalist-Magician" can use these letters and their combinations as if they were "sublime particles," similar to the fundamental particles of the physicist.[50] Lastly, the Hebrew glyphs are not only understood to be governed by "Spirit Intelligences," but to be "living intelligences" with bodies, minds and souls. The glyph itself and its vocal enunciation, comprise the physical part of its manifestation, i.e. "the 'body,' whereas in its essence it belongs to the subtle realm of *Maggidim*, the Angelic Messengers. In this subtle realm it multiplies, as it were, to create the manifested world of words, meanings and objects. In their primordial state of emanation the *Otiot* are the primordial frequencies of the Cosmos in that space (*Makom*) where all are one in the Eternal No-thing from whence all life emanates as *Light*."[51]

Having referenced the "*Sefer Shimmush Tehillim*" ("The Magical Use of Psalms"), a work attributed to Rav Hai Gaon, I should mention that whilst the current tome is not an official translation of this text, I am sharing the majority of the magical applications of the Psalms included in a number of recensions of this work. The *Sefer Shimmush Tehillim* is in fact a relatively small, anonymous, mediaeval compilation, which exists in several recensions.[52] As noted elsewhere, this work "pertains to the magical and theurgical use of Divine Names," and in many instances it is the very emphasis "on 'Divine Names' which give the Psalms their magical potencies."[53] However, in many instances it is not readily apparent why some of the Divine Names in the *Shimmush Tehillim* are listed as having been derived from a selected set of words in the biblical *Book of Psalms*. That being said, Bill Rebiger, who is certainly the greatest living authority on the *Sefer Shimmush Tehillim*, informed us that in "many cases a certain verse seems to be implicitly responsible for the listed purpose," but he also stated that in several instances the contents of a Psalm is not always evident with regard to the "purpose data."[54]

It is worth noting that the popularity of this primary text of "Jewish Magic" resulted in the Vatican having at one time included it in the "*Index Librorum Prohibitum*" ("*Index of Forbidden Books*"),[55] but, as is so often the case with "banned" books, the "*Sefer Shimmush Tehillim*" survived in a number of recensions, and its use for a great variety of "magical intentions" continues unabated to this very day. A highly sought after English translation of a certain Godfrey Selig's flawed German version of the *Sefer Shimmush Tehillim*,[56] has been doing the rounds since the late 18th century, and was eventually incorporated in a spurious magical compilation titled *"The Sixth and Seventh Books of Moses."*[57] Regarding this translation I noted elsewhere that "besides being extremely verbose, there are unfortunately many errors and corruptions of Hebrew words and Divine Names in this translation. One would have expected the translator to have cross-checked each magical prescription with its associated Psalm in the Bible, so as to ensure that the terms used were correct, especially in cases where a word clearly does not exist in Hebrew, and a quick perusal of the appropriate Psalm would have exposed it as a corruption of a well-known Hebrew term. In fact, the translator/publisher deemed it necessary to insert every now and again an 'admonition from the translator' in the text, cautioning against the incorrect use of these magical techniques, which again leaves one quite perturbed as to why these only too obvious errors were allowed into the translation."[58]

Be that as it may, in this current tome in my *"Shadow Tree Series"* of works on "Practical Kabbalah," the focus is on the broad use of biblical Psalms in "Jewish Magic," which includes the extensive magical applications and resources not addressed in the *"Sefer Shimmush Tehillim."* Amongst these we should consider the talismanic use of biblical verses. In this regard, it has been noted that "some Jews in antiquity believed that specific books were endowed with extraordinary powers, and even nowadays some Jews (both orthodox and secular) carry with them miniature Psalm booklets as amulets."[59] It should be understood that the primary intention behind Hebrew amulets is the release, so to speak, of the magical power believed to be inside the word or phrase, and in this regard the most popular material to be inscribed for amuletic purposes are deerskin parchment, paper, and metal plates. However, stones, eggshells, even a piece of plastic, etc., have been likewise viewed as good surfaces on which to write biblical verses and Divine Names. Sometimes, as I witnessed recently, the words were written on a thin wafer to be dissolved in a glass of water, or in another liquid herbal mixture, which is then imbibed by the individual requiring the "spiritual force" channeled by the words.

The same is applicable to the skin of a hard-boiled egg, or the surface of an apple employed for the purpose of writing amulets, and which is likewise consumed afterwards.

Whilst the words, or the initials of the words, were often written on a piece of parchment, or engraved on metal, to be worn on the person of the individual seeking this support, I have also witnessed biblical verses and Divine Names written on pieces of cloth or flags, and then tied to trees. In this regard, it is understood that the movement of the material in the wind, would kindle, animate, or stimulate the release of the *ruchaniyut*, i.e. the "spiritual force" inherent in the words. On one occasion I observed a very religious lady writing Divine Names on the leaves of a tree next to her home, and I have to agree with Trachtenberg who, in reference to the *Sefer Shimmush Tehillim*, noted that "every device known to magic which was calculated to cause a certain effect to occur upon or within an individual, was called into play to bring out the occult forces inherent in the verses of the Bible."[60]

B. Additional Prayers Employed with the Recitation of Psalms

Several psalms are employed in conjunction with certain prayers from within the framework of normative Judaism. For example, *Psalm 26* is conjoined with the "*Ribbono Shel Olam*" prayer, and the "*Shemoneh Esrei*" ("*Amidah*") prayer features in the magical uses of several Psalms. Another prayer which is particularly popular in "Jewish Magic" is the "*Ana B'choach*," which is aligned with *Psalm 67*, and features prominently in the annual "Counting of the *Omer*" procedure.[61] Whilst I understand perfectly well that these prayers, as well as the following "*Prayer before Reciting Psalms*," might hold no value to those with little to no interest in the Jewish faith *per se*, there might be readers who find great value in these prayers, and hence I have elected to include three of them in this tome. However, I have not shared the *Amidah* prayer here, for the simple reason that this prayer changes format at different times, i.e. changing format in accordance with certain religious rulings. Furthermore, this prayer would be of no interest to anyone other than observant Jewish religionists, who can easily access it in any good *Siddur*, i.e. a Jewish Prayer Book.[62]

1. THE PRAYER BEFORE RECITING PSALMS

It is customary amongst Jewish worshippers to enunciate the following prayer before the recitation of Psalms. I am well aware that this is not necessarily done prior to working with the Psalms in a magical manner, and it is not directly referenced in the "*Sefer Shimmush Tehillim.*" However, the importance and power of this prayer is truly remarkable, and I cannot see why it should not be employed by those who want to enhance their *Kavvanah* (focussed attention and intention), in order to, as it were, intensify the power of the magical action they intend to undertake at a specific time. However, as is the case with prayers, incantations, adjurations, or other verbal *segulot* (Magical Remedies [Spiritual Treasures]), to successfully enunciate the "*Prayer Before Reciting Psalms*" with *Kavvanah*, necessitates complete comprehension of its contents. In this regard, the following statements mentioned in the prayer should be carefully considered, since they comprise some of the most important kabbalistic teachings:

1. The said prayer requests the "insolent forces" to be cut down. We are informed this is a reference to "a kabbalistic concept denoting the evil forces that originate from the evil inclination (Satan)."[63] However, these "forces of negation and evil"[64] are referenced in the phrase from a remarkable prayer/song reading "Draw near to Me, behold My strength, for there are no harsh judgments. They are cast out, they may not enter, these [forces of evil which are likened to] insolent dogs. I herewith invite the 'Ancient of Days' at this auspicious time, and [the powers of impurity] will be utterly removed. It is His revealed will to annul all the powers."[65]

2. There is also a reference to "the briars and the thorns." This is a kabbalistic expression referencing the impure forces which frustrate our efforts Godwards, i.e. they "actively prevent us from getting closer to the Divine one."[66] In this regard, the great Rav Abraham Isaac Kook makes reference to a *Segulah*, a spiritual treasure, which is "an inner holy power" which we inherited through the "Covenant of our Forefathers," and which is said to be an unchangeable spiritual power which is "incomparably

greater and holier than the aspect of free will."[67] The good Rabbi tells us that we can reveal this special "*Inner Segulah*" through the "holiness of faith," which, for observant Jewish religionists, includes the importance of *Torah* study, as well as the increase of good deeds in this world.[68] Whilst it is indeed true that we carry within us an "inner *segulah* of holiness" passed on to us by our Patriarchs, I personally believe that everyone on this planet carry within themselves such an "inner holy power," as it were, a "spark of holiness."

However, as Rabbi Kook indicated, "at times the darkness becomes so strong that it stops the revelation of the *segulah*."[69] He further informed us that "if someone who does not have deep perceptive insight to know how to distinguish between the side of the holy *segula* quality in them and the side of malfunctioning free choice in them, which surrounds [the inner side] as the briars and thorns surround the rose, tries to befriend them, he, heaven forbid, may become corrupted, might learn from their deeds, and become attached to the evil."[70] To rectify this, it is purely a matter of *teshuvah* (rectification), i.e. aligning "free will" with the "Divine Will" within us. Yet we are reminded to be cautious lest our vaunted "holiness" leads to intolerance. In this regard, it has been noted that "an atmosphere of excessive suspicion and zeal will prevail and any deviation whatever in practice or custom will cause the doer to be branded a heretic—and to be treated accordingly. There is no end to the harm that will be caused even to pious Orthodox Jews once the attitude of exclusion reigns."[71]

3.   The "rose" surrounded by "the briars and thorns" is termed the "Celestial Rose" in the prayer. This is the *Shechinah*, the Divine Presence, "the 'Countenance of God,' or Female aspect of the Divine in manifestation."[72] She is understood to be "the divine female, *Binah's* Daughter, the Bride, Spouse, and Lover of the Holy One," whose "status becomes a litmus test for the state of divinity and cosmos. Her union with Her Lover *Tiferet* signals cosmic unity, whereas, Her separation from Him is an index of cosmic brokenness, of 'Exile'."[73] She is the "Rose of Sharon" and "the Bride of Youth" mentioned in the prayer, and she is

likewise symbolised as "the terrestrial Garden of Eden, Jerusalem, the Temple, the *Sukkah* (Canopy) of Peace, the Sea into which all rivers flow, the Royal Diadem (*Atarah*), the color *tekhelet* (bright blue), the vowel point *chiriq* and the Oral Torah. She is occasionally associated with a series of Biblical heroines, with Rachel, Leah, and Ruth, and serves as the paradigm for women, in general: 'All women in the world are contained in Her mystery',"[74] and "Her Beloved" is the Divine One, blessed is He.

4. In conclusion, we need to consider the term "*Levanon*," the word said to have been derived from the Hebrew root לבן (*lavan*—"white").[75] It is often employed "as an epithet that intimates the Sanctuary," i.e. the Holy Temple, "which used to 'whiten' the iniquities of Israel through the sacrifices of expiation of sin."[76] Whilst this is indeed the case, the word "*Levanon*" (*Lebanon*) has been employed in kabbalistic literature as a symbol for *Keter* (Crown),[77] *Chochmah* (Wisdom),[78] the upper three *sefirot*, and for *Malchut* (Kindom).[79] Elsewhere we are informed that the Cosmic Tree "has its roots in Lebanon, which are the seat of glory, blessed be he, and the Lebanon corresponds to the supernal Lebanon, and its roots are seventy-two roots."[80]

Here the *Shechinah* is once again of primal importance, and as she is aligned with *Malchut* (Kingdom), she is referenced in terms of the descent of this *Sefirah* from *Lebanon*, and in terms of her ascent to *Lebanon*., i.e. the ascent of *Malchut* (Kingdom) to *Keter* (Crown). In this regard, Moses Chaim Luzzatto wrote "in the time to come 'the mountain of the Lord's house shall be established on the top of the mountains.' This is the supernal *Keter*...."[81] Quoting *Psalm 121:1* the great Rabbi continues "'I shall lift my eyes to the hills, from whence [*me'Ayin*]comes my help'—this is the *Shekhinah*. *Ayin*—is '*Attiqa Qaddisha*'.... This is the sublime secret, as it is written 'together with me from *Lebanon*, bride, together with me from *Lebanon* you shall come.' Come and see: the *Shekhinah* is the linkage of all the ranks, as in it is the beginning of thought [and] the end of action, and everything is the linkage from the beginning [or from the head] of all to the end of all. The *Shekhinah* is the linkage of all and this is the reason why it is written: 'whence comes my help'—this is the *Ayin*, the supernal *Keter*, as from there the *Shekhinah* is dwelling, in order to link the linkages. And the secret of this issue is 'the valorous wife is the diadem of her husband.' This is the stone that is elevated endlessly....[the *Shekhinah*] is the [woman] partner to the king, indeed, as it is appropriate, and this is the meaning of 'from the *Lebanon* come with me, bride!' Despite the fact that She ascends to the Infinite, Her [sexual] linkage is with her partner, 'from the *Lebanon* come with me.' This is the reason why [it is said] 'My help is from the Lord.' This is if She is with the Lord....Come and see: when the *Shekhinah* ascends to that supernal *Keter*, it is written, 'the mountain of the Lord's house shall be established on the top of the mountains'."[82]

There is not enough space in the current tome to address these remarkable concepts in any greater detail. However, whilst keeping the information shared in mind, the traditional *"Prayer before Reciting Psalms"* could be vocalised by those who wish to do so. Observant Jewish religionists should note that this prayer is not enunciated on the Sabbath and during *Yom Tov*, i.e. the Jewish Holidays. The prayer reads:[83]

יהי רצון מלפניך יהוה אלהינו ואלהי אבותינו הבוחר
בדוד עבדו ובזרעו אחריו והבוחר בשירות ותשבחות
שתפן ברחמים אל קריאת מזמורי תהלים שאקרא
כאלו אמרם דוד המלך עליו השלום בעצמו זכותו
יגן עלינו ויעמד לנו זכות פסוקי תהלים וזכות
תבותיהם ואותיותיהם ונקודותיהם וטעמיהם והשמות
היוצאים מהם מראשי תבות ומסופי תבות לכפר
פשעינו ועוונותינו וחטאתינו ולזמר עריצים ולהכרית
כל החוחים והקוצים הסובבים את השושנה העליונה
ולחבר אשת נעורים עם דודה באהבה ואחוה ורעות
ומשם ימשך לנו שפע לנפש רוח ונשמה לטהרנו
מעוונותינו ולסלוח חטאתינו ולכפר פשעינו כמו
שסלחת לדוד שאמר מזמורים אלו לפניך כמו
שנאמר [*2 Samuel 12:13*] גם יהוה העביר חטאתך לא

תמות ואל תקחנו מהעולם הזה קדם זמננו עד מלאת
שנותינו בהם שבעים שנה באופן שנוכל לתקן את אשר
שחתנו וזכות דוד המלך עליו השלום יגן עלינו ובעדנו
שתאריך אפך עד שובנו אליך בתשובה שלמה לפניך
ומאוצר מתנת חנם חנני כדכתיב [Exodus 33:19] וחנותי
את אשר אחון ורחמתי את אשר ארחם וכשם שאנו
אומרים לפניך שירה בעולם הזה כך נזכה לומר לפניך
יהוה אלהינו שיר ושבחה לעולם הבא ועל ידי אמירת
תהלים תתעורר חבצלת השרון ולשיר בקול נעים בגילת
ורנן כבוד הלבנון נתן לה הוד והדר בבית אלהינו
במהרה בימינו אמן סלה

Transliteration:

Y'hi ratzon mil'fanecha YHVH eloheinu veilohei avoteinu habocheir b'david av'do uv'zar'o aharav v'habocheir b'shirot v'tish'bachot sheteifen b'rachamim el k'ri'at miz'morei t'hilim she'ek'ra k'ilu am'ram david hamelech alav hashalom b'atz'mo z'chuto yagein aleinu v'ya'amod lanu z'chut p'sukei t'hilim uz'chut teivoteihem v'otiyoteihem un'kudoteihem v'ta'ameihem v'hasheimot hayotz'im meihem meiroshei teivot umisofei teivot l'chapeir p'sha'einu va'avonoteinu v'chatoteinu ul'zameir aritzim ul'hach'rit kol hachochim v'hakotzim hasov'vim et hashoshanah ha'el'yonah ul'chabeir eishet n'urim im dodah b'ahavah v'ach'vah v'rei'ut umisham yimashech lanu shefa la'nefesh ru'ach u'n'shamah l'tahareinu mei'avonoteinu v'lis'lo'ach chatoteinu ul'chapeir p'sha'einu k'mo shesalach'ta l'david she'amar miz'morim eilu l'fanecha k'mo shene'emar gam YHVH he'evir chatat'cha lo tamut [2 Samuel 12:13] v'al tikacheinu meiha'olam hazeh kodem z'maneinu ad m'lot sh'noteinu bahem shiv'im shanah b'ofan shenuchal l'takein et asheir shichat'nu uz'chut david hamelech alav hashalom yagein aleinu uva'adeinu sh'ta'arich ap'cha ad shuveinu eilecha bit'shuvah sh'leimah l'fanecha umei'otzar mat'nat chinam chanei'nu k'dich'tiv [Exodus 33:19] v'chanoti et asher achon v'richam'ti et asher arachem uch'sheim she'anu om'rim l'fanecha shira ba'olam hazeh kach niz'keh lomar

*l'fanecha YHVH eloheinu shir ush'vachah la'olam haba
v'al y'dei amirat t'hilim tit'oreir chavatzelet hasharon
v'lashir b'kol na'im b'gilat v'ranein k'vod hal'vanon nitan
lah hod v'hadar b'veit eloheinu bim'heirah b'yameinu
Omein Selah*

Translation:

May it be your will *YHVH* our God and the God of our
fathers, who chose David His servant and his offspring
after him, and who chooses songs and praise, to attend with
mercy to the selected Psalms that I will recite, as if King
David, of blessed memory, may his merit protect us, had
pronounced them himself. And may the merit of the verses
of the Psalms stand in our favour, and the merit of their
words, and their letters, and their vowels, and their
cantillations, together with the Holy Names that are formed
from them, from the capitals of the words and from the
concluding letters of the words, bring atonement for our
misdeeds, iniquities, and transgressions, and to cut down
the insolent forces, and break all the briars and the thorns
which encompass the Celestial Rose, and to unite the Bride
of Youth with her Beloved in love, brotherhood, and
companionship. And from there [their union] may
abundance [a bounty] be drawn to our *Nefesh* (Instinctual
Self), *Ru'ach* (Conscious Self), and *Neshamah* (Divine
Self), to purify us of our iniquities, forgive our
transgressions, and to atone for our misdeeds, just as you
forgave David who sang these Psalms before you, as it is
said "*YHVH* also hath put away thy sin; thou shalt not die"
[*2 Samuel 12:13*]. And do not take us from This World
prematurely, until the completion of our years, seventy
years among them, that we will be able to mend what we
have ruined. And the merit of King David, of blessed
memory, will protect us and for us, so that you may bear
with us, until we return to you in complete repentance
before you, and be gracious unto us from your treasury of
undeserved grace, as it is written "and I will be gracious to
whom I will be gracious, and will show mercy on whom I
will show mercy" [*Exodus 33:19*]. And just as we recite
before you a song of praise in This World, so we will have

the privilege of reciting before you, *YHVH* our God, songs and praises in the World to Come. And through reciting the Psalms awaken the Rose of Sharon to sing with a pleasant voice, with ecstasy and joy. May the glory of the *Levanon* be given to her, majesty and splendour in the House of our God, speedily in our days. *Amen Selah.*

Conclude by enunciating *Psalm 95:1–3*:

[1] לכו נרננה ליהוה נריעה לצור ישענו

[2] נקדמה פניו בתודה בזמרות נריע לו

[3] כי אל גדול יהוה ומלך גדול על כל אלהים

Transliteration:

[1] *l'chu n'ran'nah la'YHVH nari'ah l'tzur yish'einu*

[2] *n'kad'mah panav b'todah biz'mirot nari'a lo*

[3] *ki eil gadol YHVH umelech gadol al kol elohim*

Translation:

[1] O come, let us sing unto *YHVH*; let us shout for joy to the Rock of our salvation.

[2] Let us come before His presence with thanksgiving, let us shout for joy unto Him with Psalms.

[3] For *YHVH* is a great God, and a great King above all gods.

2. *RIBONO SHEL OLAM* PRAYER

There are several prayers carrying the title "*Ribono shel Olam*" ("Master of the Universe"), i.e. the one accompanying the "Bedtime Prayer," another recited during the "Counting of the *Omer*," etc. However, the phrase "*Ribono shel Olam* prayer" usually references the supplication recited by some congregations during the utterance of the ברכת כהנים (*Birkat Kohanim*— "Priestly Blessing").[84] This prayer was lifted almost verbatim from the *Talmud* [*TB Berachot 55b*], and fundamentally pertains to dreams about which it has been said that even those "with a bad interpretation can be changed to good after being interpreted positively," and that "this is why the *Ribbono Shel Olam* prayer is formulated regarding a dream that may be good or evil."[85]

As stated in the following chapter, this prayer is recited in conjunction with *Psalm 26* by those who are in grave danger or in dangerous circumstances, and equally by women who are suffering difficult confinements. An acquaintance of mine commented that these needs have little to do with a prayer which deals mainly with bad dreams, to which I responded, with perhaps a raised eyebrow, that those who suffer such problematic circumstances might well think they are having a "bad dream"! In this regard, we are informed that this prayer could be recited "even by those who did not dream," and that one could exclude the sentence reading "I have dreamed a dream but I do not know what it indicates," and commence with the "*y'hi ratzon*" ("May it be your will") section.[86] However, as is the case with most supplicatory prayers, this one is again not recited on the Sabbath, for the simple reason that this day "is considered a delight (*oneg*), and supplication is not permitted."[87]

רבונו של עולם אני שלך וחלומותי שלך חלום חלמתי
ואיני יודע מה הוא
יהי רצון מלפניך יהוה‏ אדני‏ אלהי ואלהי אבותי
שיהיו כל חלומותי עלי ועל כל ישראל לטובה בין
שחלמתי על עצמי ובין שחלמתי על אחרים ובין שחלמו
אחרים עלי אם טובים הם חזקם ואמצם ויתקימו בי
ובהם כחלומותיו של יוסף הצדיק ואם צריכים רפואה
רפאם כחזקיהו מלך יהודה מחליו וכמרים הנביאה
מצרעתה וכנעמן מצרעתו וכמי מרה על ידי משה
רבינו וכמי יריחו על ידי אלישע וכשם שהפכת את
קללת בלעם הרשע מקללה לברכה כן תהפך כל
חלומותי עלי ועל כל ישראל לטובה ותשמרני ותחנני
ותרצני אמן

Transliteration:

Ribono shel olam ani shel'cha v'chalomotai shel'cha
chalom chalam'ti v'eini yodei'a mah hu
Y'hi ratzon mil'fanecha YHVH elohai veilohei avotai
sheyih'yu kol chalomotai alai v'al kol yis'ra'eil l'tovah
bein shechalam'ti al atz'mi uvein shechalam'ti al acheirim

uvein shechal'mu acheirim alai im tovim heim chaz'keim
v'am'tzoim v'yit'kaimu vi uvahem kuchalomotav shel yosef
hatzadik v'im tz'richim r'vu'ah r'fa'eim k'chiz'kiyahu
melech y'hudah meichol'yo uch'mir'yam han'vi'ah
mitzara'tah uch'na'aman mitzara'to uch'mei marah al
y'dei mosheh rabeinu uch'mei y'richo al y'dei elisha
uch'sheim shehafach'ta et kil'lat bil'am harasha mik'lalah
liv'rachah kein tahafoch kol chalomotai alai v'al kol
yis'ra'eil l'tovah v'tish'm'reini ut'chaneini v'tir'tzeini
Omein.

Translation:

Master of the universe, I am yours and my dreams are
yours. I have dreamed a dream but I do not know what it
indicates.

May it be your will *YHVH*, my God and God of my fathers,
that all my dreams regarding myself and regarding all of
Israel be good ones—those I have dreamed about myself,
those I have dreamed about others, and those that others
dreamed about me. If they are good, strengthen them,
fortify them, make them endure in me and in them like the
dreams of the righteous Joseph. But if they require healing,
heal them like Hezekiah, King of Judah, from his sickness;
like Miriam the prophetess from her troubles; like Naaman
from his troubles; like the waters of Marah through the
hand of Elisha. And just as you transformed the curse of
the wicked Balaam from a curse to a blessing, so may you
transform all of my dreams regarding myself and regarding
all of Israel for goodness. May you protect me, may you be
gracious to me, may you accept me. *Amen.*[88]

Readers who feel that this prayer is, as it were, misaligned with
their intentions, could skip the opening phrase, as suggested, and
commence with the "*Y'hi ratzon mil'fanecha*" ("May it be your
will") section, or they may find the bedtime "*Ribono shel Olam*"
prayer more appropriate. The latter is certainly a most beautiful
prayer of "rectification," which some might consider to be offering
a better state of preparedness prior to requesting some or other
support from the Eternal One:[89]

רבונו של עולם הריני מוחל וסולח לכל מי
שהכעיס והקניט אותי או שחטא כנגדי בין
בגופי בין בממוני בין בכבודי בין בכל אשר
לי בין באונס בין ברצון בין בשוגג בין במזיד
בין בדבור בין במעשה בין בגלגול זה בין
בגלגול אחר לכל בר ישראל ולא יענש שום
אדם בסבתי יהי רצון מלפניך יהוה‎אהדונהי
אלהי ואלהי אבותי שלא אחטא עוד ומה
שחטאתי לפניך מחק ברחמיך הרבים אבל
לא על ידי יסורין וחלאים רעים יהיו לרצון
אמרי פי והגיון לבי לפניך יהוה‎אהדונהי
צורי וגאלי

Transliteration:

> *Ribono shel olam hareini mocheil v'solei'ach l'chol mi*
> *shehich'is v'hig'nit oti o shechata k'neg'di bein b'gufi bein*
> *b'mamoni bein bich'vodi bein b'chol asher li bein b'ones*
> *bein b'ratzon bein b'shogeig bein b'meizid bein b'dibur*
> *bein b'ma'aseh bein b'gilgul zeh bein b'gilgul acheir*
> *l'chol bar yis'ra'eil v'lo yei'aneish shum adam b'sibati*
> *y'hi ratzon mil'fanecha YHVH elohai veilohei avotai shelo*
> *echeta od umah shechatati l'fanecha m'chok*
> *b'rachamecha harabim aval lo al y'dei yisurin v'chala'im*
> *ra'im yih'yu l'ratzon im'rei fi v'heg'yon libi l'fanecha*
> *YHVH tzuri v'go'ali*

Translation:

> Master of the Universe, I hereby forgive anyone who
> angered me or provoked me, or who did wrong against me,
> whether against my body, or against my property, whether
> against my honour, or whether against anything that
> belongs to me, whether done so accidentally, or whether
> willingly, whether unintentionally or whether deliberately,
> whether with words or whether through action, whether in
> this incarnation, or whether in another incarnation, by any
> person of Israel. And may no person receive retribution
> because of me. May it be your will *YHVH* my God, and
> God of my fathers, that I will not transgress again. And that
> my erstwhile transgressions before you will be erased in

your abundant mercies, though not through suffering or severe illnesses. May the words of my mouth and the thoughts of my heart find favour before you *YHVH*, my rock and my redeemer.

Readers probably observed that in both these prayers, as well as in the forty-one Psalms shared in this tome, the Ineffable Name (יהוה) is represented יהוהיאהדונהי, i.e. the latter being a combination of the Tetragrammaton and the Divine Name אדני (*Adonai*). The יאהדונהי Divine Name combination is termed the "Eight Letter Name of God." In this regard I noted elsewhere "that in Kabbalah the Ineffable Name is employed with specific reference to the sphere of *Tiferet* (Beauty) on the sefirotic Tree, whilst the Name *Adonai* pertains to the sphere of *Malchut* (Kingdom)," and that these two *sefirot* represent respectively:[90]

Tiferet	*Malchut*
יהוה (*YHVH*)	אדני (*Adonai*)
Sun (Direct Light)	Moon (Reflected Light)
King	Queen
Upper	Lower
Male Principle	Female Principle
Beloved	Lover
Husband	Bride

Conjoining the Divine Name of *Tiferet* (Beauty) with that of *Malchut* (Kingdom), is believed to facilitate "a 'sacred marriage' between *Tiferet* (King) and *Malchut* (Queen-*Shechinah*), or the male and female aspects of the Divine One," which is said to be "the most important task that the mystic assumes in his quest."[91] As mentioned before, "the sexual act itself is a physical expression of the 'sacred union' of the Divine Male and Female Principles, i.e. when undertaken with the fully focussed intention of unifying the 'Eternal One' (Divine Father) and the *Shechinah* (Divine Mother)."[92] In this regard, we are informed that "*sexual intimacy within the life of God is the paradigmatic expression of divine wholeness,*"[93] and also that "whilst we note the sexual act being employed with the intention of encouraging a 'Sacred Marriage' between the masculine and feminine aspects of the Divine One, the visualisation and mental expression of יאהדונהי (*Yahadonai* or *Yahadonahi*) is equally understood to facilitate the said 'Sacred Marriage'."[94] Thus the inclusion of יהואהדנויאהדונהי is meant to encourage the practitioner to consciously acknowledge the "Sacred Union" between the Divine One and the *Shechinah*. However, we are also informed that when we encounter this Divine Name combination in prayers, that the required intention is to focus our minds on אדון הכל היה הוה ויהיה יאהדונהי (*Adon ha-Kol hayah hoveh v'yih'yeh Yahadonahi*—"Lord of All, He was, He is, and He will be."[95]

3. *ANA BECHOACH* PRAYER

Whilst the *Ana Bechoach* prayer does not feature prominently in the magical applications of the biblical "*Book of Psalms*," the references to this remarkable prayer and the associated "Forty-two Letter Name of God" in the current study, warrant its inclusion in this tome As stated elsewhere, the *Ana Bechoach* prayer is said to have been written by the Talmudic mystic Rabbi Nechunia ben Hakanah. However, it appears it was penned at a much later date,[96] and reads:

אנא בכח גדולת ימינך תתיר צרורה
קבל רינת עמך שגבנו טהרנו נורא
נא גבור דורשי יחודך כבבת שמרם
ברכם טהרם רחמי צדקתך תמיד גמלם
חסין קדוש ברוב טובך נהל עדתך
יחיד גאה לעמך פנה זוכרי קדושתך
שועתנו קבל ושמע צעקתנו יודע תעלומות
ברוך שם כבוד מלכותו לעולם ועד

Transliteration:
Ana Bechoach G'dulat Yemincha Tatir Tz'rurah
Kabel Rinat Am'chah Sagvenu Taharenu Nora
Na Gibor Dorshei Yichudcha Kevavat Shomrem
Bar'chem Taharem Rachamei Tzidkatcha Tamid Gomlem
Chasin Kadosh B'rov Tuvcha Nahel Adatecha
Yachid Ge'eh Le'am'cha Pneh Zochrei K'dushatecha

> *Shav'atenu Kabel Ushma Tza'akatenu Yode'a Ta'alumot*
> *Baruch Shem K'vod Malchuto l'Olam Va'ed*

Translation:

> Please now with might, with the strength of your right, untie the bound.
>
> Accept our song, strengthen us, purify in awe.
>
> Awesome in grace, we who see you as One, guard from harm.
>
> Cleanse us and bless, mix mercy with justice, and always redeem.
>
> Holy power, in your great goodness, guide your people.
>
> Exalted unique, turn to us, who recall your holiness.
>
> Receive our cry, hear our plea, you know what is hidden.
>
> Blessed is the Name, glorious your kingdom, throughout space and time.[97]

This very important prayer is employed extensively in Jewish worship. It is recited every evening as part of the bedtime prayers, and daily during the *Ketoret* ("incense") section of the morning and afternoon services, the reason being that "reciting *Ketoret* removes evil thoughts during prayer," and the *Ana Bechoach* prayer is believed to have "the same remedial characteristic trait."[98] This prayer is also recited on Friday evenings after *Psalm 29*, the reason for the latter being that the *Ana Bechoach* prayer comprises "seven designations of the names of God,"[99] i.e. נורא (*Nora*— "Awesome One"), גבור (*Gibor*— "Mighty One"), חסין (*Chasin* —"Almighty"), קדוש (*Kadosh*— "Holy One"), יחיד (*Yachid*— "Unique One"), גאה (*Ge'eh*—"Exalted [proud] One"), and יודע תעלומות (*Yode'a Ta'alumot*— "Know all Secrets"). These seven designations of the Divine One are said to align with the seven "voices of God" referenced in *Psalm 29*.[100]

The *Ana Bechoach* prayer is also enunciated during the *Rosh Hashanah* ("New Year") and *Yom Kippur* services, and holds a place of prominence over the forty-nine days of the "Counting of the *Omer*." Similarly to *Psalm 67*, the "*Menorah Psalm*" of "*Omer*,"[101] the *Ana Bechoach* prayer is sometimes included in *Shiviti* plagues and Hebrew amulets in the form of a *Menorah*, i.e. the sacred seven-branched candelabrum:[102]

It should be noted that the *Ana Bechoach* prayer comprises forty-two words only, the additional six of the concluding stanza of the prayer, i.e. *Baruch Shem K'vod Malchuto l'Olam Va'ed* ("Blessed be the Name of His glorious Kingdom throughout eternity"), having been appended "as an affirmation of the entire prayer."[103] The capitals of the mentioned forty-two words of the prayer spell the "Forty-two Letter Name of God":[104]

אבגיתצ קרעשטן נגדיכש בתרצתג
חקבטנע יגלפזק שקוצית

(*Avgitatz Karastan Nagdichesh Batratztag
Chakvetna Yaglefzok Shakutzit*)

As indicated, the forty-two letters of this mysterious Divine Name are arranged into seven groups, each comprising six letters. There are a number of ways of enunciating the seven combinations, and the one shared in this series of texts on "Practical Kabbalah" was shared with me some fifty years ago.[105]

Be that as it may, the *Talmud* maintains "the forty-two lettered Name is entrusted only to him who is pious, meek, middle aged, free from bad temper, sober, and not insistent on his rights" [*TB Kiddushin 71a*], and the "secret" of the "Forty-two Letter Name of God" is said to pertain to the "Workings of Creation" (*Ma'aseh B'reshit*). As I noted elsewhere, "contemplation and meditation on this special Divine Name is said to have the power to elevate the 'Soul,' raising it from '*Olam ha-Asiyah,*' the physical 'Realm of Action,' to '*Olam ha-Yetzirah,*' the higher 'Realm of Formation'."[106] In this regard, the forty-two letters of this Divine Name construct are said to manifest as forty-two "shining lights" expressed in forty-two unique "spiritual forms." Again as stated elsewhere, "these 'forms' pertain to sets of Divine Names and associated 'Spirit Intelligences' directly related to the component letters of the 'Forty-two Letter Name.' This is viewed as a process, as it were, in which the forty-two letters are the initial 'source roots' of the spiritual forces, whilst the Divine Names and the 'Celestial Beings,' respectively associated with these letters, are the 'branches' emanating from the primordial source. All are unified in the wholeness of the 'One,' the ultimate 'Source' beyond all being."[107]

In harmony with the custom of enunciating the *Ana Bechoach* prayer as well as the "Forty-two Letter Name of God" every day at the conclusion of the bedtime prayer, I have shared elsewhere the remarkable procedure of working with the mentioned forty-two "Spiritual forms" associated with this Divine Name.[108] In conclusion, it should be noted that the "Forty-two Letter Name" relates to the *sefirah* of *Gevurah* (Strength/Severity) on the sefirotic tree, hence the popular inclusion of this Divine Name in Hebrew amulets to, as it were, invoke the special "powers of protection" believed to be inherent within the letters of this Divine Name construct.[109]

. ...The Maharal told me first to walk around the golem seven times, beginning on the right side, proceed to his head and circle around it to his legs on the left side. He told me what combinations of letters to recite as I walked around him. And thus I did seven times. When I completed the circuits, the body of the golem reddened like a glowing coal.... ... .

Chapter 2
Ma'arav — West
The Psalms of David — Book I

Prior to delineating the magical uses of Psalms, the following should be kept in mind. Firstly, the version of the "*Book of Psalms*" employed in this tome is the original included in every Hebrew Bible. It differs considerably from the one shared in the Christian Bible, in which it was seen fit to renumber Psalms chapter and verses. Secondly, it should be noted that it was conventional in days of yore, when individuals bore no surnames, to include the first names of recipients as well as those of their mothers in magical procedures. Whilst this is still customary in Jewish circles, it is not strictly necessary when everyone is readily identifiable by means of a first and a last name. Besides, in the majority of instances today we are completely oblivious of the identities of the mothers of those to be included in a magical procedure. As I have witnessed on a number of occasions, magical actions turned out to be equally effective when the names and surnames of intended "recipients" were employed. Keeping this in mind, let us now consider the magical applications of the "*Book of Psalms.*"

PSALM 1

[1] אשרי האיש אשר לא הלך בעצת רשעים ובדרך חטאים לא עמד ובמושב לצים לא ישב

[2] כי אם בתורת יהוﬞﬞﬞﬞﬞﬞﬞﬞﬞﬞﬞﬞﬞﬞﬞﬞﬞ אהﬞﬞﬞﬞﬞﬞﬞﬞﬞﬞﬞﬞﬞﬞ דﬞﬞﬞﬞﬞﬞﬞﬞﬞﬞﬞﬞﬞﬞﬞﬞﬞﬞﬞﬞﬞﬞﬞﬞ נﬞﬞﬞﬞﬞﬞﬞﬞﬞﬞﬞﬞﬞﬞﬞﬞﬞﬞﬞﬞﬞﬞﬞﬞﬞﬞﬞﬞﬞﬞﬞﬞ הﬞﬞﬞﬞﬞﬞﬞﬞﬞﬞﬞﬞﬞﬞ יﬞﬞﬞﬞﬞﬞﬞﬞﬞﬞﬞﬞﬞﬞ חפצו ובתורתו יהגה יומם ולילה

[3] והיה כעץ שתול על פלגי מים אשר פריו יתן בעתו ועלהו לא יבול וכל אשר יעשה יצליח

[4] לא כן הרשעים כי אם כמץ אשר תדפנו רוח

29

[5] על כן לא יקמו רשעים במשפט וחטאים בעדת
צדיקים

[6] כי יודע יהוהאהדונהי דרך צדיקים ודרך
רשעים תאבד

Transliteration:

[1] *ashrei ha'ish asher lo halach ba'atzat r'sha'im uv'derech chata'im lo amad uv'moshav leitzim lo yashav*
[2] *ki im b'torat YHVH chef'tzo uv'torato yeh'geh yomam valailah*
[3] *v'hayah k'eitz shatul al pal'gei mayim asher pir'yo yitein b'ito v'aleihu lo yibol v'chol asher ya'aseh yatz'liach*
[4] *lo chein har'sha'im ki im kamotz asher tid'fenu ruach*
[5] *al kein lo yakumu r'sha'im bamish'pat v'chata'im ba'adat tzadikim*
[6] *ki yodei'a YHVH derech tzadikim v'derech r'sha'im toveid*

Translation:

[1] Happy is the man that hath not walked in the counsel of the wicked, nor stood in the way of sinners, nor sat in the seat of the scornful.
[2] But his delight is in the law of *YHVH*; and in His law doth he meditate day and night.
[3] And he shall be like a tree planted by streams of water, that bringeth forth its fruit in its season, and whose leaf doth not wither; and in whatsoever he doeth he shall prosper.
[4] Not so the wicked; but they are like the chaff which the wind driveth away.
[5] Therefore the wicked shall not stand in the judgment, nor sinners in the congregation of the righteous.
[6] For *YHVH* regardeth the way of the righteous; but the way of the wicked shall perish.

Psalm 1 is the first of four Psalms recited in the Sephardic rite at the conclusion of the service on the eve of *Yom Kippur* ("Day of Atonement").[1] In terms of the six verses of the Psalm, Rabbi Abraham Chamui informs us that the "secret of this Psalm is great and awesome in the secret of the six extremities."[2] This is a kabbalistic "mystery" pertaining to the six "ends"; the "secret of the six days of creation"; the sacred Jewish "tabernacle in the desert"; the six directions "sealed" with the Name of the Ineffable One; the six *sefirot* from חסד (*Chesed*—"Loving-kindness") to יסוד (*Yesod*—"Foundation"); etc., all of which are of particular importance in Kabbalah,[3] and needs careful investigation, which the current study does not allow for lack of space.

Be that as it may, the first Psalm is ranked amongst a set of Psalms said to have the power to work rectification or restoration of the souls of those, whose wrong deeds have caused them to lose their luck, and to have become unsuccessful in whatever they do. Similar to claims made regarding Rabbi Nachman of Bratslav's well-known *Tikun ha-Klali*, it is said the mentioned group of Psalms will "sweeten the harsh judgments"; "subdue the evil inclination"; cause "mercies to arise"; and ensure the one who recite them every morning before dawn, to be "rewarded with honour, abundance, and great success."[4] I am addressing the said set of Psalms, as well as the *Tikun ha-Klali*, in the concluding part of "*The Book of Magical Psalms.*"

Whilst *Psalm 1* is certainly not the most popular Psalm amongst those included in Jewish liturgies, it is fairly extensively employed in Jewish Magic. In this regard, it should be noted that whilst the recitation of the entire first Psalm is liberally recommended to pregnant women as a protection against a difficult delivery,[5] as attested by the many entries in this regard on the world wide web, and whilst it is equally recommended as an inscription on a kosher parchment for the purpose of counteracting premature delivery, i.e. miscarriage,[6] the majority of recensions of the "*Sefer Shimmush Tehillim*" ("*Magical Use of Psalms*")[7] inform us only regarding the first three verses of *Psalm 1* being employed for this purpose in a written amulet. It has been suggested that this magical quality pertains to "the imagery of waters and fertility" in the third verse.[8]

In the current instance the instructions pertain to writing the said three verses together with a special prayer-adjuration on deerskin parchment,[9] which should be attached to the body in some or other manner, as suggested in a magical text in the Cairo Geniza,[10] or, as I noted elsewhere in terms of the prescriptions in most primary Hebrew texts, "worn as a pendant, for the purposes of preventing a pregnant woman from premature delivery or from suffering a miscarriage."[11] It should be noted that whilst deerskin parchment is referenced in some manuscripts, others simply mention "parchment" without any indication that such should be derived from a "gazelle." Another recension simply reads "Speak [the Psalm] over paper, and write."[12] In other words, any good clean surface will serve well enough in the construction of the amulet.

Also listed is a special Divine Name construct which was derived from this Psalm, and which is included in the said prayer. The associated Divine Name is אל חד (*El Chad*), which we are told was derived from the words אשרי (*ashrei*—"Happy is"): verse 1; לא כן (*lo chen*—"not so"): verse 4; יצליח (*yatzliach*—"prosper"): verse 3; and דרך רשעים (*derech r'sha'im*— "way of the wicked"): verse 6.[13] In Godfrey Selig's translation of the "*Shimmush Tehillim*," it is stated that the "Name" *El Chad* signifies "great, strong, only God."[14] Whilst the term חד (*Chad*) signifies "one" when employed in Hebrew as a prefix, and equally references "one" in Aramaic, its inclusion in the Divine Name does not really mean "great," "strong" or "only." In this instance, the Hebrew word simply means "sharp" or "acute." The translator may have arrived at the meaning "only," by seeing a connection between the words "*Chad*" and "*Echad*," the latter meaning "one." Interestingly enough, in a "*Shimmush Tehillim*" manuscript from Yemen in the Kaufmann Collection, which is located in the Oriental Collection of the Library of the Hungarian Academy of Sciences, we read regarding the Divine Name in question that "His name is *El Echad* (the One God)."[15]

As I noted elsewhere, "I cannot quite fathom why the anonymous author of the '*Shimmush Tehillim*' chose those specific words in the mentioned verses as the basis for the said Divine Name, since there are several others he might have chosen which would equally have sufficed."[16] Be that as it may, we noted that the said Divine Name construct is conjoined with a unique prayer-adjuration, the latter reading:

יהי רצון מלפניך **אל חד** שתעשה לאשה [recipient]
שלא תפיל ותרפאנה רפואה שלימה מעתה ועד עולם
אמן אמן אמן סלה סלה סלה

Transliteration:

Y'hi ratzon mil'fanecha El Chad sheta'aseh l'ishah [....name of recipient....] shelo tapil v'tir'pa'enah r'fu'ah sh'leimah mei'atah v'ad olam Omein Omein Omein Selah Selah Selah

Translation:

May it be your will *EL Chad*, to protect this woman [....name of recipient....], that she may not suffer a premature delivery, and to restore her to complete health from now on forever. *Amen Amen Amen! Selah Selah Selah!*[17]

In terms of the mentioned potential of premature delivery, I have seen a recommendation of *Psalm 1* being recited every day for the entire duration of a pregnancy.

The healing powers of the first Psalm are expanded upon in another recension of the "*Shimmush Tehillim,*" in which we are informed that the first three verses are good for halting a haemorrhage.[18] In this regard, the instruction is to write the Psalm, suspend it around the neck of the afflicted individual, and then to recite the following prayer-adjuration:

שמע קולי ובכיי יהי רצון מלפניך **אל חד** שתעצור

הדם מן [recipient] היוצא מאבר [recipient] אמן אמן

אמן נצח נצח נצח סלה סלה סלה

Transliteration:

Sh'ma koli uvich'yi y'hi ratzon mil'fanecha El Chad sheta'atzor hadam min [....name of recipient....] hayotzei mei'eiver [....name of recipient....]. Omein Omein Omein Netzach Netzach Netzach Selah Selah Selah!

Translation:

Hear my voice and my cry. May it be your will *El Chad*, that you stop the blood of [....name of recipient....], which flows from a body part of [....name of recipient....]. *Amen Amen Amen! Enduring Enduring Enduring! Selah Selah Selah!*[19]

I believe the opening statement of the incantation is a paraphrase of the portion of *Psalm 6:9* reading שמע יהוה קול בכיי [*shama*

YHVH kol bich'yi—"for *YHVH* hath heard the voice of my weeping"].

As mentioned elsewhere, the first three verses of *Psalm 1*, written on deerskin parchment, are "also recommended as an amulet to promote success in all one's endeavours," and that, "in this regard the specific reference is to the concluding phrase of verse 3 reading "and in whatsoever he doeth he shall prosper."[20] I am reminded of the saga of a certain Reb Nachum, who "had the custom of saying the first Psalm of *Tehillim* before any important undertaking, as a *segulah* for success. And why didn't he reveal this secret to his wife? It was out of bitter experience: he had told it to several friends and they had tried it—but without success. According to Reb Nachum, this was the type of *segulah* which worked only if one truly believed in it deeply. Which might boil down to willpower, according to his wife."[21]

It is worth noting that the initial letters of the seventeen words comprising *Psalm 1:3* are arranged into a Divine Name construct to be employed in an amulet for the purposes of achieving success.[22] The said Divine Name consists of a set of five Hebrew letter combinations, i.e. four tri-letter constructs and one five-letter construct, as shown below:

$$\text{וְכֹשׁ עַפֶּם אַפִּי בְּול יְוֹאֲיֵי}$$

These should be written with their vowel points, in conjunction with all the Hebrew glyphs comprising the words of the said verse, which are equally to be arranged into the following Divine Name construct incorporating twenty tri-letter combinations:[23]

$$\text{והי הכע זֶשׁת ולע לפל גים}$$
$$\text{יסא שרף ריו יתן בעת ווע להו}$$
$$\text{לאי בול וכל אשר יעש היץ ליח}$$

Divine Name constructs such as these are often concentrated upon whilst reciting the associated Psalm or verse. Otherwise they are written down to be employed as amulets.

Be that as it may, a further six-letter Divine Name construct comprising the capitals of the first six words of the verse in question, i.e. ו‎כשע‎פמ, is equally employed in Hebrew amulets for success in endeavours of all kind.[24] I have previously addressed this specific letter combination arranged in conjunction with the Divine Name שדי (*Shadai*) on a hexagram, for the purposes of "becoming a living kamea,"[25] as illustrated below:

A further magical application of verse three, pertains to the following four-letter Divine Name construct ואיי, which is the combination of the initials of the concluding four words of the verse reading יצליח יעשה אשר וכל (*v'chol asher ya'aseh yatz'liach* —"and in whatsoever he doeth he shall prosper"). It is employed in Hebrew amulets for the purpose of winning favour.[26]

Whilst the first Psalm is perhaps not reckoned amongst the most popular in the biblical "*Book of Psalms,*" the third verse of the Psalm, reading "And he shall be like a tree planted by streams of water, that bringeth forth its fruit in its season, and whose leaf doth not wither; and in whatsoever he doeth he shall prosper," is employed for other important and quite relevant magical purposes, i.e. it is recited "with planting seeds or nurturing plants"[27] and "against trees shedding their fruit."[28] This specific usage appears to have been derived from the association of *Psalm 1* with *Tu B'Shevat* (New Year for Trees), the "Jewish Arbor Day," and the planting of trees on that day.

I will address the Psalms associated with *Tu B'Shevat* in greater detail in the concluding chapter of the "*Book of Magical Psalms,*" suffice it to say that the whole of the first Psalm as well as the third verse, are employed for the planting and fertility of fruit trees, vines, the protection of vineyards, etc. Other than these usages, I have observed *Psalm 1* recommended to individuals who doubt their faith; for "*Torah* study"; to those who are "confused by the success of the wicked," and to those who are "envious of the rich."

As one might expect, magical usages of the biblical *Book of Psalms* are not limited to Jewish practitioners. In fact, they feature equally prominently in the magical literature of Christian authors, and those immersed in folk religions. Interestingly enough, the referenced use of the first Psalm to stop trees shedding fruit, is repeated in a manuscript comprising the magical use of the Psalms penned by a Christian Arab in Egypt, with an additional benefit pertaining to breaking malefic spells. In this regard, we are informed that "This (Psalm) can also be written for the tree which drops its fruit," and "the noble verses and the blessed names which are in them should also be entrusted with the protection of the tree or the vine against dropping their fruit."[29] In this instance, the magical procedure necessitates the current Psalm to be recited seven times over water, an act which is said to have an added benefit, i.e. if a bewitched individual washes his or her face in this water over a three day period, "it will break the bewitchment."[30]

In terms of the "vineyards" reference, and pertaining to a claim that "an analogical relationship generally pertains between the situation of use, or the desired outcome, and the content of the Psalm," we are informed that "the earliest evidence comes from the sixth-century medical author Aetius of Amida, who recommends *Psalm 1:3* in two different applications to protect crops from pests."[31] This verse is also listed in the Byzantine *Geoponika* for the purpose of preventing trees from dropping their fruit. In this regard it is said the fruit will be retained if you write the verse, which is afterwards tied to the tree "in a proper manner," whatever that may be.[32] The same verse is included in "the tradition of veterinary medicine, where it is recommended for inscription on the hoof of a barren mare in the Leiden *hippiatrikon*."[33]

It should be noted that many of the cross-cultural magical uses of the biblical Psalms do not align with the material shared in the "*Shimmush Tehillim*," whilst others do align. In this regard, consider *Psalm 1* as a case in point. The first three verses of this Psalm are recommended for exactly the same purpose as listed in the mentioned Jewish magical text, i.e. protection against miscarriage, in *"Le Livre d'Or, touchant les vertus et les caracteres des Pseaumes du Prophête David"* authored by a Christian hand.[34] However, in the latter instance the instructions comprise writing the first three verses of *Psalm 1*, ensuring to conclude with the phrase "and whose leaf doth not wither" (verse 3), and equally including a set of magical seals which do not feature in the original Hebrew *"Shimmush Tehillim."*

There is further instruction in the Christian text regarding the written verses and seals being fumigated with mastic.[35] However, these are not the only differences between the Jewish and Christian versions of the magical use of *Psalm 1*. There are astrological indicators included in *"Le Livre d'Or,"* the Hebrew Divine Names are corrupt, and the accompanying prayer is entirely different, and seemingly unrelated to the primary magical use of this Psalm, i.e. protection against a difficult confinement, premature delivery, and miscarriage, and the amulet is affixed to the right arm rather than worn as a pendant as per the Hebrew text.[36]

In the earlier mentioned Christian Arab manuscript, we find a related application of *Psalm 1* with a very different set of Divine Names. In this regard, we are informed that the statement in verse 3 reading "And he shall be like a tree planted by streams of water, that bringeth forth its fruit in its season," references "childbirth in the proper time."[37]

PSALM 2

[1] למה רגשו גוים ולאמים יהגו ריק

[2] יתיצבו מלכי ארץ ורוזנים נוסדו יחד על יהוה‎אדני‎אהדונהי ועל משיחו

[3] ננתקה את מוסרותימו ונשליכה ממנו עבתימו

[4] יושב בשמים ישחק אדני ילעג למו

[5] אז ידבר אלימו באפו ובחרונו יבהלמו

[6] ואני נסכתי מלכי על ציון הר קדשי

[7] אספרה אל חק יהוה‎אדני‎אהדונהי אמר אלי בני אתה אני היום ילדתיך

[8] שאל ממני ואתנה גוים נחלתך ואחזתך אפסי ארץ

[9] תרעם בשבט ברזל ככלי יוצר תנפצם

[10] ועתה מלכים השכילו הוסרו שפטי ארץ

[11] עבדו את יהוה‎אדני‎אהדונהי ביראה וגילו ברעדה

[12] נשקו בר פן יאנף ותאבדו דרך כי יבער כמעט אפו אשרי כל חוסי בו

Transliteration:

[1] *lamah rag'shu goyim ul'umim yeh'gu rik*

[2] *yit'yatz'vu mal'chei eretz v'roz'nim nos'du yachad al YHVH v'al m'shicho*

[3] *n'nat'kah et mos'roteimo v'nash'lichah mimenu avoteimo*

[4] *yosheiv bashamayim yis'chak adonai yil'ag lamo*

[5] *az y'dabeir eileimo v'apo uvacharono y'vahaleimo*

[6] *va'ani nasach'ti mal'ki al tziyon har kod'shi*

[7] *asap'rah el chok YHVH amar eilai b'ni atah ani hayom y'lid'ticha*

[8] *sh'al mimeni v'et'nah goyim nachalatecha va'achuzat'cha af'sei aretz*

[9] *t'ro'eim b'sheivet bar'zel kich'li yotzeir t'nap'tzeim*

[10] *v'atah m'lachim has'kilu hivas'ru shof'tei aretz*

[11] *iv'du et YHVH b'yir'ah v'gilu bir'adah*

[12] *nash'ku var pen ye'enaf v'tov'du derech ki yiv'ar kim'at apo ash'rei kol chosei vo*

Translation:

> [1] Why are the nations in an uproar? And why do the peoples mutter in vain?
>
> [2] The kings of the earth stand up, and the rulers take counsel together, against *YHVH*, and against His anointed:
>
> [3] 'Let us break their bands asunder, and cast away their cords from us.'
>
> [4] He that sitteth in heaven laugheth, *Adonai* hath them in derision.
>
> [5] Then will He speak unto them in His wrath, and affright them in His sore displeasure:
>
> [6] 'Truly it is I that have established My king upon Zion, My holy mountain.'
>
> [7] I will tell of the decree: *YHVH* said unto me: 'Thou art My son, this day have I begotten thee.
>
> [8] Ask of Me, and I will give the nations for thine inheritance, and the ends of the earth for thy possession.
>
> [9] Thou shalt break them with a rod of iron; thou shalt dash them in pieces like a potter's vessel.'
>
> [10] Now therefore, O ye kings, be wise; be admonished, ye judges of the earth.
>
> [11] Serve *YHVH* with fear, and rejoice with trembling.
>
> [12] Do homage in purity, lest He be angry, and ye perish in the way, when suddenly His wrath is kindled. Happy are all they that take refuge in Him

Psalm 2 is employed as a protection against storms at sea,[1] and in this regard the instructions in the "*Shimmush Tehillim*" are to simply recite the Psalm, and write it on a potsherd which is afterwards cast into the ocean, an action which is said will calm the raging waters.[2] It has been suggested that casting a potsherd into the raging waters, was inspired by "verse 9 which says 'Thou shalt break them with a rod of iron; thou shalt dash them in pieces like a potter's vessel'."[3]

For some currently obscure reason, regarding which I have personally not seen any primary manuscript sources, this procedure was expanded upon in Godfrey Selig's 1788 German, and the subsequent very verbose English, translation of the "*Shimmush Tehillim*," later incorporated in the ever popular "*The Sixth and Seventh Books of Moses*," reading:

"Should you be exposed to danger in a storm at sea, and
your life threatened, then recite this Psalm without delay
and with becoming reverence, and think respectfully of the
holiest name contained therein, namely *Shaddai*, then
immediately utter the prayer belonging thereto, after which
write everything together on a potsherd, and in full
confidence of the Omnipotent who fixes the boundary of
the sea and restrains its power, throw it into the foaming
waves, and you will see marvellous wonders, for the waves
will instantly cease their roaring and the storm will be
lulled."[4]

In this instance, it is claimed the Divine Name שׁדי (*Shadai*) is
comprised of the letters from the words רגשׁו (*rag'shu*—"agitate"
["uproar"]): verse 1; נוסדו (*nos'du*—"establish" ["take counsel"]):
verse 2; and יוצר (*yotzeir*—"potter" ["potter's vessel"]): verse 9.[5]
The mentioned prayer included in the current procedure, is equally
missing from all the primary Hebrew texts of the "*Sefer Shimmush
Tehillim*," which I have perused. It reads:

"Let it be, O Shaddai, Your holy will, that the raging of the
storm and the roaring of the waves may cease, and the
proud billows may be stilled. Lead us, oh, all-merciful
Father, to the place of our destination in safety and in good
health, for only with You is power and might. You alone
can help, and You will surely help to the honor and glory
of Your Name. Amen. *Selah*."[6]

Neither the lofty Divine Name nor the additional prayer appear to
be of importance in the procedure pertaining to "halting storms at
sea." However, it is worth noting that in the earlier mentioned
"*Shimmush Tehillim*" manuscript in the Kaufmann Collection,
there is equally no reference to the second Psalm having to be
recited prior to writing it on the potsherd.[7]

Be that as it may, we are informed that *Psalm 2* is also
employed for "health purposes," i.e. to relieve headaches.[8] In this
regard, the magical procedure is quite straightforward and
uncomplicated, requiring the first nine verses of the second Psalm

to be written up to the phrase reading "Thou shalt break them with a rod of iron," and the resultant amulet to be suspended like a pendant around the neck of the sufferer.[9]

The procedure in Selig's version of the "*Shimmush Tehillim*," necessitates writing "the first eight verses of this Psalm together with the Holy Name and appropriate prayer, upon a pure parchment, and hang it upon the neck of the patient; then pray over him the Psalm with the prayer arranged for it. Do this in humble devotion, and the sufferer will be relieved."[10] Whilst there is in this instance no indication as to what "the Holy Name and appropriate prayer" might be, there are two versions of the current use of the second Psalm in the "*Shimmush Tehillim*," both of which include a "Divine Name of the Psalm" conjoined with a related prayer-incantation.[11]

In the first instance, the instruction is to write the Psalm, suspend it around the neck of the sufferer, and to recite the following incantation which includes the Divine Name אִילָה, vocalised *Ilah*.[12] I have corrected the opening three words of the incantation reading:

יהי רצון מלפניך יהוה מלך רחמן רחמנא וחננא
יהוה שתרחם ותחנן על [....name of recipient....]
ותקל מחליו וירפא בשם **אילה** יהיה רפואה
שלימה לי'[....name of recipient....] **אמן** סלה סלה
סלה

Transliteration:

> *Y'hi ratzon mil'fanecha YHVH melech rach'man rach'mana v'chan'na YHVH shet'racheim v'tachanun al [....name of recipient....] v'takeil meichol'yo virapei b'sheim Ilah yiyeh r'fu'ah sh'leimah l'[....name of recipient....] omein selah selah selah!*

Translation:

> May it be your will *YHVH*, Merciful King, Compassionate and full of Grace, *YHVH*, that you have mercy and be gracious unto [....name of recipient....], and that you alleviate his illness, and he be cured in the name *Ilah*, and that it be complete healing for [....name of recipient....]. *Amen Selah Selah Selah!*

The mentioned second version, shared by Bill Rebiger in the Hebrew section of his superb "*Sefer Shimmush Tehillim*," appears to include the same Divine name minus the letter ' (*Yod*), i.e. אלה, which I presumed is equally vocalised "*Ilah*." In the current instance, the three component glyphs of the Divine Name construct are indicated to have been derived from: א (*Alef*) from אספרה (*asap'ra*—"let me recount" ["I will tell of"]): verse 7; ל (*Lamed*) from למה רגשו (*lamah rag'shu*—"why uproar"): verse 1; and ה (*Heh*) from the letter נ (*Nun*), the capital of נשקו בר (*nash'ku var*—"do homage" [literally "kiss the son"]): verse 12, the latter glyph having been converted by means of the א״ק בכ״ר (*Ayak Bachar*) cipher.[13] Be that as it may, the mentioned prayer-incantation reads:

יהי רצון מלפניך **אלה** רחמנא וחניא שתחון ותרחם
על זה [recipient] מכל חלי וחשישות שיש לו בראשו
מעתה ועד עולם אמן אמן אמן סלה סלה סלה

Transliteration:
> *Y'hi ratzon mil'fanecha Ilah rachamana v'chanaya shetachon ut'racheim al zeh [...name of recipient...] mikol choli v'chashishut sheyeish lo b'rosho mei'atah v'ad olam Omein Omein Omein Selah Selah Selah*

Translation:
> May it be your will *Ilah*, the Merciful and the Gracious, that you have compassion on this [....name of recipient....] from all illness and weakness which he has in his head, from now on forever. *Amen Amen Amen! Selah Selah Selah!*

There are further magical applications of single verses of the second Psalm. In this regard, *Psalm 2:5* is employed for the purpose of seeking revenge. In this instance the twenty-eight letters comprising the verse are arranged into an eight tri-letter and one four-letter Divine Name construct by combining the letters in a "straight, reverse and skipping fashion."[14] This simply means that the first set of fourteen glyphs are written in the standard fashion from right to left (אזידבראל ימובאפ), whilst the second set is written in reverse (ומל הביונורחבוו). The two sets of Hebrew glyphs are then combined, meaning the first letter of the verse is succeeded by the last; the second by the second to last; etc., finally resulting in the following Divine Name construct:[15]

אוז מיל דהב ברי

אול ניו מרו חבב אופו

Once again I have observed *Psalm 2* being employed for purposes other than those addressed thus far. In this regard, I noted the second Psalm being recited to "counteract life-threatening danger from water," which obviously stems from it being employed to calm storms at sea; for pains in the throat; for "meetings" or "councils," the latter presumably pertaining to making the right decisions; against tyranny, and to halt war. As in the case of the first Psalm, I have also seen the current Psalm recommended for those who doubt their faith.

Certain elements pertaining to the magical use of the second Psalm in Jewish sources, have found their way into the Christian magical literature, but in somewhat odd ways. In this regard, the earlier mentioned Egyptian manuscript written by a Christian Arab, having the "potsherds" in his mind, came up with a rather vengeful application of *Psalm 2*. Here the author maintains that "should anybody wish to destroy the earthenware of a potter, he is supposed to inscribe the first 9 verses on an unbaked pot which, exposed to the sun's rays, had cracked. If this pot is put into the baking oven with the other vessels, it will cause them to break into pieces."[16]

I am not sure what it is with breaking pottery in Christian magical literature dealing with the second Psalm, but a variant on the same theme appears in the earlier addressed *"Le Livre d'Or."* In this text we are informed that "if you wish to break an earthenware vessel, write this Psalm on a new tile" up to the concluding phrase of verse 9, i.e. "thou shalt dash them in pieces like a potter's vessel, after which you are to cast it onto the piece of earthenware you seek to smash." The instruction concludes with "you will be surprised at what will happen."[17] There is certainly no doubt what will happen if a tile strikes pottery.

Further instructions in "*Le Livre d'Or*" equally list the second Psalm as good for healing purposes, but of quite a different kind to the details shared in the Jewish "*Shimmush Tehillim.*" In this regard, we are told that any individual feeling "discomposed through gastronomic repletion," i.e. suffering the after-effects of gluttony, should read *Psalm 2:1–7* over pure oil. Following this action, the indisposed individual is anointed with the oil, which is said will work the cure.[18] It would seem that whilst the Jews were concerned here with pain in their heads, Christians were having to deal with gastric issues resulting from overeating!

Jokes aside, additional details maintain that if you write a specified set of magical characters "on a new tablet, wash them with the aforementioned oil and anoint your face with it," you will be welcomed by a Prince.[19] Elsewhere it is said that it is *Psalm 2:7–8* which is employed for the purpose of being "well received by Princes, Lords and others."[20]

In conclusion, and for the sake of completeness, it should be noted that the *Book of Psalms* features most prominently amongst the biblical texts employed and quoted in the so-called "Solomonic" magical systems, of which the "*Key of Solomon*" is the prime example. In this regard, *Psalm 2* is recited in conjunction with *Psalms 67* and *54* on entering the space in which a magical procedure is to be worked,[21] and likewise it is the first in a set of six Psalms recited either before or during the creation of the "magic circle," the others being *Psalms 47, 54, 67, 68* and *113*.[22]

PSALM 3

[1] מזמור לדוד בברחו מפני אבשלום בנו

[2] יהוה‏ּאדני‏ּיאהדונהי מה רבו צרי רבים קמים עלי

[3] רבים אמרים לנפשי אין ישועתה לו באלהים
סלה

[4] ואתה יהוה‏ּאדני‏ּיאהדונהי מגן בעדי כבודי ומרים
ראשי

[5] קולי אל יהוה‏ּאדני‏ּיאהדונהי אקרא ויענני מהר
קדשו סלה

[6] אני שכבתי ואישנה הקיצותי כי יהוה‏ּאדני‏ּיאהדונהי
יסמכני

[7] לא אירא מרבבות עם אשר סביב שתו עלי

[8] קומה יהוה‏ּאדני‏ּיאהדונהי הושיעני אלהי כי הכית
את כל איבי לחי שני רשעים שברת

[9] ליהוה‏ּאדני‏ּיאהדונהי הישועה על עמך ברכתך סלה

Transliteration:

[1] *miz'mor l'david b'vor'cho mip'nei av'shalom b'no*

[2] *YHVH mah rabu tzarai rabim kamim alai*

[3] *rabim om'rim l'naf'shi ein y'shu'atah lo veilohim selah*

[4] *v'atah YHVH magein ba'adi k'vodi umeirim roshi*

[5] *koli el YHVH ek'ra vaya'aneini meihar kod'sho selah*

[6] *ani shachav'ti va'ishanah hekitzoti ki YHVH yis'm'cheini*

[7] *lo irah meiriv'vot am asher saviv shatu alai*

[8] *kumah YHVH hoshi'eini elohai ki hikita et kol oy'vai lechi shinei r'sha'im shibar'ta*

[9] *laYHVH ha'y'shu'ah al am'cha vir'chatecha selah*

Translation:

[1] A Psalm of David, when he fled from Absalom his son.

[2] *YHVH*, how many are mine adversaries become! Many are they that rise up against me.

[3] Many there are that say of my soul: 'There is no salvation for him in God.' *Selah*

[4] But thou *YHVH*, art a shield about me; my glory, and the lifter up of my head.

[5] With my voice I call unto *YHVH*, and He answereth me out of His holy mountain. *Selah*

[6] I lay me down, and I sleep; I awake, for *YHVH* sustaineth me.

[7] I am not afraid of ten thousands of people, that have set themselves against me round about.

[8] Arise *YHVH*; save me, O my God; for Thou hast smitten all mine enemies upon the cheek, Thou hast broken the teeth of the wicked.

[9] Salvation belongeth unto *YHVH*; Thy blessing be upon Thy people. *Selah*

Psalm 3, from the second verse to its conclusion, is amongst the set of biblical verses which were included for Divine protection in the קְרִיאַת שמע על המיתה (*K'ri'at Shema al Hamitah*—"reciting the *Shema* at bedtime" [Bedtime Prayer]),[1] In terms of its magical use, the third Psalm is mainly employed for healing purposes.[2] As in the case of *Psalm 2*, the third Psalm is utilised to counteract headaches,[3] as well as to relieve pain in the shoulders.[4] In this regard, the instructions in the "*Shimmush Tehillim*" are to recite *Psalm 3* over olive oil, to add a little salt, and then to rub the substance over the afflicted bodily zone, i.e. the forehead or shoulders. One recension suggests the Psalm should be recited three times over the olive oil/salt mix.[5]

There are a number of variations to be found in the primary recensions, and I certainly cannot share all of them here. The techniques I include in the current tome are those which are easily executed by anyone reading this work. In this regard, it is worth noting that some uses of the third Psalm in the said recensions of the "*Shimmush Tehillim*," include a Divine Name construct and a prayer-incantation. In one instance, a manuscript maintained the third Psalm should be written and suspended around the neck of the sufferer. This action is then followed by the recitation of a prayer-incantation which includes a Divine Name construct.[6]

Curiously enough, a similar version is found in Godfrey Selig's German and its subsequent English translation of the *Shimmush Tehillim*.[7] In the latter instance, besides headaches, the third Psalm is employed to alleviate backache. The instructions further include a related Divine Name and prayer-incantation which I have not seen in any of the recensions I have perused. Be that as it may, Selig's offering is shared below, with some corrections of the listed Hebrew terms as well as of the numbering of the verses, the latter in accordance with the Hebrew Bible which I am employing in this book:

> "Whosoever is subject to severe headache and backache, let him pray this Psalm, with the leading holy names and appropriate prayer contained therein, over a small quantity of olive oil, anoint the head or back while in the act of prayer. This will afford immediate relief. The holy name is אדון (*adon*—"Lord"), and is found in the words, ואתה (*v'atah*—"and you") verse 4; בעדי (*ba'adi*—"for me"), verse 4; הקיצותי (*hekitzoti*—"I awoke") verse 6; and הושיעני (*hoshi'eini*—"save me") verse 8."[8]

The accompanying prayer reads:

> "*Adon* (Lord) of the world may it please thee to be my physician and helper. Heal me and relieve me from my severe headache and backache, because I can find help only with Thee, and only with Thee is counsel and action to be found, *amen! selah selah!*"[9]

The Divine Name אדון (*Adon*) is a standard Hebrew word meaning "sir," "master," "lord," or plain "mister," and does not derive specifically from the listed Hebrew terms in the said verses of *Psalm 3*. It seems to me more likely that the four letters comprising the "Divine Name," were turned into an anagram (*notarikon*) of the listed four words.

I believe we should briefly consider the significance of oil as a magical substance. As we have seen, in the current Psalm the intention is to pronounce the Psalm over olive oil and then to anoint the afflicted bodily part. Readers may well wonder why olive oil is used, and what makes anointing so important. The value of the olive in biblical times can be seen by the fact that it is one of seven unique products in ancient days, the consumption of which was followed by special blessings.[10] Also, the biblical saga of the flood describes how an olive branch was the first thing to be revealed after the deluge, and that this branch was retrieved by a dove which Noah dispatched from the ark.[11] To this day an olive branch universally symbolizes the return to the state of peace which preceded conditions of upheaval and conflict.[12]

Oil is the "life" of the olive, the substance used in the custom of anointing and consecrating the sacred vessels, furniture and altar of the Temple—including the pillars;[13] the anointing of individuals in need of healing, or of warriors going into battle; and the anointing and consecration of the ancient prophets, kings and priests (*Exodus 28:41; 30:26, 30; 40:9—15; 1 Samuel 9:16, 15:1; 1 Kings 1:34*; etc.).[14]

In Hebrew the word for "anoint" is מָשַׁח (*Mashach*), a term found also in Akkadian, Ugaritic, Aramaic and Arabic.[15] The basic meaning of "*Mashach*" is to smear, wipe, stroke or daub a surface, and equally to anoint with oil.[16] This is the root-word of the "*Mashiach*" meaning "anointed," which is usually translated "Messiah" in English.[17] In this regard, it is worth noting that in Judaism the "Messiah" is not a deity of any sort, and, whilst *the Messiah* references a unique human being, the fact is, as Rabbi Stuart Federow indicated, that "to anoint something is to pour oil over it on behalf of God, thus ritually dedicating it to a specific purpose or task in the world. Hence, anything anointed is *a messiah.*"[18] He further noted that "in the Bible, many things and many people are anointed," and that the anointing of Aaron and his fellow priests, meant that each of them became a messiah, and an anointed one.[19]

As it is, anointing whilst uttering an incantation, prayer, or a blessing, is a very ancient custom in the sacred traditions of many nations.[20] One might say that anointing an individual with the sacred oil, establishes a "seal of sanctity" through which that person is sympathetically, magically or mystically linked with the bounty, well-being and peace of the Eternal Living Spirit. In other words, the act of anointing a sufferer with consecrated oil, can be viewed as establishing a "Divine Channel" which links that individual with *B'reichah*, a vast spiritual resource of *Shefa* ("Abundance"), the Divine Influx.[21]

It should be further noted that anointing individuals with oil was considered to be part of a purification process. Thus, in the case of someone recovering from leprosy for example, the patient was "*kippered*" or "purified" by having oil poured over the head while incantations were uttered over the afflicted limbs.[22] However, "oil magic" was not used only for healing purposes, but for a great variety of purposes.[23] Other practices, such as a magical attempt to gain favour (the subject of *Psalm 5*), also required the practitioner to pronounce certain Psalms over oil, which was afterwards used to anoint the hands and face. In another instance, oil and *Psalm 10* are used to free an individual from demonic possession, etc.

I have personally employed *Psalm 3* for the very purpose of relieving the physical condition this Psalm is claimed to impact on, i.e. headaches, and each time the pain was relieved speedily. I have been told by my more skeptical acquaintances that this result is psychosomatic. However, in my estimation, which is entirely in harmony with the way I was instructed in the practical procedures of this great Tradition, the language of a Psalm or incantation being "Divine," aligns the practitioner of these techniques with powerful "Spiritual Forces," the "Divine Hosts" residing in the subtle realms of being, as it were, behind the words. I have also found that if you surrender yourself, i.e. open yourself, to these "Subtle Forces" during any invocation, incantation, or prayer, i.e. letting your entire being, your body, mind, soul and spirit, act in concord as a conduit for these powers, the associated "Spirit Forces" will easily flow through your body into manifestation. In other words, you literally "make the word flesh" through your very own being.

One of the most interesting and beneficial uses for healing purposes is the employment of *Psalm 3:9* in conjunction with *Leviticus 5:19*, reading אשם הוא אשם אשם ליהוה (*asham hu ashom asham la'YHVH*—"It is a guilt-offering—he is certainly guilty before *YHVH*"), for the purposes of restoring the health of one who suffers from tuberculosis. In this regard, the initials of the letters comprising the first two words of the said verse from *Leviticus* are intertwined to create the Divine Name construct אהשומא, to which is added permutations of the word אשם (*asham*), i.e. מאש משא. The full Divine Name construct reads:

אהשומא אמש מאש

The magical procedure necessitates this Divine Name construct to be read in conjunction with the said verse from the current Psalm. This is recited three times over a glass of water, which the one seeking healing from the mentioned affliction should consume afterwards. The complete incantation reads:

אהשומא אמש מאש ליהוה הישועה על עמך ברכתך
סלה

I heard the above construct vocalised "*Ah'shom'a omash ma'ash la'YHVH ha-y'shu'ah al am'cha vir'chatecha selah.*"

I chanced upon this procedure some fifty years ago, when an Israeli friend of mine recommended it to an individual who was suffering from severe asthma, and who claimed that her medical condition was cured by this technique. Three decades later I found the same procedure listed in a primary Hebrew text,[24] and following the coronavirus outbreak, I recommended this very magical procedure to a friend who is also suffering serious asthma, and who felt that this condition left her vulnerable to the said virus.

It is worth noting that illness and pain are often equated with demonic attack in medieval magical literature, and in this regard *Psalm 3* and *Psalm 91*, known as "the Song of Injuries or the Song of Afflictions," are considered potent "anti-demonic" Psalms.[25] Regarding the anti-demonic properties of these Psalms we are informed in the *Talmud* that a certain "Rabbi Yehoshua ben Levi would recite these verses to protect him from evil spirits during the night and fall asleep while saying them" [*TB Shevuot 15b:10*]. Ultimately these two anti-demonic Psalms were included in the *Kri'at Sh'ma al ha-Mitah* (Bedtime Prayer), for the purposes of spiritual protection, and are read in the order *Psalm 91* first, which is followed by *Psalm 3* from verse 2–9.[26]

It should be noted that individual verses from the third Psalm feature equally prominently in "Practical Kabbalah." In this regard, *Psalm 3:4* is directly affiliated with והו (*Vehu*), the first portion, and *Psalm 3:6* with אכא (*Acha*), the seventh portion of the "*Shem Vayisa Vayet*," i.e. "*Name of Seventy-two Names.*"[27]

However, in terms of the magical application of the biblical Psalms, not only single verses are put to magical use. Words from selected verses are equally employed for special purposes. In this regard, the three letters from the word מָגֵן (*magein*—"shield") in *Psalm 3:4*, are transposed by means of the א"ת ב"ש (*Atbash*) cipher to create the following unique Divine Name construct, which is meant to be employed as a protective shield against any kind of enemy:

$$\text{יִרָֽט}$$

This Divine Name construct is vocalised "*Yirata.*" In this regard, the opening vowels of the three words reading כִּי יָרַט הַדֶּרֶךְ (*ki yarat ha'derech*—"because your way is contrary") [*Numbers 22:32*], are respectively aligned with the three letters of this Divine Name construct,[28] which is meant to banish, distance, or shield you from any foe.

It is worth noting that the third Psalm has equally been recommended for a variety of purposes which are not specifically mentioned in, as it were, "the books." In this regard, the Psalm is recited to relieve toothache, which is part of the three debilitating conditions which can make your day most miserable, i.e. headache, toothache and backache. Otherwise this Psalm is also recited as a protection from harm, i.e. as a spiritual protection, to relieve the anxiety an individual may suffer because of enemies, as well as against torment and despair.

Regarding protection against "foes," *Psalm 3:6–7* was also referenced in Christian magical literature in terms of resisting "domestic enemies."[29] As far as further Christian applications of the third Psalm are concerned, the Arabic manuscript in the earlier mentioned Kaufmann Collection, equally extols the virtue of the Psalm against headaches, but maintains it should be recited over rose oil.[30] It is likewise employed for the same purpose in "*Le Livre d'Or*," i.e. to alleviate headaches.[31] However, in the latter instance the instructions pertain to writing *Psalm 3:1–4* in conjunction with a set of magical characters. It equally incorporates a prayer, but without any reference to oil with which to anoint the sufferer, and the amulet is thereafter tied to the head of the afflicted individual.[32]

Interestingly enough, in another Christian manuscript on the magical use of Psalms, one of Byzantine origin, the third Psalm is recommended for "sickness of the body and head."[33] In this regard, the instructions are again to prepare an amulet comprising the first four verses of the Psalm, to which is also added a set of magical characters. The amulet is afterwards bound to the forehead of the afflicted individual.[34] Alternative instructions in the same manuscript, which align more with those to be found in the *Shimmush Tehillim*, require *Psalm 3* to be read "in its entirety over pure oil," and for the magical characters to be written "on an unused tablet," following which the writing is dissolved in floral oil with which the afflicted individual is to be anointed.[35]

That is yet not the end of the instructions regarding the use of the third Psalm in magical healing. The said Byzantine manuscript lists a further application of *Psalm 3* for the purpose of curing sickness in general. In this regard, it instructs readers to write a combination of magical characters "on a newly made vessel and dissolve it with pure water and repeat this Psalm seven times each day, seven times, and put it (out) to catch the stars through the seven days, with the sick man also observing an Easter fast, and observe the seven days. Wash the sick man with that water, and he will get well."[36] The translator of this manuscript noted that the action of placing the vessel outside "to catch the stars," pertains to receiving "the emanations supposed to issue from celestial bodies, imbuing the liquid with further medicinal power."[37]

Be that as it may, in one Byzantine Christian manuscript we are informed that the third Psalm is employed "for confession."[38] In this regard, I presume that the one requiring someone to confess, would recite *Psalm 3* whilst focussing on a specific individual, or perhaps on an unfortunate situation in which someone is required to own up. Considering the "confession" claim, it is worth keeping in mind that the entire *Psalm 3* was also employed in the Roman Catholic Liturgy to exorcise demons.[39] The "confession" and Roman Catholic reference remind me of a further use of the third Psalm which is "to receive goodwill and favours from someone."[40] Here the relevant instructions are of the more, as it were, voodoo-like variety. It necessitates getting a "virgin child" of either sex to inscribe the Christian "Lord's Prayer" and *Psalm 3* on a sheet of paper on a "Wednesday at the New Moon." This is to be done with a quill plucked from the left wing of a swallow and employing a substance comprising a mixture of rosewater and saffron.

On completion, the paper is folded and placed on an infant about to receive baptism, following which the paper is retrieved and stored for later use. It is claimed the individual whose "favours" you may have lost, need only be touched by this paper, and that person "will be forced to condescend to your wish," even against his or her personal will.[41]

Mention should again be made of the fact that *Psalm 3* is also one of the Psalms which features in the "*Key of Solomon.*" In this regard, the third Psalm is amongst the set of Psalms recited during the manufacturing of the "needle and other iron instruments." The others in the set are *Psalms 8, 30, 41, 59, 50,* and *129.*[42] Curiously enough, elsewhere the third Psalm features in the construction of a "Heptacle," an amuletic device in gold, silver or wax, on which we are told "you need to engrave verses from Scripture, appropriate for the result you are aiming to achieve, along with the Names of God and the Names of the Angels necessary to get results."[43] The ritual to consecrate the item in question, which is worked on a day governed by a planetary force directly aligned with the purpose for which the said object was created, incorporates, amongst others, a "blessing prayer" comprised of *Psalm 3:2–9,* as well as of an adapted version of *Psalm 134.*[44] In conclusion it should be noted that *Psalm 3:4* is associated in one of the versions of the "*Goetia*" with the first of the "*72 Spirits of the Goetia.*"[45]

PSALM 4

[1] למנצח בנגינות מזמור לדוד

[2] בקראי ענני אלהי צדקי בצר הרחבת לי חנני
ושמע תפלתי

[3] בני איש עד מה כבודי לכלמה תאהבון ריק
תבקשו כזב סלה

[4] ודעו כי הפלה יהוה‍אדני‍יאהדונהי חסיד לו
יהוה‍אדני‍יאהדונהי ישמע בקראי אליו

[5] רגזו ואל תחטאו אמרו בלבבכם על משכבכם
ודמו סלה

[6] זבחו זבחי צדק ובטחו אל יהוה‍אדני‍יאהדונהי

[7] רבים אמרים מי יראנו טוב נסה עלינו אור פניך
יהוה‍אדני‍יאהדונהי

[8] נתתה שמחה בלבי מעת דגנם ותירושם רבו

[9] בשלום יחדו אשכבה ואישן כי אתה יהוה‍אדני‍יאהדונהי
לבדד לבטח תושיבני

Transliteration:

[1] *lam'natzei'ach bin'ginot miz'mor l'david*

[2] *b'kor'i aneini elohei tzid'ki batzar hir'chav'ta li choneini ush'ma t'filati*

[3] *b'nei ish ad meh ch'vodi lich'limah t'ehavun rik t'vak'shu chazav selah*

[4] *ud'u ki hif'lah YHVH chasid lo YHVH yish'ma b'kor'i eilav*

[5] *rig'zu v'al techeta'u im'ru vil'vav'chem al mish'kav'chem v'domu selah*

[6] *ziv'chu ziv'chei tzedek uvit'chu el YHVH*

[7] *rabim om'rim mi yar'einu tov n'sa aleinu or panecha YHVH*

[8] *natatah sim'chah v'libi mei'eit d'ganam v'tirosham rabu*

[9] *b'shalom yach'dav esh'k'vah v'ishan ki atah YHVH l'vadad lavetach toshiveini*

Translation:

[1] For the Leader; with string-music. A Psalm of David.

[2] Answer me when I call, O God of my righteousness, Thou who didst set me free when I was in distress; be gracious unto me, and hear my prayer.

[3] O ye sons of men, how long shall my glory be put to shame, in that ye love vanity, and seek after falsehood? *Selah*

[4] But know that *YHVH* hath set apart the godly man as His own; *YHVH* will hear when I call unto Him.

[5] Tremble, and sin not; commune with your own heart upon your bed, and be still. *Selah*

[6] Offer the sacrifices of righteousness, and put your trust in *YHVH*.

[7] Many there are that say: 'Oh that we could see some good!' *YHVH*, lift Thou up the light of Thy countenance upon us.

[8] Thou hast put gladness in my heart, more than when their corn and their wine increase.

[9] In peace will I both lay me down and sleep; for Thou, *YHVH*, makest me dwell alone in safety.

Whilst *Psalm 4* does not feature in the Jewish liturgy, the fifth verse is referenced in the *Talmud* in terms of the earlier mentioned *Kri'at Sh'ma al ha-Mitah* (Bedtime Prayer). In this regard, it is written that "Rabbi Joshua ben Levi says: Though a man has recited the *Shema'* in the synagogue, it is a religious act to recite it again upon his bed. Rabbi Assi says: Which verse [may be cited in support]? Tremble and sin not; commune with your own heart upon your bed, and be still, *Selah*." [*TB Berachot 4b*] However, the said verse was not incorporated into the "Bedtime Prayer," but in "Practical Kabbalah" (Jewish Magic) the whole of the fourth Psalm is said to be good for every need, i.e. any purpose whatsoever.[1] We are informed in the "*Shimmush Tehillim*" that, for general success, the fourth Psalm should be recited three times every morning,[2] prior to sunrise according to Godfrey Selig.[3] In the case of one having to conclude a business transaction, one should do this recitation in conjunction with a prayer-incantation comprising the Divine Name יה יה, following which one may pay a visit to those with whom one intends to do business, with success guaranteed.

The Divine Name construct, vocalised *"Yah Yah,"* is said to have been derived: ' (*Yod*) from תפלתי (*t'filati*—"my prayer"): verse 2; ה (*Heh*) from ודמו סלה (*v'domu selah*—"and be still Selah"): verse 5; ' (*Yod*) from לבטח תושיבני (*lavetach toshiveini* —"make me dwell in safety"): verse 9; and the concluding ה (*Heh*) from יהוה (*YHVH*): verse 6,[4] the selected glyphs being the concluding letters of the relevant words. Godfrey Selig's translation maintains the said Divine Name construct to be *"Jiheyeh* (He is and will be)."[5]

Whilst I have not seen any specific reference in the manuscript material which I have consulted, to the fourth Psalm having to be recited before sunrise, I have noted, in terms of the current use, an instruction that the Divine Name construct accompanying this Psalm should be recited before sunset. In this regard, it is said the relevant Divine Name construct should be enunciated three times before the sun goes down.[6]

As difficult as it often is to ascertain why certain biblical verses are selected for the magical purposes they are purported to influence beneficially, in the current instance the reason why *Psalm 4* is used for finding favour appears abundantly clear. The associated prayer reads:

יהי רצון מלפניך יה יה השם הגדל הגבור והנורא
שתצליח את דרכי וחישר ארחותי ותמלא משאלותי
לטובה ותעשה חפצי היום הזה אמן אמן אמן סלה
סלה סלה

Transliteration:

> *Y'hi ratzon mil'fanecha YaH YaH hashem hagadol hagibor v'hanora shetatz'li'ach et d'rachai uch'yasheir ar'chotai ut'malei mish'alotai l'tovah v'ta'aseh chef'tzi hayom hazeh Omein Omein Omein Selah Selah Selah*

Translation:

> May it be your will *YaH YaH*, the great, strong and awesome Name, for me to have success on my way, for my path to be straightened, and for my wishes for good to be fulfilled, and to grant my desire this day. *Amen Amen Amen! Selah Selah Selah!*

The fourth Psalm is equally recommended in the *Sefer Rafael ha-Malach* for the purpose of having a personal desire successfully granted by anyone,[7] whilst another prayer-incantation aligned with this Psalm, is employed for the purpose of undertaking a successful journey away from the city.[8] In the current instance the relevant Divine Name is expanded into a larger Divine Name construct, reading: יה יה הגדו הג והנ. It is said the additional three "Names" are abbreviations of three of the standard terms regularly employed in Hebrew incantations, i.e. הגדל הגבור והנורא (*ha'gadol ha'gibor v'ha'nora*—"the great, the strong, and the awesome").[9] In this regard, my personal opinion is that these abbreviations should not be read as a Divine Name, but rather enunciated in full in conjunction with the Divine Name construct of this Psalm. However, those who feel otherwise, could enunciate the complete construct "*YaH YaH Hagado Hag V'han.*"

As far as the associated procedure is concerned, the journeyman is instructed prior to leaving the city, to recite the fourth Psalm as well as the following prayer-incantation:[10]

יהי רצון מלפניך יהוה אלהי יה יה הגדול הגבור
והנורא השם הנורא והאדיר והאמיץ והחזק שתישר
אורחותי ותצליח אורחותי ודרכי אשר תאוה נפשי
ללכת בה לטות לי אני [....personal name....] שתעשה
חפצי בשם יה יה הגדול הגבור והנורא

Transliteration:

Y'hi ratzon mil'fanecha YHVH Elohai Yah Yah Hagadol Hagibor v'Hanora ha'sheim hanora v'ha'adir v'ha'amitz v'ha'chazak sheteyashar or'chotai v'tatz'liach or'chotai v'd'rachai asher t'avah naf'shi lalechet bah litot li ani [.....personal name....] sheta'aseh chef'tzi b'sheim Yah Yah Hagadol Hagibor v'Hanora.

Translation:

May it be your will *YHVH* my God, *Yah Yah Hagadol Hagibor v'Hanora*, the awesome, mighty, bold and powerful Name, that you straighten my ways [paths], and that my ways and my path, on which my soul desires to travel, will succeed for the good, me [.....personal name....]

for whom you fulfill my desire in the Name *Yah Yah Hagadol Hagibor v'Hanora.*

In terms of further instructions on the magical uses of *Psalm 4*, we are told that if you seek something from a different individual, that you should recite the Psalm as well as the following prayer:[11]

יהי רצון מלפניך יה יה השם הגדל הגבור והנורא
שתתנני לחן ולחסד ולרחמים בעיני [recipient] ותמלא
משאלותי היום הזה

Transliteration:

> *Y'hi ratzon mil'fanecha Yah Yah hasheim hagadol hagibor v'hanora shetit'neini l'chein ul'chesed ul'rachamim b'einei [....name of recipient....] ut'malei mish'alotai hayom hazeh.*

Translation:

> May it be your will *Yah Yah*, the great, strong and awesome Name, to grant me grace, kindness and compassion in the eyes of [....name of recipient....], and to fulfill my plea this day.

Amongst the easier applications of *Psalm 4* is one pertaining to requesting something from a ruler or other authorities.[12] In this regard, the instruction is to simply recite the Psalm seven times with its associated Divine Name construct, which is said will make you successful. This procedure is somewhat different from the details shared in Godfrey Selig's German/English translation, reading "if you have a cause to bring before high magistrates or princes, you must pray this Psalm and the closing prayer arranged for it, seven times in succession before the rising of the sun."[13]

In terms of the Jewish magical uses made of single verses of the fourth Psalm, it is worth considering the "amuletic" application of *Psalm 4:2* for the purpose of *She'elat Chalom* ("Dream Questioning"). As noted elsewhere, this is one of the "simpler procedures in the 'magical pantry' of Practical Kabbalah to get answers in dreams."[14] The procedure requires the practitioner to write the following word square, which is formed from the said biblical verse, on a piece of parchment or a sheet of clean white paper:

ללש	עהו	בקי
הית	נרע	קים
יחת	נחל	רבפ
צנה	יבי	אצי
דנה	אתה	ירו

The words of *Psalm 4:2* are entered into the word square in the following manner. Commence with locating the letters on the right side in the rightmost column, starting at the top and writing them downwards. Repeat the process with the rightmost letters in the centre and left columns. Continue by writing the middle letters in the right, centre and left columns in exactly the same manner. Next inscribe the remaining letters, which include those comprising the Ineffable Name, writing them horizontally as the third letters of the three blocks in each row, and concluding with an additional letter ה (*Heh*) in the left block of the bottom row. The entire phrase reads:

בקראי עניני אלהי צדקי בצר הרחבת לי חנני ושמע
תפלתי יהוה ה

Transliteration:

> *B'kor'i aneini Elohei tzid'ki batzar hir'chav'ta li choneini ush'ma t'filati YHVH H*

Translation:

> Answer me when I call, God of my righteousness, Thou who didst set me free when I was in distress; be gracious unto me, and hear my prayer *YHVH H*

After completion, the amulet is placed beneath your pillow, i.e. under your head, when you retire to sleep.[15] Personally speaking, suffice it to say that this technique works very well for me.

Be that as it may, the following Divine Name construct formed from *Psalm 4:4* is said to be good for voicing a prayer,[16] or, as I have found, vocalising it greatly increases the intensity and potency of the prayer.

וַודִי עַלְוָא כִּיַיָא הָרְפַק לְכַהי הָעִיָה
מִיחוּשׁ יהוה וַהַס הוֹהֵי יְהוֹהַד לְוַוּלִי

Transliteration:

> *Vav'dai al'va k'yaya har'fak l'chay' ha'y'ha michush*
> *YHVH vahas hohei y'hohad l'vav'li*

Ascertaining exactly how the Divine Name was constructed from the letters of the said verse is somewhat difficult. It is clear that the first ten letters, written in regular order, are intermingled with the concluding nine letters of the verse written in reverse. What transpired with the remaining letters is yet a mystery, and I am equally oblivious as to the derivation of the vowels employed in the vocalising of this Divine Name construct.

Before concluding our investigation of the magical uses of the current Psalm, we should consider the peculiar Divine Name construct דיקרנוסא (*Dikir'nosa* [also *Dikar'nosa* and *Dikeir'nosa*]), which is associated with the fourth Psalm. This important Divine Name, termed the "Name of Livelihood," is believed to be in charge of sustenance,[171] and is thus said to pertain directly to the blessings and good wishes for a prosperous New Year, hence its inclusion in some *Rosh Hashanah* liturgies.[18] It is regularly employed in Jewish Magic ("Practical Kabbalah") to encourage a good livelihood.

We are informed that this Divine Name construct was derived from the concluding phrases of two biblical verses, i.e. *Malachi 3:10* reading והריקתי לכם ברכה עד בלי די (*va'harikoti lachem b'rachah ad b'li dai*—"and pour you out a blessing, that there shall be more than sufficiency"), and from the portion of *Psalm 4:7* reading נסה עלינו אור פניך יהוה (*n'sah aleinu or panecha YHVH*—"YHVH lift Thou up the light of Thy countenance upon us").[19] The sentiments expressed in these verses are entirely in alignment with the fundamental purpose of the said Divine Name, i.e. being blessed with a good livelihood.

We are told the secret of the goodness, blessings and abundance expressed in these verses, and perforce in the

דיקרנוסא (*Dikir'nosa*) Divine Name construct, pertain directly to the Ineffable Name vowelised יְהֶוֹה (*Y'hav'ha*) in the expression in *Psalm 55:23* reading יְהֶוֹה יְהָבְךָ (*Y'hav'ha Y'hav'cha*—"burden upon *YHVH*").[20] We are also reminded that the *gematria* (numerical value) of דיקרנוסא (*Dikir'nosa*) [ד = 4 + י = 10 + ק = 100 + ר = 200 + נ = 50 + ו = 6 + ס = 60 + א = 1 = 431] is equal to that of the word מפרנס (*m'far'nes*—"breadwinner") with a *kollel*, i.e. an extra count for the word itself, [מ = 40 + פ = 80 + ר = 200 + נ = 50 + ס = 60 = 1 (*kollel*) = 431]. This is understood to confirm the affinity between דיקרנוסא (*Dikirnosa*) and פרנסה (*parnasah*— "livelihood"),[21] and it is therefore no surprise that this very important Divine Name construct should feature so prominently in Hebrew amulets and incantations for a good livelihood and financial success. I am aware of an individual who employed this Divine Name construct in conjunction with a prefix, the Divine Name חתך (*Chatach*), the latter Divine Name construct having been derived from the concluding letters of the biblical expression פותח את ידך (*Pote'ach et yadecha*—"Thou openest Thy hand") (*Psalm 145:16*), as a *hagah* (Hebrew mantra) to achieve success in a business venture.

Be that as it may, in recent years there has been some speculation around the origins of the דיקרנוסא (*Dikir'nosa*) Divine Name construct, the suggestion having been that it is a reference to "*dea carnosa*" which is purportedly the Spanish for a "portly goddess," since the term "*carnosa*" means "fleshy," i.e. fat![22] However, everybody with the least common sense knows that etymology based on a name or word having a similar sound to a word(s) in another language, is highly questionable, and that this led to many faulty assumptions over the centuries. I have to date been unsuccessful in ascertaining exactly which "goddess" was referenced "*dea carnosa*" in Spanish speaking countries, not to mention finding one who was popular to the extent that the purported "Spanish expression" was absorbed as a Divine Name into Judaism, or into "Practical Kabbalah" for that matter.

It would seem that those who are denouncing the Divine Name in question, are either oblivious or dismissive of the fact that there are variant vocalisations of the said Divine Name construct, all of which Rabbi Moses Zacutto addressed in his *"Shorshei Hashemot."*[23] Furthermore, those who insist their *Dikirnosa* = "Fat Goddess" claim is factual, have thus far offered no support, historical or otherwise, other than basing their denunciation of the said Divine Name construct on tonal similarities with Spanish words. It is fairly obvious that the issue is not about whence the Divine Name in question was derived, but rather about a serious attempt to weed Judaism of long standing, if somewhat strange sounding, Sacred Names.

As in the case of the first three Psalms, there are many magical uses of *Psalm 4* which are not listed in published sources, but which are in common use amongst many religionists. In this regard, the fourth Psalm is employed against illness in general; anxiety; insomnia; defamation (calumnies); to provide safety from fear; to protect against harm in perilous situations; to ease tribulations; to cure the depression suffered by those who have endured the heartless actions of their fellow humankind; and even against anger. The Psalm is further employed to have good fortune; for good crops; sustenance; and it is said that reciting it every day during pregnancy will ensure an easy birth. The variety of the magical applications certainly affirms the claim that *Psalm 4* is good for any purpose whatsoever.

Getting back to the magical use of the biblical *Book of Psalms*, the earlier mentioned Christian work *"Le Livre d'Or,"* maintains *Psalm 4* relieves unmentioned "afflictions," and that "he who says it in a devoted manner, will be delivered from all watery perils and from all accidents."[24] Similar to the claims in the *"Shimmush Tehillim"* pertaining to meeting with "authorities," the Christian text further states that the fourth Psalm "is also useful for obtaining the friendship of great people."[25] Additional details emphasize that this is possible when you inscribe certain magical characters on your left hand, and confidently recite the current Psalm seven times with the name of a related "Spirit Intelligence" at daybreak on a Thursday.[26] Of course, beyond having to recite the Psalm seven times for a similar purpose, none of the latter instructions feature in any primary Hebrew instructions. However, similar uses of *Psalm 4* are listed elsewhere, i.e. "to receive affection from kings and other great people."[27] In this instance, the practitioner is instructed to recite the fourth Psalm over rose oil, and then to rub his or her face three times with the oil prior to meeting with "the Squire or other Lord," from whom you will then acquire whatever you desire.[28]

We again find a reference in the earlier mentioned Byzantine Christian manuscript, which offers a two worded statement regarding the magical use of the fourth Psalm, i.e. "for unjustness."[29] Somewhat more extensive details are shared in a post-Byzantine Christian manuscript in which *Psalm 4* is recommended as a cure for insomnia. In this instance, the one requiring this service had to acquire a fragment of a tile from a church, and then to write a spell on it with a "holy spear." The fourth Psalm, as well as certain Greek characters, were added to the writing on the said tile. On conclusion of the said task, the tile fragment, now a full-fledged amulet, had to be located on the "threshold of the door" whilst uttering a further spell.[30]

Whilst there is no reference in the details shared on the Christian magical uses of the fourth Psalm for healing purposes, I have chanced upon a single reference to *Psalm 4:2–3* being employed to alleviate "a continual fever."[31] Otherwise, it is worth noting that in the *"Key of Solomon"* the fourth Psalm is listed amongst a set of Psalms recited whilst robing after having taken a ritual bath. The others are *Psalms 30, 51, 102, 114, 119:97, 126, and 139.*[32]

PSALM 5

[1] למנצח אל הנחילות מזמור לדוד

[2] אמרי האזינה יהוה^{אדני}יאהדונהי בינה הגיגי

[3] הקשיבה לקול שועי מלכי ואלהי כי אליך
אתפלל

[4] יהוה^{אדני}יאהדונהי בקר תשמע קולי בקר אערך
לך ואצפה

[5] כי לא אל חפץ רשע אתה לא יגרך רע

[6] לא יתיצבו הוללים לנגד עיניך שנאת כל
פעלי און

[7] תאבד דברי כזב איש דמים ומרמה יתעב
יהוה^{אדני}יאהדונהי

[8] ואני ברב חסדך אבוא ביתך אשתחוה אל
היכל קדשך ביראתך

[9] יהוה^{אדני}יאהדונהי נחני בצדקתך למען שוררי
הישר לפני דרכך

[10] כי אין בפיהו נכונה קרבם הוות קבר פתוח
גרנם לשונם יחליקון

[11] האשימם אלהים יפלו ממעצותיהם ברב
פשעיהם הדיחמו כי מרו בך

[12] וישמחו כל חוסי בך לעולם ירננו ותסך עלימו
ויעלצו בך אהבי שמך

[13] כי אתה תברך צדיק יהוה^{אדני}יאהדונהי כצנה רצון
תעטרנו

Transliteration:

[1] *lam'natzei'ach el han'chilot miz'mor l'david*

[2] *amarai ha'azinah YHVH binah hagigi*

[3] *hak'shivah l'kol shav'i mal'ki veilohai ki eilecha
et'palal*

[4] *YHVH boker tish'ma koli boker e'eroch l'cha
va'atzapeh*

[5] *ki lo eil chafeitz resha atah lo yegur'cha ra*

[6] *lo yit'yatz'vu hol'lim l'neged einecha saneita kol po'alei aven*

[7] *t'abeid dov'rei chazav ish damim umir'mah y'ta'eiv YHVH*

[8] *va'ani b'rov chas'd'cha avo veitecha esh'tachaveh el heichal kod'sh'cha b'yir'atecha*

[9] *YHVH n'cheini v'tzid'katecha l'ma'an shor'rai ha'y'shar l'fanai dar'kecha*

[10] *ki ein b'fihu n'chonah kir'bam havot kever patu'ach g'ronam l'shonam yachalikun*

[11] *ha'ashimeim elohim yip'lu mimo'atzoteihem b'rov pish'eihem ha'dicheimo ki maru vach*

[12] *v'yis'm'chu chol chosei vach l'olam y'raneinu v'taseich aleimo v'ya'l'tzu v'cha ohavei sh'mecha*

[13] *ki atah t'vareich tzadik YHVH katzinah ratzon ta't'renu*

Translation:

[1] For the Leader; upon the *Nehiloth*. A Psalm of David.

[2] Give ear to my words *YHVH*, consider my meditation.

[3] Hearken unto the voice of my cry, my King, and my God; for unto Thee do I pray.

[4] *YHVH*, in the morning shalt Thou hear my voice; in the morning will I order my prayer unto Thee, and will look forward.

[5] For Thou art not a God that hath pleasure in wickedness; evil shall not sojourn with Thee.

[6] The boasters shall not stand in Thy sight; Thou hatest all workers of iniquity.

[7] Thou destroyest them that speak falsehood; *YHVH* abhorreth the man of blood and of deceit.

[8] But as for me, in the abundance of Thy lovingkindness will I come into Thy house; I will bow down toward Thy holy temple in the fear of Thee.

[9] *YHVH*, lead me in Thy righteousness because of them that lie in wait for me; make Thy way straight before my face.

[10] For there is no sincerity in their mouth; their inward part is a yawning gulf, their throat is an open sepulchre; they make smooth their tongue.

[11] Hold them guilty *Elohim*, let them fall by their own counsels; cast them down in the multitude of their transgressions; for they have rebelled against Thee.

[12] So shall all those that take refuge in Thee rejoice, they shall ever shout for joy, and Thou shalt shelter them; let them also that love Thy name exult in Thee.

[13] For Thou dost bless the righteous; *YHVH*, Thou dost encompass him with favour as with a shield.

Certain Psalms feature prominently in Jewish Prayer, some less so, and others do not appear at all. In the current instance, a single verse from the fifth Psalm is particularly important because it is one of five biblical verses (three in the *Ari Siddur* [*Ari Prayer Book*]) comprising the מַה טֹבוּ (*Mah Tovuh*—"How goodly") prayer. The said five verses are *Numbers 24:5*, *Psalm 5:8*, *Psalm 26:8*, *Psalm 95:6*, and *Psalm 69:14*, and these are recited when worshippers enter the synagogue to attend the morning service. *Psalm 5:8* succinctly express the joyous, reverent mindset required upon entering the sacred abode of the Eternal One, though in the "*Ari Prayer Book*" the *Mah Tovuh* prayer is recited after the morning blessings.[1]

Regarding the magical use of the fifth Psalm, the "*Shimmush Tehillim*" informs us that reciting this entire Psalm will rid an individual from an evil spirit.[2] It has been suggested that the "evil spirit" referenced here, may well also indicate dark moods. Be that as it may, one manuscript source maintains that when an evil spirit attempts to enter you, you should recite *Psalm 5* continuously with *kavvanah*, i.e. strongly focussed intention. It is said the demonic force will depart forthwith.[3]

In another recension we find the fifth Psalm employed for the very same purpose in a somewhat more elaborate procedure. In this instance the Psalm is aligned with the Divine Name אֱלוֹהַּ (*Eloha*), which is said to have been derived from the capitals of certain words, i.e. א (*Alef*) from אֲמָרַי (*amarai*—"my words [speech]"): verse 2; ל (*Lamed*) from לֹא יִתְיַצְּבוּ (*lo yit'yatz'vu*—"shall not stand"): verse 6; ו (*Vav*) from וַאֲנִי (*va'ani*—"as for me"): verse 8; and ה (*Heh*) from הַאֲשִׁימֵם (*ha'ashimeim*—"Hold them guilty [blame them]"): verse 11. In this regard, we are informed that if you want to rid yourself from an evil spirit, that you should recite the fifth Psalm and the accompanying prayer-incantation seven times, the latter reading:

יהי רצון מלפניך **אלוה** רב ותקף רחום והנון שתרחם
עלי ותבריח מפני וממני רוח רעה כמו שהברחת
שונאי מי שהתפלל לפניך בשירה זו ביום מעתה ועד
עולם אמן אמן

Transliteration:

> *Y'hi ratzon mil'fanecha Eloha rav ut'kif rachum v'chanun shet'racheim alai v'tav'ri'ach mip'nei u'mimeni ru'ach ra'ah k'mo shehiv'rach'ta shon'ai mi shehit'paleil l'fanayich b'shirah zo ba'yom mei'atah v'ad olam Omein Omein*

Translation:

> May it be your will great *Eloha*, abundant and strong, compassionate and full of grace, to have mercy on me, and, like you expelled enemies, to divert and turn away an evil spirit from me who prayed this song before you, from now unto eternity *Amen Amen*.

Interestingly enough, the capitals of the words comprising *Psalm 5:8* are sometimes employed in amulets meant to avert attacks from evil spirits.[4] In this regard, the following amulet, composed of the entire verse, is particularly interesting, since in the current instance it is not only the construction of the amulet as an instrument of protection against invasion by demonic forces which is important, but equally the employment of the component Divine Name construct as an incantation. It is virtually functioning as an effective mini exorcism, so to speak, in order to expel an evil force which may be possessing and afflicting someone.

In terms of freeing an individual who is afflicted with an evil spirit, the said amulet is constructed from the forty-one letters of the current verse, these having been arranged into a Divine Name construct comprising thirteen tri-letter combinations, and a concluding two letter combination, as indicated overleaf:[5]

וְהִי אֵלֶךְ נֵאֵל
יֵהִק בֵּוַד רֵחֵשׁ
בֵּתָק חֵשֵׁב סָאִי
דָכֵר כָתָא אִיָת
בֵּבֵך וַ אָ

Transliteration:

VaHeiYo	AlaCha	Nu'ALa
YoHeiKo	BeiVaDa	ReiCheiShi
VeiTaCha	CheiShiBei	Sa'AYo
DaChaRei	ChaTa'A	AYoTa
VeiVeiCha	Va'A	

In the current instance, the first fourteen letters of the said verse respectively constitute the first letter of each group written in rows in the standard right to left manner. The second set of fourteen letters, encompassing the central glyphs of the tri-letter combinations, are written in reverse order from bottom to top, whilst the remaining thirteen letters, comprising the concluding letters, are written again in the standard right to left manner from top to bottom. Afterwards, the resulting Divine Name construct and amulet are employed to expel the demon. This is done by reciting the Divine Name combination in the left ear of the afflicted, following which the amulet is suspended like a necklace on the said individual.[6]

We are informed that *Psalm 5:8* was also "used in a certain sense to avert the Evil Eye." In this regard, it is said that in the days of the *Geonim*, i.e. the leaders of the great Talmudic academies in Babylonia, the ten words of this verse were utilized in a specific manner to ascertain whether a "*minyan*" was present, this being the mandatory number of male congregants required for a religious service to commence in a synagogue. In this regard, we are told that, "avoiding the necessity of pointing with the finger, or using numerals, both of which were considered harmful,"[7] the required number of male worshippers were counted by identifying each one with a word from this verse. The arrival of the tenth male was acknowledged with the tenth word of this verse, i.e. "the *Olam* is here," and the enunciation of which was believed to avert the Evil Eye. Later *Psalm 5:8* was replaced by *Psalm 18:51*.[8]

A further magical use of *Psalm 5:8* pertains to the initials of the ten words comprising this verse being combined in the Divine Name construct ובח אבא אהקב, which is employed in amulets "against evil spirits."[9] The succeeding verse, i.e. *Psalm 5:9* reading יהוה נחני בצדקתך למען שוררי הושר לפני דרכך (*YHVH n'cheini v'tzid'katecha l'ma'an shor'rai ha'y'shar l'fanai dar'kecha*—"*YHVH*, lead me in Thy righteousness because of them that lie in wait for me; make Thy way straight before my face."), was equally put to magical use of a most peculiar kind. In this regard, the capitals of the eight words comprising this verse, were combined to create the following Divine Name construct:[10]

$$\text{ינבל שהלד}$$

There is no indication on how this Divine Name construct should be pronounced, and since it has to be vocalised in a related prayer-incantation, it could either be spelled out letter by letter, or enunciated with the vowel points aligned with the letters in the mentioned verse. The Divine Name construct would then be enunciated יִנְבַל שֶׁהֲלֶדַ (*Y'n'v'l' Shohal'da*).

In terms of the magical use of this peculiar Divine Name construct, we are told that if one should spot a lot of naval ships starting to gather, I presume the reference here being to enemy vessels gathering of the coast of your own land with malevolent intentions, that you could work the following magical procedure. First you need to spy on them for a couple of days, so as to ascertain the exact number of vessels present. Then, when ready, to acquire a length of cane or cut a branch from a tree, which is placed in readiness for the magical purpose. Next utter the Divine Name מְוַם (*M'vam*) three times, prior to picking up the cane or branch with your left hand. We are reminded that the *Gematria* of this Divine Name construct [מ = 40 + ו = 6 + מ = 40 = 86] equates with that of the Divine Name אלהים (*Elohim*) [א = 1 + ל = 30 + ה = 5 + י = 10 + מ = 40 = 86].[11] As you probably know, the Divine Name *Elohim* pertains to *Gevurah* (Might) and the planet Mars on the sefirotic Tree, and, whether intentionally or not, the mentioned tri-letter Divine Name construct aligns well with the intention of the current magical act. We are also told that the vowel points employed in the enunciation of the said Divine Name construct, are those related to the Ineffable Name, the latter being often written יְהֹוָה (*Y'Ha'V'Ha*).[12]

Be that as it may, having uttered the mentioned Divine Name construct three times, and picked up the cane/branch with your left hand, you need to next cut it into pieces, the number being equivalent to that of the ships you spied in the sea, each piece representing a ship. Then, whilst holding them in your left hand, say:

מעיד אני עלי ימימיאל חמלאך הממונה על ימים
בשם הגדל מֻוַם אשר בכחו הגדול פעל משה רבינו
עליו השלום כל מה שעשה בים כשטבע פרעה
ותראה לבאים אחרינו או כנגדינו ללחום עמנו
שכל אחד מעלו החתיכות הם ספינות בעיניהם
ויראו ויפחדו מפנינו

Transliteration:

> *Mei'id ani alai Yamimi'el hamal'ach ham'muneh al yamim b'sheim hagadol M'vam asher b'kocho hagadol pa'al mosheh rabeinu alav hashalom kol ma she'asah bayam k'shetava par'oh v'teiro'eh l'ba'im achareinu o k'neg'deinu lil'chom imanu shekol echad m'eilu hachatichot heim s'finot b'eineihem v'yeira'u v'yipach'du mipaneinu.*

Translation:

> I call as witness before me *Yamimi'el*, the angel who is in charge of the days, in the great Name *M'vam*, by whose great power Moshe Rabbeinu, peace be upon him, executed everything he did at the sea when Pharaoh drowned, and show those who are coming after us, or are against us, to combat with our nation, that every single one of these pieces [wood or bamboo] are perceived to be ships in their eyes, and for them to see and be afraid of us.

Conclude the procedure by uttering the following incantation:

יהי רצון מלפניך יהוה אלהי ואלהי אבותי שתוליכנו
למקום פלוני לשלום ותשמרנו מאויבים וממשעות רעות
המתרגשות לבוא בים וביבשה ותשמרנו מרוח סועה
ומסער בשם זה המלך ינבל שהלד הנקרא אזבוגה

Transliteration:

> *Y'hi ratzon milfanecha YHVH elohai v'elohei avotai sh'tolicheinu l'makom ploni l'shalom v'tish'm'reinu m'oy'vim umisha'ot ra'ot hamit'rag'shot lavo ba'yam ubayabasha v'tish'm'reinu m'ru'ach so'ah umisa'ar b'sheim zeh hamalach Y'N'V'L' Shohal'da hanik'ra Azbugah.*

Translation:

> May it be your will *YHVH* my God and God of my father, that you transport me to a place of peace anywhere, and save us from enemies, and from the evil times we sense are coming from the sea and on land, and keep us from the winds of trouble and agitation, in the Name of this messenger *Y'N'V'L' Shohal'da* called *Azbugah*.[13]

I presume the pieces of cane or wood are afterwards cast into the sea in order to complete the intended "phantom illusion" on the enemy. Be that as it may, it should be noted that the Divine Name מֻום (*M'vam*) is the concluding tri-letter portion of the "*Shem Vayisa Vayet*," and that the entire "*Name of Seventy-two Names*" is formed from *Exodus 14:19-21*, these verses recounting the famous saga of the "Angel of *Elohim*," who protected the Israelites against the Egyptian army, as well as those of Moses, who "stretched out his hand over the sea," and in so doing divided the waters. I have addressed the "*Shem Vayisa Vayet*" in some detail in earlier volumes in this series of tomes on "Practical Kabbalah."[14]

Besides being one of the Psalms recommended to individuals for recitation in the synagogue, *Psalm 5* is also used for finding favour, and furthermore we are told it will afford success in dealings with authorities.[15] In this regard, one commentator maintains that the fifth Psalm should be simply recited three times before entering the presence of a ruler.[16] However, one manuscript instructs the Psalm should be recited at daybreak and at sunset three times over olive oil, which you should afterwards employ to anoint your face, hands and feet.[17] As mentioned, both *Psalms 4* and 5 deal with seeking the grace and favour of princes and magistrates. However, besides these two Psalms, there are others used to win favour, these being *Psalms 47, 72, 78* and *85*.

In the mentioned popular English translation of Godfrey Selig's German publication of the "*Shimmush Tehillim*," the procedure requires that you need to "think unceasingly upon the holy name of *Chananyah* (חננ׳יה—'Merciful God')" during the act of anointing your face, hands and feet, and to say "be merciful unto me, for the sake of thy great, adorable and holy name, *Chananyah*, turn the heart of my prince to me, and grant that he may regard me with gracious eyes, and let me find favor and courtesy with him. *Amen! Selah!*"[18]

As far as the Divine Name חננ׳יה (*Chananyah*) is concerned, it is claimed that it was constructed from the words חפץ (*chafetz*—"desire"): verse 5; נחנ׳ (*n'cheini*—"lead me"): verse 9; נכונה (*n'chona*—"right"): verse 10; הדיחמו (*hadicheimo* —"cast them down"): verse 11, and כצנה (*katzinah*— "as a shield"): verse 13.[19] Whilst this Divine Name construct and the associated prayer/incantation do not feature in any of the primary recensions of the "*Shimmush Tehillim*" which I have consulted, I can understand why the selected Hebrew words were employed in reference to the said Divine Name, in order to find favour with higher authorities. One could interpret the words to mean "May it be your desire (*chafetz*) to direct me (*n'cheni*) towards what is right (*n'chonah*). Cast down those (*hadichemo*) who might oppose me and be my shield (*katzinah*)."

Selig's translation has a further addition to the magical application of *Psalm 5*. He wrote "still another peculiarity of this Psalm is, when you find notwithstanding the utmost industry and care, your business does not prosper, and you have reason to fear that an evil Masal [מזל (*Mazel*)—"fortune" or "luck"], that is, an evil star, spirit or destiny is opposing you, then pray this Psalm daily, even to the last verse with great devoutness, and you will soon find yourself in more favorable circumstances."[20]

Otherwise, I have noticed that in Jewish Magic the fifth Psalm is recommended to counteract bad language; against harm and malice; against theft and thieves; to be relieved from the anxiety caused by enemies; against assassins; when an individual has to appear before a judge; against laziness and procrastination; against the Evil Eye, and, as I noted earlier, to counteract Evil Spirits, as well as dark moods. In terms of the latter, I have recommended this Psalm to an individual who was classified "bipolar," and he maintained that it brought him great relief. Be that as it may, *Psalm 5* is employed for fortune in business, and recited every day during daylight hours to cause pregnancy.

In the previously mentioned Christian literature, related instructions appear in *"Le Livre d'Or,"* in terms of "obtaining the friendship of great Lords." In this instance the practitioner is required to write the name of a Spirit Intelligence and certain magical characters on the upper side of the hand. Here we also find the instruction to recite the fifth Psalm three times over a quantity of olive oil, which in the current instance is smeared on the forehead and on top of the hand comprising the angelic name and magical seals.[21] However, there is no indication that this should be done twice a day at dawn and dusk, as per the mentioned instructions in the *"Shimmush Tehillim."*

Be that as it may, in a Syrian manuscript from the Königlichen Bibliothek zu Berlin (Sachau Collection No. 218), which equally deals with the magical use of Psalms, we find a related procedure, in which *Psalm 5* is recited "when you have to appear before the judge."[22] In this instance there is no reference to the Psalm having to be recited olive oil with which to anoint certain bodily parts.

The fifth Psalm was also employed to counter frustrating forces of the human kind. In this regard, it was noted in one of the previously mentioned Byzantine manuscripts that the current Psalm was recited when "you have become frustrated with someone," or "when you clash with your brother."[23] In a similar vein *"Le Livre d'Or,"* maintains "this Psalm is used against tempters, liars, perjurers and for the souls of the dead," adding that it is equally good "for locations or places that are being besieged."[24]

Lastly, one might be able to escape the mentioned hassles, since, according to the mentioned Byzantine manuscript, *Psalm 5* is recited in full in order "to procure invisibility."[25] Furthermore, in instances where one is suffering "fear about a judgment," we are told in a sixteenth century southern Italian manuscript that the current Psalm can be employed to alleviate such fears. However, in this instance there is a little twist in the procedure, which necessitates the practitioner to place three peony seeds in the mouth, and then to say "my words" (*Psalm 5:2*) three times, followed by reciting the entire Psalm, which is said will dispel fear.[26] On the other hand, in the earlier mentioned Syrian magical manuscript in the Sachau Collection of the Staatsbibliothek in Berlin, we are told *Psalm 5* should be recited when you have to appear before a judge.[27]

PSALM 6

[1] למנצח בנגינות על השמינית מזמור לדוד

[2] יהוה-אהדונהי אל באפך תוכיחני ואל בחמתך תיסרני

[3] חנני יהוה-אהדונהי כי אמלל אני רפאני יהוה-אהדונהי כי נבהלו עצמי

[4] ונפשי נבהלה מאד ואתה יהוה-אהדונהי עד מתי

[5] שובה יהוה-אהדונהי חלצה נפשי הושיעני למען חסדך

[6] כי אין במות זכרך בשאול מי יודה לך

[7] יגעתי באנחתי אשחה בכל לילה מטתי בדמעתי ערשי אמסה

[8] עששה מכעס עיני עתקה בכל צוררי

[9] סורו ממני כל פעלי און כי שמע יהוה-אהדונהי קול בכיי

[10] שמע יהוה-אהדונהי תחנתי יהוה-אהדונהי תפלתי יקח

[11] יבשו ויבהלו מאד כל איבי ישבו יבשו רגע

Transliteration:

[1] *lam'natzei'ach bin'ginot al hash'minit miz'mor l'david*
[2] *YHVH al b'ap'cha tochicheini v'al bachamat'cha t'yas'reini*
[3] *choneini YHVH ki um'lal ani r'fa'eini YHVH ki niv'halu atzamai*
[4] *v'naf'shi niv'halah m'od v'atah YHVH ad matai*
[5] *shuva YHVH chal'tzah naf'shi hoshi'eini l'ma'an chas'decha*
[6] *ki ein bamavet zich'recha bish'ol mi yodeh lach*
[7] *yaga'ti b'an'chati as'cheh v'chol lailah mitati b'dim'ati ar'si am'seh*
[8] *ash'shah mika'as eini at'kah b'chol tzor'rai*
[9] *suru mimeni kol po'alei aven ki shama YHVH kol bich'yi*
[10] *shama YHVH t'chinati YHVH t'filati yikach*

[11] *yeivoshu v'yibahulu m'od kol oy'vai yashuvu yeivoshu raga*

Translation:

[1] For the Leader; with string-music; on the *Sheminith*. A Psalm of David.

[2] *YHVH* rebuke me not in Thine anger, neither chasten me in Thy wrath.

[3] Be gracious unto me *YHVH*, for I languish away; heal me *YHVH*, for my bones are affrighted.

[4] My soul also is sore affrighted; and Thou *YHVH*, how long?

[5] Return *YHVH*, deliver my soul; save me for Thy mercy's sake.

[6] For in death there is no remembrance of Thee; in the nether-world who will give Thee thanks?

[7] I am weary with my groaning; every night make I my bed to swim; I melt away my couch with my tears.

[8] Mine eye is dimmed because of vexation; it waxeth old because of all mine adversaries.

[9] Depart from me, all ye workers of iniquity; for *YHVH* hath heard the voice of my weeping.

[10] *YHVH* hath heard my supplication; *YHVH* receiveth my prayer.

[11] All mine enemies shall be ashamed and sore affrighted; they shall turn back, they shall be ashamed suddenly.

Psalm 6 is the primary supplication recited in Ashkenazi communities over *Yom Kippur* (Day of Atonement) during טחנון (*Tachanun*), the "prayers of supplication."[1] Whilst this Psalm does not feature otherwise particularly prominently in Jewish liturgies, it is applied fairly extensively in Jewish Magic. In this regard, it is employed to counteract and heal diseases of the eye, or pain in the eyes.[2] In order to achieve this result, the instruction is to recite the Psalm seven times a day over a period of three successive days, doing so conjointly with a prayer-incantation comprising a unique Divine Name construct.[3] A different version has it that the Psalm should be recited the same number of times over four days,[4] and yet another maintains the sixth Psalm should be recited three times per day over a four day period.[5]

There is once again a Divine Name construct associated with the sixth Psalm, which is indicated to be יִשְׁעִי, this being a common Hebrew term vocalised "*yish'i*" meaning "my salvation." It appears in several verses in the Hebrew Bible, and some recensions of the "*Shimmush Tehillim*" indicate it to be referencing "saviour."[6] However, in terms of its current listing as a Divine Name construct, we are told that it was formed: י (*Yod*) from the initial of the phrase יְהוָה אַל בְּאַפְּךָ תוֹכִיחֵנִי (*YHVH al b'ap'cha tochicheini*—"*YHVH* rebuke me not in Thine anger*"*): verse 2; שׁ (*Shin*) from שׁוּבָה יְהוָה חַלְּצָה נַפְשִׁי (*shuva YHVH chal'tza naf'shi*—"Return *YHVH*, deliver my soul"): verse 5. ע (*Ayin*) from עָשְׁשָׁה מִכַּעַס עֵינִי (*ash'shah mika'as eini*—"Mine eye is dimmed because of vexation"): verse 8; and the concluding י (*Yod*) from יֵבֹשׁוּ וְיִבָּהֲלוּ מְאֹד (*yeivoshu v'yibahulu m'od*—"All mine enemies shall be ashamed and sore affrighted"): verse 11.[7]

Here the oft mentioned 19th century Selig German/English translation of this Psalm presents a discrepancy. It maintains the associated Divine Name construct to comprise five letters, i.e. יְשַׁעְיָה, of which it references the derivations of the first four letters shared above, without any indication as to the origins of the fifth letter. It claims the letter combination is vocalised "*Jeschayah*" or "*Jaschayah*,"[8] as it is in the Hebrew Bible in reference to יְשַׁעְיָה (*Y'sha'yah*), this being the first name of a biblical personality. It maintains this name translates "help is with the Lord."[9] The literal meaning is "*Yah* is salvation" or "*Yah* has saved."

Those meanings are not really of great importance, because the Divine Name construct in Selig's translation is flawed when compared to all the recensions and published versions of the "*Shimmush Tehillim*" which I have perused. What concerns me is his enunciation of the said Divine Name, i.e. "*Jeschayah*" ("*Jaschayah*"). Admittedly I have seen no indication regarding the pronunciation of the current Divine Name construct in any of the relevant texts, however in one recension a prayer-incantation lists the Divine Name construct צוּר יִשְׁעִי (*Tzur Yish'i*—"my Rock of Salvation"),[10] this expression comprising the concluding words of *2 Samuel 22:47*. Thus, in my estimation, the indication is clearly that the current Divine Name construct should be vocalised exactly as written in the Hebrew Bible, i.e. יִשְׁעִי (*Yish'i*), and this is the vocalisation I have included in the prayer-incantations accompanying *Psalm 6*.

In terms of a standard instruction pertaining to the current purpose, we are informed to recite the sixth Psalm seven times a day for three days, and doing so in conjunction with the referenced prayer-incantation reading:

יהי רצון מלפניך השם הגדול הגבור והנורא היוצא
מזה המזמור שהוא ישעי בעל הישועה שתושיעני
מכל צער וחולי שיש לי וחשישה שיש לי בעיני כי
לך הישועה והיכולת

Transliteration:

> *Y'hi ratzon mil'fanecha hasheim hagadol hagibor v'hanora hayotzei mizeh hamiz'mor shehu Yish'i ba'al ha'y'shu'ah shetoshi'eini mikol tza'ar v'choli sheyeish li vachashishah she'yeish li b'einai ki l'cha ha'y'shu'ah v'ha'y'cholet.*

Translation:

> May it be your will the great, strong and awesome Name that emerges from this Psalm, which is *Yish'i*, Saviour, to save me from all suffering and illness that I have, and the sickness I have in my eyes, for you have the salvation and the ability.[11]

Both the previously mentioned "*Shimmush Tehillim*" and Christian Arabic manuscripts in the Kaufmann Collection prescribe *Psalm 6* for "a pain in the eye." However, the Jewish manuscript maintains "the Psalm and the name hidden in it" should be recited seven times over the eye on a Tuesday, which is not referenced in the Arabic manuscript,[12] and which equally differs from the shared instructions in the "mainstream" versions of the "*Shimmush Tehillim*."

In terms of encouraging a speedy recovery from eye conditions, it has been suggested that the Psalm should be whispered,[13] and the accompanying prayer-incantation uttered, "seven times slowly, in a low tone, and with devotion."[14] However, the sixth Psalm is not only used to cure diseases of the eyes. In fact, it is recited to aid the cure for all manner of ill health. In this regard, the letters comprising *Psalm 6:1 to 4* are arranged into the following Divine Name construct:

אָאֵה הדרן וְוה הַאִי יתָה

כְּבִי פָהַת אֵלֶם בְּהַד לְמֵעַ

יַין נְוֹה חֲנִי יָפֶה כְּשַׁב וַיו תְּנַשׁ

חָלָה בּוּצַ לְעַל אַצְתָה מָה וְמָה

סֵהוּ יַכָה תְיַ כָנְשׁ תְּבַף מָהַן

יְפָּם נָאֵל נֵנִי חָיַנ יְיָע נְהִי רוּשַׁ

יַלְכַ כָלָד הַאָס וְנַח הִינ יָרְע

אֵמִיה

This Divine Name construct, a special prayer-incantation, as well as a set of חותמות (*chotamot*— "magical seals"), are included in a somewhat complex amulet to be written in ink on a sheet of white paper for the purpose of curing all illnesses.[15] In this regard, we are instructed to copy the Divine Name construct, then write the associated prayer-incantation below it. The latter reads:

יהי רצון מלפניך יהוה למענך ולמען שמותיך
הקדושים והטהורים אלו שתתן לי[recipient] נושא
קמיע זה עליו רפואה שלימה מלפניך ותצוה
למלאכיך הממונים על הרפואה שירפאוהו אמן
נצח סלה ועד

Transliteration:

Y'hi ratzon mil'fanecha YHVH l'ma'an'cha ul'ma'an sh'motecha hakadoshim v'hat'horim eilu shetitein l'[....name of recipient....] nosei kamea zeh alav r'fu'ah sh'leimah mil'fanecha ut'tzaveh l'mal'achecha ham'munim al har'fu'ah sheyar'pi'uhu omein netzach selah va'ed.

Translation:

> May it be your will *YHVH*, for your sake and for the sake
> of these pure and Holy Names, to grant unto [....name of
> recipient....], the bearer of this amulet complete healing
> before you, and command your angels in charge of healing
> to heal him *Amen* Enduring *Selah* forever.

Insert directly underneath the prayer incantation the following
Divine Name combination:

יוהך כלך צמרכד ייך יחוש

[*Yohach Kalach Tzamar'chad Yiyach*(?) *Yichush*(?)]

I have addressed the first three listed Divine Names in previous
volumes.[16] There is no indication of either the origins or the
enunciation of the concluding two Names, but that is of no
consequence in the current procedure. Be that as it may, locate two
hexagrams below the prayer-incantation, and insert the first two
letters of the Ineffable Name in the centre of the one to the right,
and the concluding two glyphs in the one to the left, as indicated
below:[17]

Next, the relevant text in the "*Shorshei ha-Shemot*" instructs the
following חותם (*Chotam*—"seal") should be included in the
amulet. Readers will recognise it to be the "Magic Square of the
Third Order" or "Saturn Square," which I have addressed
elsewhere:[18]

ד	ט	ב
ג	ה	ו
ח	א	ו

On the opposite side of the page, perhaps directly behind this "Magic Square," locate a further *Magen David* with the first two letters of the Ineffable Name inscribed in its centre.[19] It is believed this hexagram is drawn in the quality of mercy, which will ascend from "his three spirits,"[20] as well as allow the "spirit forces" inherent in the amulet to ascend in general into the Divine Presence of the Eternal One.[21]

It should be noted that the capitals of the words comprising *Psalm 6:2* and the first five words of verse 3, are specifically conjoined in the Divine Name construct יאבתובבתחיכאא to be employed in amulets "for mental illness."[22] On the other hand, the initials of the final five words of verse 3 as well as those of the opening three words of verse 4, are combined in the Divine Name construct ריכנע ונמ, which is employed in an amulet for bone ailments.[23]

The initials of the words comprising the opening phrase of *Psalm 6:5*, reading שובה יהוה חלצה נפשי (*shuva YHVH chal'tza naf'shi*—"Return *YHVH*, deliver my soul"), are combined in the Divine Name construct שׁיחנ, which is included in amulets equally constructed for mental ailments.[24]

The sixth Psalm is further employed for one who is in distress generally,[25] or in danger,[26] at sea or on land. In this regard, the distressed individual is instructed to recite the Psalm seven times in the evening whenever required,[27] doing so conjointly with the following prayer-incantation:

יהי רצון מלפניך ישעי בעל הישועה שתושיעני
ותצילני מכל צער כי לך הישועה והיכולת

Transliteration:

Y'hi ratzon mil'fanecha Yish'i ba'al ha'y'shu'ah shetoshi'eini v'tatzileini mikol tza'ar ki l'cha ha'y'shu'ah v'ha'y'cholet.

Translation:

May it be your will *Yish'i*, Saviour, that you save me and deliver me from any distress, for you have the salvation and the ability.[28]

As far as the healing qualities of the current Psalm is concerned, it is worth noting that *Psalm 6:5* is directly affiliated with הֲהַע (*Haha*), the twelfth portion of the "*Shem Vayisa Vayet*,"[29] and the restorative qualities of this verse is in my estimation emphasised by this affiliation with the said tri-letter portion of the "*Name of Seventy-two Names*." After all, we are taught that the ruling angelic prince of הֲהַע (*Haha*) is רפאל (*Rafa'el*), who is the angel of healing, and who is called מלאך הברית (*Malach ha-Brit—* "Angel of the Covenant").[30] In terms of its referenced healing qualities, I have seen *Psalm 6* equally recommended for diseases of the blood, and infirmity in general. Other than that, I have further observed it suggested to counteract anxieties caused by enemies; against great troubles and distress; and to bring peace of soul.

The remedial powers of the sixth Psalm is equally recognised in Christianity. In this regard it is recited during visits to the sick in Roman Catholicism.[31] However, *Psalm 6* is employed for a great variety of purposes in Christian magic. It is recited when an individual is suffering persecution at the hand of another,[32] and it is equally employed against enemies. In terms of the latter application, the instruction in the previously mentioned Byzantine Christian manuscript is to copy a set of magical characters "on skin from an unborn animal," to recite the sixth Psalm, and then to carry the written text, i.e. amulet, on the chest like a pendant. It is said there will be no longer any fear whatsoever.[33]

We are informed in "*Le Livre d'Or*" that *Psalm 6* "is good for consoling the sinner and to remove from him the grief of having offended God and this makes him look into his heart."[34] This text further noted, "that whoever recites it piously seven times in a row, will change the evil will of an ungodly Judge and will prevent him from condemning him unjustly."[35] Otherwise it is said that reciting *Psalm 6* seven times with the name of an "Intelligence" and an associated prayer, "is good for all the labours and torments of the Spirit."[36] The referenced "Intelligence" is said to be *Issi Isi*,[37] whose name is sounding very similar to the earlier mentioned Hebrew Divine Name associated with this Psalm, i.e. ישעי (*Yish'i*). In my estimation, the similarities between the two appellatives are much too close to be merely coincidental, especially when one considers that the Christian text also recommends the sixth Psalm "for sick people, who have diseased eyes."[38] Here the recitation of the Psalm seven times over a three day period with the name of the "Intelligence" equally aligns with the instructions in Jewish Magic, the only difference being that in the Christian text the name and "character" of the "Intelligence" is written on a lettuce leaf, with which the eyes are touched.[39]

It is worth noting, that the sixth Psalm is listed in the "*Key of Solomon*" amongst a set of Psalms to be recited whilst adding salt "into the vessel wherein is the Water,"[40] and in the earlier referenced version of the "*Goetia*" the fourth and fifth verses of *Psalm 6* are respectively affiliated with the fifty-eighth and the fourth of the "*72 Spirits of the Goetia.*"[41]

Psalm 7

[1] שגיון לדוד אשר שר ליהוהאדנייאהדונהי על דברי
כוש בן ימיני

[2] יהוהאדנייאהדונהי אלהי בך חסיתי הושיעני מכל
רדפי והצילני

[3] פן יטרף כאריה נפשי פרק ואין מציל

[4] יהוהאדנייאהדונהי אלהי אם עשיתי זאת אם יש
עול בכפי

[5] אם גמלתי שולמי רע ואחלצה צוררי ריקם

[6] ירדף אויב נפשי וישג וירמס לארץ חיי וכבודי
לעפר ישכן סלה

[7] קומה יהוהאדנייאהדונהי באפך הנשא בעברות
צוררי ועורה אלי משפט צוית

[8] ועדת לאמים תסובבך ועליה למרום שובה

[9] יהוהאדנייאהדונהי ידין עמים שפטני יהוהאדנייאהדונהי
כצדקי וכתמי עלי

[10] יגמר נא רע רשעים ותכונן צדיק ובחן לבות
וכליות אלהים צדיק

[11] מגני על אלהים מושיע ישרי לב

[12] אליהם שופט צדיק ואל זעם בכל יום

[13] אם לא ישוב חרבו ילטוש קשתו דרך ויכוננה

[14] ולו הכין כלי מות חציו לדלקים יפעל

[15] הנה יחבל און והרה עמל וילד שקר

[16] בור כרה ויחפרהו ויפל בשחת יפעל

[17] ישוב עמלו בראשו ועל קדקדו חמסו ירד

[18] אודה יהוהאדנייאהדונהי כצדקו ואזמרה שם
יהוהאדנייאהדונהי עליון

Transliteration:

[1] *shigayon l'david asher shar laYHVH al div'rei chush ben y'mini*

[2] *YHVH Elohai b'cha chasiti hoshi'eini mikol rod'fai v'hatzileini*

[3] *pen yit'rof k'ar'yeih naf'shi poreik v'ein matzil*

[4] *YHVH Elohai im asiti zot im yesh avel b'chapai*

[5] *im gamal'ti shol'mi ra va'achal'tzah tzor'ri reikam*

[6] *yiradof oyeiv naf'shi v'yaseig v'yir'mos la'aretz chayai uch'vodi le'afar yash'kein selah*

[7] *kumah YHVH b'apecha hinasei b'av'rot tzor'rai v'urah eilai mish'pat tzivita*

[8] *va'adat l'umim t'sov'veka v'aleha lamarom shuvah*

[9] *YHVH yadin amim shof'teini YHVH k'tzid'ki uch'tumi alai*

[10] *yig'mor na ra r'sha'im ut'chonein tzadik uvochein libot uch'layot elohim tzadik*

[11] *magini al elohim moshi'a yish'rei leiv*

[12] *elohim shofeit tzadik v'el zo'eim b'chol yom*

[13] *im lo yashuv char'bo yil'tosh kash'to darach va'yechon'nehah*

[14] *v'lo heichin k'lei mavet chitzav l'dol'kim yif'al*

[15] *hinei y'chabel aven v'harah amal v'yalad shaker*

[16] *bor karah vayach'p'reihu vayipol b'shachat yif'al*

[17] *yashuv amalo v'rosho v'al kod'kodo chamaso yeireid*

[18] *odeh YHVH k'tzid'ko va'azam'rah sheim YHVH elyon*

Translation:

[1] *Shiggaion* of David, which he sang unto *YHVH*, concerning Cush a Benjamite.

[2] *YHVH* my God, in Thee have I taken refuge; save me from all them that pursue me, and deliver me;

[3] Lest he tear my soul like a lion, rending it in pieces, while there is none to deliver.

[4] *YHVH* my God, if I have done this; if there be iniquity in my hands;

[5] If I have requited him that did evil unto me, or spoiled mine adversary unto emptiness;

[6] Let the enemy pursue my soul, and overtake it, and tread my life down to the earth; yea, let him lay my glory in the dust. *Selah*

[7] Arise *YHVH*, in Thine anger, lift up Thyself in indignation against mine adversaries; yea, awake for me at the judgment which Thou hast commanded.

[8] And let the congregation of the peoples compass Thee about, and over them return Thou on high.

[9] *YHVH* who ministerest judgment to the peoples, judge me *YHVH*, according to my righteousness, and according to mine integrity that is in me.

[10] Oh that a full measure of evil might come upon the wicked, and that Thou wouldest establish the righteous; for the righteous *Elohim* trieth the heart and reins.

[11] My shield is with *Elohim*, who saveth the upright in heart.

[12] *Elohim* is a righteous judge, yea, a God that hath indignation every day:

[13] If a man turn not, He will whet His sword, He hath bent His bow, and made it ready;

[14] He hath also prepared for him the weapons of death, yea, His arrows which He made sharp.

[15] Behold, he travaileth with iniquity; yea, he conceiveth mischief, and bringeth forth falsehood.

[16] He hath digged a pit, and hollowed it, and is fallen into the ditch which he made.

[17] His mischief shall return upon his own head, and his violence shall come down upon his own pate.

[18] I will give thanks unto *YHVH* according to His righteousness; and will sing praise to the name of *YHVH* Most High.

We are told that one should recite *Psalm 7* to win a court case, or when one has to appear in front of a tribunal; against robbers; for protection "against harm inflicted by other people"; and "to make your haters go away," i.e. to ward off enemies.[1] It is clear that the underlying motive behind the magical use of the seventh Psalm is mainly to counter the machinations of "haters," putting adversaries to flight, and ensuring that people cannot harm you. In this regard, the "*Shimmush Tehillim*" shares a procedure involving the recitation of the current Psalm, in conjunction with a simple prayer-incantation, and some recensions featuring again a special Divine Name, as well as the execution of a physical action in order to, as it were, affirm the "spell."

In the current instance, the said Divine Name is the well known אל עליון (*El El'yon*) meaning "God Most High," the first portion of which is claimed to have been derived: א (*Alef*) from שר אשר (*asher shar*—"which [he] sang"): verse 1, and ל (*Lamed*) from אודה (*odeh*—"I will thank"): verse 18, the initial of this term having been converted by means of the א״ל ב״ם (*Albam*) cipher.[2]

Whilst some recensions of the "*Shimmush Tehillim*" do not include details about an affiliated Divine Name, the Selig German/English translation took the origins of the said Divine Name much further, adding that the letters comprising the עליון (*El'yon*) portion were derived: ע (*Ayin*) from הושיעני (*hoshi'eini* —"save me"): verse 2; ל (*Lamed*) from אלי (*eilai*—"to [for] me"): verse 7; י (*Yod*) from ידין (*yadin*—"will judge"): verse 9; ו (*Vav*) from ישוב (*yashuf*—"turn"): verse 13; and the concluding נ (*Nun*) from עליון (*el'yon*—"Most High"): verse 18.[3] I have seen no primary sources to sustain this claim in any of the primary texts I have examined.

Be that as it may, in the current instance the simplest application of the seventh Psalm for the purpose of, as it were, conquering an enemy, is to take a new vessel, i.e. a bowl or pot, and fill it with water from a spring or another water source. This is followed by reciting *Psalm 7:7–18* in conjunction with the following prayer-incantation, doing so four times:

יהי רצון מלפניך אל עליון שתפיל ותכניע [recipient]
אויבי וקמי לפני אמן אמן אמן סלה סלה סלה

Transliteration:
Y'hi ratzon mil'fanecha El El'yon shetafil v'tach'niya [....name of recipient....] oy'vai v'kamai l'fanai Omein Omein Omein Selah Selah Selah

Translation:
May it be your will, *El El'yon*, that you overthrow and subjugate [....name of recipient....], my enemy and my adversary, before me. *Amen Amen Amen! Selah Selah Selah!*

It is said that an enemy would be overcome, if the water is poured out at his or her place of residence, "or at a place where he must pass over it."[4] The same instructions are shared in Rabbi Moses Zacutto's acclaimed "*Shorshei ha-Shemot*," without reference to the concluding action of dispensing the water at the abode of the enemy.[5]

More "magical effort" is required from individuals who are faced with enemies with malevolent intentions of the deadly kind, and who are pursuing them whilst they are strolling down a road. As noted, the previous procedure required water, whilst the current one is focussed on earth (dust). In this regard, the instruction is to take dust (sand) from the earth, and to recite *Psalm 7* over it. This is followed by uttering the following prayer-incantation, before scattering the dust over the path from whence you fear your pursuers may be coming from:

יהי רצון מלפניך אל עליון שתהפיך לב שונאי כמו
שהפכת אברהם אבינו בהזכירו זה השם

Transliteration:

> *Y'hi ratzon mil'fanecha El El'yon shetahafoch leiv shon'ai k'mo shehafach'ta shon'ei av'raham aveinu b'haz'kiro zeh ha'sheim.*

Translation:

> May it be your will, *El El'yon*, to turn the heart of those who hate me, as you turned the haters of Abraham, our father, when he called this name.

We are assured that they will depart and not return.[6] It is worth noting that in the current instance, a variant of the same procedure can be found in Jewish Magic, in which a very different Divine Name combination is employed. In this regard, we are equally told that when you spot robbers or enemies behind you, that you should pick up dust (sand) from the road or path you stand on, and again recite *Psalm 7* over it. Here the variant prayer-incantation reads:

> "*Jirmi'el El Hi'el* most high, turn my enemies away from me as you did the enemies of Abraham our father, peace be upon him, when he pronounced a Divine Name against his enemies, turn my enemies away from me."

It is said that the enemies will forthwith turn away behind you, but it adds the proviso that one should repeat this prayer for the entire year after the recitation of the daily עלינו לשבח (*Aleinu*

L'shabei'ach ["It is our duty (to praise God)"]) prayer.[7] The latter prayer is the most frequently recited one in the Jewish liturgy. In fact, it is enunciated at the conclusion of each of the three daily Jewish religious services.[8]

In one recension of the *"Shimmush Tehillim"* we find somewhat more complex instructions regarding the use of the seventh Psalm against enemies. Here the undertones of the prayer-incantation are most belligerent, i.e. seeking the total destruction of the enemy. In this regard, the Psalm is again whispered seven times over the dust, which is then scattered in the manner delineated above. This action is followed by enunciating the following prayer-incantation, in which there is no reference to any of the mentioned Divine Names aligned with *Psalm 7*:

אתה מלך עולם אשר מקצפך חול תחול הארץ
ומגערתך עמודי שמים ירופפו
יהי רצון מלפניך האל המושיע שתשפיל אויבי
ותפיל אימתך ופחדך על אלו האויבים הרודפים
אחרי וידמו כאבן ויגורו מפני ויחזרו לדרכם
ישובו על עקב בשתם ותכסם בושה וכלמה ואני
[....personal name....] אמלט מידם בשם האל המושיע
אמן אמן אמן סלה סלה סלה

Transliteration:

> *Atah melech olam asher mikitz'p'cha chul tachul ha'aretz u'miga'arat'cha amudei hashamayim y'rofafu*
> *Y'hi ratzon mil'fanecha el hamoshi'a shetash'pil oy'vai v'tapil eimatecha u'fach'd'cha al eilu ha'oy'vim harod'fim acharei v'yid'mu ka'aven v'yagaru mip'nei vichaz'ru l'dar'kam yashuvu al eikev bosh'tam utachasem bushah uch'limah v'ani [....personal name....] amaleit miyadam b'sheim ha'el hamoshi'a Omein Omein Omein Selah Selah Selah*

Translation:

> You are an eternal King, of whose wrath the earth shall be shaken, and from whose rebuke the pillars of heaven will tremble. May it be your will, God of Salvation, for you will humiliate my enemies, and cast your terror and dread upon these foes who pursue me. And they will be immobile like

a stone, and be afraid of me. And they will return on their way. They will turn on their heels, and cover themselves with shame and mortification. And I [....personal name....] will be delivered from their hand in the Name of the God of Salvation. *Amen Amen Amen Selah Selah Selah.*[9]

Additionally we are informed in the same manuscript that if the dust is carried to the residence of the enemy, where it is to be placed at the door or gate, the following prayer-incantation should be recited whilst performing this deed:

אתה האל הגבור והנורא באתי לפניך להפיל תחנה
שתשפיל ותכניע אויבי ואויביך הרעים ואבד גופם
ובשרם וממונם וכל אשר להם ותפטות כל עדת
ישראל ממעלליהם הרעים בשם האל יהיה הדבר
אמן אמן אמן סלה סלה סלה

Transliteration:

> *Atah ha'el hagibor v'hanora bati l'fanayich l'hapil t'chinah shetash'pil v'tach'niya oy'vai v'oy'vayich hara'im v'avad gufam ub'saram umamonam v'chol asher lahem v'tif'tor kol eidat yis'ra'eil mima'al'leihem hara'im bashem ha'el yih'yeh hadavar omein omein omein selah selah selah*

Translation:

> You are a mighty and awesome God. I have come before you to make a petition before you, that you will humiliate and subdue my enemies and your evil adversaries. Destroy their bodies, and their flesh, and their wealth, and all that they have, and deliver every Congregation of Israel from their wicked deeds. In the name of God will be the (magic) word. *Amen Amen Amen Selah Selah Selah.*[10]

The magical use of *Psalm 7* is not only about being protected against enemies, but, amongst others, also about seeking a favourable judgment in legal actions. In this regard, we are informed that anyone faced with a lawsuit, should speak the seventh Psalm in court prior to judgment, and conclude by enunciating the following prayer-incantation:[11]

יהי רצון מלפניך אל עליון שתוציאני לזכות
ותדינני לכף זכות אמן אמן

Transliteration:

> *Y'hi ratzon mil'fanecha El El'yon shetotzi'ani liz'kot*
> *v'tadineini l'chafz'chot*

Translation:

> May it be your will *El El'yon*, that I will be brought to win,
> and to judge in my favor.

The English translation of the Selig version of the "*Shimmush Tehillim*," offers the following instructions in terms of exactly how the prayer-incantation should be recited, reading:

> "If you have a case to decide before the court, and you have reasons to fear an unfavourable or partial verdict, then pray this Psalm slowly before you appear in the presence of the judge, thinking at the same time of *Eel Elijon* and of the righteousness of your cause, and as you approach the judge pray as follows, saying:
>
> 'Oh, *Eel Elijon*! turn thou the heart of the judge to favour my best interests, and grant that I may be fully justified when I depart. Give unto my words power and strength and let me find favour. Amen! Selah!'"[12]

One manuscript noted that if the ruling is unfavourable, that the individual so impacted should collect water from a spring (well), and recite the seventh Psalm seven times from verse seven to the end. The water is poured out in a specific manner over three days whilst reciting a prayer-incantation, an action which is claimed will aid the said individual in getting the verdict overturned.[13] Since this smacks of getting personal will satisfied at any cost, one may well wonder where justice enters the picture.

I am reminded of those Mafia types who suppose that if a priest can be paid to say a "Mass" for a private intention, that is the same as bribing God to do anything asked for. As I mentioned elsewhere, you cannot bribe or buy the Divine One for any price whatsoever. A deity who would be buyable would not be worth approaching anyway, because that would make nonsense out of everything. All that can be done is approach Divinity consciously, either for yourself or on behalf of someone, doing so through a chosen procedure, the idea being: "If such and such be in conformity with Your Will," and then outlining the request.[14] There is no question of influencing the Eternal Living Spirit to do what you want purely because you have gone to the trouble of dressing up specially, and saying a lot of words you think the Divine One would be glad to hear. In this regard I noted that "it is simply a straightforward matter of making a ceremonial relationship with Divinity, during which certain matters are brought into the focus of consciousness for consideration. The outcome always remains with the Superior Spirit."[15]

It should be noted that the seventh Psalm is also often recommended against intimidation and fierce persecution; for protection in perilous situations and times of trouble; anxiety caused by enemies; and for what is today commonly called post-traumatic stress disorder, i.e. the psychological damage resulting from trauma. Otherwise, it is one of the Psalms which are said to be good for headaches or other pains in the head, and for illness in general. It is equally recommended against unjust accusations, and against enemies in a court of law.

There are also again magical uses of individual verses from the current Psalm. In this regard, it should be noted that the letters comprising *Psalm 7:7* were conjoined in the following Divine Name construct, said to have the "power of revenge,"[16] which is not surprising considering the underlying sentiment expressed in the verse reading in translation, "Arise *YHVH*, in Thine anger, lift up Thyself in indignation against mine adversaries; yea, awake for me at the judgment which Thou hast commanded":

$$\text{יְהוּשׁ יְהַף יְהַט יְהַץ מוֹהַץ קָתֻוִי}$$

$$\text{כֶּהְהַר אַלְבָּא מַבִי יְהֹוָה}$$

$$\text{רְווֹצַת עֲרְבַר אוֹבִי נוֹשַׁע}$$

There is no indication as to how this Divine Name construct is enacted for the said purpose, but considering the fact that it is "vowelised," it is probably enunciated. In harmony with the sentiment of indignation highlighted in the current verse, it is worth noting that *Psalm 7:12*, specifically the portion which reads באל זעם בכל יום (*v'el zo'eim b'chol yom*—"and God hath indignation every day"), is indirectly associated with לאו (*Lav*), the seventeenth tri-letter portion of the "*Shem Vayisa Vayet*" ("*Name of Seventy-two Names*"). In this regard, we are informed that the "secret" here is "the momentary indignation of the Almighty, stirred the sea with its power."[17]

On a more positive note we might consider that *Psalm 7:18* is directly affiliated with אום (*Om*), the thirtieth tri-letter portion of the "*Shem Vayisa Vayet*."[18] This is because this tri-letter combination can be directly traced in this verse, in compliance with certain rules. This portion of the "*Name of Seventy-two Names*" is further said to incorporate two Divine Names, i.e. יהוה (*YHVH*) and אהיה (*Ehyeh*), which is due to the fact that the *gematria* of אום [א $= 1 + $ ו $= 6 + $ ם $= 40 = 47$) is equal to the collective *gematria* of the said Divine Names [י $= 10 + $ ה $= 5 + $ ו $= 6 + $ ה $= 5 + $ א $= 1 + $ ה $= 5 + $ י $= 10 + $ ה $= 5 = 47$].[19]

Psalm 7 features equally prominently in Christian magical literature for the same purposes and more. In the earlier mentioned Christian Arab manuscript in the Kaufmann collection, this Psalm is "resorted to in imploring protection against one's enemies and when one has to appear before a tribunal."[20] Virtually the same instructions regarding stopping pursuers in their tracks are found in both Christian and Jewish magical usages of the seventh Psalm, with a curious variant in the Christian presentation. "*Le Livre d'Or*" repeats the details about picking up earth, and reciting over it the Psalm, but it also instructs the user to "write the character and the Intelligence" on the soil, and then to "throw this powder along with what you have written into it, into the face of your enemies. This is said will cause them to retreat.[21]

The name of the "Intelligence" is said to be *Eliel*, which one commentator claimed to be a reference to an intelligence of the same name mentioned in "*The Stenographia of Trithemius*."[22] Beyond bearing the same appellative, there is of course no indication whether the two references pertain to one and the same "Spirit Intelligence." However, there is an obvious association between the name *Eliel* and the the Divine Name *El Elyon*, but there is really no way of ascertaining the truth of the matter. We also find in *"Le Livre d'Or"* a reference to *Psalm 7* having to be recited four times whilst drawing water from a spring, or from a river in "an earthenware vase" in the current instance. Even the accompanying prayer relates to the one listed in the *"Shimmush Tehillim,"* as does the instruction to "throw this water onto the place over which your enemies will pass and you will always vanquish them."[23]

The power of the seventh Psalm to overcome enemies is emphasized elsewhere in Christian Magic, where *Psalm 7:13–14* is listed amongst the biblical verses employed in a procedure pertaining to "binding the arrows, daggers, swords, and all Implements of War."[24] However, *"Le Livre d'Or"* maintains *Psalm 7* to be good for a lot more than getting rid of enemies. It claims this Psalm "procures the assistance of God if you say it piously when in times of need," and that "it also procures relief for prisoners and in the same way it prevents you from being cheated by whomever and it serves against enemies and against lawsuits, if you carry it upon yourself along with its character and its Intelligence."[25]

Regarding "lawsuits" we are told to simply "repeat the name of the Intelligence" when appearing before the judge, and that this is good enough to "find favour."[26] In terms of the latter, we are informed in the earlier mentioned Byzantine Christian manuscripts that this Psalm is to be used on "powerful men," and in particular when you wish to visit such individuals, e.g. "to pay court to a king."[27] In the same manuscripts we find the seventh Psalm being employed for healing purposes. In this regard, the instruction is to recite the Psalm in the ear of the sufferer.[28]

The same source maintains this Psalm to be equally useful in healing afflictions of a spiritual nature. In this regard, we are informed that *Psalm 7* is good to free a man who is "bound," i.e. his sexual prowess suffers magical constraint, which thus results in interference in his marital relations. Corrective magical measures require the practitioner to be pure for two days, then to write the current Psalm, as well as the names of the sufferer and his mother on paper. Afterwards the said practitioner should visit a spring where the paper is to be bound to the right hand of the recipient, following which it is said "that night he will bed his wife.[29] The said manuscripts also include instructions in which it is maintained that writing the current Psalm with a set of magical characters, all of which are fumigated with fragrant incenses, and buried in the corners of a residence, will ensure prosperity in that home.[30]

Psalm 7 is also employed in Christian magic for "Dream Questioning."[31] In this regard, one resource instructs individuals seeking answers in dream, to employ the seventh Psalm in conjunction with an "Intelligence" named "*Assa*," as well as its symbol, both of which are written on a laurel leaf with ink made from rose water. The procedure is to be enacted on certain days during specific planetary hours, during which the leaf is located underneath the bed directly beneath the head of the would be "dreamer." This is followed by the recitation of *Psalm 7*, anointing the forehead of the practitioner with a paste blended from a variety of substances, and the action concluded by the enunciation of a relevant prayer-incantation. It is said answers will be received in dream "without fail,"[32]

In conclusion, it should be noted that *Psalm 7:18* is aligned in the previously mentioned version of the "*Goetia*" with the fifty-second of the so-called "*72 Spirits of the Goetia*."[33]

Psalm 8

[1] למנצח על הגתית מזמור לדוד

[2] יהו‎אהדנהי‎אהדונהי אדנינו מה אדיר שמך בכל הארץ אשר תנה הודך על השמים

[3] מפי עוללים וינקים יסדת עז למען צורריך להשבית אויב ומתנקם

[4] כי אראה שמיך מעשה אצבעתיך ירח וכוכבים אשר כוננתה

[5] מה אנוש כי תזכרנו ובן אדם כי תפקדנו

[6] ותחסרהו מעט מאלהים וכבוד והדר תעטרהו

[7] תמשילהו במעשי ידיך כל שתה תחת רגליו

[8] צנה ואלפים כלם וגם בהמות שדי

[9] צפור שמים ודגי הים עבר ארחות ימים

[10] יהו‎אהדנהי‎אהדונהי אדנינו מה אדיר שמך בכל הארץ

Transliteration:

[1] *lam'natzei'ach al hagitit miz'mor l'david*

[2] *YHVH adoneinu mah adir shim'cha b'chol ha'aretz asher t'nah hod'cha al ha'shamayim*

[3] *mipi ol'lim v'yon'kim yisad'ta oz l'ma'an tzor'recha l'hash'bit oyeiv u'mit'nakeim*

[4] *ki er'eh shamecha ma'asei etz'b'otecha yarei'ach v'chochavim asher konan'ta*

[5] *mah enosh ki tiz'k'renu u'ven adam ki tif'k'denu*

[6] *vat'chas'reihu m'at mei'elohim v'chavod v'hadar t'at'reihu*

[7] *tam'shileihu b'ma'asei yadecha kol shatah tachat rag'lav*

[8] *tzoneh va'alafim kulam v'gam bahamot sadai*

[9] *tzipor shamayim ud'gei ha'yam oveir or'chot yamim*

[10] *YHVH adoneinu mah adir shim'cha b'chol ha'aretz*

Translation:

[1] For the Leader; upon the *Gittith*. A Psalm of David.

[2] *YHVH* our Lord, how glorious is Thy name in all the earth! whose majesty is rehearsed above the heavens.

[3] Out of the mouth of babes and sucklings hast Thou founded strength, because of Thine adversaries; that Thou mightest still the enemy and the avenger.

[4] When I behold Thy heavens, the work of Thy fingers, the moon and the stars, which Thou hast established;
[5] What is man, that Thou art mindful of him? and the son of man, that Thou thinkest of him?
[6] Yet Thou hast made him but little lower than the angels [*elohim*], and hast crowned him with glory and honour.
[7] Thou hast made him to have dominion over the works of Thy hands; Thou hast put all things under His feet:
[8] Sheep and oxen, all of them, yea, and the beasts of the field;
[9] The fowl of the air, and the fish of the sea; whatsoever passeth through the paths of the seas.
[10] *YHVH* our Lord, how glorious is Thy name in all the earth!

Psalm 8 is associated with ברכת הלבנה (*Birkat Halevanah*—"Blessing of the Moon"), also known as קידוש הלבנה (*Kiddush Levanah*—"Sanctification of the Moon"). The exact day when the the consecration of the New Moon should take place varies amongst Jewish communities, but all agree it should be enacted outdoors and mostly on a Saturday night, when everyone is still in the lofty Spirit of *Shabbat*, and ready to continue celebrating the *Shechinah*, the earlier mentioned Feminine Presence of the Divine One in their midst. Regarding *Psalm 8*, the very beautiful fourth verse reading "when I behold Thy heavens, the work of Thy fingers, the moon and the stars, which Thou hast established," inspired some communities to precede the "Sanctification of the Moon" with a recitation of the entire Psalm, though some enunciate only the said verse during this very special consecration.[1]

The eighth Psalm is also recited after מנחה (*Minchah*—the afternoon prayer service) of *Yom Kippur Katan*, a fast day which appears to have been introduced into Jewish worship in the sixteenth century by the Safed Kabbalists, and is celebrated on the day before *Rosh Chodesh*, i.e. the first day of the month equated with the appearance of the New Moon. However, when *Rosh Chodesh* falls on *Shabbat* or on a Sunday, the *Yom Kippur Katan* fast is celebrated on a Thursday, and the Psalm recited before the afternoon service. There are communities who standardly enunciate the eighth Psalm prior to *Minchah*.[2]

Psalm 8:2 is amongst a set of seven biblical verses which is recited during הושענא רבא (*Hoshana Raba*—"Great Supplication") on the seventh day of *Sukkot* ("Festival of Booths"). On this day, the *Torah* scrolls are taken from the Ark in the synagogue, and located on the *Bimah*, i.e. the platform with a reading desk in the centre of the synagogue, whilst the congregation trace seven circumambulations around them. A *Hoshana* is recited during each circuit, and each is completed with a recitation of a biblical verse. Collectively these seven verses represent the seven "Divine Qualities" related to the seven lower *sefirot* on the kabbalistic Tree of Life, i.e. חסד (*Chesed*— "Mercy"): *Psalm 89:3*; גבורה (*Gevurah*—"Might"): *Psalm 89:14*; תפארת (*Tif'eret*—"beauty"): *Micah 7:20*; נצח (*Netzach*— "Victory"): *Psalm 16:11*; הוד (*Hod*—"Glory"): *Psalm 8:2*; יסוד (*Yesod*—"Foundation"): *Psalm 145:17*, and מלכות (*Malchut*— "Kingdom"/"Kingship"): *Zechariah 14:9*.[3]

The performance of the seven circumambulations during *Hoshana Raba* ("Great Supplication") is in itself a "magical act" through which we seek to gain Divine favour, and the use of *Psalm 8* in Jewish Magic is to achieve this very purpose, i.e. finding favour (*limtzo chen*),[4] though not necessarily of the Divine kind only. In fact, one recension of the "*Shimmush Tehillim*" maintains this Psalm "is good for grace and favour in the eyes of all creatures."[5] In this regard, the simplest instructions are to recite the eighth Psalm seven times every evening ("sunrise" according to some recensions)[6] over a period of three days.[7] However, the most common recensions of the "*Shimmush Tehillim*" maintain the Psalm should be recited over olive oil, this substance being afterwards employed to rub the face, hands and feet.[8]

It should be noted, that not every manuscript source of the "*Shimmush Tehillim*" maintain the current Psalm should be recited seven times over three days. One recension noted it should be whispered seven times over oil, the latter substance being used to anoint the mentioned bodily parts, and then to add the following prayer-incantation which includes a related Divine Name:

אתה אלוה הבריות אדון כל תרחם עלי ותשמרני
ותתנני לחן לחסד ולרהמים בעיני כל בריותיך

שבראת בעולם הוה בשם זה יהיה הדבר ממני

[.....personal name.....] שם המזמור זה אמן אמן

אמן סלה סלה סלה

Transliteration:

> *Atah eloha habri'ot adon kol t'racheim alai v'tish'm'reini v'tit'neini l'chen l'chesed ul'rachamim b'einei kol b'ri'otecha shebarata ba'olam hazeh besheim ZaH (ZaHa). yih'yeh hadavar mimeni [.....personal name.....] sheim hamiz'mor ZaH (ZaHa). Omein Omein Omein Selah Selah Selah*

Translation:

> You are God of creatures, Lord of all. Have mercy on me, protect me and grant me grace, mercy and compassion in the eyes of all your creatures whom you have created in this world. In the name *ZaH* (*ZaHa*) will be the (magic) word for me [.....personal name.....]. The name of the Psalm is *ZaH* (*ZaHa*). *Amen Amen Amen Selah Selah Selah.*[9]

There is no indication of the derivation of the Divine Name זה (perhaps enunciated *ZaH* or *ZaHa*), and hence could inadvertently be read as the common Hebrew word meaning "this." However, the said letter combination is in the current instance indeed a Divine Name.[10] As can be seen, there are no further instances in which there is a Divine Name associated with *Psalm 8* in the primary Hebrew texts. However, a Divine Name construct is included in a prayer-incantation affiliated with the current Psalm in Selig's oft-mentioned German/English version. In this regard, we are told that "if you wish to secure the love and good will of all men in your business transactions, you should pray this Psalm three days in succession after sundown, and think continually of the holy name of רחמיאל (*Rechmial*), which signifies great and strong God of love, of grace and mercy. Pronounce at each time the appropriate prayer over a small quantity of olive oil, and anoint the face as well as the hands and feet."[11] The prayer reads "May it please thee, Oh, *Rechmial El*, to grant that I may obtain love, grace and favour in the eyes of men according to thy holy will. Amen! Selah!"[12]

We are further informed that the Divine Name was created: ר (*Resh*) from אדיר (*Adir*—"glorious"): verse 2; ח (*Chet*) from ירח (*yarei'ach*—"the moon"): verse 4; מ (*Mem*) from (*adam*— "man"): verse 5 (the word referencing "man" in the verse is אנוש [*enosh*]); י (*Yod*) from כי (*ki*—"that"): verse 5 (omitted in the English version); א (*Alef*) from מאלהום (*mei'elohim*—"than the angels"): verse 6; and תמשילהו (*tam'shileihu*—"to have dominion"): verse 7.[13]

As one might expect, *Psalm 8* is also employed for other magical intentions, e.g. to aid crying infants, or more specifically "a boy who weeps."[14] This use is added virtually as an aside in the "*Shimmush Tehillim,*" but one author appeared to have conflated the earlier instruction about reciting the Psalm over oil, and its use to stop children from crying. In this regard, we are instructed to take oil in a glass at sunset, and to recite the eighth Psalm three times consecutively over it, and then to smear some of the oil on the face, hands and feet of the child.[15] Otherwise, the Psalm is said to be good for pregnant women. It is one of the Psalms which is proposed for recitation every day during the entire length of a pregnancy; and is also recommended for children who are ill. It should be further noted that the current Psalm is further endorsed for praise and upliftment; the goodwill and love of others in business; and equally to avert any hurt which might be caused by perverted individuals.

As noted in terms of the previously addressed Psalms, there are again single verses from the current Psalm which are employed for a variety of magical purposes. In this regard, it is worth noting that the capitals of the words comprising the portion of *Psalm 8:2* reading מה אדיר שמך בכל הארץ (*mah adir shim'cha b'chol ha-aretz*—"how glorious is Thy name in all the earth"), is conjoined into the Divine Name construct מאשבה which is included in amulets for the purposes of having a request successfully granted by anyone.[16] *Psalm 8:10* is equally recommended for the same purpose.[17]

Psalm 8:2 also features in the following Divine Name construct, which is said to have the power to dispel (rebuke) impure powers which cause fevers.[18] In this regard, the Divine Name was formed from the first seven words of the said verse, six of which were conjoined with the Ineffable Name, in the following manner:

בשכמל״ו

Observing the vowel points of this Divine Name construct, which align with the vocalisation of the component letters in the said verse, as well as their conjunction with a standard enunciation of the Ineffable Name, the complete Divine Name construct reads *Y'hav'ha Y'ahadov'neihanu Y'mahah'v'ha Y'ahadiv'y'har Y'shiham'v'chaha Y'v'hachov'l'ha Y'haha'av'rehatz*. The concluding set of letters is an abbreviation of a standard Hebrew phrase employed at the end of prayers, adjurations, etc. It reads ברוך שם כבוד מלכותו לעולם ועד (*Baruch sheim k'vod mal'chuto l'olam va'ed*— "Blessed be the Name of His glorious Kingdom throughout eternity").[19]

    We are told the current Divine Name construct expresses itself in two ways, as indicated in the following arrangement:

יהוה	נוריאל	יהוה
יאהדונהנו		יאהדונהנו
ימההוה		ימההוה
יאהדויהר		יאהדויהר
ישהמוכה		ישהמוכה
יבהכולה		יבהכולה
יההאורהץ		יההאורהץ

The combination to the right is said to be "hidden" or obscure, whilst the one to the left is "open" or transparent, with the angel נוריאל (*Nuri'el*—"Flame" or "Lamp of God"), centrally balancing the powers expressed in these Divine Names.[20]

This Divine Name construct is further employed in the following prayer-incantation to encourage a good livelihood, and which we are told should be inserted at the conclusion of the תפילת העמידה (*T'filat Amidah*—"Standing Prayer"), also called the שמנה עשרה (*Shemoneh Esrei*) prayer.[21] The latter expression is the Hebrew for the word "eighteen," and thus referencing the fact that the prayer originally comprised eighteen blessings.

I am well aware that many of my readers are not Jewish, and that the *Amidah* prayer would have little if any meaning to them personally. However, I see no reason why they should not derive the mentioned benefit offered by the said prayer-incantation, if they follow the rule of reciting it in holiness and purity with *Kavvanah*, i.e. a strongly focussed intention:

יהי רצון מלפניך יְהָוָה אלהי ואלהי אבתי רבון כל
העולמים עשה למענך ולמען קדושת שמך הגדול
והנורא הקדוש וטהור יְהָוָה יְאֵהֲדֹוּנְהִי יִמָהֲהֹוָה
יְאֵהֲדֹוּיִהָר יִשְׁהָמֹוּכָה יִבְהָכֹוּלָה יְהָהָאֹוּרֵהָץ
בשכמל״ו [ברוך שם כבוד מלכותו לעולם ועד]
יְהָוָה שתמלא רצוני ומשאלותי ותזמין לי פרנסתי
ברויח ולא בצמצום ותצילני מכל חסרון כיס ומכל
צרח ומכל דבר רע ומכל מה שלבי ירא ממנו

Transliteration:
> *Y'hi ratzon mil'fanecha Y'hav'ha elohai veilohei avotai ribon kol ha'olamim aseih l'ma'an'cha ul'ma'an k'dushat shim'cha hagadol v'hanora hakadosh v'tahor Y'hav'ha Y'ahadov'neihanu Y'mahah'v'ha Y'ahadiv'y'har Y'hav'ha Y'shiham'v'chaha Y'v'hachov'l'ha Y'haha'av'rehatz baruch sheim k'vod mal'chuto l'olam va'ed Y'hav'ha shet'malei r'tzoni umish'eilotai v'taz'min li par'nasati b'revach v'lo b'tzimtzum v'tatzileini mikol chisaron kis umikol tzarah umikol davar ra umikol mah shelibi yarei mimenu*

Translation:
> May it be your will *Y'hav'ha* my God and God of my father, Lord of all the worlds, to act for your sake and for the sanctity of your great and awesome, holy and pure

name, *Y'hav'ha   Y'ahadov'neihanu   Y'mahah'v'ha Y'ahadiv'y'har   Y'shiham'v'chaha   Y'v'hachov'l'ha Y'haha'av'rehatz*, blessed be the Name of His glorious Kingdom throughout eternity. *Y'hav'ha* fulfil my will and my desires, and provide for my livelihood with profit and not with reduction, and save me from being out of pocket, and from every trouble, and from every evil thing, and from everything my heart fears.

We are admonished to be most careful not to vocalise the Divine Names aloud, but to enunciate them mentally whilst moving the throat and the lips without making any audible sound.[22]

Another verse, *Psalm 8:10*, is directly affiliated with וממב (*Umab*), the sixty-first portion of the "*Shem Vayisa Vayet.*"[23] As noted elsewhere, this tri-letter combination is said to be an acronym of the phrase ואתה מושל בכל (*v'atah moshel ba'kol*—"and Thou rulest over all*") (*I Chronicles 29:12*). We are also reminded that the *gematria* of וממב [ו = 6 + מ = 40 + ב = 2 = 48] equates with that of the word חיל (*chayil*—"strength" or "ability" [ח = 8 + י = 10 + ל = 30 = 48]).[24] This should give a clear indication what this tri-letter portion of the "*Name of Seventy-two Names*" is all about.

As far as the uses of *Psalm 8* in Christian Magic is concerned, we are informed that "an allusion to the 'mouth of babes and sucklings' in verse 2," was enough for this Psalm to be noted in the earlier mentioned Arabic Kaufmann manuscript as "an appropriate remedy to silence crying children.[25] The same purpose is listed in "*Le Livre d'Or*" where it is noted that the eighth Psalm will "prevent children crying," when it is written and tied "to the right arm of the child."[26] In the same breath it adds an oddity found nowhere else, i.e. that reciting "the first verse only from this Psalm," will afford one the ability to carry bees "to their territory."[27] Once again there are astrological considerations pertaining to these magical applications in "*Le Livre d'Or.*"[28]

In the Byzantine manuscripts *Psalm 8* is employed against "legal opponents," and for quite mischievous purposes. In this regard, it is said to be useful "for an accusation, if you accuse someone and want to take advantage of him."[29] In this regard, the practitioner should fill a new vessel with spring water, and recite the Psalm over it. The water is afterwards disposed of at the door of the judge, when the latter is away from home, and this is done whilst reciting "As this water is poured out, so too may the claim of so-and-so be dissipated."[30] The same sources states that *Psalm 8* is to be used on "powerful men."[31]

    In conclusion, *Psalm 8* features in the "*Key of Solomon*" as the first amongst a set of eight Psalms recited during the construction of "pentacles," the others being *Psalms 21, 27, 29, 32, 51, 72* and *134*.[32] It is also the fourth of nineteen Psalms recited over the wax from which ritual candles are made, the full set being *Psalms 8, 15, 22, 46, 47, 49, 51, 53, 68, 72, 84, 102, 110, 113, 126, 130, 131, 133*, and *139*.[33]

Psalm 9

[1] למנצח על מות לבן מזמור לדוד

[2] אודה יהוה‎אדני‎יאהדונהי בכל לבי אספרה כל נפלאותיך

[3] אשמחה ואעלצה בך אזמרה שמך עליון

[4] בשוב אויבי אחור יכשלו ויאבדו מפניך

[5] כי עשית משפטי ודיני ישבת לכסא שופט צדק

[6] גערת גוים אבדת רשע שמם מחית לעולם ועד

[7] האויב תמו חרבות לנצח וערים נתשת אבד זכרם המה

[8] ויהוה‎אדני‎ יאהדונהי לעולם ישב כונן למשפט כסאו

[9] והוא ישפט תבל בצדק ידין לאמים במישרים

[10] ויהי יהוה‎אדני‎יאהדונהי משגב לדך משגב לעתות בצרה

[11] ויבטחו בך יודעי שמך כי לא עזבת דרשיך יהוה‎אדני‎ יאהדונהי

[12] זמרו ליהוה‎אדני‎ יאהדונהי ישב ציון הגידו בעמים עלילותיו

[13] כי דרש דמים אותם זכר לא שכח צעקת ענוים

[14] חננני יהוה‎אדני‎יאהדונהי ראה עניי משנאי מרוממי משערי מות

[15] למען אספרה כל תהלתיך בשערי בת ציון אגילה בישועתך

[16] טבעו גוים בשחת עשו ברשת זו טמנו נלכדה רגלם

[17] נודע יהוה‎אדני‎יאהדונהי משפט עשה בפעל כפיו נוקש רשע הגיון סלה

[18] ישובו רשעים לשאולה כל גוים שכחי אלהים

[19] כי לא לנצח ישכח אביון תקות ענוים תאבד לעד

[20] קומה יהוה‎אדני‎יאהדונהי אל יעז אנוש ישפטו גוים על פניך

[21] שיתה יהוה‏אדני‏יאהדונהי מורה להם ידעו גוים אנוש
המה סלה

Transliteration:

[1] *lam'natzei'ach al mut labein miz'mor l'david*

[2] *odeh YHVH b'chol libi asap'rah kol nif'l'oteicha*

[3] *es'm'chah v'e'el'tzah vach azam'rah shim'cha el'yon*

[4] *b'shuv oy'vai achor yikash'lu v'yov'du mipanecha*

[5] *ki asita mish'pati v'dini yashav'ta l'chisei shofeit tzedek*

[6] *ga'arta goyim ibad'ta rasha sh'mam machita l'olam va'ed*

[7] *ha'oyeiv tamu choravot lanetzach v'arim natash'ta avad zich'ram heimah*

[8] *vaYHVH l'olam yeisheiv konein lamish'pat kis'o*

[9] *v'hu yish'pot teiveil b'tzedek yadin l'umim b'meisharim*

[10] *vihi YHVH mis'gav ladach mis'gav l'itot batzarah*

[11] *v'yiv't'chu v'cha yod'ei sh'mecha ki lo azav'ta dor'shecha YHVH*

[12] *zam'ru laYHVH yosheiv tziyon hagidu va'amim alilotav*

[13] *ki doreish damim otam zachar lo shachach tza'akat anavim*

[14] *chon'neini YHVH r'eih on'yi mison'ai m'rom'mi misha'arei mavet*

[15] *l'ma'an asap'rah kol t'hilatecha b'sha'arei vat tziyon agilah bishu'atecha*

[16] *tav'u goyim b'shachat asu b'reshet zu tamanu nil'k'da rag'lam*

[17] *noda YHVH mish'pat asah b'fo'al kapav nokeish rasha higayon selah*

[18] *yashuvu r'sha'im lish'olah kol goyim sh'cheichei elohim*

[19] *ki lo lanetzach yishachach ev'yon tik'vat aniyim tovad la'ad*

[20] *kumah YHVH al ya'oz enosh yishaf'tu goyim al panecha*

[21] *shitah YHVH morah lahem yeid'u goyim enosh heimah selah*

Translation:

[1] For the Leader; upon *Muthlabben*. A Psalm of David.

[2] I will give thanks unto *YHVH* with my whole heart; I will tell of all Thy marvellous works.

[3] I will be glad and exult in Thee; I will sing praise to Thy name, O Most High:

[4] When mine enemies are turned back, they stumble and perish at Thy presence;

[5] For Thou hast maintained my right and my cause; Thou sattest upon the throne as the righteous Judge.

[6] Thou hast rebuked the nations, Thou hast destroyed the wicked, Thou hast blotted out their name for ever and ever.

[7] O thou enemy, the waste places are come to an end for ever; and the cities which thou didst uproot, their very memorial is perished.

[8] But *YHVH* is enthroned for ever; He hath established His throne for judgment.

[9] And He will judge the world in righteousness, He will minister judgment to the peoples with equity.

[10] *YHVH* also will be a high tower for the oppressed, a high tower in times of trouble;

[11] And they that know Thy name will put their trust in Thee; for thou *YHVH*, hast not forsaken them that seek Thee.

[12] Sing praises to *YHVH*, who dwelleth in Zion; declare among the peoples His doings.

[13] For He that avengeth blood hath remembered them; He hath not forgotten the cry of the humble.

[14] Be gracious unto me *YHVH*, behold mine affliction at the hands of them that hate me; Thou that liftest me up from the gates of death;

[15] That I may tell of all Thy praise in the gates of the daughter of Zion, that I may rejoice in Thy salvation.

[16] The nations are sunk down in the pit that they made; in the net which they hid is their own foot taken.

[17] *YHVH* hath made Himself known, He hath executed judgment, the wicked is snared in the work of his own hands. *Higgaion. Selah*

[18] The wicked shall return to the nether-world, even all the nations that forget *Elohim*.

[19] For the needy shall not alway be forgotten, nor the expectation of the poor perish for ever.

[20] Arise *YHVH*, let not man prevail; let the nations be judged in Thy sight.

[21] Set terror over them *YHVH*; let the nations know they are but men. *Selah*

It is said that when it comes to requests and prayers, *Psalm 9* is good for everything.[1] However, in Jewish Magic the ninth Psalm is equally employed for specific purposes. Some sources maintain the Psalm will aid the healing of ill children,[2] whilst others maintain that, as in the case of the previous Psalm, the current one also supports crying children.[3] In terms of dealing with a boy afflicted with incessant tears, one recension of the "*Shimmush Tehillim*" instructs the Psalm should be written, suspended around the neck of the child, and this action concluded by saying:

יהי רצון מלפניך **אהיה** אדון כל שמע קולי ורחם
על זה הנער מנומה ושינה ותרדמה בשם **אהיה** יהיה
ל'[....name of recipient....] אמן אמן אמן סלה סלה סלה סלה

Transliteration:

> *Y'hi ratzon mil'fanecha Eh'yeh adon kol sh'ma koli v'rachem al zeh hana'ar m'numah v'sheinah v'tar'd'mah b'sheim Eh'yeh yih'yeh l'[....name of recipient....] Omein Omein Omein Selah Selah Selah*

Translation:

> May it be your will *Eh'yeh*, Lord of all. Hear my voice and have mercy on this boy with slumber, sleep and deep sleep. In the name *Eh'yeh* there will be sleep for [....name of recipient....]. *Amen Amen Amen Selah Selah Selah*.[4]

The Divine Name employed here is the well-known אהיה (*Eh'yeh*—"I am"), which in the current instance is said to have been derived: א (*Alef*) from אודה (*odeh*—"I will give thanks [give praise]"): verse 2; ה (*Heh*) from האויב (*ha'oyeiv*—"the enemy"): verse 7; ' (*Yod*) from נלכדה רגלם (*nil'k'da rag'lam* —"snared"): verse 16 by transposing the מ (*Mem*) my means of the

א״ת ב״ש (*Atbash*) cipher; and the concluding ה (*Heh*) from סלה (*Selah*): verse 21.[5]

In the published versions in which the ninth Psalm is employed to aid sick children who might be crying as a result of their indisposition, the full expression אהיה אשר אהיה (*Eh'yeh asher Eh'yeh*—"I am that I am") is listed as the associated Divine Name.[6] In this instance, it is recommended that the entire Psalm should be written and recited in conjunction with the following prayer-incantation:

יהי רצון מלפניך **אהיה אשר אהיה** השם הגדול
הגבור והנורא שתסיר ממנו זאת הבכיה תרפאהו
מבלי חשישות והסיר ממנו סבה וכל שטן ומזיק
וכל כאב וחלי מעתה ועד עולם

Transliteration:

> *Y'hi ratzon mil'fanecha Eh'yeh asher Eh'yeh hasheim hagadol hagibor v'hanora shetasir mimenu zot hab'chiyah tir'pa'eihu mib'li chashishot v'heisir mimenu sipah v'chol satan umazik v'chol k'eiv v'choli mei'atah v'ad olam.*

Translation:

> May it be your will *Eh'yeh asher Eh'yeh*, the great, strong and awesome name, that you remove this weeping from him and heal him with no weakness, and remove from him the cause (of the illness), every satan, demon and harmful spirit, every pain and every disease, for now and forever.[7]

Once again the written text is to be hung around the neck of the infant.[8] However, in the Selig German/English version of the "*Shimmush Tehillim*," it is maintained that the current Psalm and prayer-incantation should be written "upon pure parchment, with a new pen."[9] In this instance the accompanying prayer-incantation is again very different from the Hebrew version. It reads:

> "All-merciful Father! for the sake of thy mighty, adorable and holy name, *Ehyeh asher Ehyeh*, may it please thee to take away from N., son of R., the illness [here name the disease] from which he suffers, and relieve him from his pains. Make him whole in soul, body and mind, and release him during his life from all plagues, injury and danger, and by thou his helper. *Amen.*"[10]

Psalm 9 is further employed against enemies.[11] In this regard, we are told that if "haters" rise up against you, reciting this Psalm and the following accompanying prayer-incantation will save you from them:

יהי רצון מלפניך **אהיה אשר אהיה** שתצילני
מאויבי ורודפי הקמים עלי כמו שהצלת מי
שהתפלל לפניך את השירה הזאת

Transliteration:

> *Y'hi ratzon mil'fanecha Eh'yeh asher Eh'yeh shetatzileini mei'oy'vai v'rod'fai hakamim alai k'mo shehitzal'ta mi shehit'faleil l'fanecha et hashirah hazot.*

Translation:

> May it be your will *Eh'yeh asher Eh'yeh*, to save me from my enemies and my persecutors who are rising up against me, as you saved him who prayed this song [Psalm] before you.[12]

It is yet not the end of the uses of *Psalm 9*, when it comes to dealing with enemies. In fact, one manuscript shares further instructions on magical actions to be employed when an individual is harassed by a specific enemy. In this regard, the procedure repeats writing the Psalm, and suspending it around the neck whilst saying:

בשם **אלהים** חיים רחום וחנון אני נושא זה עלי
שתשפיל ותכניע ותשליך ותמגר ותפיל ארצה
לי'[....name of recipient....] **אויבי** שלא יוכל לעשות
לי רעה אני [....personal name....] בשם **אהיה** יהיה
הדבר אלי אמן אמן אמן סלה סלה סלה

Transliteration:

> *B'sheim Elohim chayim rachum v'chanun ani nose zeh alai shetash'pil v'tach'ni'a v'tash'lich v'tamager v'tapil ar'tzah l'[....name of recipient....] oy'vai shelo yochal la'asot li ra'ah ani [....personal name....] b'sheim Eh'yeh yih'yeh hadavar eilai Omein Omein Omein Selah Selah Selah*

Translation:

> In the name of the living *Elohim*, merciful and gracious, I
> bear this on me so that you will humble, and subjugate, and
> cast down, and eradicate, and confine [drop] to earth
> [....name of recipient....], my enemy, that he can no longer
> do me any evil [harm], I am [....personal name....]. In the
> name *Eh'yeh* the (magic) word will be upon me. *Amen
> Amen Amen Selah Selah Selah.*[13]

The same manuscript includes the final word on how to deal with
enemies using the ninth Psalm, i.e. getting an enemy to make peace
with you, or turning an enemy into a friend. In this regard, the
individual seeking such restitution of good relations, should go to
a flowing river without speaking or saying anything to anyone.
Then the said individual should draw water from the stream in a
pottery vessel, which should then be placed in the left hand before
reciting the Psalm three times over the water, and each time
saying:

שלא [....personal name....] יהיה דבר אלי אני

יוכל [....name of recipient....] שונאי להרע לי ולא

ידבר עוד כנגדי ויבוא וישלים עמי ולא יאכל

ולא ישתה ולא ינוח ולא ישקוט עד השלימו אתי

בשם אהיה יהיה הדבר לטובתי ולהרוחתי אמן

אמן אמן סלה סלה סלה

Transliteration:

> *Yih'yeh davar alai ani* [....personal name....] *shelo yochal*
> [....name of recipient....] *shon'ai l'hara li v'lo y'daber od
> k'neg'di v'yavo v'yash'lim imi v'lo yochal v'lo yish'teh
> v'lo yanu'ach v'lo yish'kot ad hish'limu eti b'sheim Eh'yeh
> yih'yeh hadavar l'tovati ul'haroch'ti Omein Omein Omein
> Selah Selah Selah*

Translation:

> There will be a [magic] word for me [....personal name....],
> so that [....name of recipient....], my enemy, will not hurt
> me, nor speak anymore against me. And he shall come and
> make peace with me. He shall not eat, and not drink, and
> not rest, and not be calm until he has made peace with me.

In the name *Eh'yeh* will be the (magic) word for my good and for my welfare. *Amen Amen Amen Selah Selah Selah.*[14]

I have seen references to *Psalm 9* being employed for the healing of incurable diseases, and for illness in general. It was also recommended against "slavery to sinful passions," and against anxiety caused by enemies. On the other hand, it was suggested in support of those who are oppressed, as well as to diminish poverty, and also for gratitude to the Divine One and gratitude in general.

Once again single verses from the ninth Psalm are employed in "Practical Kabbalah." As indicated elsewhere, *Psalm 9:2* is directly affiliated with דנ׳ (*Dani*), the fiftieth portion, *Psalm 9:10* with מבה (*Mebah*), the fourteenth portion, and *Psalm 9:12* with ר׳׳׳ (*Riyi*), the twenty-ninth portion of the "*Shem Vayisa Vayet.*"[15] As it is, the capitals of the first four words of *Psalm 9:10*, reading ויהי יהוה משגב לדך (*vihi YHVH mis'gav ladach*—"YHVH also will be a high tower for the oppressed"), were combined in a Divine Name construct וימל which is employed in amulets for salvation.[16] Regarding "salvation," this verse was formed into a much larger Divine Name construct which is said to aid escaping all sorts of trouble and distress:[17]

$$\text{וִהִיר הַצִיב יַהַת וְהוּת}$$
$$\text{יְהֹוה עָמָל שֶׁבְגֵג בְשְׁלָם}$$
$$\text{דִכְכֵד}$$

The construction of this Divine Name from the said verse is readily apparent. It necessitates the letters comprising the verse to be intertwined by being written in a forwards and backwards manner. In this regard, commencing with the first letter of the Divine Name construct, the letters of the first four words of the verse, except those comprising the Ineffable Name, can be traced by skipping every second letter, i.e. reading in the standard manner from right to left. This pattern is interrupted by the letters of the Ineffable Name which is divided into two pairs respectively occupying the first two glyphs of the third and fourth portions of the Divine

Name construct, and the full expression of the Ineffable Name occupying the fifth four-letter portion. The letters comprising the fifth word of the verse, the latter being simply a repeat of the third, are written in reverse, and, commencing with the concluding letter of the eighth portion of the Divine Name construct, can again be traced by reading every second letter. The same applies to the first two letters of the sixth word, but the pattern is adjusted with the last three letters of the said word, in order to fit in with the position of the earlier mentioned second two-letter portion of the Ineffable Name. The four letters comprising the concluding word in the verse can be traced by continuing to read every second letter in this reversed manner, commencing with the concluding letter of the second portion of the Divine Name construct.[18]

As far as its use in Christian magic is concerned, we find *Psalm 9*, i.e. both *Psalms 9* and *10* in the Hebrew Bible, employed in the previously mentioned Byzantine manuscripts for the purpose of being "delivered from affliction."[19] In alignment with the Jewish applications of the ninth Psalm, the same manuscripts maintain that reading the Psalm every day, will enable individuals to "subdue" their enemies.[20] On the other hand, kings, princes, and all manner of authorities, are often more "dangerous" and "threatening" than personal enemies. In this regard "*Le Livre d'Or*" advises that an individual who is seeking to be honoured by the said rulers, should write *Psalm 9* on a plate of glass in conjunction with a set of magical characters. This is followed by washing the writing with olive oil with which to rub the face of the said individual.[21]

In conclusion, as far as the Psalms employed in the "*Key of Solomon*" are concerned, it is worth noting that the ninth Psalm is listed in this text as one of seven featuring in the consecration of "the needle and other iron instruments." The others are *Psalms 3, 31, 42, 60, 51*, and *130*.[22] Otherwise, *Psalm 9:15–16* is listed in the same text in terms of recovering lost objects.[23]

Psalm 10

[1] למה יהוה‏אדני‏יאהדונהי תעמד ברחוק תעלים לעתות בצרה

[2] בגאות רשע ידלק עני יתפשו במזמות זו חשבו

[3] כי הלל רשע על תאות נפשו ובצע ברך נאץ יהוה‏אדני‏יאהדונהי

[4] רשע כגבה אפו בל ידרש און אלהים כל מזמותיו

[5] יחילו דרכו בכל עת מרום משפטיך מנגדו כל צורריו יפיח בהם

[6] אמר בלבו בל אמוט לדר ודר אשר לא ברע

[7] אלה פיהו מלא ומרמות ותך תחת לשונו עמל ואון

[8] ישב במארב חצרים במסתרים יהרג נקי עיניו לחלכה יצפנו

[9] יארב במסתר כאריה בסכה יארב לחטוף עני יחטף עני במשכו ברשתו

[10] ידכה ישח ונפל בעצומיו חל כאים

[11] אמר בלבו שכח אל הסתיר פניו בל ראה לנצח

[12] קומה יהוה‏אדני‏יאהדונהי אל נשא ידך אל תשכח ענוים

[13] על מה נאץ רשע אלהים אמר בלבו לא תדרש

[14] ראתה כי אתה עמל וכעס תביט לתת בידך עליך יעזב חלכה יתום אתה היית עוזד

[15] שבר זרוע רשע ורע תדרוש רשעו בל תמצא

[16] יהוה‏אדני‏יאהדונהי מלך עולם ועד אבדו גוים מארצו

[17] תאות ענוים שמעת יהוה‏אדני‏יאהדונהי תכין לבם תקשיב אזנך

[18] לשפט יתום ודך בל יוסיף עוד לערץ אנוש מן הארץ

Transliteration:

[1] *lamah YHVH ta'amod b'rachok ta'lim l'itot batzarah*

[2] *B'ga'avat rasha yid'lak ani yitaf'su bim'zimot zu chashavu*

[3] *ki hileil rasha al ta'avat naf'sho uvotzei'a beireich ni'eitz YHVH*

[4] *rasha k'govah apo bal yid'rosh ein elohim kol m'zimotav*

[5] *yachilu d'rachav b'chol eit marom mish'patecha mineg'do kol tzor'rav yafi'ach ba'hem*

[6] *amar b'libo bal emot l'dor va'dor asher lo v'ra*

[7] *alah pihu malei u'mir'mot va'toch tachat l'shono amal va'aven*

[8] *yeisheiv b'ma'rav chatzeirim bamis'tarim yaharog naki einav l'cheil'chah yitz'ponu*

[9] *ye'erov bamis'tar k'ar'yeih v'sukoh ye'erov lachatof ani yach'tof ani b'mosh'cho v'rish'to*

[10] *yid'keh yasho'ach v'nafal ba'atzumav cheil ka'im*

[11] *amar b'libo shachach el his'tir panav bal ra'ah lanetzach*

[12] *kuma YHVH el n'sa yadecha al tish'kach anavim*

[13] *al meh ni'eitz rasha elohim amar b'libo lo tid'rosh*

[14] *ra'itah ki atah amal vacha'as tabit lateit b'yadecha alecha ya'azov cheileicha yatom atah hayitah ozeir*

[15] *sh'vor z'ro'a rasha vara tid'rosh rish'o val tim'tza*

[16] *YHVH melech olam va'ed av'du goyim mei'ar'tzo*

[17] *ta'avat anavim shama'ta YHVH tachin libam tak'shiv oz'necha*

[18] *lish'pot yatom vadach bal yosif od la'arotz enosh min'ha'aretz*

Translation:

[1] Why standest Thou afar off *YHVH*? Why hidest Thou Thyself in times of trouble?

[2] Through the pride of the wicked the poor is hotly pursued, they are taken in the devices that they have imagined.

[3] For the wicked boasteth of his heart's desire, and the covetous vaunteth himself, though he contemn *YHVH*.

[4] The wicked, in the pride of his countenance, saith: 'He will not require'; all his thoughts are: 'There is no God.'

[5] His ways prosper at all times; Thy judgments are far above out of his sight; as for all his adversaries, he puffeth at them.

[6] He saith in his heart: 'I shall not be moved, I who to all generations shall not be in adversity.'

[7] His mouth is full of cursing and deceit and oppression; under his tongue is mischief and iniquity.

[8] He sitteth in the lurking-places of the villages; in secret places doth he slay the innocent; his eyes are on the watch for the helpless.

[9] He lieth in wait in a secret place as a lion in his lair, he lieth in wait to catch the poor; he doth catch the poor, when he draweth him up in his net.

[10] He croucheth, he boweth down, and the helpless fall into his mighty claws.

[11] He hath said in his heart: 'God hath forgotten; He hideth His face; He will never see.'

[12] Arise *YHVH*; O God, lift up Thy hand; forget not the humble.

[13] Wherefore doth the wicked contemn *Elohim*, and say in his heart: 'Thou wilt not require'?

[14] Thou hast seen; for Thou beholdest trouble and vexation, to requite them with Thy hand; unto Thee the helpless committeth himself; Thou hast been the helper of the fatherless.

[15] Break Thou the arm of the wicked; and as for the evil man, search out his wickedness, till none be found.

[16] *YHVH* is King for ever and ever; the nations are perished out of His land.

[17] *YHVH* Thou hast heard the desire of the humble: Thou wilt direct their heart, Thou wilt cause Thine ear to attend;

[18] To right the fatherless and the oppressed, that man who is of the earth may be terrible no more.

Psalm 10 is recommended in some sources to ward off hatred, and for someone who has enemies ("haters").[1] However, in the primary recensions of the "*Shimmush Tehillim*," and in the published material which references the tenth Psalm, it is employed "against obsession by evil spirits."[2] I find the term "obsession" to be very telling, since I have great misgivings about "demonic possessions" and "exorcisms." Whilst I acknowledge that "spirit possessions" do occur on occasion, in my estimation, and as I noted elsewhere, people are more likely to be "obsessed" than "possessed."[3] In this regard, I stated that "our obsessions are products of our own personalities, and while some of these are harmless enough, others might turn out to be extremely dangerous and injurious."[4] However, such obsessions are not specifically "demonic," and, as said before, it is far "too easy to invent demons where none exist in order to blame some external agency for ones own peculiarities."[5]

Be that as it may, we are informed that "Jewish exorcisms are usually 'liturgical,' using protective passages from the Psalms and other sacred texts, with *Psalms 10, 91,* and *127* particularly being lauded for their power against evil spirits."[6] In terms of employing the tenth Psalm to counteract "demon possession," the simplest procedure to be found in the manuscripts of the "*Shimmush Tehillim,*" instructs the practitioner to take a new vessel, fill it with water drawn from a spring, or perhaps from a well, etc., then to add olive oil to it, and whisper *Psalm 10* nine times over the mixture. Afterwards the entire body of the afflicted is washed with this mixture.[7] Additional actions are shared in further recensions in which the Divine Name constructs derived from the tenth Psalm are included in accompanying prayer-incantations.[8] In this regard, the most referenced Divine Name construct is written אל מץ,[9] and which is said to have been derived: א (*Alef*) from אלה פיהו (*alah pihu*—"His mouth"): verse 7; ל (*Lamed*) from למה (*lamah*—"why"): verse 1; מ (*Mem*) from ענוים (*anavim*—"the humble"): verse 17; and ץ (*Tzadi*) from אנוש מן הארץ (*enosh min'ha'aretz*—"who is of the earth"): verse 18.[10] Yitzhak Hayyim Cantarini maintains the second letter, i.e. ל (*Lamed*), was derived from חיל כאים (*cheil ka'im*—"the helpless"): verse 10.[11]

In the Selig German/English translations of the "*Shimmush Tehillim,*" the said Divine name construct is vocalised "*El Mez*" ("*El Metz*"), which he claims means "Strong God of the oppressed."[12] Other than this, there is no indication regarding the actual enunciation of this Divine Name construct. However, considering the vocalisation of the relevant Hebrew glyphs in their component verses, the letter combination אל מץ might well be vocalised *Al Metz* or perhaps *Al Matz*. This four-letter combination, appears as a single word in reference to applying "force," as in "to coerce."

In the current instance, having whispered *Psalm 10* nine times over the water/oil mixure, the following prayer-incantation is recited before bathing the demoniac in the water-oil liquid:

יהי רצון מלפניך אל מץ שתסיר כל חולי וכל

שד מגוף [....name of recipient....] מעתה ועד עולם

Transliteration:

> *Y'hi ratzon mil'fanecha El Metz (Al Metz) shetasir kol choli u'chol shed m'guf* [....name of recipient....] *mei'atah v'ad olam.*

Translation:

> May it be your will *El Metz* to remove every disease and every demon from the body of [....name of recipient....], from now and forever.[13]

The same procedure is referenced by Cantarini in his *Sefer Chayei B'Sharim*. He maintains the afflicted individual should concentrate on the Divine Name construct derived from this Psalm, whilst he/she is being washed in the oil/water, which I personally think is a very good suggestion.[14] Godfrey Selig expresses similar sentiments in his somewhat expanded version of the use of *Psalm 10*, saying:

> "If any one is plagued with an unclean, restless and evil spirit, let him fill a new earthen pot with water from the spring, and, in the name of the patient, pour into it pure olive oil, and pronounce over it this Psalm nine times, keeping in mind constantly the adorable name of *Eel Mez*, which means Strong God of the oppressed, and at each ending of the Psalm: May it be thy most holy will, Oh *Eel Mez*, to heal the body and soul of N., son of R., and free him from all his plagues and oppressions: wilt thou strengthen him in soul and body and deliver him from evil. Amen! Selah!"[15]

Be that as it may, the references in some of the prayer-incantations to the removal of "every disease," reminds me that the tenth Psalm is also recited nine times in order to be healed from all manner of illness.[16] In this regard, *Psalm 10* is referenced in the earlier mentioned Syrian magical manuscript in the Sachau Collection, in terms of it being employed for the purpose of relieving a fever. Here the one who is suffering a fever is instructed to read the Psalm three times over water, and then to wash him/herself with it."[17]

However, getting back to the use of the tenth Psalm in conjunction with a Divine Name construct incorporated in a prayer-incantation to rid the afflicted of a demonic force, one of the recensions of the *"Sefer Shimmush Tehillim"* includes a very different Divine Name construct and prayer.[18] It shares the standard instructions for an individual "who has an evil spirit in his belly," i.e. he should draw water in a new bowl, and then mix olive oil with the water. However, instead of saying the Psalm nine times, the said individual would simply recite it once, then continue with the enunciation of a prayer-incantation over the water-oil mixture. The latter includes a very different Divine Name from the one addressed earlier, and reads:

[....name of recipient....]יהוה אלהי ישראל יהוה תתן ל'

רפואה בשם אל'ימה יהיה הדבר הזה וירפא [....name

ויצא ממנו רוח הרעה אשר נכנסה בו [....of recipient

אמן אמן אמן סלה סלה סלה

Transliteration:

YHVH elohei yisra'eil YHVH titen l'[....name of recipient....] r'fu'ah b'sheim Eilimah yih'yeh hadavar hazeh virapei [....name of recipient....] vayatza mimenu ru'ach hara'ah asher nich'nesa bo Omein Omein Omein Selah Selah Selah

Translation:

YHVH God of Israel, *YHVH*, give to [....name of recipient....] healing in the name *Eilimah*, this will be the (magic) word, and [....name of recipient....] will be healed, and the evil spirit that has entered into him shall come forth. *Amen Amen Amen Selah Selah Selah.*[19]

As an aside, the combination of oil and water being used to rid an individual of baneful forces, brings to mind an important procedure which, as I noted elsewhere, is mainly employed against the Evil

Eye, but is equally used by some religious worshippers once a year on the eve of *Rosh Hashanah* (Jewish "New Year") to, as it were, "cut the ties that bind."[20] In this regard, the ritual procedure incorporates the Divine Name אגלא vocalised *Agala'a*, with a strong accent on the second syllable, i.e. "*A-GAH-la-a*," and the recitation of a biblical verse, though not one associated with the tenth Psalm. As I explained elsewhere, if you need to aid an afflicted individual to get rid of the Evil Eye, you are required to fill a bowl with spring water, in the absence of which I recommend pure, still water found in any shop, and which I can attest will serve perfectly well.[21] Furthermore, you need to acquire seven pieces of charcoal, and in the current instance the easily lit charcoal blocks which are employed in the burning of good incenses are particularly useful. These are lit in advance of the ritual-procedure, and as I mentioned before, "when these are hot and sizzling, you would loudly proclaim, even shout, *Numbers 11:2* and the Divine Name *Agala'a* as you drop a hot coal into the water, repeating this action with each coal,"[22] saying:

ויצעק העם אל משה ויתפלל משה אל יהוה ותשקע העש

Transliteration:
> *Vayitz'ak ha-am el mosheh vayitpaleil mosheh el YHVH vatishka ha-esh*

Translation:
> And the people cried unto Moses; and Moses prayed unto YHVH, and the fire abated.

It should be noted that you need to place your *Kavvanah*, your fully focussed attention and intention, on the said Divine Name, which you exclaim loudly as you drop each hot coal in the bowl of water. On conclusion of this act, pour a little olive oil three times into the mix of charcoal ash and water, pouring three times a little oil into the mix. Finally the procedure ends with a little of the charcoal, water, oil concoction consumed by the erstwhile afflicted individual, whose entire body is then smeared with the remainder of the substance. Whilst consuming this blend of unpleasant substances might sound nauseating, it is a small sacrifice to be paid in order to free oneself from malevolent forces, and "cutting the ties that bind."[23]

As far as the healing powers of *Psalm 10* are concerned, it should be noted that this Psalm is also recommended for diseases of and pain in the eyes. Otherwise, it is said to be good against the dangers of fire, storms in general, and equally to ensure good weather. It has also been suggested that the tenth Psalm is useful against the harshness of a spouse, and ultimately to aid and support those who are perplexed by injustice and the distance of the Divine One.

As in the case of other Psalms, single verses from the tenth Psalm are also employed for magical purposes. In this regard, the capitals of the four concluding words of *Psalm 10:17*, reading תכין לבם תקשיב אזנך (*tachin libam tak'shiv oz'necha*—"Thou wilt direct their heart, Thou wilt cause Thine ear to attend"), are conjoined in the Divine Name construct הלהא which is included in amulets affording protection against evil spirits.[24] Other than that, *Psalm 10:1* is directly aligned with הקם (*Hakem*), the sixteenth portion of the *"Shem Vayisa Vayet."*[25] We are informed this tri-letter portion of the "Name of Seventy-two Names" has "the power to set up (or "raise" [מהקם—*mehakem*]) Kings."[26]

The tenth Psalm does not appear to be extensively employed on its own in Christian Magic, and, as we have seen, much of its use is in conjunction with *Psalm 9*.

Psalm 11

[1] למנצח לדוד ביהוה יאהדונהי חסיתי איך
תאמרו לנפשי נודי הרכם צפור

[2] כי הנה הרשעים ידרכון קשת כוננו חצם על
יתר לירות במו אפל לישרי לב

[3] כי השתות יהרסון צדיק מה פעל

[4] יהוה יאהדונהי בהיכל קדשו יהוה יאהדונהי
בשמים כסאו עיניו יחזו עפעפיו יבחנו בני אדם

[5] יהוה יאהדונהי צדיק יבחן ורשע ואהב חמס
שנאה נפשו

[6] ימטר על רשעים פחים אש וגפרית ורוח זלעפות
מנת כוסם

[7] כי צדיק יהוה יאהדונהי צדקות אהב ישר יחזו
פנימו

Transliteration:

[1] *lam'natzei'ach l'david baYHVH chasiti eich tom'ru
l'naf'shi nudi har'chem tzipor*

[2] *ki hinei har'sha'im yid'r'chun keshet kon'nu chitzam al
yeter lirot b'mo ofel l'yish'rei leiv*

[3] *ki hashatot yeihareisun tzadik mah pa'al*

[4] *YHVH b'heichal kod'sho YHVH bashamayim kis'o
einav yechezu af'apav yiv'chanu b'nei adam*

[5] *YHVH tzadik yiv'chan v'rasha v'oheiv chamas san'ah
naf'sho*

[6] *yam'teir al r'sha'im pachim eish v'gof'rit v'ru'ach
zil'afot m'nat kosam*

[7] *ki tzadik YHVH tz'dakot aheiv yashar yechezu faneimo*

Translation:

[1] For the Leader. A Psalm of David. In *YHVH* have I
taken refuge; how say ye to my soul: 'Flee thou! to your
mountain, ye birds'?

[2] For, lo, the wicked bend the bow, they have made ready
their arrow upon the string, that they may shoot in darkness
at the upright in heart.

[3] When the foundations are destroyed, what hath the
righteous wrought?

[4] *YHVH* is in His holy temple, *YHVH*, His throne is in heaven; His eyes behold, His eyelids try, the children of men.

[5] *YHVH* trieth the righteous; but the wicked and him that loveth violence His soul hateth.

[6] Upon the wicked He will cause to rain coals; fire and brimstone and burning wind shall be the portion of their cup.

[7] For *YHVH* is righteous, He loveth righteousness; the upright shall behold His face.

We are informed *Psalm 11* affords protection against evil spirits, evil people, and all manner of danger.[1] In this regard, we are told that if individuals have trespassed in some or other manner, and in consequence fear the wicked who may make them look guilty, the said individuals should recite the eleventh Psalm seven times, and conclude with the following prayer-incantation:[2]

יהוה אלהי השמים בורא שמים וארץ אתה בראתני
ויצרתני גלוי וידוע לפניך כי הרע בעיניך עשיתי
כמה פעמים ועתה אותה וחשקה נפשי להיות ניצל
ואל אחטא עוד לפניך עם הרשעים האלה אשר
בכל מעשיהם מנאצים ומכעיסים לפניך בשם וה יה
יהיה הדבר אלי אני [.....personal name.....] אמן אמן
אמן סלה סלה סלה

Transliteration:

YHVH elohei hashamayim borei shamayim va'aretz atah b'ratani v'yatzar'tani galui vidu'a l'fanecha ki hara b'einecha asiti kameh pa'amim v'atah iv'tah v'chash'kah naf'shi lih'yot nitzal v'al echeta od l'fanecha im har'sha'im ha'eileh asher b'chol ma'aseihem mino'atzim umach'isim l'fanecha b'sheim VaH YaH yih'yeh hadavar eili ani [.....personal name.....] Omein Omein Omein Selah Selah Selah

Translation:

YHVH God in heaven, Creator of heaven and earth, you have created me and you have formed me. It is apparent and known before you that I have done what is evil in your eyes several times. And now my soul agrees and yearns to be saved, and will sin no longer before you with these wrongdoers who blaspheme before you, and mock you with all their deeds. In the name *VaH YaH* will be the (magic) word for me [.....personal name.....] *Amen Amen Amen Selah Selah Selah.*[3]

Once again the ever popular Selig German/English version of the *"Shimmush Tehillim"* shares a procedure drawn from obscure sources. It tells us the Divine Name associated with *Psalm 11* is פלא (*Pele*—"wonderful"), which it maintains to be in the words: אפל (*ofel*—"darkness"): verse 2; פעל (*pa'al*—"wrought" ["work"]): verse 3, and the name אדם ("Adam"), which appears in verse 4, though not indicated as such in Selig's text.[4] We are informed that those who daily pray the eleventh Psalm "with feelings of devotion," who focus their minds constantly on the Divine Name פלא (*Pele*), and who simultaneously recite a relevant prayer, "will be safe from all persecution, and will not have any great evil to fear."[5] The said prayer-incantation reads:

"With thee is advice, action and power, and only thou canst work wonders. Turn away from me all that is evil, and protect me from the persecution of evil men, for the sake of the great name *Pele. Amen Selah.*"[6]

Whilst relatively little is written about the magical use of the current Psalm in published sources, the eleventh Psalm is recommended against all perils, fear, paranoia, assassins, and thieves. It is said to be good in getting rid of enemies, and is also recited to ensure safety from persecution. In this regard it is employed, like the tenth Psalm, against the harshness of a spouse, and to avert domestic torment and violence. We are told *Psalm 11* is good against all kinds of "perverted activities," lies, and the danger of ruin. Otherwise, it is said to protect against vanity and pride, and is employed to maintain chastity, as well as to strengthen faith. It is further recited for charity.

Regarding the magical use of single verses, I noted elsewhere that *Psalm 11:2* is employed as a defence against an enemy at war. In this regard, the said verse is combined with *Exodus 15:3*, *Isaiah 41:2*, and the following "magical seal" (*chotam*) comprising the four letters of the Ineffable Name written in a magical script:[7]

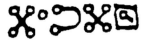

As noted previously, I am uncertain as to the exact derivation of the script, but that, "in terms of the talismanic use of this magical image, we are told it has the power to destroy the camp of the enemy in war situations."[8] To achieve the desired result, the user is instructed "to collect four fairly large stones from a dirt road or cobblestone track," on each of which will be inscribed the magical seal conjointly with specific phrases from the said verses. *Exodus 15:3* is written on the first stone with an additional concluding phrase:

יהוה איש מלחמה יהוה שמו לעולם ועד יה אמן ס
אמן אמן סלה סלה סלה

Transliteration:
> *YHVH ish mil'chamah YHVH sh'mo l'olam va'ed Yah Omein Omein Omein Selah Selah Selah*

Translation:
> *YHVH* is a man of war, *YHVH* is His Name throughout eternity *Yah Amen Amen Amen Selah Selah Selah*

The second stone comprises the phrase from *Isaiah 41:2* reading יתן כעפר חרבו (*yiten ke'afar charvo*—"his sword maketh them as the dust"), whilst the third is inscribed with the concluding phrase of the same verse reading כקש נדף קשתו (*K'kash nidaf kashto*—"his bow as the driven stubble"). The fourth stone is inscribed with the opening phrase from *Psalm 11:2* reading כי הנה הרשעים ידרכון (*Ki hineh har'sha'im yid'r'chun*—"For, lo, the wicked bend the bow"). As said previously, "having written the magical seal on all four stones conjointly with their respectively associated biblical phrases, the task is completed by casting the rocks into the arena of the enemy."[9]

In conclusion, we are informed that the portion of *Psalm 11:7* reading כי צדיק יהוה צדקות אהב (*ki tzadik YHVH tz'dakot ahev*—"for *YHVH* is righteous, He loveth righteousness"), is indirectly affiliated with חהו (*Chaho*), the twenty-fourth portion of the "*Shem Vayisa Vayet.*" In this regard, it is said that the Name חהו transposed by means of the א"ת ב"ש (*Atbash*) cipher, results in the combination סצף which is said to be the "'gate' to the Name *Chaho.*"[10] The latter statement pertains to the *gematria* of the סצף tri-letter combination (ס = 60 + צ = 90 + ף = 80 = 230), which is equal with the total numerical value of the words יהוה צדיק (*YHVH tzadik*—"*YHVH* is righteous" [י = 10 + ה = 5 + ו = 6 + ה = 5 + צ = 90 + ד = 4 + י = 10 + ק = 100 = 230]), the latter phrase being referenced in *Psalm 11:7*.[11] The main sentiment expressed here regarding the חהו Divine Name construct is that the Divine One is righteous, and loves righteousness, which is a quality everyone should pursue.

Considering the use of the eleventh Psalm in Christian magic, we are told it is used "to drive out demons."[12] Otherwise, we find a reference in the earlier mentioned Syrian magical manuscript in the Sachau Collection, to the eleventh Psalm being employed to destroy or get rid of enemies.[13] In this regard, we are informed that you should simply recite the Psalm when you have to leave your residence, which is said will aid you in defeating all your enemies.[14] However, "*Le Livre d'Or*" delineates a rather nefarious application of this Psalm against enemies. In this regard, it suggests the practitioner should write the Psalm on parchment made from the skin of a billy-goat, employing a bronze pen. This parchment is afterwards buried under the door of the enemy(ies). A second parchment is prepared in the same manner to be placed on the head of a deceased male, and, depending on the sex of the enemy, is located either in the grave of a woman or of a man. It suggests death of the enemy will ensue within a day.[15] This is more like a death-curse rather than a way in which to restrain enemies.

In conclusion, we are informed that *Psalm 11:3 and 8* are combined in an amulet meant to rescue individuals from pirates and assassins.[16]

Psalm 12

[1] למנצח על השמינית מזמור לדוד

[2] הושיעה יהוה𐤟אהדונהי כי גמר חסיד כי
פסו אמונים מבני אדם

[3] שוא ידברו איש את רעהו שפת חלקות בלב
ולב ידברו

[4] יכרת יהוה𐤟אהדונהי כל שפתי חלקות לשון
מדברת גדלות

[5] אשר אמרו ללשננו נגביר שפתינו אתנו מי אדון
לנו

[6] משד עניים מאנקת אביונים עתה אקום יאמר
יהוה𐤟אהדונהי אשית בישע יפיח לו

[7] אמרות יהוה𐤟אהדונהי אמרות טהרות כסף
צרוף בעליל לארץ מזקק שבעתים

[8] אתה יהוה𐤟אהדונהי תשמרם תצרנו מן הדור זו
לעולם

[9] סביב רשעים יתהלכון כרם זלות לבני אדם

Transliteration:

[1] *lam'natzei'ach al hash'minit miz'mor l'david*

[2] *hoshi'ah YHVH ki gamar chasid ki fasu emunim mib'nei adam*

[3] *shav y'dab'ru ish et rei'eihu s'fat chalakot b'leiv valeiv y'dabeiru*

[4] *yach'reit YHVH kol sif'tei chalakot lashon m'daberet g'dolot*

[5] *asher am'ru lil'shoneinu nag'bir s'fateinu itanu mi adon lanu*

[6] *mishod aniyim mei'en'kat ev'yonim atah akum yomar YHVH ashit b'yeisha yafi'ach lo*

[7] *im'rot YHVH amarot t'horot kesef tzaruf ba'alil la'aretz m'zukak shiv'atayim*

[8] *atah YHVH tish'm'reim titz'renu min hador zu l'olam*

[9] *saviv r'sha'im yit'halachun k'rum zulut liv'nei adam*

Translation:

[1] For the Leader; on the *Sheminith*. A Psalm of David.

[2] Help *YHVH*; for the godly man ceaseth; for the faithful fail from among the children of men.

[3] They speak falsehood every one with his neighbour; with flattering lip, and with a double heart, do they speak.

[4] May *YHVH* cut off all flattering lips, the tongue that s//eth proud things!

[5] Who have said: 'Our tongue will we make mighty; our lips are with us: who is lord over us?'

[6] 'For the oppression of the poor, for the sighing of the needy, now will I arise', saith *YHVH*; 'I will set him in safety at whom they puff.'

[7] The words of *YHVH* are pure words, as silver tried in a crucible on the earth, refined seven times.

[8] Thou wilt keep them *YHVH*; Thou wilt preserve us from this generation for ever.

[9] The wicked walk on every side, when vileness is /exalted among the sons of men.

We are informed that the Levites sang *Psalm 12* in the Temple on *Shemini Atzeret*, i.e. the eighth day of the "*Festival of Sukkot* [Booths],"[1] and the twelfth Psalm is the daily Psalm recited by Sefardic communities on the same day, and also on *Simchat Torah.*[2] Amongst other motives, we are informed that "a reason for its recitation is the number eight associated with the Psalm and holiday. The Psalm heading has the expression *al hashminit*, meaning 'upon the eighth,' an instrument having eight strings,"[3] which is understood to pertain directly to *Shemini Atzeret*, i.e. the "Eighth Assembly."[4]

It is said reciting *Psalm 12* stops individuals from weakness and trembling,[5] and we are told that enunciating the current Psalm will stop an individual from yielding to temptation and sin, and will also protect against evil counsel.[6] Whilst this is all we are told regarding the twelfth Psalm in the printed versions of the "*Shimmush Tehillim*," further details appear in one of the recensions in which we are informed that if an individual is obliged to ask for mercy over some or other matter, the said individual should repeat *Psalm 12*, as well as the following prayer-incantation, nine times inside a Synagogue:

מלך מלא רחמים המלא רחמים **אל** תפעל לי
כרוע מעללי וכרוע לבבי כי אתה **אל** מלך
רחום וחנון שומע בקול שועה וצעקה ועל כן
סמכתי על רוב רחמיך וחסדיך ובטחתי בהם
אשר הם יעזרוני ויסמכוני ויחיוני ואל אמות
ברוב עונותי אך אחיה ואשוב בתשובה שלימה
יהי רצון מלפניך מ"ה מ"ה שתכבוש עונותי
ותצלילם במעמקי ים אשר לא יזכרו ולא יפקדו
ועוד לא יעמדו לי מנגד לבטל דבר שאני רוצה
בשם **א**"ה יהיה הדבר אלי אני [....personal name....]
אמן אמן אמן סלה סלה סלה

Transliteration:

*Melech malei rachamim hamalei rachamim El tif'al li
k'ro'a ma'al'lai uk'ro'a l'vavi ki atah El melech rachum
v'chanun shomei'a b'kol shav'ah v'tz'akah v'al kein
samach'ti al rov rachamecha vachasidecha uvatach'ti
b'hem asher heim ya'az'runi v'yis'm'chuni v'y'chayuni
v'al emot b'rov avonotai ach ech'yeh v'ashuv bit'shuvah
sh'leimah y'hi ratzon mil'fanecha Mem–Heh Mem–Heh
[perhaps "Mah Mah"] shetich'bosh avonotai v'tatz'lileim
b'ma'amakei yam asher lo yizach'ru v'lo yipak'du v'od lo
ya'am'du li mineged l'vatel davar she'ani rotzeh b'sheim
Alef-Heh [perhaps "Aha"] yih'yeh hadavar eili ani
[....personal name....] Omein Omein Omein Selah Selah
Selah.*

Translation:

King full of mercy, who is full of compassion, God, you
should bring low my deed and my heart, for you are God,
a merciful and gracious King. Listen to the voice, cry for
help and wailing. Therefore I have relied on the greatness
of your mercy and your lovingkindness, and I have placed
my trust in them for they will help me, support me, and
enliven me. I will not perish from the multitude of my
offenses, but I will live and repent with complete remorse.
May it be your will, *Mem–Heh Mem–Heh* [perhaps "*Mah
Mah*"] , that you suppress my offenses, and sink them into
the depths of the sea so that they may be forgotten, that

they may not revisit [afflict] (me) or rise up against me to destroy the matter which I desire, in the name *Alef–Heh* [perhaps "*Ahah*""] the (magic) word shall be with me, I am [....personal name....]. *Amen Amen Amen Selah Selah Selah.*[7]

Whilst I have seen the letter combinations comprising the Divine Names employed in this prayer-incantation having been included in a number of Divine Name constructs employed in Jewish Magic, there is no indication on exactly how the said Divine Names should be enunciated. However, in this regard practitioners would simply spell the Divine Name, or enunciate the component glyphs with their natural respective vowels, when the actual vocalisation of a Divine Name is obscure. This action is considered as effective as if they have pronounced the Divine Name. As you may know well enough, such actions are not uncommon in "Practical Kabbalah" and Jewish meditation.[8] In the current instance the listed Divine Names would then respectively read "*Mem–Heh Mem–Heh*" or "*Meh–Heh Meh–Heh*," and "*Alef–Heh*" or "*Ah–Heh*."

That appears to be the complete instructions on the magical applications of *Psalm 12* mentioned in the available sources of the "*Shimmush Tehillim.*" However, once again Selig's German/ English versions offer details which cannot be traced to any known primary origins. In terms of the current Psalm he maintains it "possesses similar power, action and worth" as the previous Psalm. These would be to ensure safety "from all persecution," and not having "any great evil to fear."[9] In this regard, it offers a related prayer-incantation which includes the Divine Name construct אביאל, which Selig maintains is vocalised "*Avieel*" ("*Aineel*" in the English translation), and the meaning of which is said to be "Strong God! My Father!" We are informed this Divine Name construct is "found" in three words in the sixth verse, i.e. אביונים (*ev'yonim* —"the poor"), אקום (*akum*—"arise"), and לו (*lo*—"to him").[10] The prayer-incantation reads "Almighty Father, my God Alneel! grant that all conspiracies against me may be set at naught; turn away from me all danger and injury, and thine is the kingdom and the power. *Amen Selah!*"[11]

Other than these references to the magical uses of *Psalm 12* in the "*Shimmush Tehillim,*" we are told that it is good for legal trials and sentencing, i.e. reciting the Psalm before a trial will assure a good judgment.[12] However, before concluding with the use of the current Psalm in Jewish Magic, I should mention a most wonderful spiritual technique featuring the first two verses of the current Psalm, which is of particular importance to me personally, and which I make use of fairly regularly. The procedure is associated with the *Arizal* (Rabbi Isaac Luria), and references nine tri-letter portions of the "Name of Seventy-two Names," which are employed in conjunction with the first two verses of *Psalm 12* and the first five verses of *Deuteronomy 1* for the purposes of "Dream Questioning," and to cultivate a good memory.[13]

I encountered this technique the first time in the early 1970's when I visited a secondhand bookstore, and purchased a copy of a magical tome titled "*Refuah v'Chaim m'Yerushalayim*," which was published some forty years previously.[14] The work was apparently a republication of an anonymous compilation comprising, amongst others, extracts from the writings of Rabbi Moses Zacutto's acclaimed "*Shorshei ha-Shemot*," the standard published version of the "*Shimmush Tehillim*," etc. As can be expected, I was extremely excited about having found this tome, and whilst casually scanning the text, I chanced upon this remarkable technique for "Dream Questioning." I tried it several times, but somehow it did not appear to "work" for me, which I ascribed to me not being "pure" or "holy" enough in body, mind, soul, and spirit. Furthermore, whatever I did to rectify this situation, the outcome was inevitably dissatisfactory, i.e. zero!

Almost three decades later I purchased a copy of the first complete publication of Rabbi Moses Zacutto's "*Shorshei ha-Shemot*,"[15] in which there is a very different version of the same technique, as well as a listing of the original source. I decided to try working the procedure again by following, what I now believe to be, the correct version. Suffice it to say that I have not stopped employing it very regularly over the last twenty years with great success. To date I have received meaningful responses to all my "dream questions," and whilst the answers may not necessarily have been what I would have liked to hear, they were always immediate, pertinent, and unambiguous.

First let us consider the relevant nine tri-letter portions of the "Name of Seventy-two Names," i.e. from the nineteenth to the twenty-seventh, employed in working this procedure. According to *"Refuah v'Chaim m'Yerushalayim"* the array reads:[16]

לוו"י פְּהַל נַלַ"ךְ יְיָי מְלָה חַהוי נְתַה הָאֵא יְרַת

These read *senza* the additional י (*Yod*): *Lov P'hal Nalach Y'yay M'lah Chah(o) N'tah Ha'ei Y'rat*. The same tri-letter combinations are listed with differing vowel points in the following manner in the *Shorshei ha-Shemot*:[17]

לְוּו פְּהַל נַלַךְ יְיָי מְלָה חַהוּ נְתַה הָאֵאַ יְרַת

This arrangement reads in transliteration: *L'vu P'hal Nalach Y'yoya M'lah Chahu N'tah Ha'ei'a Y'rat*. There are further minor variations between the two versions, and in this regard, I found the the presentation in *"Refuah v'Chaim m'Yerushalayim"* both useful and effective.[18]

However, before we can address the actual procedure, it is important to note that anyone wishing to employ this technique is required to precede it with a ritual submersion, e.g. in a *Mikveh*, and is also required to fast on the day of action, so to speak. Only then, when ready, will the said individual commence the current action by taking a clean sheet of paper in his or her hand, and recite only the first two verses of *Psalm 12* over it.[19] The unknown author of *"Refuah v'Chaim m'Yerushalayim"* maintains the recitation of entire Psalm.[20]

Be that as it may, the paper is also prepared (marked) with the term אמת (*Emet*—"Truth"), which is in the current instance understood to be the Divine Name associated with the twelfth Psalm.[21] In this regard, the practitioner could write the said word at the top or bottom right hand corner of the sheet of paper. This is followed by reciting *Deuteronomy 1:1–5* reading:[22]

[1] אלה הדברים אשר דבר משה אל כל ישראל
בעבר הירדן במדבר בערבה מול סוף בין פארן
ובין תפל ולבן וחצרת ודי זהב

‫[2] אֶחָד עָשָׂר יוֹם מֵחֹרֵב דֶּרֶךְ הַר שֵׂעִיר עַד קָדֵשׁ‬
‫בַּרְנֵעַ‬

‫[3] וַיְהִי בְּאַרְבָּעִים שָׁנָה בְּעַשְׁתֵּי עָשָׂר חֹדֶשׁ בְּאֶחָד‬
‫לַחֹדֶשׁ דִּבֶּר מֹשֶׁה אֶל בְּנֵי יִשְׂרָאֵל כְּכֹל אֲשֶׁר צִוָּה‬
‫יְהוָה אֹתוֹ אֲלֵהֶם‬

‫[4] אַחֲרֵי הַכֹּתוֹ אֵת סִיחֹן מֶלֶךְ הָאֱמֹרִי אֲשֶׁר יוֹשֵׁב‬
‫בְּחֶשְׁבּוֹן וְאֵת עוֹג מֶלֶךְ הַבָּשָׁן אֲשֶׁר יוֹשֵׁב בְּעַשְׁתָּרֹת‬
‫בְּאֶדְרֶעִי‬

‫[5] בְּעֵבֶר הַיַּרְדֵּן בְּאֶרֶץ מוֹאָב הוֹאִיל מֹשֶׁה בֵּאֵר‬
‫אֶת הַתּוֹרָה הַזֹּאת לֵאמֹר‬

Transliteration:

[1] *eileh ha'd'varim asher diber mosheh el kol yis'ra'eil b'eiver hayar'den bamid'bar ba'aravah mol suf bein paran uvein tofel v'lavan vachatzeirot v'di zahav*

[2] *achad asar yom meichoreiv derech har sei'ir ad kadeish bar'nei'a*

[3] *vay'hi b'arba'im shanah b'ash'tei asar chodesh b'echad lachodesh diber mosheh el b'nei yis'ra'eil k'chol asher tzivah YHVH oto aleihem*

[4] *acharei hakoto eit sichon melech ha'emori asher yosheiv b'chesh'bon v'eit og melech habashan asher yosheiv b'ash'tarot b'ed're'i*

[5] *b'eiver hayar'dein b'eretz mo'av ho'il mosheh bei'eir et hatorah hazot leimor*

Translation:

[1] These are the words which Moses spoke unto all Israel beyond the Jordan; in the wilderness, in the *Arabah*, over against *Suph*, between *Paran* and *Tophel*, and *Laban*, and *Hazeroth*, and *Di-zahab*.

[2] It is eleven days journey from *Horeb* unto *Kadesh-barnea* by the way of mount Seir.

[3] And it came to pass in the fortieth year, in the eleventh month, on the first day of the month, that Moses spoke unto the children of Israel, according unto all that *YHVH* had given him in commandment unto them;

[4] after he had smitten *Sihon* the king of the Amorites, who dwelt in *Heshbon*, and *Og* the king of Bashan, who dwelt in *Ashtaroth*, at Edrei;

[5] beyond the Jordan, in the land of Moab, took Moses upon him to expound this law, saying.

Continue by uttering the following prayer-incantation:

יהי רצון מלפניך השם הגדול הגבור והנורא **אמת**
אשר היוצא מזה המזמור שתעשה למענך ולמען
ט׳ שמות של מדת גבורתך שהם לְוּוּ פֶּהַל נַלַךְ
יְיָךְ מְלֶה חַהוּ נְתַה הַאֶא יְרַת שתשיבני על
שְׁאַלְתִי שֶׁהִיא [.....state the question.....] שתשיבני
בכתב מפורש ובאר היטב בזה הניר חלק בידי
אשר אניחנו בלילה זה תחת מראשותי והבה
תמים

Transliteration:

> *Y'hi ratzon mil'fanecha hashem hagadol hagibor v'hanora Emet asher hayotzei mizeh hamiz'mor sheta'aseh l'ma'an'cha ul'ma'an 'tet' (9) sheimot shel midat g'vuratecha sheheim L'vu P'hal Nalach Y'yoya M'lah Chahu N'tah Ha'ei'a Y'rat shetashiveini al she'elati shehi [.....state the question.....] shetashiveini b'k'tav m'forash u'vei'eir heitev b'zeh han'yar cheilek b'yadi asher anichenu b'lailah zeh tachat meira'ashotai v'havah tamim.*

Translation:

> May it be your will, the great, mighty, and awesome name *Emet* that derives from this Psalm, that you will act for your sake, and for the sake of these nine names of the measure of your might which are *L'vu P'hal Nalach' Y'yoya M'lah Chahu N'tah Ha'ei'a Y'rat*, that you will answer my question which is [.....state the question.....]. Let me be answered in explicit [well expressed] and well-written text on this clean [sheet of] paper in my hand, which I have placed this night under my head, and let it be innocent [above suspicion].[23]

Afterwards, when you lie down on your bed at night, return to reciting the aforementioned verses and prayer-incantation three times. Place the paper smoothly under your head. That is where the instructions stop in the *"Shorshei ha-Shemot,"*[24] following which the practitioner should go to sleep. However, this is greatly expanded upon in the *"Refuah v'Chaim m'Yerushalayim,"* adding the recitation of *Psalm 23* seven times before locating the paper under the head.[25] Whilst I have no issue with the latter addition, I found that whether or not I included the twenty-third Psalm in the procedure made no difference to the final outcome.

Be that as it may, on waking in the morning the answer will be found either written on the paper in abbreviated format, or will be revealed in a biblical verse, or in some hidden manner in the mysterious ways of the Divine One.[26] The latter often requires a greatly expanded consciousness, in order to comprehend the intention and meaning of the response. Those who shared this technique in writing noted that sometimes responses comprise the capitals of the words comprising a verse written down with vowel points.[27] As indicated throughout this tome, many Divine Names are constructed from biblical verses in this manner.

As usual there are some magical uses of the current Psalm which are unlisted in published resources. In this regard, *Psalm 12* is said to be good for diseases of and pain in the eyes, as well as for any nervous disorder. Otherwise, it is recommended for recitation on the day of circumcision, and is said to afford safety from fear

As far as the use of the twelfth Psalm in Christian magic is concerned, it is said in the previously mentioned Byzantian Christian Magical texts that this Psalm is useful against enemies,[28] and for protecting those who are afraid on the road.[29] It is maintained in the *"Le Livre d'Or"* that the current Psalm is employed to prevent an enemy from saying "something evil about you." To affect this the Psalm and a set of magical characters are written on a glass plate, fumigated with borax, and the Psalm read over water. The glass plate is afterwards buried at the door of the enemy.[30] Other than this, *Psalm 12:6* is recommended elsewhere "to deliver a man from all infirmity."[31]

Psalm 13

[1] למנצח מזמור לדוד

[2] עד אנה יהוהאהדיאיאהדונהי תשכחני נצח עד אנה
תסתיר את פניך ממני עד אנה אשית עצות בנפשי
יגון בלבבי יומם

[3] עד אנה ירום איבי עלי

[4] הביטה עניני יהוהאהדיאיאהדונהי אלהי האירה עיני
פן אישן המות

[5] פן יאמר איבי יכלתיו צרי יגילו כי אמוט

[6] ואני בחסדך בטחתי יגל לבי בישועתך אשירה
ליהוהאהדיאיאהדונהי כי גמל עלי

Transliteration:

[1] *lam'natzei'ach miz'mor l'david*

[2] *ad anah YHVH tish'kacheini netzach ad anah tas'tir et panecha mimeni ad anah ashit eitzot b'naf'shi yagon bil'vavi yomam*

[3] *ad anah yarum oy'vi alai*

[4] *habitah aneini YHVH elohai ha'irah einai pen ishan hamavet*

[5] *pen yomar oy'vi y'chol'tiv tzarai yagilu ki emot*

[6] *va'ani b'chas'd'cha vatach'ti yageil libi bishu'atecha ashirah laYHVH ki gamal alai*

Translation:

[1] For the Leader. A Psalm of David.

[2] How long, *YHVH*, wilt Thou forget me for ever? How long wilt Thou hide Thy face from me? How long shall I take counsel in my soul, having sorrow in my heart by day?

[3] How long shall mine enemy be exalted over me?

[4] Behold Thou, and answer me, *YHVH* my God; lighten mine eyes, lest I sleep the sleep of death;

[5] Lest mine enemy say: 'I have prevailed against him'; lest mine adversaries rejoice when I am moved.

[6] But as for me, in Thy mercy do I trust; my heart shall rejoice in Thy salvation. I will sing unto *YHVH*, because He hath dealt bountifully with me.

We are informed that *Psalm 13* is recited as a protection against unnatural death,[1] i.e. accidental, violent, strange, unusual forms of death,[2] and to be saved from further calamities.[3] Amongst the "further calamities" we might consider diseases of the eyes, especially referenced in terms of the thirteenth Psalm. It appears that the expression in verse 6 reading עֵינַי הָאִירָה (*ha-irah einai* —"lighten mine eyes") inspired the belief that reciting Psalm 13 is good "for one who has an eye disease."[4]

A herb is referenced in the original instructions in terms of healing ailments of the eyes.[5] However, the Hebrew term is obscure, and does not indicate the exact identity of the plant. Rebiger suggested it might be *Calamus* (*acornus calamus*), since essential oils are obtained from its roots, which he noted are employed for healing purposes.[6] On the other hand, an acquaintance of mine made the much more likely observation in his translation of the "*Shimmush Tehillim,*" that the Hebrew appellative אוקייארד (*okiyarah*) could be referencing "*Occhio Chiaro,*" the Italian term for *Clary Sage* (*salvia sclarea*), which is commonly called "Bright Eye" because of its popular use in treating diseases of the eye.[7] Whatever the case may be, the respective Hebrew and Italian terms sound very similar, and, as per the instructions in the "*Shimmush Tehillim,*"[8] I cannot see any problem in reciting the thirteenth Psalm during the harvest of either of these herbs for the purposes of treating ailments of the eyes.

In his standard very verbose manner, Godfrey Selig again came up with a delineation of the mentioned uses of *Psalm 13* which varies greatly from primary sources. It includes a Divine Name construct עֶזְרִיאֵל (*Esri'el* [*Ezri'el*]), listed "*Essiel*" which in the English translation is said to mean "My help is the mighty God." We are informed this Divine Name construct was derived from עֵצוֹת (*eitzot*—"counsel"): verse 3; מִזְמוֹר (*mizmor*— "Psalm"): verse 1; יָרוּם (*yarum*—"exalted"): verse 3; עֲנֵנִי (*aneini* —"answer me"): verse 4; אֹיְבַי (*oy'vai*—"my enemies"): verse 5; and יָגֵל (*yagel*—"rejoice"): verse 6.[9]

In terms of using the current Psalm for the said purposes, Selig wrote that "whoever prays this Psalm daily with devotion, together with the proper prayer belonging thereto, and thinks at the same time of the powerful name of *Essiel* [*Esri'el/Ezri'el*].....will be safe for the next twenty-four hours from an unnatural death and from all bodily sufferings and punishments."[10] The "proper prayer," which he included in his instructions, reads: "Protect me according to thy good will and pleasure from violent, sudden and unnatural death, and from all other evil accidents and severe bodily afflictions, for thou art my help and my God, and thine is the power and the glory. *Amen. Selah.*"[11] He added that "according to tradition this Psalm is also a good cure for dangerous and painful diseases of the eyes." However instead of referencing the earlier mentioned herb, he simply states that "the patient must procure a plant that is good for the eyes, and with this must pray this Psalm with a suitable prayer, trusting firmly in the certain help of the mighty *Essiel* [*Esri'el/Ezri'el*], and then bind the plant upon his eyes.[12]

It should be noted that Divine Names feature in a further usage of *Psalm 13*, as delineated in one of the recensions of the "*Shimmush Tehillim.*"[13] In this instance the Psalm is employed for "Dream Questioning" when some or other calamity befell a community. In this regard the thirteenth Psalm and an associated prayer-incantation are recited eight times when lying down at night. The Divine Name directly associated with the Psalm is said to be אצנה,[14] but it does not feature anywhere in the recitation of the Psalm or the associated prayer incantation. Instead there are two Divine Name combinations listed, i.e. אהיה אשר אהיה (*Eh'yeh Asher Eh'yeh*—"I am that I am"), and the most peculiar אאצנה נצח צחן[15] comprising rather unpleasant meanings if read as common Hebrew words, i.e. אצנה (*etz'nach*—"I will fall"), נצח (*Netzach*—"endurance" or "eternity"), and צחן (*tzachan*—"stink"). The mind boggles at the meaning of this odd Divine Name combination, perhaps indicating the referenced "calamity" which beset the "community," having resulted in all and sundry having "fallen into eternal stench"! Since we really do not know how this Divine Name combination is to be enunciated, it is again a good idea, as noted previously, to either spell this strange Divine Name construct letter by letter, or to enunciate it with the natural vowel of each Hebrew glyph. Be that as it may, the said prayer-incantation reads:

יושב הכרובים ומלך עולנים לפניך באתי בבכי
ובדמעות שתשוב ותנחם על הרעה לעמיך ואל
יבואו עונותי ועונות אבותי לקטרג בי לפניך
לבל אדע את אשר בקשה נפשי לדעת על דבר
זה איך יהיה [מין] (ל)הקהל הזה מה יהיה עליהם
אם שלום אם מחלוקת או מדברים אחרים

Transliteration:

*Yosheiv ha'k'ruvim umelech olamim l'fanecha bati biv'chi
uvid'ma'ot shetashuv vatan'cheim al hara'ah l'amecha
v'el yavo'u avonotai va'avonot avotai l'kat'reig bi
l'fanecha l'val eida et asher bik'shah naf'shi l'da'at al
d'var zeh eich yih'yeh mi l'hakahal hazeh mah yih'yeh
aleihem im shalom im mach'loket o m'd'varim acheirim*

Translation:

The One who is enthroned over the *Keruvim* and King of
Eternity, I came before you with weeping and with tears,
that you may return and comfort your peoples because of
the calamity. My transgressions and the iniquities of my
fathers shall not come to accuse me before you, that I may
not perceive what my soul desired to know about this
matter, how it will be for this assembly. What will be over
them, whether it be peace, whether it be strife, or other
matters.[16]

We are told that if the querent has, as it were, a greater need, but
does not dare to ask more than one request, he should conclude the
prayer-incantation with the Divine Names *Eh'yeh asher Eh'yeh*
and *Etz'nach Netzach Tzachen*[17] by saying:

בשם אהיה אשר אהיה ובשם אצנח נצח צחן
יודע אלי הדבר ברור על שאלתי בחלום הלילה
הזה בשאלתי ראשונה בדברים אמתיים ונכוחים
אמן אמן אמן סלה סלה סלה

Transliteration:

*B'sheim Eh'yeh asher Eh'yeh ub'sheim Atz'nach Netzach
Tzachan yivada eilai hadavar barur al she'eilati bachalom
halailah hazeh b'she'eilati rishonah b'd'varim amitiyim
un'chochim Omein Omein Omein Selah Selah Selah*

Translation:

> In the name *Eh'yeh asher Eh'yeh* and in the name *Atz'nach Netzach Tzachan*, the matter shall be made clear to me concerning my request in the dream of this night, in my first request with the true and present words *Amen Amen Amen Selah Selah Selah.*[18]

Other than the details listed in the "*Shimmush Tehillim*," we are told that *Psalm 13* "is the cornerstone of longing to be close to God" and that it is thus employed for "Self Improvement."[19] Other than these uses, I have observed the thirteenth Psalm recommended for a number of additional magical applications. In this regard, it is said to be good for liver problems; diseases of, and problems with, the stomach and the heart; alleviating fevers; and for illness in general. It is said to aid against temptations, and, just in case you should falter, will protect you against suffering retribution and punishment. It is also one of the few Psalms said to afford protection against serpents, and it equally affords protection in perilous situations and in times of trouble. It is further said to offer support in moments of incredulity, i.e. disbelief.

Whilst the thirteenth Psalm does not feature in Jewish liturgies, it is fairly commonly employed in the Roman Catholic liturgy, especially in terms of exorcism, i.e. "to drive out demons."[20] Further uses of the Psalm can be found in Christian Magic which are quite different from the ones listed in terms of Jewish Magic. In the previously mentioned Byzantine Christian manuscripts we are told it is employed on "powerful men,"[21] and elsewhere in the same manuscripts it is used to cause a "distraction," literally "captivity of mind."[22] I presume this pertains to distracting those who are facing anyone with malevolent intentions.[23] It has been further noted that *Psalm 13* will aid individuals who were made "sick by an enemy," i.e. poisoned, etc., and it is equally noted that individuals who are distressed by their enemies, could redeem themselves from their attackers by repeating the current Psalm.[24]

As far as protection against enemies is concerned, the fourth and fifth verses are recommended to those who need to save themselves "from pirates and assassins."[25] Elsewhere in the "*Le Livre d'Or*" the thirteenth Psalm is also said to be effective "against rogues," and in this regard individuals are told to recite the Psalm three times if there is any concern that villains may have set a trap for them, and that this action will cause the attackers to flee.[26] Otherwise the same text maintains that if anyone happened to "have fallen asleep in a desert," the said individual should recite the current Psalm three times up to the end of the fifth verse, following which there would be nothing to fear.[27]

As can be expected, there are those who are equally seeking the goodwill of forces of the spirit kind, and, in this regard, there is a curious reference to *Psalm 13* being employed in the preparation of what is termed the "Wonderful Ring of Lucibel." We are told "Lucibel is an alternative name of Lucifer."[28] Be that as it may, the construction of the ring is performed at a definite time from silver purchased at an equally definite time. The ring itself is fashioned during the Full Moon, and the name "Lucibel" engraved on it. Afterwards the ring is tied to specially spun thread, which is attached to a hazelwood wand. The ring is then suspended over a hot spring located in a deserted place, and *"Psalm 12,"* actually *Psalm 13*, recited over it. On conclusion the item is wrapped in a "new, white silken cloth" on which is written a set of magical symbols. There are further instructions on the use of the ring, and accompanying adjurations, which have no bearing on the subject matter addressed in this tome, but are generally available to those interested in such curiosities.[29]

In conclusion, it is worth noting that in the *"Key of Solomon"* the concluding phrase of the fourth verse of *Psalm 13* is conjoined with the opening phrase of the fifth verse in the outer border of the so-called *"Fourth Pentacle of the Sun."* The latter item is said to afford an individual the ability "to see the Spirits when they appear invisible unto those who invoke them," since, when the "pentacle" is exposed "they will immediately appear visible."[30]

Psalm 14

[1] למנצח לדוד אמר נבל בלבו אין אלהים
השחיתו התעיבו עלילה אין עשה טוב

[2] יהוה‎אדני‎יאהדונהי משמים השקיף על בני אדם
לראות היש משכיל דרש את אלהום

[3] הכל סר יחדו נאלהו אין עשה טוב אין גם אחד

[4] הלא ידעו כל פעלי און אכלי עמי אכלו לחם
יהוה‎אדני יאהדונהי לא קראו

[5] שם פחדו פחד כי אלהים בדור צדיק

[6] עצת עני תבישו כי יהוה‎אדני‎יאהדונהי מחסהו

[7] מי יתן מציון ישועת ישראל בשוב יהוה‎אדני‎יאהדונהי
שבות עמו יגל יעקב ישמח ישראל

Transliteration:

[1] *lam'natzei'ach l'david amar naval b'libo ein elohim hish'chitu hit'ivu alilah ein oseih tov*

[2] *YHVH mishamayim hish'kif al b'nei adam lir'ot hayeish mas'kil doreish et elohim*

[3] *hakol sar yach'dav n'elachu ein oseih tov ein gam echad*

[4] *halo yad'u kol po'alei aven och'lei ami ach'lu lechem YHVH lo kara'u*

[5] *sham pachadu fachad ki elohim b'dor tzadik*

[6] *atzat ani tavishu ki YHVH mach'seihu*

[7] *mi yiten mitziyon y'shu'at yis'ra'eil b'shuv YHVH sh'vut amo yageil ya'akov yis'mach yis'ra'eil*

Translation:

[1] For the Leader. A Psalm of David. The fool hath said in his heart: 'There is no God'; they have dealt corruptly, they have done abominably; there is none that doeth good.

[2] *YHVH* looked forth from heaven upon the children of men, to see if there were any man of understanding, that did seek after *Elohim*.

[3] They are all corrupt, they are together become impure; there is none that doeth good, no, not one.

[4] 'Shall not all the workers of iniquity know it, who eat up My people as they eat bread, and call not upon *YHVH*?'

[5] There are they in great fear; for *Elohim* is with the righteous generation.

[6] Ye would put to shame the counsel of the poor, but *YHVH* is his refuge.

[7] Oh that the salvation of Israel were come out of Zion! When *YHVH* turneth the captivity of His people, let Jacob rejoice, let Israel be glad.

We are informed *Psalm 14* is employed against fear,[1] but it is actually against fear of being slandered, and "when one's veracity is doubted."[2] That being said, the thirteenth Psalm is employed in one of the "*Shimmush Tehillim*" manuscripts to preclude haters from doing evil,[3] i.e. halting further harm being inflicted on those who have been impacted by such harmful deeds. In this regard, those employing this procedure are instructed to go to a river or a pure spring, without talking to anyone, and collect there water in a new vessel, and to recite this Psalm seven times over the liquid.[4] Afterwards the water is sprinkled in the residence of the hater, and with each sprinkling the following prayer-incantation recited:

פהוצו שחקים לפניך באתי להזכירך כי עני ודל
ואביון אני ולא פעלתי לו רעה כמו שפועל הוא
לי על לא חמס בכפי (*Job 16:17*) וכזאת עשה לי
[....name of recipient....] הרודף אותי וכאשר הצלת
דוד מיד שאול וכף כל אויביו יהי רצון ורחמים
מלפניך שתצילני ותשפיל כל אויבי וכל שונאי
ושוטני [....personal name....] ותשיב לו גמולו
בראשו ותשיב עצתו בראשו ומחשבתו אשר חשב
עלי בשם הגדול אל שדי יהיה הדבר אלי אני
[....personal name....] אמן סלה

Transliteration:

Pahotzu shechakim l'fanecha bati l'haz'kir'cha ki ani v'dal v'evion ani v'lo pa'al'ti lo ra'ah k'mo shepo'el hu li al lo chamas b'chapai (Job 16:17) u'chazot aseih li [....name of recipient....] harodeif oti v'cha'asher hitzal'ta david m'yad sha'ul v'kaf kol oy'vav y'hi ratzon v'rachamim mil'fanecha shetatzileini v'tash'pil kol oy'vai v'chol son'ai v'sot'nai

[....personal name....] *v'tashiv lo g'mulo b'rosho v'tashiv atzato b'rosho umach'shav'to asher chashav alai b'sheim hagadol El Shadai yih'yeh hadavar eilai ani* [....personal name....] *Omein Selah*

Translation:

Disperse yourselves clouds, before you. I came to remind you that I am destitute, poor and miserable. I have done no evil to him, as he does to me, *although there is no violence in my hands* (*Job 16:17*), as he did to me, [....name of recipient....], who persecutes me, and how you have saved David from the hand of Saul and the grip of all his enemies. May it be your will and mercy to save me and humble all my enemies, and all my haters, and adversaries of [....personal name....]. You should revisit his deed back on his head. You should return his plan in his head and his thoughts about me. With the great name *El Shadai* the magic word will be to me [....personal name....], *Amen Selah.*[5]

Once again Godfrey Selig's presentation is different from every other known recension of the "*Shimmush Tehillim*," and his sources remain a mystery. According to him "whoso prays this Psalm in childlike faith and trust in the most holy name, אל אמת (*El Emet* [*Eel enunet* or *Eel summet* in the English translation]), that is, the true God, or God of Truth, and prays the prayer belonging to it daily, will find favour with all men, and will be free from slander and mistrust."[6] Other than the statement that reciting the fourteenth Psalm will grant "favour with all men," the uses listed here are the same as in the other mentioned instances. However, the Divine Name combination אל אמת (*El Emet*) does not feature anywhere other than in this version of the "*Shimmush Tehillim*." Neither do the biblical sources from which the Divine Name is said to have been derived, these being listed as אלהים (*Elohim*—"God"): verse 1; משכיל (*mas'kil*—"understanding"): verse 2; אחד (*echad*—"one"): verse 3; עמי (*ami*—"my people"): verse 4; and עצת (*atzat*—"counsel"): verse 6.[7]

In conclusion Selig added a prayer-incantation reading: "May it please thee, Oh אל אמת (*El Emet*), to grant me grace, love and favour with all men whose help I need. Grant that all may believe my words, and that no slander may be effective against me to take away the confidence of men. Thou canst do this, for thou turnest the hearts of men according to thy holy will, and liars and slanderers are an abomination to thee. Hear me for the sake of thy name. *Amen Selah!*"[8]

There are again the inevitable magical uses doing the rounds, which did not find their way into written records. In this regard, the current Psalm is said to be useful against usurers, i.e. loan sharks; for charity; and to find favour with all men. Otherwise it is said to support those who fear their words are not being heard, and is equally employed against blasphemy (sacrilege). The fourteenth Psalm is further said to be good against suffering, and for recovering from all manner of injuries.

The use of *Psalm 14* in Christian Magic appears somewhat sparse. In the Byzantine manuscripts we are told that a man should write and bury the Psalm at the entrance of his home, doing so without the knowledge of his wife, in order to prevent her from running off with another man.[9] An entirely different application of the fourteenth Psalm is mentioned in *"Le Livre d'Or,"* in which an individual seeking "to appear Majestic before someone and be respected for it,"[10] is instructed to recite the current Psalm over "pure water," and then to wash certain magical characters, which were perfumed with mastic and musk, and the resulting magically infused water poured out in front of the door of the person whose respect is being sought.[11]

In conclusion, in the *"Key of Solomon"* the fourteenth Psalm is listed amongst a set of Psalms, any of which is recommended for recitation whilst the practitioner is disrobing in preparation for taking a ritual bath. The full set comprises *Psalms 14, 53, 27, 54, 81* and *105.*[12]

Psalm 15

[1] מזמור לדוד יהוהאדני־אהדונהי מי יגור באהלך מי
ישכן בהר קדשך
[2] הולך תמים ופעל צדק ודבר אמת בלבבו
[3] לא רגל על לשנו לא עשה לרעהו רעה וחרפה לא
נשא על קרבו
[4] נבזה בעיניו נמאס ואת יראי יהוהאדני־אהדונהי יכבד
נשבע להרע ולא ימר
[5] כספו לא נתן בנשך ושחד על נקי לא לקח עשה
אלה לא ימוט לעולם

Transliteration:

[1] *miz'mor l'david YHVH mi yagur b'aholecha mi
yish'kon b'har kod'shecha*

[2] *holeich tamim ufo'el tzedek v'doveir emet bil'vavo*

[3] *lo ragal al l'shono lo asah l're'eihu ra'ah v'cher'pah
lo nasa al k'rovo*

[4] *niv'zeh b'einav nim'as v'et yir'ei YHVH y'chabeid
nish'ba l'hara v'lo yamir*

[5] *kas'po lo natan b'neshech v'shochad al naki lo lakach
oseh eileh lo yimot l'olam*

Translation:

[1] A Psalm of David. *YHVH*, who shall sojourn in Thy
tabernacle? Who shall dwell upon Thy holy mountain?

[2] He that walketh uprightly, and worketh righteousness,
and speaketh truth in his heart;

[3] That hath no slander upon his tongue, nor doeth evil to
his fellow, nor taketh up a reproach against his neighbour;

[4] In whose eyes a vile person is despised, but he
honoureth them that fear *YHVH*; he that sweareth to his
own hurt, and changeth not;

[5] He that putteth not out his money on interest, nor taketh
a bribe against the innocent. He that doeth these things
shall never be moved.

This most remarkable Psalm, which speaks of great mindfullness in meaningful living, holds a place of great importance in my heart. In commenting on *Psalm 15*, it has been noted "that the power to resolve the problem of suffering lies less with God than with the speaker,"[1] and that this Psalm informs us "that the ability to tell the truth to oneself characterizes a person worthy of entering the Tabernacle or Temple."[2] In fact, we are told categorically that material well-being is determined by the realisation "that the power to resolve the problem of suffering lies with the speaker."[3] It is thus understandable that the fifteenth Psalm is said to be "the corner stone of spiritual cleansing,"[4] good "for Self Improvement: Improving Ones Character,"[5] and that it should be recited every day by anyone who wants to "become a better person."[6]

Interestingly, that is the basis of the following Divine Name construct, which was created for "spiritual return":[7]

$$\text{יְהָךְ\ \ יְהוֹשׁ\ \ יָהוֹד\ \ יְהוֹהַק}$$
$$\text{מַרְיָה\ \ יַבְגַן\ \ וַכְשְׁרֵי\ \ בְיַאמְהָו}$$
$$\text{לַב\ כָל}$$

Vocalised "*Y'hacha Y'hosh Yahod Y'hohak Mar'yah Yav'gan Vach'sh'rai V'yam'ha'u Lav' Chal*," this Divine Name construct is derived from *Psalm 15:1*.[8] In this regard, the opening query of the verse reading יהוה מי יגור באהלך (*YHVH mi yagur b'oholecha*—"*YHVH, who shall sojourn in Thy tabernacle*"), is conjoined with the concluding query reading מי ישכן בהר קדשך (*mi yish'kon b'har kod'shecha*—"*Who shall dwell upon Thy holy mountain?*"). The latter phrase was turned around, so to speak, i.e. the letters written in reverse, and then combined with the mentioned opening query.[8] Afterwards the concluding amalgamation was subdivided into smaller groupings including a unique presentation of the Ineffable Name, as well as the word לב (*lev*—"heart"), which, as indicated in the second verse, references the locale where we should face "truth," in order to create this unique Divine Name construct.

The first four letter combinations in the upper line contains combinations of the Ineffable Name (יה יהו יהו יהוה) conjoined with the four letters of קדשׁך (*kod'sh'cha*—"your holy"), the concluding word of the verse written, as indicated, in reverse. As noted, the remaining words of the two phrases are similartly conjoined, with the inclusion of the word לב (*lev*—"heart"). However, it should be noted that this Divine Name construct appears in two formats comprising variant concluding letter combinations. I found the format which I shared here to be particularly meaningful. The alternative format does not include the additional לב (*lev*—"heart"), and concludes בִּיאַמֶּה כַלכַל (*B'amah Chalchal*). In this regard, Rabbi Moses Zacutto correctly noted that the concluding כל in the combination is superfluous.[9]

Whatever the case may be, it is said this Divine Name is said to be good for "spiritual return," i.e. what is called "atonement,"[10] and which I personally interpret "at-one-ment," as well as to counteract the יצר הרע (*yetzer ha-ra*—"evil inclination")[11] which is linked to the "desire to receive," and which I have addressed in some degree in previous volumes.[12] Above all, this Divine Name construct is employed to achieve רוח קדושה (*Ruach K'dushah*—"a spirit of holiness").[13] This probably reminds individuals of the expression רוח הקודשׁ (*Ruach haKodesh*), a term indicating "spiritual enlightenment," which is maintained to be "the level of true prophecy."[14] It is further said to be "the highest degree of godliness thought to be possible in this day and age," and that those "rare individuals credited with *ruach ha-kodesh* could foresee, forewarn, inspire, and have generally left behind remarkable works of Torah."[15] Of course, the use of the current Divine Name construct is not suddenly going to lead to "instant enlightenment," but it will support those who use this Divine Name to encourage this ideal condition of consciousness, i.e. "ultimate spiritual awakening" within themselves.

Considering the sentiments expressed thus far, it is no surprise that Jewish magical teaching maintains the enuciation of *Psalm 15* to be good for finding favour in the eyes of all people,[16] and for the one who recites it to be well received. In this regard we are informed in Godfrey Selig's version of the "*Shimmush Tehillim*," that the one who "prays this Psalm with reverence will be generally received with great favour."[17] Beyond finding favour, the *Sefer Rafael ha-Malach* maintains the fifteenth Psalm is to be employed if you want to have a request granted by anyone.[18] However, reciting *Psalm 15* is popularly recommended to slay demons,[19] which some readers might rightly observe to be a far cry from what has thus far been said about this remarkable Psalm, unless "obsession" is amongst the "demons" to be slain by this Psalm. In fact, the fifteenth Psalm is listed "against obsession."[20]

Some of the recensions of the "*Shimmush Tehillim*" recommend somewhat more complex procedures, rather than just reciting the current Psalm to put a demon to flight. In this regard, most recensions maintain the fifteenth Psalm should be recited over a new vessel filled with "drawn water."[21] The reference here is to water drawn from a fresh source like a river or spring. In my estimation, good, clean water is easily come by today, without having to hunt around for a "fresh spring" or a "clean river," the latter being rarities these days. One of the recensions of the "*Shimmush Tehillim*" maintains the Psalm should be recited over a mix of water and oil,[22] another that the Psalm should be recited ten or eleven times.[23] Almost all agree that the one in whom there is a spirit or a demon should be washed with this water.[24]

Following the recitation of the current Psalm over the "drawn water," and having washed the "possessed individual" therewith, the most popular procedure maintains that a prayer-incantation, incorporating a unique Divine Name construct, should be recited.[25] This Divine Name construct is יַלִּי, which is said to be vocalised *Yalai*,[26] and was purportedly derived: י (*Yod*) from יָגוּר (*yagur*— "sojourn" or "dwell"): verse 1; ל (*Lamed*) from רָגַל (*ragal*—"slander"): verse 3;[27] and י (*Yod*) from מ (*Mem*) in לְעוֹלָם (*l'olam*—"eternally" or "never"): verse 5, the glyph from the concluding word of the Psalm having been transposed by means of the א״ת ב״ש (*Atbash*) cipher.[28]

In the published editions of the "*Shimmush Tehillim*" a variant origin is listed in terms of the second י (*Yod*), said to have been derived from מ (*Mem*) in יִמּוֹט (*yimot*—"moved"): verse 5, which is equally noted to have been transposed by means of the א״ת ב״ש (*Atbash*) cipher.[29] The same Divine Name construct is listed in Selig's German/English version, which he transliterated "*Iali*," and his statements regarding the origins of the Divine Name

construct, align with the second claim, without reference to the
א״ת ב״ש (*Atbash*) cipher.[30]

Aside from this minor difference, most recensions of the
"*Shimmush Tehillim*" share the same simple prayer-incantation
which, as noted, is recited after having washed the "possessed
individual."[31] It reads:

יהי רצון מלפניך השם הגדול ילי שתסיר כל שד
ומזיק מגוף [....name of recipient....] אמן אמן אמן
סלה סלה סלה

Transliteration:

> *Y'hi ratzon mil'fanecha hashem hagadol Yalai shetasir kol*
> *shed umazik b'guf* [....name of recipient....] *Omein Omein*
> *Omein Selah Selah Selah*

Translation:

> May it be your will, the great Name *Yalai*, to remove every
> demon and harmful spirit from the body of [....name of
> recipient....] *Amen Amen Amen Selah Selah Selah.*

The procedure is concluded with the "demoniac" drinking of the
water, and washing his/her face, hands, and feet with it. We are
informed that this will cause the malicious spirit to flee.[32]

Another recension of the "*Shimmush Tehillim*" shares a
variant procedure of using *Psalm 15* to aid someone who has "a
demon in the belly," which includes a much larger prayer-
incantation.[33] Once again the practitioner should visit a spring,
doing so without speaking, in order to collect water in a glass
vessel. The water is then carried to the residence of the afflicted
individual, and there to recite the current Psalm eleven times. The
sufferer is then given the water to drink, and the following prayer-
incantation recited:

עליון על כל הארץ שמע בקולי וקבל תפלתי
ורחם על כל מעשיך ומפעל ידיך והנחם על
הרעה אשר עשה [....name of recipient....] ורפא
נא לו והוצא ממנו הרוח הרעה אשר בקרבו
ממאתים וארבעים ושמונה איברים שלו בשם
האל המלך הרם והנשא אלי יושב על כסא מרום

יהי דבר זה ל'[....name of recipient....] אמן אמן
אמן סלה סלה סלה

Transliteration:

*El'yon al kol ha'aretz sh'ma b'koli v'kabel t'filati
v'rachem al kol ma'asecha umif'al yadecha v'hinacheim
al hara'ah asher asah [....name of recipient....] v'r'fa na lo
v'hotzei mimenu haru'ach hara'ah asher b'kir'bo
mima'atayim v'ar'ba'im ush'monah eivarim shelo b'sheim
ha'el hamelech haram v'hanisa eili yosheiv al kisei marom
y'hi davar zeh l'[....name of recipient....] Omein Omein
Omein Selah Selah Selah*

Translation:

Most High above all the earth, hear my voice and receive
my prayer. Have mercy on all your deeds and (the) work of
your hands. Consolation for the evil that [....name of
recipient....] has done. Heal him and draw the evil spirit
that is in him out of his 248 (bodily) members, in the name
of God, the sublime and exalted King, my God, sitting on
the lofty throne. Let this (magic) word be for [....name of
recipient....] *Amen Amen Amen Selah Selah Selah.*[34]

In conclusion we need to revisit Godfrey Selig's German/English
translation of the "*Shimmush Tehillim.*" In his estimation *Psalm 15*
is employed "against the presence of an evil spirit, insanity and
melancholy."[35] In this regard, he equally notes the recitation of this
Psalm "over a new pot filled with well-water that was drawn for
this express purpose, and with this water bathe the body of the
patient."[36] He also references a prayer-incantation to be repeated
"during the process of washing," which reads as follows: "May it
be thy will, O God, to restore [....name of recipient....], who has
been robbed of his senses, and is grievously plagued by the devil,
and enlighten his name for the sake of thy holy name *Iali* Amen
Selah."[37]

I have observed the fifteenth Psalm being employed against
infirmities, fevers, rheumatism, and for diseases of the kidneys.
Other than that it has been recommended against despair, to
support retarded children, to stop thieves before they can cause any
harm, and even to get them to repent of their crimes. Considering
the importance of *Psalm 15* in terms of spiritual cleansing and

spiritual awakening, it is understandable that it is also said to be of great value in the intense self-reckoning חשבון הנפש (*Chesh'bon Hanefesh*—"Accounting of Soul") practice over *Yom Kippur* ("Day of Atonement").

In terms of the use of the fifteenth Psalm in Christian Magic, it should be noted that in the mentioned Byzantine manuscripts the psalm "is for a court judgment." In this regard, it is said that those who hold onto it will defeat their enemies.[38] Otherwise, it is suggested in the *"Le Livre d'Or"* that one should recite this Psalm when entering "into any town or approach any Prince."[39] I presume these days the latter would reference any higher authority. It is suggested that individuals should recite the psalm on entry into a city, whilst at the same time carrying a set of special magical characters on their person.[40]

Be that as it may, it should be noted in conclusion that *Psalm 15* is one of a set of seven Psalms listed in the *"Key of Solomon"* to be recited whilst being clothed in the ritual garments, and the second of nineteen Psalms recited over wax employed from which the ritual candles are made, the entire set comprising *Psalms 8, 15, 22, 46, 47, 49, 51, 53, 68, 72, 84, 102, 110, 113, 126, 130, 131, 133,* and *139.*[41]

Psalm 16

[1] מכתם לדוד שמרני אל כי חסיתי בך

[2] אמרת ליהואהדיה יאהדונהי אדני אתה טובתי בל עליך

[3] לקדושים אשר בארץ המה ואדירי כל חפצי בם

[4] ירבו עצבותם אחר מהרו בל אסיך נסכיהם מדם ובל אשא את שמותם על שפתי

[5] יהואהדיהיאהדונהי מנת חלקי וכוסי אתה תומיך גורלי

[6] הבלים נפלו לי בנעמים אף נחלת שפרה עלי

[7] אברך את יהואהדיהיאהדונהי אשר יעצני אף לילות יסרוני כליותי

[8] שויתי יהואהדיהיאהדונהי לנגדי תמיד כי מימיני בל אמוט

[9] לכן שמח לבי ויגל כבודי אף בשרי ישכן לבטח

[10] כי לא תעזב נפשי לשאול לא תתן חסידך לראות שחת

[11] תודיעני ארח חיים שבע שמחות את פניך נעמות בימינך נצח

Transliteration:

[1] *mich'tam l'david shom'reini el ki chasiti vach*

[2] *amar't laYHVH adonai atah tovati bal alecha*

[3] *lik'doshim asher ba'aretz heimah v'adirei kol chef'tzi vam*

[4] *yir'bu atz'votam acheir maharu bal asich nis'keihem midam uval esa et sh'motam al s'fatai*

[5] *YHVH m'nat chel'ki v'chosi atah tomich gorali*

[6] *chavalim naf'lu li ban'imim af nachalat shaf'rah alai*

[7] *avarech et YHVH asher y'atzani af leilot yis'runi chil'yotai*

[8] *shiviti YHVH l'neg'di tamid ki mimini bal emot*

[9] *lachein samach libi vayagel k'vodi af b'sari yish'kon lavetach*

[10] *ki lo ta'azov naf'shi lish'ol lo titein chasid'cha lir'ot shachat*

[11] *todi'eini orach chayim sova s'machot et panecha n'imot bimin'cha netzach*

Translation:

[1] *Michtam* of David. Keep me *YHVH*; for I have taken refuge in Thee.

[2] I have said unto *YHVH*: 'Thou art my Lord; I have no good but in Thee';

[3] As for the holy that are in the earth, they are the excellent in whom is all my delight.

[4] Let the idols of them be multiplied that make suit unto another; their drink-offerings of blood will I not offer, nor take their names upon my lips.

[5] *YHVH*, the portion of mine inheritance and of my cup, Thou maintainest my lot.

[6] The lines are fallen unto me in pleasant places; yea, I have a goodly heritage.

[7] I will bless *YHVH*, who hath given me counsel; yea, in the night seasons my reins instruct me.

[8] I have set *YHVH* always before me; surely He is at my right hand, I shall not be moved.

[9] Therefore my heart is glad, and my glory rejoiceth; my flesh also dwelleth in safety;

[10] For Thou wilt not abandon my soul to the nether-world; neither wilt Thou suffer Thy godly one to see the pit.

[11] Thou makest me to know the path of life; in Thy presence is fulness of joy, in Thy right hand bliss for evermore.

To my mind *Psalms 15* and *16* belong together, and could be read as one. Since I hold these special Psalms very dear, I often do read them conjointly. In this regard, it has been noted that the fifteenth Psalm pertains to "dwelling on YHWH's holy hill," whilst the sixteenth Psalm "affirms that the Psalmist dwells securely with YHWH at his right hand....thus binding the two Psalms together with the notion that YHWH is the refuge of the righteous."[1] This beautiful Psalm is recited on a Saturday prior to *Arvit* (*Ma'ariv* or Evening Service) in Sefardi communities,[2] and is also pronounced when a funeral service and the subsequent mourning falls on days when the Jewish prayers of supplication (*Tachanun* prayers) are not uttered.[3]

Be that as it may, a single phrase from *Psalm 16:8*, reading שויתי יהוה לנגדי תמיד (*shiviti YHVH l'neg'di tamid*—"I have set *YHVH* before me always"), occupies a position of particular importance in the Jewish mind. It is the header and main focus of all those phenomenal "*Shiviti*" plaques and amulets, which are named after the first word in this phrase, and which are first and foremost constructed for contemplation. A beautiful example of such items is displayed on the front cover of this tome. Amongst these amazing items is the following simple design, the amuletic virtue of which is to engender "purity of thought," and which I have addressed in detail elsewhere:[4]

It is worth noting that the whole of *Psalm 16* is employed for the purpose of awakening and sharpening intelligence.[5] However, getting back to the verse under discussion, we are told that aside from the literal meaning of *"I have set YHVH before me always,"* the "mystical understanding" of this phrase is "I see God equally before me always," which means "whatever I see is the manifestation of God."[6] Rabbi Shneur Zalman of Lyadi made it possible for his followers, and everyone else for that matter, to realise this "mystical understanding" by means of the following simple meditation, in which the mind is allowed the free flow of consciousness between אין (*Ain*—"Nothing") and עין (*Ayin*—"Eyes"). In this regard, one would read the opening phrase from *Psalm 121:1*, "I lift up mine eyes unto the mountains; from the Divine No-thing my help comes," and it is with this phrase that you commence the said meditation, which is worked in the following manner.

You are required to sit down comfortably somewhere outdoors, or in front of a window which allows you to rest your eyes gently on where earth and sky meet on the horizon.[7] If such is not possible, the great Rabbi suggested that you should "gently lift your eyes skyward so that you see nothing in particular and simply gaze at the vastness of the sky."[8] Then commence reciting אשא עיני אל ההרים מאין יבא עזרי (*esa einai el heharim, mei'ayin yavo ez'ri*—"I will lift up mine eyes unto the mountains: from whence shall my help come?") [*Psalm 121:1*]. We are told this is done purely to settle the mind, and that the repetition is ceased "when you feel settled." In this regard, you are advised not to try to "control your thoughts or even take excessive note of them," but to let go "whatever arises in your mind."[9] Furthermore, you are instructed not to "become angry with yourself if thoughts and feelings continue to arise," since "these are not under your control," and that you should rather "greet each one as another opportunity to surrender."[10]Thus you should "let it rise and fall of its own accord without active participation at all." Otherwise, "if your mind becomes agitated," you would simply focus back on repeating the "*Esa einai*" verse, without making it a "rote repetition." You are instructed to "let it go when the mind is once again calm." It is said that "in time, a sense of growing spaciousness will arise in you," and that "your mind will become as wide as the sky, making room for whatever clouds arise without identifying with any of them."[11]

This should be practised "for twenty to thirty minutes," following which you would "shift your gaze to the world around you," and "see everything from the perspective of emptiness," i.e. אִין (*Ain*), as well as "spacious mind" (*mochin d'gadlut*). Then you are advised to remind yourself שִׁוִּיתִי יהוה לְנֶגְדִּי תָמִיד (*shiviti YHVH l'neg'di tamid*), i.e. "Everything you see is a form of the formless, a manifestation of God." it is said that if you worked this meditation "several times each week, you will find that you spend more and more of your day in this state of spacious awareness, engaging form (*Yesh*) with an openness arising from emptiness (*Ayn*), and knowing both to be aspects of God."[12]

In my estimation, this meditation is magically speaking equally as effective as any of the techniques of Jewish Magic ("Practical Kabbalah"). Speaking of magical practices, it is worth noting that the capitals of the words comprising *Psalm 16:8*, are conjoined in the Divine Name construct שׁילת כמבא for inclusion in an amulet which functions as a call for help.[13] Furthermore, the term שִׁוִּיתִי (*shiviti*) itself is sometimes employed entirely on its own in Hebrew amulets.[14] As might be expected, the entire sixteenth Psalm is employed for a variety of magical purposes, amongst others, to be rescued from perilous situations.[15] We are further told that this Psalm is good for the "Opening of the Heart,"[16] this term referencing greater comprehension in spiritual studies, to make peace with enemies[17] or "change enemies into friends,"[18] and to extricate individuals from persistent problems which they have become accustomed to,[19] i.e. praying this Psalm daily will result in the dispersion of all pain and sorrow.[20] I have even heard of it being employed to call on the beneficial powers of one's ancestors.

The sixteenth Psalm is most extensively recommended for the purpose of revealing the name of a thief.[21] In this regard, the Psalm is recited in conjunction with a prayer-incantation comprising an associated Divine Name construct חִי, the latter referencing the Hebrew term "*chai*" ("live" or "alive"). However, here the term is said to have been derived: ח (*Chet*) from הבלים (*chavalim*—"lines" or "ropes"): verse 6, and י (*Yod*) from עלי

נחלת שפרה (*nachalat shaf'ra alai*—"I have a goodly heritage"): verse 6.[22]

The simplest of the procedures shared in the "*Shimmush Tehillim*" to ascertain the identity of a thief, requires the practitioner to mix and knead together sea sand and mud taken from a river bank. Following this, the names of suspects are written separately on slips of paper, after which the mud and sand mix is formed into flat cakes. One recension maintains the clay should be shaped like skulls.[23] Afterwards, the written names are respectively located inside these mud cakes, each of which is carefully placed one by one inside a water filled pottery cup or vessel. *Psalm 16* is then recited ten times over them, and each recitation concluded with the statement:

יהי רצון מלפניך חי שתודיעני מי גנב כך וכך

Transliteration:
> *Y'hi ratzon mil'fanecha Chai shetodi'eini mi ganav kach v'kach*

Translation:
> May it be your will *Chai*, that you should let me know who stole this and that.

We are informed that the mud of he one who stole will dissolve, and that the paper with the name of this individual on it will float to the surface of the water.[24] A slightly more complex procedure can be found in another recension of the "*Shimmush Tehillim*," where the one who is seeking to identify a thief, is instructed to collect "virgin earth" which has never been trodden upon, and which is said to be "clay of pottery," or "clay found in the middle of a residence" which has "never been worked."[25] Other recensions suggest the user should take clay or mud "from the hand of a potter."[26] Of course, pottery clay is easily come by, which cannot be said about such substance being taken from the centre of residences, this being found in our day only in the most remote rural regions of our planet.

Be that as it may, the practitioner is instructed to bring spring water to his/her residence, where the same procedure addressed above is enacted, except that in the current instance the sixteenth Psalm is recited twelve times with the following prayer-incantation:

יהי רצון מלפניך אלהים חי יושב מרום שוכן
שחקים שאותו האיש שגנב לי הגניבה יצא עמו
הכתוב בעגולים האלה וישוט על פני המים ואדענו
אותו אשר גנב לי ואל אחשוד הכשרים אשר לא
פשעו בדבר בשם אל חי שוכן שחקים יהיה דבר
זה אמן אמן סלה סלה

Transliteration:

*Y'hi ratzon mil'fanecha Elohim Chai yosheiv marom
shochen shechakim she'oto ha'ish sheganav li hig'nivah
yeitzei imo hakatuv ba'agulim ha'eileh v'yashut al p'nei
hamayim v'eida'enu oto asher ganav li v'el ech'shod
hak'sheirim asher lo pash'u b'davar b'sheim El Chai
shochen shechakim yih'yeh davar zeh Omein Omein Selah
Selah*

Translation:

May it be your will, *Elohim Chai*, sitting on high, dwelling
in the clouds, that this individual who stole something from
me be exposed by what is written on this flat cake, and it
will float on the surface of the water. And I will know the
one who stole (something) from me, and will not suspect
the innocent who did nothing wrong (committed no crime)
in this matter, in the name *El Chai*, who dwells in the
clouds, will be this (magic) word. *Amen Amen Selah
Selah.*[27]

Godfrey Selig's version of the "*Shimmush Tehillim*" instructs the
one who wishes to ascertain the identity of a thief, to collect and
mix together "mud or slime and sand out of a stream."[28] The names
of the suspects are again written on slips of paper, but in the
current instance the mud mixture is applied to "the reverse side of
the slips," which are afterwards placed "in a large and clean basin"
which was filled with "fresh water from the stream."[29] It is again
said that following the recitation of the *Psalm 16* and a relevant
prayer ten times, the slip of paper comprising the name of the
culprit will rise to the surface.[30] Selig's prayer-incantation includes
the Divine Name אל חי (*El Chai*), written "*Eel Caar*" in the
English translation, and reads: "Let it be thy will the Living God
to make known the name of the thief, who stole from me (here

name tht which was stolen). Grant that the name of the thief, if it is among the names, may arise before thy eyes, and thus be made known to mine and all others who are present, that thy name may be glorified: grant it for the sake of thy holy name. *Amen Selah*!"[31]

Once again the magical uses of the current Psalm are much more extensive than those listed in published sources. These range from something as mundane as finding lost keys to something as mysterious as the revelation and certitude of "secret things"; from protection against the dangers of fire, to escaping volcanoes and other public disasters. *Psalm 16* is also said to be good for illness in general, and especially for diseases of the limbs. Other than that, it is equally employed against fevers, as well as against epilepsy. It is also employed for more lofty purposes, i.e. for the forgiveness of errors and transgressions; and to turn sorrow to joy.

Single verses of the sixteenth Psalm are also used for a variety of magical purposes, and in this regard the following application is particularly interesting. It incorporates the following unique Divine Name construct which was derived from *Psalm 16:5*, reading יְהוָה מְנָת חֶלְקִי וְכוֹסִי **אַתָּה תּוֹמִיךְ גּוֹרָלִי** (*YHVH m'nat chel'ki v'chosi atah tomich gorali*—"YHVH, the portion of mine inheritance and of my cup, Thou maintainest my lot."

$$\text{יַהִי יְהַל יָהוּר יָהִוְהוּ}$$
$$\text{מַגְנְכַת יַחְמְלוּ קְתַיָהָ}$$
$$\text{וְתִכָאַוִיס}$$

Vocalised "*Yahi Y'hal Yahur Yahiv'hu Mag'n'chat Yach'm'lu K'tayaha V't'cha'avis'*," this Divine Name construct was formed from the letters of the said verse having been divided into two groups, and then combined in a unique manner, similar to a Divine Name construct addressed in the previous Psalm. The first of the two letter groups comprises the initial fifteen glyphs written in the standard manner from right to left, and the second the concluding fourteen written in reverse order, following which the two groups are conjoined letter by letter. Additionally, the upper row of the construct includes combinations of the four letters of the Ineffable Name, i.e. יְהוָה יְהוּ יְה יָה יִ, which are combined in the mentioned manner with the concluding four letters of the verse.[32]

There is not a clear, direct indication as to what this Divine Name construct is to be used for. However, it appears it is good for having requests granted. This is in fact the very purpose of the Divine Name construct יֹמחֹו, which is formed from the capitals of the first four words of *Psalm 16:5*, and popularly included in amulets for the said purpose.[33] As far as the mentioned usage of the previous Divine Name construct is concerned, the instruction is to recite the first five verses of the sixteenth Psalm, followed by enunciating the Divine Name construct seven times in the heart, and then to conclude the recitation of the remainder of the Psalm. Afterwards the practitioner has to utter the prayer-incantation comprising a petition for a request to be granted.[34] Beyond stating "May it be your will, etc.,"[35] there is no further indication as to the exact format of this prayer-incantation, but I believe the following brief one will suffice:

יהי רצון מלפניך יהוה אלהינו ואלהי אבותינו
בשם השמות האלה יַהִי יְהַל יָהוּר יַהִוְהוּ מַגִנִכַת
יַחְמְלוּ קְתַיָהָ וְתְכָאַוִיס שתצל יחוני בזה מה שארצה
מעתה ועד עולם אכיר אמן כן יהי רצון

Transliteration:

Y'hi ratzon mil'fanecha YHVH Eloheinu veilohei avoteinu b'sheim hasheimot ha'eilah Yahi Y'hal Yahur Yahiv'hu Mag'n'chat Yach'm'lu K'tayaha V't'cha'avis' sh'tatz'lichuni b'zeh mah she'ertzeh mei'atah v'ad olam omein v'chen y'hi ratzon

Translation:

May it be your will *YHVH* our God and God of our fathers, in the name of these names *Yahi Y'hal Yahur Yahiv'hu Mag'n'chat Yach'm'lu K'tayaha V't'cha'avis'*, for me to have success in this that I desire, from now unto eternity *amen* and thus be it so willed.

It should be noted that *Psalm 16:5* is also indicated to be directly related to נִיֹת (*Nit*), the fifty-fourth tri-letter portion of the "Name of Seventy-two Names,"[36] as well as to מֹנַד (*Menad*), the thirty-sixth portion of the "*Shem Vayisa Vayet*" ("*Name of Seventy-two Names*").[37]

As far as Christian Magic is concerned, the sixteenth Psalm was equally recited for the purpose of revealing the identities of thieves.[38] Otherwise, the Byzantine magical manuscripts maintain it to be good to recite this Psalm when you are afraid to travel on the road, and to counteract fear generally.[39] On the other hand, the "*Le Livre d'Or*" recommends the current Psalm for protection of a very different kind, i.e. protection "from enchantments of wicked people," and to stop them from causing harm. In this regard, users are instructed to write *Psalm 16* in conjunction with a set of magical characters, to be carried on their persons.[40] Elsewhere it is suggested that one recites verses five and six of the current Psalm in order "to prosper in all things."[41]

Psalm 17

[1] תפלה לדוד שמעה יהוהאהדונהי צדק
הקשיבה רנתי האזנה תפלתי בלא שפתי מרמה

[2] מלפניך משפטי יצא עיניך תחזינה מישרים

[3] בחנת לבי פקדת לילה צרפתני בל תמצא זמתי
בל יעבר פי

[4] לפעלות אדם בדבר שפתיך אני שמרתי ארחות
פריץ

[5] תמך אשרי במעגלותיך בל נמוטו פעמי

[6] אני קראתיך כי תענני אל הט אזנך לי שמע
אמרתי

[7] הפלה חסדיך מושיע חוסים ממתקוממים
בימינך

[8] שמרני כאישון בת עין בצל כנפיך תסתירני

[9] מפני רשעים זו שדוני איבי בנפש יקיפו עלי

[10] חלבמו סגרו פימו דברו בגאות

[11] אשרינו עתה סבבונו עיניהם ישיתו לנטות
בארץ

[12] דמינו כאריה יכסוף לטרף וככפיר ישב
במסתרים

[13] קומה יהוהאהדונהי קדמה פניו הכריעהו
פלטה נפשי מרשע חרבך

[14] ממתים ידך יהוהאהדונהי ממתים מחלד
חלקם בחיים וצפונך תמלא בטנם ישבעו בנים
והניחו יתרם לעולליהם

[15] אני בצדק אחזה פניך אשבעה בהקיץ תמונתך

Transliteration:

[1] *t'filah l'david shim'ah YHVH tzedek hak'shivah rinati ha'azinah t'filati b'lo sif'tei mir'mah*

[2] *mil'fanecha mish'pati yeitzei einecha techezenah meisharim*

[3] *bachan'ta libi pakad'ta lailah tz'raf'tani val tim'tza zamoti bal ya'avor pi*

[4] *lif'ulot adam bid'var s'fatecha ani shamar'ti or'chot paritz*

[5] *tamoch ashurai b'ma'g'lotecha bal namotu f'amai*

[6] *ani k'raticha chi ta'aneini el hat oz'n'cha li sh'ma im'rati*

[7] *haf'leih chasadecha moshi'a chosim mimit'kom'mim biminecha*

[8] *shom'reini k'ishon bat ayin b'tzeil k'nafecha tas'tireini*

[9] *mip'nei r'sha'im zu shaduni oy'vai b'nefesh yakifu alai*

[10] *chel'bamo sag'ru pimo dib'ru v'gei'ut*

[11] *ashureinu atah s'vavunu eineihem yashitu lin'tot ba'aretz*

[12] *dim'yono k'aryeih yich'sof lit'rof v'chich'fir yosheiv b'mis'tarim*

[13] *kumah YHVH kad'mah fanav ha'cheri'eihu pal'tah naf'shi meirasha char'becha*

[14] *mim'tim yad'cha YHVH mim'tim m'cheled chel'kam bachayim utz'fun'cha t'malei vit'nam yis'b'u vanim v'hinichu yit'ram l'ol'leihem*

[15] *ani b'tzedek echezeh fanecha es'b'ah v'hakitz t'munatecha*

Translation:

[1] A Prayer of David. Hear the right *YHVH*, attend unto my cry; give ear unto my prayer from lips without deceit.

[2] Let my judgment come forth from Thy presence; let Thine eyes behold equity.

[3] Thou hast tried my heart, Thou hast visited it in the night; Thou hast tested me, and Thou findest not that I had a thought which should not pass my mouth.

[4] As for the doings of men, by the word of Thy lips I have kept me from the ways of the violent.

[5] My steps have held fast to Thy paths, my feet have not slipped.

[6] As for me, I call upon Thee, for Thou wilt answer me, O God; incline Thine ear unto me, hear my speech.

[7] Make passing great Thy mercies, O Thou that savest by Thy right hand from assailants them that take refuge in Thee.

[8] Keep me as the apple of the eye, hide me in the shadow of Thy wings,

[9] From the wicked that oppress, my deadly enemies, that compass me about.

[10] Their gross heart they have shut tight, with their mouth they speak proudly.

[11] At our every step they have now encompassed us; they set their eyes to cast us down to the earth.

[12] He is like a lion that is eager to tear in pieces, and like a young lion lurking in secret places.

[13] Arise *YHVH*, confront him, cast him down; deliver my soul from the wicked, by Thy sword;

[14] From men, by Thy hand *YHVH*, from men of the world, whose portion is in this life, and whose belly Thou fillest with Thy treasure; who have children in plenty, and leave their abundance to their babes.

[15] As for me, I shall behold Thy face in righteousness; I shall be satisfied, when I awake, with Thy likeness.

Psalm 17 features prominently in the Sefardic rite over the period of *Rosh Hashanah* (New Year) and *Yom Kippur* (Day of Atonement). In this regard, it is recited over the length of a month prior to the Jewish High Holy Days, and every day over the ten days between *Rosh Hashanah* and *Yom Kippur*.[1] It should be noted that in Jewish mystical tradition, the days of awe are extended to הושענא רבא (*Hoshana Raba*—"Great Supplication"), the earlier mentioned seventh day of the festival of *Sukkot* (Festival of Booths), and hence the seventeenth Psalm is recited over this period as well.[2]

In Jewish Magic ("Practical Kabbalah") the current Psalm is recited when undertaking a journey,[3] which the author of the *Rafael ha-Malach* affirms is about having success on your way.[4] Further details are offered in the "*Shimmush Tehillim*," in which *Psalm 17* is recited in conjunction with a simple prayer-incantation, the latter incorporating the Divine Name יה (*Yah*).[5] This Divine Name is said to have been derived: י (*Yod*) from שדוני (*shaduni*—"oppress me"): verse 9, and ה (*Heh*) from מרמה (*mir'mah*—"deceit"): verse 1.[6] The prayer-incantation reads:

יהי רצון מלפניך יה השם הגבור והנורא שמצליח
דרכי ותיישר ארחותי אמן אמן אמן סלה סלה סלה

Transliteration:

> *Y'hi ratzon mil'fanecha Yah hasheim hagibor v'hanora*
> *shematz'li'ach d'rachai ut'yasheir or'chotai Omein Omein*
> *Omein Selah Selah Selah.*

Translation:

> May it be your will *Yah*, the great, strong and awesome
> Name, to make my journey prosperous and to straighten
> my path *Amen Amen Amen Selah Selah Selah.*[7]

A somewhat expanded version of this prayer-incantation appears
in one of the recensions of the "*Shimmush Tehillim*," which
includes a plea for protection from hateful onslaughts of enemies
you may encounter on your way, and for them to be constrained.
It reads:

יהי רצון מלפניך יה השם הגדול והנורא שבו
בראת שמים וארץ שתצילני מכף אויב ואורב
בדרך ועני עטי אויבי ורודפי בסיורים ותצליח
דרכי ותישר אורחותי אמן אמן אמן סלה סלה
סלה

Transliteration:

> *Y'hi ratzon mil'fanecha Yah hasheim hagadol v'hanora*
> *sh'vo barata shamayim v'aretz shetatzileini mikaf oyeiv*
> *v'oreiv baderech v'ani iti oy'vai v'rod'fai b'siyurim*
> *v'tatz'liach d'rachai ut'yasheir or'chotai Omein Omein*
> *Omein Selah Selah Selah*

Translation:

> May it be your will *Yah*, the great and awesome Name with
> which you created heaven and earth, that you will deliver
> me from the hand of the enemy, and an ambush on the way,
> and suppress and plague my enemy and highwaymen on
> the journey, and make my journey prosperous and
> straighten my path *Amen Amen Amen Selah Selah Selah.*[8]

There is yet a further version of the seventeenth Psalm being
employed to ensure a successful trip. In this instance, the one
seeking this support is instructed to repeat the Psalm as well as an

associated prayer-incantation four times. We are informed the recitation "four times" aligns with "four clouds" mentioned in the prayer-incantation, and possibly with the "four cardinal points in which a journey can take place."[9]

The relevant Divine Name associated with this Psalm is said to be וה (*Vah* [?]),[10] which I believe should be יה (*Yah*), as this is the format employed in every other recension and published version of the *"Shimmush Tehillim."* Maybe the author of this manuscript misread a *"Yod"* for a *"Vav"* in a poorly written primary source, or else chose to replace the first two glyphs of the *Tetragrammaton*, with the concluding two. However, there is no indication why this variant was included in this specific manuscript. The prayer-incantation reads:

יהי רצון מלפניך וה [יה] שוכן ארבעה שחקים
ברום עליות שתוליכני קוממיות לארצי ותצעידני
לשלום ותשמרני מכל אויב ואורב בדרך ותצליח
דרכי ומעללי ומחשבותי לטובה ואל יעמוד לי
מנגד שום בריה לבטל מחשבותי אך אהיה מעולה
בשם וה [יה] אמן אמן אמן סלה סלה סלה

Transliteration

> *Y'hi ratzon mil'fanecha Vah [Yah] shochen ar'ba'ah shechakim b'rom aliyot shetolicheini kom'miyut l'ar'tzi v'tatz'ideini l'shalom v'tish'm'reini mikol oyeiv v'oreiv baderech v'tatz'li'ach d'rachai uma'al'lai umach'sh'votai l'tovah v'al ya'amod li mineged shum b'riyah l'vatel mach'sh'votai ach eh'yeh m'uleh b'shem Vah [Yah] Omein Omein Omein Selah Selah Selah*

Translation:

> May it be your will *Vah [Yah]*, who lives in the four clouds, at the loftiest Heights, that you may lead me fearlessly into my countries and lead me to peace, protect me from every enemy and highwayman on the way and let my ways, actions and thoughts turn out for good. Let no creature rise up against me to extinguish my thoughts. I will be distinguished in the name *Vah [Yah] Amen Amen Amen Selah Selah Selah.*[11]

Finally there is Selig's version of the magical use of *Psalm 17*, in which he informs as that "a traveller, who prays this Psalm early in the morning, with ardour, together with the proper prayer, in the name of יה (*Jah*), will be secure from all evil for twenty-four hours."[12] He lists the same origins for this Divine Name as mentioned in other recensions of the "*Shimmush Tehillim*," but he inexplicably references "*Jah Jenora*" as the Divine Name in his version of the prayer-incantation.[13] The latter is equally untraceable in any of the known primary sources referencing the magical use of the current Psalm. It reads "May it be thy holy will, Oh, *Jah, Jenora*, to make my journey prosperous, to lead me in pleasant paths, to protect me from all evil, and to bring me safely back to my loved ones, for thy mighty and adorable name's sake. *Amen*."[14]

Whilst the current Psalm is mainly employed in Jewish Magic for protection and success "on the road," it is also one of the Psalms employed against fevers. Otherwise I have seen it recommended for magical use against the dangers of fire, dangers from the sea, floods, lightning, volcanoes, and against storms in general. It is equally used to banish pests and insects, and in this regard I have witnessed a farmer blasting a recording of the seventeenth Psalm recited in Hebrew through speakers placed in his agricultural fields, in order to protect the crops against an onslaught of locusts. Be that as it may, we are told that *Psalm 17* is good against pride and ignorance, that it will counter anxiety caused by enemies, that it works against unjust accusations, offers security from evil, and is recited "for a good death." Ultimately it is recited to express gratitude for good fortune, and interestingly is said to be good for sportsmen!

As far as the use of single verses are concerned, the initials of the words comprising *Psalm 17:8* are conjoined in the following Divine Name construct שכבע בכת, which is included in amulets to ensure "success on the road."[15] Furthermore, the entire verse, reading שמרני כאישון בת עין בצל כנפיך תסתירני (*sham'reini ke'ishon bat ayin b'tzel k'nafeicha tas'tireini*—"Keep me as the apple of the eye, hide me in the shadow of Thy wings"), was employed in the construction of the following Divine Name construct:[16]

שַׁנְבִּי מִיצֶנ רֵעָלֵר
נתכי יַבָּנתָ כנפֶס
אוּיתַ ישֹׁךָ

This Divine Name construct was created by intertwining the letters of the verse in, as it were, a forwards and backwards manner. The first eight letters comprise the capitals of the eight letter combinations, and changing direction, i.e. writing backwards, the succeeding eight glyphs respectively comprise the second letters of the eight letter combinations of this Divine Name construct. Changing direction again, and writing in the standard manner from right to left, the third letter in each of the eight combinations comprise the third set of letters comprising the verse. Reversing direction one final time, the seven letters of the last word of this verse become the concluding glyphs of the first seven four-letter combinations.[17]

This unique Divine Name construct is employed in an amulet for the protection of the bearer against damage of any kind in the world, and against all manner of evil.[18] In this regard, having first established a condition of personal purity and after fasting, an individual would copy this Divine Name construct, as well as the *chotam* (magical seal) below, on a kosher deerskin parchment.[19] As noted before, a sheet of good and clean white paper will serve equally well:

ד	ף	מ
מ	ד	ף
ף	מ	ד

The construction of this amulet is concluded by reciting the following prayer-incantation:

יהי רצון מלפניך יהוה אלהינו ואלהי אבותינו
אהיה למענך ולמען שמותיך שתשלח מלאכיך
הממונים על השמירה ויהיו עמי בעזרי

Transliteration:

>*Y'hi ratzon mil'janecha YHVH Eloheinu veilohei avoteinu*
>*Eh'yeh l'ma'an'cha ul'ma'an sh'motecha shetish'lach*
>*malachecha hamemonim al hash'mirah vayih'yu imi*
>*b'ez'ri*

Translation:

> May it be your will *YHVH* our God and God of our fathers,
> *Eh'yeh*, for your sake and for the sake of your Names, to
> send your Angels in charge of protection, to be with me for
> my support.

Having completed the enunciation of this prayer-incantationm, the amulet is tied to the right arm of the bearer.[20]

A further magical use of a single verse from the seventeenth Psalm pertains to חבו (*Chavu*), the sixty-eighth tri-letter portion of the "*Shem Vayisa Vayet.*" We are told this tri-letter portion is an acronym of the section in *Psalm 17:14* reading חלקם בחיים וצפונך (*chel'kam ba'chayim utz'fun'cha* —"whose portion is in this life, and Thy treasure").[21] It is said this portion of "Name of Seventy -two Names" has the power to free souls who ended up in the realm of the *Klipot* (demonic shards) because of the semen they spilled during nocturnal emissions.[22]

In the magical material shared in the previously mentioned Byzantian Christian manuscripts, *Psalm 17* is recited for the destruction of "an enemy anywhere."[23] Further uses of the seventeenth Psalm are listed in these manuscripts, i.e. it is recited to cause a distraction,[24] and it is also maintained that a woman suffering pain in a breast should enunciate the Psalm whilst taking the "sacrament from the holy mysteries," following which she should anoint the breast which is said will heal.[25] Yet another application of the current Psalm is listed, one which pertains to ascertaining the identity of a thief in the magical use of the previous Psalm in Jewish magic.[26] The instructions are virtually identical, i.e. write the names of the suspects on slips of paper, in the current instance including the words "*Marana sarba*. The one who ate my bread has gravely supplanted me," the latter phrase being a paraphrase of *Psalm 41:10*;[27] collect "dirt from the hands of a potter"; repeat the Psalm, seven times in the current instance;[28]

roll the pieces of paper separately inside the clay; then submerge them in water, and the one which surfaces first will reveal the identity of the thief.[29]

In conclusion, the oft-mentioned "*Le Livre d'Or*" maintains *Psalm 17* should be recited seven times, and a set of special magical characters carried on your person, "if you wish to avoid scandal and strife."[30]

Psalm 18

[1] למנצח לעבד יהוה^{אדני}יאהדונהי לדוד אשר
דבר ליהוה^{אדני} יאהדונהי את דברי השירה הזאת
ביום הציל יהוה^{אדני}יאהדונהי אותו מכף כל אוביו
ומיד שאול

[2] ואמר ארחמך יהוה^{אדני}יאהדונהי חזקי

[3] יהוה^{אדני}יאהדונהי סלעי ומצודתי ומפלטי
אלי צורי אחסה בו מגני וקרן ישעי משגבי

[4] מהלל אקרא יהוה^{אדני}יאהדונהי ומן איבי אושע

[5] אפפוני חבלי מות ונחלי בליעל יבעתוני

[6] חבלי שאול סבבוני קדמוני מוקשי מות

[7] בצר לי אקרא יהוה^{אדני}יאהדונהי ואל אלהי
אשוע ישמע מהיכלו קולי ושועתי לפניו תבוא
באזניו

[8] ותגעש ותרעש הארץ ומוסדי הרים ירגזו
ויתגעשו כי חרה לו

[9] עלה עשן באפו ואש מפיו תאכל גחלים בערו
ממנו

[10] ויט שמים וירד וערפל תחת רגליו

[11] וירכב על כרוב ויעף וידא על כנפי רוח

[12] ישת חשך סתרו סביבותיו סכתו חשכת מים
עבי שחקים

[13] מנגה נגדו עביו עברו ברד וגחלי אש

[14] וירעם בשמים יהוה^{אדני}יאהדונהי ועליון יתן
קלו ברד וגחלי אש

[15] וישלח חציו ויפיצם וברקים רב ויהמם

[16] ויראו אפיקי מים ויגלו מוסדות תבל מגערתך
יהוה^{אדני} יאהדונהי מנשמת רוח אפך

[17] ישלח ממרום יקחני ימשני ממים רבים

[18] יצילני מאיבי עז ומשנאי כי אמצו ממני

[19] יקדמוני ביום אידי ויהי יהוה^{אדני}יאהדונהי
למשען לי

[20] ויוציאני למרחב יחלצני כי חפץ בי

[21] יגמלני יהוה־אדני כצדקי כבר ידי
ישיב לי

[22] כי שמרתי דרכי יהוה־אדני ולא רשעתי
מאלהי

[23] כי כל משפטיו לנגדי וחקתיו לא אסיר מני

[24] ואהי תמים עמו ואשתמר מעוני

[25] וישב יהוה־אדני לי כצדקי כבר ידי
לנגר עיניו

[26] עם חסיד תתחסד עם גבר תמים תתמם

[27] עם נבר תתברר ועם עקש תתפתל

[28] כי אתה עם עני תושיע ועינים רמות תשפיל

[29] כי אתה תאיר נרי יהוה־אדני אלהי יגיה
חשכי

[30] כי בך ארץ גדוד ובאלהי אדלג שור

[31] האל תמים דרכו אמרת יהוה־אדני צרופה
מגן הוא לכל החסים בו

[32] כי מי אלוה מבלעדי יהוה־אדני ומי צור
זולתי אלהינו

[33] האל המאזרני חיל ויתן תמים דרכי

[34] משוה רגלי כאילות ועל במתי יעמידני

[35] מלמד ידי למלחמה ונחתה קשת נחושה זרועתי

[36] ותתן לי מגן ישעך וימינך תסעדני וענותך
תרבני

[37] תרחיב צעדי תחתי ולא מעדו קרסלי

[38] ארדוף אויבי ואשיגם ולא אשוב עד כלותם

[39] אמחצם ולא יכלו קום יפלו תחת רגלי

[40] ותאזרני חיל למלחמה תכריע קמי תחתי

[41] ואיבי נתתה לי ערף ומשנאי אצמיתם

[42] ישועו ואין מושיע על יהוה־אדני ולא ענם

[43] ואשחקם כעפר על פני רוח כטיט חוצות אריקם

[44] תפלטני מריבי עם תשימני לראש גוים עם לא
ידעתי יעבדוני

[45] לשמע אזן ישמעו לי בני נכר יכחשו לי

[46] בני נכר יבלו ויחרגו ממסגרותיהם

[47] חי יהוהאדניאהדונהי וברוך צורי וירום אלוהי
ישעי

[48] האל הנותן נקמות לי וידבר עמים תחתי

[49] מפלטי מאיבי אף מן קמי תרוממני מאיש חמס
תצילני

[50] על כן אודך בגוים יהוהאדניאהדונהי ולשמך
אזמרה

[51] מגדל ישועות מלכו ועשה חסד למשיחו לדוד
ולזרעו עד עולם

Transliteration:

[1] *lam'natzei'ach l'eved YHVH l'david asher diber la'YHVH et div'rei ha'shirah ha'zot b'yom hitzil YHVH oto mikaf kol oy'vav umiyad sha'ul*

[2] *vayomar er'cham'cha YHVH chiz'ki*

[3] *YHVH sal'i um'tzudati um'fal'ti eili tzuri echeseh bo magini v'keren yish'i mis'gabi*

[4] *m'hulal ek'ra YHVH umin oy'vai ivashei'a*

[5] *afafuni chev'lei mavet v'nachalei v'liya'al y'va'atuni*

[6] *chev'lei she'ol s'vavuni kid'muni mok'shei mavet*

[7] *batzar li ek'ra YHVH v'el elohai ashavei'a yish'ma m'heichalo koli v'shav'ati l'fanav tavo v'oz'nav*

[8] *vatig'ash vatir'ash ha'aretz umos'dei harim yir'gazu vayit'ga'ashu ki charah lo*

[9] *alah ashan b'apo v'eish mipiv tocheil gechalim ba'aru mimenu*

[10] *vayet shamayim vayeirad va'arafel tachat rag'lav*

[11] *vayir'kav al k'ruv va'ya'of vayeide al kan'fei ru'ach*

[12] *yashet choshech sit'ro s'vivotav sukato chesh'chat mayim avei shechakim*

[13] *minogah neg'do avav av'ru barad v'gachalei esh*

[14] *vayar'eim ba'shamayim YHVH v'el'yon yitein kolo barad v'gachalei esh*

[15] *vayish'lach chitzav vay'fitzeim uv'rakim rav vay'humeim*

[16] *vayeira'u afikei mayim vayigalu mos'dot teiveil miga'arat'cha YHVH minish'mat ru'ach apecha*

[17] *yish'lach mimarom yikacheini yam'sheini mimayim rabim*

[18] *yatzileini mei'oy'vi az umison'ai ki am'tzu mimeni*

[19] *y'kad'muni v'yom eidi vay'hi YHVH l'mish'an li*

[20] *vayotzi'eini lamer'chav y'chal'tzeini ki chafeitz bi*

[21] *yig'm'leini YHVH k'tzid'ki k'vor yadai yashiv li*

[22] *ki shamar'ti dar'chei YHVH v'lo rasha'ti mei'elohai*

[23] *ki chol mish'patav l'neg'di v'chukotav lo asir meni*

[24] *va'ehi tamim imo va'esh'tameir mei'avoni*

[25] *vayashev YHVH li ch'tzid'ki k'vor yadai l'neged einav*

[26] *im chasid tit'chasad im g'var tamim titamam*

[27] *im navar tit'barar v'im ikeish tit'patal*

[28] *ki atah am ani toshi'a v'einayim ramot tash'pil*

[29] *ki atah ta'ir neiri YHVH elohai yagiha chosh'ki*

[30] *ki v'cha arutz g'dud uveilohai adaleg shur*

[31] *ha'eil tamim dar'ko im'rat YHVH tz'rufah magein hu l'chol hachosim bo*

[32] *ki mi eloha mi bal'adei YHVH umi tzur zulati eloheinu*

[33] *ha'eil ham'az'reini chayil vayitein tamim dar'ki*

[34] *m'shaveh rag'lai ka'ayalot v'al bamotai ya'amideini*

[35] *m'lameid yadai lamil'chamah v'nichatah keshet n'chushah z'ro'otai*

[36] *vatiten li magein yish'echa vimin'cha tis'adeini v'an'vat'cha tar'beini*

[37] *tar'chiv tza'adi tach'tai v'lo ma'adu kar'sulai*

[38] *er'dof oy'vai v'asigeim v'lo ashuv ad kalotam*

[39] *em'chatzeim v'lo yuch'lu kum yip'lu tachat rag'lai*

[40] *vat'az'reini chayil lamil'chamah tach'ri'a kamai tach'tai*

[41] *v'oy'vai natatah li oref um'san'ai atz'miteim*

[42] *y'shav'u v'ein moshi'a al YHVH v'lo anam*

[43] *v'esh'chakeim k'afar al p'nei ru'ach k'tit chutzot arikeim*

[44] *t'fal'teini meirivei am t'simeini l'rosh goyim am lo yada'ti ya'av'duni*

[45] *l'sheima ozen yisham'u li b'nei neichar y'chachashu li*

[46] *b'nei neichar yibolu v'yach'r'gu mimis'g'roteihem*

[47] *chai YHVH uvaruch tzuri v'yarum elohei yish'i*

[48] *ha'el hanotein n'kamot li vayad'beir amim tach'tai*
[49] *m'fal'ti mei'oy 'vai af min kamai t'rom 'moini moi'ish chamas tatzileini*
[50] *al kein od'cha vagoyim YHVH ul'shim'cha azameira*
[51] *mag'dil y'shu'ot mal'ko v'oseh chesed lim'shicho l'david ul'zar'o ad olam*

Translation:

[1] For the Leader. A Psalm of David the servant of *YHVH*, who spoke unto *YHVH* the words of this song in the day that *YHVH* delivered him from the hand of all his enemies, and from the hand of Saul;

[2] And he said: I love thee *YHVH*, my strength.

[3] *YHVH* is my rock, and my fortress, and my deliverer; my God, my rock, in Him I take refuge; my shield, and my horn of salvation, my high tower.

[4] Praised, I cry, is *YHVH*, and I am saved from mine enemies.

[5] The cords of Death compassed me, and the floods of *Belial* assailed me.

[6] The cords of *Sheol* surrounded me; the snares of Death confronted me.

[7] In my distress I called upon *YHVH*, and cried unto my God; out of His temple He heard my voice, and my cry came before Him unto His ears.

[8] Then the earth did shake and quake, the foundations also of the mountains did tremble; they were shaken, because He was wroth.

[9] Smoke arose up in His nostrils, and fire out of His mouth did devour; coals flamed forth from Him.

[10] He bowed the heavens also, and came down; and thick darkness was under His feet.

[11] And He rode upon a cherub, and did fly; yea, He did swoop down upon the wings of the wind.

[12] He made darkness His hiding-place, His pavilion round about Him; darkness of waters, thick clouds of the skies.

[13] At the brightness before Him, there passed through His thick clouds hailstones and coals of fire.

[14] *YHVH* also thundered in the heavens, and the Most High gave forth His voice; hailstones and coals of fire.

[15] And He sent out His arrows, and scattered them; and He shot forth lightnings, and discomfited them.

[16] And the channels of waters appeared, and the foundations of the world were laid bare, at Thy rebuke *YHVH*, at the blast of the breath of Thy nostrils.

[17] He sent from on high, He took me; He drew me out of many waters.

[18] He delivered me from mine enemy most strong, and from them that hated me, for they were too mighty for me.

[19] They confronted me in the day of my calamity; but *YHVH* was a stay unto me.

[20] He brought me forth also into a large place; He delivered me, because He delighted in me.

[21] *YHVH* rewarded me according to my righteousness; according to the cleanness of my hands hath He recompensed me.

[22] For I have kept the ways of *YHVH*, and have not wickedly departed from my God.

[23] For all His ordinances were before me, and I put not away His statutes from me.

[24] And I was single-hearted with Him, and I kept myself from mine iniquity.

[25] Therefore hath *YHVH* recompensed me according to my righteousness, according to the cleanness of my hands in His eyes.

[26] With the merciful Thou dost show Thyself merciful, with the upright man Thou dost show Thyself upright;

[27] With the pure Thou dost show Thyself pure; and with the crooked Thou dost show Thyself subtle.

[28] For Thou dost save the afflicted people; but the haughty eyes Thou dost humble.

[29] For Thou dost light my lamp; *YHVH* my God doth lighten my darkness.

[30] For by Thee I run upon a troop; and by my God do I scale a wall.

[31] As for God, His way is perfect; the word of *YHVH* is tried; He is a shield unto all them that take refuge in Him.

[32] For who is God, save *YHVH*? And who is a Rock, except our God?

[33] The God that girdeth me with strength, and maketh my way straight;

[34] Who maketh my feet like hinds', and setteth me upon my high places;

[35] Who traineth my hands for war, so that mine arms do bend a bow of brass.

[36] Thou hast also given me Thy shield of salvation, and Thy right hand hath holden me up; and Thy condescension hath made me great.

[37] Thou hast enlarged my steps under me, and my feet have not slipped.

[38] I have pursued mine enemies, and overtaken them; neither did I turn back till they were consumed.

[39] I have smitten them through, so that they are not able to rise; they are fallen under my feet.

[40] For Thou hast girded me with strength unto the battle; Thou hast subdued under me those that rose up against me.

[41] Thou hast also made mine enemies turn their backs unto me, and I did cut off them that hate me.

[42] They cried, but there was none to save; even unto *YHVH*, but He answered them not.

[43] Then did I beat them small as the dust before the wind; I did cast them out as the mire of the streets.

[44] Thou hast delivered me from the contentions of the people; Thou hast made me the head of the nations; a people whom I have not known serve me.

[45] As soon as they hear of me, they obey me; the sons of the stranger dwindle away before me.

[46] The sons of the stranger fade away, and come trembling out of their close places.

[47] *YHVH* liveth, and blessed be my Rock; and exalted be the God of my salvation;

[48] Even the God that executeth vengeance for me, and subdueth peoples under me.

[49] He delivereth me from mine enemies; yea, Thou liftest me up above them that rise up against me; Thou deliverest me from the violent man.

[50] Therefore I will give thanks unto Thee *YHVH*, among the nations, and will sing praises unto Thy name.

[51] Great salvation giveth He to His king; and showeth mercy to His anointed, to David and to his seed, for evermore.

Psalm 18 is not only of great value in "Practical Kabbalah," but is particularly important in understanding certain primary beliefs underpinning the Jewish "Days of Awe," i.e. the ten days from *Rosh Hashanah* (New Year) to *Yom Kippur* ("Day of Atonement"). In this regard, we should consider the Divine Name construct אשעלים (perhaps vocalised "*Eishelim*"), which is said to have been derived from *Psalm 18:1*, and which we are told is the name of the "Prince of the Sea," i.e. the angelic ruler of the sea.[1] To date I have been unable to ascertain exactly how this Divine Name construct was extracted from the said verse, but the Divine Name as well as the "Spirit Intelligence" whom it references, are said to protect individuals against persistent enemies.[2] In fact, it is maintained that the Divine Name construct is a *Notarikon* (acronym) of ים שעל אויבים (*oy'vim she'al yam*—"enemies at sea").[3] We are further informed that this pertains to the opening statement in *Isaiah 40:12* reading [מים] בשעלו מדד מי (*mi madad b'sho'olo* [*mayim*]—"who hath measured the waters"), regarding which we are told that individuals "who measures their own water" shall gain the respect of those who rise up against them.[4]

To my mind this simply means that if you mind your own business, and keep your nose out of the affairs of others, you will be respected and have no enemies. That is however a personal opinion, and the "measuring of the waters" statement pertains to important beliefs in Judaism regarding our existence and actions in this world. In this regard, we are told that *Psalm 18:31* is the origin of a Divine Name construct/angelic name סַרְפִיאֵל (*Sarif'eil*), which is said to be "in charge of the *Torah*" and of "peace in the world."[5] We are further informed that this Divine Name construct pertains to סֹפְרִיאֵל (*Saf'ri'el*),[6] the angel who measures and records human merits and sins,[7] is "in charge of the *Book of Life*,"[8] and who is said to be directly associated with peace.[9] Curiously enough, in "Jewish Magic" this "spirit intelligence" is adjured "to make known" anything an individual is seeking, such knowledge being afterwards ascertained by means of a special divinatory procedure.[10]

Both "peace" and the angel סּפריאל (*Saf'ri'el*) are the underlying factors of the prayers recited over the mentioned ten "Days of Awe" from *Rosh Hashanah* to *Yom Kippur* ("Day of Atonement").[11] Furthermore, "peace" is the primary principle of the שׂים שׁלום (*Sim Shalom*—"grant peace") prayer, recited by Sephardic communities during all services at the conclusion of the *Amidah* prayer, and by Ashkenazim, as well as by some Sefardic Chasidim, during the morning service (*Shacharit*) and *Musaf*. The latter term references the additional prayer-service following *Shacharit*, which is enunciated on *Shabbat* and holidays in alignment with the "additional sacrifices" in the ancient הּמקדׁש בּית (*Beit haMikdash*—"Holy Temple").[12] The *Sim Shalom* prayer is in fact the final blessing to be pronounced immediately following the *Birkat haKohanim* ("Priestly Blessing") [*Numbers 6:24-26*] at the conclusion of the oft-mentioned *Amidah* prayer.[13] It has been noted that "the body of *Sim Shalom* is not formulated as a blessing but rather as an entreaty for the effectiveness of the Priestly Blessing," and that only at the conclusion of its recitation, "is the prayer concluded and sealed, so to speak, when we bless God, who is the source of the blessing of peace."[14]

However, the *Birkat haKohanim* and the *Sim Shalom* prayer-blessing are closely aligned. In this regard, it has been observed that the latter prayer "is a kind of echo and reformulation of the Priestly Blessing,"[15] and that the "*Sim Shalom* prayer-blessing, in its repetition of almost every element of the Priestly Blessing—its particular echoing of the illumined face of God, and its parallel conclusion with the blessing of peace—can be seen as a kind of extended adaptation of the Priestly Blessing for the lay practitioner."[16] We are reminded that a rationale for reciting the *Sim Shalom* prayer-blessing immediately following the *Birkat Kohanim*, is that that they parallel each other in six attributes. In the Priestly Blessing these attributes are "bless you," "keep you," "make shine," "be gracious unto you," "the Lord turn," and "peace." In *Sim Shalom* the six attributes are "peace," "goodness," "blessing," "graciousness," "kindness," and "compassion."[17] We are further informed that *Sim Shalom* "has the substance of *Birkat Kohanim*," i.e. "grant peace" aligns with "and grant you peace";

"bless us, our Father" aligns with "bless you"; and "the light of Your countenance" aligns with "the Lord make shine His countenance."[18]

Readers may well wonder what all of this has to do with the earlier mentioned Divine Name construct סרפיאל (*Sarif'eil*) derived from *Psalm 18:31*, and perforce with the angelic name ספריאל (*Saf'ri'el*). As noted, the latter "Spirit Intelligence" is said to be in charge of the סרפ חיים (*Sefer Chayim*—"Book of Life"), and in this regard, the *Sim Shalom* prayer-blessing recited during the period between *Rosh Hashanah* and *Yom Kippur*, includes the statement:

בספר חיים ברכה ושלום ופרנסה טובה נזכר
ונכתב לפניך אנחנו וכל עמך בית ישראל לחיים
טובים ולשלים

Transliteration:

B'sefer chayim b'rachah v'shalom ufar'nasah tovah nizacheir v'nikateiv l'fanecha anach'nu v'chol am'cha beit Yis'ra'eil l'chayim tovim ul'shalom.

Translation:

In the Book of Life, blessing, and peace, and good livelihood, may we be remembered and inscribed before You—we and your entire people the Family of Israel—for a good life and for peace.[19]

The mentioned Divine/Angelic Names and relevant concepts do not only relate to this blessing, but specifically to the concluding phrase of the *Sim Shalom* prayer-blessing, which is adjusted, in the Ashkenazi liturgy for recitation during the morning service (*Shacharit*) and additional *Musaf* services over the ten "Days of Awe," to read ברוך אתה יהוה עוןֹשה השלום (*baruch atah YHVH [Adonai] oseh haShalom*— "Blessed are you *YHVH* (*Adonai*) who makes peace").[20] The format עשה השלום (*oseh haShalom*) also features in a most meaningful and "magical" procedure in the "*Mourner's Kaddish*" included in the *Yom Kippur* liturgy.[21] In this regard, the worshipper is instructed to take three steps backwards, bow left and say עשה]ה[שלום במרומיו (*oseh*

[*ha*]*shalom bim'romav*—"He who makes [the] peace in his heights"). The action is continued by bowing to the right and saying עלינו שלום יעשה הוא (*hu ya'aseh shalom aleinu*—"may he make peace upon us"), and the statement concluded by bowing centrally and saying אמן ישראל כל ועל (*v'al kol yis'ra'eil v'im'ru Omein*—"and upon all Israel *Amen*"). The worshipper is finally enjoined to "remain standing in place for a few moments," and then to advance three steps forwards.[22] Commenting on the phrase "may he make peace upon us," Rabbi Nosson Scherman noted that "if the Heavenly forces require God to make peace among them, surely human beings who are so prone to jealousy, hatred, and fractious conduct require God's mercy to bring peaceful harmony into their relationship."[23]

Be that as it may, we are informed the *gematria* of the words עש[ו]ה (*Oseh*) [ע = 70 + ו = 6 + ש = 300 + ה = 5 = 381] and השלום (*haShalom*) [ה = 5 + ש = 300 + ל = 30 + ו = 6 + מ = 40 = 381], equates with those of the Divine/Angelic Names ספריאל/סרפיאל (*Sarif'eil/Saf'ri'el*) [ס = 60 + פ = 80 + ר = 200 + י = 10 + א = 1 + ל = 30 = 381],[24] as well as with the *gematria* of the word צרופה (*tzerufah*—"tried") in the expression from the thirty-first verse of the current Psalm reading צרופה יהוה אמרת (*im'rat YHVH tzerufah*—"the word of *YHVH* is tried"].[25]

In terms of the magical applications of *Psalm 18*, we are told it is enunciated to escape from evil kings,[26] and that it is further employed against robbers and bandits, as well as for protection against all manner of illness.[27] In this regard, all the popular publications of the "*Shimmush Tehillim*" instructs that if you should see robbers approaching you, you should recite the Psalm, and this will cause them to flee.[28] The action also includes a brief prayer-incantation, as well as a relevant Divine Name construct אליה (*El Yah*), which is said to have been derived from the Psalm: א (*Alef*) from דבר אשר (*asher diber*—"who spoke"): verse 1; ל (*Lamed*) from (*Sha'ul*—"Saul"): verse 1; י (*Yod*) from מ (*mem*) in תתמם (*titamam*—"upright"): verse 26, the said glyph transposed by means of the א"ת ב"ש (*Atbash*) cipher; and ה (*Heh*) from הנותן האל (*ha'el hanoten*—"the God that executeth [gave]"): verse 48.[29]

One recension maintains the concluding ה (*Heh*) of the Divine Name construct to have been extracted from ע (*Ayin*) in עם חסיד (*im chasid*—"with the merciful"): verse 26, the letter having been transposed by means of the א״ל ב״מ (*Albam*) cipher.[30] On the other hand, Selig's German/English translation generally agree with the derivation of the letters of the Divine Name construct, except for the letter י (*Yod*) which it claims to have been gleaned from תמים (*tamim*— "straight"): verse 33.[31] The mentioned prayer-incantation reads:

יהי רצון מלפניך אליה שתצילני מכל אויבי ומכל שונאי ומכל פגע רע

Transliteration:
> *Y'hi ratzon mil'fanecha El'yah shetatzileini mikol oy'vai umikol shon'ai umikol pega ra.*

Translation:
> May it be your will *El'yah* that you rescue me from all my enemies, from all my haters and from every evil calamity.[32]

The instructions in Godfrey Selig's usual verbose German/English translation of the "*Shimmush Tehillim*," maintains those about to be attacked by robbers, should "pray this Psalm quickly but fervently, with the prayer belonging to it, with confidence in the holiest name of *Eel Jah*, that is, mighty, all-merciful and compassionate God." This he said will cause the robbers to depart "suddenly without inflicting the slightest injury." The mentioned prayer reads: "Mighty, all-merciful and compassionate God, *El Jah* [*Eel Jah* in the English translation], may it be pleasing to thy most holy will, to defend me against approaching robbers, and protect me against all enemies, opposers and evil circumstances, for thine is the power and thou canst help. Hear me for the sake of thy most holy name, *El Jah. Amen Selah!*"[33]

That is yet not the long and short of it as far as this specific application of the eighteenth Psalm is concerned, since an expanded version is shared in one of the recensions of the "*Shimmush Tehillim*." In this regard, the instruction is again to recite *Psalm 18* if you should be accosted by robbers along the way, but doing so six times.[34] Considering the length of the Psalm, you might be reduced to a blabbering blob of protoplasm by the attackers halfway through the first declamation. Furthermore, the practitioner is exhorted to follow on each recitation with the enunciation of the following prayer-incantation *senza* the earlier mentioned Divine Name construct:

יהי רצון מלפניך יהוה אלהי שתצילני מן
הלסטים האלה אשר פגעוני ומתירא אני מהם
פן יהרגוני אני בוטח בחסדיך שתשוב מחרון אפך
ואל תזכור לי עונותי ותשיבני בתשובה שלימה
לפניך ואל יקטרגוני עונותי והשיבני בזאת כי
אתה (Exodus 34:6) יהוה אל רחום וחנון ארך
אפים ורב חסד ונחם על הרעה (Joel 2:13) ככתוב
וינחם יהוה על הרעה אשר דבר לעשות לעמו
(Exodus 32:14) אמן אמן אמן סלה סלה סלה

Transliteration:

Y'hi ratzon mil'fanecha YHVH Elohai shetatzileini min halis'tim ha'eileh asher p'ga'uni umit'yarei ani meihem pen yahar'guni ani bote'ach b'chas'decha shetashuv meicharon apecha v'al tiz'kor li avonotai v'tishiveini b't'shuvah sh'leimah l'fanecha v'al yikat'r'guni avonotai v'hashiveini b'zot ki atah (Exodus 34:6) YHVH El rachum v'chanun erech apayim v'rav chesed v'nicham al hara'ah (Joel 2:13) kakatuv vayinachem YHVH al hara'ah asher d'ber la'asot l'amo (Exodus 32:14) Omein Omein Omein Selah Selah Selah

Translation:

May it be your will *YHVH* my God, that you will save me from these robbers who attack me, and whom I fear, so that they will not murder me. I trust in your grace that you will repent of your (divine) wrath, and that you will not remind me of my offenses, that you will let me repent to you in complete repentance, and that you will not accuse me of my transgressions. Answer me on this matter, for you are "*YHVH* God, merciful and gracious" (*Exodus 34:6*), "long-suffering, and abundant in mercy, and repenteth Him of the evil" (*Joel 2:13*), as it is written "And *YHVH* repented of the evil which He said He would do unto His people" (*Exodus 32:14*). *Amen Amen Amen Selah Selah Selah.*[35]

Psalm 18 is also employed for healing purposes, and in this regard the practitioner is advised to speak the Psalm over water and oil, with which to anoint the sick, whom we are told will recover.[36] In Godfrey Selig's version of the "*Shimmush Tehillim*" it is noted that in the case of a sick person "with whom the usual bodily remedies have failed," the practitioner should "fill a small flask with olive oil and water, pronounce over it, with reverence, the eighteenth Psalm, anoint all the limbs of the patient, and pray a suitable prayer in the name of *El Jah*." It is maintained that the sufferer will recover speedily.[37] A further variant technique, maintains the Psalm is employed against fever, and in this regard instructs the user to write the Psalm down, and then to suspend it on the person of the sufferer.[38]

    Psalm 18 is said to be good for "human sciences" and to aid in coping with natural disasters. It is also used to encourage donations, and, as in the case of the previous Psalm, the current one is employed to express gratitude in general, for good fortune, and especially to the Divine One. Otherwise, *Psalm 18:29* has been recommended for lighting candles, and other single verses from the eighteenth Psalm are equally employed for magical purposes. In this regard, the following Divine Name construct is derived from *Psalm 18:46*, reading ממסגרותיהם ויחרגו יבלו נכר בני (*b'nei nechar yibolu v'yach'r'gu mimis'g'roteihem*— "The sons of the stranger fade away, and come trembling out of their close places").[39]

$$\text{יֵרְ֒דוּ \quad בְּנֵי \quad בְּנֵי}$$
$$\text{וּם \quad יָּה \quad וְמָ}$$

Considering the sentiments expressed in this verse, it should come as no surprise that this Divine Name construct is employed in adjurations and Hebrew amulets meant to control "external spirit forces,"[40] the latter being perhaps of the demonic variety, or, for that matter, of the human kind.

    The formulation of this Divine Name construct from the said verse is somewhat tricky, but readily explicable. The first בְּנֵי references the first word of the verse. The second בְּנֵי is derived from the capitals of the first three words of the verse, whilst יֵרְדוּ, the third tri-letter combination, comprises the concluding letters of the said three words. The combination וֹמ was derived from the capitals of the concluding two words of the verse, and the final וֹם from the concluding letters of the same words. The Divine Name יֹה penultimate comprises the penultimate letters of the concluding word of the verse.[41] The vowels included in the Divine Name construct are exactly those employed in the enunciation of their respectively associated letters in *Psalm 18:46*.

The very next verse is aligned with with אִֽיעַ (*Iya*), the sixty-seventh portion of the "*Shem Vayisa Vayet*, and the fiftieth verse with נְלַךְ (*Nelach*), the twenty-first portion."[42] However, *Psalm 18:49* is employed in "Practical Kabbalah" for a rather unpleasant purpose, i.e. revenge. In this regard, the verse reading מפלטי מאיבי אף מן קמי תרוממני מאיש חמס תצילני (*m'falti mei'oy'vai af min kamai t'rom'meini mei'ish chamas tatzileini*—"He delivereth me from mine enemies; yea, Thou liftest me up above them that rise up against me; Thou deliverest me from the violent man"), is arranged into the following Divine Name construct:[43]

$$\text{וִי נֹם הַת לִח אֶת הִי}$$
$$\text{תְו וִי מֹד קָב נִר נְעַ חֶם}$$
$$\text{לִי}$$

As in the current instance, Divine Name constructs are often listed to be respectively useful for some or other purpose without offering any instructions as far as the actual procedures involved. However, in most instances it is simply a matter of focussing on the, as it were, "target of ones intentions," and then to utter the Divine Name construct like a magic spell, to affect the desired outcome.

Psalm 18 also features in Christian Magic, and in this regard it is equally recommended in the previously mentioned Byzantine Christian manuscripts "when you are attacked by someone."[44] However, we are informed in the same manuscripts that the eighteenth Psalm is useful for finding favour, and in this regard it maintains the Psalm should be recited seven times per day over a period of seven days. Following this, the practitioner is instructed to write the Psalm down, and to fumigate the paper with seven grains of mastic. The paper, now a fully fledged amulet, is bound to the right hand, following which it is said "your heart will always have favour."[45] The instructions conclude with a remark that repeating the latter action every day "is much better," and this lengthy instruction is concluded with a prayer.[46]

In alignment with one of the uses of the eighteenth Psalm in the "*Shimmush Tehillim*," the Christian "*Le Livre d'Or*" recommends it to heal "any sick people in any one place."[47] In this regard, the instructions include filling a new pottery bowl with pure water, and then to read the Psalm over it. This is followed by copying a set of magical characters to be located in the corners of a residence. This action is said will cause those who are ill to be healed.[48] A similar use is seen in *A Treatise of Mixed Cabalah*, where *Psalm 18:5, 6* and *36* are suggested "to deliver a sick man from all infirmity."[49]

In conclusion, it should be noted that *Psalm 18:8* features in the "*Key of Solomon*" in the outer border of the "*Seventh Pentacle of Saturn*," which we are told "is fit for exciting earthquakes."[50]

Psalm 19

[1] למנצח מזמור לדוד

[2] השמים מספרים כבוד אל ומעשה ידיו מגיד הרקיע

[3] יום ליום יביע אמר ולילה ללילה יחוה דעת

[4] אין אמר ואין דברים בלי נשמע קולם

[5] בכל הארץ יצא קום ובקצה תבל מליהם לשמש שם אהל בהם

[6] והוא כחתן יצא מחפתו ישיש כגבור לרוץ ארח

[7] מקצה השמים מוצאו ותקופתו על קצותם ואין נסתר מחמתו

[8] תורת יהוה‌אדני‌יאהדונהי תמימה משיבת נפש עדות יהוה‌אדני‌יאהדונהי נאמנה מחכימת פתי

[9] פקודי יהוה‌אדני‌יאהדונהי ישרים משמחי לב מצות יהוה‌אדני‌יאהדונהי ברה מאירת עינים

[10] יראת יהוה‌אדני‌יאהדונהי טהורה עומדת לעד משפטי יהוה‌אדני‌יאהדונהי אמת צדקו יחדו

[11] הנחמדים מזהב ומפז רב ומתוקים מדבש ונפת צופים

[12] גם עבדך נזהר בהם בשמרם עקב רב

[13] שגיאות מי יבין מנסתרות נקני

[14] גם מזדים חשך עבדך אל ימשלו בי אז איתם ונקיתי מפשע רב

[15] יהיו לרצון אמרי פי והגיון לבי לפניך יהוה‌אדני‌יאהדונהי צורי וגאלי

Transliteration:

[1] *lam'natzei'ach miz'mor l'david*

[2] *hashamayim m'sap'rim k'vod el uma'aseih yadav magid haraki'a*

[3] *yom l'yom yabi'a omer v'lailah l'lailah y'chaveh da'at*

[4] *ein omer v'ein d'varim b'li nish'ma kolam*

[5] *b'chol ha'aretz yatza kavam uvik'tzeih teiveil mileihem lashemesh sam ohel bahem*

[6] *v'hu k'chatan yotzei meichupato yasis k'gibor larutz orach*

[7] *mik'tzeih hashamayim motza'o ut'kufato al k'tzotam v'ein nistar meichamato*

[8] *torat YHVH t'mimah m'shivat nafesh eidut YHVH ne'emanah mach'kimat peti*

[9] *pikudei YHVH y'sharim m'sam'chei leiv mitz'vat YHVH barah m'irat einayim*

[10] *yir'at YHVH t'horah omedet la'ad mish'p'tei YHVH emet tzad'ku yach'dav*

[11] *hanechemadim mizahav umipaz rav um'tukim mid'vash v'nofet tzufim*

[12] *gam av'd'cha niz'har bahem b'shom'ram eikev rav*

[13] *sh'gi'ot mi yavin minis'tarot nakeini*

[14] *gam mizeidim chasoch av'decha al yim'sh'lu vi az eitam v'nikeiti mipesha rav*

[15] *yih'yu l'ratzon im'rei fi v'heg'yon libi l'fanecha YHVH tzuri v'go'ali*

Translation:

[1] For the Leader. A Psalm of David.

[2] The heavens declare the glory of God, and the firmament showeth His handiwork;

[3] Day unto day uttereth speech, and night unto night revealeth knowledge;

[4] There is no speech, there are no words, neither is their voice heard.

[5] Their line is gone out through all the earth, and their words to the end of the world. In them hath He set a tent for the sun,

[6] Which is as a bridegroom coming out of his chamber, and rejoiceth as a strong man to run his course.

[7] His going forth is from the end of the heaven, and his circuit unto the ends of it; and there is nothing hid from the heat thereof.

[8] The law of *YHVH* is perfect, restoring the soul; the testimony of *YHVH* is sure, making wise the simple.

[9] The precepts of *YHVH* are right, rejoicing the heart; the commandment of *YHVH* is pure, enlightening the eyes.

[10] The fear of *YHVH* is clean, enduring for ever; the ordinances of *YHVH* are true, they are righteous altogether;

[11] More to be desired are they than gold, yea, than much fine gold; sweeter also than honey and the honeycomb.
[12] Moreover by them is Thy servant warned; in keeping of them there is great reward.
[13] Who can discern his errors? Clear Thou me from hidden faults.
[14] Keep back Thy servant also from presumptuous sins, that they may not have dominion over me; then shall I be faultless, and I shall be clear from great transgression.
[15] Let the words of my mouth and the meditation of my heart be acceptable before Thee *YHVH*, my Rock, and my Redeemer.

We are told that this Psalm was "instituted by the Men of the Great Assembly as the first of the additional Psalms recited on Sabbath and festivals," and that it was chosen in "remembrance of creation" as "embodied in the Sabbath." It was further noted that *Psalm 19* "alludes to the first of the ten sayings" with which the world was created, i.e. "God said 'Let there be Light" [*Genesis 1:3*].[1] Whatever way one may interpret this, or whichever of the four levels of "*Torah* knowledge" one may apply to achieve greater understanding, i.e. "*Pardes*"—*Peshat* (literal), *Remez* (symbolical), *Drash* (allegorical), and *Sod* (mystical [secret]), to me this is metaphorically all about "Consciousness awakening unto Itself." Thus I fully understand why the nineteenth Psalm is recited to encourage greater memory,[2] to attain wisdom,[3] "to awaken intelligence,"[4] or, in the words of one commentator, "for awakening/sharpening one's intellect to help remember his Torah learning."[5] All of this conjoins in the "Opening of the Heart" concept, to which I have made brief reference earlier in terms of *Psalm 16*, and which is particularly focused upon in the current Psalm.

Whilst it is said that one can achieve this condition of expanded consciousness by simply reciting *Psalm 19* once,[6] or seven times according to one commentator,[7] much greater effort is required according to the "*Shimmush Tehillim*." In this regard, we are informed that those who desire the "Opening of the Heart," must first purify, i.e. cleanse, themselves. Following this, they should recite the Psalm seven times over a cup full of wine mixed with honey, with an associated Divine Name. The action, is concluded by consuming the wine, and uttering a relevant prayer-incantation which includes the said Divine Name, which is ´ה (יהוה [*Hashem* or *Adonai*]) in all the published versions of the "*Shimmush Tehillim*,"[8] whilst there are variances in some manuscripts. One source claims the Divine Name is יה (*Yah*),[9] whilst another maintains it is the Divine Name construct הי which it states was derived: ה (*Heh*) from השמים (*hashamayim*—"the heavens"): verse 2; and י (*Yod*) from וגאלי (*v'go'ali*—"and my Redeemer"): verse 15.[10] The same Divine Name construct and its origins can be found in Selig's version of the "*Shimmush Tehillim*," though the English translation of his text mistakenly assigns the origins of the second letter to the sixth verse instead of the fifteenth.[11] Be that as it may, the said prayer-incantation reads:

יהי רצון מלפניך יהוה [or יה] שתפתח לבי
[or לב] [....name of recipient....] בתורתך ובכל
חכמה שלא ישכח לעולם מה שילמוד אמן
אמן אמן סלה סלה סלה סלה

Transliteration:

    Y'hi ratzon mil'fanecha YHVH [or *Yah*] *shetif'tach libi* [or *leiv*] [....name of recipient....] *b'toratecha uv'chol choch'mah shelo yish'kach l'olam mah sheyil'mod Omein Omein Omein Selah Selah Selah*

Translation:

    May it be your will *YHVH* [or *Yah*], that you open my heart [or the heart of] [....name of recipient....], for your *Torah* and all the wisdom, so that he never forgets what he will learn. *Amen Amen Amen Selah Selah Selah*.[12]

As indicated, this prayer-incantation can be uttered for oneself or for another individual. In this regard, Godfrey Selig's German/ English presentation asks "do you desire your son to possess an open and broad heart, so that he may become an apt student and understand the lessons placed before him readily, then speak this Psalm over a cup filled with wine and honey, pronounce also the holy name and an appropriate prayer over it, and let the lad drink of it, and your desires will be realized."[13] In this instance, the

Divine Name is listed as יהוה הי (*YHVH Hei*), but Selig included no relevant prayer with these instructions.[14]

Be that as it may, in terms of working the procedure for oneself, there is again an expanded version of this "Opening of the Heart," and "kidneys" for that matter, to be found elsewhere.[15] Without referencing the need for personal purification, it instructs the user to locate a small bowl filled with honey in a larger bowl filled with wine. In this instance, the nineteenth Psalm is recited thirteen times over the liquid, and each recitation is followed by uttering the following prayer-incantation:[16]

יהי רצון מלפניך הי בורא שמים וארץ שתפתחו
לבי וכליותי כדי שאוכל להבחין דברי תורתיך
ואקיים ואשמור ואלמוד מצוותיך גם לאחרים
אלמד בשמך רחום וחנון יהיה הדבר אלי אני
[....personal name....] ויפתח לבי וכליותי כדי
ללמוד הקל והחמור וכל סתרי תורה והסיר
ממני לב טפש ושים בקרבי לב פתוח בשם אהי
אמן אמן אמן סלה סלה סלה סלה

Transliteration:

> *Y'hi ratzon mil'fanecha Hei borei shamayim va'aretz shetifat'chu libi v'kil'yotai k'dei she'uchal l'hav'chin div'rei torateicha v'akayeim v'ish'mor v'el'mod mitz'votecha gam l'acheirim alamed b'shim'cha rachum v'chanun yih'yeh hadavar eilai ani [....personal name....] v'yif'tach libi v'kil'yotai k'dei lil'mod hakal v'hachomer v'chol sit'rei torah v'heisir mimeni lev tipeish v'sim b'kir'bi lev patu'ach b'shem Eihi Omein Omein Omein Selah Selah Selah*

Translation:

> May it be your will *Hei*, Creator of heaven and earth, that you open my heart and my kidneys for me, so that I may explore the words of your *Torah*, and keep, preserve and learn your commandments. I will also teach others. With your merciful and gracious name this matter will be done for me [....personal name....]. He will open my heart and my kidneys so that I may learn the simple, the difficult, and

all the secrets of the *Torah*. Remove a foolish heart from me, and give me an open heart in your name *Eihi*. *Amen Amen Amen Selah Selah Selah.*

Whether it was done intentionally or not, the Divine Name construct employed in this procedure appears in two formats, i.e. הי ("*Hei*") and איהי ("*Eihi*"[?]).[17] In terms of the claim that these Divine Names were fashioned from letters taken from selected words in the current Psalm, it should be noted that the following much larger Divine Name construct was composed from the capitals of all the words contained in *Psalm 19:8* and *10* for related purposes, i.e. to be able to learn, understand, and remember:[18]

$$תעימ \quad ייי \quad תנטא$$
$$ממעצ \quad נפלי$$

The formulation of this Divine Name construct is pretty straightforward. The said two verses comprise exactly twenty words, and the capitals of these words are formulated into the set of five four-letter combinations comprised by the current Divine Name construct. Hence the five combinations are composed of the capitals of the twenty words applied in exact order in a sort of skipping manner. In this regard, the first letters of the five sets incorporate the capitals of the first five words of the said verses, whilst the second letters in the five sets comprise the capitals of the second group of five words, etc.[19]

Individuals who wish to magically increase their intellectual capacity as well as their ability to recollect, are instructed to slice an apple into five round pieces. These slices are afterwards roasted in a fire, prior to writing the five four-letter combinations of the Divine Name construct on them. Next the entire Hebrew Alphabet is copied on the inside of a new cup.[20] In this regard, it is a lot easier to write the twenty-two glyphs on a slip of clean, white paper, which is then located inside the cup.

Continue by reciting the nineteenth Psalm from the second verse to the end of the Psalm, as well as the following prayer-incantation, doing so twenty-one times. The prayer-incantation reads:

יהי רצון מלפניך יהוה אלהינו ואלהי אבותינו
שתצליחוני בלימודי כמו דוד שעשה המזמור
הזה [recite *Psalm 19:8–10*]

Transliteration:

> *Y'hi ratzon mil'fanecha YHVH Eloheinu veilohei avoteinu
> sh'tatz'lichuni b'limudi k'mo david she'asah hamiz'mor
> hazeh* [recite *Psalm 19:8–10*]

Translation:

> May it be your will *YHVH* our God and God of our fathers,
> that I may succeed in my studies like David did this Psalm
> [recite *Psalm 19:8–10*]

Following this action, pour wine in the cup, and dissolve therewith the twenty-two letters of Hebrew alphabet copied on the inside of the cup. Then consume the five apple slices, and drink the wine.[21]

As one might expect there is yet a further technique involving the nineteenth Psalm for the purpose of the "Opening of the Heart." In this regard, the letters comprising *Psalm 19:8* and *15*, as well as *Psalm 16:11*, are conjoined in the following Divine Name construct:[22]

הין	יוע	תגי	ראד		ולו	תית
מהי	יוח	מהח	תצר	הוא		ורי
נלש	תפע	בנב	שיש	מכמ		היי
תית	ווא	דנת	עלו	שבח		פימ
איע	נפנ	היכ	ווי	ההנ		יגפ
כצמ	חוי	מנב	האת	נמו		מרמ
ייח	תהצ	פינ	תוכ	מלנ		ירי

Discarding a single ' (*Yod*) in the first verse, in order to arrive at the required number of letters, the Divine Name construct was created by writing the letters of the said verse in the standard manner from right to left, the second in reverse directly underneath, and the third, written again in the standard right to left manner, directly beneath the second line. Reading the letter combinations in columns of three letters each, will reveal the forty-two tri-letter combinations comprising this Divine Name construct.

Be that as it may, *Psalm 19* is employed for quite a diverse set of purposes. We are informed that anyone who is in danger, or in dangerous circumstances, should recite *Psalm 19:8–10* six times.[23] Furthermore, I have heard the complete Psalm verbalised on the day of a wedding for the purpose of ensuring a happy marriage. Talking of marriage, the nineteenth Psalm is also employed to ease delivery for a woman who is encountering difficulties during childbirth.[24] In this regard, the easiest instruction to ease a difficult confinement, or to ensure a peaceful birth experience, is for the midwife, or whoever else might be offering support to the woman in labour, to place her/his hand on the abdomen of the said woman, and to recite *Psalm 19:6* seven times.[25]

The sixth verse is listed for the very same purpose in the "*Shimmush Tehillim*," but the procedure involved is very different. In the current instance we are informed that when a woman suffers difficulties during childbirth, she could be helped by collecting clay (soil) at a crossroad, and the first six verses of the Psalm written on it.[26] Another recension maintains that verse six, as well as the opening phrase of verse seven should be written seven times on a new pottery shard found at a crossroad, following it having been first cleansed in running, bubbling, or drawn water.[27] In my estimation, it is much more likely to find clay at a dirt-track crossroad, than it is a "new pottery shard." Both versions instruct the clay/pottery shard to be placed on the "womb" of the woman in labour. However, the second recension recommends the recitation of the following prayer-incantation prior to placing the pottery shard on her belly:[27]

יהי רצון מלפניך יהוה הנוטה כדוק שמים
[....name of recipient....] עֲל [*Isaiah 40:22*]
היולדת ותתיר חבליה ותלד מהרה בקרוב
זמן אמן אמן אמן סלה סלה סלה

Transliteration:

Y'hi ratzon mil'fanecha YHVH hanoteh chadok shamayim [Isaiah 40:22] al [....name of recipient....] hayoledet v'tatir chavaleha v'teiled m'heirah b'karov z'man Omein Omein Omein Selah Selah Selah.

Translation:

> May it be your will *YHVH* who stretches the heavens like
> a veil [*Isaiah 40:22*] over [....name of recipient....] the
> mother. Induce her contractions, and let her give birth
> shortly and speedily. *Amen Amen Amen Selah Selah Selah.*

As noted, this prayer-incantation is included only in one
manuscript. Otherwise in the published versions of this procedure,
and in most manuscripts, the clay is to be located on the belly of
the woman in labour, following which *Psalm 19* is recited seven
times.[28] There is however a proviso that the clay/pottery shard be
removed forthwith after the birth of the infant,[29] in order to
forestall the intestines of the mother from exiting her body as
well.[30]

In conclusion it is worth noting Godfrey Selig's
German/English versions of the "*Shimmush Tehillim*" also include
a prayer-incantation in terms of the current usage of the nineteenth
Psalm. In this regard, it instructs the entire Psalm to be recited
"seven times in succession, with the proper holy name of God and
the appropriate prayer,"[31] the latter reading "Lord of heaven and
earth! May it please thee graciously to be with this parturient, N.,
daughter of R., who is fluctuating between life and death;
ameliorate her sufferings, and help her and the fruit of her body
that she may soon be delivered. Keep her and her child in perfect
health and grant her life, for the sake of the holy name הי (*Hei*)
Amen Selah![32]

Psalm 19 is further said to be "good against evil spirits."[33]
In this regard, we are told that those who seek to free anyone who
is burdened with an evil spirit, should recite this Psalm seven
times, then conclude with the following prayer-incantation,
following which we are told the evil spirit will flee:

יהי רצון מלפניך הי השם הגדול הגבור והנורא
שתבריח מ׳ [....name of afflicted....] זה רוח רעה

Transliteration:

> *Y'hi ratzon mil'fanecha Hei hashem hagadol hagibor
> v'hanora shetav'ri'ach m'[....name of afflicted....] zeh
> ru'ach ra'ah.*

Translation:

> May it be your will *Hei*, the great, strong, and awesome name, that you put this evil spirit to flight from [....name of afflicted....]. [34]

Selig's version of this procedure incorporates all the mentioned elements. In this regard, he wrote "pray this Psalm, with the holy name and an appropriate prayer, seven times over the person possessed of the evil spirit,"[35] without including an actual prayer-incantation. It also does not incorporate the brief addendum found in most of the traditional recensions of the "*Shimmush Tehillim*," in which it is noted that the nineteenth Psalm should also be written down, and hung on the person of the individual who was afflicted by the evil spirit.[36] Regarding this amuletic use of the current Psalm, some recensions include an additional inscription reading "against fever."[37] This is particularly interesting, since *Psalm 19* is maintained to have the power to reduce fevers.[38] In this regard, those who require this support are also instructed to write down the entire Psalm, but to include the following Divine Name construct, which was composed from the letters comprising the Psalm:[39]

ליא   מהי   אוי   המכ   למל
ותם   היק   נקב   ודב   דאא   ולי
מהם   כלא   ימי   בוכ   לשא
פפי   ינם   מנע   תית   ונמ   ועק
אצי   למי   יטע   מעי   מיב   ימל
שמי   בער   ענב   וצג   רומ   המו
מרי   אאו   איב   מחע   מנג
הסלה

Conclude by adding the following incantation-prayer:

יהי רצון מלפניך רופא חנם ומלא רחמים שתרפא
[recipient] נושא קמיע זה מן הקדחת אמן

Transliteration:

> *Y'hi ratzon mil'fanecha rofei chinam umalei rachamim shet'rapei* [....name of recipient....] *nosei kamea zeh min hakadachat Omein*

Translation:

> May it be your will, compassionate and merciful healer, to cure [....name of recipient....] the bearer of this amulet from the fever *Amen.*[40]

Besides the listed uses, I have observed the nineteenth Psalm being employed to express praise, for upliftment, and when there are doubts about personal faith. It is also recommended for success in business, and when you are out in nature, i.e. when you are moved to express praise to the Divine One for the beauty you are observing around you.

As far as any further applications of single verses from the current Psalm are concerned, it should be noted that the initials of the words comprising the opening phrase of *Psalm 19:8*, the latter reading שפנ תביׁשמ המימת הוהי תרות (*torat YHVH t'mimah m'shivat nafesh*—"The law of *YHVH* is perfect, restoring the soul"), are combined in the Divine Name construct היתׁרמנ which is ermployed in amulets for mental ailments.[41] On the other hand, the capitals of the words comprising *Psalm 19:15* are combined in the Divine Name construct ילאפולל יצו, which is included in amulets employed as a call for help.[42]

The nineteenth Psalm does not appear to have been extensively employed in Christian Magic. A reference appears in the Byzantian Christian magical manuscripts, in which it is suggested that this Psalm be read prior to sunrise, in order to find favour "for the entire day."[43] An altogether different application of the current Psalm is listed in the previously mentioned Syrian magical manuscript in the Sachau Collection, in which it is recommended to anyone suffering from headaches.[44] Other than that, *Psalm 19* is listed in "*Le Livre d'Or*" for the very purpose of easing a difficult childbirth, which we have already addressed in terms of Jewish Magic. However, in the current instance the Psalm is copied up to the phrase in verse 6 reading "and rejoiceth as a strong man." The writing is then placed under the feet of the woman in confinement. The instant she has given birth, the said portion of the nineteenth Psalm is again copied, though this time conjointly with some magical characters on a sheet of glass. After fumigating the latter writing with aloes, the inscription is dissolved in holy water, a portion of which is to be consumed by the woman, and some rubbed on her stomach as the Psalm is enunciated.[45]

Psalm 20

[1] למנצח מזמור לדוד

[2] יענך יהוהﭏﬓﬨ﬩שׁשׂשּׁשּׂאַ﬷יאהדונהי ביום צרה ישגבך שם
אלהי יעקב

[3] ישלח עזרך מקדש ומציון יסעדך

[4] יזכר כל מנחתך ועולתך ידשנה סלה

[5] יתן לך כלבבך וכל עצתך ימל**א**

[6] נרננה בישועתך ובשם **אלהינו** נדגל ימל**א**
יהוהﭏﬓﬨ﬩שׁשׂשּׁשּׂאַ﬷יאהדונהי כל משאלותיך

[7] עתה ידעתי כי הושיע יהוהﭏﬓﬨ﬩שׁשׂשּׁשּׂאַ﬷יאהדונהי משיחו
יענהו משמי קדשו בגברות ישע ימינו

[8] אלה ברכב ואלה בסוסים ואנחנו בשם
יהוהﭏﬓﬨ﬩שׁשׂשּׁשּׂאַ﬷יאהדונהי אלהינו נזכיר

[9] המה פרעו ונפלו ואנחנו קמנו ונתעודד

[10] יהוהﭏﬓﬨ﬩שׁשׂשּׁשּׂאַ﬷יאהדונהי הושיעה המלך יעננו ביום קראנו

Transliteration:

[1] *Lam'natze'ach mizmor l'david*

[2] *ya'an'cha YHVH b'yom tzarah y'sagev'cha sheim elohei ya'akov*

[3] *yish'lach ez'r'cha mikodesh umitziyon yis'adeka*

[4] *yiz'kor kol min'chotecha v'olat'cha y'dash'neh selah*

[5] *yiten l'cha chil'vavecha v'chol atzat'cha y'malei*

[6] *n'ran'nah bishu'atecha uv'sheim eloheinu nid'gol y'malei YHVH kol mish'alotecha*

[7] *atah yada'ti ki hoshi'a YHVH m'shicho ya'aneihu mish'mei kod'sho big'vurot yeisha y'mino*

[8] *eileh varechev v'eileh vasusim va'anach'nu b'sheim YHVH eloheinu naz'kir*

[9] *heimah kar'u v'nafalu va'anach'nu kam'nu vanit'odad*

[10] *YHVH hoshi'ah hamelech ya'aneinu v'yom kor'einu*

Translation:

> [1] For the Leader. A Psalm of David.
> [2] *YHVH* answer thee in the day of trouble; the name of the God of Jacob set thee up on high;
> [3] Send forth thy help from the sanctuary, and support thee out of Zion;
> [4] Receive the memorial of all thy meal-offerings, and accept the fat of thy burnt-sacrifice; *Selah*
> [5] Grant thee according to thine own heart, and fulfil all thy counsel.
> [6] We will shout for joy in thy victory, and in the name of our God we will set up our standards; *YHVH* fulfil all thy petitions.
> [7] Now know I that *YHVH* saveth His anointed; He will answer him from His holy heaven with the mighty acts of His saving right hand.
> [8] Some trust in chariots, and some in horses; but we will make mention of the name of *YHVH* our God.
> [9] They are bowed down and fallen; but we are risen, and stand upright.
> [10] Save, *YHVH*; let the King answer us in the day that we call

Looking closely at *Psalms 18* to *21*, we notice the figure of the pious king to be particularly prominent in these Psalms. Being the one who keeps the *Torah*, he is said to be "the exemplar for the people."[1] In this regard, these four Psalms highlight kingship and personal piety, i.e. the total dependence of the king upon the strength of *Hashem* (*YHVH*) "in the face of challenges,"[2] and with the emphasis on "kingship" and "*Torah*," *Psalm 18, 20* and *21* are considered "royal Psalms," and are thus often addressed together. However, I believe all four listed Psalms should be considered conjointly, especially so since *Psalm 20* and *21* are "integrally linked" with *Psalm 18*, which is in turn closely aligned with *Psalm 19*.[3] In fact, the correlation between *Psalm 18* and *19* is evident in the attribution of certain qualities to *Hashem* in the eighteenth Psalm, with the exact same qualities assigned to the *Torah* in the nineteenth Psalm. In *Psalm 18* the Divine One is delineated as pure, perfect, and the giver of light, whilst in *Psalm 19* the *Torah* is depicted as perfect, pure, and giving light.[4]

As noted, the king and his, or Israel's, total dependence upon *Hashem*, is a theme common to all four Psalms, and to my mind, the very power of these "royal Psalms," is in the absolute faith and trust in the Divine One, "and a rejection of anything which would detract from that commitment."[5] In this regard, we are informed that *Psalm 20* and *21* are associated with kingship dependent upon *Hashem*, with the king delighting in the *Torah* of the Eternal One, the latter being the theme of *Psalm 19*. Hence it has been said that *Psalm 18, 20* and *21* are effectively "a small group of royal Psalms which has been divided by a torah Psalm."[5] In terms of the "pious king," what is particularly important here is the introduction of the figure of the מָשִׁיחַ (*M'shi'ach*— "Messiah") in *Psalm 20:7* reading הוֹשִׁיעַ יְהוָה מְשִׁיחוֹ (*hoshi'a YHVH m'shicho*—"*YHVH* saveth His anointed"). I believe this is primary to the position of importance held by the twentieth Psalm in Jewish liturgies, i.e. it being recited prior to the וּבָא לְצִיּוֹן (*Uva L'tziyon*—"and a redeemer shall come to Zion") concluding prayer of the daily service.[6]

As far as the magical uses of *Psalm 20* are concerned, it is enunciated for a woman suffering labour pains by those who believe in the "miraculous powers" of the twentieth Psalm, yet disapproves of Jewish Magic, as well as by those who acknowledge the "magical powers" of the current Psalm. In this regard, the difference between "magic" and "miracle" is merely a question of which side of the fence you are on, i.e. getting down to semantics in which, to rephrase Shakespeare, "sweet rose by any other name would smell like fish"! However, both sides agree that "the nine verses in the Psalm," i.e. without the superscription comprising verse 1, "correspond to the nine months of pregnancy, and the seventy words in the Psalm correspond to the seventy pangs of a woman in labor."[7] Thus we are informed that Jews have recited *Psalm 20* for the purpose of easy delivery since the Gaonic period, i.e. the year 589 to 1038.[8]

In this regard, a simple instruction is for the woman in labour, or her husband, to recite the current Psalm twelve times.[9] There are sources in which it is maintained that the twentieth Psalm should be enunciated nine times.[10] In this regard, we are informed that anyone giving support to a woman suffering a difficult confinement, could enunciate *Psalm 20* provided the woman in question can hear the recitation. We are further told that if this action did not bring relief to the said woman, that the Psalm should be recited a further nine times. If this is yet not easing the birth process, the one who is supporting her should request the aid of an "angelic force," saying "I conjure you, *Armisael*, angel who governs the womb, that you help this woman and the child in her body to life and peace. Amen, Amen, Amen'."[11]

Elsewhere we are informed the "mother-to-be" should recite *Psalm 20* three times herself whilst in labour, and to vary the vowels of the five appearances of the Ineffable Name in the Psalm, doing so in specific ways.[12] If this did not work in getting the said woman to give birth forthwith, the midwife is to utter a prayer-incantation, focussing on שמשיאל (*Shamshi'el*), as well as on "all unknown angels," whose support is called upon in the name of אגלא אהיה אשר אהיה אנקתם פסתם פספסים דיונסים (*Agala'a Eh'yeh asher Eh'yeh Anak'tam Pas'tam Pas'pasim Dion'sim*).[13]

Whilst these instructions are complex, there are others far more difficult to execute by a woman suffering a difficult confinement. In one instance the said woman is expected to recite a set of twenty-three Psalms, followed by the enunciation of the current Psalm twelve times. She then has to spell the letters of her personal name by reciting the relevant verses from the acrostic *Psalm 119*, including those spelling the קרע שטן (*K'ra Satan*) portion of the "Forty-two Letter Name of God," and finally conclude with lengthy prayer-incantations.[14] I have no idea how any woman would manage this, especially when she has to focus an enormous amount of attention on the process of giving birth. Of course, I am sure her husband, or other intimates, would be willing to recite this Psalm for her with equal fervency. In this regard, the most uncomplicated instruction suggests reciting *Psalm 20* during delivery, and *Psalm 139* immediately following the birth.

Be that as it may, in the current instance the simplest procedure of all is, as noted, to recite the twentieth Psalm twelve times. Further instruction maintains a pregnant woman should recite the twentieth Psalm every day from the beginning of the ninth month until the day on which she is giving birth.[15] It is worth

noting that the current Psalm was sometimes employed in amulets
for the purpose of protecting women during childbirth.[16] In this
regard, the following Divine Name construct was formulated from
Psalm 20, as a kind of amulet to be contemplated for the purpose
of easing childbirth.[17] The vowels employed are those of the
sounding of the names of the letters themselves, e.g. "*La*" for ל
(Lamed), "*Yo*" for י (*Yod*); "*Nu*" for נ (*Nun*), etc.[18]

לְמֶלְיֵיבֶצ שַׁאָיֵיעֶם וְיֵיכָמֵי
סִילְכוּעֵי נְבוּאָנְיֵי כְמֶעָיכֶהֵי
מֵיְמֶקְבֵיֵי אָבוּבֶוּבֵי אַנְהְכְוּוְק
וְיֶהֶיֶבֶק

We are told all of these letters are interchangeable with those
comprising the Ineffable Name, i.e. י (*Yod*), ה (*Hei*) and ו (*Vav*).[19]
In order to ascertain the exact manner in which this is done,
attention is focussed again on the enunciation of the various
Hebrew glyphs, and in this regard the vowels "*ei*" and "*ee*" align
with י (*Yod*), the vowel "*ah*" with ה (*Hei*), "*oh*" and "*oo [u]*" with
ו (*Vav*). Thus, in terms of the current Divine Name construct, the
letters ב (*Bet*), ה (*Hei*), מ (*Mem*), and ש (*Shin*) are interchangeable
with י (*Yod*); א (*Alef*), ו (*Vav*), כ (*Kaf*), ל (*Lamed*), ס (*Samech*), ע
(*Ayin*), and צ (*Tzadi*) with ה (*Hei*); and י (*Yod*), נ (*Nun*) and ק
(*Kof*) with ו (*Vav*).[20] By interchanging the letters of the current
Divine Name construct in this manner, we are presented with the
combination:

היהוויה ויהווהי הווהידו
הוההההו ויההווו היהודיו
יייייוו היהידיו הוהיההו
הויייוין

It is said the power of this Divine Name construct is, as it were,
revealed in its arrangement on the sefirotic Tree:[21]

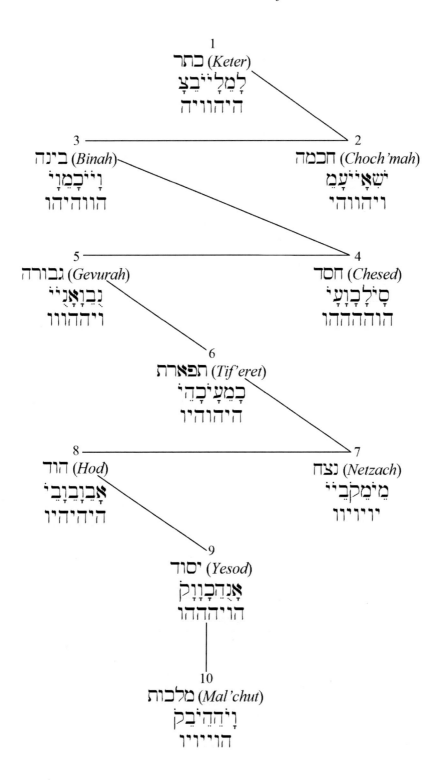

1
כתר (*Keter*)
לְמֶלְיֵّבֶצ
היהוויה

3
בינה (*Binah*)
וְיֵّכְמֵרֵי
הווהיהו

2
חכמה (*Choch'mah*)
יֵשָׁאֵّי'עֶם
ויהוודי

5
גבורה (*Gevurah*)
נֶבֶנֵّאֶנֵّי'
ויהווו

4
חסד (*Chesed*)
סֵילֶכָּעֵי'
הוההההו

6
תפארת (*Tif'eret*)
כָּמֶעִّי'כֵהֵי'
היהודיו

8
הוד (*Hod*)
אֶבֶנֶבֶّי'
היהיהיו

7
נצח (*Netzach*)
מֵיّמֶקֶّבֵי'
יויייוו

9
יסוד (*Yesod*)
אֶנֶהֶבֶוֶ'ק
הויהההו

10
מלכות (*Mal'chut*)
וְיֵّהֶהֵיّבֶק
הוייייו

One of the most remarkable meditation practices is based on this special arrangement of the twentieth Psalm, but being dedicated to the magical uses of Psalms, this book does not afford enough space for additional excursions into the wonderful world of "Kabbalistic Meditation." As noted, in "Practical Kabbalah" this sefirotic arrangement of the Divine Name construct, as well as its transcribed format, are employed to support a woman who is suffering a difficult childbirth. In this regard, whilst focussing on each of the ten *sefirot* successively, the associated Divine Name combinations are respectively whispered into the ear of the woman in labour. This is believed will ease and speed up delivery.[22]

It should be noted that the current Psalm is not only recited during a difficult confinement, or to ensure an easy birth.I have observed it equally suggested for recitation every day over the entire length of a pregnancy, and it is also recommended to prevent the divorce of infertile couples. Be that as it may, amongst the dangers a woman might encounter during pregnancy are jealousy, resentment, etc., i.e. the Evil Eye, and we are informed in the "*Shimmush Tehillim*" that the twentieth Psalm is good for countering the Evil Eye.[23] In this regard, practitioners are instructed to whisper the Psalm once over water and salt, following which the substance is passed on to the individual requiring this support.[24] Whilst there is no direct indication as to what the said individual should do with this water/salt mix, the application is in all likelihood the same as when the twentieth Psalm is whispered over rose or olive oil with which the nose, face, hands or feet are anointed afterwards.[25] In one such usage this Psalm is enunciated to induce favourable outcomes in judicial matters, i.e. to get a good judgment.[26] With this purpose in mind, users are instructed in the "*Shimmush Tehillim*" to whisper the twentieth Psalm seven times over rose oil, water, and salt, and then to anoint therewith their faces and hands [feet according to one recension]. Afterwards the mixture is sprinkled on personal clothing, and this is said will save them from every distress or hardship.[27] In the current instance we are told the Divine Name construct יהו (*YHV*) is associated with this Psalm, and that it was derived: י (*Yod*) from יענך (*ya'an'cha* —"answer thee"): verse 2; ה (*Heh*) from סלה (*Selah*): verse 4; and ו (*Vav*) from קראנו (*kor'einu*—"we call"): verse 10.[28]

There is again no indication on how this Divine Name is vocalised, but it is probably focussed upon in the usual manner during the recitation of the Psalm. In this regard, Selig's German/English version of the magical use of the current Psalm includes the same Divine Name construct and its listed origins.[29] However, it expands upon the details shared, i.e. instructing the practitioner to pray over the rose oil, water and salt mix, "seven times in the most holy name יהו (*Jeho*), this Psalm and a suitable prayer, in a low voice and with reverence."[30] It equally shares the procedure of anointing the face and hands, as well as sprinkling it on clothes," which it says will ensure freedom "from danger and suffering for that day."[31] It equally affirms the use of the nineteenth Psalm in judicial matters, and included an additional prayer-incantation reading: "Lord and judge of all the World! Thou holdest the hearts of all men in thy power and movest them according to thy holy will; grant that I may find grace and favour in the sight of my judges and those placed above me in power, and dispose their hearts to my best interests. Grant that I may be favoured with a reasonable and favourable verdict, that I may be justified by it, and that I may freely go from hence. Hear me, merciful, beloved Father, and fulfil my desire, for the sake of thy great and adorable name, יהו (*Jeho*) *Amen Selah*."[32]

It would seem the statement regarding the self-anointing lasting for a single day only, as well the prayer-incantation shared above, were composed by Selig himself, since I have found no reference to these, as it were, additional material in any primary or, for that matter, other secondary sources. However, I have seen references to *Psalm 20* protecting against all manner of danger and suffering,[33] and that reciting the twentieth Psalm twelfth times consecutively is good "to prevent all kinds of trouble."[34] In this regard, it was reported that Rav Moshe Sternbuch *shlit"a* affirmed "that this is tried and tested," and that "during numerous times of distress, a group of people performed this *segula*," i.e. reciting *Psalm 20* "twelve times together one *pasuk* [verse] at a time," and that "they saw wonders."[35]

Psalm 20 is also employed for the purpose of healing. In this regard, the instruction is to recite this Psalm twelve times in conjunction with a relevant prayer.[36] We find the twentieth Psalm being listed for the same purpose in the *"Shimmush Tehillim,"* in which we are instructed to enunciate the Psalm fourteen times over olive oil. The following prayer-incantation is added to each recitation:

יהי רצון מלפניך אלהי וַהִי יַהִי שייקל חולי זה
מעל [....name of recipient....] וירחק החולי ממנו
וירפא ממנו מהרה בשם והי יהי שירפא

Transliteration:

> *Y'hi ratzon mil'fanecha elohai Vahi Yahi sheyakeil choli zeh mei'al [....name of recipient....] virachak hacholi mimenu virape mimenu m'heirah b'shem Vahi Yahi sheyeirapei*

Translation:

> May it be your will my God, *Vahi Yahi*, to lighten this disease from [....name of recipient....], and remove the illness from him, and heal him speedily in the name *Vahi Yahi* which shall heal.

The chest [breasts] of the sufferer should afterwards be annointed three or more times a day with this oil.[37]

As far as healing is concerned, we are told that reciting *Psalm 20:2* twelve times, and then to follow this with a blessing of the name of the sufferer, as well as of that of his/her mother, is a most effective magical procedure.[38] The capitals of the words comprising the second verse, reading ישגבך שם אלהי יעקב יענך יהוה ביום צרה (*ya'an'cha YHVH b'yom tzarah y'sagev'cha sheim elohei ya'akov*—"*YHVH* answer thee in the day of trouble; the name of the God of Jacob set thee up on high"), are conjoined into the Divine Name construct ייבץ ישאו (in some instances only ישאי, these glyphs being the capitals of the last four words). These Divine Name constructs are employed in amulets as a call for help.[39] In the case of the one formed from the complete verse, the initial of the concluding word, i.e. י (*Yod*) of יעקב (*Ya'akov*— "Jacob"), was for some obscure reason changed to a ו (*Vav*).[40]

Regarding the uses of the nineteenth Psalm which are again not listed in the printed sources, there are references to this Psalm being good for those who have lost children or their parents, and equally for relatives or friends who are having to deal with difficulties. In fact, we are told it is good to recite for the well-being of loved ones in general. Otherwise, *Psalm 20* is one of the Psalms recommended for any problem whatsoever, and in this regard it is recited fifteen times consecutively. It is also enunciated against any crisis in Israel, and whilst it has been suggested for all manner of spiritual troubles, it is equally employed for atonement (repentance), self improvement, achieving a good character, for success in business, and to bring peace of mind.

It should be noted, that the capitals of the words comprising *Psalm 20:10*, reading יהוה הושיעה המלך יעננו ביום קראנו (*YHVH hoshi'ah ha-melech ya'aneinu b'yom kor'einu*—"Save, *YHVH*; let the King answer us in the day that we call"), are conjoined in a variety of Divine Name constructs, i.e. יההיבק, היבק and יבק, all of which are equally employed in amulets as "a call for help."[41] We are informed that four verses in the twentieth Psalm pertain directly to the יבק Divine Name construct:

1. The *Gematria* (numerical value) of the initials of the four words comprising the opening phrase of the second verse ייבצ [י = 10 + י = 10 + ב = 2 + צ = 90 = 112] is equal to that of יבק [י = 10 + ב = 2 + ק = 100 = 112].[42]

2. The capitals of the three words in the seventh verse, reading קדשו בגברות ישע (*kad'sho big'vurot yeisha*—"His holy mighty acts saving"), conjoin in the Divine Name construct קבי, which is clearly a permutation of יבק.[43]

3. The initials of the words in the ninth verse, reading ואנחנו קמנו ונתעודד (*va'anachnu kam'nu va-nit'odad*—"but we are risen, and stand upright") [ו = 6 + ק = 100 + ו = 6 = 112], share the same *Gematria*;[44]

4. pertains to the earlier mentioned concluding phrase of the Psalm from whence the יבק Divine Name construct was derived.[45]

All of this is said to plainly mean that the "Ineffable One will answer you" (יהוה יַעַנְךָ—*ya'un'cha IHVH*) by diverting away all distress, and to bring salvation closer "on the day that we call" (יַעֲנֵנוּ בְיוֹם קָרְאֵנוּ—*ya'aneinu b'yom kor'einu*).[46]

It is worth noting that the permutation בַּקֶר, is employed in amulets for protection.[47] In terms of this purpose, we might consider the use of *Psalm 20* for safety and protection on the road. Here the actual procedure is somewhat strange. In this regard, we are instructed before entering a vehicle, to recite a verse from the Psalm of which the first and concluding letters are the same as those comprising similarly located letters in your personal name. Thus, for example, if your name is אֱלִיעֶזֶר (*Eliezer*) you would read *Psalm 20:8* which begins with the letter א (*Alef*) and ends with ר (*Resh*).[48] As might be expected, this does not work with every Hebrew personal name, or, for that matter, every other name transliterated into Hebrew. In this regard, a sort of proximation of the location of the first and concluding letters of your first name at the beginning and conclusion of a verse will suffice. Even then it is going to be difficult, if not impossible, in many instances to find suitable verses in the twentieth Psalm.

Whilst we are addressing the current Psalm being employed for protection, we should consider the following Divine Name construct:

$$\text{זָן עִי חֶס לַעֲ שֶׁד יְךָ}$$
$$\text{דֻשׁ קֶם מִצָ כָי רוּ}$$

Derived from *Psalm 20:3*, יִשְׁלַח עֶזְרְךָ מִקֹדֶשׁ וּמִצִיוֹן יִסְעָדֶךָ (*yishlach ezr'cha mikodesh u'mitziyon yis'adeka* — "Send forth thy help from the sanctuary, and support thee out of Zion"), this Divine Name construct is said to have the power to give guidance in times of trouble, and to aid one neither to be afraid, nor to be under the impact of the Evil Eye.[49] It is most effective when worn on your person as an amulet. Other than that, the letters comprising *Psalm 20:5* were employed in the following Divine Name construct, which was composed for the purpose of finding grace:[50]

יכולא תבכם נבלי
ללעכ ככצת

As indicated, this Divine Name construct comprises a set of five and four letter combinations. As mentioned, it was formulated from the twenty-one letters comprising the fifth verse of the current Psalm reading יתן לך כלבבך וכל עצתך ימלא (*yiten l'cha chil'vavecha v'chol atzat'cha y'malei*—"Grant thee according to thine own heart, and fulfil all thy counsel"). This Divine Name construct was created by arranging the letters into five groups. Focusing on the first five letters, these are respectively arranged as the first glyphs of the five sets, whilst the second five written in reverse order, i.e. commencing with the last letter and concluding with the first, comprise the second letters, and the third group of five, placed again from first to fifth, respectively comprise the third letters of the five sets, etc.

The initials of the four words comprising the concluding phrase of *Psalm 20:6* reading ימלא יהוה כל משאלותיך (*y'malei YHVH kol mish'alotecha*—"YHVH fulfil all thy petitions"), are conjoined in the Divine Name construct ייכם, which is employed in amulets for finding grace, compassion, and salvation.[51] In a similar vein all the letters comprising *Psalm 20:6* were formulated into a Divine Name construct in the same manner as in the case of *Psalm 20:3*, but in the current instance the purpose is finding grace and affection (love) in the eyes of a king, or of any high authority:[52]

נאי רלה נמו ניה הלב
בגל ידמ שנש ווא ענל תיו
כהת ולי באב שמ

As might be expected, the twentieth Psalm was also employed in Christian Magic, but nowhere near as extensively as in Jewish Magic. The Christian Byzantine magical manuscripts inform us that this Psalm is good to alleviate distress, and that it should be recited over a child who "sees his dear one," i.e. is suffering an epileptic fit, which is said will afford immediate relief.[53] Further details in the same manuscripts maintain that if you find yourself in a court action, reciting the current Psalm six times, and carrying on your person a specific set of Greek letters, will ensure that "your suit will happen quickly and you will get what you seek without obstacle."[54] Furthermore, the same source maintains that you can get out of prison if you recite the Psalm nineteen times per day.[55]

   In conclusion, it is worth noting that that "*Le Livre d'Or*" maintains that one who seeks Divine blessing, should recite *Psalm 20* three times a day, and carry a unique set of magical glyphs on his or her person.[56] It is further said, that if this Psalm is read over a person who is sick, that individual will either become more calm and restful, or expire forthwith![57] Curiously enough, one source maintains that the sixth and initial phrase of the seventh verse is employed to "know whether a sick person will die or live." It is maintained that "if he is to survive, you will receive your reply within the day; if not, he will die."[58] On the other hand, the oft mentioned Syrian magical manuscript in the Sachau Collection recommends the twentieth Psalm for those who suffer from a broken heart.[59]

Psalm 21

[1] למנצח מזמור לדוד

[2] יהוה⁧אדני⁩יאהדונהי בעזך ישמח מלך ובישועתך מה יגל מאד

[3] תאות לבו נתתה לו וארשת שפתיו בל מנעת סלה

[4] כי תקדמנו ברכות טוב תשית לראשו עטרת פז

[5] חיים שאל ממך נתתה לו ארך ימים עולם ועד

[6] גדול כבודו בישועתך הוד והדר תשוה עליו

[7] כי תשיתהו ברכות לעד תחדהו בשמחה את פניך

[8] כי המלך בטח ביהוה⁧אדני⁩יאהדונהי ובחסד עליון בל ימוט

[9] תמצא ידך לכל איביך ימינך תמצא שנאיך

[10] תשיתמו כתנור אש לעת פניך יהוה⁧אדני⁩יאהדונהי באפו יבלעם ותאכלם אש

[11] פרימו מארץ תאבד וזרעם מבני אדם

[12] כי נטו עליך רעה חשבו מזמה בל יוכלו

[13] כי תשיתמו שכם במיתריך תכונן על פניהם

[14] רומה יהוה⁧אדני⁩יאהדונהי בעזך נשירה ונזמרה גבורתך

Transliteration:

[1] *lam'natzei'ach miz'mor l'david*

[2] *YHVH b'oz'cha yis'mach melech uvishu'at'cha mah yagel m'od*

[3] *ta'avat libo natatah lo va'areshet s'fatav bal mana'ta selah*

[4] *ki t'kad'menu bir'chot tov tashit l'rosho ateret paz*

[5] *chayim sha'al mim'cha natatah lo orech yamim olam va'ed*

[6] *gadol k'vodo bishu'atecha hod v'hadar t'shaveh alav*

[7] *ki t'shiteihu v'rachot la'ad t'chadeihu v'simchah et panecha*

[8] *ki ha'melech botei'ach baYHVH uv'chesed el'yon bal yimot*

[9] *tim'tza yad'cha l'chol oy'vecha y'min'cha tim'tza son'echa*

[10] *t'shiteimo k'tanur esh l'eit panecha YHVH b'apo y'val'eim v'toch'leim esh*

[11] *pir'yamo mei'eretz t'abeid v'zar'am mib'nei adam*

[12] *ki natu alecha ra'ah chash'vu m'zimah bal yuchalu*

[13] *ki t'shiteimo shechem b'meitarecha t'chonein al p'neihem*

[14] *rumah YHVH v'uzecha nashirah un'zam'rah g'vuratecha*

Translation:

[1] For the Leader. A Psalm of David.

[2] *YHVH* in Thy strength the king rejoiceth; and in Thy salvation how greatly doth he exult!

[3] Thou hast given him his heart's desire, and the request of his lips Thou hast not withholden. *Selah*

[4] For Thou meetest him with choicest blessings; Thou settest a crown of fine gold on his head.

[5] He asked life of Thee, Thou gavest it him; even length of days for ever and ever.

[6] His glory is great through Thy salvation; honour and majesty dost Thou lay upon him.

[7] For Thou makest him most blessed for ever; Thou makest him glad with joy in Thy presence.

[8] For the king trusteth in *YHVH*, yea, in the mercy of the Most High; he shall not be moved.

[9] Thy hand shall be equal to all thine enemies; thy right hand shall overtake those that hate thee.

[10] Thou shalt make them as a fiery furnace in the time of thine anger; *YHVH* shall swallow them up in His wrath, and the fire shall devour them.

[11] Their fruit shalt thou destroy from the earth, and their seed from among the children of men.

[12] For they intended evil against thee, they imagined a device, wherewith they shall not prevail.

[13] For thou shalt make them turn their back, thou shalt make ready with thy bowstrings against the face of them.

[14] Be Thou exalted *YHVH*, in Thy strength; so will we sing and praise Thy power.

Whilst the twentieth Psalm is a veritable cornucopia of information, both in terms of its liturgical and magical uses, *Psalm 21* is more, as it were, reserved in its magical applications. It is said to be good to recite this Psalm in order "to maintain oneself" before entering the presence of "a spiritual or temporal authority,"[1] or before appearing before "one's master or rabbi."[2] However, in the "*Shimmush Tehillim*" there appears to be more than just reciting the twenty-first Psalm before appearing before some or other authority. In fact, depending on which recension you are consulting, this text maintains that if you want to go before a lord, master, prince, king, or senior authority, that you should say this Psalm with its associated Divine Name over olive oil, doing so six times (seven according to some sources), and then to anoint your face therewith.[3] One manuscript maintains you should anoint your face, hands, and feet.[4]

Once again Godfrey Selig's German/English translation of the "*Shimmush Tehillim*" includes material not found in any known primary source. In this regard, we are told that "if you have a petition to present to the king, or to some other person in high power, pronounce this Psalm over a mixture of olive oil and resin, and at the same time think of the holy name of יהך (*Jehach*), anoint your face, and pray in faith and in confidence a prayer suitable to your circumstances, and then you may comfort yourself with the assurance that you will be favourably received and receive."[5] It should be noted that the Divine Name combination יהך is included in most recensions of the "*Shimmush Tehillim*."[6] In one published version a *patach* (vowel "*ah*") is added to the concluding glyph, as if to emphasize that the enunciation of this Divine Name construct should be "*Y'hacha*,"[7] i.e. in alignment with the sounding of the component glyphs in the words from whence they derive. However, some sources claim the Divine Name associated with this Psalm to be יה (*Yah*).[8]

All published versions of the "*Shimmush Tehillim*"[9] agree that the יהך Divine Name construct was derived: י (*Yod*) from יהוה בעזך (*YHVH b'oz'cha* —"YHVH in Thy strength"): verse 2; ה (*Heh*) from רומה (*rumah*[10] [incorrectly listed "*dumah*"[11]]— "be exalted"): verse 14; and ך from במיתריך (*b'meitarecha*— "with thy bowstrings"): verse 13. One source maintains the concluding glyph to have been derived from כי תשיתמו (*ki t'shiteimo*—"For thou shalt make"): verse 13.[12]

Whilst the entire twenty-first Psalm is recited for the purpose of finding favour with kings and other higher authorities, it should be noted that the letters comprising *Psalm 21:2* were arranged into the following Divine Name construct, to be employed in amulets for the same purpose:[13]

יתכ העמ ווה השי ביג עבי
זול ככמ ילא שמד מח

This Divine Name construct is formulated in exactly the same manner as were some of the Divine Name constructs addressed in the previous Psalm. However, *Psalm 21* is also said to be good for protection against storms at sea.[14] In this regard, the instruction is to whisper the Psalm six times over rose oil, water and salt. To this is added the following prayer-incantation reading:[15]

יהי רצון מלפניך השם הגדול הגבור והנורא
היוצא מזה המזמור שתשקיט הים מזעפו כי
אתה מושל בגאות הים שאון גליו אתה תשבחם
אמן אמן אמן סלה סלה סלה

Transliteration:

> *Y'hi ratzon mil'fanecha hasheim hagadol hagibor v'hanora hayotzei mizeh hamizmor shetash'kit hayam miza'afo ki atah mosheil b'gei'ot hayam sh'on galav atah t'shab'cheim Omein Omein Omein Selah Selah Selah*

Translation:

> May it be your will, the great, strong and terrible Name that emerges from this Psalm, that you may calm the sea in its tumult. For you control the tides of the sea; you will break the roar of its waves. *Amen Amen Amen Selah Selah Selah.*

Once again Godfrey Selig's version of this application includes additional details not find elsewhere. Thus he instructs those who encounter a dangerous storm at sea, to "mix rose-oil, water, salt and resin," and then to "pronounce over it slowly this Psalm, and

the holy name *Jehach* ("*Jehaen*" in the English publication)."[16]
This is followed by pouring "the consecrated salve into the
foaming sea" whilst enunciating a prayer incantation which more
or less aligns with the one found in the Hebrew texts, but is
somewhat more verbose. It reads: "Lord of the world! Thou rulest
the pride of the foaming and roaring sea, and calmest the terrible
noise of the waves. May it please thee, for the sake of thy most
holy name, *Jehach*, to calm the storm, and to deliver us mercifully
from this danger *Amen Selah!*"[17]

To conclude the use of *Psalm 21* in "Jewish Magic," it is
worth noting that in one of the recensions of the "*Shimmush
Tehillim*" this Psalm is recommended to individuals who wish to
repent of their misdeeds, and who hence wish to perform good
deeds. In this regard, the recitation of the current Psalm is followed
by uttering the following prayer-incantation:[18]

יהי רצון מלפניך שתפתח לי שערי תשובה לבקש
רחמים על חטאי אשר עשיתי ואוכל להתענות
ולהתודות עליו כל ימי חיי בשם יהוה אמן אמן
אמן סלה סלה סלה

Transliteration:
> *Y'hi ratzon mil'fanecha shetif'tach li sha'arei t'shuvah
> l'vakeish rachamim al chata'ai asher asiti v'uchal
> l'hit'anot ul'hit'vadot alav kol y'mei chayai b'shem YHVH
> Omein Omein Omein Selah Selah Selah*

Translation:
> May it be your will that you open for me the gates of
> repentence, to seek mercy for my sins I have committed. I
> will be able to bow down, and confess to him all the days
> of my life in the name of *YHVH Amen Amen Amen Selah
> Selah Selah.*

The twenty-first Psalm is equally employed for a number of
purposes unlisted in "official" literature. I have witnessed it
recommended for anaemia, ailments of the chest, heart, stomach,
bones, incurable diseases, and to heal bites. Contrastingly, it is
advocated for self improvement and the development of a good
character, to express gratitude, to alleviate poverty, and encourage
giving alms to the poor. Furthermore, the twenty-first Psalm is
suggested for recitation before crossing a lake or the ocean.

In Christian Magic we find *Psalm 21* equally listed for the purposes of finding favour with a "higher power." In this regard, it is stated in the Byzantine magical manuscripts that the current Psalm should be recited before appearing in front of a judge or a ruler.[19] Here there are also references to rose-oil, but rather than it being employed to calm stormy seas, the twenty-first Psalm is recited over it, following which the face is anointed or washed with this substance, in order to make an individual greatly loved amongst all people.[20] To affect this purpose, the said individual also has to carry a set of magical characters, which one source claims should be written "with saffron on Friday in the first hour at the new moon, and with the Psalm carry also the characters."[21]

We find similar instructions in *"Le Livre d'Or,"* in which the current Psalm is equally recommended to be enunciated over rose oil, seven times in the current instance, in order to be well received by all and sundry "regardless of how your character or status may be."[22] This is certainly not a nice prospect for those who were blinded to the true nature of an individual who resorted to this form of, as it were, "psychic imposition." Be that as it may, in the current instance the face of the practitioner is also anointed with the oil, and so is the set of magical characters which is to be carried on his/her person in order to "receive many honours."[23] Elsewhere, we find *Psalm 21:14* recommended for similar purposes, i.e. "to be raised up with Dignity by everyone."[24]

The mentioned Christian Byzantine manuscripts noted that repeating *Psalm 21* will ensure that "you will have work for the whole day," and that it is also good for journeys.[25] On the other hand, the Syrian magical manuscript in the Sachau Collection suggests you say it over olive oil and anoint your body therewith, when you need to appear before "rulers."[26] It also recommends it to be written for sheep, and hung around the neck of a lamb,[27] presumably for protection.

In the *"Key of Solomon"* the twenty-first Psalm is listed the second amongst a set of eight Psalms to be recited during the construction of "pentacles," the others being *Psalms 8, 27, 29, 32, 51, 72* and *134.*[28]

Psalm 22

[1] למנצח על אילת השחר מזמור לדוד

[2] אלי אלי למה עזבתני רחוק מישועתי דברי שאגתי

[3] אלהי אקרא יומם ולא תענה ולילה ולא דמיה לי

[4] ואתה קדוש יושב תהלות ישראל

[5] בך בטחו אבתינו בטחו ותפלטמו

[6] אליך זעקו ונמלטו בך בטחו ולא בושו

[7] ואנכי תולעת ולא איש חרפת אדם ובזוי עם

[8] כל ראי ילעגו לי יפטירו בשפה יניעו ראש

[9] גל אל יהוה‎אהדונהי יפלטהו יצילהו כי חפץ בו

[10] כי אתה גחי מבטן מבטיחי על שדי אמי

[11] עליך השלכתי מרחם מבטן אמי אלי אתה

[12] אל תרחק ממני כי צרה קרובה כי אין עוזר

[13] סבבוני פרים רבים אבירי בשן כתרוני

[14] פצו עלי פיהם אריה טרף ושאג.

[15] כמים נשפכתי והתפרדו כל עצמותי היה לבי כדונג נמס בתוך מעי

[16] יבש כחרש כחי ולשוני מדבק מלקוחי ולעפר מות תשפתני

[17] כי סבבוני כלבים עדת מרעים הקיפוני כארי ידי ורגלי

[18] אספר כל עצמותי המה יביטו יראו בי

[19] יחלקו בגדי להם ועל לבושי יפילו גורל

[20] ואתה יהוה‎אהדונהי אל תרחק אילותי לעזרתי חושה

[21] הצילה מחרב נפשי מיד כלב יחידתי

[22] הושיעני מפי אריה ומקרני רמים עניתני

[23] אספרה שמך לאחי בתוך קהל אהללך

[24] יראי יהוה‎אהדונהי הללוהו כל זרע יעקב כבדוהו וגורו ממנו כל זרע ישראל

[25] כי לא בזה ולא שקץ ענות עני ולא הסתיר
פניו ממנו ובשועו אליו שמע

[26] מאתך תהלתי בקהל רב נדרי אשלם נגד
יראיו

[27] יאכלו ענוים וישבעו יהללו יהוהאדני-יאהדונהי
דרשיו יחי לבבכם לעד

[28] יזכרו וישבו אל יהוהאדני-יאהדונהי כל אפסי
ארץ וישתחוו לפניך כל משפחות גוים

[29] כי ליהוהאדני יאהדונהי המלוכה ומשל בגוים

[30] אכלו וישתחוו כל דשני ארץ לפניו יכרעו
כל יורדי עפר ונפשו לא חיה

[31] זרע יעבדנו יספר לאדני לדור

[32] יבאו ויגידו צדקתו לעם נולד כי עשה

Transliteration:

[1] *lam'natzei'ach al ayelet hashachar miz'mor l'david*

[2] *eili eili lamah azav'tani rachok mi shu'ati div'rei sha'agati*

[3] *elohai ek'ra yomam v'lo ta'aneh v'lailah v'lo dumiyah li*

[4] *v'atah kadosh yosheiv t'hilot yisra'eil*

[5] *b'cha bat'chu avoteinu bat'chu vat'fal'teimo*

[6] *eilecha za'aku v'nim'latu b'cha vat'chu v'lo voshu*

[7] *v'anochi tola'at v'lo ish cher'pat adam uv'zui am*

[8] *kol ro'ai yal'igu li yaf'tiru v'safah yani'u rosh*

[9] *gol el YHVH y'fal'teihu yatzileihu ki chafeitz bo*

[10] *ki atah gochi mibaten mav'tichi al sh'dei imi*

[11] *alecha hosh'lach'ti meirachem mibeten imi eili atah*

[12] *al tir'chak mimeni ki tzarah k'rovah ki ein ozeir*

[13] *s'vavuni parim rabim abirei vashan kit'runi*

[14] *pa'tzu alai pihem ar'yeih toreif v'sho'eig*

[15] *kamayim nish'pach'ti v'hit'par'du kol atz'motai hayah libi kadonag nameis b'toch mei'ai*

[16] *yavesh kacheres kochi ul'shoni mud'bak mal'kochai v'la'afar mavet tish'p'teini*

[17] *ki sevavuni k'lavim adat m'rei'im hikifuni ka'ari yadai v'rag'lai*

[18] *asapeir kol atz'motai heimah yabitu yir'u vi*

[19] *y'chal'ku v'gadai lahem v'al l'vushi yapilu goral*
[20] *v'atah YHVH al tir'chak eyaluti l'ez'rati chu'shah*
[21] *hatzilah meicherev naf'shi miyad kelev y'chidati*
[22] *hoshi'eini mipi ar'yeih umikar'nei reimim anitani*
[23] *asap'rah shim'cha l'echai b'toch kahal ahal'leka*
[24] *yir'ei YHVH hal'luhu kol zera ya'akov kab'duhu v'guru mimenu kol zera yis'ra'eil*
[25] *ki lo vazah v'lo shikatz enut ani v'lo his'tir panav mimenu uv'shav'o eilav shamei'a*
[26] *mei'it'cha t'hilati b'kahal rav n'darai ashaleim neged y'rei'av*
[27] *yoch'lu anavim v'yis'ba'u y'hal'lu YHVH dor'shav y'chi l'vav'chem la'ad*
[28] *yiz'k'ru v'yashuvu el YHVH kol af'sei aretz v'yish'tachavu l'fanecha kol mish'p'chot goyim*
[29] *ki la'YHVH ham'lucha umosheil bagoyim*
[30] *ach'lu vayish'tachavu kol dish'nei eretz l'fanav yich'r'u kol yor'dei afar v'naf'sho lo chiyah*
[31] *zera ya'av'denu y'supar la'adonai lador*
[32] *yavo'u v'yagidu tzid'kato l'am nolad ki asah*

Translation:

[1] For the Leader; upon *Ayelet ha-Shahar*. A Psalm of David.

[2] My God, my God, why hast Thou forsaken me, and art far from my help at the words of my cry?

[3] O my God, I call by day, but Thou answerest not; and at night, and there is no surcease for me.

[4] Yet Thou art holy, O Thou that art enthroned upon the praises of Israel.

[5] In Thee did our fathers trust; they trusted, and Thou didst deliver them.

[6] Unto Thee they cried, and escaped; in Thee did they trust, and were not ashamed.

[7] But I am a worm, and no man; a reproach of men, and despised of the people.

[8] All they that see me laugh me to scorn; they shoot out the lip, they shake the head:

[9] 'Let him commit himself unto *YHVH*! let Him rescue him; let Him deliver him, seeing He delighteth in him.'

[10] For Thou art He that took me out of the womb; Thou madest me trust when I was upon my mother's breasts.

[11] Upon Thee I have been cast from my birth; Thou art my God from my mother's womb.

[12] Be not far from me; for trouble is near; for there is none to help.

[13] Many bulls have encompassed me; strong bulls of Bashan have beset me round.

[14] They open wide their mouth against me, as a ravening and a roaring lion.

[15] I am poured out like water, and all my bones are out of joint; my heart is become like wax; it is melted in mine inmost parts.

[16] My strength is dried up like a potsherd; and my tongue cleaveth to my throat; and Thou layest me in the dust of death.

[17] For dogs have encompassed me; a company of evil-doers have inclosed me; like a lion, they are at my hands and my feet.

[18] I may count all my bones; they look and gloat over me.

[19] They part my garments among them, and for my vesture do they cast lots.

[20] But Thou *YHVH*, be not far off; O Thou my strength, hasten to help me.

[21] Deliver my soul from the sword; mine only one from the power of the dog.

[22] Save me from the lion's mouth; yea, from the horns of the wild-oxen do Thou answer me.

[23] I will declare Thy name unto my brethren; in the midst of the congregation will I praise Thee.

[24] 'Ye that fear *YHVH*, praise Him; all ye the seed of Jacob, glorify Him; and stand in awe of Him, all ye the seed of Israel.

[25] For He hath not despised nor abhorred the lowliness of the poor; neither hath He hid His face from him; but when he cried unto Him, He heard.'

[26] From Thee cometh my praise in the great congregation; I will pay my vows before them that fear Him.

[27] Let the humble eat and be satisfied; let them praise *YHVH* that seek after Him; may your heart be quickened for ever!

[28] All the ends of the earth shall remember and turn unto *YHVH*; and all the kindreds of the nations shall worship before Thee.

[29] For the kingdom is *YHVH*'s; and He is the ruler over the nations.

[30] All the fat ones of the earth shall eat and worship; all they that go down to the dust shall kneel before Him, even he that cannot keep his soul alive.

[31] A seed shall serve him; it shall be told of *Adonai* unto the next generation.

[32] They shall come and shall declare His righteousness unto a people that shall be born, that He hath done it.

Psalm 22 is in Sefardic tradition the "daily Psalm" of the "Festival of *Purim*," when Jews everywhere celebrate the escape from the machinations of the evil Haman, an official in the Persian court, who seek the downfall and destruction of the Jewish populace.[1] As readers know probably well enough, the central figure of this festival is the Jewish Queen Esther, the favourite wife of the Persian King Ahasuerus. According to the "*Sefer ha-Zohar*" this wondrous queen is symbolising the *Shechinah*, the Feminine Presence of the Divine One in manifestation.[2] Furthermore, a close affiliation is recognised between the twenty-second Psalm and Queen Esther. In this regard, the Talmud [*TB Yoma 29a*] recognises the words אילת השחר (*ayelet hashachar*—"morning star") in *Psalm 22:1* to be referencing Queen Esther, which we are told is the reason why the current Psalm was chosen to be recited over the period or *Purim*.[3]

Tradition has it that Queen Esther herself sung this Psalm when she entered the presence of the Persian King [*TB Megillah 15b*], and the daily recitation of the twenty-second Psalm over *Purim* goes back to ancient days. In this regard, we are told that the "Sephardi custom of reciting *Psalm 22* before the evening service on the night of Purim is thus documented in one of the Geniza manuscripts that reflect the early custom of the inhabitants of Eretz Yisrael."[4] As might be expected, several reasons are given for the recitation of the current Psalm during *Purim*, amongst which is one pertaining to *Notarikon* (anagrams), which is one of several Kabbalistic methods employed to interpret sacred writ. In the current instance the capitals of the six words comprising *Psalm 22:21* reading יחידתי כלב מיד נפשי מחרב הצילה (*hatzilah mei'cherev naf'shi mi'yad kelev y'chidati*—"Deliver my soul from the sword; mine only one from the power of the dog"). The said glyphs spell מכי המן (*Haman Maki*) which, viewed from biblical perspectives, could be read "strike down Haman." The reference in this verse to "the sword" and the "power of the dog," is thus understood to be the evil Haman himself.[5] Anyone interested in the connections between the biblical "*Book of Esther*" and *Psalm 22*, would do well to peruse the extensive exposition on the twenty-second Psalm in *Midrash Tehillim*.[6]

Aligning with the sentiments expressed in this delineation, we are informed in Jewish Magic that the twenty-second Psalm is good for all manner of problematic issues, i.e. against every kind of trouble[7] and "against all grief."[8] At the time of the writing of the "*Shimmush Tehillim*" one of these issues was to be able to cross a river[9] or a port,[10] or to step over a snake[11] in safety, and all of which are referenced in different recensions of the same text, as are dangerous animals and bumping into a vicious foe.[12] In this regard, the instruction is to recite *Psalm 22*, following which there need be no fear.[13] It is worth considering that as far as dealing with enemies is concerned, the Divine Name construct תַּעְשָׁשׁ (*Ta'eshashu*), alternatively תָּיְשָׁשׁ (*Tay'shashu*), was formulated for this purpose from selected letters in *Psalm 22:20*. The suffix שׁוּבה (*shuvah*—"return") was added to the verse which reads שׁוּבה

וְאַתָּה יְהוה אַל תִּרְחָק אֱיָלוּתִי לְעֶזְרָתִי חוּשָׁה (*v'atah YHVH al tir'chak eyaluti l'ez'rati chu'sha shuvah*—"But Thou *YHVH*, be not far off; O Thou my strength, hasten to help me return"). The power of this Divine Name construct is said to be its ability to save you from an enemy, particularly when you intentionally focus on this Divine Name construct whilst reciting the associated verse.[14] It is also worth noting that *Psalm 22:20* is directly affiliated with יְלִי (*Yeli*), the second portion of the "*Shem Vayisa Vayet*" ("*Name of Seventy-two Names*").[15]

The *"Shimmush Tehillim"* equally references a Divine Name construct associated with the twenty-second Psalm. This is said to be אֵה (perhaps enunciated *"Eiha"*) which it claims was derived: א (*Alef*) from אֵלִי (*eli*—"my God"): verse 2, and ה (*Heh*) from עָשָׂה (*asah*—"He hath done"): verse 32.[16] Godfrey Selig shares the same details in his version of the *"Shimmush Tehillim,"* and maintains the Divine Name construct should be vocalised *"Aha."*[17] This is one of the rare instances in which his version actually aligns with the details shared in primary recensions of the *"Shimmush Tehillim."* In the current instance water, beasts, and harmful humans enter the picture, but more as an aside, so to speak, rather than in a direct manner. Thus Selig informs us that "if a traveler prays this Psalm seven times daily, with the appropriate divine name אֵה (*Aha*), and a prayer arranged according to surrounding circumstances, in full trust in the mighty protection of our exalted and most merciful God, no misfortune will happen to him. Should he travel by water neither pirates nor storms can harm him, and if he travels by land he will be safe from harm by beasts and men."[18]

Whilst there is no indication in the original recensions of the *"Shimmush Tehillim"* that *Psalm 22* should be recited seven times for the mentioned purposes, users are instructed to recite the Psalm that number of times when they wish to purify themselves from all that is unclean.[19] Other than that, we are informed that the twenty-second Psalm is good for "opening the heart,"[20] or, as some commentators noted, "to sharpen intelligence,"[21] and it is further said that a woman in labour could ease the birth experience by reciting this Psalm.[22] Besides being good for trouble of every kind, it is also recited in dealing with all temporal affairs. It is further said to protect against humiliation, and to aleviate fear and anxiety, especially when caused by enemies. We are also informed that the twenty-second Psalm contains and halts fires.

In alignment with the use of the current Psalm in Jewish Magic, *Psalm 22:12–20* are employed in Christian Magic in order "to be deliverd from all trials and tribulations,"[23] and in the Christian Byzantine manuscripts the twenty-second Psalm is employed against enemies who "contrive unjustness against you."[24] Furthermore, continuing on the theme of controlling enemies by magical means, "*Le Livre d'Or*" maintains that if you fear the malice of "petty people," you should recite *Psalm 22* seven times, and bury a set of magical characters at the entrance of the residence of your enemy.[25] Regarding an "enemy" of a different sort, the Syrian magical manuscript in the Sachau Collection recommends the twenty-second Psalm be written down and laid down with cattle, which is believed will ensure that no wolves will come near them.[26]

Lastly, the current Psalm is listed in the "*Key of Solomon*" as one of a set of Psalms to be recited over the wax from which ritual candles are constructed, the full compliment being *Psalms 8, 15, 22, 46, 47, 49, 51, 53, 68, 72, 84, 102, 110, 113, 126, 130, 131, 133*, and *139*.[27] We also find the concluding phrase of *Psalm 22:15* located in the outer border of the "*Fifth Pentacle of Venus*," which is said to incite and excite love "when it is only showed unto any person soever."[28] Furthermore, the concluding three words of the seventeenth verse of the same Psalm, conjointed with the first three words of the succeeding verse, features in the outer border of the "*Sixth Pentacle of Jupiter*," which is said to protect "against all earthly dangers."[29]

Psalm 23

[1] מזמור לדוד יהוה‎אהדי‎יאהדונהי רעי לא אחסר

[2] בנאות דשא ירביצני על מי מנחות ינהלני

[3] נפשי ישובב ינחני במעגלי צדק למען שמו

[4] גם כי אלך בגיא צלמות לא אירא רע כי אתה
עמדי שבטך ומשענתך המה ינחמני

[5] תערך לפני שלחן נגד צררי דשנת בשמן ראשי
כוסי רויה

[6] אך תוב וחסד ירדפוני כל ימי חיי ושבתי בבית
יהוה‎אהדי‎ יאהדונהי לארך ימים

Transliteration:

[1] *Mizmor l'david YHVH ro'i lo ech'sar*

[2] *bin'ot deshe yar'bitzeini al mei m'nuchot y'nahaleini*

[3] *naf'shi y'shoveiv yan'cheini v'ma'g'lei tzedek l'ma'an sh'mo*

[4] *gam ki eileich b'gei tzal'mavet lo ira ra ki atah imadi shiv't'cha umish'antecha heimah y'nachamuni*

[5] *ta'aroch l'fanai shul'chan neged tzor'rai dishanta vashemen roshi kosi r'vaya*

[6] *Ach tov vachesed yir'd'funi kol y'mei hayay v'shav'ti b'veit YHVH l'orech yamim*

Translation:

[1] A Psalm of David. *YHVH* is my shepherd; I shall not want.

[2] He maketh me to lie down in green pastures; He leadeth me beside the still waters.

[3] He restoreth my soul; He guideth me in straight paths for His name's sake.

[4] Yea, though I walk through the valley of the shadow of death, I will fear no evil, for Thou art with me; Thy rod and Thy staff, they comfort me.

[5] Thou preparest a table before me in the presence of mine enemies; Thou hast anointed my head with oil; my cup runneth over.

[6] Surely goodness and mercy shall follow me all the days of my life; and I shall dwell in the house of *YHVH* for ever.

Psalm 23 is recited in Sefardic traditions on Friday night, and some say it during *Yom Kippur* (Day of Atonement).[1] It is also customary amongst Sefardim and Kabbalists to enunciate this Psalm after the weekday evening service, and at funerals and at the dedication of tombstones.[2] Very importantly the twenty-third Psalm is said when washing hands before meals. In this regard, we are informed that an individual should say a prayer for a good פרנסה (*parnasah*—"livelihood") before starting a meal. Naturally, this could be any personal prayer suitable for this purpose, but in this regard *Psalm 23* is absolutely ideal since it speaks of goodness, blessedness, well-being, and total trust in Divine Providence. Hence the recitation of this magnificent Psalm between washing hands and המוציא (*Hamotzi*), the blessing of the bread,[3] which is said to be a good *Segulah* ("magical virtue") to ensure that there will be no shortage of food in the home.[4] Some readers might wonder what is to be done in our day when many meals are consumed in public locales, and in many instances dietary requirements restrict the intake of bread. In my estimation, since the Psalm comprises only six verses which can be memorised quite easily, it could be recited whilst washing hands prior to participation in any meal.

Be that as it may, we are told that the twenty-third Psalm comprises fifty-seven words which correspond to the *Gematria* (numerical value) of the word זן (*zan*—"nourishes" or "to nurture") [ז = 7 + נ = 50 = 57],[5] and also to that of the word דגים (*Dagim*—"Fishes") [ד = 4 + ג = 3 + י = 10 + ם = 40 = 57]. We are told that this is hinted in the word דשא (*deshe*—"pastures") from the second verse, the letters of which are said to reference an anagram: ד (*Dalet*) for דגים (*Dagim*—"Fishes"); ש (*Shin*) for שבת (*Shabbat*—"Sabbath"); and א (*Alef*) for (*Adam*—"man" or "humankind").[6] Furthermore, whilst the spellings of certain words in the Psalm can be varied, we are informed that there are two hundred and twenty-seven letters in *Psalm 23*, and that this figure is the *gematria* (numerical value) of the word ברכה (*b'rachah*—"blessing") [ב = 2 + ר = 200 + כ = 20 + ה = 5 = 227].[7] Thus it should come as no surprise that this Psalm is called the *Mizmor ha-Parnasah*, i.e. the sustenance-Psalm,[8] and that it is believed to have the power to encourage a good livelihood.

In the *"Shimmush Tehillim"* the focus is mainly on the oneiromantic uses of *Psalm 23*, i.e. for שאלת חלום (*She'elat Chalom*—"Dream Questioning"),[9] or to understand a dream.[10] In this regard, the procedure is to purify yourself and to fast[11] for a single day.[12] Before retiring to sleep at night, recite the twenty-third Psalm seven times, each time concluding with *Psalm 10:17* which reads תאות ענוים שמעת יהוה תכין לבם תקשיב אזנך (*ta'avat anavim shama'ta YHVH tachin libam tak'shiv oz'necha*—"*YHVH* Thou hast heard the desire of the humble: Thou wilt direct their heart, Thou wilt cause Thine ear to attend").[13] Afterwards it is simply a question of getting into bed and going to sleep. However, we are informed that there is a Divine Name construct associated with the twenty-third Psalm, which is י'ה (*Yah*) said to have been derived: י (*Yod*) from יהוה רעי (*YHVH ro'i*—"*YHVH* is my Shepherd"): verse 1, and ה (*Heh*) from נ (*Nun*) in נפשי (*naf'shi*—"my soul"): verse 3, the second letter having been transposed by means of the א"י ק בח"ר (*Ayak Bachar*) cipher.[14]

The magical use of *Psalm 23* is absent in several of the published versions of the *"Shimmush Tehillim,"* but it does appear in manuscripts, some published editions of this text, and equally in Godfrey Selig's ever popular German/English translation.[15] It aligns with the primary recensions in terms of the Divine Name and its derivation, as well as the necessary self purification and fasting prior to working the procedure.[16] It also agrees that the Psalm should be recited seven times, following which there are major differences between the primary sources and Selig's offering. For one thing, the enunciation of *Psalm 10:17* after each recitation of the current Psalm, is replaced with a prayer reading "Lord of the World! notwithstanding thy unutterable mighty power, exaltation and glory, thou wilt still lend a listening ear to the prayer of thy humblest creature, and wilt fulfil his desires, Hear my prayer also, loving Father, and let it be pleasing to thy most holy will to reveal unto me in a dream, whether (here the affair of which a correct knowledge is deserved must be plainly stated) as thou didst often reveal through dreams the fate of our forefathers. Grant me my petition for the sake of thy adorable name י'ה *Jah Amen Selah!*"[17] It is readily apparent that Selig chopped and changed the procedure, as he was wont to do throughout his very flawed version of the *"Shimmush Tehillim."*

Be that as it may, a variant and a somewhat tricky procedure involving *Psalm 23* employed for the same purpose, is listed in one of the recensions of the "*Shimmush Tehillim*."[18] In this instance the individual wishing to employ the technique of dream incubation, is instructed to fast for three days. On the night of the fourth day, the said individual is to recite the Psalm next to his/her bed, conjoining the Divine Name combination אל שדי (*El Shadai*) with יהוה (*YHVH*) every time the Ineffable Name is mentioned in the Psalm. For example, the first verse of the Psalm would then read מזמור לדוד יהוה אל שדי רעי לא אחסר (*Mizmor l'david YHVH El Shadai ro'i lo ech'sar*—"A Psalm of David. *YHVH El Shadai* is my shepherd; I shall not want"). In the current instance, the Psalm is recited once only, which is followed by the following prayer-incantation, commencing with the Divine Name combination יהוה אל שדי (*YHVH El Shadai*), and including an additional Divine Name, i.e. והו:[19]

יהוה אל שדי יהי רצון מלפניך יהוה אלהי ואלהי
אבותי והו השם הגדול והנקי והטהור שתודיעני
שאלתי [....insert petition....] הדבר שאני שואל ממך
הלילה הזאת בחלום בדברים ערבים ונעמים
וערוכים על מערכתם בשם יהוה אלהי ישראל אמן
אמן אמן סלה סלה סלה

Transliteration:

> *YHVH El Shadai, y'hi ratzon milfanecha YHVH elohai veilohei avotai VHV (Vehu/Vaho[?]) hashem hagadol v'hanaki v'hatahor shetodi'eini hadavar she'ani sho'el mim'cha [....insert petition....] she'eilati halailah hazot bachalom b'd'varim areivim v'n'imim v'aruchim al ma'arachatam b'shem YHVH Elohei Yis'ra'eil Omein Omein Omein Selah Selah Selah.*

Translation:

> May it be your will *YHVH* my God and God of my Father, *VHV (Vehu/Vaho[?])*, the great, clean and pure name, that you will let me know the thing I am asking of you [....insert petition....], and answer my query this night in a dream with sweet, pleasant and prepared words about their

arrangement. In the name of *YHVH* God of Israel. *Amen Amen Amen Selah Selah Selah.*

Interestingly enough, a somewhat similar procedure for a dream inquiry is listed amongst the magical texts found in the Cairo Geniza, which was claimed to be "good, fitting, tested and true."[20] In this instance, the practitioner is likewise instructed to fast for three days. On the third night, the said individual is required to refrain from eating anything, to dress in clean clothing, to stay in a residence where there is no women, and, prior to going to sleep, to recite *Psalm 23* seven times. This is followed by uttering the following adjuration:[21]

משביע אני עליכם שתראו לי מה שאני מבקש
ותודיעו שאלתי ובקשתי

Transliteration:
>   *Mash'bi'a ani aleichem sheteira'u li mah she'ani m'vakeish v'todi'u she'eilati ubakashati*

Translation:
>   I adjure you to show me what I am asking for, and answer my query and my request.

Afterwards the instruction reads "go to sleep and you will see a wondrous being that will come to you and tell you what you want and what you request."[22] In a comment on this procedure we are told that "research on rituals of abstinence in magical texts has shown that such rituals seek to accomplish a temporary transformation of the body through an extraordinary degree of purification. By avoiding all contact with women, the man avoids all traces of menstrual purity. By restricting his diet, he becomes 'like the ministering angels' who do not eat or drink. Only then is he fit for the company of divine beings, who have an extreme intolerance of impurity."[23]

>   *Psalm 23* is equally employed for dream incubation, i.e. "to acquire knowledge of that which is secret and hidden,"[24] in conjunction with the seven tri-letter portions of the "*Shem Vayisa Vayet*" reading מנד אני חעם רהע ייז ההה מיכ (*Menad Ani Cha'am Reho Yeyiz Hahah Mich*) in *She'elat Chalom* ("dream questioning"). In this regard, the seven tri-letter Divine Name constructs are recited and written conjointly with the whole of the

twenty-third Psalm, "in order to experience great revelations."[25] We are told that all of this should be done on a Wednesday evening or on Thursday, and that the writing should be with ink on sheets of pure white cloth.

When the writing and enunciation of the Psalm is concluded, the set of seven tri-letter portions of the "*Shem Vayisa Vayet*" ("*Name of Seventy-two Names*") are enunciated seven times, and the written sheets located under the pillow of the one working the "dream questioning." The procedure is then concluded by uttering the following adjuration prior to falling asleep:

יהי רצון מלפניך יהוה אלהי ואלהי אבותי ומלפניכם
אותיות קדושות ונוראות שתראו לי הלילה בדבר
[.....add details.....] או הן או לאו

Transliteration:
> *Y'hi ratzon mil'fanecha YHVH elohai veilohei avotai, umilif'nechem otiot k'doshot v'nor'ot, shetiru li halailah bid'var* [.....add details.....], *o hen o lav*

Translation:
> May it be your will *YHVH* my God and God of my father, and from before your face, for me to be shown holy and sublime signs, that you should reveal to me this night regarding [....add details.....], whether yes or no.

The instructions insist that the intake of food be halted from the middle of the day intended for the ritual procedure, and to usher in this "dream question" action with prayer and a ritual bath, e.g. visit a *mikveh*.[26] Whilst this procedure is only slightly more labour intensive than the others listed in terms of the mentioned use of the current Psalm, the following one is much more complex. In this regard, *Psalm 23* is employed in conjunction with the "Magic Square of the Third Order," Divine and Angelic Names, as well as an adjuration, again for the purpose of *She'elat Chalom* (Dream Questioning)."[27] We are told that the procedure should be worked in a condition of holiness and purity on the eve of *Shabbat*, i.e. on a Thursday evening.[28]

When properly prepared for the task at hand, practitioners commence the magical action by writing the "magic square" in question on a piece of parchment, ensuring that the letter/numbers comprising this *chotam* are inscribed in their exact letter order in *ashurit* (the Hebrew letters employed by scribes). The latter glyphs are considered of primary importance, sincc, as I noted elsewhere "this is considered an important action in the process of, as it were, 'triggering the spiritual powers' behind the magical seal."[29] In this regard, special reference is made to the letter ח (*chet*), which we are told should be written like a "hunchback," i.e. חּ, this being the manner in which this glyph appears in Holy Writ.[30] Using *sofer* script, i.e. Jewish scribal calligraphy in which the Hebrew glyphs are adorned with "*tagin*" (crownlets), the magic square would appear as shown below:

ד	ט	ב
ג	ה	ז
ח	א	ו

When ready to retire to bed for the night, the completed magical seal is tied to the forehead of the practitioner, with the writing correctly positioned so as to be visible to any onlooker. This action is followed by reciting *Psalm 23* seven times, doing so in a unique manner. As in the earlier mentioned procedure in which the Ineffable Name was enunciated in conjunction with the Divine Name *El Shadai*, the combination שדי רוע (*Shadai ro'i*) is added to each of the two appearances of יהוה (*YHVH*) in the Psalm, the entire combination reading יהוה שדי רוע (*YHVH Shadai ro'i*). There is a further instruction regarding the Divine Name אל אלהים (*El Elohim*) having to be included after the word אתה (*atah*) in the fourth verse,[31] which would then read:

גם כי אלך בגיא צלמות לא אירא רע כי אתה
אל אלהים עמדי שבטך ומשענטך המה ינחמני

Transliteration:
*Gam ki eleich b'gei tzal'mavet lo ira ra ki atah El Elohim
imadi shiv't'cha umish'an'techa heimah y'nachamuni*

Translation:

> Yea, though I walk through the valley of the shadow of death, I will fear no evil, for Thou *El Elohim* art with me; Thy rod and Thy staff, they comfort me.

Having readied themselves in this manner, practitioners then proceed to recite the twenty-third Psalm, ensuring that the second phrase of the first verse is repeated seven times, thus reading:

[Verse 1] מזמור לדוד יהוה שדי רעי לא אחסר

יהוה שדי רעי לא אחסר יהוה שדי רעי לא אחסר

יהוה שדי רעי לא אחסר יהוה שדי רעי לא אחסר

יהוה שדי רעי לא אחסר יהוה שדי רעי לא אחסר

Transliteration:

> [Verse 1] *Miz'mor l'david YHVH Shadai ro'i lo ech'sar, YHVH Shadai ro'i lo ech'sar, YHVH Shadai ro'i lo ech'sar, YHVH Shadai ro'i lo ech'sar, YHVH Shadai ro'i lo ech'sar, YHVH Shadai ro'i lo ech'sar, YHVH Shadai ro'i lo ech'sar*

Translation:

> [Verse 1] A Psalm of David. *YHVH Shadai* is my shepherd; I shall not want, *YHVH Shadai* is my shepherd; I shall not want, *YHVH Shadai* is my shepherd; I shall not want, *YHVH Shadai* is my shepherd; I shall not want, *YHVH Shadai* is my shepherd; I shall not want, *YHVH Shadai* is my shepherd; I shall not want, *YHVH Shadai* is my shepherd; I shall not want.

After concluding the recitation of the Psalm in the manner delineated, practitioners are further advised to enunciate the following set of Angelic Names seven times, whilst keeping their *kavvanah*, i.e. their personal intention and attention, pertaining to the dream question, firmly focused in mind:[32]

צופיאל צדקיאל רפאל רזיאל

(*Tzofi'el Tzadki'el Rafa'el Razi'el*)

Afterwards both hands are placed on the "magic seal" on the forehead, followed by uttering the following adjuration:[33]

בזכות החותם הזה הנקרא חותם יה ובזכות השמות
שהזכרתי שתודיעני הלילה הזה תשובת שאלתי
בבירור שהי כך וכך

Transliteration:

> *Biz'chut hachotam hazeh hanikra chotam Yah v'biz'chut hashemot shehiz'kar'ti shetodi'eini halailah hazeh t'shuvat she'elati b'beirur shehi kach v'kach.*

Translation:

> In the merit of this seal, called the seal of *Yah*, and in the merit of the Names I mentioned, that you reveal to me this night the answer to my question, in a manner which is clear and certain.

The procedure is concluded by practitioners getting into bed, and ensuring that they sleep on their left side, and to turn over onto their right side if they should wake up after midnight.[34]

Before concluding, this discusion of the use of *Psalm 23* in Jewish Magic, it should be noted that *Psalm 23:1* is listed as being good for calming storms at sea. In this regard the practitioner is instructed to recite the phrase יהוה רעי לא אחסר (*YHVH ro'i lo ech'sar*—"*YHVH* is my shepherd; I shall not want*") thirteen times, followed by enunciating the Divine/Angelic Name עַל בְּבִיאֵל (*Al'b'vi'eil*) thirty-six times.[35] There is no indication whence this Divine or Angelic Name was derived.

Whilst the listed magical applications of the current Psalm might appear to be quite limited, it is worth noting that besides having been recommended to encourage a good livelihood, the twenty-third Psalm is recommended for financial prosperity, and to express gratitude for good fortune, as well as for gratitude generally. It is further suggested for illness and healing in general; against anxiety and for safety from fear; for protection in perilous situations and in times of trouble; and for protection from harm. Furthermore, for those who are religious and seek to live a more spiritual life, it was as noted proposed that *Psalm 23* be recited after hand-washing, before the blessing of a meal, also as a statement of faith, against blasphemy, and to increase trust in the

Divine One. Otherwise, it is used on the day of a funeral, during a time of mourning, to ensure longevity, and when in need of comfort. Furthermore, it is recommended to instil obedience in rebellious children.

In conclusion, it is worth noting that the *Psalm 23* is one amongst a group of Psalms which are sometimes arranged in the format of the *Menorah* for inclusion in *Shiviti* plaques and amulets, as indicated below:[36]

As far as the use of *Psalm 23* in Christian Magic is concerned, we are told in "*Le Livre d'Or*" that those who are leaving with sadness, or who are departing on a journey, should recite this Psalm in order to preclude their enemies from restraining them.[37] Furthermore, if they should get lost on the way, they should recite the twenty-third Psalm over "good oil," an act which will ensure they will find their way back.[38] Talking of journeys, elsewhere we are informed that *Psalm 23:3–4* recited with the prefix "the Lord is my shepherd," will ensure you are protected "when passing through dubious and dangerous places."[39] On the other hand, reciting the fifth and sixth verse will aid you in finding food and accomodation.[40]

Psalm 24

[1] לדוד מזמור ליהוה_{אדני}יאהדונהי הארץ ומלואה תבל וישבי בה

[2] כי הוא על ימים יסדה ועל נהרות יכוננה

[3] מי יעלה בהר יהוה_{אדני}יאהדונהי ומי יקום במקום קדשו

[4] נקי כפים ובר לבב אשר לא נשא לשוא נפשי ולא נשבע למרמה

[5] ישא ברכה מאת יהוה_{אדני}יאהדונהי וצדקה מאלהי ישעו

[6] זה דור דרשו מבקשי פניך יעקב סלה

[7] שאו שערים ראשיכם והנשאו פתחי עולם ויבוא מלך הכבוד

[8] מי זה מלך הכבוד יהוה_{אדני}יאהדונהי עזוז וגבור יהוה_{אדני}יאהדונהי גבור מלחמה

[9] שאו שערים ראשיכם ושאו פתחי עולם ויבא מלך הכבוד

[10] מי הוא זה מלך הכבוד יהוה_{אדני}יאהדונהי צבאות הוא מלך הכבוד סלה

Transliteration:

[1] *l'david miz'mor laYHVH ha'aretz um'lo'ah teiveil v'yosh'vei vah*

[2] *ki hu al yamim y'sadah v'al neharot y'chon'nehah*

[3] *mi ya'aleh v'har YHVH umi yakum bim'kom kod'sho*

[4] *n'ki chapayim uvar leivav asher lo nasa lashav naf'shi v'lo nish'ba l'mir'mah*

[5] *yisa v'rachah mei'eit YHVH utz'dakah mei'elohei yish'o*

[6] *zeh dor dor'shav m'vak'shei fanecha ya'akov selah*

[7] *s'u sh'arim rasheichem v'hinas'u pit'chei olam v'yavo melech hakavod*

[8] *mi zeh melech hakavod YHVH izuz v'gibor YHVH gibor mil'chamah*

[9] *s'u sh'arim rasheichem us'u pit'chei olam v'yavo melech hakavod*

[10] *mi hu zeh melech hakavod YHVH tz'va'ot hu melech hakavod selah*

Translation:

[1] A Psalm of David. The earth is *YHVH*'s, and the fulness thereof; the world, and they that dwell therein.

[2] For He hath founded it upon the seas, and established it upon the floods.

[3] Who shall ascend into the mountain of *YHVH*? and who shall stand in His holy place?

[4] He that hath clean hands, and a pure heart; who hath not taken My name in vain, and hath not sworn deceitfully.

[5] He shall receive a blessing from *YHVH*, and righteousness from the God of his salvation.

[6] Such is the generation of them that seek after Him, that seek Thy face, even Jacob. *Selah*

[7] Lift up your heads, O ye gates, and be ye lifted up, ye everlasting doors; that the King of glory may come in.

[8] 'Who is the King of glory?' '*YHVH* strong and mighty, *YHVH* mighty in battle.'

[9] Lift up your heads, O ye gates, yea, lift them up, ye everlasting doors; that the King of glory may come in.

[10] 'Who then is the King of glory?' '*YHVH* of hosts; He is the King of glory.' *Selah*

In the time of the Second Temple in Jerusalem it was customary for the Levites to enunciate a unique "Psalm of the Day" for every day of the week, a custom which is now part of the morning synagogal service. *Psalm 24* is the יום של שיר (*shir shel yom*— "Psalm of the Day") for the first day of the week, i.e. Sunday.[1] In this regard, "It has been taught: R. Judah said in the name of R. Akiba: On the first day [of the week] what [Psalm] did they [the Levites] say? [The one commencing] 'The earth is the Lord's and the fullness thereof,' because He took possession and gave possession and was [sole] ruler in His universe."[2] This quote is from *TB Rosh Hashanah 31a*.

Talking of *Rosh Hashanah* (Jewish New Year), it is customary amongst the Ashkenazic and Oriental Sefardic communities to recite the twenty-fourth Psalm on *Rosh Hashanah* and *Yom Kippur* (Day of Atonement).[3] Kabbalists, taking their cue from the pronouncements of Rabbi Chaim Vital, maintain that chanting the current Psalm over the High Holy Days, doing so with *Kavvanah*, i.e. fully focussed concentration and intention, and "with a sweet niggun (tune),"[4] is a *Segulah* ("Magical virtue") for a good livelihood. It is said this action will ensure that there is no lack of sustenance throughout the coming year.[5] In many Sefardic synagogues it is customary to recite the current Psalm verse by verse with the *Aron Kodesh* (the Holy Ark in which the sacred biblical scrolls are kept) open. In this regard, each verse of the Psalm is enunciated first by the *Chazan* (Cantor), and then repeated by the congregation.[6]

Considering these details, it is no surprise that *Psalm 24* is called *Miz'mor haParnasah*, i.e. "The Psalm of Livelihood," in Moroccan Jewish communities, and equally why they use the expression *petichat haheichal shel haparnasah* ("opening the ark of livelihood") in reference to the privilege of opening the ark in the synagogue.[7] It should be noted that there are Jewish communities who do not accept these Kabbalistic pronouncements, and hence do not align with the custom of reciting the Psalm over this period.[8] However, in Ashkenazi tradition the Psalm is also recited weekdays when the *Torah* scroll is returned to ark, on *Rosh Chodesh*, i.e. the ushering in of a month at the first sign of the New Moon, etc.[9] Jewish religionists who align with the custom of enunciating *Psalm 24* at these designated times, are instructed to do so after the *Amidah* prayer.[10] In my estimation "Divine Blessing" and the "Divine Glory" are the primary functional factors of "The Psalm of Livelihood." This is affirmed in the fifth verse, and by the term כָּבוֹד (*Kavod*—"glory") which is a synonym for the *Shechinah*, the earlier mentioned Feminine Presence of the Eternal One in manifestation. As it is, the term *Kavod* appears five times in *Psalm 24*, which has been said to be a reference to the five books comprising the *Torah*.[11]

The utterance of the twenty-fourth Psalm after the "Eighteen-fold Prayer" (*Shemoneh Ez'rei/Amidah*), is also referenced in the "*Shimmush Tehillim*." In this regard, it is noted in some recensions that "it is good to pray (the Psalm) every day after his eighteen petitions (prayers)," to which one recension added "pray it, and your Creator will answer you."[12] It would seem the figure eighteen spilled over in a greater manner in a magical use of *Psalm 24*. In this regard, some recensions of the "*Shimmush*

Tehillim" advise practitioners, that to achieve success and grace with any cause whatsoever, they should recite the current Psalm and an associated prayer-incantation eighteen times.[13] This prayer-incantation includes the special Divine Name מ"ץ, which is said to a transposition of the Name י"ה (*Yah*) by means of the א"ת ב"ש (*Atbash*) cipher.[14] Vocalised "*Matza*,"[15] it is in fact the first portion of the Divine Name מצפ"ץ (*Matz'patz* or *Matzapatza*), which is equally a transposition of יהוה" (*YHVH*) by means of the same cipher. As I noted elsewhere, this transposed Divine Name is claimed to be meaning "*God protect*," and that "in the *Sefer ha-Zohar* the Name *Matz'patz* is said to pertain to the concept of 'mercy'," which is corroborated by "the *gematria* of מצפ"ץ (*Matz'patz* [מ = 40 + צ = 90 + פ = 80 + צ = 90 = 300) which is equal to that of ברחמי"ם (*b'rachamim*—"with mercy" [ב = 2 + ר = 200 + ח = 8 + מ = 40 + י = 10 + ם = 40 = 300)."[16] I further noted that "it is in this respect, i.e. divine Mercy, that the name *Matz'patz* is employed in Hebrew magical incantations and *Kame'ot* (amulets)."[17] Be that as it may, the earlier mentioned prayer-incantation which is recited in conjunction with *Psalm 24* reads:

יהי רצון מלפניך מ"ץ מ"ץ השם הנקי והזך והטהור
שאצליח בדבר זה בשם יהוה אלהי ישראל ובשם
הנקי והזך מ"ץ מ"ץ אמן אמן אמן סלה סלה סלה

Transliteration:
> *Y'hi ratzon mil'fanecha Matza Matza hanaki v'hazach v'hatahor she'atz'liach bid'var zeh b'shem YHVH elohei Yisra'eil ub'shem hanaki v'hazach Matza Matza Omein Omein Omein Selah Selah Selah.*

Translation:
> May it be your will *Matza Matza*, the clean, pure and unblemished name, that I will succeed in this matter in the name of the *YHVH* God of Israel, and by the clean and pure name *Matza Matza. Amen Amen Amen Selah Selah Selah.*[18]

As one might expect, for most people the expression "a good livelihood" equates with success in business. In this regard, we are told that an individual seeking such success, should recite *Psalm*

24 three times, following which he/she should enunciate the following prayer-incantation which concludes with *Psalm 19:15*:

יהי רצון מלפניך יהוה אלהי ואלהי אבותי שבכח
השם [contemplate *YHVH* in your heart] הקדוש והטהור
שאצליח בעניז [....name of client....] [....business matter....]
למעז שמך הגדול אלהי השמים ואלהי הארץ אמז
נצח סלה ועד
[*Psalm 19:15*] יהיו לרצון אמרי פי והגיון לבי לפניך
יהוה צורי וגאלי

Transliteration:

> *Y'hi ratzon mil'fanecha YHVH elohai v'elohei avotai sheb'cho'ach hasheim* [contemplate *YHVH* in your heart] *hakadosh v'hatahor she'atz'li'ach b'inyan* [....name of client....] [....business matter....] *l'ma'an shim'cha hagadol elohei hashamayim veilohei ha'aretz Omein Netzach Selah va'ed*
>
> [*Psalm 19:15*] *yih'yu l'ratzon im'rei fi v'heg'yon libi l'fanecha YHVH tzuri v'go'ali*

Translation:

> May it be your will *YHVH* my God and God of my father, by the power of the holy and pure Name [contemplate *YHVH* in your heart], that I will succeed in the matter [....include the name of the client....] [....reference the business matter....]. For the sake of your great Name, God of the heavens, and God of the earth *Amen* Enduring *Selah* forever.
>
> [*Psalm 19:15*] Let the words of my mouth and the meditation of my heart be acceptable before Thee *YHVH*, my Rock, and my Redeemer.[19]

It is somewhat surprising that little of the magical applications found in the various recensions of the "*Shimmush Tehillim*," actually found their way into the popular printed editions of this most primary text on the magical uses of Psalms. Instead, we are informed that the current Psalm is good to recite every day,[20] following which the main emphasis is on it being employed for the purpose of being rescued from, or protected against, floods and whirlpools,[21] or to survive a storm at sea.[22] Of course, there is nothing wrong with the twenty-fourth Psalm being employed for this purpose, but we are informed on this magical application in a rather abrupt manner in exactly nine words. Even Godfrey Selig's standard annoying reworking of the "*Shimmush Tehillim*" sounds more exciting in the current instance, despite the fact that he addressed *Psalms 24* and *25* conjointly, and claimed that whilst "the contents of these two Psalms differ materially, in respect to their mystical uses, they are equal and alike in power and action."[23] There is certainly no redeeming quality in the remainder of Selig's presentation. In this regard, he noted that "whosoever repeats these Psalms daily in the morning with feelings of devotion, will escape from the greatest danger, and the devastating flood will not harm him,"[24] but he included an associated Divine Name construct without indicating that the latter applies specifically to the twenty-fifth Psalm.

Be that as it may, in another magical application of the *Psalm 24* we find all the letters comprising the Psalm converted into the following Divine Name construct, which is said to have the power to aid those who are plagued with שֵׁדִים (*Shedim*—"demons"):

$$
\begin{array}{cccccc}
\text{יְמִי} & \text{יוֹן} & \text{הֶעָיָ} & \text{וְבָכ} & \text{הָוֹה} & \text{לְמַל} \\
\text{וְנִל} & \text{נָלָנ} & \text{לַאל} & \text{נְכוּ} & \text{יָבָק} & \text{בִּיוּ} \\
\text{שָׁרוּ} & \text{יַסֵשׁ} & \text{דְּמָפ} & \text{יֻזֵד} & \text{יוּם} & \text{יִבְמֶ} \\
\text{שַׁשַׁר} & \text{יַגְמ} & \text{יֵעוּ} & \text{זְמֶה} & \text{מַהַמ} & \text{פְּעוּ} \\
\text{צְֽהַם} & \text{מֶהִי} & \text{מְהוּ} & \text{וְמֶה} & & \text{וְפַע} \\
& & & & & \text{הַסֶלָה}
\end{array}
$$

In order to get rid of these demonic forces, the individual so influenced is required to write this Divine Name construct on the inside of a bowl. The writing is then dissolved by filling the bowl with water, some of which is consumed and a portion saved, I presume for later use when required.[25] Other than this procedure, we are informed that *Psalm 24:5* is directly affiliated with יהה (*Yahah*), the sixty-second portion of the "*Shem Vayisa Vayet.*"[26]

There is again greater diversity in the magical uses of *Psalm 24* external to the applications listed in the official literature.

In this regard it is employed against enemies; the danger of ruin, and as a protection against danger in general; against despair; but equally to be uplifted. As noted, the twenty-fourth Psalm is recited for livelihood, but it is equally employed to ensure sustenance; to facilitate choice in life, and for an individual to recover his or her heritage. The latter action might necessitate having to open many "doors," figuratively speaking, but curiously enough, the current Psalm is said to open literal doors in spite of a lost key. I suspect the latter use derives from the reference to the current Psalm being employed in this regard in the *"Key of Solomon."*[27]

In Christian Magic the oft mentioned Byzantine manuscripts, the procedure pertaining to the application of the current Psalm appears to align more with the use of *Psalm* 23 in Jewish Magic,[28] without specific reference to "Dream Questioning." In this regard, we are told that if the twenty-fourth Psalm is enunciated "seven times each night or also during the day at midday" in front of the home iconostasis, i.e. the wooden stand or wall on which one or more icons are displayed, doing so "from the ninth day of the moon until the 29th," each time fumigating your reading "with one pure grain of mastic," and lighting a single candle, there will appear to you in the middle of the day "a white spirit in a form like that of a woman. Do not be afraid at all, only start asking first of all her name, then the question that you seek to know."[29] On the other hand, in a charm from the post-Byzantine-period we read "that when someone has a terrifying enemy, he should recite the entire *Psalm 24*," then write a set of magical characters, "and invoke the archangels to send them fleeing."[30]

Elsewhere, we are told in the *"Le Livre d'Or"* that if someone has an intense desire to be loved and to appear gracious, that individual should write down *Psalm 24* from the first to the conclusion of the opening phrase in the eighth verse, doing so with a set of magical characters. Afterwards the writing is fumigated with mastic, saffron and rose water, following which it is carried like an amulet on the person of the one eliciting this magical support.[31]

An altogether different application of the current Psalm is listed in the *"Key of Solomon."* In this regard, *Psalm 24:7* features in the outer border of the *"Fifth Pentacle of Mercury,"* which we are informed serves "to open doors in whatever way they may be closed, and nothing it may encounter can resist it."[32]

Psalm 25

[1] לדוד אליך יהוהאדני-יאהדונהי נפשי אשא

[2] אלהי בך בטחתי אל אבושה אל יעלצו אויבי לי

[3] גם כל קויך לא יבשו יבשו הבוגדים ריקם

[4] דרכיך יהוהאדני-יאהדונהי הודיעני ארחותיך למדני

[5] הדריכני באמתך ולמדני כי אתה אלהי ישעי
אותך קויתי כל היום

[6] זכר רחמיך יהוהאדני-יאהדונהי וחסדיך כי מעולם
המה

[7] חטאות נעורי ופשעי אל תזכר כחסדך זכר לי
אתה למען טובך יהוהאדני-יאהדונהי

[8] טוב וישר יהוהאדני-יאהדונהי על כן יורה חטאים
בדרך

[9] ידרך ענוים במשפט וילמד ענוים דרכו

[10] כל ארחות יהוהאדני-יאהדונהי חסד ואמת לנצרי
בריתיו ועדתיו

[11] למען שמך יהוהאדני-יאהדונהי וסלחת לעוני כי רב
הוא

[12] מי זה האיש ירא יהוהאדני-יאהדונהי יורנו בדרך
יבחר

[13] נפשו בטוב תלין וזרעו יירש ארץ

[14] סוד יהוהאדני-יאהדונהי ליראיו ובריתו להודיעם

[15] עיני תמיד אל יהוהאדני-יאהדונהי כי הוא יוציא
מרשת רגלי

[16] פנה אלי וחנני כי יחיד ועני אני

[17] צרות לבבי הרחיבו ממצוקותי הוציאני

[18] ראה עניי ועמלי ושא לכל חטאותי

[19] ראה אויבי כי רבו ושנאת חמס שנאוני

[20] שמרה נפשי והצילני אל אבוש כי חסיתי בך

[21] תם וישר יצרוני כי קויתיך

[22] פדה אלהים את ישראל מכל צרותיו

Transliteration:

[1] *l'david eilecha YHVH naf'shi esa*

[2] *elohai b'cha vatach'ti al evoshah al ya'al'tzu oy'vai li*

[3] *gam kol kovecha lo yeivoshu yeivoshu habog'dim reikam*

[4] *d'rachecha YHVH hodi'eini or'chotecha lam'deini*

[5] *had'richeini va'amitecha v'lam'deini ki atah elohei yish'i ot'cha kiviti kol hayom*

[6] *z'chor rachamecha YHVH vachasadecha ki mei'olam heimah*

[7] *chatot n'urai uf'sha'ai al tiz'kor k'chas'd'cha z'chor li atah l'ma'an tuv'cha YHVH*

[8] *tov v'yashar YHVH al kein yoreh chata'im badarech*

[9] *yad'reich anavim bamish'pat vilameid anavim dar'ko*

[10] *kol or'chot YHVH chesed v'emet l'notz'rei v'rito v'eidotav*

[11] *l'ma'an shim'cha YHVH v'salach'ta la avoni ki rav hu*

[12] *mi zeh ha'ish y'rei YHVH yorenu b'derech yiv'char*

[13] *naf'sho b'tov talin v'zar'o yirash aretz*

[14] *sod YHVH li rei'av uv'rito l'hodi'am*

[15] *einai tamid el YHVH ki hu yotzi meireshet rag'lai*

[16] *p'neih eilai v'choneini ki yachid v'ani ani*

[17] *tzarot l'vavi hir'chivu mim'tzukotai hotzi'eini*

[18] *r'eih on'yi va'amali v'sa l'chol chatotai*

[19] *r'eih oy'vai ki rabu v'sin'at chamas s'nei'uni*

[20] *sham'ra naf'shi v'hatzileini al eivosh ki chasiti vach*

[21] *tom vayosher yitz'runi ki kiviticha*

[22] *p'deih elohim et yis'ra'eil mikol tzarotav*

Translation:

[1] A Psalm of David. Unto Thee *YHVH*, do I lift up my soul.

[2] O my God, in Thee have I trusted, let me not be ashamed; let not mine enemies triumph over me.

[3] Yea, none that wait for Thee shall be ashamed; they shall be ashamed that deal treacherously without cause.

[4] Show me Thy ways *YHVH*; teach me Thy paths.

[5] Guide me in Thy truth, and teach me; for Thou art the God of my salvation; for Thee do I wait all the day.

[6] Remember *YHVH*, Thy compassions and Thy mercies; for they have been from of old.

[7] Remember not the sins of my youth, nor my transgressions; according to Thy mercy remember Thou me, for Thy goodness' sake *YHVH*.

[8] Good and upright is *YHVH*; therefore doth He instruct sinners in the way.

[9] He guideth The humble in justice; and He teacheth the humble His way.

[10] All the paths of *YHVH* are mercy and truth unto such as keep His covenant and His testimonies.

[11] For Thy name's sake *YHVH*, pardon mine iniquity, for it is great.

[12] What man is he that feareth *YHVH*? him will He instruct in the way that He should choose.

[13] His soul shall abide in prosperity; and his seed shall inherit the land.

[14] The counsel of *YHVH* is with them that fear Him; and His covenant, to make them know it.

[15] Mine eyes are ever toward *YHVH*; for He will bring forth my feet out of the net.

[16] Turn Thee unto me, and be gracious unto me; for I am solitary and afflicted.

[17] The troubles of my heart are enlarged; O bring Thou me out of my distresses.

[18] See mine affliction and my travail; and forgive all my sins.

[19] Consider how many are mine enemies, and the cruel hatred wherewith they hate me.

[20] O keep my soul, and deliver me; let me not be ashamed, for I have taken refuge in Thee.

[21] Let integrity and uprightness preserve me, because I wait for Thee.

[22] Redeem Israel, *Elohim*, out of all his troubles.

An acrostic Psalm which has been termed "an alphabet of prayer and meditation, the utterance of a humble yet confident faith,"[1] *Psalm 25* is one of ten additional Psalms in פְּסוּקֵי דְזִמְרָא (*pesukei d'zim'ra*— "Verses of Singing"), i.e. the *Zemirot* (songs) section recited in the Sefardi rite on *Yom Kippur* ("Day of Atonement").[2] The twenty-fifth Psalm is also recited by Sefardim and some Chassidic communities in שחנון (*Tachanun*), i.e. prayers of supplication.[3] Whilst *Tachanun* is not uttered by reform Jews, and whilst some consider it optional, I personally find it a most powerful supplicatory action. Yet, I should mention that, personally speaking, I do not believe in an anthropomorphised deity residing somewhere in the vast expanse of the heavens, who is spending a lot of time passing judgment on even the least of actions of every single human on this planet. Neither do I believe that this deity is meeting out reward and punishment on us. In other words, I believe we are punished *by* our sins, not *for* them. Hence when I pray for "mercy" from the Eternal Living Spirit, I am attempting to rectify my position of imbalance whilst aligning with the, as it were, natural "Forces of Correction" within the vast ocean of Collective Consciousness which we all share, and in which the "laws of cause and effect," or, perhaps better, the "process of rectification" functions automatically. In this regard, I noted elsewhere "that 'sin' is obviously wrongful behaviour which damages us by the doing in such a way, that we fail to achieve anything like the 'Intention of God' in ourselves for our period of incarnation. Therefore, in 'falling short' of the mark by so far, we hinder our progression towards 'Perfection' by that much. In sinning against ourselves, we sin against the 'God-in-us'."[4]

I find the manner in which these prayers for supplication (*Tachanun*) are executed in Sefardic communities particularly fascinating, powerful, and trance inducing. In this regard, the prayer is done seated, and in the Ashkenazic rite it is customary to lower the head, burying it in the crook of the arm, or resting on the left hand, or on the right by those who are wearing *Tefillin* (phylacteries) on the left.[5] On the other hand, the Sefardim do not rest the head on the arm or hand, but bend down and lower their heads towards the ground,[6] an action, which in some instances, results in the worshipper having his head virtually between his knees. In my now remote youth I found this specific action absolutely electrifying and mind altering. I rarely felt so focused and alert, and, as is my nature, I incorporated the procedure into the numerous prayers, incantations, Divine Names, etc., which I have uttered over the many decades as a dedicant to "Practical Kabbalah." Besides, it reminded me of the oft mentioned custom of the "Riders of the Chariot" (*Yordei Merkabah*) of old, who placed their heads between the knees in order to traverse the "heavenly halls."[7] I thought of it as a useful imitation of the so-called "prophetic" meditation position, which is not only "an expression of 'subjugation and humility, so that the prayer will be better received',"[8] but was employed, as Aryah Kaplan noted, "for the intense concentration of spiritual energy."[9] Furthermore, it is reported that the great Rabbi Levi Yitzchak of Berdichev taught "that in the order of the Sefirot, the two knees represent the Sefirot Victory (*Netzach*) and Splendor (*Hod*), and that placing the knees in conjunction with the head releases the spiritual energy of these Sefirot to the mind."[10]

Be that as it may, in terms of Jewish Magic the twenty-fifth Psalm is recommended to counteract distress;[11] against all manner of danger, and to be saved from any form of stress, tension, oppression or pressure;[12] for protection in times of trouble, and against harm in perilous situations;[13] to ward off misfortune;[14] and ultimately for everything![15] In this regard, the "*Shimmush Tehillim*" instructs practitioners to recite the Psalm every morning whenever they encounter problems, which is said will ensure that they are saved. It lists an associated Divine Name construct, which is אֱלִי (*Eli*): א (*Alef*) from אֵלֶיךָ (*eilecha*—"unto Thee"): verse 1; ל (*Lamed*) from לְמַעַן שִׁמְךָ (*l'ma'an shim'cha*—"for Thy name's sake"): verse 11; and י (*Yod*) from מ (*Mem*) in מִי זֶה (*mi zeh*—"who is this" ["what"]): verse 12,[16] the said glyph having been transposed by means of the אָ״ת ב״ש (*Atbash*) cipher.[17] Selig's version includes the same Divine Name constructs, but, as noted earlier, he addressed the previous and current Psalm conjointly without mentioning that the "escape from the greatest danger" pertains to *Psalm 25*, and being protected from "the devastating flood" relates to *Psalm 24*.[18]

Considering the application of the twenty-fifth Psalm to overcome a range of dangers and obstacles, it is worth noting that the letters comprising *Psalm 25:19* were arranged into the following Divine Name construct which is employed in conjunction with the "Forty-letter Name of God," as well as with *Leviticus 27:29*, this verse being equally enunciated in reverse for the purpose of blocking and destroying hatred:

תְּאַנְשׂוּ סָמְחַ יְנוּאֻנֵשׂ
הְאֵר יְבַיְוֹא יְךָ וּבֻרָ

Vocalised *"Y'nivu'uneis' S'macha T'an'siv' Ubura Yichi Y'vay'vo'o H'eir'*," this Divine Name construct was formatted by writing *Psalm 25:19* in reverse. The same method is applied here to the letters comprising the seven six-letter groupings of the "Forty-two Letter Name of God," which is likewise written in reverse, and vocalised in the following unique manner:

צְתֹיַ גֶבַּא נְטַשׂ עְרֹקַ שַׁכֵיַ דַגִנָ גְתַצָ רֹטַב
עְנְט בַּקֶח קֶזֻף לְגַי תְיָץ וַקֹשׁ

In this instance the "Forty-two Letter Name of God" is vocalised *"Tzitoya Gebi'a N'tasa 'roka Shacheiyei Dagina G'tatza Rotavi In'ti Vakeche Keiz'f' Ligaya T'yatzo Vakoshu."* Next, we need to consider *Leviticus 27:29* reading:

כל חרם אשר יחרם מן האדם לא יפדה מות יומת

Transliteration:
> *kol cheirem asher yocharam min ha'adam lo yipadeh mot yumat*

Translation:
> None devoted, that may be devoted of men, shall be ransomed; he shall surely be put to death.

The verse is likewise enunciated backwards in the following manner:

תְּמָוּי תֹּוֹם הְדֶפָי אֵל מְדָאֲהָ נֶם מְרַחְדָ רְשֶׁא
מְרֶח לְךָ

Here the verse is vocalised *"t'ma'uyu tomo h'depayi 'lo m'da'aha n'mi m'rachayo r'she'a m're'chei l'cho.*"[19] The easiest manner in which to employ the Divine Name constructs and associated verse for the mentioned purpose, is to simply enunciate them whilst focussing on the issue at hand, and/or writing them down to be carried as an amulet.

It is worth noting that there are alternative uses of the twenty-fifth Psalm listed in some recensions of the *"Shimmush Tehillim."* In this regard, we are told that to have success in learning, studying, or in having a *Mitzvah*, i.e. successfully fulfilling a religious duty or commandment (also a good deed), the practitioner should recite the Psalm, followed by the following prayer-incantation.[20] It includes two Divine Name combinations, i.e. אל חי (*El Chai*—"Living God") and the unusual אי יה (perhaps enunciated *"Ei Yah"*):

אתה יהוה אלהי אל אלהי ואלהי אבותי אל חי
יהי רצון מלפניך מלכי ואלהי אי יה אמן סלה

Transliteration:
> *Atah YHVH Elohai El Elohai v'elohei avotai El Chai y'hi ratzon mil'fanecha mal'ki v'elohai Ei Yah Omein Selah.*

Translation:
> You are *YHVH*, my God, *El* my God, and God of my Father *El Chai*. May it be your will my king and my God *Ei Yah Amen Selah.*

As in the case of all the previous Psalms, I have witnessed the current Psalm being employed for a variety of other purposes. It was suggested to individuals who are suffering loneliness, or find themselves in some or other difficulty. It is employed against anxiety caused by enemies; against "occult intrigues"; as well as against unjust accusations, and wrongful or unfavourable judgments. The twenty-fifth Psalm is further suggested for illness and healing in general, and for protection against floods. Lastly we are told that the current Psalm offers support to those who suffer confusion in their faith, and who might be burdened by having commited a sin. It is also recommended for recitation in order to encourage forgiveness, and when visiting the graves of loved ones.

In conclusion, *Psalm 25:6* is directly affiliated with עמם (*Omem*), the fifty-second portion of the *"Name of Seventy-two Names,"*[21] and indirectly with מיך (*Mich*), the forty-second portion of the *"Shem Vayisa Vayet."*[22] In terms of the latter tri-letter combination from the "*Name of Seventy-two Names*," we are informed the *gematria* of this Name [מ = 40 + י = 10 + כ = 20 = 70] equates with that of the word סוד (*sod*—"counsel," "assembly," or "secret" [ס = 60 + ו = 6 + ד = 4 = 70]). This is said to pertain to סוד יהוה ליראיו (*Sod YHVH lirei'av*—"The counsel of *YHVH* is with them that fear Him") (*Psalm 25:14*).[23]

In Christian magic we are informed in the Byzantine magical manuscripts that *Psalm 25* is good for dealing with those who "contrive injustice (against you) in hostile fashion," and equally when legal actions is taken against you.[24] Elsewhere, in different recensions of the same manuscript, the twenty-fifth Psalm is said to be good "for thoughts of lethargy," and it is recommended to be recited seven times a day over a period of seven days, in order to banish evil from a residence.[25]

"*Le Livre d'Or*" maintains that an individual who is ill and as a result has difficulty sleeping, should locate this Psalm under his/her head, following which it is said sleep will ensue.[26] Elsewhere *Psalm 25:13* and *15* are referenced in terms of a similar purpose, i.e. "to make a sick man rest,"[27] and for those who have to leave their homes for any reason, i.e. everyone alive, the Syrian magical manuscript in the Sachau Collection maintains that reading the twenty-fifth Psalm before departure, will secure you divine protection against all manner of danger.[28]

Psalm 26

[1] לדוד שפטני יהוה־אהדונהי כי אני בתמי הלכתי וביהוה־יאהדונהי בטחתי לא אמעד

[2] בחנני יהוה־אהדונהי ונסני צרפה כליותי ולבי

[3] כי חסדך לנגד עיני והתהלכתי באמתך

[4] לא ישבתי עם מתי שוא ועם נעלמים לא אבוא

[5] שנאתי קהל מרעים ועם רשעים לא אשב

[6] ארחץ בנקיון כפי ואסבבה את מזבחך יהוה־יאהדונהי

[7] לשמע בקול תודה ולספר כל נפלאותיך

[8] יהוה־יאהדונהי אהבתי מעון ביתך ומקום משכן כבודך

[9] אל תאסף עם חטאים נפשי ועם אנשי דמים חיי

[10] אשר בידיהם זמה וימינם מלאה שחד

[11] ואני בתמי אלך פדני וחנני

[12] רגלי עמדה במישור במקהלים אברך יהוה־יאהדונהי

Transliteration:

[1] *l'david shof'teini YHVH ki ani b'tumi halach'ti uva'YHVH ba'tach'ti lo em'ad*

[2] *b'chaneini YHVH v'naseini tzar'fa chil'yotai v'libi*

[3] *ki chas'd'cha l'neged einai v'hit'halach'ti ba'amitecha*

[4] *lo yashav'ti im m'tei shav v'im na'alamim lo avo*

[5] *saneiti k'hal m'rei'im v'im r'sha'im lo eisheiv*

[6] *er'chatz b'nikayon kapai va'asov'vah et miz'bachacha YHVH*

[7] *lash'mi'a b'kol todah ul'sapeir kol nif'l'otechah*

[8] *YHVH ahav'ti m'on beitecha um'kom mish'kan k'vodecha*

[9] *al te'esof im chata'im naf'shi v'im an'shei damim chayai*

[10] *asher bideihem zimah viminam mal'ah shochad*

[11] *va'ani b'tumi eileich p'deini v'choneini*

[12] *rag'li am'dah v'mishor b'mak'heilim avareich YHVH*

Translation:

[1] A Psalm of David. Judge me *YHVH*, for I have walked in mine integrity, and I have trusted in *YHVH* without wavering.

[2] Examine me *YHVH*, and try me; test my reins and my heart.

[3] For Thy mercy is before mine eyes; and I have walked in Thy truth.

[4] I have not sat with men of falsehood; neither will I go in with dissemblers.

[5] I hate the gathering of evil doers, and will not sit with the wicked.

[6] I will wash my hands in innocency; so will I compass Thine altar *YHVH*,

[7] That I may make the voice of thanksgiving to be heard, and tell of all Thy wondrous works.

[8] *YHVH* I love the habitation of Thy house, and the place where Thy glory dwelleth.

[9] Gather not my soul with sinners, nor my life with men of blood;

[10] In whose hands is craftiness, and their right hand is full of bribes.

[11] But as for me, I will walk in mine integrity; redeem me, and be gracious unto me.

[12] My foot standeth in an even place; in the congregations will I bless *YHVH*.

The truly "Magical" ceremony of הושענא רבא (*Hoshana Raba* —"Great Supplication"), which we noted includes the seven הקפות (*hakafot*— "circumambulations") around the central reading desk (*Bimah*) of the synagogue, is performed, as noted earlier, on the seventh day of the festival of *Sukkot* (Feast of Tabernacles). Worshippers carry *Lulavim* (palm fronds) and *Etrogim* (yellow citrons), and utter *Hoshana* prayer-invocations for forgiveness and salvation, as they tread the seven circuits around the *Torah* scrolls held on the *Bimah* by fellow congregants.[1] It is said the seven *hakafot* (circumambulations) relate to the seven words of *Psalm 26:6* reading כפי ואסבבה את מזבחך יהוה ארחץ בנקיון (*er'chatz b'nikayon kapai va'asov'va et miz'bachacha YHVH*—"I will wash my hands in innocency; so will I compass Thine altar *YHVH*"). The *Hoshanot* prayers are introduced in some Sefardic communities by the recitation of this verse, whilst in others by the enunciation of the sixth and and seventh verses of the Psalm.[2]

In terms of Jewish Magic, *Psalm 26* is indicated to be advantageous in times of trouble, misfortune, or danger.[3] In fact, we are told that the twenty-sixth Psalm is useful as a protection against harm in all perilous situations,[4] whether it be trouble at sea or on land,[5] and equally beneficial for those who are in distress, captivity, or imprisoned.[6] Whilst some sources would suggest the simple recitation of the current Psalm when anyone should find him or herself in any of these unfortunate circumstances, others insist on additional measures. In this regard, we are informed that those who are in danger, or finding themselves in dangerous circumstances, should recite *Psalm 26* in conjunction with the "*Ribono shel Olam*" prayer[7] which I shared in the first chapter. The same is recommended for women who are having problems during childbirth.[8] The current Psalm is listed amongst those which are traditionally recited when a woman is suffering a difficult confinement.[9]

Psalm 26 is recommended in the "*Shimmush Tehillim*" for individuals who are in need, whether at sea or on land, and for those who are in captivity.[10] In this regard, we are told in some recensions of this text, that those who recite the Psalm with its relevant Divine Name construct, אלהי (*Elohai*—"My God"), will be saved. We are further informed that this Divine Name was derived: א (*Alef*) from אשר בידיהם (*asher bideihem*—"in whose hands"): verse 10; ל (*Lamed*) from לשמע (*lash'mi'a*—"to hear"): verse 7 (incorrectly listed לשמוע in the published versions); ה (*Heh*) from ל (*Lamed*) in לא ישבתי (*lo yashav'ti*—"I have not sat"): verse 4, the letter having been transposed by means of the אח״ס בט״ע (*Achas Betah*) cipher; and י (*Yod*) from כ (*Kaf*) in כי חסדך (*ki chas'd'cha*—"For Thy mercy"): verse 3, the letter having been transposed by means of the system of letter exchange of adjacent glyphs in the Hebrew alphabet, i.e. א (*Alef*) with ב (*Bet*), י (*Yod*) with כ (*Kaf*), etc.[11]

Godfrey Selig's version of the magical use of the twenty-sixth Psalm shares the same Divine Name construct to be employed in conjunction with the current Psalm, i.e. אלהי (which he noted is vocalised "*Elohe*"), but, as indicated in all the published versions as well as in some manuscripts, the concluding glyph of this Divine Name construct is claimed to have been derived from חטאים (*chata'im*—"sinners"): verse 9.[12] However, a major difference between the mentioned recensions, Selig's offering, and the published versions, is the associated Divine Name construct in all the publications of the "*Shimmush Tehillim*," which is said to be אלהכי. There is no indication as to how it should be enunciated, except for noting that the penultimate letter כ (*Kaf*) was derived from כפי (*kapai*—"my hands"): verse 6.[13] I personally believe that those who seek to employ *Psalm 26* for the listed purposes, would do well to focus on the Divine Name found in the manuscript recensions, rather than on the one in the published versions.

Be that as it may, Selig maintained that if those who are incarcerated prayed the twenty-sixth Psalm "with the indicated holy names...., and with an appropriate prayer," they "may confidently look forward to an early release from prison."[14] In this instance the format of the "appropriate prayer" is left in the hands of the practitioner. However, in one recension of the "*Shimmush Tehillim*" we find the recitation of the current Psalm for emergencies at sea or on land in conjunction with the following prayer-incantation, without reference to a specific Divine Name construct derived from the Psalm. In this instance, the prominent Divine Name employed is אל חי (*El Chai*):

אתה אלהי אל אלהי ואלהי אבותי אל חי לפניך
באתי בבכי ובדמעות שתצילני מזאת הצרה ואל
נא תעשה לי כרוע מעללי ואל יעמדו לי עונותי
מנגד להשפילני בשם אל חי אמן אמן אמן סלה
סלה סלה

Transliteration:

> *Atah elohai El elohai v'elohei avotai El Chai l'fanecha bati biv'chi uvid'ma'ot shetatzileini mizot hatzarah v'al na ta'aseh li k'ro'a ma'al'lai v'al ya'am'du li avonotai mineged l'hash'pileini b'sheim El Chai Omein Omein Omein Selah Selah Selah.*

Translation:

> You are my God, *El* my God and God of my fathers *El Chai* (Living God). I come before you with weeping and with tears, that you might deliver me from this plight. Please do not destroy my actions. My offenses shall not stand against me to humiliate me. In the Name *El Chai. Amen Amen Amen Selah Selah Selah.*[15]

In terms of the listed magical uses of the current Psalm, it should be noted that the capitals of the seven words comprising *Psalm 26:8*, i.e. יהוה אהבתי מעון ביתך ומקום משכן כבודך (*YHVH ahav'ti m'on beitecha u'm'kom mish'kan k'vodecha*—"*YHVH* I love the habitation of Thy house, and the place where Thy glory dwelleth"), are conjoined in the Divine Name construct יאמב ומכ which is employed in amulets for wearers "to be saved from trouble."[16] Curiously enough, the same verse is said to be directly aligned with מנד (*Menad*), the thirty-sixth portion of the "*Shem Vayisa Vayet*."[17]

Lastly, *Psalm 26* is generally recommended against enemies, betrayal (treachery), as well as against theft, thieves and all kinds of brigands, but is also employed to ensure safety from fear. As far as religious matters are concerned, the twenty-sixth Psalm is recommended for personal recitation in the synagogue, and is employed to encourage fidelity to religion, justice and righteousness. *Psalm 26:6* is recommended for recitation whilst washing hands, and, in terms of persuing goodness, the current Psalm is enunciated for the well-being of orphans.

As far as Christian magic is concerned, the Byzantine Christian manuscripts recommend *Psalm 26* when anyone is afraid to speak whilst on a journey.[18] Some manuscripts maintain the Psalm to be good for "enchantments and magical bindings." In this regard, the instruction is to recite it seven times, which will ensure that you cannot be harmed.[19] Elsewhere it says that to "loose magic," the practitioner should recite the twenty-sixth Psalm over water at daybreak whilst fasting, and, commencing on the Christian celebration of Epiphany, this Psalm should be repeated three times over a period of three days, following which the water is consumed. It is further maintained, that the Psalm should be written with a set of magical characters, to be carried on the person requiring this support.[20]

Similar instructions can be found in "*Le Livre d'Or*," in which we are told that if an individual wishes "to destroy the workings of enchantments and fancies," that the said individual should write down the Psalm, and that this will preclude the "enchanter" from working anything against him/her.[21] The same text maintains that if a person recites *Psalm 26* "in the midst" of adversaries, that individual will be protected from assault.[22] We find the same application listed elsewhere, where we are informed that *Psalm 26:11–12* should be recited "amidst enemies" in order to be delivered from those foes.[23]

Psalm 27

[1] לדוד יהוה־אדני־אהדונהי אורי וישעי ממי אירא
יהוה־אדני־אהדונהי מעוז חיי ממי אפחד

[2] בקרב עלי מרעים לאכל את בשרי צרי ואיבי
לי המה כשלו ונפלו

[3] אם תחנה עלי מחנה לא יירא לבי אם תקום עלי
מלחמה בזאת אני בוטח

[4] אחת שאלתי מאת יהוה־אדני־אהדונהי אותה אבקש
שבתי בבית יהוה־אדני־אהדונהי כל ימי היי לחזות בנעם
יהוה־אדני־אהדונהי ולבקר בהיכלו

[5] כי יצפנני בסכה ביום רעה יסתרני בסתר אהלו
בצור ירוממני

[6] ועתה ירום ראשי על איבי סבובותי ואזבחה
באהלו זבחי תרועה אשירה ואזמרה ליהוה־אדני־אהדונהי

[7] שמע יהוה־אדני־אהדונהי קולי אקרא וחנני וענני

[8] לך אמר לבי בקשו פנו את פניך יהוה־אדני־אהדונהי
אבקש

[9] אל תסתר פניך ממני אל תט באף עבדך עזרתי
היית אל תטשני ואל תעזבני אלהי ישעי

[10] כי אבי ואמי עזבוני ויהוה־אדני־אהדונהי יאספני

[11] הורני יהוה־אדני־אהדונהי דרכך ונחני בארח
מישור למען שוררי

[12] אל תתנני בנפש צרי כי קמו בי עדי שקר ויפח
חמס

[13] לולא האמנתי לראות בטוב יהוה־אדני־אהדונהי
בארץ חיים

[14] קוה אל יהוה־אדני־אהדונהי חזק ויאמץ לבך וקוה
אל יהוה־אדני־אהדונהי

Transliteration:
[1] *l'david YHVH ori v'yish'i mimi ira YHVH ma'oz chayai
mimi ef'chad*
[2] *bik'rov alai m'rei'im le'echol et b'sari tzarai v'oy'vai
li heimah chash'lu v'nafalu*

[3] *im tachaneh alai machaneh lo yira libi im takum alai mil'chamah b'zot ani vote'ach*

[4] *achat sha'al'ti mei'eit YHVH otah avakeish shiv'ti b'veit YHVH kol y'mei chayai la'chazot b'no'am YHVH ul'vaker b'heichalo*

[5] *ki yitz'p'neini b'sukoh b'yom ra'ah yas'tireini b'seiter aholo b'tzur y'rom'meini*

[6] *v'atah yarum roshi al oy'vai s'vivotai v'ez'b'chah v'aholo ziv'chei t'ru'ah ashirah va'azam'rah laYHVH*

[7] *sh'ma YHVH koli ek'ra v'choneini va'aneini*

[8] *l'cha amar libi bak'shu fanai et panecha YHVH avakesh*

[9] *al tas'teir panecha mimeni al tat b'af av'decha ez'rati ha'yitah al tit'sheini v'al ta'az'veini elohei yish'i*

[10] *ki avi v'imi azavuni va'YHVH ya'as'feini*

[11] *horeini YHVH dar'kecha un'cheini b'orach mishor l'ma'an shor'rai*

[12] *al tit'neini b'nefesh tzarai ki kamu vi eidei sheker vifei'ach chamas*

[13] *lulei he'eman'ti lir'ot b'tuv YHVH b'eretz chayim*

[14] *kaveih el YHVH chazak v'ya'ameitz libecha v'kaveih el YHVH*

Translation:

[1] A Psalm of David. *YHVH* is my light and my salvation; whom shall I fear? *YHVH* is the stronghold of my life; of whom shall I be afraid?

[2] When evil-doers came upon me to eat up my flesh, even mine adversaries and my foes, they stumbled and fell.

[3] Though a host should encamp against me, my heart shall not fear; though war should rise up against me, even then will I be confident.

[4] One thing have I asked of *YHVH*, that will I seek after: that I may dwell in the house of *YHVH* all the days of my life, to behold the graciousness of *YHVH*, and to visit early in His temple.

[5] For He concealeth me in His pavilion in the day of evil; He hideth me in the covert of His tent; He lifteth me up upon a rock.

[6] And now shall my head be lifted up above mine enemies round about me; and I will offer in His tabernacle

sacrifices with trumpet-sound; I will sing, yea, I will sing praises unto *YHVH*.

[7] Hear *YHVH*, when I call with my voice, and be gracious unto me, and answer me.

[8] In Thy behalf my heart hath said: 'Seek ye My face'; Thy face *YHVH*, will I seek.

[9] Hide not Thy face from me; put not Thy servant away in anger; Thou hast been my help; cast me not off, neither forsake me, O God of my salvation.

[10] For though my father and my mother have forsaken me, *YHVH* will take me up.

[11] Teach me Thy way *YHVH*; and lead me in an even path, because of them that lie in wait for me.

[12] Deliver me not over unto the will of mine adversaries; for false witnesses are risen up against me, and such as breathe out violence.

[13] If I had not believed to look upon the goodness of *YHVH* in the land of the living!—

[14] Wait on *YHVH*; be strong, and let thy heart take courage; yea, wait thou for *YHVH*.

Psalm 27 is recited daily in both the Ashkenazic and Sefardic rites during the period commencing on the second day of *Rosh Chodesh Elul*, the New Moon marking the beginning of the twelfth and final month of the Hebrew Calendar, and concluding on the Jewish holiday of שמיני עצרת (*Shemini Atzeret*).[1] In the Ashkenazi rites the Psalm is recited at the end of the morning (*Shacharit*) and evening (*Arvit*) services, whilst in the Sefardi rites it is likewise said at *Shacharit*, and following that it is again recited during the afternoon prayer service (*Minchah*).[2] Whilst the *Shemini Atzeret* holiday marks the conclusion of *Sukkot*, this being the reason for it being called the "Eighth day of Solemn Assembly," it is a separate holiday.[3] As far as reciting the twenty-seventh Psalm over this period is concerned, we are informed that אורי (*ori*—"my light") [verse 1] alludes to *Rosh Hashanah* ("New Year"); ישעי (*yish'i*—"my salvation") [verse 9] suggests *Yom Kippur* ("Day of Atonement"); כי יצפנני בסכה (*ki yitz'p'neini b'sukoh* —"For He concealeth me in His pavilion [tabernacle]") [verse 5] references *Sukkot* ("Festival of Tabernacles); and מִמִּי אִירָא (*mimi ira*—"whom shall I fear") pertains to *Hoshana Rabah* ("Great Supplication").[4] It was further indicated that the Ineffable Name appears thirteen times in the current Psalm, which is said to reference the "Thirteen Attributes of Mercy," and that the "thirteen Holy Names awaken the thirteen mercies that are said to be dealt out in days of judgment,"[5] these "days" being a reference to the Holy Days beginning with *Rosh Hashanah* and concluding with *Shemini Atzeret*. It should be noted that the saga of the seven *hakafot* (circumambulations) of the "Great Supplication" (*Hoshana Rabah*), which I addressed in terms of *Psalms 8* and *26*, is completed by dancing the seven circuits (*hakafot*) of the "Great Jubilation" of שמחת תורה (*Simchat Torah*—"Rejoicing with the Torah") on *Shemini Atzeret*.[6]

As far as the magical applications of *Psalm 27* are concerned, the Psalm is recommended to control wild, dangerous animals, and stubborn cattle.[7] In this regard, the instruction is to recite this Psalm "on the way," and the beast will be conquered.[8] In one recension of the "*Shimmush Tehillim*" the "dangerous animal" is a human who wants to bewitch someone.[9] In this regard, we are told that the current Psalm can be employed against such bewitchment, and that the afflicted individual should recite the Psalm and the following prayer-incantation reading:

מלך מלא רחמים הושיעני והצילני מן הברייה
הרעה שלא תוכל להרע לי ולא להזיק אחד
מרמ"ח [ממאתים וארבעים ושמונה] איברים
שבי ולא אפחד ממנה בשם מה אלי אמן אמן
סלה

Transliteration:

> *Melech malei rachamim hoshi'eini v'hatzileini min haberiyah hara'ah shelo tuchal l'hara li v'lo l'hazik echad mi'resh-mem-chet* [*mima'atayim v'ar'ba'im ush'monah*] *eivarim shebi v'lo af'chad mimenah b'shem Mah Eili. Omein Omein Selah.*

Translation:

> King full of mercy, redeem and deliver me from the evil creature, so that she (he) may do me no harm, nor injure

any of the 248 limbs that are in me, and I will not be afraid
of her (him). In the name *Mah Eili. Amen Amen Selah.*

In this instance, the prayer-incantation includes a Divine Name
combination מה אלי (*Mah Eili*), which could be translated "what
is my God."[10] Be that as it may, the same instruction pertaining to
controlling "stubborn cattle" by means of *Psalm 27*, is said to
apply in conquering a city.[11] and this is the focus of Godfrey
Selig's version of the "*Shimmush Tehillim,*" in which it is noted "if
you wish to be well and kindly received in a strange city, and
desire to be hospitably entertained, repeat this Psalm upon your
journey again and again, with reverence, and in full confidence that
God will dispose the hearts of men to receive and entertain you
kindly."[12]

In terms of further magical applications of the twenty-
seventh Psalm, we are informed that it is a *Segulah* ("Magical
virtue") for anyone to recite the Psalm from *Rosh Hashanah*
(Jewish New Year) onwards, in order to ensure that the coming
year will be favourable and sweet. It is further noted that a person
who follows this practice, "will strip all the celestial accusers," and
though there might be a "bad decree issued" against the said
individual, he/she will abolish it, and be found just by the "celestial
tribunal."[13] Other than this procedure, it is worth noting that the
capitals of the words comprising *Psalm 27:7* are conjoined in the
Divine Name construct שׁיקאוו, which is included in amulets
which function as a call for help,[14] and *Psalm 27:13* is directly
affiliated with לאו (*Lov*), the eleventh portion of the "*Shem
Vayisa Vayet.*"[15]

The twenty-seventh Psalm is also recommended for illness
and healing in general. Other than this, it is said to be a safeguard
from harm, and, as in the case of the previous Psalm, it affords
protection in perilous situations and in times of trouble. The
special shielding qualities of this Psalm is particularly emphasised
in it being recommended as a protection against invading armies.
I have also seen *Psalm 27* recommended to those who are feeling
forsaken and abandoned, and it is further suggested for recitation
during a period of mourning. In conclusion, as again in the case of
the previous Psalm, the current Psalm is suggested for private
recitation in the synagogue.

Christian Magic informs us that the twenty-seventh Psalm is useful when individuals are "off to war or to an army camp." In this regard, we are told in the byzantine magical manuscripts that individuals who find themselves in such circumstances, should write the Psalm on paper with an ink made from saffron and rose oil. The item is then fumigated with "man-orchid and peony," and the Psalm engraved on their swords, which was the favourite weapon of war at the time.[16] The same manuscripts maintains that "if you have an enemy at your door and he is disgracing you," that you should recite the Psalm, and carry it on your person with a set of "signs," including the names "*Sabaoth Adonai Eloi Eloi Samouel* Jesus Christ," which will preclude you from being defeated by the enemy.[17] In fact, we are told *Psalm 27* is useful against enemies, and, in this regard, the Psalm should be recited and carried as an amulet on the right hand.[18] The same sources inform us that this Psalm is good to recite by those who are suffering "dispair,"[19] and by those who are obliged to file defamation charges against someone.[20]

We are also told that *Psalm 27:1–2* is a good vermifuge. In this regard, the said verses are employed in conjunction with rhubarb to rid someone from an infestation of worms. The instruction is to crush the rhubarb and other substances, and add "holy water" to mix. This is followed by writing the said two verses of the twenty-seventh Psalm, before imbibing the liquid mixture.[21] Curiously enough we find similar instructions in "*Le Livre d'Or*" in which we are told that *Psalm 27:2–3* is good for "children suffering with worms." However, it instructs that the said verses should be written up to the phrase "even mine adversaries and my foes, they stumbled and fell," which is the conclusion of verse 2. Be that as it may, to this writing should be added three times the *Pater Noster* and *Ave Maria* prayers.[22] The same text also maintains that if you intend to plant a grapevine, you should write down *Psalm 27* during the New Moon, then dissolve the writing in the spring from which you intend to water the vine. This is said will ensure that the vine "will be protected from all that is invisible."[23]

In conclusion, it should be noted that in the "*Key of Solomon*" the twenty-seventh Psalm is listed amongst the set employed in the construction of "pentacles." The others are *Psalms*

8, 21, 29, 32, 51, 72 and *134.*[24] It is also one of the Psalms, any of which is recommended for recitation whilst the practitioner is disrobing in preparation for taking a ritual bath. The others are *Psalms 14, 53, 27, 54, 81* and *105.*[25]

Psalm 28

[1] לדוד אליך יהוה‏אדני‏אהדונהי אקרא צורי אל
תחרש ממני פן תחשה ממני ונמשלתי עם יורדי בור

[2] שמע קול תחנוני בשועי אליך בנשאי ידי אל
דביר קדשך

[3] **אל תמשכני** עם רשעים ועם **פעלי** פעלי **און**
דברי שלום עם רעיהם ורעה בלבבם

[4] תן להם כפעלם וכרע מעלליהם כמעשה ידיהם
תן להם השב גמולם להם

[5] כי לא יבינו אל פעלת יהוה‏אדני‏אהדונהי ואל
מעשה ידיו יהרסם ולא יבנם

[6] ברוך יהוה‏אדני‏אהדונהי כי שמע קול תחנוני

[7] יהוה‏אדני‏אהדונהי עזי ומגני בו בטח לבי ונעזרתי
ויעלז לבי ומשירי אהודנו

[8] יהוה‏אדני‏אהדונהי עז למו ומעוז ישועות משיחו הוא

[9] הושיעה את עמך וברך את נחלתך ורעם ונשאם
עד העולם

Transliteration:

[1] *l'david eilecha YHVH ek'ra tzuri al techerash mimeni pen techesheh mimeni v'nim'shal'ti im yor'dei vor*

[2] *sh'ma kol tachanunai b'shav'i eilecha b'nos'i yadai el d'vir kod'shecha*

[3] *al tim sh'cheini im r'sha'im v'im po'alei aven dov'rei shalom im rei'eihem v'ra'ah bil'vavam*

[4] *ten lahem k'fa'olam uch'ro'a ma'al'leihem k'ma'aseih y'deihem tein lahem hasheiv g'mulam lahem*

[5] *ki lo yavinu el p'ulot YHVH v'el ma'aseih yadav yeher'seim v'lo yiv'neim*

[6] *baruch YHVH ki shama kol tachanunai*

[7] *YHVH uzi umagini bo vatach libi v'ne'ezar'ti vaya'aloz libi umishiri ahodenu*

[8] *YHVH oz lamo uma'oz y'shu'ot m'shicho hu*

[9] *hoshi'ah et amecha uvarech et nachaletecha ur'eim v'nas'eim ad ha'olam*

Translation:

[1] Psalm of David. Unto thee *YHVH*, do I call; my Rock, be not Thou deaf unto me; lest, if Thou be silent unto me, I become like them that go down into the pit.
[2] Hear the voice of my supplications, when I cry unto Thee, when I lift up my hands toward Thy holy Sanctuary.
[3] Draw me not away with the wicked, and with the workers of iniquity; who speak peace with their neighbours, but evil is in their hearts.
[4] Give them according to their deeds, and according to the evil of their endeavours; give them after the work of their hands; render to them their desert.
[5] Because they give no heed to the works of *YHVH*, nor to the operation of His hands; He will break them down and not build them up.
[6] Blessed be *YHVH*, because He hath heard the voice of my supplications.
[7] *YHVH* is my strength and my shield, in Him hath my heart trusted, and I am helped; therefore my heart greatly rejoiceth, and with my song will I praise Him.
[8] *YHVH* is a strength unto them; and He is a stronghold of salvation to His anointed.
[9] Save Thy people, and bless Thine inheritance; and tend them, and carry them for ever.

Psalm 28 does not feature in any great manner in Jewish Liturgies, and its magical uses are equally limited in "Practical Kabbalah," in which we are told that it is good to recite this Psalm if you want to ensure a prayer to be heard.[1] Otherwise, it is used "to appease an enemy,"[2] i.e. if you wish a "hater" (enemy) to make peace with you."[3] In this regard, we are instructed to recite the twenty-eighth Psalm, with its associated Divine Name which is said to be הי (*HY*).[4] Considering the enunciation of a related Divine Name construct in one of the recensions of the "*Shimmush Tehillim*," the pronunciation of this Divine Name construct could be *"Hayi."*[5] However, we are informed that this is a Divine Name construct which was derived: ה (*Heh*) from ל (*Lamed*) in לדוד (*l'david* —"of David"): verse 1, by exchanging the letters, though there is no reference to the specific kabbalistic cipher involved. The letter

' (*Yod*) is said to be derived from the מ (*Mem*) at the conclusion of the Psalm עד העולם (*ad ha'olam*— "for ever"): verse 9, this glyph having been transposed by means of the א״ת ב״ש (*Atbash*) cipher.[6]

The Godfrey Selig version of the "*Shimmush Tehillim*" shares the same details, except that it maintains the Psalm should be enunciated "with a suitable prayer, trusting in the power and readiness of the Great Ruler of hearts, and so your wish will be fully realised."[7] Curiously enough, we find a "suitable prayer" included in a recension of the "*Shimmush Tehillim*" which differs from the instructions pertaining to *Psalm 28* shared in the standard published versions.[8] Here the Psalm is simply recited "against enemies" without any intention of seeking reconciliation or establishing peace. The practitioner is told to recite the Psalm, and then to conclude with the following prayer-incantation:

שומע צעקת נרדפים שמעני והצילני נא מיד אויבים
הרעים האלו והורידהו מגדולה שהגדיל עלי
[....name of recipient....] ואל ישמח [....personal name....]
אשר יבקש ממני סליחה וכפרה על אשר חטא לי בשם
הֵי הָא

Transliteration:

> *Shomei'a tza'ak'ta nir'dafim shemei'ani v'hatzileini na miyad oy'vim hara'im ha'eilu v'horiduhu mig'dolah shehig'dil alai* [....personal name....] *v'el yis'mach* [....name of recipient....] *asher y'vakeish mimeni s'lichah v'chaparah al asher chata li b'sheim Hayi Ha.*

Translation:

> Hearer of the cry of the persecuted, please hear and deliver me from the hand of these evil enemies, and bring down for him the power which he magnified over me [....personal name....], and let not [....name of recipient....] rejoice that he ask me for forgiveness from me and atonement for that transgression against me, in the name *Hayi Ha*.[9]

Other than the listed applications of *Psalm 28* in published sources, we find the current Psalm employed to be healed from nervous disorders; against pride; and for protection against lightning and storms in general.

We find the same use of the twenty-eighth Psalm in the Christian "*Le Livre d'Or*," in which it is equally maintained that this Psalm "reconciles us to our enemies."[10] However, to affect this outcome the practitioner is instructed to recite the Psalm three times in conjunction with the name of a "[Spirit] Intelligence," as well as crossing the middle fingers and tracing a magical character with them, whilst staring at the enemy. It is said this should be done twice, following which peace will be established.[11] The same text maintains that those who are suffering the effects of their misdeeds, "can obtain all they need from God" if they recite the Psalm "every day with devotion."[12] It further claims that *Psalm 28* is good for those who are abused by their children and loved ones, and equally for those who benefit the poor so as to multiply their possessions on earth and in heaven.[13]

Elsewhere, in the Byzantine manuscripts, practitioners are instructed to enunciate the twenty-eighth Psalm seven times, doing so over rose oil in the morning and evening for three days. The face is then anointed with this oil prior to being seen by anyone, which, we are told, will ensure practitioners "will be loved by kin and strangers, men and women included."[14] Elsewhere in the same manuscripts we find the Psalm recommended to free a demoniac. In this regard, *Psalm 28* is recited three times into the ear of the sufferer, following which it is said "the demon will yield."[15]

Psalm 29

[1] מזמור לדוד הבו ליהוה־אדני יאהדונהי בני אלים
הבו ליהוה־אדני יאהדונהי כבוד ועז

[2] הבו ליהוה־אדני יאהדונהי כבוד שמו השתחוו
ליהוה־אדני יאהדונהי בהדרת קדש

[3] קול יהוה־אדני־יאהדונהי על המים אל הכבוד
הרעים יהוה־אדני־יאהדונהי על מים רבים

[4] קול יהוה־אדני־יאהדונהי בכח קול יהוה־אדני־יאהדונהי
בהדר

[5] קול יהוה־אדני־יאהדונהי שבר ארזים וישבר
יהוה־אדני יאהדונהי את ארזי הלבנון

[6] וירקידם כמו עגל לבנון ושרין כמו בן ראמים

[7] קול יהוה־אדני־יאהדונהי חצב להבות אש

[8] קול יהוה־אדני יאהדונהי יחיל מדבר יחיל
יהוה־אדני יאהדונהי מדבר קדש

[9] קול יהוה־אדני־יאהדונהי יחולל אילות ויחשף יערות
ובהיכלו כלו אמר כבוד

[10] יהוה־אדני־יאהדונהי למבול ישב וישב יהוה־אדני־יאהדונהי
מלך לעולם

[11] יהוה־אדני־יאהדונהי עז לעמו יתן יהוה־אדני־יאהדונהי
יברך את עמו בשלום

Transliteration:

[1] *miz'mor l'david havu laYHVH b'nei eilim havu laYHVH kavod va'oz*

[2] *havu laYHVH k'vod sh'mo hish'tachavu laYHVH b'had'rat kodesh*

[3] *kol YHVH al hamayim el hakavod hir'im YHVH al mayim rabim*

[4] *kol YHVH bako'ach kol YHVH behadar*

[5] *kol YHVH shoveir arazim vay'shaber YHVH et ar'zei hal'vanon*

[6] *vayar'kideim k'mo eigel l'vanon v'sir'yon k'mo ven r'eimim*

[7] *kol YHVH chotzeiv lahavot eish*

[8] *kol YHVH yachil mid'bar yachil YHVH mid'bar kadesh*
[9] *kol YHVH y'choleil ayalot vayechesof y'arot uv'heichalo kulo omeir kavod*
[10] *YHVH lamabul yashav vayeishev YHVH melech l'olam*
[11] *YHVH oz l'amo yitein YHVH yivareich et amo bashalom*

Translation:

[1] A Psalm of David. Ascribe unto *YHVH*, O ye sons of might, ascribe unto *YHVH* glory and strength.

[2] Ascribe unto *YHVH* the glory due unto His name; worship *YHVH* in the beauty of holiness.

[3] The voice of *YHVH* is upon the waters; the God of glory thundereth, even *YHVH* upon many waters.

[4] The voice of *YHVH* is powerful; the voice of *YHVH* is full of majesty.

[5] The voice of *YHVH* breaketh the cedars; yea, *YHVH* breaketh in pieces the cedars of *Lebanon*.

[6] He maketh them also to skip like a calf; *Lebanon* and *Sirion* like a young wild-ox.

[7] The voice of *YHVH* heweth out flames of fire.

[8] The voice of *YHVH* shaketh the wilderness; *YHVH* shaketh the wilderness of *Kadesh*.

[9] The voice of *YHVH* maketh the hinds to calve, and strippeth the forests bare; and in His temple all say: 'Glory.'

[10] *YHVH* sat enthroned at the flood; yea, *YHVH* sitteth as King for ever.

[11] *YHVH* will give strength unto His people; *YHVH* will bless his people with peace.

Psalm 29 is recited in the Sefardic tradition on *Shabbat*, and during the morning service (*Shacharit*) on festivals.[1] In fact, it is the last of six Psalms recited prior to the evening service (*Arvit*), i.e. during קבלת שבת (*Kabbalat Shabbat*—"Reception of the Sabbath").[2] It is said the six Psalms, comprising *Psalms 95* to *99* as well as *Psalm 29*, represent "the six working days of the week, the six days of creation," or the six blasts of the שופר (*Shofar*—ram's horn) "that were sounded on Friday afternoon to announce the ushering in of the Sabbath."[3] We are also informed that the *Gematria* (numerical value) of the initials of the first word of each of the six Psalms [ל = 30 + שׁ = 300 + י = 10 + מ = 40 + י = 10 + מ = 40 = 430], is equal to that of the word נֶפֶשׁ (*Nefesh*—"soul"/ Instinctual Self) [נ = 50 + פ = 80 + שׁ = 300 = 430]. This is said to signify "the soulful inspiration derived from these Psalms on the eve of Shabbat."[4] However, there is yet more to this affirmation of meaningfulness by means of concepts coalescing in the vast, as it were, "'NOW' kaleidoscope" of the Eternal Living Spirit. In this regard, we are told that the six Psalms comprise a total of 702 words, and that this is the *Gematria* of שַׁבָּת *Shabbat* [שׁ = 300 + ב = 2 + ת = 400 = 702]. Furthermore, it is noted that there are collectively 65 verses in these Psalms, and that this figure is the *Gematria* of אֲדֹנָי (*Adonai*) [א = 1 + ד = 4 + נ = 50 + י = 10 = 65],[5] the Divine Name traditionally associated with *Malchut* (Kingdom) on the sefirotic Tree.

As far as the uniqueness of *Psalm 29* is concerned, we are told that the renowned Kabbalist Rabbi Isaac Luria, "for whom the process of creation and redemption, and the idea of a divine spark in everything, was important,"[6] used to go out into the open fields to watch the setting of the sun and welcome the arrival of *Shabbat*, during which he would recite *Psalm 29*.[7] We are informed the great Rabbi "walked around the table while reciting the Psalm in commemoration of the *Mizbayah* ('altar'), a practice still prevalent in Jerusalem."[8] It is also said that the good Rabbi stressed that the Psalm should be enunciated "slowly, with much concentration and joy,"[9] and we are told that the remarkable qualities embodied in the twenty-ninth Psalm, results in תִּקּוּנִים (*Tikunim*—"corrections"/ "restorations") of cosmic proportions being enacted in the celestial realms through the enunciation of twenty-ninth Psalm on the arrival of *Shabbat*.[10]

In this regard, Rabbi Alexander Susskind of Grodno, the remarkable Lithuanian Kabbalist, maintained that "before he begins to recite this Psalm let a man be ready to receive the additional Sabbath soul." He further wrote that through the recitation of the expression הָבוּ לַיהוה (*havu la'YHVH*—"Give [Ascribe] unto *YHVH* [enunciated "*Adonai*"]), "a special *tikkun* is performed in the worlds on high," whilst another is enacted through the enunciation of the word קוֹל (*kol*—"voice") seven times in this Psalm.[11] It has been suggested that these seven appearances of the word "voice" in the Psalm, pertain to seven different kinds of voices related to the seven *Middot* (Divine "Emotive Qualities" or "Measures"), i.e. Kindness, Severity, Harmony, Endurance, Humility, Foundation, and Royalty, which are referencing the seven lower *sefirot* of חסד (*Chesed*— "Lovingkindness"), גבורה (*Gevurah*—"Might"), תפארת (*Tif'eret* —"beauty"), נצח (*Netzach*— "Victory"), הוד (*Hod*—"Glory"), יסוד (*Yesod*—"Foundation"), and מלכות (*Malchut*—"Kingdom"/ "Kingship").[12]

Kabbalists have also aligned the initials of the previously mentioned seven six-letter constructs formed from the seven lines of the *Ana Bechoach* prayer, the latter following the recitation of *Psalm 29* in the service, with the seven appearances of the "voice of *YHVH*" mentioned in the current Psalm.[13] Collectively these seven glyphs comprise the Divine Name construct אקנבחיש (vocalised *Akanavachayasha*), which is included in Hebrew amulets for the purposes of countering baseless enmity or envy, rescue, protection, etc.[14] Be that as it may, it is further said that the seven appearances of the "voice of *YHVH*," which King David enunciated over the waters, align with the seven-blessing *Shabbat Amidah*,[15] and equally with the seven *hakafot*, i.e. the circumambulations around the *Bimah* (central reading desk) on הושענא רבא (*Hoshanah Rabah*—"Great Supplication"), and on שמחת תורה (*Simchat Torah*— "Rejoicing with the *Torah*"). This was cited to be the reason why some recite the twenty-ninth Psalm after the seven circuits on *Hoshana Raba* ("Great Supplication").[16] As noted earlier, it is customary to vocalise verses from the "*Book of Psalms*" as well as other relevant poems between circuits, and some communities enunciate *Psalms 29* and *113* whilst the circumambulations are proceeding.[17]

It should be noted that the recitation of the Ineffable Name eighteen times in the twenty-ninth Psalm, is said to result in another special celestial *Tikkun* ("restoration") being enacted.[18] We are informed it is especially significant that the eighteen appearances of the Ineffable Name in the Psalm align with "the eighteen-blessing *Amidah*."[19] In this regard, it is maintained that every time the Ineffable Name (*Adonai*) is enunciated in the current Psalm, "we advance one more blessing in the *Amidah*,"[20] thus it is said that "as *Psalm 29* ends with 'May *Adonai* bless his people with shalom,' so the final blessing of the *Amidah* ends with '"*Adonai* who blesses his people with *shalom*'."[21] Furthermore, we are informed that the eighteen appearances of the Ineffable Name in the Psalm comprises seventy-two letters (4 x 18), which we are told relate to the "Name of Seventy-two Names."[22] This number also aligns with the first of the four expanded spellings of the Ineffable Name known as עַב (*Av*) extension, i.e. יוד הי ויו הי (*Yod-vav-dalet Heh-yod Vav-yod-vav Heh-yod*), called the "Seventy-Two Letter Name of God," and which relates to אצילות (*Atzilut* —"Emanation") the highest of the "Four Worlds" of Kabbalah.[23] We are further reminded that the *Gematria* (numerical value) of חסד (*Chesed*— "Lovingkindness") [ח = 8 + ס = 60 + ד = 4 = 72],[24] and that the Divine One gave the Sabbath to Israel "as an act of *chesed*."[25]

As many readers of kabbalistic works know well enough, the *sefirah* of *Chesed* represents love, joy, expansiveness, etc., and thus Rabbi Alexander Susskind of Grodno instructed that consequently *Psalm 29* should be recited "with great deliberation and with a most powerful joy. He should have in mind that his intention in reciting this Psalm is in order to perform great *tikkunim* in the worlds on high and to give satisfaction to the Creator, blessed and exalted be He for ever. Then it will undoubtedly be accounted to him as if he had had all the intentions in mind."[26] Regarding these "intentions," the great Rabbi reminds us that "the All-Merciful desires the heart."[27] Reciting the twenty-ninth Psalm in this manner, is as if one is fulfilling the sacred obligation of Kabbalah expressed in the statement:

לשם יחוד קודשא בריך הוא ושכינתיה בדחילו
ורחימו ליחד שם י"ה בו"ה ביחודא שלים

Transliteration:

> *l'shem yichud kud'sha b'rich hu ush'chinteih bid'chilu
> ur'chimu l'yacheid shem Y"H b'V"H b'yichuda sh'lim*

Translation:

> For the sake of unifying the Holy One, blessed be He and
> the *Shechinah*, in awe and reverence, to unify *YH* and *VH*
> in complete unity.

In this regard, we are informed that the verses in *Psalm 29* are
equal in number to the *Gematria* of ו‎ה (*VH*) [ו‎ = 6 + ה‎ = 5 = 11],
the concluding letters of the Ineffable Name. Furthermore, it has
been indicated that the conjoined *Gematria* of the Divine Names
יהוה (*YHVH*) [י‎ = 10 + ה‎ = 5 + ו‎ = 6 + ה‎ = 5 = 26] and אדני
(*Adonai*) [א‎ = 1 + ד‎ = 4 + נ‎ = 50 + י‎ = 10 = 65], equates with the
ninety-one words of the Psalm.[28] Thus we are told that "praying the
Psalm with the proper intention integrates the two names, a process
known as a *yichud*. This process corresponds to the union of 'The
Holy one, blessed be He' (*Tiferet*) and his bride, the *Shechinah*"[29]
in *Malchut*. I have addressed some of the teachings regarding the
Divine One and the *Shechinah* in fair detail in previous volumes.[30]

　　In terms of magical applications, it has been noted in the
Talmud as far back as the 6th or 7th centuries [*TB Pesachim 112a*],
that *Psalm 29.3–10* will protect individuals who need to drink
water during the nights when evil spirits are particularly active. It
was believed that demons will infest water left next to the bed,
hence we are told that one "must not drink water either on the
nights of the fourth days [Wednesdays], or on the nights of a
Sabbath,"[31] when demonic forces were said to be especially active.
However, those who need to consume water during those nights,
could do so after reciting the said verses from the twenty-ninth
Psalm, i.e. those comprising the earlier mentioned seven references
to קול יהוה (*kol YHVH*—the "voice of *YHVH*").[32] As it is, *Psalm
29* is generally employed in Jewish Magic as a protection against
evil spirits,[33] and water is included in several of the procedures to
combat demonic forces.

　　Whilst the magical use of the twenty-ninth Psalm is missing
in a number of published editions of the "*Shimmush Tehillim*," in
those where it does feature we are told that the individual needing
support to counter the onslaught of an evil spirit, should collect
water which has not seen the sun, doing so in a pot or new vessel.
Following this the next action would be to take seven willow rods

and seven leaves from a palm which does not produce fruit, and to place them in the vessel with water.[34] Next, the practitioner has to recite the Psalm ten times[35] (three times according to one recension)[36] over the water in the evening, and then place the vessel on the earth under the stars. At "the end of the day" i.e. at the next sunset, the water should be poured out at the "gate" or entrance of the residence of the afflicted.[37] The associated Divine Name construct is said to be ה"א (*Heh-Alef*), but there is no indication as to how it should be enunciated. However, it is not strictly necessary to know this, since the practitioner needs only to concentrate on the letter combination whilst reciting the Psalm. However, we are informed that in the case of this Divine Name construct, the letter ה (*Heh*) was derived from הבו (*havu*—"give"/ "ascribe"): verse 1, and א (*Alef*) from י (*Yod*) in יהוה עז (*YHVH oz*—"*YHVH* strength"): verse 11, the concluding letter having been transposed by means of the א"יק בכ"ר (*Ayak Bachar*) cipher.[38]

    This is one of those instances in which Godfrey Selig's German/ English version of the "*Shimmush Tehillim*" more or less aligns with the Hebrew edition in print at the time. According to him the Psalm is employed "for casting out an evil spirit," i.e. to free a demoniac from possession, and that, besides the "seven leaves of a date palm that never bore fruit," the individual working this procedure should collect "seven splinters of the osier,"[39] the latter being a relatively small willow found mainly in wetlands. Otherwise, Selig maintains the associated Divine Name construct to be אה, which he noted is vocalised "*Aha*," and regarding its origins, the only difference is his claim that the letter ה (*Heh*) was derived from the term הבו (*havu* [listed "*habre*" in the English translation]) in the second instead of the first verse.[40]

    As one might expect by now, a variant to this procedure is shared in another recension of the "*Shimmush Tehillim*," which is employed to free an individual who "has a spirit that dwells."[41] The instructions are virtually the same as listed in the previous paragraphs, but the following brief prayer-incantation is included in the procedure:

מלכי ואלהי בך חסיתי כי תעזרני ותרפאני ותסר

הרוח אשר חונה עלי בשם יָה יְהו

Transliteration:

> *Mal'ki vellohai b'cha chasiti ki ta'az'reini v'tir'pa'eini*
> *v'taseir haruach asher choneh alai b'shem Yah Y'h[o].*

Translation:

> My King and my God, I have taken refuge in you, for you
> will help me and heal me, and you will remove the spirit
> that is upon me. In the name *Yah Y'h[o]*.

The Psalm and said prayer-incantation should be recited three
times in the morning and three times at night. Here it is not the pot
with the willow rods and palm leaves soaked in water which is
placed under the stars, but the individual who is working the
procedure who "should rest in a place where the stars can be seen."
The next morning the Psalm should be recited three more times,
and the water imbibed by the afflicted individual.[42]

It should be noted that there is more to the association of
the twenty-ninth Psalm with water. We are told that reciting this
Psalm ten times in the evening, will afford "protection against
trouble at sea or on land."[43] *Psalm 29* is also employed in
conjunction with the Divine Name אדירירון (*Adiriron* or
Adir'yaron), which is said to mean "the Mighty One sings,"[44] for
the purpose of calming a stormy sea. In this regard, the recitation
of the Psalm is concluded by enunciating the said Divine Name.
This is done ten times.[45] The twenty-ninth Psalm is further aligned
with the Divine/Angelic Name אכתריאל (*Achatri'el*), referencing
the unique "Spirit Intelligence," whom I noted elsewhere is "the
leader of the first 'Angelic Host' in charge of the 'Element of
Water'."[45] We are informed that the central "power" of *Achatri'el*
and his angelic host is "the great Name *Vuho'u* (והו),"[46] which is
the first tri-letter portion of the "*Shem Vayisa Vayet*," and which is
noted to incorporate within itself:[47]

1.   the potency of עזא (*Aza* [perhaps "Mighty One"]), who is
        the ruler over water;
2.   the combined strength of the entire angelic camp
        overseeing Water, of which אכתריאל (*Achatri'el*) is the
        leader.

3.   the might of מטטרון (*Metatron*), the Prince of the Face; and

4.   the power of the Holy Names which are said to be engraved on the "Throne of Glory," of which the first eighteen triplets of the "Name of Seventy-two Names" are listed with a set of vowels, regarding which I was told the following enunciations are correct:

וֵהוּ (*VaHeiVo*), יְלִי (*YeLeYa*), סִיַת (*SoYaTa*), עָלֶם (*AL'Mo*), מֹהֶשׁ (*MoHeSh'*), לְלָהּ (*L'LoHa*), אָכָא (*ECha'A*), כָהַת (*K'HaTu*), הֵזִי (*HiZaYa*), אָלָד (*ALaDa*), לְאָו (*L'AVa*), הֲהֶע (*HaHe'E*), יְזָל (*YaZaLe*), מָבָה (*MaV'He*), הָרִי (*HaRaYa*), הָקֶם (*HaKiMa*), לְאָו (*L'UVa*), and כָלִי (*KaLiY'*).

In order to align oneself with the power of אכתריאל (*Achatri'el*), we are instructed to recite *Psalm 29* six times.[48] However, as I noted before, "whilst this is the standard procedure," I was taught to work this action "with the prefix אכתריאל יה (*Achatri'el Yah*) added to the Ineffable Name, wherever the latter Divine Name appears in the said Psalm."[49]

    Be that as it may, the twenty-ninth Psalm is also employed in conjunction with a special adjuration to the "Princes of the Cup," to ascertain the identity of a thief. In this regard, the procedure necessitates the services "of two boys who have not encountered a pollution," in front of whom the magical procedure is to be executed, and who will submerge themselves in water prior to the enunciation of the adjuration.[50] The practitioner is instructed to take sesame oil with which to anoint a cup "from inside and from outside," as well as along the edge. Following this, a wax candle is lit and stuck "to the edge of the cup in front of the boys."[51] Further instruction has it that the practitioner "shall place the cup on a dish and turn it on its mouth towards the sun," following which he should recite *Psalm 29*, and then enunciate the following adjuration nine or more times:

אשבענא עליכון שרי כוס הממונים על הכוס בעלאה
ותתאה ובכל מיני משתיא בשם הוי״ה [יְהֹוָה] ברוך
הוא ובשם עשר ספירות בשם **אגף נגף שגף אגף**
מגף שחף אגף נגף שחף שתראוני מי גנב הגניבה של
[....name of victim....] כשם שאתם אמתיים כן תשיבונו
ותראונו ראייה אמתית

Transliteration:

> *Ash'ba'ana aleichon sarei kos ham'munim al hakos*
> *b'ila'ah v'tata'ah uv'chol minei mash'taya b'sheim*
> *Havayah [YHVH] baruch hu uv'sheim eser s'firot b'sheim*
> *Agaf Nagaf Shagaf Agaf Magaf Shachaf Agaf Nagaf*
> *Shachaf shetir'uni mi ganav hag'neivah shel [....name of*
> *victim....] k'sheim she'atem amitiyim kein t'shivuni*
> *v'tir'uni r'iyah amitit.*

Translation:

> I adjure you princes of the cup who are appointed on the
> cup above and below, and in all kinds of drinks, in the
> name of *YHVH*, blessed be He, and in the name of the ten
> *Sefirot*, in the name of *Agaf Nagaf Shagaf Agaf Magaf*
> *Shachaf Agaf Nagaf Shachaf*, that you shall show me who
> has stolen the stolen object from [....name of victim....]. As
> you are true so you shall answer us, and show us a true
> showing.[52]

I have observed the current Psalm being endorsed for diseases and
healing in general, and it has been noted to be particularly good to
counteract sea-sickness. It has been suggested that the use of this
Psalm in expelling evil spirits, includes the expulsion of bad or
dark moods. The twenty-ninth Psalm has been further proposed
against all manner of tribulation; for protection in perilous
situations; and to support those who are dealing with spiritual
troubles, as well as with internal desolation. The current Psalm is
also recited to ensure a happy old age and retirement, as well as to
realise the awesomeness of the Divine One.

As far as the use of *Psalm 29* in Christian magic is
concerned, we find it recommended in Byzantine magical
manuscripts for an individual who has "an evil demon in his
house." In this regard, he or she is instructed to recite the Psalm for

seven days, which is said will cause the malevolent force to flee.[53] However, the same manuscripts also maintain that *Psalm 29* is good "for dispelling magic and the like," and thus to ensure that "the sorcerer or magician will not be able to do you harm," the practitioner should recite the current Psalm seven times.[54] It is further maintained that if you should find yourself "surrounded by your enemies," reciting the Psalm in this manner, will place them "at your mercy," and ensure that "they will not be able to harm you."[55] Otherwise, we are informed that the twenty-ninth Psalm is good to use against blasphemy.[56]

The Syrian magical manuscript in the Sachau Collection, suggests that individuals read *Psalm 29* and anoint themselves with it "for the sake of an (evil) spirit,"[57] perhaps to heal their own distressed spirits. Be that as it may, this Psalm is listed in the Christian *"Le Livre d'Or"* for healing purposes. In this regard, the procedure involves the Psalm being recited into "the ear of a sick man" whilst he is imbibing barley beer, which is said will result in his recovery.[58] It is further noted, that writing down the Psalm in conjunction with a set of magical characters, which is afterwards fumigated with nutmeg, and then buried "in the corners of a house," will ensure that the occupants "will enjoy great blessings from it."[59]

In conclusion, as mentioned before, *Psalm 29* is listed the fourth amongst a set of eight Psalms recited during the construction of "pentacles" in the *"Key of Solomon."* The others are *Psalms 8, 21, 27, 32, 51, 72* and *134.*[60]

Psalm 30

[1] מזמור שיר חנכת הבית לדוד

[2] ארוממך יהוה‏אדני‏אהדונהי כי דליתני ולא שמחת
איבי לי

[3] יהוה‏אדני‏אהדונהי אלהי שועתי אליך ותרפאני

[4] יהוה‏אדני‏אהדונהי העלית מן שאול נפשי חייתני
מירדי בור

[5] זמרו ליהוה‏אדני‏אהדונהי חסידיו והודו לזכר
קדשו

[6] כי רגע באפו חיים ברצונו בערב ילין בכי
ולבקר רנה

[7] ואני אמרתי בשלוי בל אמוט לעולם

[8] יהוה‏אדני‏אהדונהי ברצונך העמדתה להררי עז
הסתרת פניך הייתי נבהל

[9] אליך יהוה‏אדני‏אהדונהי אקרא ואל אדני אתחנן

[10] מה בצע בדמי ברדתי אל שחת היודך עפר
היגיד אמתך

[11] שמע יהוה‏אדני‏אהדונהי וחנני יהוה‏אדני‏אהדונהי
היה עזר לי

[12] הפכת מספדי למחול לי פתחת שקי ותאזרני
שמחה

[13] למען יזמרך כבוד ולא ידם יהוה‏אדני‏אהדונהי
אלהי לעולם אודך

Transliteration:

[1] *miz'mor shir chanukat habayit l'david*

[2] *aromim'cha YHVH ki dilitani v'lo simach'ta oy'vai li*

[3] *YHVH elohai shiva'ti eilecha vatir'pa'eini*

[4] *YHVH he'elita min sh'ol naf'shi chiyitani miyor'di vor*

[5] *zam'ru la'YHVH chasidav v'hodu l'zeicher kod'sho*

[6] *ki rega b'apo chayim bir'tzono ba'erev yalin bechi v'laboker rinah*

[7] *va'ani amar'ti v'shal'vi bal emot l'olam*

[8] *YHVH bir'tzon'cha he'emad'tah l'har'ri oz his'tar'ta fanecha hayiti niv'hal*

[9] *eilecha YHVH ek'ra v'el adonai et'chanan*

[10] *ma betza b'dami b'rid'ti el shachat hayod'cha afar hayagid amitecha*

[11] *sh'ma YHVH v'choneini YHVH he'yeih ozeir li*

[12] *hafach'tah mis'p'di l'machol li pitach'ta saki vat'az'reini sim'chah*

[13] *l'ma'an y'zamer'cha chavod v'lo yidom YHVH elohai l'olam odeka*

Translation:

[1] A Psalm; a Song at the Dedication of the House; of David.

[2] I will extol thee *YHVH*, for Thou hast raised me up, and hast not suffered mine enemies to rejoice over me.

[3] *YHVH* my God, I cried unto Thee, and Thou didst heal me;

[4] *YHVH*, Thou broughtest up my soul from the nether-world; Thou didst keep me alive, that I should not go down to the pit.

[5] Sing praise unto *YHVH*, O ye His godly ones, and give thanks to His holy name.

[6] For His anger is but for a moment, His favour is for a life-time; weeping may tarry for the night, but joy cometh in the morning.

[7] Now I had said in my security: 'I shall never be moved.'

[8] Thou hadst established *YHVH*, in Thy favour my mountain as a stronghold—Thou didst hide Thy face; I was affrighted.

[9] Unto Thee *YHVH*, did I call, and unto *Adonai* I made supplication:

[10] 'What profit is there in my blood, when I go down to the pit? Shall the dust praise Thee? shall it declare Thy truth?

[11] Hear *YHVH*, and be gracious unto me; *YHVH*, be Thou my helper.'

[12] Thou didst turn for me my mourning into dancing; Thou didst loose my sackcloth, and gird me with gladness;

[13] So that my glory may sing praise to Thee, and not be silent; *YHVH* my God, I will give thanks unto Thee for ever.

Psalm 30 was at first enunciated by Sefardic communities over חנוכה (*Chanukah*), the eight day "Festival of Lights" when Jews everywhere commemorate the rededication of the second Temple in Jerusalem.[1] Whilst it is difficult to ascertain exactly when the Psalm entered the daily liturgy, it appears to have featured initially in the Sefardic and Yemenite *Siddurim* (Prayer Books) "where it was included in the Sabbath prayer only."[2] In fact, it would seem the thirtieth Psalm was introduced into the morning service by kabbalists,[3] whom we are told "revealed some of the hidden aspects and meanings of the Psalm."[4] In this regard, we are told that the thirtieth Psalm comprises "thirteen verses aligned with thirteen מכילן דרחמי (*Mechilan d'Rachamei*—Qualities of Mercy), and thirteen *Middot* (Virtues)."[5]

We are further informed that commencing at the first appearance of the Ineffable Name in the Psalm, and counting from thence to the conclusion of the Psalm, there are ninety-one words which correspond with the conjoint *Gematria* of the Ineffable Name [י = 10 + ה = 5 + ו = 6 + ה = 5 = 26] and the Divine Name אדני (*Adonai*) [א = 1 + ד = 4 + נ = 50 + י = 10 = 65]."[6] As it is, both of these Divine Names feature in the Psalm, the Ineffable Name nine times, and the Name אדני (*Adonai*) once, and these ten appearances of the Name of the Eternal One are said to align with the Ten Commandments,[7] and equally with the ten *Sefirot*. In this regard, we are informed that *Psalm 30* "has nine *Havayot* (Essences or Modes of Being), and one Lord [*Adonai*] of ten mountains."[8] Otherwise, it appears that it was from the Kabbalistic order of prayers, i.e. the *Nusach Ari*, that the current Psalm was eventually included into other prayer books,[9] and that from about the seventeenth century it has became customary to recite it every day prior to פסוקי דזמרא (*Pesukei d'Zimra*—"Verses of Song") comprising the second section of the morning service.[10]

As far as its use in Jewish Magic is concerned, *Psalm 30* is generally employed against "every bad thing," or as a protection against evil.[11] The current Psalm is listed in the "*Shimmush Tehillim*" as useful against all manner of evil, when employed in conjunction with the Divine Name אל, the latter said to be a Divine Name construct derived: א (*Alef*) from ארוממך (*aromim'cha*—"I will extol thee"): verse 2; and ל (*Lamed*) from

לְמַעַן יְזַמֶּרְךָ (*l'ma'an y'zamer'cha*—"may sing praise to Thee"): verse 13.[12]

Psalm 30 is also said to be good for health and healing, and hence we find in one recension of the "*Shimmush Tehillim*" the Psalm listed for the said purpose, and the recitation succeeded by the statement:[13]

רפאם וחזקם כאשר רפאת הזקיהו מלך יהודה
מחליו רפאם בשם הגדול מהש

Transliteration:

....*r'fa'eim v'chaz'keim ka'asher rafata chiz'kiyahu melech y'hudah meichol'yo r'fa'eim b'sheim hagadol Mahash.*

Translation:

....heal and strengthen, as you healed Hezekiah king of Judah from his illness, so heal with the great name *Mahash*.

In terms of the restoration of health, it should be noted that the following Divine Name construct derived from *Psalm 30:3–4*, is employed in an amulet for healing:[14]

אמי   הנש   ושפ   האן   יול
עהי   והנ   שעת   ילי   היי   לתח
כאב   יני   ליד   איר   יהי   תומ
            תרר   ופו

The Divine Name construct was formulated by dividing the fifty-seven letters of the said verses into three nineteen tri-letter combinations. The first nineteen letters comprise the capitals of the nineteen tri-letter combinations of the Divine Name construct; the second nineteen written in reverse, encompass the central glyphs; and the concluding nineteen glyphs include the third letters in the set written in the standard manner from right to left.[15]

Regarding the earlier mentioned protection against evil, it is worth noting that *Psalm 30:12* was written in reverse in order to create the following Divine Name construct, which is considered unique in expelling an evil spirit:[16]

יקש   ינרזאתו   ההמש

תחתפ יל לוחמל ידפסמ

תכפה

In one recension of the "*Shimmush Tehillim*" we find the thirtieth Psalm employed for the purpose of being saved from a different kind of "evil," i.e. nightmares.[17] In this regard, the practitioner is instructed to fast before retiring to sleep. On waking in the morning he/she should recite the Psalm twenty-one times in conjunction with the following prayer-incantation:[18]

יהי רצון מלפניך שומע תפילות שישמע תפלתי

וצעקתי וירחם עלי ויושיעני ויצילני מחלום רע

Transliteration:

> *Y'hi ratzon mil'fanecha shomei'a t'filot sheyish'ma t'filati v'tza'akati virachem alai v'yoshi'eini v'yatzileini meichalom ra.*

Translation:

> May it be your will, Hearer of Prayers that you may hear my prayer and my cry, and have mercy on me, and deliver me and rescue me from a bad dream.

Whilst the instructions are somewhat confusing, it would seem that in the case of a good dream, the practitioner should recite the thirtieth Psalm, and conclude with:[19]

חזקהו וקיימהו כאשר קיימת חלומות יוסף בן יעקב

Transliteration:

> *....chaz'keihu v'kayameihu ka'asher kiyam'ta chalomot Yoseif ben Ya'akov.*

Translation:

> ....empower and sustain it, as the dreams of Josef son of Jacob were sustained.

The twenty-five glyphs comprising *Psalm 30:12* were also divided into three groups, and then written forwards and backwards, in the manner delineated in terms of a previously mentioned Divine Name construct. In the current instance, the same technique is applied in order to formulate the eight tri-letter combinations in the following Divine Name construct, which is employed to ensure that a prayer is heard when an individual seeks a favourable outcome in a request for benefaction from someone:[20]

$$\text{יִיע} \quad \text{עהה} \quad \text{מַוְיָ} \quad \text{שְׁהֶהּ}$$
$$\text{וְחָלִי} \quad \text{הֶנֶר} \quad \text{וְנֶוָ} \quad \text{הִיו}$$

In employing this Divine Name construct, you have to be purified first, and then pray the *Amidah* prayer with the congregation or community, i.e. in the synagogue. When you get to the blessing commencing with the phrase "Hear our voice Lord our God," focus your mind on your personal prayer-request. Following the conclusion of the *Amidah*, recite the Divine Name construct, then conclude the procedure with the following prayer-incantation:[21]

יהי רצון מלפניך יהוה למענך ולמען שמותיך
[....name of recipient...] אלה שתעזרני היום ותן בלב
עלי חן וחסד ורחמים לתת את שאלתי ובקשתי
ועזרני עליו ואל יענה עלי בדבר הזה ובכל מה
שאני מבקש ממנו וקשור פיו מלדבר רע לפני
חניאל חסדיאל רחמיאל אהביאל היו עמי ועזרוני
בשאלתי זאת שאשאל היום ותצליח בעזרת האל
וישועתו

Transliteration:

> *Y'hi ratzon mil'fanecha YHVH l'ma'an'cha ul'ma'an sh'motecha eileh sheta'az'reini hayom v'tein b'lev [....name of recipient...] alai chen v'chesed v'rachamim lateit et she'elati uvakashati v'az'reini alav v'al ya'aneh alai bid'var hazeh uv'chol mah she'ani m'vakeish mimenu uk'shor pif mil'daber ra l'fanai chani'el chasdi'el rach'mi'el ahavi'el hayu imi v'az'runi b'she'eilati zot she'esh'al hayom v'tatz'liach b'ez'rat ha'el vishu'ato*

Translation:

> May it be your will *YHVH* for your sake, and for the sake
> of these your names, that you should help me today by
> placing in the heart of [....name of recipient...] grace, mercy
> and compassion for me, to grant me my request, and to aid
> me with him that he may not spurn me on this matter, and
> on whatever I may request from him, and may you bind his
> mouth from speaking ill of me. *Chani'el Chasdi'el
> Rach'mi'el Ahavi'el* be with me in this request I will
> petition today, and will succeed with the help of the Divine
> One and His salvation.

It is important to note that this magical procedure is specifically
written for observant Jewish religionists, and, whilst it might be
uncomfortable for some readers to hear this, it is the sincerity of
the believer which affirms the validity of the profound Jewish
religious sentiments expressed in the *Amidah* prayer. Hence this
procedure will not work for those to whom the sacred principles
honoured by the Jewish worshipper are meaningless, or cannot be
acknowledged, and thus hold no value in their daily lives. That
being said, there are related procedures found throughout this
tome, which can be applied by all who approach this remarkable
Tradition with honesty of heart, sincerity of soul, and ultimately
with respect.

Returning to the magical uses of single verses, it is worth
noting that the initials of the words comprising the opening phrase
of *Psalm 30:11*, reading וחנני יהוה שמע (*sh'ma YHVH
v'choneini*—"Hear *YHVH*, and be gracious unto me*"), are
combined in the Divine Name construct שיו which is employed in
amulets as a call for help.[22] Elsewhere we find the capitals of the
eight words comprising *Psalm 30:4*, with an additional ה (*Heh*)
prefix to the word שאול (*Sh'ol*—"nether-world"), thus avoiding
any direct reference to the realm of, as it were, "outer darkness,"
were combined into the Divine Name construct יהמהנחמב,
which is included in amulets "for life" and "for mental illness."[23]
Otherwise, what remains to be said is that מחי (*Machi*), the sixty-
fourth tri-letter portion of the "*Shem Vayisa Vayet*," is directly
aligned with *Psalm 30:11*.[24]

Be that as it may, *Psalm 30* is often recited for the purpose of being saved from difficulties, as well as for protection in perilous situations and in times of trouble. It is also employed against all bad things and circumstances, and is enunciated against enemies, hatred, malice, threats, and also against betrayal and treachery. It is especially used against religious persecution in foreign lands. Otherwise, this Psalm is recited to diminish poverty, and to counteract depression and sadness. On a more positive note, it is recited against vanity, to strengthen will and a love of study. In conclusion, the thirtieth Psalm is suggested to women to recite before they have a union with their husbands, and, as in the case of the previous Psalm, the current one is recommended for enunciation to ensure a good old age and a happy retirement.

Similarly to the previous Psalm, the current one is recommended in the Christian *"Le Livre d'Or"* for an individual who is suffering serious illness. In this regard, the suggestion is to recite the thirtieth Psalm seven times over "pure water," which is afterwards employed for washing the person of the afflicted. Following this action, the Psalm should be enunciated a further seven times over "good oil," in which a set of magical characters are to be washed, and the sufferer anointed therewith.[25] Elsewhere we find *Psalm 30:3–4* recommended "against a malevolent fever.[26]

Dealing with affliction of a different sort, the earlier mentioned Syrian magical manuscript in the Sachau Collection notes that reading *Psalm 30* will drive away evil,[27] and that it should be read three times and written down for an individual who is demon possessed. In this regard, the instruction is to read the Psalm over olive oil, and then to anoint the entire body of the demoniac.[28] The same text recommends the recitation of the Psalm at bedtime, doing so in the name of a child and his/her mother, in order to encourage the child to advance in his/her education.[29]

In conclusion it should be noted that in the *"Key of Solomon"* the thirtieth Psalm is listed amongst the set of Psalms recited whilst robing after taking a ritual bath. The others are *Psalms 4, 51, 102, 114, 119:97, 126,* and *139.*[30]

Psalm 31

[1] למנצח מזמור לדוד

[2] בך יהוהאדניאהדונהי חסיתי אל אבושה לעולם
בצדקתך פלטני

[3] הטה אלי אזנך מהרה הצילני היה לי לצור
מעוז לבית מצודות להושיעני

[4] כי סלעי ומצודתי אתה ולמען שמך תנחני ותנהלני

[5] תוציאני מרשת זו טמנו לי כי אתה מעוזי

[6] בידך אפקיד רוחי פדית אותי יהוהאדניאהדונהי
אל אמת

[7] שנאתי השמרים הבלי שוא ואני אל יהוהאדניאהדונהי
בטחתי

[8] אגילה ואשמחה בחסדך אשר ראית את עניי ידעת
בצרות נפשי

[9] ולא הסגרתני ביד אויב העמדת במרחב רגלי

[10] חנני יהוהאדניאהדונהי כי צר לי עששה בכעס עיני
נפשי ובטני

[11] כי כלו ביגון חיי ושנותי באנחה כשל בעוני כחי
ועצמי עששו

[12] מכל צררי הייתי חרפה ולשכני מאד ופחד למידעי
ראי בחוץ נדדו ממני

[13] נשכחתי כמת מלב הייתי ככלי אבד

[14] כי שמעתי דבת רבים מגור מסביב בהוסדם יחד
עלי לקחת נפשי זממו

[15] ואני עליך בטחתי יהוהאדניאהדונהי אמרתי אלהי אתה

[16] בידך עתתי הצילני מיד אויבי ומרדפי

[17] האירה פניך על עבדך הושיעני בחסדך

[18] יהוהאדניאהדונהי אל אבושה כי קראתיך יבשו
רשעים ידמו לשאול

[19] תאלמנה שפתי שקר הדברות על צדיק עתק בגאוה
ובוז

[20] מה רב טובך אשר צפנת ליראיך פעלת לחסים בך
נגד בני אדם

[21] תסתירם בסתר פניך מרכסי איש תצפנם בסכה
מריב לשנות

[22] ברוך יהוה‎אהדונהי כי הפליא חסדו לי בעור
מצור

[23] ואני אמרתי בחפזי נגרזתי מנגד עיניך אכן שמעת
קול תחנוני בשועי אליך

[24] אהבו את יהוה‎אהדונהי כל חסידיו אמונים נצר
יהוה‎אהדונהי ומשלם על יתר עשה גאוה

[25] חזקו ויאמץ לבבכם כל המיחלים ליהוה‎אהדונהי

Transliteration:

[1] *lam'natzei'ach miz'mor l'david*

[2] *b'cha YHVH chasiti al evoshah l'olam b'tzid'kat'cha fal'teini*

[3] *hateih eilai oz'necha m'heirah hatzileini heyeih li l'tzur ma'oz l'veit m'tzudot l'hoshi'eini*

[4] *ki sal'i um'tzudati atah ul'ma'an shim'cha tan'cheini ut'nahaleini*

[5] *totzi'eini m'reishet zu tam'nu li ki atah ma'uzi*

[6] *b'yad'cha af'kid ruchi padita oti YHVH el emet*

[7] *saneiti hashom'rim hav'lei shav va'ani el YHVH batach'ti*

[8] *agilah v'es'm'cha b'chas'decha asher ra'ita et on'yi yada'ta b'tzarot nafshi*

[9] *v'lo his'gar'tani b'yad oyeiv he'emad'ta vamer'chav rag'lai*

[10] *choneini YHVH ki tzar li ash'shah v'cha'as eini naf'shi uvit'ni*

[11] *ki chalu v'yagon chayai ush'notai ba'anachah kashal ba'avoni chochi va'atzamai asheishu*

[12] *mikol tzor'rai hayiti cher'pah v'lish'cheinai m'od ufachad lim'yuda'ai ro'ai bachutz nad'du mimeni*

[13] *nish'kach'ti k'meit mileiv hayiti kich'li oveid*

[14] *ki shama'ti dibat rabim magor misaviv b'hivas'dam yachad alai lakachat naf'shi zamamu*

[15] *va'ani alecha vatach'ti YHVH amar'ti elohai atah*

[16] *b'yad'cha itotai hatzileini miyad oy'vai umeirod'fai*

[17] *ha'ira fanecha al av'decha hoshi'eini v'chas'decha*

[18] *YHVH al eivoshah ki k'raticha yeivoshu r'sha'im yid'mu lish'ol*

[19] *tei'alam'na sif'tei shaker hadov'rot al tzadik atak b'ga'avah vavuz*

[20] *mah rav tuv'cha asher tzafan'ta lirei'echa pa'al'ta lachosim bach neged b'nei adam*

[21] *tas'tireim b'seter panecha meiruch'sei ish titz'p'neim b'sukah meiriv l'shonot*

[22] *baruch YHVH ki hif'li chas'do li b'ir matzor*

[23] *va'ani amarti v'chof'zi nig'raz'ti mineged einecha achein shama'ta kol tachanunai b'shav'i eilecha*

[24] *ehevu et YHVH kol chasidav emunim notzeir YHVH um'shaleim al yeter oseih ga'avah*

[25] *chiz'ku v'ya'ameitz l'vav'chem kol ham'yachalim la YHVH*

Translation:

[1] For the Leader. A Psalm of David.

[2] In thee *YHVH*, have I taken refuge; let me never be ashamed; deliver me in Thy righteousness.

[3] Incline Thine ear unto me, deliver me speedily; be Thou to me a rock of refuge, even a fortress of defence, to save me.

[4] For Thou art my rock and my fortress; therefore for Thy name's sake lead me and guide me.

[5] Bring me forth out of the net that they have hidden for me; for Thou art my stronghold.

[6] Into Thy hand I commit my spirit; Thou hast redeemed me *YHVH*, Thou God of truth.

[7] I hate them that regard lying vanities; but I trust in *YHVH*

[8] I will be glad and rejoice in Thy lovingkindness; for Thou hast seen mine affliction, Thou hast taken cognizance of the troubles of my soul,

[9] And Thou hast not given me over into the hand of the enemy; Thou hast set my feet in a broad place.

[10] Be gracious unto me *YHVH*, for I am in distress; mine eye wasteth away with vexation, yea, my soul and my body.

[11] For my life is spent in sorrow, and my years in sighing; my strength faileth because of mine iniquity, and my bones are wasted away.

[12] Because of all mine adversaries I am become a reproach, yea, unto my neighbours exceedingly, and a dread to mine acquaintance; they that see me without flee from me.

[13] I am forgotten as a dead man out of mind; I am like a useless vessel.

[14] For I have heard the whispering of many, terror on every side; while they took counsel together against me, they devised to take away my life.

[15] But as for me, I have trusted in Thee *YHVH*; I have said: 'Thou art my God.'

[16] My times are in Thy hand; deliver me from the hand of mine enemies, and from them that persecute me.

[17] Make Thy face to shine upon Thy servant; save me in Thy lovingkindness.

[18] *YHVH* let me not be ashamed, for I have called upon Thee; let the wicked be ashamed, let them be put to silence in the nether-world.

[19] Let the lying lips be dumb, which speak arrogantly against the righteous, with pride and contempt.

[20] Oh how abundant is Thy goodness, which Thou hast laid up for them that fear Thee; which Thou hast wrought for them that take their refuge in Thee, in the sight of the sons of men!

[21] Thou hidest them in the covert of Thy presence from the plottings of man; Thou concealest them in a pavilion from the strife of tongues.

[22] Blessed be *YHVH*; for He hath shown me His wondrous lovingkindness in an entrenched city.

[23] As for me, I said in my haste: 'I am cut off from before Thine eyes'; nevertheless Thou heardest the voice of my supplications when I cried unto Thee.

[24] O love *YHVH*, all ye His godly ones; *YHVH* preserveth the faithful, and plentifully repayeth him that acteth haughtily.

[25] Be strong, and let your heart take courage, all ye that wait for *YHVH*.

Other than the occasional verses, i.e. the phrase from verse 6 reading "Into Thy hand I commit my spirit" included in the bedtime prayer, and verses 8 to 11 being enunciated when worshippers cover their heads with the טלית (*Talit*—"Prayer Shawl"), *Psalm 31* does not feature in Jewish liturgies.[1] I suspect this is because of the somber nuances and tragedy expressed in this Psalm. This dark undertone led to verses from the thirty-first *Psalm* being applied in malevolent ways, e.g. *Psalm 31:11* was employed in a most sinister and evil manner to bring conflict, and provoke a separation between individuals; etc. Thus, whilst it is my intention to share the magical uses of Psalms in a fairly comprehensive and definitive manner, abhorrent procedures meant to engender hate and discord have no place in this study.

The thirty-first Psalm is generally recommended as a protection against the Evil Eye.[2] In this regard, my Jewish readers might note that the recitation of *Psalm 31* whilst wearing the "*Talit Katan*," i.e. the fringed shirtlike-garment traditionally worn by religious Jewish males under (or over) their clothing, is equally recommended as a magical virtue (*segulah*) for protection against the Evil Eye. In this case, it was suggested that the enunciation of the current Psalm should be conjoined with the well-known "Priestly Blessing," reading:

יברכך יהוה וישמרך
יאר יהוה פניו אליך ויחנך
יסע יהוה פניו אליך וישם לך שלום

Transliteration:
> *Y'varech'cha YHVH v'yishm'recha*
> *Ya'eir YHVH panav eilecha vichuneka*
> *Yisa YHVH panav eilecha v'yasem l'cha shalom*

Translation:
> *YHVH* bless thee, and keep thee,
> *YHVH* make His face to shine upon thee, and be gracious unto thee,
> *YHVH* lift up His countenance upon thee, and give thee peace.[3]

As in the case of *Psalm 29*, the magical use of *Psalm 31* is not listed in some of the published versions of the "*Shimmush*

Tehillim." However, where it is included, it is noted as useful against the Evil Eye when whispered over olive oil whilst focusing on the associated Divine Name construct יָה (*Yah*), which is said to have been derived: י (*Yod*) from בצדקתך פלטני (*b'tzid'kat'cha fal'teini*—"deliver me in Thy righteousness"): verse 2, and ה (*Heh*) from המיחלים ליהוה (*ham'yachalim la YHVH*—"all ye that wait for *YHVH*"): verse 25.[4] The same Divine Name construct is included in Godfrey Selig's German/English version of the "*Shimmush Tehillim,*" though he got the scriptural derivations of the letters somewhat mixed up. In this instance, there is no direct reference to the Psalm being employed to avert the Evil Eye *per se*. Instead Selig wrote "would you escape slanders, and are you desirous that evil tongues may do you no harm or cause you vexation, repeat this Psalm in a low voice, with commendable devotion, over a small quantity of pure olive oil, and anoint your face and hands with it in the name of *Jah*."[5]

Those who would be concerned with the "Evil Eye" surfacing in certain situations, might consider the following Divine Name construct and procedure. In this instance the letters comprising *Psalm 31:21* are conjoined in a Divine Name construct reading:[6]

תשסי   תאיי   רסמך   ברסם

תכרי   פנתת   צופן   נשמל

בבסי   כרהם

This Divine Name was created by dividing the forty letters comprising the said verse into two unequal portions, i.e. twenty-two letters in the first portion, and eighteen in the second. Each of these are in turn split into two equal portions. Hence there are four portions, the first and second of which comprise eleven letters each, whilst the third and fourth are respectively composed of nine letters. From these four sections the Divine Name construct was composed by conjoining the first and second parts, i.e. the first letter of the first part with the concluding letter of the second part, etc. The same, as it were, skipping method was applied in formulating the concluding eighteen letters from the third and fourth portions. Afterwards the forty glyphs were divided into ten four-letter combinations, and thus we have this remarkable Divine Name construct which is recited in conjunction with the said verse, in order "to see and not be seen," i.e. to be able to witness anything whilst being personally invisible.[7]

Whilst addressing the use of the current Psalm to avert the "Evil Eye" and silence the "Evil Tongue," it should be noted that the thirty-seven letters comprising *Psalm 31:19*, the latter reading

תֵּאָלַמְנָה שִׂפְתֵי שָׁקֶר הַדֹּבְרוֹת עַל צַדִּיק עָתָק בְּגַאֲוָה וָבוּז

(*t'alam'na sif'tei shaker ha'dov'rot al tzadik atak b'ga'ava vavuz* —"let the lying lips be dumb, which speak arrogantly against the righteous, with pride and contempt"), were formulated into the following Divine Name construct for the purpose of binding the tongue of an individual from speaking evil:[8]

תֵּיק אָדְעָ לַצֶתָ מֶלְק
נָעַב הֵתַג שׁוֹא פֶּרְן
תֵּבְה יֵדְן שָׁהַב קֶרוּז

Whilst we are addressing the tethering of the unbridled "spirit of evil" emanating from the tongue of a slanderer, it is worth noting that the capitals of the nine words comprising the same verse are conjoined in the Divine Name construct תֵּשְׁשָׁהַ עַצַעָעְבַן (vocalised *Teisishaha Atza'av'va*), which is said to have the power to adjure all the well-known angels for the purpose of keeping a "spirit" from causing injury when it exists the body of an individual it occupied.[9]

One recension of the "*Shimmush Tehillim*" includes a variant use of *Psalm 31*, in which it is enunciated for the purpose of being saved from imprisonment, and to escape from it when already captured. In this regard, those who find themselves in this dire situation are instructed to recite the Psalm every morning, followed by the following prayer-incantation. The latter includes a Divine Name which I have not seen listed anywhere else:[10]

צוּר אֱלֹהֵי עוֹלָם חָסִיתִי בָךְ מִיַּד כָּל אוֹיְבַי הַצִּילֵנִי
וּמִכָּל רַע תִּנְצְרֵנִי וְרַחֲמֶיךָ וַחֲסָדֶיךָ תָּמִיד יִנְצְרוּנִי

יסובבוני ותשמרני מכל תפיסה רעה ומכל דברים
רעים ואם בעונותי אכשל ואהיה נמאס ביד אכזר
רחמיך וחסדיך ישמרוני בעת צרה ותוציאני מאפילה
לאורה ומצרה לרוחה ותוריני עם כל אסירי ישראל
בשם הטהור והקדוש יְדָוִי

Transliteration:

> *Tzur Elohei olam chasiti vach miyad kol oy'vai hatzileini umikol ra tin'tz'reini v'rachamecha v'chasadecha tamid yin'tz'runi y'sovavuni v'tish'm'runi michol t'fisah ra'ah umikol d'varim ra'im v'im ba'avonotai ikashel v'eh'yeh nim'as b'yad ach'zar rachamecha v'chasadecha yish'm'runi b'eit tzarah v'totzi'eini mei'afeilah l'orah umitzarah lir'v'chah v'toreini im kol asirei yis'ra'eil b'shem hatahor v'hakadosh Yidavi.*

Translation:

> Rock, Eternal God, I have taken refuge in you. Deliver me from the hand of all my enemies, and preserve me from all evil, and your mercy and your kindness will always preserve me, surround me, and protect me from every terrible imprisonment, and from all evil things. If I stumble with my transgressions, and be persecuted by the hand of the cruel, your mercy and your kindness will always protect me in the time of trouble. You will lead me out of darkness into light, and out of need to prosperity. You shall enlighten me with all the captives of Israel, with the pure and holy name *Yidavi*.

Several of the verses of the current Psalm are equally employed for other purposes in Jewish Magic. In this regard, the capitals of the words comprising the opening phrase of *Psalm 31:4*, are conjoined in the Divine Name construct בסוא, which is employed in amulets for life and rescue.[11] It should be obvious to everyone that the principles of "life" and "rescue" naturally include the processes of digestion and defecation. In this regard, the initials of the five words comprising the concluding phrase of *Psalm 31:10*, reading עששה בכעס עיני נפשי ובטני [*ash'sha v'cha'as eini naf'shi uvit'ni*—"mine eye wasteth away with vexation, yea, my soul and

my body"], are combined in the Divine Name construct עבעוב,
which is included in amulets for ailments associated with the
digestive tract,[12] e.g. indigestion, constipation, food poisoning,
diarrhea, etc. I can personally vouch for the efficacy of not only
this amulet, but of reciting the entire verse when experiencing the
discomfort of disorders in the digestive system. Other than this, the
capitals of the concluding five words of *Psalm 31:11* are combined
in the Divine Name construct כבבוע, which is employed in an
amulet for weakness and bone disease,[13] and the initials of the
opening three words of *Psalm 31:13* are conjoined in the Divine
Name construct נכם, which is included in amulets for heart
ailments.[14] It is also worth noting that *Psalm 31:15* is directly
affiliated with לכב (*Lekav*), the thirty-first portion of the "*Shem
Vayisa Vayet.*"[15]

Psalm 31 is one of the most used in my personal "spiritual
pharmacopeia," and much of the best applications of this Psalm are
found in "magical recipes" shared in person by elderly Jewish
ladies and gentlemen, who grew up with the magical uses of sacred
writ being their "staple spiritual diet," so to speak, rather than
relying exclusively on magical practices shared in official
publications. Of course, I fully acknowledge the invaluable
material shared in the published magical records, whilst also
sharing the folk customs of our forebears. That being said, it is
worth noting that the current Psalm is equally employed against
illness in general as well as to facilitate healing. It has been
recommended for those who suffer from rheumatism, and, believe
it or not, against bites of any kind. In this regard I witnessed many
years ago an elderly Jewish lady taking some hair from a dog who
bit her grandchild, and, whilst reciting *Psalm 31*, she lightly
touched the wound with the hair. I recall my horror at the thought
of that unhygienic substance touching the skin of the child, but the
rather rapid healing put paid to my fears.

Being a devotee of "Practical Kabbalah" for nearly fifty
years, and having dedicated myself to sharing as much of this
remarkable Tradition as far as possible from primary perspectives,
I have found the recommendation of the thirty-first Psalm to
encourage the love of study; for the revelation and certitude of
"secret things"; as well as to counteract fatigue, to be very useful

indeed. What is more, the current Psalm offers protection in perilous situations and in times of trouble; protection against floods; all troubles and distress; and against harm in general. It is also recited against witchcraft and bewitchment; as well as to alleviate anxiety caused by enemies. We are further informed that *Psalm 31* is good to be recited by a man for a marriage; to ensure sustenance when the weather is unsuitable for agriculture; to alleviate personal rage; for penitence; and to find peace of soul.

As far as its use in Christian Magic is concerned, the oft-mentioned Byzantine manuscripts recommend the recitation of the thirty-first Psalm from the first verse to the conclusion of the opening phrase in verse ten, reading "Be gracious unto me *YHVH*, for I am in distress." No purpose is listed in this instance, but perhaps the primary intention behind the utterance is the sentiments expressed in the said phrase from the tenth verse.[16] The same verses are recommended in *"Le Livre d'Or"* for the purpose of being freed from imprisonment. In this regard, the said verses are recited twice during the day and once at night, and certain magical characters are written on bread to be consumed by the prisoner, whom we are told "will be freed from prison immediately."[17] Elsewhere in the mentioned Byzantine manuscripts *Psalm 31* is recommended "for a grudge."[18]

In conclusion, *Psalm 31* is listed in the *"Key of Solomon"* as one of seven Psalms employed in the consecration of "the needle and other iron instruments." The others are *Psalms 3, 9, 42, 60, 51,* and *130.*[19]

Psalm 32

[1] לדוד משכיל אשרי נשוי פשע כסוי חטאה

[2] אשרי אדם לא יחשב יהוה‌אדני‌אהדונהי לו עון ואין ברוחו רמיה

[3] כי החרשתי בלו עצמי בשאגתי כל היום

[4] כי יומם ולילה תכבד עלי ידך נהפך לשדי בחרבני קיץ סלה

[5] חטאתי אודיעך ועוני לא כסיתי אמרתי אודה עלי פשעי ליהוה‌אדני‌אהדונהי ואתה נשאת עון חטאתי סלה

[6] על זאת יתפלל כל חסיד אליך לעת מצא רק לשטף מים רבים אליו לא יגיעו

[7] אתה סתר לי מצר תצרני רני פלט תסובבני סלה

[8] אשכילך ואורך בדרך זו תלך איעצה עליך עיני

[9] אל תהיו כסוס כפרד אין הבין במתג ורסן עדיו לבלום בל קרב אליך

[10] רבים מכאובים לרשע והבוטח ביהוה‌אדני‌אהדונהי חסד יסובבנו

[11] שמחו ביהוה‌אדני‌אהדונהי וגילו צדיקים והרנינו כל ישרי לב

Transliteration:

[1] *l'david mas'kil ash'rei n'sui pesha k'sui chata'ah*
[2] *ash'rei adam lo yach'shov YHVH lo avon v'ein b'rucho r'miya*
[3] *ki he'cherash'ti balu atzamai b'sha'agati kol hayom*
[4] *ki yomam valailah tich'bad alai yadecha neh'pach l'shadi b'char'vonei kayitz Selah*
[5] *chatati odi'acha va'avoni lo chisiti amar'ti odeh alei f'sha'ai laYHVH v'atah nasata avon chatati Selah*
[6] *al zot yit'paleil kol chasid eilecha l'eit m'tzo rak l'sheitef mayim rabim eilav lo yagi'u*
[7] *atah seiter li mitzar titz'reini ranei faleit t'sov'veini Selah*

[8] *as 'kil 'cha v 'or 'cha b 'derech zu teileich i 'atzah alecha eini*

[9] *al tih 'yu k 'sus k 'fered ein ha 'vin b 'meteg varesen ed 'yo liv 'lom bal k 'rov eilecha*

[10] *rabim mach 'ovim larasha v 'habotei 'ach ba 'YHVH chesed y 'sov 'venu*

[11] *sim 'chu vaYHVH v 'gilu tzadikim v 'har 'ninu kol yish 'rei leiv*

Translation:

[1] A Psalm of David. *Maschil.* Happy is he whose transgression is forgiven, whose sin is pardoned.

[2] Happy is the man unto whom *YHVH* counteth not iniquity, and in whose spirit there is no guile.

[3] When I kept silence, my bones wore away through my groaning all the day long.

[4] For day and night Thy hand was heavy upon me; my sap was turned as in the droughts of summer. *Selah*

[5] I acknowledged my sin unto Thee, and mine iniquity have I not hid; I said: 'I will make confession concerning my transgressions unto *YHVH*'—and Thou, Thou forgavest the iniquity of my sin. *Selah*

[6] For this let every one that is godly pray unto Thee in a time when Thou mayest be found; surely, when the great waters overflow, they will not reach unto him.

[7] Thou art my hiding-place; Thou wilt preserve me from the adversary; with songs of deliverance Thou wilt compass me about. *Selah*

[8] 'I will instruct thee and teach thee in the way which thou shalt go; I will give counsel, Mine eye being upon thee.'

[9] Be ye not as the horse, or as the mule, which have no understanding; whose mouth must be held in with bit and bridle, that they come not near unto thee.

[10] Many are the sorrows of the wicked; but he that trusteth in *YHVH*, mercy compasseth him about.

[11] Be glad in *YHVH*, and rejoice, ye righteous; and shout for joy, all ye that are upright in heart.

Psalm 32 is included in the זמירות (*Zemirot* —"Hymns") section of Sefardic rites,[1] and also by the Sefardic communities in London and Amsterdam during the afternoon prayer service (*Minchah*) on the eve of *Yom Kippur*.[2] It has been suggested that the latter recitation was prompted by the second verse reading "Happy is the man unto whom *YHVH* counteth not iniquity, and in whose spirit there is no guile."[3]

In Jewish Magic the thirty-second Psalm is employed for the purpose of finding רחמים (*rachamim*—"mercy" or "compassion").[4] In this regard, Godfrey Selig noted in his version of the "*Shimmush Tehillim*" that "whoever prays this Psalm daily receives grace, love and mercy."[5] However, we find a proviso in all the other published versions, in which it is noted that to affect mercy, the Psalm should be recited every day after prayers,[6] the latter referencing, according to Rebiger, the "eighteen petitions" (*Amidah* prayer).[7] Since there is no indication as to exactly which "prayers" are referenced, i.e. personal morning prayers on waking, or the synagogal prayers, it is difficult to verify this suggestion.

Be that as it may, one recension of the "*Shimmush Tehillim*" includes a larger offering in terms of "a plea for mercy from the Name of God." In this instance *Psalm 32* is recited four times whilst concentrating on the Divine Name והו עלם (*V'hu Ilam*), and each recitation is succeeded by the following prayer-incantation:[8]

מלך אמיץ כח ורב עלילה נא אל תפן לרוע מעללי
ואל תפן לחטאי ואל תבקש לעוני ואל תפעליני
כמשפטי ואל תדינני כמעללי אכן בחסד וברחמים
תדינני ועל כסא רחמים תשב בבואי למשפט ובאתי
בתחנון לפניך לבקש מלפניך מחילה על צרכי
בשמך הנכבד והנורא עלם יהיה לי הדבר הזה בשם
הנכבד אלהי ישראל אמן אמן אמן אמן סלה סלה סלה

Transliteration:

*Melech amitz ko'ach v'rav alilah na al teifen l'ro'a
ma'al'lai v'al teifen l'chat'ai v'al t'vakeish la'avonai v'al
taf'ileini k'mish'patai v'al t'dineini k'ma'al'lai achein
b'chesed uvarachamim t'dineini v'al kisei rachamim*

teisheiv b'vo'i l'mish'pat ubati b'tachanun l'fanecha l'vakeish mil'fa'necha m'chilah al tzar'chai b'shim'cha hanich'bad v'hanora Ilam yih'yeh li hadavar hazeh b'sheim hanich'bad elohei yis'ra'eil Omein Omein Omein Selah Selah Selah.

Translation:

> King of valiant strength and great deeds, please do not turn unto my wicked deeds, and do not turn unto my sins, and do not enquire after my iniquity, and do not judge in accordance with my ordinances, and do not judge me in terms of my deeds, but judge me instead with compassion and mercy, and you will sit on the throne of mercy when I am brought to trial. I have come before you with supplications to find forgiveness because of my needs, in your honoured and awesome name *Ilam*. This will be to me the word in your honoured Name God of Israel, *Amen Amen Amen Selah Selah Selah.*

I have seen the recitation of the thirty-second Psalm for the purpose of attracting a spouse, and, whilst we are on the subject of finding a life partner, one of the recensions of the *"Shimmush Tehillim"* lists the use of this Psalm for the purpose of precluding a possible miscarriage. In this regard, the procedure necessitates the Psalm to be written with its magical Name, which is afterwards suspended around the neck of the pregnant woman. This is followed by uttering the following prayer-incantation:[9]

יהי רצון מלפניך אלהים חיים שתרחם ותחוס עיניך עלי
ותשמע אלי ותשמור הבריה הזות [...Name of Recipient....]
שלא יארע לה שום רעה ולא שדין ולילין ולא ינגפו
הולד אשר במעיה ולא יצא מגופה עד השעה הראויה
ללדת ולא תפיל מהריונה זה בשם הבורא עֲלָם אמן
אמן אמן סלה סלה סלה

Transliteration:

> *Y'hi ratzon mil'fanecha elohim chayim shet'racheim v'tachos einecha alai v'tish'ma eilai v'tish'mor haberiyah hazot* [....Name of Recipient...] *shelo ye'era lah shum ra'ah v'lo sheidin v'lilin v'lo yinag'fu hav'lad asher*

b'mei'eha v'lo yetzei migufah ad hasha'ah har'uyah
laledet v'lo tapil meiherionah zeh b'shem haborei Ilam
Omein Omein Omein Selah Selah Selah

Translation:

> May it be your will Living God, that you should have
> mercy, and let your eye rest upon me, and listen to me and
> protect this creature [....Name of Recipient...], so that no
> evil be done to her, and no demons and *Lilin* shall strike
> the child that is in her belly, and it should not come out of
> her body until that moment in time when it is good for
> giving birth, and she should not miscarry during her
> pregnancy. In the name of the creator *Ilam. Amen Amen
> Amen Selah Selah Selah.*

It should also be noted that *Psalm 32:7* is included in an amulet for
the purpose of protecting a woman in labour. In this regard, the
practitioner is instructed to write the verse conjointly with a set of
Divine Names, reading אדון מדון נדון נכדן נשטן נשקט
(*Adon Madon Nadon Nachudan Nash'tan Nash'kat*), as well as
אזבוגה (*Azbugah*), on kosher parchment, a sheet of paper, or
something of a similar nature, in the following manner:[10]

+---+
| אָדוֹן מָדוֹן נָדוֹן נַכְדָן נַשְׁטָן נַשְׁקַט |
| אתה סתר לי מצר תצרני רני פלט תסובבני סלה |
| סלה תסובבני פלט רני תצרני מצר לי סתר אתה |
| אזבוגה |
+---+

On completion the amulet is placed inside a bag, which is located
either on top or underneath the pillow of the woman in labour.[11] As
noted elsewhere, "in Judaism it is understood that it takes a while
for a woman to regain her 'purity' following birth....the
instructions accompanying this amulet maintain that the said
woman should carry the amulet with her, until she regained her
ritual purity."[12]

   Psalm 32:7 is very popular in Jewish Magic, and is
employed in Hebrew incantations, amulets for protection, Divine

Name constructs, etc. The letters comprising this verse, reading אתה סתר לי מצר תצרני רני פלט תסובבני סלה (*atah seiter li mitzar titz'reini ranei falet t'sov'veini Selah*—"Thou art my hiding-place; Thou wilt preserve me from the adversary; with songs of deliverance Thou wilt compass me about. *Selah*"), were conjoined in a unique manner to formulate the following Divine Name construct, which is said to be good for literally everything:[13]

הסה	תלל	אהם
רבו	תנם	סית
צתי	יוב מסנ	לבב
צפט	תלל	רמפ
רית	ננג ירי	ריר
לתי	פצנ ירר	ננצ
סמר	תצצ	טרמ
נתת	בלי ברס	ויל
לתת	סהא	יסר
	האה	

In formulating this Divine Name construct, the words and letters comprising *Psalm 32:7* were inscribed in three rows. The first row comprises the verse written in the usual manner from right to left, i.e. אתה סתר לי, etc., whilst in the second all the letters of the verse are written entirely in reverse, i.e. from left to write, e.g. יל רתם התא, etc. The third row is made up of the words of the verse written in reverse, e.g. לי סתר אתה, etc. and the Divine Name construct is revealed by reading the rows of letters vertically, i.e. in columns. However, whilst Rabbi Moses Zacutto shared this Divine Name construct in the "*Shorshei ha-Shemot*," he stated that a different arrangement appears in all the books he examined. In this regard, the letter ו (*Vav*) was excluded from the arrangement, which he noted should read:[14]

אהם	תלל	הסה
סית	תנס	רבב
לבב	יסן מתי	צטפ
רלל	תפט	ציר
רנן	נרי ייח	רנצ
נרר	יצן פתי	לרם
טצצ	תמר	סיל
בלי	ברס נתת	יסר
סהא	לתת	האה

The astute Rabbi offered no reason why he addressed two versions of this Divine Name construct in his acclaimed book on the "Roots of Divine Names,"[15] without clarifying which should be considered the correct version. Be that as it may, the capitals of the nine words comprising *Psalm 32:7* were conjoined in the following Divine Name construct:[16]

$$\text{אֲסֵל מִתְרָ פַּתֶס}$$

Enunciated "*Aseili Mitira Pat'seh*," this Divine Name construct is delineated a "great and holy Name," which is employed for the same purpose as listed in the previous Divine Name construct incorporating the entire verse.[17] It is also good for protection, and it is said that one of the powers of this Divine Name is for someone to defeat all demonic forces which may be afflicting his or her person.[18] Curiously enough, the whole of *Psalm 32* has been listed as good "against the evil eye,"[19] and it is also said that anyone reciting *Psalm 32:7* three times every day without the concluding word סלה (*Selah*), will be saved from a "strange death."[20] Here it should be mentioned, that the initials of the first five words of the current verse, i.e. אתה סתר לי מצר תצרני (*atah seiter li mitzar titz'reini*—"Thou art my hiding-place; Thou wilt preserve me"), with the addition of the letter צ (*Tzadi*) from the fourth word, were compiled into the Divine Name construct אסל מ מצרת, which is employed in amulets for general protection.[21]

It is also worth nothing that this verse, as well as others, are associated with the "Name of Seventy-two Names." In this regard, *Psalm 32:22* is directly affiliated with סאל (*Se'al*), the forty-fifth portion, of the "*Shem Vayisa Vayet*,"[22] whilst *Psalm 32:7* is indirectly associated with מצר (*Metzer*), the sixtieth portion of the said Divine Name. In this regard, doubling the *gematria* of מצר [מ = 40 + צ = 90 + ר = 200 = 330], is equal to that of the term סתר (*seiter*—"shelter" or "secret" [ס = 60 + ת = 400 + ר = 200 = 660]). As noted elsewhere, "we are informed that the Name מצר is meant to be used as a protection against the 'evil eye'," and that this pertains to *Psalm 32:7*, the main sentiments of which is Divine protection.[23] You will notice that both the mentioned terms, i.e. סתר (*Seiter*—"hiding-place" or "shelter") and מצר (*Mitzar*—"distress" or "straits," translated "adversary"), are present in the said verse.

Another verse, *Psalm 32:10*, is said to be indirectly aligned with אלד (*Elad*), the tenth portion of the "*Shem Vayisa Vayet*," and, again as I noted before, it is of particular significance that the *Gematria* of אלד is equal to that of אגלא (*Agala'a* [א = 1 + ג = 3 + ל = 30 + א = 1 = 35]), a very important Divine Name construct whose power is in גבורה (*Gevurah*—"Might").[24] I also indicated that the *Gematria* of אלד [א = 1 + ל = 30 + ד = 4 = 35] with the *kolel*, i.e. an additional count for the word itself, is equal to that of the word והבוטח [ו = 6 + ה = 5 + ב = 2 + ו = 6 + ט = 9 + ח = 8 = 36],[25] which we are told relates directly to the first word of the concluding phrase in *Psalm 32:10* reading והבוטח ביהוה חסד יסובבנו (*v'haboteach ba'YHVH chesed y'sov'venu*—"But he that trusteth in *YHVH*, mercy compasseth him about").[26]

There are again a number of magical applications of the current Psalm which were passed on by word of mouth, and which are still in use amongst common folk everywhere. In this regard, it is worth noting that *Psalm 32* is employed for illness and healing in general, and, interestingly enough, to preserve the voice. It is recommended to find your way when lost during a journey, and equally to find "lost" treasures. Whilst we noted that this Psalm is recited for protection in general, it is directly referenced as one of the Psalms suggested for protection in perilous situations and times of trouble. It is especially recommended for protection of the fatherland, and for universal brotherhood. As far as ones personal nature is concerned, the thirty-second Psalm is said to be good for atonement (repentance), especially after having used it to relief oneself from the burden of misdeeds (sin), and to request mercy from the Divine One. Lastly, it is recommended to encourage charity and good deeds, and, as in the case of the previous Psalm, is recommended for a man to recite on his marriage.

The use of the *Psalm 32* in the Byzantine Christian magical manuscripts, align somewhat with an earlier mentioned application of the Psalm shared in one of the recensions of the *"Shimmush Tehillim."* We are informed in the said Christian magical texts that *Psalm 32*, when used in conjunction with *Psalm 31*, "is useful for a woman who does not conceive." In this regard, the woman who seeks to fall pregnant, is instructed to copy the two Psalms on a parchment or a sheet of paper, which she then has to place on her pillow "where she sleeps," and doing so for three Thursdays. She is further instructed to "place also ivy leaves at the full moon,"[27] and this is believed will aid her in falling pregnant.

The magical use of the thirty-second Psalm in *"Le Livre d'Or"* will definitely preclude pregnancy. This text instructs those who are "tempted by the spirit of fornication" to enunciate *Psalm 32* seven times "over holy water at the Epiphany of the Lord."[28] They are further instructed to wash themselves with the water, then to copy a set of magical characters, which are afterwards perfumed with mastic prior to being tied to the right arm, following which it is maintained the "desires will be extinguished."[29] This use is quite contrary to the employment of the current Psalm in Jewish Magic for the purpose of finding kindness and compassion. Be that as it may, elsewhere we find *Psalm 32:9* used as a protection against being bitten by a dog or a snake,[30] and the Syrian magical manuscript in the Sachau Collection maintains it should be read five times in order to be protected against all evil.[31]

In conclusion, in the *"Key of Solomon"* Psalm 32 the current Psalm is listed fifth in a set of eight Psalms recited during the construction of "pentacles," the others being *Psalms 8, 21, 27, 29, 51, 72,* and *134.*[32]

Psalm 33

[1] רננו צדיקים ביהוה יאהדונהי לישרים נאוה
תהלה

[2] הודו ליהוה יאהדונהי בכנור בנבל עשור זמרו לו

[3] שירו לו שיר חדש היטיבו נגן בתרועה

[4] כי ישר דבר יהוהיאהדונהי וכל מעשהו באמונה

[5] אהב צדקה ומשפט חסד יהוהיאהדונהי מלאה
הארץ

[6] בדבר יהוהיאהדונהי שמים נעשו וברוח פיו כל
צבאם

[7] כנס כנד מי הים נתן באוצרות תהומות

[8] ייראו מיהוה יאהדונהי כל הארץ ממנו יגורו
כל ישבי תבל

[9] כי הוא אמר ויהי הוא צוה ויעמד

[10] יהוהיאהדונהי הפיר עצת גוים הניא מחשבות
עמים

[11] עצת יהוהיאהדונהי לעולם תעמד מחשבות
לבו לדר ודר

[12] אשרי הגוי אשר יהוהיאהדונהי אלהיו העם
בחר לנחלה לו

[13] משמים הביט יהוהיאהדונהי ראה את כל בני
האדם

[14] ממכון שבתו השגיח אל כל ישבי הארץ

[15] היצר יחד לבם המבין אל כל מעשיהם

[16] אין המלך נושע ברב חיל גבור לא ינצל ברב
כח

[17] שקר הסוס לתשועה וברב חילו לא ימלט

[18] הנה עין יהוהיאהדונהי אל יראיו למיחלים
לחסדו

[19] להציל ממות נפשם ולחיותם ברעב

[20] נפשנו חכתה ליהוה יאהדונהי עזרנו ומגננו הוא

[21] כי בו ישמח לבנו כי בשם קדשו בטחנו

[22] יהי חסדך יהוהיאהדונהי עלינו כאשר יחלנו לך

Transliteration:

[1] *ran'nu tzadikim baYHVH lay'sharim navah t'hilah*

[2] *hodu laYHVH b'chinor b'neivel asor zam'ru lo*

[3] *shiru lo shir chadash heitivu nagein bit'ru'a*

[4] *ki yashar d'var YHVH v'chol ma'aseihu b'emunah*

[5] *oheiv tzedakah umish'pat chesed YHVH mal'ah ha'aretz*

[6] *bid'var YHVH shamayim na'asu uv'ru'ach piv kol tz'va'am*

[7] *koneis kaneid mei hayam notein b'otzarot t'homot*

[8] *yir'u mei'YHVH kol ha'aretz mimenu yaguru kol yosh'vei teiveil*

[9] *ki hu amar vayehi hu tzivah vaya'amod*

[10] *YHVH hefir atzat goyim heini mach'sh'vot amim*

[11] *atzat YHVH l'olam ta'amod mach'sh'vot libo l'dor va'dor*

[12] *ash'rei hagoi asher YHVH elohav ha'am ba'char l'nachalah lo*

[13] *mishamayim hibit YHVH ra'ah et kol b'nei ha'adam*

[14] *mim'chon shiv'to hish'gi'ach el kol yosh'vei ha'aretz*

[15] *hayotzer yachad libam hameivin el kol ma'aseihem*

[16] *ein hamelech nosha b'rov chayil gibor lo yinatzel b'rov ko'ach*

[17] *sheker hasus lit'shu'ah uv'rov cheilo lo y'maleit*

[18] *hinei ein YHVH el y'rei'av lam yachalim l'chas'do*

[19] *l'hatzil mimavet naf'sham ul'chayotam bara'av*

[20] *naf'sheinu chik'tah la'YHVH ez'reinu umagineinu hu*

[21] *ki vo yis'mach libeinu ki v'sheim kod'sho vatach'nu*

[22] *y'hi chas'd'cha YHVH aleinu ka'asher yichal'nu lach*

Translation:

[1] Rejoice in *YHVH*, O ye righteous, praise is comely for the upright.

[2] Give thanks unto *YHVH* with harp, sing praises unto Him with the psaltery of ten strings.

[3] Sing unto Him a new song; play skilfully amid shouts of joy.

[4] For the word of *YHVH* is upright; and all His work is done in faithfulness.

[5] He loveth righteousness and justice; the earth is full of the lovingkindness of *YHVH*.

[6] By the word of *YHVH* were the heavens made; and all the host of them by the breath of His mouth.

[7] He gathereth the waters of the sea together as a heap; He layeth up the deeps in storehouses.

[8] Let all the earth fear *YHVH*; let all the inhabitants of the world stand in awe of Him.

[9] For He spoke, and it was; He commanded, and it stood.

[10] *YHVH* bringeth the counsel of the nations to nought; He maketh the thoughts of the peoples to be of no effect.

[11] The counsel of *YHVH* standeth for ever, the thoughts of His heart to all generations.

[12] Happy is the nation whose God is *YHVH*; the people whom He hath chosen for His own inheritance.

[13] *YHVH* looketh from heaven; He beholdeth all the sons of men;

[14] From the place of His habitation He looketh intently upon all the inhabitants of the earth;

[15] He that fashioneth the hearts of them all, that considereth all their doings.

[16] A king is not saved by the multitude of a host; a mighty man is not delivered by great strength.

[17] A horse is a vain thing for safety; neither doth it afford escape by its great strength.

[18] Behold, the eye of *YHVH* is toward them that fear Him, toward them that wait for His mercy;

[19] To deliver their soul from death, and to keep them alive in famine.

[20] Our soul hath waited for *YHVH*; He is our help and our shield.

[21] For in Him doth our heart rejoice, because we have trusted in His holy name.

[22] Let Thy mercy *YHVH*, be upon us, according as we have waited for Thee.

Psalm 33 is one of the special Psalms which are recited only during the morning prayers (*Shaharit*) on *Shabbat* and festivals.[1] We are told the reason why this Psalm is included in the said service is because the Sabbath is "the memorial to creation," and this aligns with the sentiments expressed in *Psalm 33:6* reading "by the word of *YHVH* were the heavens made; and all the host of them by the breath of His mouth."[2] It is further said that this verse relates to the so-called ten "*Ma'amarot*" ("Sayings") with which the Eternal Living Spirit is said to have "created the heavens and the earth and all creatures in them."[3] The "Ten Sayings" reference the ten "*Elohim* said...." verses in the first chapter of *Genesis*,[4] which are in turn said to be referencing ten primal substances created on the "first day" of creation.[5] In this regard, I noted elsewhere that "whether referred to as 'Ten Sayings,' 'Ten Substances' or 'Ten Attributes,' these were considered of fundamental importance in the creation of heaven and earth."[6] I also noted that "the notion of the ten *Ma'amarot* and ten creative potencies ultimately found their way into the primary texts of the early Kabbalists, in the form of the doctrine of the ten *Sefirot*."[7]

We are informed that the twenty-two verses of *Psalm 33* align with "the twenty-two letters of the Hebrew alphabet with which the Torah was written, and with which God created the world."[8] In this regard, I noted elsewhere and reiterated in the previous chapter, that "in its primal state of emanation, the Hebrew Alphabet is understood to represent the primordial vibrations of the cosmos in that space (*Makom*) where all are one."[9] In this regard I stated that "by employing these glyphs in magic and meditation one attempts to reach as close an affinity with Divine Emanations as one possibly can," and that in order to achieve this "we have to apply the three traditional methods of *mivta*—the articulation of the names and letters, *michtav*—writing them, and *mashav*—their contemplation."[10] All three of these methods feature in the magical uses of the biblical "*Book of Psalms*."

In Jewish Magic the primary purpose of *Psalm 33* is to support and protect a woman "whose children die young."[11] In this regard, we are informed in the published versions of the "*Shimmush Tehillim*," that the Psalm should be recited with an associated Divine Name over olive oil, following which the woman should be anointed therewith.[12] The referenced Divine Name is יהוה (*YHVH*), which in the current instance is said to have been derived: י (*Yod*) from ביהוה (*ba'YHVH*—"in *YHVH*"):

verse 1; ה (*Heh*) from חודו (*hodu*—"Give thanks"): verse 2; ו (*Vav*) from עצת (*atzat*—"The counsel"): verse 11, through exchange with ע"ו [ר"ב ש"א] (*Ashbar*) cipher]; and ה (*Heh*) from היצר (*hayotzer*—"the fashioner"): verse 15.[13]

The procedure of reciting the thirty-third Psalm over olive oil to aid a woman whose children are dying, are greatly expanded upon in a different recension of the "*Shimmush Tehillim*."[14] In this regard, the practitioner is instructed to whisper the Psalm with its associated Divine Name nine times over olive oil, and at the conclusion of which to recite the following prayer-incantation. In this instance, the Divine Name is indicated to be אל חי יהוה (*El Chai YHVH*):[15]

צור מלכי זאת האשה ברוב עונינו וברוב פשעינו
עוליה מועטים והולכים ומתים ונענשים רחם עליה
ורפאה ושמע קול בכיה ותחנוניה ושמור הריונה
והולדות אשר תלד מבלי היות שוממין ולא מתים
בשם אל חי יהוה שיהיה דבר זה אמן אמן אמן סלה
סלה סלה

Transliteration:

> *Tzur mal'ki zot ha'ishah b'rov avoneinu ub'rov p'sha'einu olaleha mo'atim v'hol'chim umeitim v'ne'enashim rachem aleha ur'fa'ah ush'ma kol b'chiyah v'tach'nuneiha ush'mor herionah v'hav'ladot asher teled mib'li heyot shom'min v'lo meitim b'sheim El Chai YHVH sheyih'yeh davar zeh Omein Omein Omein Selah Selah Selah*

Translation:

> Rock, my King, this woman, for the multitude of our transgressions, and for the multitude of our iniquities, have few infants who are languishing, dying, and punished. Have mercy on her, and heal her, and hear the sound of weeping, and her supplications, and protect her pregnancy and children whom she will bear, without which they will be abandoned, and that they will not die. Let this be in the name of *El Chai YHVH*.

In conclusion, the oil is offered to the woman in question, of which she should imbibe a little every day with her food and drink for the duration of her pregnancy. It is further said that it is equally good to anoint the newborn with this oil, and to include a little of it in the food and drink of the infant.[16]

Psalm 33 is equally included in amulets constructed for the very same purpose. In this regard, the following Divine Name construct, being an abbreviation of the entire Psalm, was formulated by conjoining the capitals of all the words of the Psalm into the following fifty-four tri-letter combinations written with vowels:

רַצֵּב לָנָת הֹלַב בְּעָז לְשֵׁל שְׁחָה נַבְכ יָדְי וְמַב אֹצּוּ
הֵיְמ הָבִּי שָׁנַוּ פִּכְצ כֹּכֶּם הַנֹב תִּיֶמ כָּהְמ יָכְי תֶכָה
אָוַה צְוִי הֵעַג הֶמַע עַיְל תַמַל לְוָא הַאַי אֶהָב לְלֹם
הִיְר אֶכְב הָמְשׁ הָאֵב יְהָה יַלְה אֶכֶם אֶהַנ בְּחָג
לִיְב כֹּשֶׁה לֹוחֵ לִיְה לֹיַל לְמִנ וּבָנ חָלַע וְהֹב
בִּיל כְּבֹק בָיְח יָעַב יְחַל

Vocalised "*ratzaba lanat' holab' b'aza losilo sichahei nabiki yad'y' v'mabe otz'u che'y'ma habiy' sana'u pichatz' kokamei hanob' t'yimei kahami yakayo teikihu avahu tzivay' hei'ago heima'a ay'l' tamali l'va'a ha'ay' ehaba l'lomi hiy'ra ebab' hamishi hi'eba yohaha yaliha ekama eihano b'chagi loyib' koseha li'uchei loy'hi eiy'e y'lal' l'mina ubana chila'e uhuki boyili kiv'ka vay'cha y'aka yichala,*" this Divine Name construct is employed as an amulet to aid women who suffer miscarriages, or who cannot fall pregnant. This abbreviation of the current Psalm is written either on the inside of a bowl, or on parchment to be located inside the bowl. The writing is then dissolved in water poured in the bowl, and afterwards consumed by the woman seeking spiritual protection or to fall pregnant, and this is done on the night of her *Mikveh* (ritual bath).[17]

The same Divine Name construct is also employed in conjunction with a set of additional Divine Names, the names of eleven "Spirit Intelligences," as well as the following letter square constructed from the capitals of the words in *Exodus 23:26* reading לֹא תִהְיֶה מְשַׁכֵּלָה וַעֲקָרָה בְּאַרְצֶךָ (*Lo tih'yeh m'shakelah va'akarah b'artzecha*—"None shall miscarry, nor be barren, in thy land"), for the purpose of supporting a woman who has suffered a miscarriage, or who has lost her sons in infancy:[18]

בְּ	וָ	מֶ	תִ	לְ
לְ	בְּ	וָ	מֶ	תִ
תִ	לְ	בְּ	וָ	מֶ
מֶ	תִ	לְ	בְּ	וָ
וָ	מֶ	תִ	לְ	בְּ

The Angelic Names included with the letter square are יופיאל (*Yofi'el*), נוריאל (*Nuri'el*), ותקיאל (*Vat'ki'el*), ברוכיאל (*Baruchi'el*), תושיאל (*Tushi'el*), אוריאל (*Ori'el*), סתריאל (*Sat'ri'el*), תומיאל (*Tav'mi'el*), רחמיאל (*Rach'miel*), צדקיאל (*Tzad'ki'el*), and יושעאל (*Yoshu'el*).

The amulet is formulated by inscribing the *chotam* (magical seal), i.e. the letter square and associated Angelic Names, at the top of a deerskin parchment, kosher scroll, or clean sheet of paper. This is followed by copying the following incantation below the letter square:

יהי רצון מלפניך שומר נפשות חסידיו שתשמור פרי
בטנה של נושאת קמיע זה עליה מכל נזק ומקרה רע
ומהפסד היסודות כי אין שומר ורופא מבלעדיך
כדכתיב אם יהוה לא יבנה בית שוא עמלו בוניו בו
אנא מלא רחמים חוס וחמול ורחם עליה ולא תשכל
פרי בטנה עוד אמן נצח סלה ועד אמן כן יהי רצון

Transliteration:
Y'hi ratzon mil'fanecha shomer nefashot chasidav shetishmor pri bit'nah shel noset kamea zeh aleah mikol

> nezek umik'reh ra v'mehef'sed hayesodot ki ein shomer
> v'rofe mibil'adecha k'dek'tiv (*Psalm 127:1*) im YHVH lo
> yif'neh vayit shav am'lu vonav bo ana male rachamim chus
> v'chamol v'rachem aleah v'lo teshakel pri bit'nah od
> Omein Netzach Selah va'ed Omein ken y'hi ratzon

Translation:

> May it be your will, He who protects the souls of His
> devotees, to safeguard with this amulet the fruit of her belly
> she is carrying on her, from all harm and bad incidents,
> from the loss of the foundations, since there is nobody else
> who protects and heals besides You, as it is written (*Psalm
> 127:1*) "Except *YHVH* build the house, they labour in vain
> that build it." Please grant compassion, protect and have
> pity and mercy on her, that she will no more loose the fruit
> of her belly. *Amen* enduring *Selah* forever. *Amen* thus be it
> so willed.

Next append the earlier listed abbreviation of *Psalm 33* with
vowels to the incantation, and conclude by adding the following
Divine and Angelic Names:

סנוי סנסנוי סמנגלף יאהקותה בדפטיאל
פדפדס שמרירון עזרירון אנרנל צמרכד
עששיי

Sanoi San'sanoi Seman'gelof, YAHKVTH (combination of the
Ineffable Name and אקה), *B'daf'ti'el, Pad'padas, Sham'riron,
Az'riron, Enar'nal, Tzamar'chad, Ash'tzei.*[19] Since the lack of
space in the current volume precludes me from explaining these
Divine Names here, it should be noted that I have elucidated them
to some degree in previous volumes of this *"Shadow Tree Series"*
of texts on Jewish Magic.[20] Be that as it may, the following rather
complex arrangement of all the letters comprising *Psalm 33*, is
equally employed in an amulet to prevent any danger befalling an
unborn fetus, as well as preventing miscarriages:[21]

רו צם בה לם נה תה הו לה בר בל ער זו
לו שו לו שר חש הו נן בה כי יר דר יה
ול מו בה אב צה וט חד יה מה הץ בר יה
שם נו וח פו כל צם כס כד מי הם נן בת
תת יו מה כל הץ מו יו כל יי תל כי הא
אר וי הא צה וד יה הר עת גם הא מת עם
מת עם עת יה לם תד מת לו לר ור אי הי
אר יה או הם בר לה לו מם הט יה רה את
כל בי תם מן שו הח אל כל יי הץ הר יד
לם הן אל כל מם אן הך נע בב חל גר לא
יל בב כח שר הס לה וב חו לא יט הה עץ
יה אל יו לם לו לל מת נם ום בב נו חה
לה עו וו הא כי בו יח לו כי בם קו בו
יי חך יה עו כר יו לך

Inscribing these very large Divine Name constructs formulated for amuletic purposes from the letters comprising the thirty-third Psalm, might be somewhat daunting for those practitioners who are not exactly accomplished Hebrew scribes. However, the first and last letters of the six words of *Psalm 33:1*, are conjoined in the Divine Name construct רו צם בה למ נה תה, which is equally employed in amulets for countering miscarriage.[22] It is certainly much easier to write down!

As far as other uses of the current Psalm are concerned, *Psalm 33* is recommended for recitation "in times of difficulty and sorrow."[23] In this regard, we are informed that it is spoken against epidemics,[24] or to be safeguarded during a pandemic, this condition having been prevalent globally at the time when this tome was being written. The "*Shimmush Tehillim*" states succinctly that the inhabitants of an area where there is distress should recite *Psalm 33*.[25] Selig's version of this text instructs that "at the time of a general famine, the inhabitants of the afflicted district should pray this Psalm with united hearts and powers, and they will surely be heard."[26]

The thirty-third Psalm is also popularly employed to, as it were, "empower" the acclaimed, if somewhat infamous, "redstring," so popular amongst followers of a modern–day Kabbalah cult. As I noted elsewhere, "many of the current 'Kabbalistic' claims being made in terms of the 'red string,' are plain nonsense. There are certainly no exclusive traditional Kabbalistic associations to the practice, and neither does it find it's origins in Kabbalah *per se*."[27] In this regard, I mentioned that "those who purchase these readily available little bracelets, are not following the procedure of acquiring a length of red string cut from a red string wound around the tomb of the Matriarch Rachel in Bethlehem."[28] As it is, any red string can be, and was in fact, employed by many ultra-religionists down the centuries, provided it was long enough to wind seven times around your left wrist whilst uttering *Psalm 33* as well as the *Ana Becho'ach* prayer."[29] In this regard, I stated that "none of these details are being fulfilled by those to whom it appears traditional teachings are quite secondary to exploitive monetary objectives."[30]

As indicated, in "official literature" the main focus of the current Psalm is on protection of mothers and their offspring. However, the thirty-third Psalm is also amongst the group recommended for illness and healing in general, with special reference to diseases of the bones. Furthermore, it is recited for success in business; to express gratitude for good fortune; and to give praise. It is equally employed in adversity; against lies; and against unjust, as well as to be freed from, imprisonment. On a more spiritual level, this Psalm is recommended for recitation as a statement of faith.

As we have already noted, individual verses of the current Psalm are separately employed for magical purposes. In this regard, the capitals of the words comprising *Psalm 33:6* are combined in the Divine Name construct בישונופכץ, which is used in amulets for success.[31] On the other hand, *Psalm 33:18* is used to improve livelihood. In this regard, those wishing to work this procedure are instructed to raise their eyes to heaven after the morning prayers, and to recite the said verse three times.[32] The same verse is directly affiliated with נָא (*Nena*), the fifty-third portion of the "*Shem Vayisa Vayet.*"[33] Furthermore, the opening phrase of *Psalm 33:9* relate indirectly to לוּו (*Lov*), the nineteenth portion of the "*Shem Vayisa Vayet.*" In this regard, we are informed that the *gematria* of this Name [ל = 30 + ו = 6 + ו = 6] is 42, which is said to pertain to the "Forty-two Letter Name." which I mentioned elsewhere is believed to be the Divine Name with which the world was created. I further noted that in this regard the "secret" is said to be כִּי הוּא אָמַר וַיְהִי (*Ki hu amar va'yehi*—'For He spoke, and it was')," i.e. the opening phrase of the said verse from the thirty-third Psalm, and it has also been noted that the *gematria* of the opening words כִּי הוּא [כ = 20 + י = 10 + ה = 5 + ו = 6 + א = 1 = 42] is equal to that of לוּו.[34]

In Christian Magic *Psalm 33* appears to apply in both, as it were, love and war! The Psalm is recommended against sterility. In this regard, "*Le Livre d'Or*" suggests copying it in conjunction with a set of magical characters, all of which is to be perfumed with mastic and incense, and then tied to the right arm of the woman prior to engaging in the procreative act, which will ensure that she falls pregnant.[35] On the other hand, the current Psalm is recommended for recitation in conditions of war, especially by those who find themselves in the middle of a battle.[36]

Psalm 34

[1] לדוד בשנותו את טעמו לפני אבימלך ויגרשהו וילך

[2] אברכה את יהוﬣﬡﬢﬢ﬩﬩יאהדונהי בכל עת תמיד תהלתו בפי

[3] ביהוﬣﬡﬢﬢ﬩﬩יאהדונהי תתהלל נפשי ישמעו ענוים וישמחו

[4] גדלו ליהוﬣﬡﬢﬢ﬩﬩יאהדונהי אתי ונרוממה שמו יחדו

[5] דרשתי את יהוﬣﬡﬢﬢ﬩﬩יאהדונהי וענני ומכל מגורותי הצילני

[6] הביטו אליו ונהרו ופניהם אל יחפרו

[7] זה עני קרא ויהוﬣﬡﬢﬢ﬩﬩יאהדונהי שמע ומכל צרותיו הושיעו

[8] חנה מלאך יהוﬣﬡﬢﬢ﬩﬩יאהדונהי סביב ליראיו ויחלצם

[9] טעמו וראו כי טוב יהוﬣﬡﬢﬢ﬩﬩יאהדונהי אשרי הגבר יחסה בו

[10] יראו את יהוﬣﬡﬢﬢ﬩﬩יאהדונהי קדשיו כי אין מחסור ליראיו

[11] כפירים רשו ורעבו ודרשי יהוﬣﬡﬢﬢ﬩﬩יאהדונהי לא יחסרו כל טוב

[12] לכו בנים שמעו לי יראת יהוﬣﬡﬢﬢ﬩﬩יאהדונהי אלמדכם

[13] מי האיש החפץ חיים אהב ימים לראות טוב

[14] נצר לשונך מרע ושפתיך מדבר מרמה

[15] סור מרע ועשה טוב בקש שלום ורדפהו

[16] עיני יהוﬣﬡﬢﬢ﬩﬩יאהדונהי אל צדיקים ואזניו אל שועתם

[17] פני יהוﬣﬡﬢﬢ﬩﬩יאהדונהי בעשי רע להכרית מארץ זכרם

[18] צעקו ויהוﬣﬡﬢﬢ﬩﬩יאהדונהי שמע ומכל צרותם הצילם

[19] קרוב יהוﬣﬡﬢﬢ﬩﬩יאהדונהי לנשברי לב ואת דכאי רוח יושיע

[20] רבות רעות צדיק ומכלם יצילנו יהוה‎אדני‎יאהדונהי

[21] שמר כל עצמותיו אחת מהנה לא נשברה

[22] תמותת רשע רעה ושנאי צדיק יאשמו

[23] פדה יהוה‎אדני‎יאהדונהי נפש עבדיו ולא יאשמו כל
החסים בו

Transliteration:

[1] *l'david b'shanoto et ta'mo lif'nei avimelech vay'garsheihu vayeilach*

[2] *avar'cha et YHVH b'chol eit tamid t'hilato b'fi*

[3] *baYHVH tit'haleil naf'shi yish'm'u anavim v'yis'machu*

[4] *gad'lu laYHVH iti un'rom'mah sh'mo yach'dav*

[5] *darash'ti et YHVH v'anani umikol m'gurotai hitzilani*

[6] *hibitu eilav v'naharu uf'neihem al yech'paru*

[7] *zeh ani kara vaYHVH shamei'a umikol tzarotav hoshi'o*

[8] *choneh mal'ach YHVH saviv lirei'av vay'chal'tzeim*

[9] *ta'amu ur'u ki tov YHVH ash'rei hagever yeche'seh bo*

[10] *yir'u et YHVH k'doshav ki ein mach'sor lirei'av*

[11] *k'firim rashu v'ra'eivu v'dor'shei YHVH lo yach's'ru chol tov*

[12] *l'chu vanim shim'u li yir'at YHVH alamed'chem*

[13] *mi ha'ish hechafetz chayim oheiv yamim lir'ot tov*

[14] *n'tzor l'shon'cha meira us'fatecha midabeir mir'mah*

[15] *sur meira va'aseih tov bakeish shalom v'rod'feihu*

[16] *einei YHVH el tzadikim v'oz'nav el shav'atam*

[17] *p'nei YHVH b'osei ra l'hach'rit mei'eretz zich'ram*

[18] *tza'aku va'YHVH shamei'a umikol tzarotam hitzilam*

[19] *karov YHVH l'nish'b'rei leiv v'et dak'ei ru'ach yoshi'a*

[20] *rabot ra'ot tzadik umikulam yatzilenu YHVH*

[21] *shomeir kol atz'motav achat meiheinah lo nish'barah*

[22] *t'moteit rasha ra'ah v'son'ei tzadik ye'shamu*

[23] *podeh YHVH nefesh avadav v'lo ye'sh'mu kol hachosim bo*

Translation:

[1] A Psalm of David; when he changed his demeanour before Abimelech, who drove him away, and he departed.

[2] I will bless *YHVH* at all times; His praise shall continually be in my mouth.

[3] My soul shall glory in *YHVH*; the humble shall hear thereof, and be glad.

[4] O magnify *YHVH* with me, and let us exalt His name together.

[5] I sought *YHVH*, and He answered me, and delivered me from all my fears.

[6] They looked unto Him, and were radiant; and their faces shall never be abashed.

[7] This poor man cried, and *YHVH* heard, and saved him out of all his troubles.

[8] The angel of *YHVH* encampeth round about them that fear Him, and delivereth them.

[9] O consider and see that *YHVH* is good; happy is the man that taketh refuge in Him.

[10] O fear *YHVH*, ye His holy ones; for there is no want to them that fear Him.

[11] The young lions do lack, and suffer hunger; but they that seek *YHVH* want not any good thing.

[12] Come, ye children, hearken unto me; I will teach you the fear of *YHVH*.

[13] Who is the man that desireth life, and loveth days, that he may see good therein?

[14] Keep thy tongue from evil, and thy lips from speaking guile.

[15] Depart from evil, and do good; seek peace, and pursue it.

[16] The eyes of *YHVH* are toward the righteous, and His ears are open unto their cry.

[17] The face of *YHVH* is against them that do evil, to cut off the remembrance of them from the earth.

[18] They cried, and *YHVH* heard, and delivered them out of all their troubles.

[19] *YHVH* is nigh unto them that are of a broken heart, and saveth such as are of a contrite spirit.

[20] Many are the ills of the righteous, but *YHVH* delivereth him out of them all.

[21] He keepeth all his bones; not one of them is broken.

[22] Evil shall kill the wicked; and they that hate the righteous shall be held guilty.

[23] *YHVH* redeemeth the soul of His servants; and none of them that take refuge in Him shall be desolate.

Psalm 34 is recited during the morning service (*Shacharit*) on *Shabbat* and festivals, as well as at the earlier mentioned *hakafot* (circumambulations) during שמחת תורה (*Simchat Torah—* "Rejoicing with the *Torah*").[1] It is said King David sang this Psalm on *Shabbat*, and thus it was determined by the "Men of the Great Assembly" that it should be recited on *Shabbat*.[2] The Psalm itself is an acrostic Psalm, i.e. the verses are arranged alphabetically, except that in the current instance the verse for the letter ו (*Vav*) appears to be missing, and an extra verse commencing with the letter פ (*Peh*) is added at the end of the Psalm. It has been speculated that the letter ו (*Vav*) is referenced by the word ופניהם (*uf'neihem*—"and their faces") in verse 6, thus both the letters ה (*Heh*) and ו (*Vav*) are referenced in this verse.[3] On the other hand, it has been said that the letter פ (*Peh*) appears twice in the Psalm, because this letter is substituting ו (*Vav*) in the א״ת ב״ש (*Atbash*) cipher.[4]

    Psalm 3:4 reading גדלו יהוה אתי ונרוממה שמו יחדו (*gad'lu la'YHVH iti un'rom'ma sh'mo yach'dav—*"O magnify *YHVH* with me, and let us exalt His name together") is particularly significant in Jewish worship. Whilst it is selected to be recited in the synagogue when the *Torah* scroll is taken from the ark, it is also used to call three or more adults who are about to participate in a communal meal, to say grace collectively.[5] We are informed the six words comprising this verse aligns with the "six paces of those who bore the ark [of the covenant]" as written in *2 Samuel 6:13* reading ויהי כי צעדו נשאי ארון יהוה ששה צעדים (*vay'hi ki tza'ado nos'ei aron YHVH shishah tz'adim—*"And it was so, that they who bore the ark of *YHVH* had gone six paces").[6] Furthermore, we are told the fourth verse of the current Psalm comprises twenty-six letters, this number being equal the gematria of the Ineffable Name[7] [י = 10 + ה = 5 + ו = 6 + ה = 5 = 26]. It is also recognized that this verse conceals, so to speak, one of the permutations of the Ineffable Name, i.e. the concluding letters of the first four words spell והיו, which is the permutation associated with the Hebrew month of טבת (*Tevet*). I have addressed this in some detail elsewhere.[8]

In terms of its use in Jewish Magic, *Psalm 34* is recited when undertaking a roadtrip or a voyage,[9] or "to have success on your way," i.e. during a journey.[10] In this regard, the "*Shimmush Tehillim*" maintains the Psalm should be recited "with its Name" when en route to some or other destination, and affirms that "you will succeed."[11] Godfrey Selig shares the same instructions in his version of the "*Shimmush Tehillim*" with some additional emphasis on the stance of the excursionist, saying "this Psalm is highly recommended to each traveller, for if he prays it diligently he will surely finish his journey in safety."[12] The associated Divine Name is said to be פלא (*Pele*), which is a standard Hebrew term meaning "wonder," but which is indicated in the current instance to be a Divine Name construct derived: פ (*Peh*) from פדה יהוה (*podeh YHVH*— "YHVH redeemeth"): verse 23; ל (*Lamed*) from לכו בנים (*l'chu vanim*—"Come, ye children"): verse 12; and א (*Alef*) from בשנותו את טעמו (*b'shanoto et ta'mo*—"when he changed his demeanour"): verse 1.[13] Selig claims the letters ל (*Lamed*) and א (*Alef*) in the said Divine Name construct, were respectively derived from לפני (*lif'nei*—"before"): verse 1; and from קרא (*kara*—"cried"): verse 7.[14] In this regard, there is nothing to be found in primary Hebrew sources to substantiate this claim.

The thirty-fourth Psalm is also considered good for finding favour in the eyes of authorities.[15] In this regard, the Psalm is employed to succeed in having a request granted.[16] The "*Shimmush Tehillim*" maintains the Psalm should again be recited with the earlier mentioned Divine Name construct, before meeting with a prince or ruler in order to find favour.[17] Elsewhere it is maintained that *Psalm 34* should be recited seven times prior to appearing before a ruler.[18] Furthermore, we are informed that the current Psalm could be recited to benefit someone else who finds him/herself in a stressful situation, and hence needs to meet with an authority. Thus it is written that "if you wish to release your friend from pressure, say it and go with him to a distinguished (person)."[19]

In a different recension of the "*Shimmush Tehillim*" the current Psalm is employed against every affliction by persecutors.

In this regard, you are required to write the Psalm down with its associated Divine Name אל פלה יועץ גבור (*El Peleh Yo'eitz Gibor*), and suspended around your neck. This action is followed by uttering the following prayer-incantation:[20]

בשם יהוה אלהי ישראל רחום וחנון אני עושה זה
הכתב ל[....Name of Recipient....] אלהים חיים ומלך
עולם ירחם עלי ויוציאני מכף כל רודפי וישפיל
אותם למטה למטה ואותי ירים למעלה למעלה
בשם אל פלה יועץ גבור אמן אמן אמן סלה
סלה סלה

Transliteration:

> *B'shem YHVH elohei yis'ra'el rachum v'chanun ani oseh zeh hak'tav l'[....Name of Recipient....] elohim chayim umelech olam y'rachem alai va'yotzi'eini mikaf kol rod'fai v'yash'pil otam lamateh lamateh v'oti yarim l'ma'lah l'ma'lah b'shem El Peleh Yo'eitz Gibor Omein Omein Omein Selah Selah Selah*

Translation:

> In the name of *YHVH*, God of Israel, merciful and gracious, I am preparing this writing for [....Name of Recipient....] Living God and eternal King have mercy on me, and lead me out of the hand of all my persecutors, and humble them all the way down, but raising me all the way up. With the name *El Peleh Yo'eitz Gibor* [*El Peleh*—"Heroic Counselor"]. *Amen Amen Amen Selah Selah Selah.*

We are advised in the same text that *Psalm 34* is also good for preaching, i.e. for giving a sermon.[21] In this regard, I should mention that I enunciated *Psalm 34* when I was particularly anxious prior to the presentation of a public lecture, and thought that if it works for "preachers," it should work for those who are required to speak publically. Hence I can testify to its efficacy.

The current Psalm is also employed for healing purposes. It has been suggested that that the thirty-fourth Psalm be whispered over olive oil, and the sick individual be anointed therewith, in order to alleviate a fever.[22] As it is, individual verses from the Psalm are equally employed for healing purposes. The capitals of the words comprising *Psalm 34:18* are conjoined to formulate the Divine Name construct צָוַשָׁוּצָהּ (*Tzavasha'utzahi*), which is employed in amulets meant to heal the sick,[23] and to save the bearer from all manner of trouble.[24] The special qualities of deliverance and healing of this verse are further emphasised in the very next verse, i.e. *Psalm 34:19*. The initials of the first six words of this verse are combined into the Divine Name construct קילּוד, which is employed in amulets for salvation, and to benefit heart and mental ailments.[25] On the other hand, the capitals of the words comprising the opening phrase of *Psalm 34:21*, reading שמר כל עצמותיו (*shomeir kol atz'motav*—"He keepeth all his bones"), are conjoined in the Divine Name construct שכע which is included in amulets to alleviate bone ailments.[26]

The initials of the six words comprising *Psalm 34:8* were combined in the Divine Name construct חמיסלו which is employed in amulets as a "call for help."[27] However, this combination represents the first six letters of a much larger Divine Name construct formed from the initials of the words comprising *Psalm 34:8–9*:

חמי סלו טוב טיא היב

This set of Divine Names is sometimes employed in amulets in conjunction with *Psalm 121* in support of infants who cry incessantly.[28] In this regard, the following letter squares were constructed from the same two verses of the thirty-fourth Psalm, equally for inclusion in an amulet for the very same purpose:

יי	רר	יש	לא	הו	נו	ום	חע
ור	וב	יג	אה	כב	או	לא	מר
צה	לס	חח	יי	הב	וו	הט	יי
נסו	אמן	טו	מב	בה	יו	בה	סי

Delineating the formulation of these letter squares is somewhat difficult. The words of the said two verses are written in a single line, with the inclusion of two additional letters in two words, i.e. in verse 8, i.e. ו (*Vav*) in the word חונה (*choneh*), and י (*Yod*) in ליריאיו (*lirei'av*). The total number of letters comprising both verses are then divided in two groups of thirty letters each, i.e the first half concludes with the opening letter ט (*Tet*) of the second verse, and the second half comprises the remainder of this verse. Next the thirty glyphs in each section are arranged into seven four-letter combinations and one two-letter combination. These are then located inside the letter square, i.e. the first four glyphs of the first set comprise the rightmost letters top right, whilst the first four glyphs of the second set are located adjacent those of the first set, etc. Having completed this task, the term אמן (*Omein*) and the standard abbreviation נצח סלה ועד] נס"ו (*Netzach Selah va'ed* —"Enduring, *Selah* forever") are entered into the two remaining cells bottom left.[29] Other than the Divine Name constructs derived from the said verses, I should mention that *Psalm 34:5* is directly associated with נטה (*Netah*), the twenty-fifth tri-letter portion of the "*Shem Vayisa Vayet*."[30] Furthermore, *Psalm 34:16* is also directly aligned with עלם (*Elem*), the fourth portion,[31] and *Psalm 34:17* with מצר [*Metzer*], the sixtieth tri-letter portion of the "*Name of Seventy-two Names*."[32]

There are again a number of magical applications of the current Psalm for purposes not found in published sources. Whilst the *Psalm 34* is recited against persecution, it is equally employed against invading armies, as well as against malice, betrayal (treachery), and against witchcraft and bewitchment. As noted, this Psalm is used to find favour with authorities, but equally to be received favourably by friends. In conclusion, it is recited by widows and widowers, also when visiting the graves of loved ones, for the well-being of orphans, and to diminish and alleviate poverty.

As far as Christian Magic is concerned, we are informed in the Byzantine magical manuscripts that *Psalm 34:1—21* "is for a person who has fallen and broken his leg."[33] Here the instruction is to recite the Psalm over olive oil, and then to rub the broken leg with it, which is said will facilitate healing speedily.[34] Curiously enough, in *"Le Livre d'Or"* the same verses are equally listed for a broken bone, but also for toothache. In this regard, the individual requiring healing is instructed to carry date stones to a crossroad where the said verses are recited seven times, following which his/her face is perfumed with smoke, and this is believed will facilitate healing.[35] Elsewhere *Psalm 34:13* and *21* are recited for the same purposes.[36]

We find in the Byzantine *"Geoponika"* the opening phrase in *Psalm 34:9*, reading טעמו וראו כי טוב יהוה (*ta'amu ur'u ki tov YHVH*—"consider and see that *YHVH* is good") being inscribed on barrels, in order to ensure that the wine is well preserved until the following harvest and wine production.[37] It is claimed this practice started with the Christian historian Sextus Julius Africanus.[38] However, it is not the Hebrew text, but rather the Latin words reading *"Gustate et videte quod bonus est Dominus"* ("Taste and see that the Lord is good") which was inscribed on the barrels.[39] In this regard, the words טעמו וראו (*ta'amu u'r'u*—"consider and see") were reinterpreted "taste and see," or as it has been popularly rendered later in German "schmecket und sehet.[40]

In conclusion, the previously mentioned Syrian magical manuscript in the Sachau Collection recommends reading *Psalm 34* for sorcery to be thwarted. In this regard, you should recite it over water, and it is said that if "you glow with head," that you should wash your face with it.[41] Otherwise, the same text suggests this Psalm be read to encourage love between a man and a woman. It is further said, that the Psalm should also be written for the same purpose inside a cistern, i.e. (a water storage facility), and to let the couple drink from it.[42]

Psalm 35

[1] לדוד ריבה יהוה_{אדני}יאהדונהי את יריבי לחם את לחמי

[2] החזק מגן וצנה וקומה בעזרתי

[3] והרק חנית וסגר לקראת רדפי אמר לנפשי ישעתך אני

[4] יבשו ויכלמו מבקשי נפשי יסגו אחור ויחפרו חשבי רעתי

[5] יהיו כמץ לפני רוח ומלאך יהוה_{אדני}יאהדונהי דוחה

[6] יהי דרכם חשך וחלקלקת ומלאך יהוה_{אדני}יאהדונהי רדפם

[7] כי חנם טמנו לי שחת רשתם חנם חפרו לנפשי

[8] תבואהו שואה לא ידע ורשתו אשר טמן תלכדו בשואה יפל בה

[9] ונפשי תגיל ביהוה_{אדני} יאהדונהי תשיש בישועתו

[10] כל עצמותי תאמרנה יהוה_{אדני}יאהדונהי מי כמוך מציל עני מחזק ממנו ועני ואביון מגזלו

[11] יקומון עדי חמס אשר לא ידעתי ישאלוני

[12] ישלמוני רעה תחת טובה שכול לנפשי

[13] ואני בחלותם לבושי שק עניתי בצום נפשי ותפלתי על חיקי תשוב

[14] כרע כאה לי התהלכתי כאבל אם קדר שחותי

[15] ובצלעי שמחו ונאספו נאספו עלי נכים ולא ידעתי קרעו ולא דמו

[16] בחנפי לעגי מעוג חרק עלי שנימו

[17] אדני כמה תראה השיבה נפשי משאיהם מכפירים יחידתי

[18] אודך בקהל רב בעם עצום אהללך

[19] אל ישמחו לי איבי שקר שנאי חנם יקרצו עין

[20] כי לא שלום ידברו ועל רגעי ארץ דברי מרמות יחשבון

[21] וירחיבו עלי פיהם אמרו האח האח ראתה עיננו

[22] ראיתה יהוהאדניאהדונהי אל תחרש אדני אל תרחק
ממני

[23] העירה והקיצה למשפטי אלהי ואדני לריבי

[24] שפטני כצדקך יהוהאדניאהדונהי אלהי ואל ישמחו
לי

[25] אל יאמרו בלבם האח נפשנו אל יאמרו בלענוהו

[26] יבשו ויחפרו יחדו שמחי רעתי ילבשו בשת וכלמה
המגדילים עלי ירנו וישמחו חפצי צדקי

[27] ויאמרו תמיד יגדל יהוהאדניאהדונהי החפץ שלום
עבדו

[28] ולשוני תהגה צדקך כל היום תהלתך

Transliteration:
[1] *l'david rivah YHVH et y'rivai l'cham et lochamai*
[2] *hachazeik magein v'tzinah v'kumah b'ez'rati*
[3] *v'hareik chanit us'gor lik'rat rod'fai emor l'naf'shi y'shu'ateich ani*
[4] *yeivoshu v'yikal'mu m'vak'shei naf'shi yisogu achor v'yach'p'ru chosh'vei ra'ati*
[5] *yih'yu k'motz lif'nei ru'ach umal'ach YHVH docheh*
[6] *y'hi dar'kam choshech va'chalak'lakot umal'ach YHVH rod'fam*
[7] *ki chinam tam'nu li shachat rish'tam chinam chaf'ru l'naf'shi*
[8] *t'vo'eihu sho'ah lo yeida v'rish'to asher taman til'k'do b'sho'ah yipol bah*
[9] *v'naf'shi tagil baYHVH tasis bishu'ato*
[10] *kol atz'motai tomar'na YHVH mi chamocha matzil ani meichazak mimenu v'ani v'ev'yon migoz'lo*
[11] *y'kumun eidei chamas asher lo yada'ti yish'aluni*
[12] *y'shal'muni ra'ah tachat tovah sh'chol l'nafshi*
[13] *va'ani bachalotam l'vushi sak ineiti vatzom naf'shi ut'filati al cheiki tashuv*
[14] *k'rei'a k'ach li hit'halach'ti ka'avel eim kodeir shachoti*
[15] *uv'tzal'i sam'chu v'ne'esafu ne'es'fu alai neichim v'lo yada'ti kar'u v'lo damu*
[16] *b'chan'fei la'agei ma'og charok alai shineimo*

[17] *adonai kamah tir'eh hashivah naf'shi misho'eihem mik'firim y'chidati*

[18] *od'cha b'kahal rav b'am atzum ahal'lekah*

[19] *al yis'm'chu li oy'vai sheker son'ai chinam yik'r'tzu ayin*

[20] *ki lo shalom y'dabeiru v'al rig'ei eretz div'rei mir'mot yachashovun*

[21] *vayar'chivu alai pihem am'ru he'ach he'ach ra'ata eineinu*

[22] *ra'itah YHVH al techerash adonai al tir'chak mimeni*

[23] *ha'irah v'hakitzah l'mish'pati elohai vadonai l'rivi*

[24] *shof'teini ch'tzid'k'chah YHVH elohai v'al yis'm'chu li*

[25] *al yom'ru v'libam he'ach naf'sheinu al yom'ru bila'anuhu*

[26] *yeivoshu v'yach'p'ru yach'dav s'meichei ra'ati yil'b'shu voshet uch'limah hamag'dilim alai yaronu v'yis'm'chu chafeitzei tzid'ki*

[27] *v'yom'ru tamid yig'dal YHVH he'chafeitz sh'lom av'do*

[28] *ul'shoni teh'geh tzid'kecha kol hayom t'hilatecha*

Translation:

[1] A Psalm of David. Strive *YHVH*, with them that strive with me; fight against them that fight against me.

[2] Take hold of shield and buckler, and rise up to my help.

[3] Draw out also the spear, and the battle-axe, against them that pursue me; say unto my soul: 'I am Thy salvation.'

[4] Let them be ashamed and brought to confusion that seek after my soul; let them be turned back and be abashed that devise my hurt.

[5] Let them be as chaff before the wind, the angel of *YHVH* thrusting them.

[6] Let their way be dark and slippery, the angel of *YHVH* pursuing them.

[7] For without cause have they hid for me the pit, even their net, without cause have they digged for my soul.

[8] Let destruction come upon him unawares; and let his net that he hath hid catch himself; with destruction let him fall therein.

[9] And my soul shall be joyful in *YHVH*; it shall rejoice in His salvation.

[10] All my bones shall say: '*YHVH*, who is like unto Thee, who deliverest the poor from him that is too strong for him, yea, the poor and the needy from him that spoileth him?'

[11] Unrighteous witnesses rise up; they ask me of things that I know not.

[12] They repay me evil for good; bereavement is come to my soul.

[13] But as for me, when they were sick, my clothing was sackcloth, I afflicted my soul with fasting; and my prayer, may it return into mine own bosom.

[14] I went about as though it had been my friend or my brother; I bowed down mournful, as one that mourneth for his mother.

[15] But when I halt they rejoice, and gather themselves together; the abjects gather themselves together against me, and those whom I know not; they tear me, and cease not;

[16] With the profanest mockeries of backbiting they gnash at me with their teeth.

[17] *Adonai* how long wilt Thou look on? Rescue my soul from their destructions, mine only one from the lions.

[18] I will give Thee thanks in the great congregation; I will praise Thee among a numerous people.

[19] Let not them that are wrongfully mine enemies rejoice over me; neither let them wink with the eye that hate me without a cause.

[20] For they speak not peace; but they devise deceitful matters against them that are quiet in the land.

[21] Yea, they open their mouth wide against me; they say: 'Aha, aha, our eye hath seen it.'

[22] Thou hast seen *YHVH*; keep not silence; *Adonai* be not far from me.

[23] Rouse Thee, and awake to my judgment, even unto my cause, my God and my Lord.

[24] Judge me *YHVH* my God, according to Thy righteousness; and let them not rejoice over me.

[25] Let them not say in their heart: 'Aha, we have our desire'; let them not say: 'We have swallowed him up.'

[26] Let them be ashamed and abashed together that rejoice at my hurt; let them be clothed with shame and confusion that magnify themselves against me.

[27] Let them shout for joy, and be glad, that delight in my righteousness; yea, let them say continually: 'Magnified be *YHVH*, who delighteth in the peace of His servant.'

[28] And my tongue shall speak of Thy righteousness, and of Thy praise all the day.

Psalm 35 does not appear to have been used in any prominent manner at any time in Jewish liturgies. In this regard, I believe it is the belligerent tone of the Psalm which makes it unsuitable for synagogal worship. Its employment in Jewish Magic is equally sparse, and in accordance with the rule of not sharing in this series of texts on "Practical Kabbalah" (Jewish Magic) any magical procedures seeking to curse or destroy any of our fellow humankind, I have excluded certain practices related to this Psalm.

As indicated by the first verse of the current Psalm reading ריבה יהוה את יריבי לחם את לחמי (*rivah YHVH et y'rivai l'cham et lo chamai*—"Strive *YHVH*, with them that strive with me; fight against them that fight against me"), the thirty-fifth Psalm is employed, in the words of one commentator, "against mischievous busybodies,"[1] or rather against belligerent people or adversaries rising up against you.[2] In this regard, the "*Shimmush Tehillim*" maintains the Psalm should be recited three times each morning,[3] whilst we are told elsewhere that "if someone oppresses you or hates you, say it in your prayers three days, three times a day."[4] Here the "*Shimmush Tehillim*" references the well-known Divine Name יה (*Yah*), which should clearly be concentrated on whilst reciting the current Psalm. In this instance the Divine Name is said to have been derived: י (*Yod*) from לחם את לחמי (*l'cham et lochamai*—"fight against them that fight against me"): verse 1, and ה (*Heh*) from חחזק מגן וצנה (*ha'chazeik magein v'tzinah*—"Take hold of shield and buckler"): verse 2,[5] both phrases indicating the aggressive undertones of the magical application.

Godfrey Selig's German/English version of the "*Shimmush Tehillim*" maintains a somewhat different use of *Psalm 35* pertaining more to legal action against combatants. In this regard, he wrote "have you a lawsuit pending in which you are opposed by unrighteousness, revengeful and quarrelsome people, then, pray this Psalm with its holy name *Jah*, early in the morning for three successive days, and you will surely win your case." He equally shares the same origins of the Divine Name construct.[6] There is validity to his "litigation" claims here, since we are informed elsewhere that the thirty-fifth Psalm is employed to win a lawsuit.[7]

Single verses from the current Psalm are employed in a much less antagonistic manner. In this regard, *Psalm 35:18* reading אהללך בעם עצום רב בקהל אודך (*od'cha b'kahal rav b'am atzum ahal'lekah*—"I will give Thee thanks in the great congregation; I will praise Thee among a numerous people"), is recommended for recitation whilst "gazing at crowds and passersby."[8] Other than that, *Psalm 35:24* is directly aligned with שאה (*Sha'ah*), the twenty-eighth portion of the "*Shem Vayisa Vayet.*"[9]

As noted earlier, the listed magical applications of the current Psalm are somewhat sparse. However, more was passed on orally, and in this regard *Psalm 35* is employed against harm and being hurt; for protection against enemies; as well as to alleviate any anxiety caused by enemies. As in the case of the previous Psalm, the thirty-fifth Psalm is recited against betrayal, as well as against exploitation, and to locate criminals. In conclusion, we are told this Psalm is good for ensuring a safe pregnancy, and for protecting children. It is even recommended for the protection of animals, both wild and domestic.

The application of *Psalm 35* in Christian Magic is somewhat more diverse. In the Byzantine magical manuscripts it is equally employed "to defeat someone."[10] Continuing the theme of protection against contenders, we are informed elsewhere that *Psalm 35:5* and *6* offers protection "against persecution from powerful men and from tyrants."[11] When it comes to a time when you require ultimate protection, so to speak, you are instructed in the Syrian magical manuscript in the Sachau Collection to recite the Psalm three times when you are off to war.[12] However, we are also informed in the mentioned Byzantine magical manuscripts, that the current Psalm, as well as the following one, are efficacious when "spoken with compunction and contrition of heart," and that doing so until midday will establish peace and favour with all who "are at odds with you."[13] In the same manuscripts reference is made to the current Psalm being employed to expel demons from a residence. In this regard, it is maintained that the demons will flee when the Psalm is recited over a seven day period.[14] Curiously enough, the thirty-fifth Psalm is employed in Roman Catholic exorcisms.[15] In this regard, it is worth noting that in Christianity sexual appetites, other than the reproductive variety, are often delineated "demonic," and hence it should come as no surprise that *Psalm 35* is recommended in the Byzantine magical manuscripts to those who "struggle against fornication."[16]

According to *"Le Livre d'Or"* you should enunciate the current Psalm seven times, concluding with a related oration, if you should "fall into need."[17] It also suggests that you write the Psalm which is afterwards tied to your arm, if you "wish to have access to a Prince or to your enemies."[18]

Psalm 36

‫[1] למנצח לעבד יהוהאדניאהדונהי לדוד‬

‫[2] נאם פשע לרשע בקרב לבי אין פחד אלהים‬
‫לנגד עיניו‬

‫[3] כי החליק אליו בעיניו למצא עונו לשנא‬

‫[4] דברי פיו און ומרמה חדל להשכיל להיטיב‬

‫[5] און יחשב על משכבו יתיצב על דרך לא טוב‬
‫רע לא ימאס‬

‫[6] יהוהאדניאהדונהי בהשמים חסרך אמונתך עד‬
‫שחקים‬

‫[7] צדקתך כהררי אל משפטיך תהום רבה אדם‬
‫ובהמה תושיע יהוהאדניאהדונהי‬

‫[8] מה יקר חסדך אלהים ובני אדם בצל כנפיך‬
‫יחסיון‬

‫[9] ירוין מדשן ביתך ונחל עדניך תשקם‬

‫[10] כי עמך מקור חיים באורך נראה אור‬

‫[11] משך חסדך לידעיך וצדקתך לישרי לב‬

‫[12] אל תבאני רגל גאוה ויד רשעים אל תנדני‬

‫[13] שם נפלו פעלי און דחו ולא יכלו קום‬

Transliteration:

[1] *lam'natzei'ach l'eved YHVH l'david*

[2] *n'um pesha larasha b'kerev libi ein pachad elohim l'neged einav*

[3] *ki hechelik eilav b'einav lim'tzo avono lis'no*

[4] *div'rei fiv aven umir'ma chadal l'has'kil l'heitiv*

[5] *aven yach'shov al mish'kavo yit'yatzeiv al derech lo tov ra lo yim'as*

[6] *YHVH b'hashamayim chas'decha emunat'cha ad sh'chakim*

[7] *tzid'kat'cha k'har'rei eil mish'patecha t'hom rabah adam uv'heimah toshi'a YHVH*

[8] *mah yakar chas'd'cha elohim uv'nei adam b'tzeil k'nafecha yechesayun*

[9] *yir'v'yun mideshen beitecha v'nachal adanecha tash'keim*

[10] *ki im'cha m'kor chayim b'or'cha nir'eh or*
[11] *m'shoch chas'd'cha l'yod'echa v'tzid'kat'cha l'yish'rei leiv*
[12] *al t'vo'eini regel ga'avah v'yad r'sha'im al t'nideini*
[13] *sham naf'lu po'alei aven dochu v'lo yach'lu kum*

Translation:

[1] For the Leader. A Psalm of David the servant of *YHVH*.
[2] Transgression speaketh to the wicked, methinks—there is no fear of *Elohim* before his eyes.
[3] For it flattereth him in his eyes, until his iniquity be found, and he be hated.
[4] The words of his mouth are iniquity and deceit; he hath left off to be wise, to do good.
[5] He deviseth iniquity upon his bed; he setteth himself in a way that is not good; he abhorreth not evil.
[6] Thy lovingkindness *YHVH*, is in the heavens; Thy faithfulness reacheth unto the skies.
[7] Thy righteousness is like the mighty mountains; Thy judgments are like the great deep; man and beast Thou preservest *YHVH*.
[8] How precious is Thy lovingkindness *Elohim*, and the children of men take refuge in the shadow of Thy wings.
[9] They are abundantly satisfied with the fatness of Thy house; and Thou makest them drink of the river of Thy pleasures.
[10] For with Thee is the fountain of life; in Thy light do we see light.
[11] O continue Thy lovingkindness unto them that know Thee; and Thy righteousness to the upright in heart.
[12] Let not the foot of pride overtake me, and let not the hand of the wicked drive me away.
[13] There are the workers of iniquity fallen; they are thrust down, and are not able to rise.

As in the case of the previous Psalm, the current one does not feature in Jewish liturgy except for a single verse, *Psalm 36:7*, which is one of three verses from the "*Book of Psalms*" which include the word צדקתך (*Tzid'kat'cha*—"Thy righteousness"), i.e. *Psalm 36:7, 71:19*, and *119:42*. These verses are recited during the afternoon prayer service (*Minchah*) of *Shabbat*, in reversed order in the Ashkenazi liturgy, and in ascending order in the Sefardi liturgy.[1]

It should be noted that worship in the synagogue is not a random "sunday-go-to-church" affair where congregants stand to stretch their legs whilst singing a hymn, or sit down to listen to the often fearsome ministrations of clergymen. Jewish worship is "magical," so to speak, in the sense that sitting, standing, and bowing in the synagogue, are in many instances predetermined for spiritual reasons. Even the order of the recitation of biblical verses is often filled with infinite, though perhaps hidden, meaning. This is especially applicable in the mentioned three verses being recited in ascending order in the Sefardi rite, regarding which we are informed that the concluding words of these verses are expressed in the phrase in *Jeremiah 10:10* reading יהוה אלהים אמת (*YHVH Elohim Emet*—"*YHVH* is a true God").[2]

There are several reasons posited for reading these three verses on *Shabbat*. In this regard, we are told that the *Torah* was offered to the Jews on the Sabbath, and thus these verses are recited on this day because *Psalm 36:7* comprises ten words, aligning with the Decalogue (Ten Commandments); there are forty letters in *Psalm 71:19*, referencing the time spent by Moses on the mountain to acquire the two לחות הברית (*Luchot ha'Brit*— "Tablets of the Covenant") comprising the "Ten Commandments"; and because there are five words in *Psalm 119:42* which are said to pertain to the Pentateuch, i.e. the "Five Books of Moses."[3]

In a more mystical vein, we are informed in the *Sefer ha-Zohar* that Moses departed from the world at "a time of favour" during *Minchah* (afternoon service) of *Shabbat*.[4] We are also told that "there are three who departed the world at this time....One is Moses, supernal faithful one, another, Joseph the Righteous; another King David."[5] In the current instance, these three personages are symbolically aligned:

> a. Moses the Faithful Prophet who "grasps all sides, right and left," with *Tif'eret* (Beauty), the Sun, the "*Written Torah*," and "Thy righteousness also *Elohim*, which reacheth unto high heaven; Thou who hast done great things *YHVH*, who is like unto Thee?" (*Psalm 71:19*).

b. Josef the Righteous who is "like all those towering mountains" with *Yesod* (Foundation), and "Thy righteousness is like the mighty mountains; Thy judgments are like the great deep; man and beast Thou preservest *YHVH*." (*Psalm 36:7*).

c. King David with *Shechinah–Malchut* (Kingdom), the Moon, the "*Oral Torah*," and "Thy righteousness is an everlasting righteousness, and Thy law is the truth." (*Psalm 119.142*).[6]

We are told that Joseph the Righteous, symbolizing *Yesod*, "conveys the flow of the sefirotic *mountains*, namely *Hesed* through *Yesod* itself," whilst Moses the Faithful Prophet "attained *the heights* of *Tif'eret* and accomplished *great things* by grasping the polar opposites *Hesed* and *Gevurah*, on the right and left."[7] Furthermore, Josef the Righteous and King David are said to be "included in Moses" symbolising *Tif'eret* uniting with the *Shechinah* "via His extension, *Yesod*."[8] Lastly, King David symbolises the *Shechinah* recognised as both צדק (*Tzedek*— "Righteousness"), and עולם (*Olam*—"world"), which are said to be "indicated by the phrase צדק לעולם (*Tzedek l'Olam*— "Everlasting Righteousness").[9] However, whilst there is much more to be said about the profundity of meaning surrounding the occasion when Moses the Faithful Prophet, Josef the Righteous, and King David departed our domain of mortal existence, suffice it to say that reciting the mentioned verses during *Minchah* (afternoon service) of *Shabbat*, is a kind of צידוק הדין (*Tziduk ha-Din*—"justification of judgment), i.e. an acknowledgment of Divine Righteousness, and "an acceptance of the justice of the divine decree of death (imposed on Moses, David, and Joseph)."[10]

Psalm 36 is employed in "Practical Kabbalah" (Jewish Magic) for the purpose of annihilating the wicked or evil ones.[11] The magical use of the thirty-sixth Psalm does not appear in every published edition of the "*Shimmush Tehillim*," but in those where it is listed, we are told that it is good against every "evil decree," i.e. "evil tidings,"[12] and I would think it would be equally good against an "evil spell" or "curse." In this regard, Godfrey Selig maintains in his version of the "*Shimmush Tehillim*," that this Psalm is used "against all evil and slanderous libels," and that you should "pray this Psalm, and they will cause you no injury."[13] We are further informed that there is a Divine Name associated with this Psalm which is אמת (*Emet*—"Truth").[14] The Selig version claims this Divine Name was derived from: "*arven*" (in the English translation), which was corrected in a recent publication to און (*aven*—"iniquity" [evil]): verse 13 (incorrectly listed "verse 6"); משפטיך (*mish'patecha*—"Thy judgments"): verse 7; and תהום (*t'hom*— "the deep"): verse 7.[15]

In a different recension of the "*Shimmush Tehillim*," we are informed that the thirty-sixth Psalm is good for shutting the mouths of evil doers, as well as the jaws of vicious beasts. In this regard, the practitioner is instructed to recite the Psalm with its Name, and conclude with the following prayer-incantation:

צור אלהי עולם מצעקתי אל תתעלם אך שמע
צעקתי ותפילתי והצילני מחיות רעות בשם
אֵלָד

Transliteration:

> *Tzur Elohei olam mitza'akati al tit'alam ach sh'ma tza'akati v't'filati v'hatzileini meichayot ra'ot b'shem Eilad.*

Translation:

> Rock, God of the world, do not ignore my cries, but hear my cry and my prayer. Rescue me from evil beasts in the Name *Eilad*.

The practitioner is further instructed to recite the Psalm in the morning when seeing the beasts. It is said that enunciating the Psalm every morning with the accompanying prayer-incantation, will ensure safety "from every evil beast."[16] Whilst we are focussing on a magical procedure for protection against "evil beasts," it should be noted that the Divine Name construct דְּמֵעָה (*D'mei'ah*) was derived from the concluding letters of the words from *Psalm 36:7* reading אדם ובהמה תושיע (*adam u'v'heimah toshi'a*—"man and beast Thou preservest"), for the purpose of protection during a horsedrawn carriage ride, to ensure that the traveller is not thrown from the vehicle, and equally that the said person would not be injured if he/she should fall from the carriage.[17] The vowels employed in the enunciation of this Divine Name are those applying to the word בְּהֵמָה (*b'heimah*—"animal" or "beast"). It was suggested that the current verse should be recited three times during the carriage ride, each time with its associated Divine Name construct.[18] Of course, the kind of "carriages" we are travelling in today, are very different from the average horsedrawn carriage of the late nineteenth century. The modern motorised vehicles are "daunting beasts" whose power is still measured in terms of the "horse"....actually many horses! I cannot see why the same procedure involving the said verse and associated Divine Name construct, could not be applied for the same purpose when travelling in our current transportation facilities.

The thirty-sixth Psalm is also recited for success in business, and to find leniency with debtors. It is enunciated for the protection of fields and gardens; for good crops; and to find relief from famines. It is also recommended to encourage fruitfulness in women who are barren, and to ensure conception. Otherwise, it is used as a protection against killers and assassins; against theft, thieves and robbers; against persecution; for freedom from all evil; to remove animosity after arguments; to alleviate the frustration arising from the wickedness of others; against anger, as well as for peace.

In conclusion, it should be noted that *Psalm 36:9* is indirectly affliated with דמב (*Dameb*), the sixty-fifth portion of the "*Shem Vayisa Vayet*."[19] In this regard we are informed that a permutation of the full spelling of the glyphs comprising this Divine Name combination, i.e. ד(לל)ה מ(ם)ב(י"ת), reveals the word מתת (*matat*—a "gift" or "present"). We are told that the *gematria* of מתת [מ = 40 + ת = 400 + ת = 400 = 840] equates with that of the term תשקם (*tash'kem*—"they drink from" [ת = 400 + ש = 300 + ק = 100 + ם = 40 = 840]), which is said to relate to the phrase in current verse reading וְנַחַל עֲדָנֶיךָ תַשְׁקֵם (*v'nachal adanecha tash'kem*—"and Thou makest them drink of the river of Thy pleasures."[20]

As noted earlier, in the oft mentioned Byzantine Christian magical manuscripts *Psalms 35* and *36* are employed conjointly, to establish peace and favour with "all who are at odds with you."[21]

A similar use is made of the thirty-third Psalm in the Syrian magical manuscript in the Sachau Collection, in which it is said that whoever has scheming neighbours, should write down the current Psalm, and carry it on his or her person. We are told that this will ensure that the said individual and the unpleasant neighbours will be separated from one another.[22] And regarding "enemies" of the insect kind, the Latin phrase "*Ibi ceciderunt, expulsi sunt inimici meï*" ("They die there. My enemies are expelled"), derived from *Psalm 36:13*, was recommended to rid a granary of weevil bugs. In this regard, it was suggested that the said phrase "should be written on slips of paper that are placed at the four corners of the granary holding wheat, or in the wheat itself, to drive away the weevils."[23]

    Psalm 36 is also employed in Christian Magic for healing purposes. In this regard, we are told that the Psalm should be read for someone who has a very severe fever, and that the individual concerned will be healed with Divine support.[24] Elsewhere, in "*Le Livre d'Or*," it is said that a safe pregnancy could be secured until birth, by writing the thirty-sixth Psalm and fixing it inside the hood of the garment worn by the mother-to-be, or else tying it to her right arm.[25] When it comes to a pregnant woman going into labour, *Psalm 36:8* and *10* were conjoined for the purpose of ensuring a painless birth.[26]

Psalm 37

[1] לדוד אל תתחר במרעים אל תקנא בעשי עולה

[2] כי כחציר מהרה ימלו וכירק דשא יבולון

[3] בטח ביהוה יאהדונהי ועשה טוב שכן ארץ ורעה אמונה

[4] והתענג על יהוה יאהדונהי ויתן לך משאלת לבך

[5] גול על יהוה יאהדונהי דרכך ובטח עליו והוא יעשה

[6] והוציא כאור צדקך ומשפטך כצהרים

[7] דום ליהוה יאהדונהי והתחולל לו אל תתחר במצליח דרכו באיש עשה מזמות

[8] הרף מאף ועזב חמה אל תתחר אך להרע

[9] כי מרעים יכרתון וקוי יהוה יאהדונהי המה יירשו ארץ

[10] ועוד מעט ואין רשע והתבוננת על מקומו ואיננו

[11] וענוים יירשו ארץ והתענגו על רב שלום

[12] זמם רשע לצדיק וחרק עליו שניו

[13] אדני ישחק לו כי ראה כי יבא יומו

[14] חרב פתחו רשעים ודרכו קשתם להפיל עני ואביון לטבוח ישרי דרך

[15] חרבם תבוא בלבם וקשתותם תשברנה

[16] טוב מעט לצדיק מהמון רשעים רבים

[17] כי זרועות רשעים תשברנה וסומך צדיקים יהוה יאהדונהי

[18] יודע יהוה יאהדונהי ימי תמימם ונחלתם לעולם תהיה

[19] לא יבשו בעת רעה ובימי רעבון ישבעו

[20] כי רשעים יאבדו ואיבי יהוה יאהדונהי כיקר כרים כלו בעשן כלו

[21] לוה רשע ולא ישלם וצדיק חונן ונותן

[22] כי מברכיו יירשו ארץ ומקלליו יכרתו

[23] מיהוה יאהדונהי מצעדי גבר כוננו ודרכו יחפץ

[24] כי יפל לא יוטל כי יהוהאדניאהדונהי סומך ידו

[25] נער הייתי גם זקנתי ולא ראיתי צדיק נעזב
וזרעו מבקש לחם

[26] כל היום חונן ומלוה וזרעו לברכה

[27] סור מרע ועשה טוב ושכן לעולם

[28] כי יהוהאדניאהדונהי אהב משפט ולא יעזב את
חסידיו לעולם נשמרו וזרע רשעים נכרת

[29] צדיקים יירשו ארץ וישכנו לעד עליה

[30] פי צדיק יהגה חכמה ולשונו תדבר משפט

[31] תורת אלהיו בלבו לא תמעד אשריו

[32] צופה רשע לצדיק ומבקש להמיתו

[33] יהוהאדניאהדונהי לא יעזבנו בידו ולא ירשיענו
בהשפטו

[34] קוה אל יהוהאדניאהדונהי ושמר דרכו וירוממך
לרשת ארץ בהכרת רשעים תראה

[35] ראיתי רשע עריץ ומתערה כאזרח רענן

[36] ויעבר והנה איננו ואבקשהו ולא נמצא

[37] שמר תם וראה ישר כי אחרית לאיש שלום

[38] ופשעים נשמדו יחדו אחרית רשעים נכרתה

[39] ותשועת צדיקים מיהוהאדניאהדונהי מעוזם בעת
צרה

[40] ויעזרם יהוהאדניאהדונהי ויפלטם יפלטם מרשעים
ויושיעם כי חסו בו

Transliteration:

[1] *l'david al tit'char bam'rei'im al t'kanei b'osei av'lah*
[2] *ki chechatzir m'heirah yimalu uch'yerek deshe yibolun*
[3] *b'tach baYHVH va'aseih tov sh'chon eretz ur'eih emunah*
[4] *v'hit'anag al YHVH v'yiten l'cha mish'alot libecha*
[5] *gol al YHVH dar'kecha uv'tach alav v'hu ya'aseh*
[6] *v'hotzi cha'or tzid'kecha u'mish'patecha katzohorayim*
[7] *dom laYHVH v'hit'choleil lo al tit'char b'matz'li'ach dar'ko b'ish oseh m'zimot*
[8] *heref mei'af va'azov cheimah al tit'char ach l'harei'a*
[9] *ki m'rei'im yikaretun v'kovei YHVH heimah yir'shu aretz*

[10] *v'od m'at v'ein rasha v'hit'bonan'ta al m'komo v'einenu*

[11] *va'anavim yir'shu aretz v'hit'an'gu al rov shalom*

[12] *zomeim rasha latzadik v'choreik alav shinav*

[13] *adonai yis'chak lo ki ra'ah ki yavo yomo*

[14] *cherev pat'chu r'sha'im v'dar'chu kash'tam l'hapil ani v'ev'yon lit'vo'ach yish'rei darech*

[15] *char'bam tavo v'libam v'kash'totam tishavar'nah*

[16] *tov m'at latzadik meihamon r'sha'im rabim*

[17] *ki z'ro'ot r'sha'im tishavar'nah v'someich tzadikim YHVH*

[18] *yodei'a YHVH y'mei t'mimim v'nachalatam l'olam tih'yeh*

[19] *lo yeivoshu b'eit ra'ah uvimei r'avon yis'ba'u*

[20] *ki r'sha'im yoveidu v'oy'vei YHVH kikar karim kalu ve'ashan kalu*

[21] *loveh rasha v'lo y'shaleim v'tzadik chonein v'notein*

[22] *ki m'vorachav yir'shu aretz um'kulalav yikareitu*

[23] *meiYHVH mitz'adei gever konanu v'dar'ko yech'patz*

[24] *ki yipol lo yutal ki YHVH someich yado*

[25] *na'ar hayiti gam zakan'ti v'lo ra'iti tzadik ne'ezav v'zar'o m'vakesh la'chem*

[26] *kol hayom chonein umal'veh v'zar'o liv'rachah*

[27] *sur meira va'aseih tov ush'chon l'olam*

[28] *ki YHVH oheiv mish'pat v'lo ya'azov et chasidav l'olam nish'maru v'zera r'sha'im nich'rat*

[29] *tzadikim yir'shu aretz v'yish'keinu la'ad aleha*

[30] *pi tzadik yeh'geh choch'mah ul'shono t'dabeir mish'pat*

[31] *torat elohav b'libo lo tim'ad ashurav*

[32] *tzofeh rasha latzadik um'vakeish laha'mito*

[33] *YHVH lo ya'az'venu v'yado v'lo yar'shi'enu b'hishaf'to*

[34] *kaveih el YHVH ush'mor dar'ko viromim'cha lareshet aretz b'hikaret r'sha'im tir'eh*

[35] *ra'iti rasha aritz umit'areh k'ez'rach ra'anan*

[36] *vaya'avor v'hineih einenu va'avak'shei'hu v'lo nim'tza*

[37] *sh'mor tam ur'eih yashar ki acharit l'ish shalom*

[38] *ufosh'im nish'm'du yach'dav acharit r'sha'im nich'ratah*

[39] *ut'shu'at tzadikim meiYHVH ma'uzam b'eit tzarah*

[40] *vaya'z'reim YHVH vay'fal'teim y'fal'teim meir'sha'im v'yoshi'eim ki chasu vo*

Translation:

[1] A Psalm of David. Fret not thyself because of evil-doers, neither be thou envious against them that work unrighteousness.

[2] For they shall soon wither like the grass, and fade as the green herb.

[3] Trust in *YHVH*, and do good; dwell in the land, and cherish faithfulness.

[4] So shalt thou delight thyself in *YHVH*; and He shall give thee the petitions of thy heart.

[5] Commit thy way unto *YHVH*; trust also in Him, and He will bring it to pass.

[6] And He will make thy righteousness to go forth as the light, and thy right as the noonday.

[7] Resign thyself unto *YHVH*, and wait patiently for Him; fret not thyself because of him who prospereth in his way, because of the man who bringeth wicked devices to pass.

[8] Cease from anger, and forsake wrath; fret not thyself, it tendeth only to evil-doing.

[9] For evil-doers shall be cut off; but those that wait for *YHVH*, they shall inherit the land.

[10] And yet a little while, and the wicked is no more; yea, thou shalt look well at his place, and he is not.

[11] But the humble shall inherit the land, and delight themselves in the abundance of peace.

[12] The wicked plotteth against the righteous, and gnasheth at him with his teeth.

[13] *Adonai* doth laugh at him; for He seeth that his day is coming.

[14] The wicked have drawn out the sword, and have bent their bow; to cast down the poor and needy, to slay such as are upright in the way;

[15] Their sword shall enter into their own heart, and their bows shall be broken.

[16] Better is a little that the righteous hath than the abundance of many wicked.

[17] For the arms of the wicked shall be broken; but *YHVH* upholdeth the righteous.

[18] *YHVH* knoweth the days of them that are wholehearted; and their inheritance shall be for ever.

[19] They shall not be ashamed in the time of evil; and in the days of famine they shall be satisfied.

[20] For the wicked shall perish, and the enemies of *YHVH* shall be as the fat of lambs—they shall pass away in smoke, they shall pass away.

[21] The wicked borroweth, and payeth not; but the righteous dealeth graciously, and giveth.

[22] For such as are blessed of Him shall inherit the land; and they that are cursed of Him shall be cut off.

[23] It is of *YHVH* that a man's goings are established; and He delighted in his way.

[24] Though he fall, he shall not be utterly cast down; for *YHVH* upholdeth his hand.

[25] I have been young, and now am old; yet have I not seen the righteous forsaken, nor his seed begging bread.

[26] All the day long he dealeth graciously, and lendeth; and his seed is blessed.

[27] Depart from evil, and do good; and dwell for evermore.

[28] For *YHVH* loveth justice, and forsaketh not His saints; they are preserved for ever; but the seed of the wicked shall be cut off.

[29] The righteous shall inherit the land, and dwell therein for ever.

[30] The mouth of the righteous uttereth wisdom, and his tongue speaketh justice.

[31] The law of his God is in his heart; none of his steps slide.

[32] The wicked watcheth the righteous, and seeketh to slay him.

[33] *YHVH* will not leave him in his hand, nor suffer him to be condemned when he is judged.

[34] Wait for *YHVH*, and keep His way, and He will exalt thee to inherit the land; when the wicked are cut off, thou shalt see it.

[35] I have seen the wicked in great power, and spreading himself like a leafy tree in its native soil.

[36] But one passed by, and, lo, he was not; yea, I sought him, but he could not be found.

[37] Mark the man of integrity, and behold the upright; for there is a future for the man of peace.

[38] But transgressors shall be destroyed together; the future of the wicked shall be cut off.

[39] But the salvation of the righteous is of *YHVH*; He is their stronghold in the time of trouble.

[40] And *YHVH* helpeth them, and delivereth them; He delivereth them from the wicked, and saveth them, because they have taken refuge in Him.

Whilst *Psalm 37* does not feature in Jewish liturgies, it is recommended in Jewish Magic "against drunkenness," and "to cure a drunkard."[1] In this regard, we are instructed in the "*Shimmush Tehillim*" to fill a glass (a jug seems more suitable in the current instance) with water.[2] One recension of this text suggests adding some salt.[3] Next recite (whisper according to another recension) the current Psalm with its associated Divine Name over the water, and let the drunkard drink a little of this substance, before pouring the rest over his head and face. It is no wonder it is said he will forthwith wake up, and his intoxication will instantly disappear.[4] Whilst the instruction references a drunken man, I certainly cannot see why the same technique should not work for a woman.

    Be that as it may, in this instance the associated Divine Name is said to be הא, (*Ha'a* [?]), א (*Alef*) from אל תתחר (*al tit'char*—"Fret not"): verse 1, and ה (*Heh*) from the ו (*Vav*) in ויעזרם (*vaya'z'reim*—"helpeth them"): verse 40, the letter having been transposed by means of the א"ב ב"מ (*Aibat*) cipher.[5] There is no indication as to how this Divine Name construct should be enunciated, but considering the vowels associated with the letters from which it is said to have been derived, the enunciation might simply be "*ha'a*."

    In another recension of the "*Shimmush Tehillim*" we find a somewhat expanded version of this procedure. In this instance the instruction is likewise to take water and salt, whisper the current Psalm over it with its associated Divine Name, and to let the drunkard imbibe some, but here the face and cheeks are sort of daubed with the remainder of the water, which is said will cause his drunkenness to depart. Afterwards the procedure is concluded by uttering the following prayer-incantation:

אל רחום וחנון ארך אפים רחם על האיש הזה
[....Name of Recipient....] והחזיר לו דעתו מיושבת
עליו כבראשונה ואל יהי עוד שכור אך יצא מזה
השכרות כאילו לא שתה בשם אל עליון אה יהיה
הדבר הזה אמן אמן אמן סלה סלה סלה סלה

Transliteration:

El rachum v'chanun erech apayim racheim al ha'ish hazeh [....Name of Recipient....] v'hechazer lo da'ato m'yoshevet alav kabarishonah v'al y'hi od shikor ach yetzei mizeh hasich'rut k'ilo lo shatah b'shem El El'yon Aha yih'yeh hadavar hazeh. Omein Omein Omein Selah Selah Selah.

Translation:

Merciful, gracious, long-suffering God, have mercy on this man [....Name of Recipient....], and give him back his level-headed mind as before, and he should no longer be a drunkard, but emerge from this drunkenness as if he had not been drinking. In the name *El El'yon Aha* will be this word. *Amen Amen Amen Selah Selah Selah.*[6]

In the current instance the Divine Name combination comprises the well-known אל עליון [*El El'yon*] conjoined with אה (*Aha* [?]), the reverse of the Divine Name referenced earlier.

That is the full extent of the listed applications of *Psalm 37* in Jewish magical literature. However, once again we see the current Psalm being extensively enunciated for a great variety of reasons amongst those Jewish folk who are accustomed to reciting Psalms on a daily basis, and who are happy to pass along their oral heritage to receptive ears. In this regard we are told that the current Psalm is particularly good for healing in general, and especially for anaemia; cancer; fever; weakness and trembling generally; for diseases of, and pain in, the eyes; loss of hearing (deafness); broken bones; gangrene; and for the healing of wounds, with special reference to those who were seriously wounded by criminals. As far as the latter types are concerned, we are told that the thirty-seventh Psalm is employed against oppressors and anger; against witchcraft and bewitchment; to be saved from defamation, slander and gossip; for protection in perilous situations; and in times of trouble.

The current Psalm is further recommended for the healing of nervous disorders, especially if these conditions were brought on by the hazards of living in troubled times. For those who reside in rural areas, the hazards of life sometimes include serpents from which, it is said, one could also find protection by reciting the thirty-seventh Psalm. It is further recommended to those who are doubting their faith, and equally to anyone who is confused by the success of the wicked. In this regard, the current Psalm is enunciated to halt envy of evil people, and, for that matter, envy of the rich. If someone should lose his or her faith in life and in the Divine One, this Psalm is enunciated for penitence; forgiveness of errors and transgressions; to maintain *Torah* principles; and ultimately to find "Peace of Soul."

Not much remains to be said about the thirty-seventh Psalm as far as its use in Jewish Magic is concerned, except that *Psalm 37:4* is directly aligned with ענו (*Anu*), the sixty-third portion of the "*Shem Vayisa Vayet.*"[7]

In Christian Magic the uses of the current Psalm is somewhat more diverse. In this regard, we are informed in the Byzantine magical manuscripts that it is employed in "a struggle against fornication,"[8] whilst we are told elsewhere in the same manuscripts that the Psalm is recited "if you wish to teach someone."[9] In "*Le Livre d'Or*" the thirty-seventh Psalm is employed for a much more sinister purpose, i.e. to destroy an enemy.[10] As far as "enemies" are concerned, it is worth noting that *Psalm 37:15* features in the "*Key of Solomon*" in the outer border of the "*Sixth Pentacle of Mars*," the virtue of which is said to be so great "that being armed therewith, if thou art attacked by any one, thou shalt neither be injured nor wounded when thou fightest with him, and his own weapons shall turn against him."[11]

Psalm 38

‏[1] מזמור לדוד להזכיר‎

‏[2] יהוה‏אדני‏יאהדונהי אל בקצפך תוכיחני ובחמתך‎
‏תיסרני‎

‏[3] כי חציך נחתו בי ותנחת עלי ידך‎

‏[4] אין מתם בבשרי מפני זעמך אין שלום בעצמי‎
‏מפני חטאתי‎

‏[5] כי עונתי עברו ראשי כמשא כבד יכבדו ממני‎

‏[6] הבאישו נמקו חבורתי מפני אולתי‎

‏[7] נעויתי שחתי עד מאד כל היום קדר הלכתי‎

‏[8] כי כסלי מלאו נקלה ואין מתם בבשרי‎

‏[9] נפוגותי ונדכיתי עד מאד שאגתי מנהמת לבי‎

‏[10] אדני נגדך כל תאותי ואנחתי ממך לא נסתרה‎

‏[11] לבי סחרחר עזבני כחי ואור עיני גם הם אין אתי‎

‏[12] אהבי ורעי מנגד נגעי יעמדו וקרובי מרחק עמדו‎

‏[13] וינקשו מבקשי נפשי ודרשי רעתי דברו הוות‎
‏ומרמות כל היום יהגו‎

‏[14] ואני כחרש לא אשמע וכאלם לא יפתח פיו‎

‏[15] ואהי כאיש אשר לא שמע ואין בפיו תוכחות‎

‏[16] כי לך יהוה‏אדני‏יאהדונהי הוחלתי אתה תענה אדני‎
‏אלהי‎

‏[17] כי אמרתי פן ישמחו לי במוט רגלי עלי הגדילו‎

‏[18] כי אני לצלע נכון ומכאובי נגדי תמיד‎

‏[19] כי עוני אגיד אדאג מחטאתי‎

‏[20] ואיבי חיים עצמו ורבו שנאי שקר‎

‏[21] ומשלמי רעה תחת טובה ישטנוני תחת רדפי טוב‎

‏[22] אל תעזבני יהוה‏אדני‏יאהדונהי אלהי אל תרחק ממני‎

‏[23] חושה לעזרתי אדני תשועתי‎

Transliteration:
[1] *miz'mor l'david l'haz'kir*
[2] *YHVH al b'ketz'p'cha tochicheini uvachamat'cha t'yas'reini*
[3] *ki chitzecha nichatu vi vatin'chat alai yadecha*

[4] *ein m'tom biv'sari mip'nei za'mecha ein shalom ba'atzamai mip'nei chatati*

[5] *ki avonotai av'ru roshi k'masa chaveid yich'b'du mimeni*

[6] *hiv'ishu namaku chaburotai mip'nei ival'ti*

[7] *na'aveiti shachoti ad m'od kol hayom kodeir hilach'ti*

[8] *ki ch'salai mal'u nik'leh v'ein m'tom biv'sari*

[9] *n'fugoti v'nid'keiti ad m'od sha'ag'ti minahamat libi*

[10] *adonai neg'd'cha chol ta'avati v'an'chati mim'cha lo nistarah*

[11] *libi s'char'char azavani chochi v'or einai gam heim ein iti*

[12] *ohavai v'rei'ai mineged nig'i ya'amodu uk'rovai meirachok amadu*

[13] *vay'nak'shu m'vak'shei naf'shi v'dor'shei ra'ati dib'ru havot umir'mot kol hayom yeh'gu*

[14] *va'ani ch'cheireish lo esh'ma uch'ileim lo yif'tach piv*

[15] *va'ehi k'ish asher lo shomei'a v'ein b'fiv tochachot*

[16] *ki l'cha YHVH hochal'ti atah ta'aneh adonai elohai*

[17] *ki amar'ti pen yis'm'chu li b'mot rag'li alai hig'dilu*

[18] *ki ani l'tzela nachon umach'ovi neg'di tamid*

[19] *ki avoni agid ed'ag meichatati*

[20] *v'oy'vai chayim atzeimu v'rabu son'ai shaker*

[21] *um'shal'mei ra'ah tachat tovah yis't'nuni tachat rod'fi tov*

[22] *al ta'az'veini YHVH elohai al tir'chak mimeni*

[23] *chushah l'ez'rati adonai t'shu'ati*

Translation:

[1] A Psalm of David, to make memorial.

[2] *YHVH* rebuke me not in Thine anger; neither chasten me in Thy wrath.

[3] For Thine arrows are gone deep into me, and Thy hand is come down upon me.

[4] There is no soundness in my flesh because of Thine indignation; neither is there any health in my bones because of my sin.

[5] For mine iniquities are gone over my head; as a heavy burden they are too heavy for me.

[6] My wounds are noisome, they fester, because of my foolishness.

[7] I am bent and bowed down greatly; I go mourning all the day.

[8] For my loins are filled with burning; and there is no soundness in my flesh.

[9] I am benumbed and sore crushed; I groan by reason of the moaning of my heart.

[10] *Adonai*, all my desire is before Thee; and my sighing is not hid from Thee.

[11] My heart fluttereth, my strength faileth me; as for the light of mine eyes, it also is gone from me.

[12] My friends and my companions stand aloof from my plague; and my kinsmen stand afar off.

[13] They also that seek after my life lay snares for me; and they that seek my hurt speak crafty devices, and utter deceits all the day.

[14] But I am as a deaf man, I hear not; and I am as a dumb man that openeth not his mouth.

[15] Yea, I am become as a man that heareth not, and in whose mouth are no arguments.

[16] For in Thee *YHVH*, do I hope; Thou wilt answer *Adonai* my God.

[17] For I said: 'Lest they rejoice over me; when my foot slippeth, they magnify themselves against me.'

[18] For I am ready to halt, and my pain is continually before me.

[19] For I do declare mine iniquity; I am full of care because of my sin.

[20] But mine enemies are strong in health; and they that hate me wrongfully are multiplied.

[21] They also that repay evil for good are adversaries unto me, because I follow the thing that is good.

[22] Forsake me not *YHVH*; O my God, be not far from me.

[23] Make haste to help me *Adonai*, my salvation.

This Psalm does not feature in Jewish liturgies, but *Psalm 38:16* is amongst a set of biblical verses comprising the ותתפלל חנה (*Vatit'paleil Chanah*—"and Hannah prayed") prayer, which is recited in the Syrian, Moroccan, and Judeo-Spanish traditions during the morning service (*Shacharit*). Whilst the authorship of this prayer is unknown, it has been speculated that "its recital was instituted by the kabbalists from the time of R. Isaac Luria (*Ari*)."[1]

As far as the use of *Psalm 38* in "Practical Kabbalah" (Jewish Magic) is concerned, we are told that it affords protection against bad advice,[2] and equally against defamation.[3] In this regard, we are informed that in order to be saved from slander, or if an evil king,[4] or an "evil person" according to others,[5] plans something against you, that you need to rise in the morning, go outdoors, and there in the open pray the Psalm.[6] In this instance, the associated Divine Name is also said to be אֲהָ (*Aha* [?]).[7] Be that as it may, in dealing with *Psalms 38* and *39* conjointly, Godfrey Selig puts a somewhat different slant on the slander issue in the expanded procedure he shared in his version of the "*Shimmush Tehillim*."[8] Thus he wrote "if you have been so much slandered that the king and the officers of the law have been turned against you, and are taking measures to punish you, arise early, at the break of day and go out into the fields. Pray these Psalms and their holy name seven times with great devotion, and fast the entire day."[9] The "holy name" is the listed one, but which Selig maintains was derived from certain words in verses from the following Psalm.

If it should come to anyone having to take legal action, e.g. against the "slanderer," or having to face some or other litigation, it is worth noting that the concluding letters of the words comprising *Psalm 38:14* and *15*, were conjoined into the following Divine Name construct for the purpose of ensuring success when one has to appear before a judge.

יששאע מאחו ישרא עניח

To achieve the said aim, the practitioner is required to recite the said verses followed by the Divine Name construct.[10]

In a different recension of the "*Shimmush Tehillim*" we find the thirty-eighth Psalm listed as good for confessing, i.e. admitting transgressions.[11] In this regard, the instruction is to recite the Psalm with its associated Divine Name four times a day after rising in the morning, and to conclude with the following prayer-incantation:

יהוה יהוה אל רחום וחנון ארך אפים ורב חסד

ואמת [*Exodus 34:6*] לפניך באתי בבכי ובתחנונים

להודות על חטאי ופשעי וזדונותי ושגגותי בשם

יהוה יהוה אל רחום וחנון ארך אפים ורב חסד

ואמת [*Exodus 34:6*] אמן אמן אמן סלה סלה סלה סלה

Tranliteration:

> *YHVH YHVH El rachum v'chanun erech apayim v'rav*
> *chesed v'emet* [*Exodus 34:6*] *l'fanecha bati b'bechi*
> *b'tach'nunim l'hodot al chat'ai up'sha'ai uz'donotai*
> *ush'gagotai b'sheim YHVH YHVH El rachum v'chanun*
> *erech apayim v'rav chesed v'emet* [*Exodus 34:6*].

Translation:

> *YHVH YHVH El* merciful and gracious, long-suffering, and
> abundant in goodness and truth. [*Exodus 34:6*] I came
> before you with weeping and supplication to admit my
> sins, and my transgressions, and my wickedness and my
> errors, in the name *YHVH YHVH El* merciful and gracious,
> long-suffering, and abundant in goodness and truth.
> [*Exodus 34:6*] *Amen Amen Amen Selah Selah Selah.*[12]

As far as the magical use of single verses from the current Psalm
is concerned, it should be noted that the capitals from the phrase in
Psalm 38:4 reading אין מתם בבשרי (*ein m'tom biv'sari*—"There
is no soundness in my flesh"), are formulated into the Divine
Name construct אמב which is employed as an amulet "for
ailments of the skin and muscles."[13] The capitals of the first three
words of *Psalm 38:6* reading הבאישו נמקו חבורתי (*hiv'ishu
namaku chaburotai*—"My wounds are noisome, they fester") are
combined in the Divine Name construct הנה, which is likewise
employed in amulets created to counteract skin diseases in
general.[14] Yet the healing powers of the thirty-eighth Psalm extend
further than the skin. The initials of the opening four words of
Psalm 38:11, reading לבי סחרחר עזבני כחי (*libi s'char'char
azavani chochi*—"My heart fluttereth, my strength faileth me"),
are combined into the Divine Name construct לסעב which is
employed in amulets for heart and bone ailments.[15] Lastly, it is
worth noting that *Psalm 38:22* is directly aligned with ערי (*Ari*),
the forty-sixth portion of the "*Shem Vayisa Vayet.*"[16]

As far as "healing powers" are concerned, we find *Psalm 38* listed amongst the many employed for the healing of illness in general, and in the current instance specifically for pain in the jaws. It is recommended for all manner of suffering, and for affliction and the afflicted, with special reference to the dumb. The current Psalm is also one of the many enunciated for protection in perilous situations and in times of trouble. In this regard, it is recommended as a support to exiles and refugees. It is further enunciated against threats; to alleviate anxiety caused by enemies; to overcome a fear of dying; and ultimately for a "good death." On a more positive note, the thirty-eighth Psalm is recited against apathy (indifference); to overcome spiritual troubles; to find a mate; and to engender, receive and increase love.

In Christian Magic the current Psalm is equally employed for healing purposes. In this regard the Syrian magical manuscript in the Sachau Collection notes its use against headaches.[17] On the other hand, "*Le Livre d'Or*" maintains the thirty-eighth Psalm to be good for "pain in the eyes."[18] In this regard, it suggests the Psalm be recited "over holy water at Christmas," and the eyes washed therewith. Afterwards, a set of associated magical characters are to be written down, fumigated with mastic and incense, and worn around the neck by the sufferer.[19] Elsewhere we find *Psalm 38:11* recommended against "blindness," and *Psalm 38:4–5* against "muteness."[20]

Psalm 39

[1] למנצח לידותון מזמור לדוד

[2] אמרתי אשמרה דרכי מחטוא בלשוני אשמרה לפי מחסום בעד רשע לנגדי

[3] נאלמתי דומיה החשיתי מטוב וכאבי נעכר

[4] חם לבי בקרבי בהגיגי תבער אש דברתי בלשוני

[5] הודיעני יהוה‏אדני‏ה‏ קצי ומדת ימי מה היא אדעה מה חדל אני

[6] הנה טפחות נתתה ימי וחלדי כאין נגדך אך כל הבל כל אדם נצב סלה

[7] אך בצלם יתהלך איש אך הבל יהמיון יצבר ולא ידע מי אספם

[8] ועתה מה קויתי אדני תוחלתי לך היא

[9] מכל פשעי הצילני חרפת נבל אל תשימני

[10] נאלמתי לא אפתח פי כי אתה עשית

[11] הסר מעלי נגעך מתגרת ידך אני כליתי

[12] בתוכחות על עון יסרת איש ותמס כעש חמודו אך הבל כל אדם סלה

[13] שמעה תפלתי יהוה‏אדני‏ה‏ ושועתי האזינה אל דמעתי אל תחרש כי גר אנכי עמך תושב ככל אבותי

[14] השע ממני ואבליגה בטרם אלך ואינני

Transliteration:

[1] *lam'na'tzei'ach lidutun miz'mor l'david*

[2] *amar'ti esh'm'rah d'rachai m'chato vil'shoni esh'm'rah l'fi mach'som b'od rasha l'neg'di*

[3] *ne'elam'ti dumiyah hechesheiti mitov uch'eivi ne'kar*

[4] *cham libi b'kir'bi bahagigi tiv'ar eish dibar'ti bil'shoni*

[5] *hodi'eini YHVH kitzi umidat yamai mah hi eid'ah meh chadeil ani*

[6] *hineih t'fachot natatah yamai v'chel'di ch'ayin neg'decha ach kol hevel kol adam nitzav selah*

[7] *ach b'tzelem yit'halech ish ach hevel yehemayun yitz'bor v'lo yeida mi os'fam*

[8] *v'atah mah kiviti adonai tochal'ti l'cha hi*

[9] *mikol p'sha'ai hatzileini cher'pat naval al t'simeini*

[10] *ne'elam'ti lo ef'tach pi ki atah asita*

[11] *haseir mei'alai nig'echa mitig'rat yad'cha ani chaliti*

[12] *b'tochachot al avon yisar'ta ish vatemes ka'ash chamudo ach hevel kol adam selah*

[13] *shim'ah t'filati YHVH v'shav'ati ha'azinah el dim'ati al techerash ki geir anochi imach toshav k'chol avotai*

[14] *hasha mimeni v'av'ligah b'terem eileich v'eineni*

Translation:

[1] For the Leader, for Jeduthun. A Psalm of David.

[2] I said: 'I will take heed to my ways, that I sin not with my tongue; I will keep a curb upon my mouth, while the wicked is before me.'

[3] I was dumb with silence; I held my peace, had no comfort; and my pain was held in check.

[4] My heart waxed hot within me; while I was musing, the fire kindled; then spoke I with my tongue:

[5] *YHVH* make me to know mine end, and the measure of my days, what it is; let me know how short-lived I am.

[6] Behold, Thou hast made my days as hand-breadths; and mine age is as nothing before Thee; surely every man at his best estate is altogether vanity. *Selah*

[7] Surely man walketh as a mere semblance; surely for vanity they are in turmoil; he heapeth up riches, and knoweth not who shall gather them.

[8] And now *Adonai*, what wait I for? My hope, it is in Thee.

[9] Deliver me from all my transgressions; make me not the reproach of the base.

[10] I am dumb, I open not my mouth; because Thou hast done it.

[11] Remove Thy stroke from off me; I am consumed by the blow of Thy hand.

[12] With rebukes dost Thou chasten man for iniquity, and like a moth Thou makest his beauty to consume away; surely every man is vanity. *Selah*

[13] Hear my prayer *YHVH*, and give ear unto my cry; keep not silence at my tears; for I am a stranger with Thee, a sojourner, as all my fathers were.

[14] Look away from me, that I may take comfort, before I go hence, and be no more.'

Psalm 39 is said to be good for someone who is fasting.[1] However, there is no indication in the published version of the "*Shimmush Tehillim*" of this Psalm relating "to any specific ailment or situation."[2] It instructs the practitioner to rise at dawn and to go out into the open, where the Psalm is to be recited seven times with its associated Divine Name construct.[3] The latter is indicated to be הי, which is said to have been derived: ה (*Heh*) from הׁשע ממני (*hasha mimeni*—"look away from me"): verse 14; and י (*Yod*) from אמרתי (*amar'ti*—"I said"): verse 2.[4]

The fact that there is no clear application to be found in the printed editions of the "*Shimmush Tehillim*," resulted in an assumption that the thirty-ninth Psalm is good for everything. However, in one recension of the said text *Psalm 39* is indicated as good for שאלת חלום (*she'elat chalom*—"Dream Questioning"). In this regard, the practitioner is instructed to fast, to get into bed alone, doing so between white sheets, and to recite the Psalm fifteen times during the night, each time concluding with the following prayer incantation:

להתחנן ולהתפלל לפני אלהי עולם באתי בלילה
הזאת ושפכתי לב לפניו כמים פרשתי כפי אל אל
בשמים אשר ברחמיו וחסדיו ישמעני ויטה אזנו אלי
לשמוע צעקתי ויבוא אלי בעל החלום בלילה הזאת
ויגיד שאלתי זאת שאני שואל לדעת דבר זה אם
יהיה כך או כך ויפרש שאלתי בכל הצורך בשם
המלך הנורא והקדוש יודע אלי זה הדבר שאני שואל
הלילה בשינתי זאת ראשונה אמן אמן אמן סלה
סלה סלה

Transliteration:

l'hit'chanein ul'hit'palel lif'nei elohei olam bati balailah hazot v'shafach'ti leiv l'fanav kamayim paras'ti kapai el eil bashamayim asher barachamav v'chasadav yish'ma'eini v'yateh oz'no alai lish'mo'a tza'akati v'yavo alai ba'al hachalom balailai hazot v'yagid she'eilati zot she'ani sho'el lada'at davar zeh im yih'yeh kaf o kaf v'yif'ros she'eilati b'chol hatzorech b'sheim hamelech hanora v'hakadosh yivada eilai zeh hadavar she'ani sho'el

*halailah b'sheinati zot rishonah Omein Omein Omein
Solah Selah Seluh*

Translation:

> To supplicate and pray I have come this night before the
> eternal God, and I have poured out my heart like water
> before Him. I have declared myself to God in heaven, who
> will hear me with his mercy and grace, and will incline his
> ear to hear my cry, and the Lord of the dream will come to
> me this night, and He will answer my question I ask in
> order to know this matter, whether it will be one way or the
> other. And He shall explain my question sufficiently. In the
> name of the King, awesome and holy, this matter which I
> inquire shall become known to me this night in my first
> sleep. *Amen Amen Amen Selah Selah Selah.*[5]

We are informed in the "*Jewish Encyclopedia*" that the "*Shimmush
Tehillim*" recommends the thirty-ninth Psalm "against evil design
on the part of the king."[6] I do not know whence this attribution was
derived, since there is no reference to such an application in any
recension of the "*Shimmush Tehillim*" that I am aware of. In fact,
this magical application pertains more to the previous Psalm rather
than the current one. However, *Psalm 39:2* is employed against an
evil spirit. In this regard the following Divine Name construct was
created by writing the said verse in reverse, and then reciting the
letters of the resulting phrase with the Hebrew vowel points *sh'va*,
kamatz, and *cholam*,[7] as indicated below. These vowels are
respectively aligned with גבורה (*Gevurah*—"Might"), חסד
(*Chesed*—"Lovingkindness"), and תפארת (*Tif'eret*—"beauty")
on the sefirotic Tree:

ידגנל עשר דועב מוסחם
יפל הרמשא ינושלב
אוטחם יכרד הרמשא
יתרמא

Transliteration:

> *Y'dagon'la   osh'ra   dov'avo   m'vasoch'ma   yof'la
> hor'masho'   yanov'shalov'   avot'cha'mo   y'charod'
> harom'sha'o y't'rom'a.*[8]

Psalm 39 is one of the Psalms recommended against defamation, slander and gossip, as well as against verbal abuse and suffering. Should such abuse result in dismissal at a workplace, the current Psalm is enunciated when an individual is laid off work. However, it is equally recited against unemployment; poverty; to find work; to make debtors more lenient; and also to be relieved from depressions brought on by unemployment. The current Psalm is also one of the many recommended for protection in perilous situations, as well as in times trouble, and on a more positive note, it is said to ensure success in spiritual matters.

As far as the use of further single verses from the current Psalm in "Practical Kabbalah" is concerned, it is worth noting that לאו (*Lav*), the seventeenth tri-letter portion of the "*Shem Vayisa Vayet*," is indirectly related to the phrase in *Psalm 39:12* reading אך הבל כל אדם סלה (*ach hevel kol adam selah*—"surely every man is breath [vanity], *selah*"). In this regard, it is said the *gematria* of לאו [ל = 30 + א = 1 + ו = 6 = 37] is equal to that of להב (*lahav*—a "flame" [ל = 30 + ה = 5 + ב = 2 = 37]). We are informed that this is a reference to the *Neshamah*, the "Higher Spirit Self," which is "the 'breath' of the Almighty, permeating the body with the flame of life."[9] Furthermore, the *gematria* of לאו equally equates with that of הבל (*Hevel*—"breath"), the letters of this term being a permutation of the mentioned Hebrew word להב (*lahav*), and is likewise noted to be a direct reference to the said opening phrase of *Psalm 39:12*.[10]

In Christian magic we find a reference in the Byzantine magical manuscripts that the thirty-ninth Psalm is employed against anyone "who is hostile to you." In this regard, it recommends the recitation of the current Psalm over three olive leaves, whilst fasting, and that the leaves be located underneath the door of the enemy.[11] Otherwise, when it comes to "torment" of a different kind, i.e. bad dreams, the "*Le Livre d'Or*" suggests writing this Psalm on the right side of your face, doing so without speaking, which we are told will ensure that "you will have no more bad dreams."[12]

Psalm 40

[1] למנצח לדוד מזמור

[2] קוה קויתי יהוהאדני־יאהדונהי ויט אלי וישמע שועתי

[3] ויעלני מבור שאון מטיט היון ויקם על סלע
רגלי כונן אשרי

[4] ויתן בפי שיר חדש תהלה לאלהינו יראו רבים
וייראו ויבטחו ביהוהאדני־יאהדונהי

[5] אשרי הגבר אשר שם יהוהאדני־יאהדונהי מבטחו ולא
פנה אל רהבים ושטי כזב

[6] רבות עשית אתה יהוהאדני־יאהדונהי אלהי נפלאתיך
ומחשבתיך אלינו אין ערך אליך אגידה ואדברה
עצמו מספר

[7] זבח ומנחה לא חפצת אזנים כרית לי עולה וחטאה
לא שאלת

[8] אז אמרתי הנה באתי במגלת ספר כתוב עלי

[9] לעשות רצונך אלהי חפצתי ותורתך בתוך מעי

[10] בשרתי צדק בקהל רב הנה שפתי לא אכלא
יהוהאדני־יאהדונהי אתה ידעת

[11] צדקתך לא כסיתי בתוך לבי אמונתך ותשועתך
אמרתי לא כחדתי חסדך ואמתך לקהל רב

[12] אתה יהוהאדני־יאהדונהי לא תכלא רחמיך ממני חסדך
ואמתך תמיד יצרוני

[13] כי אפפו עלי רעות עד אין מספר השיגוני עונתי
ולא יכלתי לראות עצמו משערות ראשי ולבי עזבני

[14] רצה יהוהאדני־יאהדונהי להצילני יהוהאדני־יאהדונהי
לעזרתי חושה

[15] יבשו ויחפרו יחד מבקשי נפשי לספותה יסגו
אחור ויכלמו חפצי רעתי

[16] ישמו על עקב בשתם האמרים לי האח האח

[17] ישישו וישמחו בך כל מבקשיך יאמרו תמיד יגדל
יהוהאדני־יאהדונהי אהבי תשועתך

[18] ואני עני ואביון אדני יחשב לי עזרתי ומפלטי
אתה אלהי אל תאחר

Transliteration:

[1] *lam'natzei'ach l'david miz'mor*

[2] *kavoh kiviti YHVH vayeit eilai vayish'ma shav'ati*

[3] *vaya'aleini mibor sha'on mitit hayavein vayakem al sela rag'lai konein ashurai*

[4] *vayitein b'fi shir chadash t'hilah leiloheinu yir'u rabim v'yira'u v'yiv't'chu baYHVH*

[5] *ash'rei hagever asher sam YHVH miv'tacho v'lo fanah el r'havim v'satei chazav*

[6] *rabot asita atah YHVH elohai nif'l'otecha umach'sh'votecha eileinu ein aroch eilecha agidah va'adabeirah atz'mu misapeir*

[7] *zevach umin'chah lo chafatz'ta oz'nayim karita li olah vachata'ah lo sha'al'ta*

[8] *az amar'ti hinei vati bim'gilat seifer katuv alai*

[9] *la'asot r'tzon'cha elohai chafatz'ti v'torat'cha b'toch mei'ai*

[10] *bisar'ti tzedek b'kahal rav hineih s'fatai lo ech'la YHVH atah yada'ta*

[11] *tzid'kat'cha lo chisiti b'toch libi emunat'cha ut'shu'at'cha amar'ti lo chichad'ti chas'd'cha va'amit'cha l'kahal rav*

[12] *atah YHVH lo tich'la rachamecha mimeni chas'd'cha va'amit'cha tamid yitz'runi*

[13] *ki af'fu alai ra'ot ad ein mis'par hisiguni avonotai v'lo yachol'ti lir'ot atz'mu misa'arot roshi v'libi azavani*

[14] *r'tzeih YHVH l'hatzileini YHVH l'ez'rati chushah*

[15] *yeivoshu v'yach'p'ru yachad m'vak'shei naf'shi lis'potah yisogu achor v'yikal'mu chafeitzei ra'ati*

[16] *yashomu al eikev bosh'tam ha'om'rim li he'ach he'ach*

[17] *yasisu v'yis'm'chu b'cha kol m'vak'shecha yom'ru tamid yig'dal YHVH ohavei t'shu'atecha*

[18] *va'ani ani v'ev'yon adonai yachashov li ez'rati um'fal'ti atah elohai al t'achar*

Translation:

[1] For the Leader. A Psalm of David.

[2] I waited patiently for *YHVH*; and He inclined unto me, and heard my cry.

[3] He brought me up also out of the tumultuous pit, out of the miry clay; and He set my feet upon a rock, He established my goings.

[4] And He hath put a new song in my mouth, even praise unto our God; many shall see, and fear, and shall trust in *YHVH*.

[5] Happy is the man that hath made *YHVH* his trust, and hath not turned unto the arrogant, nor unto such as fall away treacherously.

[6] Many things hast Thou done *YHVH* my God, even Thy wonderful works, and Thy thoughts toward us; there is none to be compared unto Thee! If I would declare and speak of them, they are more than can be told.

[7] Sacrifice and meal-offering Thou hast no delight in; mine ears hast Thou opened; burnt-offering and sin-offering hast Thou not required.

[8] Then said I: 'Lo, I am come with the roll of a book which is prescribed for me;

[9] I delight to do Thy will, O my God; yea, Thy law is in my inmost parts.'

[10] I have preached righteousness in the great congregation, lo, I did not refrain my lips; *YHVH* Thou knowest.

[11] I have not hid Thy righteousness within my heart; I have declared Thy faithfulness and Thy salvation; I have not concealed Thy mercy and Thy truth from the great congregation.

[12] Thou *YHVH*, wilt not withhold Thy compassions from me; let Thy mercy and Thy truth continually preserve me.

[13] For innumerable evils have compassed me about, mine iniquities have overtaken me, so that I am not able to look up; they are more than the hairs of my head, and my heart hath failed me.

[14] Be pleased *YHVH*, to deliver me; *YHVH* make haste to help me.

[15] Let them be ashamed and abashed together that seek after my soul to sweep it away; let them be turned backward and brought to confusion that delight in my hurt.

[16] Let them be appalled by reason of their shame that say unto me: 'Aha, aha.'

[17] Let all those that seek Thee rejoice and be glad in Thee; let such as love Thy salvation say continually: '*YHVH* be magnified.'

[18] But, as for me, that am poor and needy, *Adonai* will account it unto me; Thou art my help and my deliverer; O my God, tarry not.

Psalm 40, according to the "*Shimmush Tehillim*," is good for being rescued from, or protected against, an evil spirit.[1] In the current instance there is again a Divine Name, יָהּ (*Yah*), to concentrate on whilst reciting the Psalm. In this instance, it is maintained that this Divine Name was derived: י (*Yod*) from שׁוֹעְתִי (*shav'ati*—"my cry"): verse 2; and ה (*Heh*) from לעזרתי חושה (*l'ez'rati chushah*—"make haste to help"): verse 14.[2] I have observed some speculation that the expression "evil spirit" might also be referencing a "dark mood," which was recognised at one time as an "evil spirit." That would mean that the fortieth Psalm would be good to recite by individuals who are bipolar.

Be that as it may, in another recension we find the current Psalm recited in order to be redeemed from the hand of a prince, judge, king, or any ruling authority for that matter. In this regard, the individual requiring this support, is instructed to recite the current Psalm with its associated Divine Name early in the morning. This action is concluded by enunciating the following prayer-incantation:

מלך רם ונשא על כל נשאים ורם על כל רמים
לפניך באתי בדמעות ובבכי ובקול מר שתשמע
אלי ותעשה חפצי ורצוני והצילני מיד השר הזה
אשר בא אלי בעלילות רשע להפילני ולכשילני
ולגזול ממני ממוני על לא המס בכפי (*Job 16:17*)
ועל לא דין ומשפט על כן אלהי פלטיני והצילני
והושיעני מידו ותשמעני כי אתה שומע צעקת
העניים והאביונים בשם המסלה סיט עלם יהיה
הדבר אמן אמן אמן אמן סלה סלה סלה סלה

Transliteration:

> *Melech ram v'nisa al kol nasa'im v'ram al kol ramim l'fanecha bati bid'ma'ot ub'bechi uv'kol mar sh'tish'ma eilai v'ta'aseh chef'tzi ur'tzoni v'hatzileini miyad hasar hazeh asher ba elai b'alilot resha l'hapileini v'lich'shileini v'lig'zol mimeni mamuni al lo chamas b'chapai (Job 16:17) v'al lo din umish'pat al kein elohai pal'teini v'hatzileini v'hoshi'eini miyado v'tash'mi'eini ki atah shomei'a tza'akat ha'aniyim v'ha'ev'yonim b'sheim Ham'silah[?] Sit Elem yih'yeh hadavar Omein Omein Omein Selah Selah Selah*

Translation:

> High and lofty King above all the exalted, and raised over all the elevated, I have come before you with tears, weeping and a bitter voice, so that you hear me and fulfill my desires and my will. Deliver me from the hand of this prince, who came to me with wicked acts to overthrow me, to make me stumble, and to steal my possessions, *although there is no violence in my hands (Job 16:17)*, and no trial or judgment. Therefore my God will let me escape, save me and deliver me from his hand. You shall hear me, for you hear the cry of the poor and the wretched. In the name *Ham'silah[?] Sit Elem* will be the word. *Amen Amen Amen Selah Selah Selah.*[3]

The curious Divine Name combination המסלה סיט עלם (*Ham'silah[?] Sit Elem*) includes the third and fourth tri-letter portions from the "Name of Seventy-two Names." Interestingly enough, a similar use is made of *Psalm 14* to halt an individual who seeks to inflict harm on your person, and it likewise includes *Job 16:17* in the associated prayer incantation. Be that as it may, it should be noted that other than the mentioned magical applications of the current Psalm, there is a reference to *Psalm 40:2* being directly affiliated with לוו (*Lov*), the nineteenth portion of the "*Shem Vayisa Vayet.*"[4]

As is the case with every Psalm addressed thus far, there are again a number of applications of *Psalm 40* which are shared external to official publications. In harmony with the use of the current Psalm to be saved from the hands of a king, judge or ruling authority, the fortieth Psalm is recited to prevent discord after disagreements between employers and employees. In this regard, it is worth noting that this Psalm is equally recommended for wrong and upsetting love; as a protection from harm; and against unforseen disasters. On a more positive note, it is employed as a statement of faith, and to express appreciation of the Divine One.

The use of the current Psalm in Christian magic is somewhat more diverse. In this regard it is suggested in the Byzantine magical manuscripts that *Psalm 40* should be recited "if you see a person transgressing,"[5] whilst in the Syrian magical manuscript in the Sachau Collection it is read over wool and oil, these substances being employed in the anointing of the body of a sick person.[6] The healing theme also features in "*Le Livre d'Or,*" in which we are told that it should be written with a set of associated magical characters, and afterwards carried on the right arm by a woman who suffers the risk of miscarriage.[7]

In conclusion, it should be noted that *Psalm 40:14* features in the "*Key of Solomon*" in the outer border of the "*Third Pentacle of Moon,*" regarding which it is said that "carried on your person during a journey, will protect the bearer against all attacks by night, and against every kind of danger and peril by Water."[8]

Psalm 41

[1] למנצח מזמור לדוד

[2] **אשרי** משכיל אל דל ביום רעה ימלטהו
יהוה יאהדונהי

[3] **יהוה**יאהדונהי ישמרהו ויחיהו ואשר בארץ
ואל תתנהו בנפש איביו

[4] **יהוה**יאהדונהי יסעדנו על ערש דוי כל משכבו
הפכת בחליו

[5] **אני** אמרתי יהוהיאהדונהי חנני רפאה נפשי כי
חטאתי לך

[6] **אויבי** יאמרו רע לי מתי ימות ואבד שמו

[7] **ואם** בא לראות שוא ידבר לבו יקבץ און לו **יצא**
לחוץ ידבר

[8] **יחד** עלי יתלחשו כל שנאי עלי יחשבו רעה לי

[9] **דבר** בליעל יצוק בו ואשר שכב לא יוסיף לקום

[10] **גם** איש שלומי אשר בטחתי בו אוכל לחמי הגדיל
עלי עקב

[11] **ואתה** יהוהיאהדונהי חנני והקימני ואשלמה להם

[12] **בזאת** ידעתי כי חפצת בי כי לא יריע איבי עלי

[13] **ואני** בתמי תמכת בי ותציבני לפניך לעולם

[14] **ברוך** יהוהיאהדונהי אלהי ישראל מהעולם ועד
העולם אמן ואמן

Transliteration:

[1] *lam'natzei'ach miz'mor l'david*

[2] *ash'rei mas'kil el dal b'yom ra'ah y'mal'teihu YHVH*

[3] *YHVH yish'm'reihu vi'chayeihu v'ushar ba'aretz v'al tit'neihu b'nefesh oy'vav*

[4] *YHVH yis'adenu al eres d'vai kol mish'kavo ha'fach'ta v'chol'yo*

[5] *ani amar'ti YHVH choneini r'fa'ah naf'shi ki chatati lach*

[6] *oy'vai yom'ru ra li matai yamut v'avad sh'mo*

[7] *v'im ba lir'ot shav y'dabeir libo yik'botz aven lo yeitzei lachutz y'dabeir*

[8] *yachad alai yit'lachashu kol son'ai alai yach'sh'vu ra'ah li*

[9] *d'var b'liya'al yatzuk bo va'asher shachav lo yosif lakum*

[10] *gam ish sh'lomi asher batach'ti vo ocheil lach'mi hig'dil alai akeiv*

[11] *v'atah YHVH choneini vahakimeini va'ashal'mah lahem*

[12] *b'zot yada'ti ki chafatz'ta bi ki lo yari'a oy'vi alai*

[13] *va'ani b'tumi tamach'ta bi vatatziveini l'fanecha l'olam*

[14] *baruch YHVH elohei yis'ra'eil meiha'olam v'ad ha'olam omein v'omein*

Translation:

[1] For the Leader. A Psalm of David.

[2] Happy is he that considereth the poor; *YHVH* will deliver him in the day of evil.

[3] *YHVH* preserve him, and keep him alive, let him be called happy in the land; and deliver not Thou him unto the greed of his enemies.

[4] *YHVH* support him upon the bed of illness; mayest Thou turn all his lying down in his sickness.

[5] As for me, I said: '*YHVH* be gracious unto me; heal my soul; for I have sinned against Thee.'

[6] Mine enemies speak evil of me: 'When shall he die, and his name perish?'

[7] And if one come to see me, he speaketh falsehood; his heart gathereth iniquity to itself; when he goeth abroad, he speaketh of it.

[8] All that hate me whisper together against me, against me do they devise my hurt:

[9] 'An evil thing cleaveth fast unto him; and now that he lieth, he shall rise up no more.'

[10] Yea, mine own familiar friend, in whom I trusted, who did eat of my bread, hath lifted up his heel against me.

[11] But Thou, *YHVH* be gracious unto me, and raise me up, that I may requite them.

[12] By this I know that Thou delightest in me, that mine enemy doth not triumph over me.

[13] And as for me, Thou upholdest me because of mine integrity, and settest me before Thy face for ever.
[14] Blessed be *YHVH* the God of Israel, from everlasting and to everlasting. Amen, and Amen.

Psalm 41 is recommended to those who have been fired from their place of employment.[1] In this regard, we are informed in the published version of the *"Shimmush Tehillim"* that you should recite *Psalms 41–43* conjointly three times a day when you have been dismissed from your work place, and someone else was appointed in your stead.[2] As usual, Godfrey Selig embroidered extensively on this theme in his version of the *"Shimmush Tehillim,"* of which little appears in any of the standard published versions. Thus he wrote "If your enemies have despoiled you of credit and caused you to be mistreated, and thereby reduce your earnings, or perhaps, deprive you of your office and installed another in your place, you should pray these three times a day for three successive days, together with a prayer that is appropriate to your circumstances, and by doing this you will perceive incredible things. Your enemies will be put to shame and you will be unscathed."[3]

Whilst one recension of the *"Shimmush Tehillim"* relates the details shared in the previous paragraph, another maintains the forty-first Psalm should be recited to halt you from going idle in your profession. In this regard, it suggests that the Psalm be enunciated with an associated Divine Name three times a day, each recitation concluding with the following prayer-incantation:

יהי רצון מלפניך **אל** חי שוכן שחק שאנצל מן
הבטלה כי הבטלה מביאה לידי שעמום כאשר
אמרו רבותינו זכרונם לברכה במסכת כתובות
על כן באתי לפניך **אל** חי שוכן שחק שתצילני
מן הבטלה כי יגורתי שמא לא ארויח במלאכתי
כדי שאוכל להפיק רצוני ומזוני על כן תשמע
אלי והצילני מן הרעה הזאת **אמן** נצח סלה ועד

Transliteration:
> *Y'hi ratzon mil'fanecha El Chai Shochein Shachak*
> *sh'enatzel min habatalah ki habatalah m'vi'ah lidei*

shi'imum ka'asher am'ru raboteinu zich'ronam liv'rachah b'm'sechet ketubot al kein bati l'fanecha El Chai Shochein Shachak shetatzileini min habatalah ki yagur'ti shema lo ar'vi'ach b'malach'ti k'deishe'uchal l'hafik r'tzoni um'zonai al kein tish'ma elai v'hatzileini min hara'ah hazot Omein Netzach Selah va'ed

Translation:

> May it be your will, *El Chai Shochein Shachak* [*El Chai* who resides in the heavens (clouds)], that I be kept from idleness, for idleness leads to foolishness, as our rabbis of blessed memory said in *Tractate Ketubot*,[155] Wherefore I came before you *El Chai Shochein Shachak*, so that you might save me from idleness, because I feared that I might not earn (enough) from my work to finance my needs and my food. Therefore you shall hear me and deliver me from this evil. *Amen* enduring *Selah* forever.[4]

It should be noted that *Psalm 41* is also important in dealing with illness. In this regard, we are informed that sufferers will be empowered if they work the following procedure with all their strength and heartfelt passion, i.e. with *Kavvanah* (focussed intention). Commence by reciting:

[*Psalm 25:18*] ראה עניי ועמלי ושא לכל חטאותי

[*Jeremiah 17:14*] רפאני יהוה וארפא הושיעני

ואושעה כי תהלתי אתה

Transliteration:

> *r'eih on'yi va'amali v'sa l'chol chatotai*
> *r'fa'eini YHVH v'eirafei hoshi'eini v'ivashei'ah ki t'hilati atah*

Translation:

> Witness my suffering and travail and all my fallibilities [sins].
> Heal me *YHVH*, and I shall be healed; save me, and I shall be saved; for Thou art my praise.

Next the practitioner is required to focus on the Divine Name ריו (*Riv*) which is said to be beneficial for healing. This Divine Name construct was derived from the capitals of the first three words of

Jeremiah 17:14, i.e. ר (*Resh*) from רפאני (*r'fa'eini*—"heal me");
י (*Yod*) from יהוה (*YHVH*); and ו (*Vav*) from וארפא (*v'eirafei*—
"and heal"). This portion of the procedure is worked whilst reciting
Psalm 41 three times every day. In conclusion, we are informed
regarding this healing procedure, that it is written:

כי שמע אלהים אל קול הנער באשר [*Genesis 21:17*]
הוא שם

Transliteration:
   ki shama elohim el kol hana'ar ba'asher hu sham
Translation:
   for *Elohim* hath heard the voice of the lad where he is.

This is interpreted to mean that the Divine *Shechinah* was present
above the head of the individual needing healing.[5]
     As far as the magical employment of single verses are
concerned, the initials of the words comprising *Psalm 41:4* are
conjoined to form the Divine Name construct ייעעדכמהב
which is included in amulets as a call for help.[6] This appears to
align well with the magical use of the succeeding verse, i.e. *Psalm
41:5*, in which the capitals of the words comprising the opening
phrase reading יהוה חנני רפאה נפשי (*YHVH choneini r'fa'ah
naf'shi*—"YHVH be gracious unto me; heal my soul"), are
conjoined to form the Divine Name construct יחרנ, which is
employed in amulets to control mental illness.[7] The initials of the
five concluding words of this verse are likewise combined in the
Divine Name construct רנכהל, and is also included in amulets
for mental ailments.[8] Otherwise, the same verse is employed in an
amulet to stop a child from crying incessantly due to some or other
ailment. In this regard, the letters comprising the said verse are
arranged into the following Divine Name construct comprising
eleven tri-letter portions:

אפש ננ יהכ אאי
מפח ררט תיא ינת
יני החל והך

This Divine Name construct was composed by dividing the thirty-three glyphs of this verse into three groups of eleven letters each. The first eleven glyphs form the initials of the eleven tri-letter portions, whilst the second eleven written in reverse comprise the middle letters. The remaining eleven letters, written in the standard right to left manner, respectively comprise the concluding glyphs of the eleven tri-letter portions. Using the directions shared in *"Sefer Shorshei Hashemot"* as a guide,[9] I constructed the said amulet in the following manner. Commence by inscribing the Divine Name construct at the top of a clean sheet of paper, or a kosher parchment if you prefer. Then, directly below it, write the following opening statement:

יהי רצון מלפניך יהוה אלהי ואלהי אבותי שבכח השמות

Transliteration:
> *Y'hi ratzon mil'fanecha YHVH elohai v'elohei avotai sheb'choach hashemot*

Translation:
> May it be your will *YHVH* my God and God of my father, by the power of the Names

Next insert the following magical seal as well a set of Divine and Angelic Names directly underneath the opening statement:

רפאל שמריאל

אנקתם פסתם פספסים דיונסים יהו יוהך כלך

(Rafa'el Sham'ri'el Anak'tam Pas'tam Pas'pasim Dion'sim Yehu Yohach Kalach)

Roll up the paper, tie it with a length of string, and suspend it around the neck of the infant.[10]

Other than the listed magical applications of single verses from the forty-first Psalm, it is worth noting that the capitals of the words of *Psalm 41:14*, excluding the prefix ו (*Vav*) of the concluding word, are combined in the Divine Name construct ביאימוהאא which is employed in an amulet by those who are looking "for a new apartment,"[11] or any other residence for that matter.

In conclusion, we need to acknowledge again those applications of the current Psalm which do not feature in published works. We noted that *Psalms 41–43* are recommended to those who have been dismissed from their place of work, hence it should come as no surprise that the current Psalm is itself recommended against unemployment; for sustenance; and against despair. *Psalm 41* is recited against betrayal (treachery); against enemies who cause loss; and is equally enunciated by those who have fears of being hurt. In this regard, it is again one of the many Psalms employed for protection in perilous situations, and in times of trouble.

It is likewise employed for the protection of the fatherland, and to support exiles and refugees. The forty-first Psalm is also employed when encountering spiritual troubles, and especially when calling on the Eternal Presence of the Divine One. Other than that, it is recited to ensure the successful delivery of a premature child.

In Christian magic *Psalm 41* is equally listed to be good "if someone has brought you down."[12] In this regard, the Byzantine magical manuscripts instruct the user to write the Psalm on the hands of your enemy "and destroy him,"[13] which is a pretty impossible task if you ask me, unless you knock him out first! Jokes aside, the translator of those manuscripts noted that "a relatively easy emendation.....would yield 'write it on your hands and efface it'."[14] The magical use of the current Psalm in "*Le Livre d'Or*" is equally belligerent,[15] stating that if you have a partner "whom you hate or you mistrust," you should recite the Psalm seven times over rose oil, then anoint your face therewith, "and you will overcome her."[16] Additional details require the writing of a set of magical characters with the name of the partner on parchment made from the "skin of a young billy-goat," which is perfumed with saffron and rose oil. Afterwards this item is buried "in front of her door."[17] Rather unpleasant actions!

The healing potential of the current Psalm is equally emphasised in Christian Magic. Thus there is an instruction in the Syrian magical manuscript in the Sachau Collection regarding the current Psalm being read three times when an individual is experiencing violent pains.[18] Elsewhere we are told that *Psalm 41:4–5* is employed against fever,[19] and the third verse is said to be used to elevate the user "with dignity by everyone."[20]

. ...Now the Maharal ordered his student, Rabbi Yaakov Sasson, to complete the seven circuits as well and gave him other combinations of letters. When his circuits were done, the fire departed, for water had come into the body and vapor began wafting from the golem. Then he grew hair like a man of thirty and nails formed at the tips of his fingers. After this, the Maharal began his seven circuits. When he was done, all three of us recited in unison the verse: 'He breathed into his nostrils the breath of life and the man became a living creature,' for even the atmosphere we inhale must contain fire, water, and air, which are the three elements mentioned in the *Book of Creation*... ... .

Index of Magical Applications

1. General

2. Health, Healing & General Physical Well-being

Blood [diseases]: 6
Bones [diseases]: 6:3-4; 21; 31:11; 33; 34:21; 38:11
Broken limbs: 37

Cancer: 37
Chest [diseases of]: 21
Constipation [to alleviate]: 31:10

Deafness [loss of hearing]: 37
Diarrhea [to alleviate]: 31:10
Digestive Tract [ailments of]: 31:10
Diseases [general]: 29
Diseases [incurable]: 9; 21
Dumb [for the]: 38

Epilepsy: 16; 37
Eyes [diseases of & pain in the]: 6; 10; 12; 13; 37

Fatigue (languor/lethargy): 31
Fever [against]: 8:2; 13; 15; 16; 17; 18; 19; 34; 37
Food Poisoning [to alleviate]: 31:10

Gangrene: 37

Headaches & Pains in the Head [Against]: 2; 3; 7
Haemorrhage & Loss of Blood [to halt]: 1:1–3
Heart [ailments & problems]: 13; 21; 31:11; 34:19; 38:11

Illness & Healing [in general]: 4; 6; 6:1–4; 7; 9; 10; 13; 16; 18; 20; 23; 25; 27; 29; 30; 30:3; 31; 32; 33; 34:18; 37; 38; 39; 41
Indigestion [to alleviate]: 31:10
Infirmity: 6; 15

Jaws [pain in]: 38

Kidneys [diseases of]: 15; 19

Limbs [diseases of]: 16
Liver Problems: 13

Muscles [ailments of]: 38:4

Plagues (Epidemics/Pandemics) [to be saved & protected from]: 33

Rheumatism: 15; 31

Shoulders [pain]: 3
Skin [ailments of]: 38:4
Sportsmen: 17
Stomach [diseases of]: 13; 21

Toothache [pains in teeth & gums]: 3
Throat [pains in]: 2
Tuberculosis: 3:9

Voice [preservation of]: 32

Weakness & Trembling [generally & due to illness]: 12; 31:11; 37
Wounds [healing of]: 37

3. Mental & Emotional Well-being
Anxiety: 4; 22; 23
Anxiety [caused by enemies]: 3; 5; 6; 7; 9; 17; 22; 25; 31; 35; 38
Apathy [indifference/disinterest]: 38

Character [for self improvement & a good]: 13; 15; 20; 21
Chastity [to maintain]: 11; 123
Choice [in life]: 24
Comfort [in need of]: 23
Confusion [resulting from the success of the wicked]: 1; 37

Depression (brought on by unemployment) [to relieve]: 39
Depression [to counteract]: 30
Despair [against]: 3; 15; 24; 41
Difficulties & Sorrow [to be saved from]: 30; 33;
Difficulty [for a person in]: 25; 26
Drunkeness [against & for loss of reason due to]: 37
Drunkards [to cure]: 37

Evil Counsel (bad advice) [protection against]: 12; 38
Evil Inclination/Desire to Receive [(הרע יצר—*yetzer hara*) against]: 15

Fear (Paranoia) [against]: 11; 14; 20:3
Fear [safety from]: 4; 11; 12; 20:3; 22; 23; 26
Forgiveness: 25
Forsaken [feeling]: 27
Frustration [with wickedness of others]: 36

Gratitude: 9; 17; 18; 21; 23; 33

Incredulity [disbelief]: 13
Injustice [perplexed by]: 10
Internal desolation: 29
Insanity [against]: 15

Laziness & Procrastination [against]: 5
Loss of Reason [due to alcohol]: 37

Melancholy [against]: 15
Mental Ailments [against]: 6:2–3; 6:5; 19:8; 34:19;
Mentally Ill [dangerously insane]: 12
Mood (Ruach Ra/Evil Spirit) [against a bad/dark]: 5; 29; 40

Nervous Disorders [to be healed from]: 12; 28; 37

Obsession [against]: 15

Peace of Mind: 20
Peace of Soul: 6; 31; 37
Perverted Activities [against all kinds of]: 11
Post-traumatic Stress Disorder [psychological damage resulting from trauma]: 7
Pride [against]: 11; 17; 28
Purification [against all that is unclean]: 22

Ruin [danger of]: 11; 24

Sadness: 30
Sensitive Individuals [for depression brought on by heartless persons]: 4
Sinful Passions [against slavery to]: 9–10; 59
Sorrow to Joy [turning]: 16

Temptation [against & for relief from]: 12; 13; 25
Tragedy & Calamaties [protection against]: 13
Troubles & Distress: 6; 9:10; 20; 25; 31; 34; 34:18
Trouble & Tribulations [against all manner of]: 4; 16; 22; 25; 29

Uplifted [to be]: 8; 19; 24

Vanity [against]: 11; 30

4. Sleep & Dreams

Dream Question (*She'elat Chalom*) [receiving answers in]: 4:2; 12; 13; 23; 39

Insomnia [inability to sleep]: 4

Nightmares: 30:3

5. Intelligence, Study, Memory, Speech & Secret Sciences

Ignorance [against]: 17
Intelligence [to awaken]: 16; 19; 19:8–10
Intelligence [to sharpen & increase]: 16; 19; 19:8–10; 22
Intuition: 16

Memory [for a good]: 12; 19; 19:8–10

Occult Intrigues: 25

Preaching (sermons/lectures): 34

Sciences [human]: 18
Study [love of]: 30; 31
Success [in studying & learning]: 25

Will [force of]: 30; 50
Wisdom [to encourage]: 19

6. Journeys & Travel

Accidents [protection against & during chariot & motor-vehicle]: 36:7

Journeys [external to cities to be successful]: 4
Journeys [when undertaking]: 17; 34

Lost when Traveling [to find your way]: 32

Protection [against enemies on the road]: 17

River [to ford/cross]: 22

Safety [against danger at sea & on land]: 22; 26; 29
Sea [against storms at]: 2; 21; 23:1; 24; 29
Sea [danger from the]: 17
Sea/Lake [before crossing]: 21
Sea-sickness [against]: 29

Travel [for success on the road]: 17:8; 34
Travel [to say on the road]: 17; 20

7. Success

Desires [successfully granted]: 4

Governmental Officials [before meeting with]: 34

Need [for every purpose/requirement]: 4

Requests [granted]: 4; 8:2; 8:10; 15; 16:1–5; 16:5; 34
Requests [from higher authorities fulfilled]: 4; 21:2; 34

Success [in dealings with authorities]: 5
Success [in general & in all endeavours]: 1; 1:1–3; 1:3; 4; 24; 33:6

8. Career, Trade, Transactions, Financial Success
Livelihood, Good Fortune & Charity

Business [goodwill & love of others in]: 8
Business [success in]: 19; 20; 33; 36
Business Transactions [to conclude]: 4

Charity & Good Deeds: 14; 21; 25; 32
Councils &Meetings [business]: 2

Debtors: 36; 39
Dismissed [when laid off]: 39; 41
Donations: 18

Employer & Employee [to prevent discord after disagreements]: 40
Enemies [who cause loss]: 41

Financial Success: 4:7; 24
Fortune [in business]: 5

Good Fortune: 4
Good Fortune [gratitude for]: 17; 18; 23; 33

Idleness in a Profession [against]: 41

Livelihood [anxious concern about]: 23
Livelihood (*Dikir'nosa*) [name of]: 4:7
Livelihood [for a good]: 8:2; 23; 24; 33:18

Misdeeds [to repent of]: 21
Misfortune [against bad luck]: 5; 22; 25; 26

Poverty [against & for diminishing of]: 9; 30; 34; 39
Poverty [to encourage alms to the poor]: 21
Prosperity [financial]: 23

Rich [against envy of the]: 1; 37

Treasures: 32
Trip [success on a business]: 17; 17:8

Unemployment [against]: 39; 41
Usurers [against loan sharks]: 14

Work [to find]: 39

9. Food, Agriculture, Plant Growth, Fisheries, Animal Husbandry & Nature

Animals [protection of]: 35
Animals [protection of domestic]: 35

Beasts [protection against wild, dangerous & savage]: 22; 27; 36
Bites: 21; 31

Cattle & Livestock [to control stubborn]: 27
Crops: 4; 36

Famine [relief from a]: 33; 36
Fertility of Vines & Trees: 1; 1:3
Fields [protection of]: 36
Fire [*dangers of*]: 10; 16; 17
Fire [to contain & halt]: 22
Floods [protection against]: 17; 24; 25; 31
Floods [to be rescued from]: 24
Fruit Trees: 1

Gardens [protection of]: 36
Good Weather: 10

Land or Water [for need or danger on]: 6; 26; 29
Lightning/Thunderbolts [protection against]: 17; 28

Natural Disaster: 18
Nature [when in]: 19

Pests & Insects: 17
Planting Seeds, Vines & Trees: 1; 1:3
Plants [nurturing]: 1; 1:3

Serpents [protection against]: 13; 22; 37

Storms [in general]: 10; 17; 28
Sustenance: 4; 24; 41
Sustenance [during unsuitable weather for agriculture]: 31

Trees [against shedding fruit]: 1; 1:3

Vines & Vineyards [protection of]: 1; 1:3
Volcanoes: 16; 17

Water [against life-threatening danger from]: 2; 26

10. Human Interaction, Friendship, Brotherhood, & Reconciliation

City (New Environment) [to conquer a strange & to be kindly received in a]: 27
Crowds & Passersby [when gazing at]: 35:18

Enemies [reconciliation with]: 9; 28
Enemies [turning into friends]: 9; 16
Exploitation [against being taken advantage of]: 35

Favour & Grace [of princes, magistrates & authorities]: 5; 20:6; 34
Favour [to find]: 1:3; 4; 5; 8
Favour [with all men]: 14; 15
Friends [to be received favourably]: 34

Grace & Mercy [to receive]: 20:5; 20:6; 32

Harm [protection from]: 3; 5; 7; 14; 20; 23; 27; 31; 35; 40
Humiliation [against]: 22
Hurt [against being]: 35; 41
Hurt [by perverted individuals]: 8

Kings [to be rescued from evil]: 18; 38; 39
Kings, Judges & Ruling Authorities [to be saved from]: 40

Maintaining Self [before a spiritual/temporal authority]: 21; 21:2
Mercy/Compassion [to request]: 12; 32

11. Relationships, Love, Marriage, Family & Homes

12. Pregnancy, Childbirth & Children

Barren Women [for]: 36

Childbirth [difficult confinement or dangerous delivery]: 1; 1:1–3; 19; 19:6; 26
Childbirth [during confinement]: 1–4; 20; 21–24; 22; 32:7; 33
Children [for crying]: 8; 9; 34:8–9; 41:5
Children [for retarded]: 15
Children [for sick]: 8; 9
Children [protection of]: 35
Children [restoring health of]: 9
Circumcision [on the day]: 12
Conception [to ensure]: 36

Delivery of a Child [successful]: 19; 20
Delivery of a Premature Child [successful]: 41

Miscarriage [against]: 1; 1:1–3; 32; 33; 33:1

Pregnancy [to ensure a safe]: 1; 4; 8; 20; 33; 35
Pregnancy [to cause]: 5; 33
Premature Delivery [against]: 1; 1:1–3;
Rebellious Children [to instill obedience in]: 23

Woman in labour [support for]: 20

13. Dying, Death, Orphans, Old Age & Life Extension

Children [for a woman whose offspring died]: 33
Children [loss of]: 20

Death [against an unnatural & strange]: 13 (good for one day); 32:7
Death [fear of]: 38
Death [for a good]: 17; 38
Death [protecting infants & children from]: 33

Funeral [on the day]: 23

Longevity: 23

Mourning [during time of]: 23; 27

Old Age & Retirement [happy]: 29; 30
Orphans: 26; 34

Parents [loss of]: 20

Visiting the Graves [of loved ones]: 25; 34

Widows/Widowers: 34

14. Religion & Spirituality

Accounting of the Soul [*Chesh'bon Hanefesh*]: 15
Atonement/Repentance [חשובה—*teshuvah* (spiritual return)]: 6;
15; 20; 25; 32; 38

Blasphemy [against]: 14; 23

Candle-lighting [with]: 18:29
Celestial Accusers [to be recited from *Rosh Hashanah* (New Year)
onwards to strip]: 27
Celestial Decrees [to be recited from *Rosh Hashanah* (New Year)
onwards to abolish bad]: 27
Confused Religiously: 25

Divine One [awesomeness of the]: 29
Divine One [calling on the Eternal Presence of the]: 41
Divine One [perplexed by distance of the]: 10

Faith [for doubts about]: 1; 2; 19; 37
Faith [to strengthen]: 11
Fasting [for one who is]: 39
Fidelity [to religion, justice & righteousness]: 26

Good spirits [loyalty of]: 26
Good Year [to be recited from *Rosh Hashanah* (New Year)
onwards to ensure a]: 27

Gratitude [to the Divine One]: 9; 18

Hands [after washing]: 23
Hands [with washing]: 26:6

Israel [for crisis in]: 20

Meal [reciting before the blessing of a]: 23
Meditations: 16:8
Mercy [request for Divine]: 32

Opening the Heart [greater comprehension of spiritual studies]: 16; 22

Penitence: 6; 31; 37
Persecution [against religious persecution in foreign lands]: 30
Prayers [to voice, empower, or ensure being heard]: 4:4; 28; 30:12

Religious Commandments [for success in performing a *Mitzvah*]: 25

Salvation: 34:18
Spiritual Cleansing: 15
Spiritual Awakening [to achieve a spirit of holiness]: 15
Spiritual Matters [success in]: 39
Spiritual Troubles: 20; 29; 38; 41
Statement of Faith: 23; 33
Statement of Faith & Appreciation of the Divine One: 40
Synagogue [in the]: 5; 26; 27
Torah Principles [to maintain]: 37
Torah study (Opening the Heart) [prior to]: 1; 16; 19
Trust in the Divine One [increasing]: 23

15. Malevolent Spirit Forces, Ghosts & Evil Spells

Angels [for protection against possible injury during exorcism]: 31:19

16. Hatred, Jealousy, Evil Eye, Enemies, Adversity & Animosity

Enemies [protection against persistent]: 18:1
Enemies [protective shield against against]: 3:4
Enemies [to conquer]: 7:7–18
Enemies [to get rid of]: 11
Enemies [to preclude harm being inflicted by]: 14
Evil Decrees & Evil Tidings [against]: 36
Evil Eye (Ayin Hara) [against & to avert the]: 5; 5:8; 20; 20:3; 31; 32
Evil People [not to envy]: 37
Evil People [protection against]: 11; 38

Hate [for haters to depart]: 7
Hatred [against]: 10; 25:19; 30; 35

Intimidation [against]: 7

Jealousy & Resentment [against]: 20

Malice [against]: 5; 30; 34

Peace [to establish with enemies]: 16; 28

Trouble & Danger [against]: 20; 25; 26; 26:8

17. Slander, Falsehood & Wrongdoing

Bad Language: 5
Busybodies [against mischievous]: 35

Defamation, Slander & Gossip [against & to be saved from]: 4; 14; 31; 37; 38, 39

Evil & Slanderous Libel [against]: 36
Evil Doers [for the annihilation of]: 36

Forgiveness [of errors & transgressions]: 16; 31; 37

Lies [against]: 11; 33

Sin [after committing & being burdened with]: 25; 32
Sin [to discourage transgression]: 12

Tongue [binding an evil]: 31; 31:19

Unjust Accusations [against]: 7; 17; 25

Wicked Men [against]: 11
Wrongdoing [victim of]: 39

18. Robbery, Theft & Common Criminality
Criminals [to locate]: 35

Robbers & Bandits [to flee]: 18:1

Theft, Thieves & Robbers [against]: 5; 7; 11; 18:1; 26; 36
Thiefs [to discover identity of]: 16; 29
Thiefs [to halt burglars before harm & to cause repentance of]: 15

19. Justice, Legal Matters, Law Suits & Judgment
Court of Law [in a]: 20
Court of Law [against enemies in a]: 7; 38:14–15

Judge [appearing before a]: 5
Judgment [for good]: 20
Judgment [for wrongful or unfavourable]: 7; 12; 25; 38
Judicial Matters [general]: 20

Lawsuit [success in a]: 7; 35; 38:14–15
Lawsuit [winning against the unrighteous, quarrelsome & vengeful]: 35; 38:14–15

Trials & Sentencing: 12
Tribunals [when having to appear before]: 7

20. Punishment, Vengeance & Imprisonment

Imprisonment: 31
Imprisonment [against unjust & to be freed from]: 31; 33
Imprisonment [liberation from]: 31

Prisoners [for release of]: 31; 26
Punishment [against suffering]: 13

Revenge [to seek]: 2:5; 7:7; 18:49

21. Anger, Rage, Belligerence, Violence, War & Peace

Abuse [against verbal]: 39
Anger [against]: 4; 36; 37
Armies [protection against invading]: 27; 34
Assassins [against]: 5; 11; 26; 36
Attackers [who intend to kill]: 7

Enemy at War [defence against]: 11:2
Exiles & Refugees [to support]: 38; 41

Fatherland [protection of]: 32; 41

Naval Ships [against attacks from]: 5:9

Oppression [against]: 35
Oppressed [for those who are]: 9; 35
Oppressors [against]: 35; 37

Peace: 36
Perilous Situations & Times of Trouble [protection in]: 4; 6; 7; 9; 13; 16; 18; 20; 20:3; 23; 25; 26; 27; 29; 30; 31; 32; 33; 37; 38; 39; 41
Perils [against all]: 11
Persecution [safety from]: 11; 12
Persecution [against fierce]: 7; 34; 36

Rage [alleviate personal]: 31

Threats [against]: 30; 38
Torment [against]: 3
Tyranny [against]: 2

War [to halt]: 2
Wounded [seriously by criminals]: 37

"In the year 5340 (1580), on the 20th Adar, at four hours after midnight the three of us left for the Moldau River on the outskirts of Prague. By its banks we looked for and found an area with loam and clay, from which we made the form of a man, three cubits long, lying on his back, and then shaped a face, arms, and legs.

Then all three of us stood at the golem's feet, staring at his face. The Maharal told me first to walk around the golem seven times, beginning on the right side, proceed to his head and circle around it to his legs on the left side. He told me what combinations of letters to recite as I walked around him. And thus I did seven times. When I completed the circuits, the body of the golem reddened like a glowing coal.

Now the Maharal ordered his student, Rabbi Yaakov Sasson, to complete the seven circuits as well and gave him other combinations of letters. When his circuits were done, the fire departed, for water had come into the body and vapor began wafting from the golem. Then he grew hair like a man of thirty and nails formed at the tips of his fingers. After this, the Maharal began his seven circuits. When he was done, all three of us recited in unison the verse: 'He breathed into his nostrils the breath of life and the man became a living creature,' for even the atmosphere we inhale must contain fire, water, and air, which are the three elements mentioned in the *Book of Creation*.

Then the golem opened his eyes and gazed at us in wonder. Now the Maharal called to him in an insistent voice: 'Stand on your feet!'... ... ."

— Yudl Rosenberg
(The Golem and the Wondrous
Deeds of the Maharal of Prague)

REFERENCES
&
BIBLIOGRAPHY

INTRODUCTION

1. **Swart, J.G.:** *The Book of Seals & Amulets*, The Sangreal Sodality Press, Johannesburg 2014.
2. **Vital, Chaim:** *Sefer Sha'arei Kedusha*, quoted in **Kaplan, A.:** *Meditation and Kabbalah*, Samuel Weiser Inc., York Beach 1988.
3. **Trachtenberg, J.:** *Jewish Magic and Superstition: A Study in Folk Religion*, Behrman's Jewish Book House Publishers, New York 1939.

CHAPTER 1

1.   **Finkelman, S.:** *Living the Parashah: Bereishis*, Mesorah Publications, Brooklyn 2007.
2.   **Friedman, H.H.:** *Heaven Forbid: The Talmudic Attitude Towards the Spoken Word*, privately published electronic essay. **Lebovits, M.D.:** *Opening One's Mouth to the Satan*, Halachically Speaking Vol. 13 Issue 10, Brooklyn 2017.
3.   *Ibid.*
4.   *Ibid.*
5.   **Trachtenberg, J.:** *Jewish Magic and Superstition, Op. Cit.*
6.   *Ibid.*
7.   *Ibid.*
8.   **Friedman, H.H.:** *Heaven Forbid, Op. Cit..* **Lebovits, M.D.:** *Opening One's Mouth to the Satan, Op. Cit.*
9.   **Trachtenberg, J.:** *Jewish Magic and Superstition, Op. Cit.*
10.   *Ibid.*
11.   *Ibid.*
12.   *Ibid.*
13.   *Ibid.*
14.   *Ibid.*
15.   **Mathers, S.L. Macgregor:** *Key of Solomon the King: Clavicula Salomonis*, Routledge & Kegan Paul, London 1974. **Mathers, S.L. MacGregor:** *The Book of Sacred Magic of Abramelin the Mage*, Thorsons Publishers Limited, Wellingborough, Northamptonshire 1976. **Dehn, G.:** *The Book of Abramelin*, Ibis Press, Lake Worth 2006. **Skinner, S. & Rankine, D.:** *The Veritable Key of Solomon*, Golden Hoard Press Pty. Ltd., Singapore 2015. **Waite, A.E.:** *The Book of Black Magic and of Pacts: Including the Rites and Mysteries of Goëtic Theurgy, Sorcery, and Infernal Necromancy*, The de Laurence Co., Chicago 1910. **Butler, E.M.:** *Ritual Magic, Cambridge University Press*, Cambridge, London, New York & Melbourne 1946. **Bilardi, C.R.:** *The Red Church Or the Art of Pennsylvania German Braucherei*, Pendraig Publishing, Sunland 2009. **Alvarado, D.:** *Voodoo Hoodoo Spellbook*, Weiser Books, San Francisco &Newburyport 2011. **Miss Michaele & Poterfield, C.:** *Hoodoo Bible Magic: Sacred Secrets of Scriptural Sorcery*, Missionary Independent Spiritual Church, Forestville 2014.

Casas, S.: *Old Style Conjure: Hoodoo, Rootwork, & Folk magic*, Weiser Books, Newburyport 2017.

Donmoyer, P.J.: *Powwowing in Pennsylvania: Braucherei and the Ritual of Everyday Life*, Pennsylvania German Cultural Heritage Center, Kutztown University of Pennsylvania, Pennsburg 2018.

Orth, R.L.T: *Folk Religion of the Pennsylvania Dutch: Witchcraft, Faith Healing and Related Practices*, McFarland & Company Inc. Publishers, Jefferson 2018.

Taren S.: *Hoodoo in the Psalms: God's Magick*, MOON Books, 2019.

Gary, G.: *The Black Toad: West Country Witchcraft and Magic*, Llewellyn Publications, Woodbury 2020.

—*The Charmers' Psalter*, Llewellyn Publications, Woodbury 2020;

16.   **Idel, M.:** *Old worlds, New mirrors: On Jewish Mysticism and Twentieth-century Thought*, University of Pennsylvania Press, Philadelphia 2015.

17.   **Trachtenberg, J.:** *Jewish Magic and Superstition, Op. Cit.*

18.   **Magonet, J.:** *A Rabbi Reads the Psalms*, SCM Press, London 1994.

19.   *Ibid.*

20.   *Ibid.*

21.   **Swart, J.G.:** *The Book of Self Creation*, The Sangreal Sodality Press, Johannesburg 2009.

—*The Book of Sacred Names*, The Sangreal Sodality Press, Johannesburg 2011.

22.   *Ibid.*

23.   *Ibid.*

24.   *Ibid.*

25.   *Ibid.*

26.   *Ibid.*

27.   **Vital, Chaim:** *Sha'ar Ru'ach ha-Kodesh*, quoted in **Fine, L.:** *Physician of the Soul, Healer of the Cosmos: Isaac Luria and His Kabbalistic Fellowship*, Stanford University Press, Stanford 2003.

28.   **Swart, J.G.:** *The Book of Self Creation, Op. Cit.*

29.   *Ibid.*

30.   *Ibid.*

31.   *Ibid.*

32.   *Ibid.*

33.   *Ibid.*

34.   *Ibid.*

35.   *Ibid.*

36. *Ibid.*
37. *Ibid.*
38. *Ibid.*
39. **Swart, J.G.:** *The Book of Sacred Names, Op. Cit.*
40. *Ibid.*
41. *Ibid.*
42. *Ibid.*
43. *Ibid.*
44. *Ibid.*
45. *Ibid.*
46. *Ibid.*
47. *Ibid.*
48. *Ibid.*
49. *Ibid.*
50. **Swart, J.G.:** *The Book of Self Creation, Op. Cit.*
51. **Swart, J.G.:** *The Book of Sacred Names, Op. Cit.*
52. **Swart, J.G.:** *The Book of Seals & Amulets, Op. Cit.*
53. *Ibid.*
54. **Rebiger, B.:** *Die Magische Verwendung von Psalmen im Judentum,* in **Zenger, E.:** *Ritual und Poesie: Formen und Orte Religiöser Dichtung im Alten Orient, im Judentum und im Christentum,* Herders Biblische Studien 36, Freiburg 2003.
55. **Foreiro, F.:** *Novus Index Librorum Prohibitorum, juxta decretum Sacrae Congregationis Illustriss. S.R.E. Cardinalium à S.D.N. Urbano Papa VIII Sanctaq. Sedé Apostolica publicatum, Romae 4 Febr. 1627 auctus; primum auctoritate Pij IV. P.M. editus, deinde à Sixto Vampliatus, tertio à Clemente VIII recognitus; praefixis regulis, ac modo exéquendae prohibitionis per R.P. Franciscum Foretium Ord. Praed. à deputatione S.S. Trid. Synodi Secretarium; ante quemlibet librum noviter prohibitum praefixum est signun,* Apud Antonii Boetzeri Haeredes, Coloniae Agrippinae 1627.
56. **Selig, G.:** *Sepher Schimmusch Tehillim. Oder: Gebrauch der Psalme zum leiblichen Wohl der Menschen,* Johann Andreas Kunze, Berlin 1788/ Verlag E. Schubert, Bilfingen 1972.
    —*Secrets of the Psalms: A Fragment of the Practical Kabala, with Extracts from other Kabalistic writings, as translated by the author,* Dorene, Arlington 1929.
57. *The Sixth and Seventh Books of Moses or, Moses' Magical Spirit-art, known as the Wonderful Arts of the Old Wise Hebrews, taken from the Mosaic books of the Cabala and the Talmud, for the good of mankind. Translated from the German, word for word, according to Old Writings, with Numerous Engravings,* The Arthur Westbrook Co., 1870.

Peterson, J.H.: *The Sixth and Seventh Books of Moses or Moses' Magical Spirit-Art: Known as the Wonderful Arts of the Old Wise Hebrews, Taken from the Mosaic Books of the Kabbalah and the Talmud, for the Good of Mankind*, Ibis Press, Newburyport 2008.

58. **Swart, J.G.**: *The Book of Seals & Amulets, Op. Cit.*
59. **Saar, O.P.**: *Jewish Love Magic: From Late Antiquity to the Middle Ages*, Koninklijke Brill NV, Leiden & Boston, 2017.
60. **Trachtenberg, J.**: *Jewish Magic and Superstition, Op. Cit.*
61. **Swart, J.G.**: *The Book of Immediate Magic - Part 2*, The Sangreal Sodality Press, Johannesburg 2018.
62. **Churba, A.**: *Siddur Keter Shelomo: Complete Weekday and Shabbat Siddur with linear English translation according to the customs of Aram Soba*, Congregation Shaare Rachamim, Brooklyn 2011.
    Scherman, N. & Zlotowitz, G.: *Siddur Kol Sim'chah: The Artscroll Sephardic Siddur*, The Schottenstein Edition, Mesorah Publications, Brooklyn 2019.
63. **Rabinowitz, G. ben L.**: *Tiv HaTehillos: Essence of Praises, a Commentary on Sefer Tehillim*, Feldheim Publishers, Jerusalem & New York 2005.
64. **Buxbaum, Y.**: *Jewish Spiritual Practices*, Rowman & Littlefield Publishers, Inc., Lanham 2005.
65. **Steinsaltz, A.**: *The Miracle of the Seventh Day: A Guide to the Spiritual Meaning, Significance, and Weekly Practice of the Jewish Sabbath*, Jossey-Bass, San Francisco 2003.
    Wexelman, D.M.: *Kabbalah: The Splendor of Judaism*, Jason Aronson, Northvale 2000.
66. **Rabinowitz, G. ben L.**: *Tiv HaTehillos: Essence of Praises, Op. Cit.*
67. **Kook, A.I. & Feldman, T.**: *Rav A.Y. Kook: Selected Letters*, Ma'aliot Publications of Yeshivat Birkat Moshe, Ma'aleh Adumim 1986.
68. *Ibid.*
69. *Ibid.*
70. *Ibid.*
71. **Lamm, N. & Wurzburger, W.S.**: *A Treasury of "Tradition"*, Vol. 40 Part 1, Hebrew Publishing Company, New York 1967.
72. **Swart, J.G.**: *The Book of Self Creation, Op. Cit.*
73. **Ginsburg, E.K.**: *The Sabbath in the Classical Kabbalah*, State University of New York Press, Albany 1989.
74. *Ibid.*

75. **Kaplan, A.**: *The Bahir: An Ancient Kabbalistic Text attributed to Rabbi Nehuniah ben HaKana*, Samuel Weiser Inc., New York 1979.

76. **Rabinowitz, G. ben L.**: *Tiv HaTehillos: Essence of Praises, Op. Cit.*

77. **Idel, M.**: *The Privileged Divine Feminine in Kabbalah*, Walter de Gruyter GmbH & Co, Berlin 2020.

78. **Idel, M.**: *Kabbalah*: New Perspectives, Yale University Press, New Haven & London 1988.

79. **Idel, M.**: *The Privileged Divine Feminine in Kabbalah, Op. Cit.*

80. **Idel, M.**: *Kabbalah*: New Perspectives, *Op. Cit.*

81. **Luzzatto, M.Ch.**: *Sefer ha-Kelalim*, quoted in **Idel, M.**: *The Privileged Divine Feminine in Kabbalah, Op. Cit.*

82. *Ibid.*

83. *Seder Tefilot Tikun Ezra: kolel tefilot kol hashanah*, Taubstummen Instituts Druckerei, Wien 1815.
    Aramah, M. ben Y.: *Sefer Meir Tehilot*, Warsaw 1898.
    Ronen, D.: *Tehilim Kavvanot ha-Lev*, Machon Shirah Chadashah, Petah Tikva 2013.
    Landsberg, M.: *Sefer Tehillim im Peirush Rashi Metzudat David Metzudat Tziyon v'alav sovev Peirush Divrei Mosheh*, S.D. Friedman, Brooklyn 2015.
    Rabinowitz, G. ben L.: *Tiv HaTehillos: Essence of Praises, Op. Cit.*

84. **Gold, A. & Scherman, N.**: *Birkas Kohanim: The Priestly Blessings background translation and commentary anthologized from Talmudic, Midrashic, and Rabbinic Sources*, Mesorah Publications Ltd., Brooklyn 1981.

85. **Weiss, Y.A.**: *Limud Yomi: A Daily Dose of Torah* Vol. 2, Mesorah Publications Ltd., Brooklyn 2008.

86. **Nulman, M.**: *The Encyclopedia of Jewish Prayer*, Jason Aronson, Northvale 1993.

87. *Ibid.*

88. **Gold, A.; Zlotowitz, M. & Scherman, N.**: *The Complete ArtScroll Machzor: Pesach*, Mesorah Publications, Brooklyn 1990.
    Gold, A. & Scherman, N.: *Birkas Kohanim: The Priestly Blessings, Op. Cit.*

89. **Churba, A.**: *Siddur Keter Shelomo, Op. Cit.*
    Scherman, N. & Zlotowitz, G.: *Siddur Kol Sim'chah, Op. Cit.*

90. **Swart, J.G.**: *The Book of Seals & Amulets, Op. Cit.*

91. **Ariel, D.S.**: *The Mystic Quest*, Schocken Books Inc., New York 1992.

92. **Swart, J.G.**: *The Book of Seals & Amulets, Op. Cit.*

93.   **Eilberg-Schwartz, H.:** *People of the Body: Jews and Judaism from an Embodied Perspective*, State University of New York Press, Albany 1992.

94.   **Swart, J.G.:** *The Book of Seals & Amulets, Op. Cit.*

95.   **Scherman, N. & Zlotowitz, G.:** *Siddur Kol Sim'chah, Op. Cit.*

96.   **Swart, J.G.:** *The Book of Sacred Names, Op. Cit.*
        —*The Book of Seals & Amulets, Op. Cit.*

97.   *Ibid.*

98.   **Nulman, M.:** *The Encyclopedia of Jewish Prayer, Op. Cit.*

99.   *Ibid.*

100.   *Ibid.*

101.   **Swart, J.G.:** *The Book of Immediate Magic - Part 2, Op. Cit.*

102.   **Swart, J.G.:** *The Book of Sacred Names, Op. Cit.*
        —*The Book of Seals & Amulets, Op. Cit.*

103.   *Ibid.*

104.   *Ibid.*

105.   *Ibid.*

106.   *Ibid.*

107.   **Swart, J.G.:** *The Book of Sacred Names, Op. Cit.*

108.   *Ibid.*

109.   *Ibid.*

        Swart, J.G.: *The Book of Seals & Amulets, Op. Cit.*
        —*The Book of Immediate Magic - Part 1*, The Sangreal Sodality Press, Johannesburg 2015.

CHAPTER 2

Psalm 1

1. **Nulman, M.:** *The Encyclopedia of Jewish Prayer*, *Op. Cit.*
2. **Chamui, A.S.H:** *Sefer Yemalet Nafsho*, Defus Eliyahu Mosheh Devich Hakohen, Calcutta 1884.
3. **Eleazer ben Yehudah of Worms:** *Perush al Sefer Yetzirah*, Przemysl 1883 [facsimile copy Brooklyn 1978].
   Posquieros, A. ben David: *Sefer Yetzirah*, Horodna 1806.
   Donnolo, S.: *Sefer Chachmoni hu Perush al Sefer Yetzirah*, Hotsa'at Backal, Jerusalem 1994.
   Mordell, P: *Sefer Yetsirah*, P. Mordell, Philadelphia, 1914.
   Stenring, K.: *The Book of Formation*, KTAV, New York 1968.
   Kalisch, I.: *The Sepher Yetzirah: A Book of Creation*, L.H. Frank & Co., New York (Reprinted by the AMORC, San Jose, California, 1974.)
   Westcott, W.W.: *Sepher Yetzirah*, Occult Research Press, New York, 1887. Reprinted by Samuel Weiser, New York 1975.
   Suares, C.: *The Sepher Yetzirah: Including the Original Astrology according to the Qabala and its Zodiac,"* Shambhala Publications Inc., Boulder 1976.
   Friedman, I.: *The Book of Creation: Sefer Yetzirah*, Samuel Weiser Inc., New York 1977.
   Blumenthal, D.R.: *Understanding Jewish Mysticism: A Source Reader*, Volume I, KTAV Publishing House Inc., New York 1978.
   Kaplan, A.: *Sefer Yetzirah: The Book of Creation In Theory and Practice*, Samuel Weiser Inc., York Beach 1990 (Revised edition with index 1997).
   Hyman, A.P.: *Sefer Yesira*, Mohr Siebeck, Tübingen 2004.
   Cordovero, M.: *Pardes Rimmonim*, Yarid ha-Sefarim, Jerusalem 2000.
   Horowitz, S.S. ben A.: *Shefa Tal*, Hanau, 1612.
4. **Chamui, A.S.H:** *Sefer Yemalet Nafsho*, *Op. Cit.*
5. *Le Livre des Psaumes Hébreu-Français et Phonétique: Traduction Français et Transcription Phonétique du Livre des Psaumes. Prières pour les malades, la subsistance. Prières prononcées sur la tombe des tsadikim, hachkavot, différents kaddich, allumage des bougies. Message du Ramban et autre prières*, Nouvelle Edition, Editions Sinai, Tel Aviv 2006.

Azulai, H.Y.D.: *Sefer Tehillim Sha'arei Rachamim: im Segulot v'Tefilot ha'Chida*, Agudat Zichron Rachamim, Jerusalem 1997.

Ronen, D.: *Tehilim Kavvanot ha-Lev, Op. Cit.*

6.   **Grünwald, M.:** *Ueber den Einfluss der Psalmen auf die Katholische Liturgie, mit steter Rücksichtnahme auf die Talmudisch-Midraschische Literatur*, Commissions-Verlag von J. Kauffmann, Frankfurt am Main 1891.

Klein, M.: *A Time to Be Born: Customs and Folklore of Jewish Birth*, The Jewish Publication Society, Philadelphia 2000.

7.   **Kimchi, D. ben Y.:** *Sefer Tehillim: im Perush Rabbi David Kimchi*, Amsterdam 1731.

Sefer Shimmush Tehillim, Éliás Békéscsaba Klein, Budapest.

Seder Tefilot Tikun Ezra, Op. Cit.

Refuah v'Chayim m'Yerushalayim im Shimush Tehilim, Defus Yehudah vi-Yerushalayim, Jerusalem 1931.

Landsberg, M.: *Sefer Tehillim im Peirush Rashi, Op. Cit.*

Singer, I. & Adler, C.: *The Jewish Encyclopedia, Op. Cit.*

Selig, G.: *Sepher Schimmusch Tehillim, Op. Cit.*

The Sixth and Seventh Books of Moses, Op. Cit.

Peterson, J.H.: *The Sixth and Seventh Books of Moses, Op. Cit.*

Fodor, A.: *The Use of Psalms in Jewish and Christian Arabic Magic*, in Apor, E.: *Jubilee Volume of the Oriental Collection 1951–1976*, Magyar Tudományos Akadémia Könyvtára, Budapest 1978.

Rebiger, B.: *Sefer Shimmush Tehillim: Buch vom magischen Gebrauch der Psalmen, Edition, Übersetzung und Kommentar*, TSAJ 137 (Tübingen: Mohr Siebeck, 2010.

Brauner, R.: *Synopsis of Sefer Shimush Tehillim, containing protections against numerous calamities: attributed to Rav Hai Gaon*, Reuven Brauner sixth edition, Raanana 2012.

Swart, J.G.: *The Book of Seals & Amulets, Op. Cit.*

Hai ben Sherira Gaon & Varady, A.N.: *Shimush Tehillim (the Theurgical Use of Psalms)*, document shared on Creative Commons Attribution-ShareAlike (CC BY-SA) 4.0 International, May 4th 2015.

Dennis, G.W.: *The Encyclopedia of Jewish Myth, Magic and Mysticism*, Llewellyn Publications, Woodbury 2007.

8.   **Fodor, A.:** *The Use of Psalms in Jewish and Christian Arabic Magic, Op. Cit.*

Gillingham, S.: *A Journey of Two Psalms: The Reception of Psalms 1 and 2 in Jewish and Christian Tradition*, Oxford University Press, Oxford 2013.

9.　　**Kimchi, D. ben Y.:** *Sefer Tehillim, Op. Cit.*
Sefer Shimmush Tehillim, Op. Cit.
Seder Tefilot Tikun Ezra, Op. Cit.
Refuah v'Chayim m'Yerushalayim im Shimush Tehilim, Op. Cit.
Landsberg, M.: *Sefer Tehillim im Peirush Rashi, Op. Cit.*
Singer, I. & Adler, C.: *The Jewish Encyclopedia, Op. Cit.*
Selig, G.: *Sepher Schimmusch Tehillim, Op. Cit.*
The Sixth and Seventh Books of Moses, Op. Cit.
Peterson, J.H.: *The Sixth and Seventh Books of Moses, Op. Cit.*
Rebiger, B.: *Sefer Shimmush Tehillim, Op. Cit.*
Brauner, R.: *Synopsis of Sefer Shimush Tehillim, Op. Cit.*
Fodor, A.: *Ibid.*
Hai ben Sherira Gaon & Varady, A.N.: *Shimush Tehillim (the Theurgical Use of Psalms), Op. Cit.*
Dennis, G.W.: *The Encyclopedia of Jewish Myth, Magic and Mysticism, Op. Cit.*

10.　　**Isaacs, H.D. & Baker, C.F.:** *Medical and Para-medical Manuscripts in the Cambridge Genizah Collections*, Cambridge University Press, Cambridge 1994.
Baker, C.F. & Polliack, M.: *Arabic and Judaeo-Arabic Manuscripts in the Cambridge Genizah Collections*, Vol. 1, Cambridge University Press, Cambridge 2001.

11.　　**Swart, J.G.:** *The Book of Seals & Amulets, Op. Cit.*

12.　　**Rebiger, B.:** *Sefer Shimmush Tehillim, Op. Cit.*

13.　　**Kimchi, D. ben Y.:** *Sefer Tehillim, Op. Cit.*
Sefer Shimmush Tehillim, Op. Cit.
Seder Tefilot Tikun Ezra, Op. Cit.
Refuah v'Chayim m'Yerushalayim im Shimush Tehilim, Op. Cit.
Landsberg, M.: *Sefer Tehillim im Peirush Rashi, Op. Cit.*
Selig, G.: *Sepher Schimmusch Tehillim, Op. Cit.*
The Sixth and Seventh Books of Moses, Op. Cit.
Peterson, J.H.: *The Sixth and Seventh Books of Moses, Op. Cit.*
Rebiger, B.: *Sefer Shimmush Tehillim, Op. Cit.*
Brauner, R.: *Synopsis of Sefer Shimush Tehillim. Op. Cit.*
Fodor, A.: *The Use of Psalms in Jewish and Christian Arabic Magic, Op. Cit.*
Hai ben Sherira Gaon & Varady, A.N.: *Shimush Tehillim (the Theurgical Use of Psalms), Op. Cit.*

14.　　**Selig, G.:** *Ibid.*
The Sixth and Seventh Books of Moses, Ibid.
Peterson, J.H.: *Ibid.*

15.　　**Fodor, A.:** *The Use of Psalms in Jewish and Christian Arabic Magic, Op. Cit.*

16.　　**Swart, J.G.:** *The Book of Seals & Amulets, Op. Cit.*

17.   *Ibid.*
        Kimchi, D. ben Y.: *Sefer Tehillim, Op. Cit.*
        Sefer Shimmush Tehillim, Op. Cit.
        Seder Tefilot Tikun Ezra, Op. Cit.
        Refuah v'Chayim m'Yerushalayim im Shimush Tehilim, Op. Cit.
        Landsberg, M.: *Sefer Tehillim im Peirush Rashi, Op. Cit.*
        Selig, G.: *Sepher Schimmusch Tehillim, Op. Cit.*
        The Sixth and Seventh Books of Moses, Op. Cit.
        Peterson, J.H.: *The Sixth and Seventh Books of Moses, Op. Cit.*
        Rebiger, B.: *Sefer Shimmush Tehillim, Op. Cit.*
        Hai ben Sherira Gaon & Varady, A.N.: *Shimush Tehillim (the Theurgical Use of Psalms), Op. Cit.*
        Sienna, N.: *Jewish Magic in Theory and Practice*, Essay published by the University of Minnesota, NHC Summer Institute 2016.
18.   **Rebiger, B.:** *Sefer Shimmush Tehillim, Op. Cit.*
19.   *Ibid.*
20.   **Swart, J.G.:** *The Book of Seals & Amulets, Op. Cit.*
21.   **Weinbach, S. & Ehrlich-Klein, T.:** *Salt, Pepper and Eternity: Stories that Last Forever*, Targum Press, Southfield 2001.
22.   **Zacutto, M.:** *Shorshei ha-Shemot, Op. cit.*
        Davis, E. & Frenkel, D.A.: *Ha-Kami'a ha-Ivri, Op. Cit.*
        Green, A.: *Judaic Artifacts: Unlocking the Secrets of Judaic Charms and Amulets*, Astrolog Publishing House, Hod Hasharon 2004.
        Swart, J.G.: *The Book of Seals & Amulets, Op. Cit.*
        —*The Book of Immediate Magic - Part 1, Op. Cit.*
23.   **Zacutto, M.:** *Ibid.*
24.   **Davis, E. & Frenkel, D.A.:** *Ha-Kami'a ha-Ivri, Op. Cit.*
        Green, A.: *Judaic Artifacts, Op. Cit.*
25.   **Swart, J.G.:** *The Book of Immediate Magic - Part 1, Op. Cit.*
26.   **Davis, E. & Frenkel, D.A.:** *Ha-Kami'a ha-Ivri, Op. Cit.*
        Green, A.: *Judaic Artifacts, Op. Cit.*
27.   **Weintraub, S.Y.:** *Healing Activities and P'sukim from Tehillim: Words of Psalms in/as Jewish Meditations for Healing*, essay published by UJA Federation of New York, 2000.
28.   **Heim, R.:** *Incantamenta Magica Graeca Latina: Collegit, disposuit, edidit R. Heim*, B.G. Teubneri, Lipsiae 1892.
        Singer, I. & Adler, C.: *The Jewish Encyclopedia, Op. Cit.*
        Fodor, A.: *The Use of Psalms in Jewish and Christian Arabic Magic, Op. Cit.*
        Magonet, J.: *A Rabbi Reads the Psalms, Op. Cit.*

29. **Fodor, A.:** *The Use of Psalms in Jewish and Christian Arabic Magic, Op. Cit.*
30. *Ibid.*
31. **Zellmann-Rohrer, M.:** *"Psalms Useful for Everything:" Byzantine and Post-Byzantine Manuals for the Amuletic Use of the Psalter,* Dumbarton Oaks Research Library and Collection, Washington 2019.
32. *Ibid.*
    Owen, T.: *Geoponika: Agricultural Pursuits,* Vol. 2, J. White, London 1806.
33. **Zellmann-Rohrer, M.:** *Ibid.*
34. **Rankine, D. & Barron, P.H.:** *The Book of Gold: A 17th Century Magical Grimoire of Amulets, Charms, Prayers, Sigils and Spells using the Biblical Psalms of King David,* Avalonia, London 2010.
    Marty, J. & MacParthy, F.: *Usage Mago-Théurgiques des Psaumes: Selon la kabbala Judaique et Chrétienne: Sefer Shimoush Théhilim & Le Livre d'Or,* Sesheta Publications, Brestot 2018.
35. *Ibid.*
36. *Ibid.*
37. **Fodor, A.:** *The Use of Psalms in Jewish and Christian Arabic Magic, Op. Cit.*

Psalm 2

1. **Kimchi, D. ben Y.:** *Sefer Tehillim, Op. Cit.*
   Sefer Shimmush Tehillim, Op. Cit.
   Le Livre des Psaumes Hébreu-Français et Phonétique, Op. Cit.
   Azulai, H.Y.D.: *Sefer Tehillim Sha'arei Rachamim: im Segulot v'Tefilot ha'Chida, Op. Cit.*
   Ronen, D.: *Tehilim Kavvanot ha-Lev, Op. Cit.*
   Grünwald, M.: *Ueber den Einfluss der Psalmen auf die Katholische Liturgie, Op. Cit.*
   Seder Tefilot Tikun Ezra, Op. Cit.
   Refuah v'Chayim m'Yerushalayim im Shimush Tehilim, Op. Cit.
   Landsberg, M.: *Sefer Tehillim im Peirush Rashi, Op. Cit.*
   Singer, I. & Adler, C.: *The Jewish Encyclopedia, Op. Cit.*
   Selig, G.: *Sepher Schimmusch Tehillim, Op. Cit.*
   The Sixth and Seventh Books of Moses, Op. Cit.
   Peterson, J.H.: *The Sixth and Seventh Books of Moses, Op. Cit.*
   Fodor, A.: *Ibid.*
   Rebiger, B.: *Sefer Shimmush Tehillim, Op. Cit.*
   Brauner, R.: *Synopsis of Sefer Shimush Tehillim. Op. Cit.*

404

Hai ben Sherira Gaon & Varady, A.N.: *Shimush Tehillim (the Theurgical Use of Psalms), Op. Cit.*
Gillingham, S.: *A Journey of Two Psalms, Ibid.*

2. *Sefer Shimmush Tehillim, Ibid.*
   The Sixth and Seventh Books of Moses, Ibid.
   Selig, G.A.: *Ibid.*
   Peterson, J.H.: *Ibid.*
   Fodor, A.: *Ibid.*
   Rebiger, B.: *Sefer Shimmush Tehillim, Op. Cit.*
   Swart, J.G.: *The Book of Seals & Amulets, Op. Cit.*
   Hai ben Sherira Gaon & Varady, A.N.: *Ibid.*

3. **Fodor, A.:** *Ibid.*

4. **Selig, G.:** *Sepher Schimmusch Tehillim, Op. Cit.*
   The Sixth and Seventh Books of Moses, Op. Cit.
   Peterson, J.H.: *The Sixth and Seventh Books of Moses, Op. Cit.*

5. *Ibid.*

6. *Ibid.*

7. **Fodor, A.:** *The Use of Psalms in Jewish and Christian Arabic Magic, Op. Cit.*

8. **Kimchi, D. ben Y.:** *Sefer Tehillim, Op. Cit.*
   Sefer Shimmush Tehillim, Op. Cit.
   Seder Tefilot Tikun Ezra, Op. Cit.
   Refuah v'Chayim m'Yerushalayim im Shimush Tehilim, Op. Cit.
   Landsberg, M.: *Sefer Tehillim im Peirush Rashi, Op. Cit.*
   Selig, G.: *Sepher Schimmusch Tehillim, Op. Cit.*
   The Sixth and Seventh Books of Moses, Op. Cit.
   Peterson, J.H.: *The Sixth and Seventh Books of Moses, Op. Cit.*
   Rebiger, B.: *Sefer Shimmush Tehillim, Op. Cit.*
   Swart, J.G.: *The Book of Seals & Amulets, Op. Cit.*
   Gillingham, S.: *A Journey of Two Psalms, Op. Cit.*

9. *Ibid.*

10. *The Sixth and Seventh Books of Moses, Ibid.*
    Selig, G.A.: *Ibid.*
    Peterson, J.H.: *Ibid.*

11. **Rebiger, B.:** *Sefer Shimmush Tehillim, Op. Cit.*

12. *Ibid.*

13. *Ibid.*

14. **Zacutto, M.:** *Shorshei ha-Shemot, Op. Cit.*

15. *Ibid.*

16. **Fodor, A.:** *The Use of Psalms in Jewish and Christian Arabic Magic, Op. Cit.*

17. **Rankine, D. & Barron, P.H.:** *The Book of Gold, Op. Cit.*
    Marty, J. & MacParthy, F.: *Usage Mago-Théurgiques des Psaumes, Op. Cit.*

405

18.   *Ibid.*
19.   *Ibid.*
20.   *Ibid.*
      Skinner, S. & Rankine, D.: *A Collection of Magical Secrets: taken from Peter de Abano, Cornelius Agrippa and from other famous Occult Philosophers, and a Treatise of Mixed Cabalah which comprises the Angelic Art taken from Hebrew Sages*, Avalonia, London 2009.
21.   **Skinner, S. & Rankine, D.:** *The Veritable Key of Solomon, Op. Cit.*
22.   *Ibid.*
      Mathers, S.L. Macgregor: *Key of Solomon the King, Op. Cit.*

Psalm 3

1.   **Nulman, M.:** *The Encyclopedia of Jewish Prayer, Op. Cit.*
      Eisenberg, R.L.: *The JPS Guide to Jewish Traditions*, Jewish Publication Society, Philadelphia 2008.
2.   **Kimchi, D. ben Y.:** *Sefer Tehillim, Op. Cit.*
      Sefer Shimmush Tehillim, Op. Cit.
      Seder Tefilot Tikun Ezra, Op. Cit.
      Refuah v'Chayim m'Yerushalayim im Shimush Tehilim, Op. Cit.
      Landsberg, M.: *Sefer Tehillim im Peirush Rashi, Op. Cit.*
      Singer, I. & Adler, C.: *The Jewish Encyclopedia, Op. Cit.*
      Selig, G.: *Sepher Schimmusch Tehillim, Op. Cit.*
      The Sixth and Seventh Books of Moses, Op. Cit.
      Peterson, J.H.: *The Sixth and Seventh Books of Moses, Op. Cit.*
      Fodor, A.: *The Use of Psalms in Jewish and Christian Arabic Magic, Op. Cit.*
      Rebiger, B.: *Sefer Shimmush Tehillim, Op. Cit.*
      Brauner, R.: *Synopsis of Sefer Shimush Tehillim. Op. Cit.*
3.   *Ibid.*
      Le Livre des Psaumes Hébreu-Français et Phonétique, Op. Cit.
      Ronen, D.: *Tehilim Kavvanot ha-Lev, Op. Cit.*
4.   **Kimchi, D. ben Y.:** *Sefer Tehillim, Op. Cit.*
      Sefer Shimmush Tehillim, Op. Cit.
      Azulai, H.Y.D.: *Sefer Tehillim Sha'arei Rachamim: im Segulot v'Tefilot ha'Chida, Op. Cit.*
      Seder Tefilot Tikun Ezra, Op. Cit.
      Refuah v'Chayim m'Yerushalayim im Shimush Tehilim, Op. Cit.
      Landsberg, M.: *Sefer Tehillim im Peirush Rashi, Op. Cit.*
      Singer, I. & Adler, C.: *The Jewish Encyclopedia, Op. Cit.*
      Fodor, A.: *The Use of Psalms in Jewish and Christian Arabic Magic, Op. Cit.*

Rebiger, B.: *Sefer Shimmush Tehillim, Op. Cit.*
Brauner, R.: *Synopsis of Sefer Shimush Tehillim. Op. Cit.*
5. **Rebiger, B.**: *Ibid.*
6. *Ibid.*
7. **Selig, G.**: *Sepher Schimmusch Tehillim, Op. Cit.*
    The Sixth and Seventh Books of Moses, Op. Cit.
    Peterson, J.H.: *The Sixth and Seventh Books of Moses, Op. Cit.*
8. *Ibid.*
9. *Ibid.*
10. **ha-Kohen, I.M. & Orenstein, A.**: *Mishnah Berurah: The Classic Commentary to Shulchan Aruch Orach Chayim, comprising the Laws of Daily Jewish Conduct,* Vol. 2 (C): *Laws concerning Miscellaneous Blessings, the Minchah Service, the Ma'ariv Service and Evening Conduct,* Pisgah Foundation, Jerusalem 1989.
11. **Daniels, C.L. & Stevans, C.M.**: *Encyclopaedia of Superstitions, Folklore, and the Occult Sciences of the World,* Vol 2, J.H. Yewdale & Sons, Chicago 1903.
    Impelluso, L.: *Nature and Its Symbols,* transl. Sartarelli, S., The J. Paul Getty Museum, Los Angeles 2003.
    Quiles, J.L., Ramírez-Tortosa, M.C., & Yaqoob, P.: *Olive Oil and Health,* CABI, Oxfordshire & Cambridge 2006.
12. *Ibid.*
    Efe, R., Ozturk, M. & Ghazanfar, S.: Environment and Ecology in the Mediterranean Region, Cambridge Scholars Publishing, Newcastle upon Tyne 2012.
    Angus, J.: *Olive Odyssey: Searching for the Secrets of the Fruit That Seduced the World,* Greystone Books, Vancouver & Berkeley 2014.
13. **Guggenheimer, H.W.**: *The Jerusalem Talmud: Fourth Order: Neziqin, Tractates Sanhedrin, Makkot, and Horaiot,* Walter de Gruyter GmbH & Co. KG, Berlin & New York 2010.
    Federow, S.: *Judaism and Christianity: A Contrast,* iUniverse Inc., Bloomington 2012.
    Schrager, A.J.: *The Lives of Abraham and Moses According to Josephus,* Exlibris, Philadelphia 2006.
    Bloom, M.: *Jewish Mysticism and Magic: An Anthropological Perspective,* Routledge, London 2010.
14. **Bloom, M.**: *Ibid.*
    Jennings, D.: *Jewish Antiqities: or a Course of Lectures on the Three first books of Godwin's Moses and Aaron,* William Baynes and Son, Edinburgh 1825.
    Patai, R.: *On Jewish Folklore,* Wayne State University Press, Detroit 1983.

15. **Unger, M.F. & White, W.:** *Nelson's Expository Dictionary of the Old Testament*, Thomas Nelson Publishers, Nashville 1980.
— **& Vine, W.E.:** *Vine's Complete Expository Dictionary of Old and New Testament Words: with Topical Index*, Thomas Nelson, 2000.

16. *Ibid.*

17. *Ibid.*

18. **Federow, S.:** *Judaism and Christianity, Op. Cit.*

19. *Ibid.*

20. **Wilkinson, J.G.:** *A Second Series of the Manners and Customs of the Ancient Egyptians*, Vol. 2, John Murray, London 1841.
McClintock, J. & Strong, J.: *Cyclopaedia of Biblical, Theological, and Ecclesiastical Literature*, Vol. 1, Harper & Brothers Publishers, New York 1883.
Malamat, A.: *Mari and the Bible*, Koninklijke Brill NV, Leiden 1998.
Fried, L.S.: *The Priest and the Great King: Temple-palace Relations in the Persian Empire*, Eisenbrauns, Winona Lake 2004.

21. **Swart, J.G.:** *The Book of Immediate Magic - Part 1, Op. Cit.*

22. **Milgrom, J.:** *Studies in the Cultic Theology and Terminology*, Vol. 36, E.J. Brill, Leiden 1983.
Botterweck, G.J. & Ringgren, H.: *Theological Dictionary of the Old Testament*, Vol. 5, William B. Eerd3mans Publishing Company, Grand Rapids & Cambridge 1986.
Gorman, F.H.: *Divine Presence and Community: A Commentary on the Book of Leviticus*, Wm. B. Eerdmans Publishing Co. & The Handsel Press Ltd, Grand Rapids & Edinburgh 1997.

23. **Daiches, J.:** *Babylonian Oil Magic in the Talmud and in the Later Jewish Literature*, Jews' College, London 1913.

24. **Zacutto, M.:** *Shorshei ha-Shemot, Op. Cit.*

25. **Bischoff, E. & Linden, A. von der:** *Geheime Wissenschaften: Eine Sammlung seltener älterer und neuerer Schriften über Alchemie, Magie, Kabbalah, Rosenkreuzerei, Freimaurerei, Hexen- und Teufelswesen usw., Zweiter Band: Die Elemente der Kabbalah: Magische Wissenschaft—Magische Künste*, Hermann Barsdorf Verlag, Berlin 1914.
Trachtenberg, J.: *Jewish Magic and Superstition, Op. Cit.*
Numbers, R.L. & Amundsen, D.W.: *Caring and Curing: Health and Medicine in the Western Religious Traditions*, Macmillan, New York 1986.
Penner, J.: *Patterns of Daily Prayer in Second Temple Period Judaism*, Koninklijke Brill NV, Leiden & Boston 2012.

Harari, Y.: *The Sages and the Occult,* in Safrai, S.; Safrai, Z., Schwartz, J. & Tomson, P.J.: *The Literature of the Sages Part 2,* Royal Van Gorcum & Fortress Press, Assen 2006.
—*Jewish Magic before the Rise of Kabbalah,* Wayne State University Press, Detroit 2017.
Frankfurter, D.: *Guide to the Study of Ancient Magic,* Koninklijke Brill NV, Leiden & Boston 2019.

26. **Nulman, M.:** *The Encyclopedia of Jewish Prayer, Op. Cit.*
27. **Hanover, N.N. ben M.:** *Sefer Sha'arei Tzion,* Zolkiev 1816.
     Zacutto, M.: *Shorshei ha-Shemot, Op. Cit.*
     Kratchin, B. Beinish: *Amtachat Binyamin,* Hotza'at Backal, Jerusalem 1966.
     Reuchlin, J.: *De Arte Cabalistica: On the Art of the Kabbalah,* transl. M. & S. Goodman, Abaris Books Inc., New York 1983.
     Kircher, A.: *Oedipus Aegyptiacus,* Rome 1653.
     Swart, J.G.: *The Book of Sacred Names, Op. Cit.*
     —*The Book of Immediate Magic - Part 1, Op. Cit.*
28. **Zacutto, M.:** *Shorshei ha-Shemot, Op. Cit.*
29. **Skinner, S. & Rankine, D.:** *A Collection of Magical Secrets, Op. Cit.*
30. **Fodor, A.:** *The Use of Psalms in Jewish and Christian Arabic Magic, Op. Cit.*
31. **Rankine, D. & Barron, P.H.:** *The Book of Gold, Op. Cit.*
     Marty, J. & MacParthy, F.: *Usage Mago-Théurgiques des Psaumes, Op. Cit.*
32. *Ibid.*
33. **Zellmann-Rohrer, M.:** *Psalms Useful for Everything, Op. Cit.*
34. *Ibid.*
35. *Ibid.*
36. *Ibid.*
37. *Ibid.*
38. *Ibid.*
39. **Grünwald, M.:** *Ueber den Einfluss der Psalmen auf die Katholische Liturgie, Op. Cit.*
     Singer, I.: *The Jewish Encyclopedia, Op. Cit.*
40. **Skinner, S. & Rankine, D.:** *A Collection of Magical Secrets, Op. Cit.*
41. *Ibid.*
42. **Mathers, S.L. Macgregor:** *Key of Solomon the King, Op. Cit.*
     Skinner, S. & Rankine, D.: *The Veritable Key of Solomon, Op. Cit.*
     Rankine, D. & Barron, P.H.: *The Book of Gold, Op. Cit.*
43. **Skinner, S. & Rankine, D.:** *A Collection of Magical Secrets, Op. Cit.*

44. *Ibid.*
45. **Skinner, S. & Rankine, D.:** *The Goetia of Dr Rudd*, Golden Hoard Press Ltd., Singapore 2007.

Psalm 4

1. *Le Livre des Psaumes Hébreu-Français et Phonétique, Op. Cit.*
    Azulai, H.Y.D.: *Sefer Tehillim Sha'arei Rachamim: im Segulot v'Tefilot ha'Chida, Op. Cit.*
    Ronen, D.: *Tehilim Kavvanot ha-Lev, Op. Cit.*
2. **Kimchi, D. ben Y.:** *Sefer Tehillim, Op. Cit.*
    Sefer Shimmush Tehillim, Op. Cit.
    Seder Tefilot Tikun Ezra, Op. Cit.
    Refuah v'Chayim m'Yerushalayim im Shimush Tehilim, Op. Cit.
    Landsberg, M.: *Sefer Tehillim im Peirush Rashi, Op. Cit.*
    Grünwald, M.: *Ueber den Einfluss der Psalmen auf die Katholische Liturgie, Op. Cit.*
    Rebiger, B.: *Sefer Shimmush Tehillim, Op. Cit.*
    Hai ben Sherira Gaon & Varady, A.N.: *Shimush Tehillim* (*the Theurgical Use of Psalms*), *Op. Cit.*
3. **Selig, G.:** *Sepher Schimmusch Tehillim, Op. Cit.*
    The Sixth and Seventh Books of Moses, Op. Cit.
    Peterson, J.H.: *The Sixth and Seventh Books of Moses, Op. Cit.*
4. *Ibid*
    Kimchi, D. ben Y.: *Sefer Tehillim, Op. Cit.*
    Sefer Shimmush Tehillim, Op. Cit.
    Seder Tefilot Tikun Ezra, Op. Cit.
    Refuah v'Chayim m'Yerushalayim im Shimush Tehilim, Op. Cit.
    Landsberg, M.: *Sefer Tehillim im Peirush Rashi, Op. Cit.*
    Rebiger, B.: *Sefer Shimmush Tehillim, Op. Cit.*
    Hai ben Sherira Gaon & Varady, A.N.: *Shimush Tehillim* (*the Theurgical Use of Psalms*), *Op. Cit.*
    Sienna, N.: *Jewish Magic in Theory and Practice, Op. Cit.*
5. **Selig, G.:** *Sepher Schimmusch Tehillim, Op. Cit.*
    The Sixth and Seventh Books of Moses, Op. Cit.
    Peterson, J.H.: *The Sixth and Seventh Books of Moses, Op. Cit.*
6. **Rebiger, B.:** *Sefer Shimmush Tehillim, Op. Cit.*
7. **Rosenberg, Y.Y.:** *Rafael ha-Malach*, Asher Klein, Jerusalem 2000.
8. **Rebiger, B.:** *Sefer Shimmush Tehillim, Op. Cit.*
9. *Ibid.*
10. *Ibid.*
11. *Ibid.*
    Kimchi, D. ben Y.: *Sefer Tehillim, Op. Cit.*
    Sefer Shimmush Tehillim, Op. Cit.

Seder Tefilot Tikun Ezra, Op. Cit.
Refuah v'Chayim m'Yerushalayim im Shimush Tehilim, Op. Cit.
Landsberg, M.: *Sefer Tehillim im Peirush Rashi, Op. Cit.*
Brauner, R.: *Synopsis of Sefer Shimush Tehillim. Op. Cit.*
Hai ben Sherira Gaon & Varady, A.N.: *Shimush Tehillim (the Theurgical Use of Psalms), Op. Cit.*
Sienna, N.: *Jewish Magic in Theory and Practice, Op. Cit.*
12. *Ibid.*
13. **Selig, G.:** *Sepher Schimmusch Tehillim, Op. Cit.*
The Sixth and Seventh Books of Moses, Op. Cit.
Peterson, J.H.: *The Sixth and Seventh Books of Moses, Op. Cit.*
14. **Swart, J.G.:** *The Book of Seals & Amulets, Op. Cit.*
15. *Ibid.*
16. **Zacutto, M.:** *Shorshei ha-Shemot, Op. Cit.*
17. *Ibid.*
18. *Ibid.*
19. *Ibid.*
20. *Ibid.*
21. *Ibid.*
22. **Faur, Y.:** *Anti-Maimonidean Demons*, in **Avery-Peck, A.:** *Review of Rabbinic Judaism: Ancient, Medieval, and Modern*, Vol. 6 Issue 1, Leiden Koninklijke Brill NV, Leiden & Boston 2003.
23. **Zacutto, M.:** *Shorshei ha-Shemot, Op. Cit.*
24. **Rankine, D. & Barron, P.H.:** *The Book of Gold, Op. Cit.*
Marty, J. & MacParthy, F.: *Usage Mago-Théurgiques des Psaumes, Op. Cit.*
25. *Ibid.*
26. *Ibid.*
27. **Skinner, S. & Rankine, D.:** *A Collection of Magical Secrets, Op. Cit.*
28. *Ibid.*
29. **Zellmann-Rohrer, M.:** *Psalms Useful for Everything, Op. Cit.*
30. **Tselikas, A.:** *Spells and Exorcisms in Three Post-Byzantine Manuscripts*, in **Petropoulos, J.:** *Greek Magic, Ancient, Medieval, and Modern*, Routledge, London 2008.
Lecouteux, C.: *Dictionary of Ancient Magic Words and Spells from Abraxas to Zoar*, transl. Graham, J.E., Inner Traditions, Rochester & Toronto 2014.
31. **Skinner, S. & Rankine, D.:** *A Collection of Magical Secrets, Op. Cit.*
32. **Mathers, S.L. Macgregor:** *Key of Solomon the King, Op. Cit.*

411

Psalm 5

1.   **Nulman, M.:** *The Encyclopedia of Jewish Prayer, Op. Cit.*
2.   **Kimchi, D. ben Y.:** *Sefer Tehillim, Op. Cit.*
      Sefer Shimmush Tehillim, Op. Cit.
      Le Livre des Psaumes Hébreu-Français et Phonétique, Op. Cit.
      Azulai, H.Y.D.: *Sefer Tehillim Sha'arei Rachamim: im Segulot v'Tefilot ha'Chida, Op. Cit.*
      Seder Tefilot Tikun Ezra, Op. Cit.
      Refuah v'Chayim m'Yerushalayim im Shimush Tehilim, Op. Cit.
      Landsberg, M.: *Sefer Tehillim im Peirush Rashi, Op. Cit.*
      Ronen, D.: *Tehilim Kavvanot ha-Lev, Op. Cit.*
      Singer, I. & Adler, C.: *The Jewish Encyclopedia, Op. Cit.*
      Selig, G.: *Sepher Schimmusch Tehillim, Op. Cit.*
      The Sixth and Seventh Books of Moses, Op. Cit.
      Peterson, J.H.: *The Sixth and Seventh Books of Moses, Op. Cit.*
      Rebiger, B.: *Sefer Shimmush Tehillim, Op. Cit.*
      Brauner, R.: *Synopsis of Sefer Shimush Tehillim. Op. Cit.*
      Hai ben Sherira Gaon & Varady, A.N.: *Shimush Tehillim (the Theurgical Use of Psalms), Op. Cit.*
3.   **Rebiger, B.:** *Ibid.*
4.   **Davis, E. & Frenkel, D.A.:** *Ha-Kami'a ha-Ivri, Op. Cit.*
      Green, A.: *Judaic Artifacts, Op. Cit.*
5.   **Zacutto, M.:** *Shorshei ha-Shemot, Op. Cit.*
6.   *Ibid.*
7.   **Singer, I. & Adler, C.:** *The Jewish Encyclopedia, Op. Cit.*
8.   *Ibid.*
9.   **Schrire, T.:** *Hebrew Amulets, Op. Cit.*
      Green, A.: *Judaic Artifacts, Op. Cit.*
10.   **Zacutto, M.:** *Shorshei ha-Shemot, Op. Cit.*
11.   *Ibid.*
12.   *Ibid.*
13.   *Ibid.*
14.   **Swart, J.G.:** *The Book of Sacred Names, Op. Cit.*
      —*The Book of Seals & Amulets, Op. Cit.*
      —*The Book of Immediate Magic - Part 1, Op. Cit.*
15.   **Rosenberg, Y.Y.:** *Rafael ha-Malach, Op. Cit.*
16.   **Grünwald, M.:** *Ueber den Einfluss der Psalmen auf die Katholische Liturgie, Op. Cit.*
17.   **Kimchi, D. ben Y.:** *Sefer Tehillim, Op. Cit.*
      Sefer Shimmush Tehillim, Op. Cit.
      Seder Tefilot Tikun Ezra, Op. Cit.
      Refuah v'Chayim m'Yerushalayim im Shimush Tehilim, Op. Cit.

Landsberg, M.: *Sefer Tehillim im Peirush Rashi, Op. Cit.*
Singer, I. & Adler, C.: *The Jewish Encyclopedia, Op. Cit.*
Selig, G.: *Sepher Schimmusch Tehillim, Op. Cit.*
The Sixth and Seventh Books of Moses, Op. Cit.
Peterson, J.H.: *The Sixth and Seventh Books of Moses, Op. Cit.*
Rebiger, B.: *Sefer Shimmush Tehillim, Op. Cit.*
Brauner, R.: *Synopsis of Sefer Shimush Tehillim. Op. Cit.*
Hai ben Sherira Gaon & Varady, A.N.: *Shimush Tehillim (the Theurgical Use of Psalms), Op. Cit.*

18. **Selig, G.**: *Sepher Schimmusch Tehillim, Op. Cit.*
     The Sixth and Seventh Books of Moses, Op. Cit.
     Peterson, J.H.: *The Sixth and Seventh Books of Moses, Op. Cit.*
19. *Ibid.*
20. *Ibid.*
21. **Rankine, D. & Barron, P.H.**: *The Book of Gold, Op. Cit.*
     Marty, J. & MacParthy, F.: *Usage Mago-Théurgiques des Psaumes, Op. Cit.*
22. **Zellmann-Rohrer, M.**: *Psalms Useful for Everything, Op. Cit.*
23. *Ibid.*
24. **Rankine, D. & Barron, P.H.**: *The Book of Gold, Op. Cit.*
     Marty, J. & MacParthy, F.: *Usage Mago-Théurgiques des Psaumes, Op. Cit.*
25. **Zellmann-Rohrer, M.**: *Psalms Useful for Everything, Op. Cit.*
     Pradel, F.: *Griechische und Süditalienische Gebete, Beschwörungen und Rezepte des Mittelalters,* Alfred Topelmann, Giessen 1907.
26. **Skinner, S. & Rankine, D.**: *A Collection of Magical Secrets, Op. Cit.*
27. **Kayser, C.**: *Gebrauch von Psalmen zur Zauberei,* in Windisch, E.: *Zeitschrift der Deutschen Morgenländischen Gesellschaft,* Vol. 42, F.A. Brockhaus Leipzig 1888.

Psalm 6

1. **Hoffman, L.A.**: *My People's Prayer Book: Traditional Prayers, Modern Commentaries: Vol. 6—Tachanun and Concluding Prayers,* Jewish Lights Publishing, Woodstock 2002.
2. **Kimchi, D. ben Y.**: *Sefer Tehillim, Op. Cit.*
    Sefer Shimmush Tehillim, Op. Cit.
    Seder Tefilot Tikun Ezra, Op. Cit.
    Le Livre des Psaumes Hébreu-Français et Phonétique, Op. Cit.
    Azulai, H.Y.D.: *Sefer Tehillim Sha'arei Rachamim: im Segulot v'Tefilot ha'Chida, Op. Cit.*

Ronen, D.: *Tehilim Kavvanot ha-Lev, Op. Cit.*
Grünwald, M.: *Ueber den Einfluss der Psalmen auf die Katholische Liturgie, Op. Cit.*
Refuah v'Chayim m'Yerushalayim im Shimush Tehilim, Op. Cit.
Landsberg, M.: *Sefer Tehillim im Peirush Rashi, Op. Cit.*
Singer, I. & Adler, C.: *The Jewish Encyclopedia, Op. Cit.*
Selig, G.: *Sepher Schimmusch Tehillim, Op. Cit.*
The Sixth and Seventh Books of Moses, Op. Cit.
Peterson, J.H.: *The Sixth and Seventh Books of Moses, Op. Cit.*
Rebiger, B.: *Sefer Shimmush Tehillim, Op. Cit.*
Brauner, R.: *Synopsis of Sefer Shimush Tehillim. Op. Cit.*
Hai ben Sherira Gaon & Varady, A.N.: *Shimush Tehillim (the Theurgical Use of Psalms), Op. Cit.*

3.   *Ibid.*
4.   **Rebiger, B.:** *Ibid.*
5.   *Ibid.*
6.   *Ibid.*
7.   *Ibid.*
       Kimchi, D. ben Y.: *Sefer Tehillim, Op. Cit.*
Sefer Shimmush Tehillim, Op. Cit.
Seder Tefilot Tikun Ezra, Op. Cit.
Refuah v'Chayim m'Yerushalayim im Shimush Tehilim, Op. Cit.
Landsberg, M.: *Sefer Tehillim im Peirush Rashi, Op. Cit.*
Hai ben Sherira Gaon & Varady, A.N.: *Shimush Tehillim (the Theurgical Use of Psalms), Op. Cit.*

8.   **Selig, G.:** *Sepher Schimmusch Tehillim, Op. Cit.*
       The Sixth and Seventh Books of Moses, Op. Cit.
       Peterson, J.H.: *The Sixth and Seventh Books of Moses, Op. Cit.*
9.   *Ibid.*
10.   **Rebiger, B.:** *Sefer Shimmush Tehillim, Op. Cit.*
11.   *Sefer Shimmush Tehillim, Op. Cit.*
       Rebiger, B.: *Sefer Shimmush Tehillim, Op. Cit.*
       Hai ben Sherira Gaon & Varady, A.N.: *Shimush Tehillim (the Theurgical Use of Psalms), Op. Cit.*
12.   **Fodor, A.:** *The Use of Psalms in Jewish and Christian Arabic Magic, Op. Cit.*
13.   **Kimchi, D. ben Y.:** *Sefer Tehillim, Op. Cit.*
       Sefer Shimmush Tehillim, Op. Cit.
       Seder Tefilot Tikun Ezra, Op. Cit.
       Refuah v'Chayim m'Yerushalayim im Shimush Tehilim, Op. Cit.
       Landsberg, M.: *Sefer Tehillim im Peirush Rashi, Op. Cit.*
       Rebiger, B.: *Sefer Shimmush Tehillim, Op. Cit.*
       Hai ben Sherira Gaon & Varady, A.N.: *Shimush Tehillim (the Theurgical Use of Psalms), Op. Cit.*

14. **Selig, G.:** *Sepher Schimmusch Tehillim, Op. Cit.*
    The Sixth and Seventh Books of Moses, Op. Cit.
    Peterson, J.H.: *The Sixth and Seventh Books of Moses, Op. Cit.*
15. **Zacutto, M.:** *Shorshei ha-Shemot, Op. Cit.*
16. *Ibid.*
17. *Ibid.*
18. *Ibid.*
19. *Ibid.*
20. *Ibid.*
21. *Ibid.*
22. **Davis, E. & Frenkel, D.A.:** *Ha-Kami'a ha-Ivri, Op. Cit.*
    Green, A.: *Judaic Artifacts, Op. Cit.*
23. *Ibid.*
24. *Ibid.*
25. **Rebiger, B.:** *Sefer Shimmush Tehillim, Op. Cit.*
26. **Singer, I. & Adler, C.:** *The Jewish Encyclopedia, Op. Cit.*
27. *Ibid.*
    Kimchi, D. ben Y.: *Sefer Tehillim, Op. Cit.*
    Sefer Shimmush Tehillim, Op. Cit.
    Seder Tefilot Tikun Ezra, Op. Cit.
    Refuah v'Chayim m'Yerushalayim im Shimush Tehilim, Op. Cit.
    Landsberg, M.: *Sefer Tehillim im Peirush Rashi, Op. Cit.*
    Selig, G.: *Sepher Schimmusch Tehillim, Op. Cit.*
    The Sixth and Seventh Books of Moses, Op. Cit.
    Peterson, J.H.: *The Sixth and Seventh Books of Moses, Op. Cit.*
    Rebiger, B.: *Sefer Shimmush Tehillim, Op. Cit.*
    Brauner, R.: *Synopsis of Sefer Shimush Tehillim. Op. Cit.*
    Hai ben Sherira Gaon & Varady, A.N.: *Shimush Tehillim (the
    Theurgical Use of Psalms), Op. Cit.*
28. **Rebiger, B.:** *Ibid.*
29. **Zacutto, M.:** *Shorshei ha-Shemot, Op. Cit.*
    Swart, J.G.: *The Book of Sacred Names, Op. Cit.*
30. *Ibid.*
31. **Grünwald, M.:** *Ueber den Einfluss der Psalmen auf die
    Katholische Liturgie, Op. Cit.*
32. **Zellmann-Rohrer, M.:** *Psalms Useful for Everything, Op. Cit.*
33. *Ibid.*
34. **Rankine, D. & Barron, P.H.:** *The Book of Gold, Op. Cit.*
    Marty, J. & MacParthy, F.: *Usage Mago-Théurgiques des
    Psaumes, Op. Cit.*
35. *Ibid.*
36. *Ibid.*

37. *Ibid.*
38. *Ibid.*
39. *Ibid.*
40. **Mathers, S.L. Macgregor:** *Key of Solomon the King, Op. Cit.*
41. **Skinner, S. & Rankine, D.:** *The Goetia of Dr Rudd, Op. Cit.*

Psalm 7

1. *Sefer Shimmush Tehillim, Op. Cit.*
   Le Livre des Psaumes Hébreu-Français et Phonétique, Op. Cit.
   Azulai, H.Y.D.: *Sefer Tehillim Sha'arei Rachamim: im Segulot v'Tefilot ha'Chida, Op. Cit.*
   Ronen, D.: *Tehilim Kavvanot ha-Lev, Op. Cit.*
   Selig, G.: *Sepher Schimmusch Tehillim, Op. Cit.*
   The Sixth and Seventh Books of Moses, Op. Cit.
   Peterson, J.H.: *The Sixth and Seventh Books of Moses, Op. Cit.*
   Rosenberg, Y.Y.: *Rafael ha-Malach, Op. Cit.*
   Grünwald, M.: *Ueber den Einfluss der Psalmen auf die Katholische Liturgie, Op. Cit.*
   —*Mitteilungen der Gesellschaft für Jüdische Volkskunde*, Vol. 1, Hamburg 1900.
   Singer, I. & Adler, C.: *The Jewish Encyclopedia, Op. Cit.*
   Fodor, A.: *The Use of Psalms in Jewish and Christian Arabic Magic, Op. Cit.*
   Rebiger, B.: *Sefer Shimmush Tehillim, Op. Cit.*
   Brauner, R.: *Synopsis of Sefer Shimush Tehillim. Op. Cit.*
   Hai ben Sherira Gaon & Varady, A.N.: *Shimush Tehillim* (*the Theurgical Use of Psalms*), *Op. Cit.*
2. *Sefer Shimmush Tehillim, Ibid.*
   Selig, G.: *Ibid.*
   The Sixth and Seventh Books of Moses, Ibid.
   Peterson, J.H.: *Ibid.*
   Rebiger, B.: *Ibid.*
   Hai ben Sherira Gaon & Varady, A.N.: *Ibid.*
3. **Selig, G.:** *Ibid.*
   The Sixth and Seventh Books of Moses, Ibid.
   Peterson, J.H.: *Ibid.*
4. *Ibid.*
   Sefer Shimmush Tehillim, Op. Cit.
   Rebiger, B.: *Sefer Shimmush Tehillim, Op. Cit.*
   Hai ben Sherira Gaon & Varady, A.N.: *Shimush Tehillim* (*the Theurgical Use of Psalms*), *Op. Cit.*
5. **Zacutto, M.:** *Shorshei ha-Shemot, Op. Cit.*

6. *Ibid.*
   Sefer Shimmush Tehillim, Op. Cit.
   Rebiger, B.: *Sefer Shimmush Tehillim, Op. Cit.*
   Hai ben Sherira Gaon & Varady, A.N.: *Shimush Tehillim (the Theurgical Use of Psalms), Op. Cit.*
7. **Grünwald, M.:** *Mitteilungen der Gesellschaft für Jüdische Volkskunde, Op. Cit.*
8. **Nulman, M.:** *The Encyclopedia of Jewish Prayer, Op. Cit.*
9. **Rebiger, B.:** *Sefer Shimmush Tehillim, Op. Cit.*
10. *Ibid.*
11. *Ibid.*
    Peterson, J.H.: *The Sixth and Seventh Books of Moses, Op. Cit.*
    Hai ben Sherira Gaon & Varady, A.N.: *Shimush Tehillim (the Theurgical Use of Psalms), Op. Cit.*
12. *Sefer Shimmush Tehillim, Op. Cit.*
    Selig, G.: *Sepher Schimmusch Tehillim, Op. Cit.*
    The Sixth and Seventh Books of Moses, Op. Cit.
13. **Rebiger, B.:** *Sefer Shimmush Tehillim, Op. Cit.*
14. **Swart, J.G.:** *The Book of Sacred Names, Op. Cit.*
15. *Ibid.*
16. **Zacutto, M.:** *Shorshei ha-Shemot, Op. Cit.*
17. *Ibid.*
    Swart, J.G.: *The Book of Sacred Names, Op. Cit.*
    —*The Book of Immediate Magic - Part 1, Op. Cit.*
18. *Ibid.*
19. *Ibid.*
20. **Fodor, A.:** *The Use of Psalms in Jewish and Christian Arabic Magic, Op. Cit.*
21. **Rankine, D. & Barron, P.H.:** *The Book of Gold, Op. Cit.*
    Marty, J. & MacParthy, F.: *Usage Mago-Théurgiques des Psaumes, Op. Cit.*
22. **Mclean, A.:** *Steganographia of Trithemius*, Magnum Opus Hermetic Sourceworks, Edinburgh 1982.
23. **Rankine, D. & Barron, P.H.:** *The Book of Gold, Op. Cit.*
    Marty, J. & MacParthy, F.: *Usage Mago-Théurgiques des Psaumes, Op. Cit.*
24. **Gollancz, H.:** *The Book of Protection: being a Collection of Charms*, Oxford University Press/Henry Frowde, London 1912.
25. **Rankine, D. & Barron, P.H.:** *The Book of Gold, Op. Cit.*
    Marty, J. & MacParthy, F.: *Usage Mago-Théurgiques des Psaumes, Op. Cit.*
26. *Ibid.*

27. **Zellmann-Rohrer, M.:** *Psalms Useful for Everything, Op. Cit.*
28. *Ibid.*
29. *Ibid.*
30. *Ibid.*
31. **Skinner, S. & Rankine, D.:** *A Collection of Magical Secrets, Op. Cit.*
32. *Ibid.*
33. **Skinner, S. & Rankine, D.:** *The Goetia of Dr Rudd, Op. Cit.*

Psalm 8

1. **Nulman, M.:** *The Encyclopedia of Jewish Prayer, Op. Cit.*
   Posner, R.: *Jewish Liturgy: Prayer and Synagogue Service Through the Ages*, Keter Publishing House, Jerusalem 1975.
   Scherman, N.; Goldwurm, H. & Gold, A.: *Rosh Hashanah: Its Significance, Laws, and Prayers: Presentation anthologized from Talmudic and Traditional Sources*, Mesorah Publications, Ltd., Brooklyn 1983.
2. *Ibid.*
3. **Ross, L.K.:** *Celebrate! The Complete Jewish Holidays Handbook*, Rowman & Littlefield Publishers, Inc., Lanham 1994.
4. **Kimchi, D. ben Y.:** *Sefer Tehillim, Op. Cit.*
   Sefer Shimmush Tehillim, Op. Cit.
   Le Livre des Psaumes Hébreu-Français et Phonétique, Op. Cit.
   Azulai, H.Y.D.: *Sefer Tehillim Sha'arei Rachamim: im Segulot v'Tefilot ha'Chida, Op. Cit.*
   Seder Tefilot Tikun Ezra, Op. Cit.
   Refuah v'Chayim m'Yerushalayim im Shimush Tehilim, Op. Cit.
   Landsberg, M.: *Sefer Tehillim im Peirush Rashi, Op. Cit.*
   Ronen, D.: *Tehilim Kavvanot ha-Lev, Op. Cit.*
   Grünwald, M.: *Ueber den Einfluss der Psalmen auf die Katholische Liturgie, Op. Cit.*
   Singer, I. & Adler, C.: *The Jewish Encyclopedia, Op. Cit.*
   Selig, G.: *Sepher Schimmusch Tehillim, Op. Cit.*
   The Sixth and Seventh Books of Moses, Op. Cit.
   Peterson, J.H.: *The Sixth and Seventh Books of Moses, Op. Cit.*
   Fodor, A.: *The Use of Psalms in Jewish and Christian Arabic Magic, Op. Cit.*
   Rebiger, B.: *Sefer Shimmush Tehillim, Op. Cit.*
   Brauner, R.: *Synopsis of Sefer Shimush Tehillim. Op. Cit.*
   Hai ben Sherira Gaon & Varady, A.N.: *Shimush Tehillim (the Theurgical Use of Psalms), Op. Cit.*

5. **Rebiger, B.:** *Ibid.*
6. *Ibid.*
7. *Ibid.*
   Brauner, R.: *Synopsis of Sefer Shimush Tehillim. Op. Cit.*
   Hai ben Sherira Gaon & Varady, A.N.: *Shimush Tehillim (the Theurgical Use of Psalms), Op. Cit.*
8. **Rebiger, B.:** *Ibid.*
   Kimchi, D. ben Y.: *Sefer Tehillim, Op. Cit.*
   Sefer Shimmush Tehillim, Op. Cit.
   Seder Tefilot Tikun Ezra, Op. Cit.
   Refuah v'Chayim m'Yerushalayim im Shimush Tehilim, Op. Cit.
   Landsberg, M.: *Sefer Tehillim im Peirush Rashi, Op. Cit.*
   Selig, G.: *Sepher Schimmusch Tehillim, Op. Cit.*
   The Sixth and Seventh Books of Moses, Op. Cit.
   Peterson, J.H.: *The Sixth and Seventh Books of Moses, Op. Cit.*
9. **Rebiger, B.:** *Ibid.*
10. *Ibid.*
11. **Selig, G.:** *Sepher Schimmusch Tehillim, Op. Cit.*
    The Sixth and Seventh Books of Moses, Op. Cit.
    Peterson, J.H.: *The Sixth and Seventh Books of Moses, Op. Cit.*
12. *Ibid.*
13. *Ibid.*
14. **Kimchi, D. ben Y.:** *Sefer Tehillim, Op. Cit.*
    Sefer Shimmush Tehillim, Op. Cit.
    Seder Tefilot Tikun Ezra, Op. Cit.
    Singer, I. & Adler, C.: *The Jewish Encyclopedia, Op. Cit.*
    Refuah v'Chayim m'Yerushalayim im Shimush Tehilim, Op. Cit.
    Landsberg, M.: *Sefer Tehillim im Peirush Rashi, Op. Cit.*
    Fodor, A.: *The Use of Psalms in Jewish and Christian Arabic Magic, Op. Cit.*
    Rebiger, B.: *Sefer Shimmush Tehillim, Op. Cit.*
    Brauner, R.: *Synopsis of Sefer Shimush Tehillim. Op. Cit.*
    Hai ben Sherira Gaon & Varady, A.N.: *Shimush Tehillim (the Theurgical Use of Psalms), Op. Cit.*
15. **Eliram (Amslam), S.:** *Sefer Segulot, Terufot u'Mazalot,* Eliram–Sifre Kodesh, Jerusalem 2002.
16. **Davis, E. & Frenkel, D.A.:** *Ha-Kami'a ha-Ivri, Op. Cit.*
    Green, A.: *Judaic Artifacts, Op. Cit.*
17. **Green, A.:** *Ibid.*
    Rosenberg, Y.Y.: *Rafael ha-Malach, Op. Cit.*
18. **Zacutto, M.:** *Shorshei ha-Shemot, Op. Cit.*
19. *Ibid.*

20.   *Ibid.*
21.   *Ibid.*
      **Ba'al Shem, E.; Ba'al-Shem, J.; ha-Kohen, N. ben Isaac; &
      Katz, N.:** *Mifalot Elokim*, Mechon Bnei Yishachar, Jerusalem
      1994.
22.   *Ibid.*
23.   **Zacutto, M.:** *Shorshei ha-Shemot, Op. Cit.*
      Swart, J.G.: *The Book of Sacred Names, Op. Cit.*
24.   *Ibid.*
25.   **Fodor, A.:** *The Use of Psalms in Jewish and Christian Arabic
      Magic, Op. Cit.*
26.   **Rankine, D. & Barron, P.H.:** *The Book of Gold, Op. Cit.*
      Marty, J. & MacParthy, F.: *Usage Mago-Théurgiques des
      Psaumes, Op. Cit.*
27.   *Ibid.*
28.   *Ibid.*
29.   **Zellmann-Rohrer, M.:** *Psalms Useful for Everything, Op. Cit.*
30.   *Ibid.*
31.   *Ibid.*
32.   **Mathers, S.L. Macgregor:** *Key of Solomon the King, Op. Cit.*
33.   *Ibid.*

Psalm 9

1.   **Eliram (Amslam), S.:** *Sefer Segulot, Terufot u'Mazalot, Op.
      Cit.*
2.   *Sefer Shimmush Tehillim, Op. Cit.*
      Le Livre des Psaumes Hébreu-Français et Phonétique, Op. Cit.
      Azulai, H.Y.D.: *Sefer Tehillim Sha'arei Rachamim: im Segulot
      v'Tefilot ha'Chida, Op. Cit.*
      Ronen, D.: *Tehilim Kavvanot ha-Lev, Op. Cit.*
      Selig, G.: *Sepher Schimmusch Tehillim, Op. Cit.*
      The Sixth and Seventh Books of Moses, Op. Cit.
      Peterson, J.H.: *The Sixth and Seventh Books of Moses, Op. Cit.*
      Dennis, G.W.: *The Encyclopedia of Jewish Myth, Magic and
      Mysticism, Op. Cit.*
      Rebiger, B.: *Sefer Shimmush Tehillim, Op. Cit.*
3.   **Grünwald, M.:** *Ueber den Einfluss der Psalmen auf die
      Katholische Liturgie, Op. Cit.*
      Singer, I. & Adler, C.: *The Jewish Encyclopedia, Op. Cit.*
      Brauner, R.: *Synopsis of Sefer Shimush Tehillim. Op. Cit.*
      Rebiger, B.: *Sefer Shimmush Tehillim, Op. Cit.*
      Eliram (Amslam), S.: *Sefer Segulot, Terufot u'Mazalot, Op.
      Cit.*

Hai ben Sherira Gaon & Varady, A.N.: *Shimush Tehillim (the Theurgical Use of Psalms), Op. Cit.*
4. **Rebiger, B.**: *Sefer Shimmush Tehillim, Op. Cit.*
5. *Ibid.*
   Sefer Shimmush Tehillim, Op. Cit.
   Grünwald, M.: *Ueber den Einfluss der Psalmen auf die Katholische Liturgie, Op. Cit.*
   Selig, G.: *Sepher Schimmusch Tehillim, Op. Cit.*
   The Sixth and Seventh Books of Moses, Op. Cit.
   Peterson, J.H.: *The Sixth and Seventh Books of Moses, Op. Cit.*
6. *Ibid.*
   Hai ben Sherira Gaon & Varady, A.N.: *Shimush Tehillim (the Theurgical Use of Psalms), Op. Cit.*
7. *Ibid.*
8. *Ibid.*
9. **Selig, G.**: *Sepher Schimmusch Tehillim, Op. Cit.*
   The Sixth and Seventh Books of Moses, Op. Cit.
   Peterson, J.H.: *The Sixth and Seventh Books of Moses, Op. Cit.*
10. *Ibid.*
11. *Ibid.*
   Sefer Shimmush Tehillim, Op. Cit.
   Grünwald, M.: *Ueber den Einfluss der Psalmen auf die Katholische Liturgie, Op. Cit.*
   Singer, I. & Adler, C.: *The Jewish Encyclopedia, Op. Cit.*
   Brauner, R.: *Synopsis of Sefer Shimush Tehillim. Op. Cit.*
   Rebiger, B.: *Sefer Shimmush Tehillim, Op. Cit.*
   Hai ben Sherira Gaon & Varady, A.N.: *Shimush Tehillim (the Theurgical Use of Psalms), Op. Cit.*
12. *Ibid.*
13. **Rebiger, B.**: *Sefer Shimmush Tehillim, Op. Cit.*
14. *Ibid.*
15. **Zacutto, M.**: *Shorshei ha-Shemot, Op. Cit.*
   Swart, J.G.: *The Book of Sacred Names, Op. Cit.*
16. **Davis, E. & Frenkel, D.A.**: *Ha-Kami'a ha-Ivri, Op. Cit.*
   Green, A.: *Judaic Artifacts, Op. Cit.*
17. **Zacutto, M.**: *Shorshei ha-Shemot, Op. Cit.*
18. *Ibid.*
19. **Zellmann-Rohrer, M.**: *Psalms Useful for Everything, Op. Cit.*
20. *Ibid.*
21. **Rankine, D. & Barron, P.H.**: *The Book of Gold, Op. Cit.*
   Marty, J. & MacParthy, F.: *Usage Mago-Théurgiques des Psaumes, Op. Cit.*
22. **Mathers, S.L. Macgregor**: *Key of Solomon the King, Op. Cit.*

23. **Skinner, S. & Rankine, D.:** *A Collection of Magical Secrets, Op. Cit.*

Psalm 10

1. *Le Livre des Psaumes Hébreu-Français et Phonétique, Op. Cit.*
   Azulai, H.Y.D.: *Sefer Tehillim Sha'arei Rachamim: im Segulot v'Tefilot ha'Chida, Op. Cit.*
   Ronen, D.: *Tehilim Kavvanot ha-Lev, Op. Cit.*
   Rebiger, B.: *Sefer Shimmush Tehillim, Op. Cit.*
2. **Rebiger, B.:** *Ibid.*
   Cantarini, I.H.: *Sefer Chayei Besarim*, British Library Manuscript Or 10357 [Gaster Codex 443.83].
   Singer, I. & Adler, C.: *The Jewish Encyclopedia, Op. Cit.*
   Refuah v'Chayim m'Yerushalayim im Shimush Tehilim, Op. Cit.
   Selig, G.: *Sepher Schimmusch Tehillim, Op. Cit.*
   The Sixth and Seventh Books of Moses, Op. Cit.
   Peterson, J.H.: *The Sixth and Seventh Books of Moses, Op. Cit.*
   Brauner, R.: *Synopsis of Sefer Shimush Tehillim. Op. Cit.*
   Daiches, J.: *Babylonian Oil Magic in the Talmud and in the Later Jewish Literature, Op. Cit.*
3. **Swart, J.G.:** *The Book of Self Creation, Op. Cit.*
   —*The Book of Seals & Amulets, Op. Cit.*
4. *Ibid.*
5. *Ibid.*
6. **Laycock, J.P.:** *Spirit Possession around the World: Possession, Communion, and Demon Expulsion across Cultures*, ABC-CLIO, LLC, Santa Barbara & Denver 2015.
7. **Rebiger, B.:** *Sefer Shimmush Tehillim, Op. Cit.*
8. *Ibid.*
   Trachtenberg, J.: *Jewish Magic and Superstition, Op. Cit.*
9. **Selig, G.:** *Sepher Schimmusch Tehillim, Op. Cit.*
   The Sixth and Seventh Books of Moses, Op. Cit.
   Peterson, J.H.: *The Sixth and Seventh Books of Moses, Op. Cit.*
   Refuah v'Chayim m'Yerushalayim im Shimush Tehilim, Op. Cit.
   Rebiger, B.: *Sefer Shimmush Tehillim, Op. Cit.*
10. *Ibid*
11. **Cantarini, I.H.:** *Sefer Chayei Besarim, Op. Cit.*
    Daiches, J.: *Babylonian Oil Magic in the Talmud and in the Later Jewish Literature, Op. Cit.*
12. **Selig, G.:** *Sepher Schimmusch Tehillim, Op. Cit.*
    The Sixth and Seventh Books of Moses, Op. Cit.
    Peterson, J.H.: *The Sixth and Seventh Books of Moses, Op. Cit.*

13.   **Rebiger, B.:** *Sefer Shimmush Tehillim, Op. Cit.*
        Refuah v'Chayim m'Yerushalayim im Shimush Tehilim, Op. Cit.
        Goldish, M.: *Spirit Possession in Judaism: Cases and Contexts from the Middle Ages to the Present*, Wayne State University Press, Detroit 2003.
14.   **Cantarini, I.H.:** *Sefer Chayei Besarim, Op. Cit.*
15.   **Selig, G.:** *Sepher Schimmusch Tehillim, Op. Cit.*
        The Sixth and Seventh Books of Moses, Op. Cit.
        Peterson, J.H.: *The Sixth and Seventh Books of Moses, Op. Cit.*
16.   **Brauner, R.:** *Synopsis of Sefer Shimush Tehillim. Op. Cit.*
17.   **Kayser, C.:** *Gebrauch von Psalmen zur Zauberei, Op. Cit.*
18.   **Rebiger, B.:** *Sefer Shimmush Tehillim, Op. Cit.*
19.   *Ibid.*
20.   **Swart, J.G.:** *The Book of Sacred Names, Op. Cit.*
21.   *Ibid.*
22.   *Ibid.*
23.   *Ibid.*
24.   **Rosenberg, Y.Y.:** *Rafael ha-Malach, Op. Cit.*
        Green, A.: *Judaic Artifacts, Op. Cit.*
25.   **Zacutto, M.:** *Shorshei ha-Shemot, Op. Cit.*
        Swart, J.G.: *The Book of Sacred Names, Op. Cit.*
26.   *Ibid.*

Psalm 11

1.   *Sefer Shimmush Tehillim, Op. Cit.*
        Grünwald, M.: *Ueber den Einfluss der Psalmen auf die Katholische Liturgie, Op. Cit.*
        Singer, I. & Adler, C.: *The Jewish Encyclopedia, Op. Cit.*
        Le Livre des Psaumes Hébreu-Français et Phonétique, Op. Cit.
        Azulai, H.Y.D.: *Sefer Tehillim Sha'arei Rachamim: im Segulot v'Tefilot ha'Chida, Op. Cit.*
        Ronen, D.: *Tehilim Kavvanot ha-Lev, Op. Cit.*
        Brauner, R.: *Synopsis of Sefer Shimush Tehillim. Op. Cit.*
        Rebiger, B.: *Sefer Shimmush Tehillim, Op. Cit.*
        Hai ben Sherira Gaon & Varady, A.N.: *Shimush Tehillim (the Theurgical Use of Psalms), Op. Cit.*
2.   **Rebiger, B.:** *Sefer Shimmush Tehillim, Op. Cit.*
3.   *Ibid.*
4.   **Selig, G.:** *Sepher Schimmusch Tehillim, Op. Cit.*
        The Sixth and Seventh Books of Moses, Op. Cit.
        Peterson, J.H.: *The Sixth and Seventh Books of Moses, Op. Cit.*
5.   *Ibid.*
6.   *Ibid.*

7. **Zacutto, M.:** *Shorshei ha-Shemot, Op. Cit.*
—*The Book of Seals & Amulets, Op. Cit.*
8. *Ibid.*
9. *Ibid.*
10. *Ibid.*
Swart, J.G.: *The Book of Sacred Names, Op. Cit.*
—*The Book of Immediate Magic - Part 1, Op. Cit.*
11. *Ibid.*
12. **Grünwald, M.:** *Ueber den Einfluss der Psalmen auf die Katholische Liturgie, Op. Cit.*
13. **Kayser, C.:** *Gebrauch von Psalmen zur Zauberei, Op. Cit.*
14. *Ibid.*
15. **Rankine, D. & Barron, P.H.:** *The Book of Gold, Op. Cit.*
Marty, J. & MacParthy, F.: *Usage Mago-Théurgiques des Psaumes, Op. Cit.*
16. **Skinner, S. & Rankine, D.:** *A Collection of Magical Secrets, Op. Cit.*

Psalm 12

1. **Katz, M. & Gershon Schwartz, G.:** *Swimming in the Sea of Talmud: Lessons for Everyday Living*, The Jewish Publication Society, Philadelphia 1997.
2. **Nulman, M.:** *The Encyclopedia of Jewish Prayer, Op. Cit.*
Gelbard, S.P.: *Rite and Reason: 1050 Jewish Customs and Their Sources*, Vol. 1, transl. Bulman, N., Mifal Rashi Publications, Petach Tikvah 1995.
Hacham, A.H. & Berman, I.V.: *Psalms with the Jerusalem Commentary*, Mosad Harav Kook, Jerusalem 2003.
3. *Ibid.*
4. *Ibid.*
5. *Le Livre des Psaumes Hébreu-Français et Phonétique, Op. Cit.*
Azulai, H.Y.D.: *Sefer Tehillim Sha'arei Rachamim: im Segulot v'Tefilot ha'Chida, Op. Cit.*
Ronen, D.: *Tehilim Kavvanot ha-Lev, Op. Cit.*
6. **Kimchi, D. ben Y.:** *Sefer Tehillim, Op. Cit.*
Sefer Shimmush Tehillim, Op. Cit.
Seder Tefilot Tikun Ezra, Op. Cit.
Grünwald, M.: *Ueber den Einfluss der Psalmen auf die Katholische Liturgie, Op. Cit.*
Singer, I. & Adler, C.: *The Jewish Encyclopedia, Op. Cit.*
Refuah v'Chayim m'Yerushalayim im Shimush Tehilim, Op. Cit.
Landsberg, M.: *Sefer Tehillim im Peirush Rashi, Op. Cit.*
Brauner, R.: *Synopsis of Sefer Shimush Tehillim. Op. Cit.*

Rebiger, B.: *Sefer Shimmush Tehillim, Op. Cit.*

Hai ben Sherira Gaon & Varady, A.N.: *Shimush Tehillim (the Theurgical Use of Psalms), Op. Cit.*

7. **Rebiger, B.:** *Ibid.*
8. **Blumenthal, D.:** *Understanding Jewish Mysticism: A Source Reader - The Philosophic Mystical Tradition and the Chassidic Tradition,* Volume II, KTAV Publishing House Inc., New York 1982.

    Kaplan, A.: *Meditation and Kabbalah,* Samuel Weiser Inc., York Beach 1988.

    Idel, M.: *The Mystical Experience in Abraham Abulafia,* SUNY Press, Albany 1988.

    —*Golem: Jewish Magical and Mystical Traditions on the Artificial Anthropoid,* SUNY Press, Albany 1990.

    Besserman, P.: *The Shambhala Guide to Kabbalah and Jewish Mysticism,* Shambhala, Berkeley, 1997.

    Swart, J.G.: *The Book of Immediate Magic - Part 2, Op. Cit.*

    Martin, M.J.: *Spelling the Divine Name: Observations on Jewish Alphabetical Inscriptions,* essay published in Abgadiyat No. 2, Koninklijke Brill NV & Bibliotheca Alexandrine Calligraphy Centre, Leiden 2007.

    Dennis, G.W.: *The Encyclopedia of Jewish Myth, Magic and Mysticism,* Llewellyn Publications, Woodbury 2007.

9. **Selig, G.:** *Sepher Schimmusch Tehillim, Op. Cit.*

    The Sixth and Seventh Books of Moses, Op. Cit.

    Peterson, J.H.: *The Sixth and Seventh Books of Moses, Op. Cit.*

10. *Ibid.*
11. *Ibid.*
12. **Palagi, C.:** *Refuah ha-Chayim,* Jerusalem 1908.

    Eliram (Amslam), S.: *Sefer Segulot, Terufot u'Mazalot, Op. Cit.*

13. **Zacutto, M.:** *Shorshei ha-Shemot, Op. Cit.*
14. *Refuah v'Chayim m'Yerushalayim im Shimush Tehilim, Op. Cit.*
15. **Zacutto, M.:** *Shorshei ha-Shemot, Op. Cit.*
16. *Refuah v'Chayim m'Yerushalayim im Shimush Tehilim, Op. Cit.*
17. **Zacutto, M.:** *Shorshei ha-Shemot, Op. Cit.*
18. *Refuah v'Chayim m'Yerushalayim im Shimush Tehilim, Op. Cit.*
19. **Zacutto, M.:** *Shorshei ha-Shemot, Op. Cit.*
20. *Refuah v'Chayim m'Yerushalayim im Shimush Tehilim, Op. Cit.*
21. **Zacutto, M.:** *Shorshei ha-Shemot, Op. Cit.*

    Refuah v'Chayim m'Yerushalayim im Shimush Tehilim, Op. Cit.

22. *Ibid.*
23. *Ibid.*

24. **Zacutto, M.:** *Shorshei ha-Shemot, Op. Cit.*
25. *Refuah v'Chayim m'Yerushalayim im Shimush Tehilim, Op. Cit.*
26. **Zacutto, M.:** *Shorshei ha-Shemot, Op. Cit.*
27. *Ibid.*
28. **Zellmann-Rohrer, M.:** *Psalms Useful for Everything, Op. Cit.*
29. *Ibid.*
30. **Rankine, D. & Barron, P.H.:** *The Book of Gold, Op. Cit.*
    Marty, J. & MacParthy, F.: *Usage Mago-Théurgiques des Psaumes, Op. Cit.*
31. *Ibid.*

Psalm 13

1. **Kimchi, D. ben Y.:** *Sefer Tehillim, Op. Cit.*
   Sefer Shimmush Tehillim, Op. Cit.
   Seder Tefilot Tikun Ezra, Op. Cit.
   Grünwald, M.: *Ueber den Einfluss der Psalmen auf die Katholische Liturgie, Op. Cit.*
   Refuah v'Chayim m'Yerushalayim im Shimush Tehilim, Op. Cit.
   Landsberg, M.: *Sefer Tehillim im Peirush Rashi, Op. Cit.*
   Brauner, R.: *Synopsis of Sefer Shimush Tehillim. Op. Cit.*
   Rebiger, B.: *Sefer Shimmush Tehillim, Op. Cit.*
   Hai ben Sherira Gaon & Varady, A.N.: *Shimush Tehillim* (*the Theurgical Use of Psalms*), *Op. Cit.*
   Selig, G.: *Sepher Schimmusch Tehillim, Op. Cit.*
   The Sixth and Seventh Books of Moses, Op. Cit.
   Peterson, J.H.: *The Sixth and Seventh Books of Moses, Op. Cit.*
2. **Singer, I. & Adler, C.:** *The Jewish Encyclopedia, Op. Cit.*
   Refuah v'Chayim m'Yerushalayim im Shimush Tehilim, Op. Cit.
   Le Livre des Psaumes Hébreu-Français et Phonétique, Op. Cit.
   Azulai, H.Y.D.: *Sefer Tehillim Sha'arei Rachamim: im Segulot v'Tefilot ha'Chida, Op. Cit.*
   Ronen, D.: *Tehilim Kavvanot ha-Lev, Op. Cit.*
3. **Grünwald, M.:** *Ueber den Einfluss der Psalmen auf die Katholische Liturgie, Op. Cit.*
   Brauner, R.: *Synopsis of Sefer Shimush Tehillim. Op. Cit.*
   Rebiger, B.: *Sefer Shimmush Tehillim, Op. Cit.*
   Hai ben Sherira Gaon & Varady, A.N.: *Shimush Tehillim* (*the Theurgical Use of Psalms*), *Op. Cit.*
4. **Kimchi, D. ben Y.:** *Sefer Tehillim, Op. Cit.*
   Sefer Shimmush Tehillim, Op. Cit.
   Seder Tefilot Tikun Ezra, Op. Cit.

Grünwald, M.: *Ueber den Einfluss der Psalmen auf die Katholische Liturgie, Op. Cit.*
Refuah v'Chayim m'Yerushalayim im Shimush Tehilim, Op. Cit.
Landsberg, M.: *Sefer Tehillim im Peirush Rashi, Op. Cit.*
Brauner, R.: *Synopsis of Sefer Shimush Tehillim. Op. Cit.*
Rebiger, B.: *Sefer Shimmush Tehillim, Op. Cit.*
Hai ben Sherira Gaon & Varady, A.N.: *Shimush Tehillim (the Theurgical Use of Psalms), Op. Cit.*

5. *Ibid.*
6. **Rebiger, B.**: *Sefer Shimmush Tehillim, Op. Cit.*
7. **Raz, U.**: *The Magical Use of Psalms*, unpublished manuscript.
8. *Sefer Shimmush Tehillim, Op. Cit.*
    Grünwald, M.: *Ueber den Einfluss der Psalmen auf die Katholische Liturgie, Op. Cit.*
    Rebiger, B.: *Sefer Shimmush Tehillim, Op. Cit.*
    Hai ben Sherira Gaon & Varady, A.N.: *Shimush Tehillim (the Theurgical Use of Psalms), Op. Cit.*
9. **Selig, G.**: *Sepher Schimmusch Tehillim, Op. Cit.*
    The Sixth and Seventh Books of Moses, Op. Cit.
    Peterson, J.H.: *The Sixth and Seventh Books of Moses, Op. Cit.*
10. *Ibid.*
11. *Ibid.*
12. *Ibid.*
13. **Rebiger, B.**: *Sefer Shimmush Tehillim, Op. Cit.*
14. *Ibid.*
15. *Ibid.*
16. *Ibid.*
17. *Ibid.*
18. *Ibid.*
19. **Spiegel, J.**: *Dancing with Angels: Jewish Kabbalah Meditation from Torah to Self-improvement to Prophecy*, electronic document version 3.
20. **Grünwald, M.**: *Ueber den Einfluss der Psalmen auf die Katholische Liturgie, Op. Cit.*
    Singer, I. & Adler, C.: *The Jewish Encyclopedia, Op. Cit.*
21. **Zellmann-Rohrer, M.**: *Psalms Useful for Everything, Op. Cit.*
22. *Ibid.*
23. *Ibid.*
24. *Ibid.*
25. **Skinner, S. & Rankine, D.**: *A Collection of Magical Secrets, Op. Cit.*
26. **Rankine, D. & Barron, P.H.**: *The Book of Gold, Op. Cit.*
    Marty, J. & MacParthy, F.: *Usage Mago-Théurgiques des Psaumes, Op. Cit.*

27. *Ibid.*
28. **Skinner, S. & Rankine, D.:** *A Collection of Magical Secrets, Op. Cit.*
29. *Ibid.*
30. **Mathers, S.L. Macgregor:** *Key of Solomon the King, Op. Cit.*

Psalm 14

1. *Le Livre des Psaumes Hébreu-Français et Phonétique, Op. Cit.*
   Azulai, H.Y.D.: *Sefer Tehillim Sha'arei Rachamim: im Segulot v'Tefilot ha'Chida, Op. Cit.*
   Ronen, D.: *Tehilim Kavvanot ha-Lev, Op. Cit.*
2. **Kimchi, D. ben Y.:** *Sefer Tehillim, Op. Cit.*
   Sefer Shimmush Tehillim, Op. Cit.
   Seder Tefilot Tikun Ezra, Op. Cit.
   Singer, I. & Adler, C.: *The Jewish Encyclopedia, Op. Cit.*
   Grünwald, M.: *Ueber den Einfluss der Psalmen auf die Katholische Liturgie, Op. Cit.*
   Refuah v'Chayim m'Yerushalayim im Shimush Tehilim, Op. Cit.
   Landsberg, M.: *Sefer Tehillim im Peirush Rashi, Op. Cit.*
   Brauner, R.: *Synopsis of Sefer Shimush Tehillim. Op. Cit.*
   Rebiger, B.: *Sefer Shimmush Tehillim, Op. Cit.*
   Hai ben Sherira Gaon & Varady, A.N.: *Shimush Tehillim (the Theurgical Use of Psalms), Op. Cit.*
   Selig, G.: *Sepher Schimmusch Tehillim, Op. Cit.*
   The Sixth and Seventh Books of Moses, Op. Cit.
   Peterson, J.H.: *The Sixth and Seventh Books of Moses, Op. Cit.*
3. **Rebiger, B.:** *Ibid.*
4. *Ibid.*
5. *Ibid.*
6. **Selig, G.:** *Sepher Schimmusch Tehillim, Op. Cit.*
   The Sixth and Seventh Books of Moses, Op. Cit.
   Peterson, J.H.: *The Sixth and Seventh Books of Moses, Op. Cit.*
7. *Ibid.*
8. *Ibid.*
9. **Zellmann-Rohrer, M.:** *Psalms Useful for Everything, Op. Cit.*
10. **Rankine, D. & Barron, P.H.:** *The Book of Gold, Op. Cit.*
    Marty, J. & MacParthy, F.: *Usage Mago-Théurgiques des Psaumes, Op. Cit.*
11. *Ibid.*
12. **Mathers, S.L. Macgregor:** *Key of Solomon the King, Op. Cit.*

Psalm 15

1. **Schonfield, J.:** *Undercurrents of Jewish Prayer*, Liverpool University Press, Liverpool 2008.
2. *Ibid.*
3. *Ibid.*
4. **Spiegel, J.:** *Dancing with Angels, Op. Cit.*
5. *Ibid.*
6. *Ibid.*
7. **Zacutto, M.:** *Shorshei ha-Shemot, Op. Cit.*
8. *Ibid.*
9. *Ibid.*
10. *Ibid.*
11. *Ibid.*
12. **Swart, J.G.:** *The Book of Self Creation, Op. Cit.*
    —*The Book of Sacred Names, Op. Cit.*
    —*The Book of Immediate Magic - Part 1, Op. Cit.*
    —*The Book of Immediate Magic - Part 2, Op. Cit.*
13. **Zacutto, M.:** *Shorshei ha-Shemot, Op. Cit.*
14. **Kaplan, A.:** *Meditation and The Bible*, Samuel Weiser, York Beach, Maine 1988.
    —*Innerspace: Introduction to Kabbalah, Meditation and Prophecy*, Moznaim Publishing Corporation, Jerusalem 1990.
15. **Glinert, L.:** *The Joys of Hebrew*, Oxford University Press, Oxford 1992.
16. **Kimchi, D. ben Y.:** *Sefer Tehillim, Op. Cit.*
    Sefer Shimmush Tehillim, Op. Cit.
    Seder Tefilot Tikun Ezra, Op. Cit.
    Refuah v'Chayim m'Yerushalayim im Shimush Tehilim, Op. Cit.
    Landsberg, M.: *Sefer Tehillim im Peirush Rashi, Op. Cit.*
    Brauner, R.: *Synopsis of Sefer Shimush Tehillim. Op. Cit.*
    Rebiger, B.: *Sefer Shimmush Tehillim, Op. Cit.*
    Hai ben Sherira Gaon & Varady, A.N.: *Shimush Tehillim* (*the Theurgical Use of Psalms*)*, Op. Cit.*
17. **Selig, G.:** *Sepher Schimmusch Tehillim, Op. Cit.*
    The Sixth and Seventh Books of Moses, Op. Cit.
    Peterson, J.H.: *The Sixth and Seventh Books of Moses, Op. Cit.*
18. **Rosenberg, Y.Y.:** *Rafael ha-Malach, Op. Cit.*
19. *Sefer Shimmush Tehillim, Op. Cit.*
    Le Livre des Psaumes Hébreu-Français et Phonétique, Op. Cit.
    Azulai, H.Y.D.: *Sefer Tehillim Sha'arei Rachamim: im Segulot v'Tefilot ha'Chida, Op. Cit.*
    Ronen, D.: *Tehilim Kavvanot ha-Lev, Op. Cit.*

Brauner, R.: *Synopsis of Sefer Shimush Tehillim. Op. Cit.*
Hai ben Sherira Gaon & Varady, A.N.: *Shimush Tehillim (the Theurgical Use of Psalms), Op. Cit.*

20. Singer, I. & Adler, C.: *The Jewish Encyclopedia, Op. Cit.*
21. Kimchi, D. ben Y.: *Sefer Tehillim, Op. Cit.*
    Seder Tefilot Tikun Ezra, Op. Cit.
    Refuah v'Chayim m'Yerushalayim im Shimush Tehilim, Op. Cit.
    Landsberg, M.: *Sefer Tehillim im Peirush Rashi, Op. Cit.*
    Rebiger, B.: *Sefer Shimmush Tehillim, Op. Cit.*
22. Rebiger, B.: *Ibid.*
23. *Ibid.*
24. *Ibid.*
    Kimchi, D. ben Y.: *Sefer Tehillim, Op. Cit.*
    Seder Tefilot Tikun Ezra, Op. Cit.
    Refuah v'Chayim m'Yerushalayim im Shimush Tehilim, Op. Cit.
    Landsberg, M.: *Sefer Tehillim im Peirush Rashi, Op. Cit.*
25. *Ibid.*
26. Rebiger, B.: *Sefer Shimmush Tehillim, Op. Cit.*
27. *Ibid.*
    Kimchi, D. ben Y.: *Sefer Tehillim, Op. Cit.*
    Seder Tefilot Tikun Ezra, Op. Cit.
    Refuah v'Chayim m'Yerushalayim im Shimush Tehilim, Op. Cit.
    Landsberg, M.: *Sefer Tehillim im Peirush Rashi, Op. Cit.*
28. Rebiger, B.: *Ibid.*
29. *Ibid.*
    Kimchi, D. ben Y.: *Sefer Tehillim, Op. Cit.*
    Seder Tefilot Tikun Ezra, Op. Cit.
    Refuah v'Chayim m'Yerushalayim im Shimush Tehilim, Op. Cit.
    Landsberg, M.: *Sefer Tehillim im Peirush Rashi, Op. Cit.*
30. Selig, G.: *Sepher Schimmusch Tehillim, Op. Cit.*
    The Sixth and Seventh Books of Moses, Op. Cit.
    Peterson, J.H.: *The Sixth and Seventh Books of Moses, Op. Cit.*
31. Rebiger, B.: *Sefer Shimmush Tehillim, Op. Cit.*
    Kimchi, D. ben Y.: *Sefer Tehillim, Op. Cit.*
    Seder Tefilot Tikun Ezra, Op. Cit.
    Refuah v'Chayim m'Yerushalayim im Shimush Tehilim, Op. Cit.
    Landsberg, M.: *Sefer Tehillim im Peirush Rashi, Op. Cit.*
32. *Ibid.*
33. Rebiger, B.: *Sefer Shimmush Tehillim, Op. Cit.*
34. *Ibid.*
35. Selig, G.: *Sepher Schimmusch Tehillim, Op. Cit.*
    The Sixth and Seventh Books of Moses, Op. Cit.
    Peterson, J.H.: *The Sixth and Seventh Books of Moses, Op. Cit.*

36. *Ibid.*
37. *Ibid.*
38. **Zellmann-Rohrer, M.**: *Psalms Useful for Everything, Op. Cit.*
39. **Rankine, D. & Barron, P.H.**: *The Book of Gold, Op. Cit.*
    Marty, J. & MacParthy, F.: *Usage Mago-Théurgiques des Psaumes, Op. Cit.*
40. *Ibid.*
41. **Mathers, S.L. Macgregor**: *Key of Solomon the King, Op. Cit.*

Psalm 16

1. **Owens, D.C.**: *Portraits of the Righteous in the Psalms: An Exploration of the Ethics of Book I*, Pickwick Publications, Eugene 2013.
2. *Siddur Kol Yaakov*, edited Bitton, D., Sephardic Heritage Foundation Inc., New York 1985,
   Nulman, M.: *The Encyclopedia of Jewish Prayer, Op. Cit.*
3. **Nulman, M.**: *Ibid.*
   Silverman, M.: *Tefilot v'Nichunim: Prayers of Consolation, for Shiva, Yahrzeit and Kever Avot: with Readings and Meditations, Traditional Mincha, Ma'ariv and Shachris Service*, Prayer Book Press, Hartford 1961.
   Hoffman, L.A.: *My People's Prayer Book: Traditional Prayers, Modern Commentaries, Vol. 9—Welcoming the Night: Minchah and Ma'ariv (Afternoon and Evening Prayer)*, Jewish Lights Publication, Woodstock 2005.
4. **Swart, J.G.**: *The Book of Seals & Amulets, Op. Cit.*
5. **Singer, I. & Adler, C.**: *The Jewish Encyclopedia, Op. Cit.*
   Brauner, R.: *Synopsis of Sefer Shimush Tehillim. Op. Cit.*
6. **Shneur Zalman (of Lyady)**: *Tanya, the Masterpiece of Hasidic Wisdom: Selections Annotated & Explained*, transl. Shapiro, R., SkyLight Paths Publishing, Woodstock 2010.
7. *Ibid.*
8. *Ibid.*
9. *Ibid.*
10. *Ibid.*
11. *Ibid.*
12. *Ibid.*
13. **Davis, E. & Frenkel, D.A.**: *Ha-Kami'a ha-Ivri, Op. Cit.*
    Green, A.: *Judaic Artifacts, Op. Cit.*
14. **Schrire, T.**: *Hebrew Amulets, Op. Cit.*
    Green, A.: *Judaic Artifacts, Op. Cit.*
15. **Rosenberg, Y.Y.**: *Rafael ha-Malach, Op. Cit.*

16. **Kimchi, D. ben Y.:** *Sefer Tehillim, Op. Cit.*
Sefer Shimmush Tehillim, Op. Cit.
Seder Tefilot Tikun Ezra, Op. Cit.
Grünwald, M.: *Ueber den Einfluss der Psalmen auf die Katholische Liturgie, Op. Cit.*
Refuah v'Chayim m'Yerushalayim im Shimush Tehilim, Op. Cit.
Landsberg, M.: *Sefer Tehillim im Peirush Rashi, Op. Cit.*
Rebiger, B.: *Sefer Shimmush Tehillim, Op. Cit.*
Hai ben Sherira Gaon & Varady, A.N.: *Shimush Tehillim (the Theurgical Use of Psalms), Op. Cit.*

17. *Ibid.*
Brauner, R.: *Synopsis of Sefer Shimush Tehillim. Op. Cit.*

18. **Selig, G.:** *Sepher Schimmusch Tehillim, Op. Cit.*
The Sixth and Seventh Books of Moses, Op. Cit.
Peterson, J.H.: *The Sixth and Seventh Books of Moses, Op. Cit.*

19. **Kimchi, D. ben Y.:** *Sefer Tehillim, Op. Cit.*
Sefer Shimmush Tehillim, Op. Cit.
Seder Tefilot Tikun Ezra, Op. Cit.
Grünwald, M.: *Ueber den Einfluss der Psalmen auf die Katholische Liturgie, Op. Cit.*
Refuah v'Chayim m'Yerushalayim im Shimush Tehilim, Op. Cit.
Landsberg, M.: *Sefer Tehillim im Peirush Rashi, Op. Cit.*
Brauner, R.: *Synopsis of Sefer Shimush Tehillim. Op. Cit/.*
Rebiger, B.: *Sefer Shimmush Tehillim, Op. Cit.*
Hai ben Sherira Gaon & Varady, A.N.: *Shimush Tehillim (the Theurgical Use of Psalms), Op. Cit.*

20. **Selig, G.:** *Sepher Schimmusch Tehillim, Op. Cit.*
The Sixth and Seventh Books of Moses, Op. Cit.
Peterson, J.H.: *The Sixth and Seventh Books of Moses, Op. Cit.*

21. **Kimchi, D. ben Y.:** *Sefer Tehillim, Op. Cit.*
Sefer Shimmush Tehillim, Op. Cit.
Seder Tefilot Tikun Ezra, Op. Cit.
Le Livre des Psaumes Hébreu-Français et Phonétique, Op. Cit.
Azulai, H.Y.D.: *Sefer Tehillim Sha'arei Rachamim: im Segulot v'Tefilot ha'Chida, Op. Cit.*
Grünwald, M.: *Ueber den Einfluss der Psalmen auf die Katholische Liturgie, Op. Cit.*
Singer, I. & Adler, C.: *The Jewish Encyclopedia, Op. Cit.*
Refuah v'Chayim m'Yerushalayim im Shimush Tehilim, Op. Cit.
Landsberg, M.: *Sefer Tehillim im Peirush Rashi, Op. Cit.*
Ronen, D.: *Tehilim Kavvanot ha-Lev, Op. Cit.*
Brauner, R.: *Synopsis of Sefer Shimush Tehillim. Op. Cit.*
Rebiger, B.: *Sefer Shimmush Tehillim, Op. Cit.*

Hai ben Sherira Gaon & Varady, A.N.: *Shimush Tehillim (the Theurgical Use of Psalms)*, *Op. Cit.*
Dennis, G.W.: *The Encyclopedia of Jewish Myth, Magic and Mysticism*, *Op. Cit.*

22. **Kimchi, D. ben Y.:** *Ibid*
   Sefer Shimmush Tehillim, *Ibid.*
   Seder Tefilot Tikun Ezra, *Op. Cit.*
   Grünwald, M.: *Ibid.*
   Refuah v'Chayim m'Yerushalayim im Shimush Tehilim, *Ibid.*
   Landsberg, M.: *Ibid.*
   Rebiger, B.: *Ibid.*
   Hai ben Sherira Gaon & Varady, A.N.: *Ibid.*
   Selig, G.: *Sepher Schimmusch Tehillim*, *Op. Cit.*
   The Sixth and Seventh Books of Moses, *Op. Cit.*
   Peterson, J.H.: *The Sixth and Seventh Books of Moses*, *Op. Cit.*

23. **Rebiger, B.:** *Sefer Shimmush Tehillim*, *Op. Cit.*

24. **Kimchi, D. ben Y.:** *Sefer Tehillim*, *Op. Cit.*
   Sefer Shimmush Tehillim, *Op. Cit.*
   Seder Tefilot Tikun Ezra, *Op. Cit.*
   Grünwald, M.: *Ueber den Einfluss der Psalmen auf die Katholische Liturgie*, *Op. Cit.*
   Refuah v'Chayim m'Yerushalayim im Shimush Tehilim, *Op. Cit.*
   Landsberg, M.: *Sefer Tehillim im Peirush Rashi*, *Op. Cit.*
   Hai ben Sherira Gaon & Varady, A.N.: *Shimush Tehillim (the Theurgical Use of Psalms)*, *Op. Cit.*
   Selig, G.: *Sepher Schimmusch Tehillim*, *Op. Cit.*
   The Sixth and Seventh Books of Moses, *Op. Cit.*
   Peterson, J.H.: *The Sixth and Seventh Books of Moses*, *Op. Cit.*

25. **Rebiger, B.:** *Sefer Shimmush Tehillim*, *Op. Cit.*

26. *Ibid.*

27. *Ibid.*

28. **Selig, G.:** *Sepher Schimmusch Tehillim*, *Op. Cit.*
   The Sixth and Seventh Books of Moses, *Op. Cit.*
   Peterson, J.H.: *The Sixth and Seventh Books of Moses*, *Op. Cit.*

29. *Ibid.*

30. *Ibid.*

31. *Ibid.*

32. **Zacutto, M.:** *Shorshei ha-Shemot*, *Op. Cit.*

33. **Davis, E. & Frenkel, D.A.:** *Ha-Kami'a ha-Ivri*, *Op. Cit.*
   Green, A.: *Judaic Artifacts*, *Op. Cit.*

34. **Zacutto, M.:** *Shorshei ha-Shemot*, *Op. Cit.*

35. *Ibid.*

36. **Zacutto, M.:** *Shorshei ha-Shemot*, *Op. Cit.*

Swart, J.G.: *The Book of Sacred Names, Op. Cit.*

37. *Ibid.*
38. **Männlingen, J.C.:** *Denkwürdigen Kuriositäten derer sowohl Inn- als Ausländischer Abergläubischer Albertäten,* Frankfurt & Leipzig 1713.
     Rubin, S.: *Geschichte des Aberglaubens,* transl. Stern, J., E. Thiele, Leipzig 1888.
     Singer, I. & Adler, C.: *The Jewish Encyclopedia, Op. Cit.*
39. **Zellmann-Rohrer, M.:** *Psalms Useful for Everything, Op. Cit.*
40. **Rankine, D. & Barron, P.H.:** *The Book of Gold, Op. Cit.*
     Marty, J. & MacParthy, F.: *Usage Mago-Théurgiques des Psaumes, Op. Cit.*
41. **Skinner, S. & Rankine, D.:** *A Collection of Magical Secrets, Op. Cit.*

Psalm 17

1. **Feld, E.:** *Machzor Lev Shalem for Rosh Hashanah and Yom Kippur,* Rabbinical Assembly of America, New York 2010.
2. *Ibid.*
3. **Kimchi, D. ben Y.:** *Sefer Tehillim, Op. Cit.*
     Sefer Shimmush Tehillim, Op. Cit.
     Seder Tefilot Tikun Ezra, Op. Cit.
     Le Livre des Psaumes Hébreu-Français et Phonétique, Op. Cit.
     Azulai, H.Y.D.: *Sefer Tehillim Sha'arei Rachamim: im Segulot v'Tefilot ha'Chida, Op. Cit.*
     Grünwald, M.: *Ueber den Einfluss der Psalmen auf die Katholische Liturgie, Op. Cit.*
     Singer, I. & Adler, C.: *The Jewish Encyclopedia, Op. Cit.*
     Refuah v'Chayim m'Yerushalayim im Shimush Tehilim, Op. Cit.
     Landsberg, M.: *Sefer Tehillim im Peirush Rashi, Op. Cit.*
     Ronen, D.: *Tehilim Kavvanot ha-Lev, Op. Cit.*
     Brauner, R.: *Synopsis of Sefer Shimush Tehillim. Op. Cit.*
     Rebiger, B.: *Sefer Shimmush Tehillim, Op. Cit.*
     Hai ben Sherira Gaon & Varady, A.N.: *Shimush Tehillim (the Theurgical Use of Psalms), Op. Cit.*
     Selig, G.: *Sepher Schimmusch Tehillim, Op. Cit.*
     The Sixth and Seventh Books of Moses, Op. Cit.
     Peterson, J.H.: *The Sixth and Seventh Books of Moses, Op. Cit.*
4. **Rosenberg, Y.Y.:** *Rafael ha-Malach, Op. Cit.*
5. **Kimchi, D. ben Y.:** *Sefer Tehillim, Op. Cit.*
     Sefer Shimmush Tehillim, Op. Cit.
     Seder Tefilot Tikun Ezra, Op. Cit.
     Grünwald, M.: *Ueber den Einfluss der Psalmen auf die*

Katholische Liturgie, Op. Cit.
Refuah v'Chayim m'Yerushalayim im Shimush Tehilim, Op. Cit.
Landsberg, M.: *Sefer Tehillim im Peirush Rashi, Op. Cit.*
Rebiger, B.: *Sefer Shimmush Tehillim, Op. Cit.*
Hai ben Sherira Gaon & Varady, A.N.: *Shimush Tehillim* (*the Theurgical Use of Psalms*), *Op. Cit.*

6. *Ibid.*
7. *Ibid.*
8. **Rebiger, B.:** *Sefer Shimmush Tehillim, Op. Cit.*
9. *Ibid.*
10. *Ibid.*
11. *Ibid.*
12. **Selig, G.:** *Sepher Schimmusch Tehillim, Op. Cit.*
    The Sixth and Seventh Books of Moses, Op. Cit.
    Peterson, J.H.: *The Sixth and Seventh Books of Moses, Op. Cit.*
13. *Ibid.*
14. *Ibid.*
15. **Rosenberg, Y.Y.:** *Rafael ha-Malach, Op. Cit.*
    Davis, E. & Frenkel, D.A.: *Ha-Kami'a ha-Ivri, Op. Cit.*
    Green, A.: *Judaic Artifacts, Op. Cit.*
16. **Zacutto, M.:** *Shorshei ha-Shemot, Op. Cit.*
17. *Ibid.*
18. *Ibid.*
19. *Ibid.*
20. *Ibid.*
21. *Ibid.*
    Swart, J.G.: *The Book of Sacred Names, Op. Cit.*
22. *Ibid.*
23. **Zellmann-Rohrer, M.:** *Psalms Useful for Everything, Op. Cit.*
24. *Ibid.*
25. *Ibid.*
26. *Ibid.*
27. *Ibid.*
28. *Ibid.*
29. *Ibid.*
30. **Rankine, D. & Barron, P.H.:** *The Book of Gold, Op. Cit.*
    Marty, J. & MacParthy, F.: *Usage Mago-Théurgiques des Psaumes, Op. Cit.*

Psalm 18

1. **Zacutto, M.:** *Shorshei ha-Shemot, Op. Cit.*
2. *Ibid.*
3. *Ibid.*

4. *Ibid.*
5. *Ibid.*
6. *Ibid.*
   Scherman, N.: *Machzor Zichron Yosef l'Yom Kipur*, Mesorah Publications Ltd., Brooklyn 1986.
7. *Ibid.*
8. *Ibid.*
9. *Ibid.*
10. **Tishby, I.:** *Messianic Mysticism: Moses Hayim Luzzatto and the Padua School*, The Littman Library of Jewish Civilization, London 2008.
11. **Nulman, M.:** *The Encyclopedia of Jewish Prayer, Op. Cit.*
    Scherman, N.: *Machzor Zichron Yosef l'Yom Kipur, Op. Cit.*
12. **Posner, R.:** *Jewish Liturgy: Prayer and Synagogue Service Through the Ages*, Keter Publishing House, Jerusalem 1975.
    Kadden, B. & Kadden, B.B.: *Teaching Tefilah: Insights and Activities on Prayer*, A.R.E. Publishing Inc., Denver 2004.
    Golinkin, D.: *The Restoration of Sacrifices in Modern Jewish Liturgy*, in Alberdina, H.; Poorthuis, M.; Schwartz J. and Turner, Y.: *The Actuality of Sacrifice: Past and Present*, Koninklijke Brill NV, Leiden & Boston 2014.
13. *Ibid.*
14. **Carmy, S.:** *From Paternal Prerogative to Priestly Obligation: The Genealogy of Birkat Kohanim* in **Birnbaum, D. & Cohen, M.S.:** *Birkat Kohanim*, New Paradigm Matrix, New York 2016.
15. **Jacobson-Maisels, J.:** *Receptivity, Dependence, Love and the Healing Power of Blessing*, in **Birnbaum, D. & Cohen, M.S.:** *Birkat Kohanim, Op. Cit.*
16. **Kadden, B. & Kadden, B.B.:** *Teaching Tefilah: Insights and Activities on Prayer, Op. Cit.*
17. **Nulman, M.:** *The Encyclopedia of Jewish Prayer, Op. Cit.*
18. *Ibid.*
19. **Scherman, N.:** *Machzor Zichron Yosef l'Yom Kipur, Op. Cit.*
20. *Ibid.*
    Nulman, M.: *The Encyclopedia of Jewish Prayer, Op. Cit.*
21. *Ibid.*
22. *Ibid.*
23. **Scherman, N.:** *Kaddish: The Kadish Prayer, a New Translation with a Commentary Anthologized from Talmudic, Midrashic, and Rabbinic Sources*, Mesorah Publications Ltd., Brooklyn 1991.
24. **Nulman, M.:** *The Encyclopedia of Jewish Prayer, Op. Cit.*
    Scherman, N.: *Machzor Zichron Yosef l'Yom Kipur, Op. Cit.*

25. **Zacutto, M.**: *Shorshei ha-Shemot, Op. Cit.*
26. *Le Livre des Psaumes Hébreu-Français et Phonétique, Op. Cit.*
    Azulai, H.Y.D.: *Sefer Tehillim Sha'arei Rachamim: im Segulot v'Tefilot ha'Chida, Op. Cit.*
    Ronen, D.: *Tehilim Kavvanot ha-Lev, Op. Cit.*
27. **Kimchi, D. ben Y.**: *Sefer Tehillim, Op. Cit.*
    Sefer Shimmush Tehillim, Op. Cit.
    Seder Tefilot Tikun Ezra, Op. Cit.
    Grünwald, M.: *Ueber den Einfluss der Psalmen auf die Katholische Liturgie, Op. Cit.*
    Singer, I. & Adler, C.: *The Jewish Encyclopedia, Op. Cit.*
    Refuah v'Chayim m'Yerushalayim im Shimush Tehilim, Op. Cit.
    Landsberg, M.: *Sefer Tehillim im Peirush Rashi, Op. Cit.*
    Brauner, R.: *Synopsis of Sefer Shimush Tehillim. Op. Cit.*
    Rebiger, B.: *Sefer Shimmush Tehillim, Op. Cit.*
    Hai ben Sherira Gaon & Varady, A.N.: *Shimush Tehillim (the Theurgical Use of Psalms), Op. Cit.*
28. *Ibid.*
29. *Ibid.*
30. **Rebiger, B.**: *Sefer Shimmush Tehillim, Op. Cit.*
31. **Selig, G.**: *Sepher Schimmusch Tehillim, Op. Cit.*
    The Sixth and Seventh Books of Moses, Op. Cit.
    Peterson, J.H.: *The Sixth and Seventh Books of Moses, Op. Cit.*
32. **Kimchi, D. ben Y.**: *Sefer Tehillim, Op. Cit.*
    Sefer Shimmush Tehillim, Op. Cit.
    Seder Tefilot Tikun Ezra, Op. Cit.
    Grünwald, M.: *Ueber den Einfluss der Psalmen auf die Katholische Liturgie, Op. Cit.*
    Refuah v'Chayim m'Yerushalayim im Shimush Tehilim, Op. Cit.
    Landsberg, M.: *Sefer Tehillim im Peirush Rashi, Op. Cit.*
    Rebiger, B.: *Sefer Shimmush Tehillim, Op. Cit.*
    Hai ben Sherira Gaon & Varady, A.N.: *Shimush Tehillim (the Theurgical Use of Psalms), Op. Cit.*
33. **Selig, G.**: *Sepher Schimmusch Tehillim, Op. Cit.*
    The Sixth and Seventh Books of Moses, Op. Cit.
    Peterson, J.H.: *The Sixth and Seventh Books of Moses, Op. Cit.*
34. **Rebiger, B.**: *Sefer Shimmush Tehillim, Op. Cit.*
35. *Ibid.*
36. **Kimchi, D. ben Y.**: *Sefer Tehillim, Op. Cit.*
    Sefer Shimmush Tehillim, Op. Cit.
    Seder Tefilot Tikun Ezra, Op. Cit.
    Grünwald, M.: *Ueber den Einfluss der Psalmen auf die Katholische Liturgie, Op. Cit.*

Refuah v'Chayim m'Yerushalayim im Shimush Tehilim, Op. Cit.
Landsberg, M.: *Sefer Tehillim im Peirush Rashi, Op. Cit.*
Rebiger, B.: *Sefer Shimmush Tehillim, Op. Cit.*
Hai ben Sherira Gaon & Varady, A.N.: *Shimush Tehillim (the Theurgical Use of Psalms), Op. Cit.*

37. **Selig, G.:** *Sepher Schimmusch Tehillim, Op. Cit.*
     The Sixth and Seventh Books of Moses, Op. Cit.
     Peterson, J.H.: *The Sixth and Seventh Books of Moses, Op. Cit.*
38. **Rebiger, B.:** *Sefer Shimmush Tehillim, Op. Cit.*
39. **Zacutto, M.:** *Shorshei ha-Shemot, Op. Cit.*
40. *Ibid.*
41. *Ibid.*
42. *Ibid.*
     Swart, J.G.: *The Book of Sacred Names, Op. Cit.*
     —*The Book of Immediate Magic - Part 1, Op. Cit.*
43. **Zacutto, M.:** *Shorshei ha-Shemot, Op. Cit.*
44. **Zellmann-Rohrer, M.:** *Psalms Useful for Everything, Op. Cit.*
45. *Ibid.*
46. *Ibid.*
47. **Rankine, D. & Barron, P.H.:** *The Book of Gold, Op. Cit.*
     Marty, J. & MacParthy, F.: *Usage Mago-Théurgiques des Psaumes, Op. Cit.*
48. *Ibid.*
49. **Skinner, S. & Rankine, D.:** *A Collection of Magical Secrets, Op. Cit.*
50. **Mathers, S.L. Macgregor:** *Key of Solomon the King, Op. Cit.*

Psalm 19

1. **Nulman, M.:** *The Encyclopedia of Jewish Prayer, Op. Cit.*
2. **Eliram (Amslam), S.:** *Sefer Segulot, Terufot u'Mazalot, Op. Cit.*
3. *Le Livre des Psaumes Hébreu-Français et Phonétique, Op. Cit.*
     Azulai, H.Y.D.: *Sefer Tehillim Sha'arei Rachamim: im Segulot v'Tefilot ha'Chida, Op. Cit.*
     Ronen, D.: *Tehilim Kavvanot ha-Lev, Op. Cit.*
     Singer, I. & Adler, C.: *The Jewish Encyclopedia, Op. Cit.*
4. **Dennis, G.W.:** *The Encyclopedia of Jewish Myth, Magic and Mysticism, Op. Cit.*
5. **Brauner, R.:** *Synopsis of Sefer Shimush Tehillim. Op. Cit.*
6. *Le Livre des Psaumes Hébreu-Français et Phonétique, Op. Cit.*
     Azulai, H.Y.D.: *Sefer Tehillim Sha'arei Rachamim: im Segulot v'Tefilot ha'Chida, Op. Cit.*
     Ronen, D.: *Tehilim Kavvanot ha-Lev, Op. Cit.*

7.   **Brauner, R.:** *Synopsis of Sefer Shimush Tehillim. Op. Cit.*

8.   **Kimchi, D. ben Y.:** *Sefer Tehillim, Op. Cit.*
Sefer Shimmush Tehillim, Op. Cit.
Seder Tefilot Tikun Ezra, Op. Cit.
Grünwald, M.: *Ueber den Einfluss der Psalmen auf die Katholische Liturgie, Op. Cit.*
Landsberg, M.: *Sefer Tehillim im Peirush Rashi, Op. Cit.*
Rebiger, B.: *Sefer Shimmush Tehillim, Op. Cit.*
Hai ben Sherira Gaon & Varady, A.N.: *Shimush Tehillim* (*the Theurgical Use of Psalms*), *Op. Cit.*

9.   **Rebiger, B.:** *Sefer Shimmush Tehillim, Op. Cit.*

10.   *Ibid.*

11.   **Selig, G.:** *Sepher Schimmusch Tehillim, Op. Cit.*
The Sixth and Seventh Books of Moses, Op. Cit.
Peterson, J.H.: *The Sixth and Seventh Books of Moses, Op. Cit.*

12.   **Kimchi, D. ben Y.:** *Sefer Tehillim, Op. Cit.*
Sefer Shimmush Tehillim, Op. Cit.
Seder Tefilot Tikun Ezra, Op. Cit.
Grünwald, M.: *Ueber den Einfluss der Psalmen auf die Katholische Liturgie, Op. Cit.*
Refuah v'Chayim m'Yerushalayim im Shimush Tehilim, Op. Cit.
Landsberg, M.: *Sefer Tehillim im Peirush Rashi, Op. Cit.*
Rebiger, B.: *Sefer Shimmush Tehillim, Op. Cit.*
Hai ben Sherira Gaon & Varady, A.N.: *Shimush Tehillim* (*the Theurgical Use of Psalms*), *Op. Cit.*

13.   **Selig, G.:** *Sepher Schimmusch Tehillim, Op. Cit.*
The Sixth and Seventh Books of Moses, Op. Cit.
Peterson, J.H.: *The Sixth and Seventh Books of Moses, Op. Cit.*

14.   *Ibid.*

15.   **Rebiger, B.:** *Sefer Shimmush Tehillim, Op. Cit.*

16.   *Ibid.*

17.   *Ibid.*

18.   **Zacutto, M.:** *Shorshei ha-Shemot, Op. Cit.*

19.   *Ibid.*

20.   *Ibid.*

21.   *Ibid.*

22.   *Ibid.*

23.   **Eliram (Amslam), S.:** *Sefer Segulot, Terufot u'Mazalot, Op. Cit.*

24.   **Singer, I. & Adler, C.:** *The Jewish Encyclopedia, Op. Cit.*
Brauner, R.: *Synopsis of Sefer Shimush Tehillim. Op. Cit.*
Hai ben Sherira Gaon & Varady, A.N.: *Shimush Tehillim* (*the Theurgical Use of Psalms*), *Op. Cit.*

Weisberg, C.: *Expecting Miracles: Finding Meaning and Spirituality in Pregnancy through Judaism*, Urim Publications, Jerusalem 2004.

25. **Eliram (Amslam), S.:** *Sefer Segulot, Terufot u'Mazalot, Op. Cit.*
Avizohar-Hagai, C. & Harari, Y.: *Childbirth Magic in Amulets and Recipes from the Gross Family Collection*, in **Sabar, S., Schrijver, E. & Wiesemann, F.:** *Windows on Jewish Worlds: Essays in Honor of William Gross*, Walburg Pers B.V., Uitgeverij, Amsterdam 2019.

26. **Kimchi, D. ben Y.:** *Sefer Tehillim, Op. Cit.*
Sefer Shimmush Tehillim, Op. Cit.
Seder Tefilot Tikun Ezra, Op. Cit.
Grünwald, M.: *Ueber den Einfluss der Psalmen auf die Katholische Liturgie, Op. Cit.*
Landsberg, M.: *Sefer Tehillim im Peirush Rashi, Op. Cit.*
Selig, G.: *Sepher Schimmusch Tehillim, Op. Cit.*
The Sixth and Seventh Books of Moses, Op. Cit.
Peterson, J.H.: *The Sixth and Seventh Books of Moses, Op. Cit.*

27. **Rebiger, B.:** *Sefer Shimmush Tehillim, Op. Cit.*
28. *Ibid.*
Kimchi, D. ben Y.: *Sefer Tehillim, Op. Cit.*
Sefer Shimmush Tehillim, Op. Cit.
Seder Tefilot Tikun Ezra, Op. Cit.
Grünwald, M.: *Ueber den Einfluss der Psalmen auf die Katholische Liturgie, Op. Cit.*
Landsberg, M.: *Sefer Tehillim im Peirush Rashi, Op. Cit.*
Selig, G.: *Sepher Schimmusch Tehillim, Op. Cit.*
The Sixth and Seventh Books of Moses, Op. Cit.
Peterson, J.H.: *The Sixth and Seventh Books of Moses, Op. Cit.*

29. *Ibid.*
30. **Rebiger, B.:** *Sefer Shimmush Tehillim, Op. Cit.*
31. **Selig, G.:** *Sepher Schimmusch Tehillim, Op. Cit.*
The Sixth and Seventh Books of Moses, Op. Cit.
Peterson, J.H.: *The Sixth and Seventh Books of Moses, Op. Cit.*

32. *Ibid.*
33. **Singer, I. & Adler, C.:** *The Jewish Encyclopedia, Op. Cit.*
Dennis, G.W.: *The Encyclopedia of Jewish Myth, Magic and Mysticism, Op. Cit.*
Brauner, R.: *Synopsis of Sefer Shimush Tehillim. Op. Cit.*
Hai ben Sherira Gaon & Varady, A.N.: *Shimush Tehillim (the Theurgical Use of Psalms), Op. Cit.*

34. **Kimchi, D. ben Y.:** *Sefer Tehillim, Op. Cit.*
Sefer Shimmush Tehillim, Op. Cit.
Seder Tefilot Tikun Ezra, Op. Cit.
Landsberg, M.: *Sefer Tehillim im Peirush Rashi, Op. Cit.*
Rebiger, B.: *Sefer Shimmush Tehillim, Op. Cit.*
35. **Selig, G.:** *Sepher Schimmusch Tehillim, Op. Cit.*
The Sixth and Seventh Books of Moses, Op. Cit.
Peterson, J.H.: *The Sixth and Seventh Books of Moses, Op. Cit.*
36. **Kimchi, D. ben Y.:** *Sefer Tehillim, Op. Cit.*
Sefer Shimmush Tehillim, Op. Cit.
Seder Tefilot Tikun Ezra, Op. Cit.
Landsberg, M.: *Sefer Tehillim im Peirush Rashi, Op. Cit.*
Brauner, R.: *Synopsis of Sefer Shimush Tehillim. Op. Cit.*
Rebiger, B.: *Sefer Shimmush Tehillim, Op. Cit.*
Hai ben Sherira Gaon & Varady, A.N.: *Shimush Tehillim (the Theurgical Use of Psalms), Op. Cit.*
37. **Rebiger, B.:** *Sefer Shimmush Tehillim, Op. Cit.*
38. **Zacutto, M.:** *Shorshei ha-Shemot, Op. Cit.*
39. *Ibid.*
40. *Ibid.*
41. **Davis, E. & Frenkel, D.A.:** *Ha-Kami'a ha-Ivri, Op. Cit.*
Green, A.: *Judaic Artifacts, Op. Cit.*
42. *Ibid.*
43. **Zellmann-Rohrer, M.:** *Psalms Useful for Everything, Op. Cit.*
44. **Kayser, C.:** *Gebrauch von Psalmen zur Zauberei, Op. Cit.*
45. **Rankine, D. & Barron, P.H.:** *The Book of Gold, Op. Cit.*
Marty, J. & MacParthy, F.: *Usage Mago-Théurgiques des Psaumes, Op. Cit.*

Psalm 20

1. **Grant, J.A.:** *The King as Exemplar: The Function of Deuteronomy's Kingship Law in the Shaping of the Book of Psalms*, Society of Biblical Literature, Atlanta 2004.
2. *Ibid.*
3. *Ibid.*
4. *Ibid.*
5. *Ibid.*
6. **Nulman, M.:** *The Encyclopedia of Jewish Prayer, Op. Cit.*
7. *Ibid.*
Tirshom, J. ben E.: *Shoshan Yesod Olam* in *Collectanea of Kabbalistic and Magical Texts*, Bibliothèque de Genève: Comites Latentes 145, Genève.
Eisenstein, J.D.: *Otzar Dinim Uminhagim*, Hebrew Publishing Company, New York 1917.

Pollack, H.: *Jewish Folkways in Germanic Lands* (*1648-1806*), Institute of Technology Press, Cambridge 1971.

Folmer, M.: *A Jewish Childbirth Amulet from the Bibliotheca Rosenthaliana* in **Peursen, W.Th. van & Dyk, J.W.:** *Tradition and Innovation in Biblical Interpretation: Studies Presented to Professor Eep Talstra on the Occasion of his Sixty-Fifth Birthday*, Koninklijke Brill NV, Leiden 2011.

8. **Klein, M.:** *A Time to Be Born, Op. Cit.*
9. *Ibid.*

HaCohen, H. ben A.: *Sefer Sha'arei Rachamim*, Thessaloniki 1741.

Beinish, B.: *Amtachat Binyamin, Op. Cit.*

Azulai, H.Y.D.: *Sefer Avodat ha-Kodesh*, Jerusalem 1847.

Modina, A.B. ben M.: *Sefer Ma'avar Yabok*, Vilna 1860.

Weisberg, C.: *Expecting Miracles, Op. Cit.*

Hillel, Y.M.: *Roni Akara: A Guide for the Childless in Accordance with Torah Hashkafah, based upon the Teachings of Our Sages and Other Rabbinic Sources*, Ahavat Shalom Publications, Jerusalem 2005.

10. **Klein, M.:** *A Time to Be Born, Op. Cit.*
11. **Trachtenberg, J.:** *Jewish Magic and Superstition, Op. Cit.*
12. **Klein, M.:** *A Time to Be Born, Op. Cit.*

Ba'al Shem, Elijah; Ba'al-Shem, Joel; ha-Kohen, N. ben Isaac; & Katz, N.: *Sefer Toldot Adam*, Machon Bnei Yishaschar, Jerusalem 1994.

Cardin, N.B.: *Out of the Depths I call to You: A Book of Prayers for the Married Jewish Woman*, Jason Aronson Inc., Northvale 1992.

13. *Ibid.*
14. **HaCohen, H. ben A.:** *Sefer Sha'arei Rachamim, Op. Cit.*

Beinish, B.: *Amtachat Binyamin, Op. Cit.*

Klein, M.: *A Time to Be Born, Op. Cit.*

Hillel, Y.M.: *Roni Akara: A Guide for the Childless, Op. Cit.*

15. **Klein, M.:** *Ibid.*
16. **Folmer, M.:** *A Jewish Childbirth Amulet from the Bibliotheca Rosenthaliana, Op. Cit.*
17. **Zacutto, M.:** *Shorshei ha-Shemot, Op. Cit.*
18. *Ibid.*
19. *Ibid.*
20. *Ibid.*
21. *Ibid.*
22. *Ibid.*
23. **Rebiger, B.:** *Sefer Shimmush Tehillim, Op. Cit.*

24. *Ibid.*
25. *Ibid.*
26. *Ibid.*
    Le Livre des Psaumes Hébreu-Français et Phonétique, Op. Cit.
    Azulai, H.Y.D.: *Sefer Tehillim Sha'arei Rachamim: im Segulot v'Tefilot ha'Chida, Op. Cit.*
    Singer, I. & Adler, C.: *The Jewish Encyclopedia, Op. Cit.*
    Ronen, D.: *Tehilim Kavvanot ha-Lev, Op. Cit.*
    Brauner, R.: *Synopsis of Sefer Shimush Tehillim. Op. Cit.*
27. **Kimchi, D. ben Y.**: *Sefer Tehillim, Op. Cit.*
    Sefer Shimmush Tehillim, Op. Cit.
    Seder Tefilot Tikun Ezra, Op. Cit.
    Grünwald, M.: *Ueber den Einfluss der Psalmen auf die Katholische Liturgie, Op. Cit.*
    Refuah v'Chayim m'Yerushalayim im Shimush Tehilim, Op. Cit.
    Landsberg, M.: *Sefer Tehillim im Peirush Rashi, Op. Cit.*
    Rebiger, B.: *Sefer Shimmush Tehillim, Op. Cit.*
    Hai ben Sherira Gaon & Varady, A.N.: *Shimush Tehillim* (*the Theurgical Use of Psalms*)*, Op. Cit.*
28. *Ibid.*
29. **Selig, G.**: *Sepher Schimmusch Tehillim, Op. Cit.*
    The Sixth and Seventh Books of Moses, Op. Cit.
    Peterson, J.H.: *The Sixth and Seventh Books of Moses, Op. Cit.*
30. *Ibid.*
31. *Ibid.*
32. *Ibid.*
33. **Folmer, M.**: *A Jewish Childbirth Amulet from the Bibliotheca Rosenthaliana, Op. Cit.*
34. *Advice & Segulos From Our Sages On Avoiding Epidemics,* Electronic Essay of Machon Asifas Zikainim Inc., Lakewood 2020.
35. *Ibid.*
36. **Lipshitz, S. ben Y.Y.**: *Segulot Yisrael*, Kahn & Fried, Munkatch 1905.
    Eliram (Amslam), S.: *Sefer Segulot, Terufot u'Mazalot, Op. Cit.*
37. **Rebiger, B.**: *Sefer Shimmush Tehillim, Op. Cit.*
38. **Eliram (Amslam), S.**: *Sefer Segulot, Terufot u'Mazalot, Op. Cit.*
39. **Davis, E. & Frenkel, D.A.**: *Ha-Kami'a ha-Ivri, Op. Cit.*
    Green, A.: *Judaic Artifacts, Op. Cit.*
40. *Ibid.*
41. **Zacutto, M.**: *Shorshei ha-Shemot, Op. Cit.*

42. *Ibid.*
43. *Ibid.*
44. *Ibid.*
45. *Ibid.*
46. *Ibid.*
47. *Ibid.*
48. **Lipshitz, S. ben Y.Y.:** *Segulot Yisrael, Op. Cit.*
    Eliram (Amslam), S.: *Sefer Segulot, Terufot u'Mazalot, Op. Cit.*
49. **Zacutto, M.:** *Shorshei ha-Shemot, Op. Cit.*
50. *Ibid.*
51. **Davis, E. & Frenkel, D.A.:** *Ha-Kami'a ha-Ivri, Op. Cit.*
    Green, A.: *Judaic Artifacts, Op. Cit.*
52. **Zacutto, M.:** *Shorshei ha-Shemot, Op. Cit.*
53. **Zellmann-Rohrer, M.:** *Psalms Useful for Everything, Op. Cit.*
54. *Ibid.*
55. *Ibid.*
56. **Rankine, D. & Barron, P.H.:** *The Book of Gold, Op. Cit.*
    Marty, J. & MacParthy, F.: *Usage Mago-Théurgiques des Psaumes, Op. Cit.*
57. *Ibid.*
58. **Skinner, S. & Rankine, D.:** *A Collection of Magical Secrets, Op. Cit.*
59. **Kayser, C.:** *Gebrauch von Psalmen zur Zauberei, Op. Cit.*

Psalm 21

1. *Le Livre des Psaumes Hébreu-Français et Phonétique, Op. Cit.*
   Azulai, H.Y.D.: *Sefer Tehillim Sha'arei Rachamim: im Segulot v'Tefilot ha'Chida, Op. Cit.*
   Singer, I. & Adler, C.: *The Jewish Encyclopedia, Op. Cit.*
   Ronen, D.: *Tehilim Kavvanot ha-Lev, Op. Cit.*
2. **Brauner, R.:** *Synopsis of Sefer Shimush Tehillim. Op. Cit.*
3. **Kimchi, D. ben Y.:** *Sefer Tehillim, Op. Cit.*
   Sefer Shimmush Tehillim, Op. Cit.
   Seder Tefilot Tikun Ezra, Op. Cit.
   Grünwald, M.: *Ueber den Einfluss der Psalmen auf die Katholische Liturgie, Op. Cit.*
   Refuah v'Chayim m'Yerushalayim im Shimush Tehilim, Op. Cit.
   Landsberg, M.: *Sefer Tehillim im Peirush Rashi, Op. Cit.*
   Rebiger, B.: *Sefer Shimmush Tehillim, Op. Cit.*
   Hai ben Sherira Gaon & Varady, A.N.: *Shimush Tehillim (the Theurgical Use of Psalms), Op. Cit.*
4. **Rebiger, B.:** *Ibid.*

5.   **Selig, G.:** *Sepher Schimmusch Tehillim, Op. Cit.*
       The Sixth and Seventh Books of Moses, Op. Cit.
       Peterson, J.H.: *The Sixth and Seventh Books of Moses, Op. Cit.*
6.   *Ibid.*
       Kimchi, D. ben Y.: *Sefer Tehillim, Op. Cit.*
       Sefer Shimmush Tehillim, Op. Cit.
       Seder Tefilot Tikun Ezra, Op. Cit.
       Refuah v'Chayim m'Yerushalayim im Shimush Tehilim, Op. Cit.
       Landsberg, M.: *Sefer Tehillim im Peirush Rashi, Op. Cit.*
       Rebiger, B.: *Sefer Shimmush Tehillim, Op. Cit.*
       Hai ben Sherira Gaon & Varady, A.N.: *Shimush Tehillim (the Theurgical Use of Psalms), Op. Cit.*
7.   *Sefer Shimmush Tehillim, Op. Cit.*
       Hai ben Sherira Gaon & Varady, A.N.: *Shimush Tehillim (the Theurgical Use of Psalms), Op. Cit.*
8.   **Grünwald, M.:** *Ueber den Einfluss der Psalmen auf die Katholische Liturgie, Op. Cit.*
       Rebiger, B.: *Sefer Shimmush Tehillim, Op. Cit.*
9.   **Kimchi, D. ben Y.:** *Sefer Tehillim, Op. Cit.*
       Sefer Shimmush Tehillim, Op. Cit.
       Seder Tefilot Tikun Ezra, Op. Cit.
       Grünwald, M.: *Ueber den Einfluss der Psalmen auf die Katholische Liturgie, Op. Cit.*
       Refuah v'Chayim m'Yerushalayim im Shimush Tehilim, Op. Cit.
       Landsberg, M.: *Sefer Tehillim im Peirush Rashi, Op. Cit.*
       Rebiger, B.: *Sefer Shimmush Tehillim, Op. Cit.*
       Hai ben Sherira Gaon & Varady, A.N.: *Shimush Tehillim (the Theurgical Use of Psalms), Op. Cit.*
       Selig, G.: *Sepher Schimmusch Tehillim, Op. Cit.*
       The Sixth and Seventh Books of Moses, Op. Cit.
       Peterson, J.H.: *The Sixth and Seventh Books of Moses, Op. Cit.*
10.   *Refuah v'Chayim m'Yerushalayim im Shimush Tehilim, Op. Cit.*
       Landsberg, M.: *Sefer Tehillim im Peirush Rashi, Op. Cit.*
       Rebiger, B.: *Sefer Shimmush Tehillim, Op. Cit.*
11.   **Kimchi, D. ben Y.:** *Sefer Tehillim, Op. Cit.*
       Sefer Shimmush Tehillim, Op. Cit.
       Seder Tefilot Tikun Ezra, Op. Cit.
       Grünwald, M.: *Ueber den Einfluss der Psalmen auf die Katholische Liturgie, Op. Cit.*
       Rebiger, B.: *Sefer Shimmush Tehillim, Op. Cit.*
       Hai ben Sherira Gaon & Varady, A.N.: *Shimush Tehillim (the Theurgical Use of Psalms), Op. Cit.*

Selig, G.: *Sepher Schimmusch Tehillim, Op. Cit.*
The Sixth and Seventh Books of Moses, Op. Cit.
Peterson, J.H.: *The Sixth and Seventh Books of Moses, Op. Cit.*
12.   Rebiger, B.: *Ibid.*
Selig, G.: *Sepher Schimmusch Tehillim, Op. Cit.*
The Sixth and Seventh Books of Moses, Op. Cit.
Peterson, J.H.: *The Sixth and Seventh Books of Moses, Op. Cit.*
13.   Zacutto, M.: *Shorshei ha-Shemot, Op. Cit.*
14.   *Ibid.*
Kimchi, D. ben Y.: *Sefer Tehillim, Op. Cit.*
Sefer Shimmush Tehillim, Op. Cit.
Seder Tefilot Tikun Ezra, Op. Cit.
Refuah v'Chayim m'Yerushalayim im Shimush Tehilim, Op. Cit.
Landsberg, M.: *Sefer Tehillim im Peirush Rashi, Op. Cit.*
Hai ben Sherira Gaon & Varady, A.N.: *Shimush Tehillim (the Theurgical Use of Psalms), Op. Cit.*
15.   *Ibid.*
16.   Selig, G.: *Sepher Schimmusch Tehillim, Op. Cit.*
The Sixth and Seventh Books of Moses, Op. Cit.
Peterson, J.H.: *The Sixth and Seventh Books of Moses, Op. Cit.*
17.   *Ibid.*
18.   Rebiger, B.: *Sefer Shimmush Tehillim, Op. Cit.*
19.   Zellmann-Rohrer, M.: *Psalms Useful for Everything, Op. Cit.*
20.   *Ibid.*
21.   *Ibid.*
22.   Rankine, D. & Barron, P.H.: *The Book of Gold, Op. Cit.*
Marty, J. & MacParthy, F.: *Usage Mago-Théurgiques des Psaumes, Op. Cit.*
23.   *Ibid.*
24.   Skinner, S. & Rankine, D.: *A Collection of Magical Secrets, Op. Cit.*
25.   Zellmann-Rohrer, M.: *Psalms Useful for Everything, Op. Cit.*
26.   Kayser, C.: *Gebrauch von Psalmen zur Zauberei, Op. Cit.*
27.   *Ibid.*
28.   Mathers, S.L. Macgregor: *Key of Solomon the King, Op. Cit.*

Psalm 22

1.   Fendel, Z.: *Purim: Season of Miracles*, Hashkafah Publications, New York 2005.
2.   Matt, D.C.: *The Zohar: Pritzker Edition*, Vol. 5, Stanford University Press, Stanford 2005
Novick, L.: *On the Wings of Shekhinah: Rediscovering Judaism's Divine Feminine*, Quest Books, Wheaton 2008.

3.   **Kimchi, D. ben Y.:** *Sefer Tehillim, Op. Cit.*
Cohen, A.: *The Psalms*, The Soncino Press, London 1960.
Nulman, M.: *The Encyclopedia of Jewish Prayer, Op. Cit.*

4.   **Fleischer, E.:** *Tefillah u-Minhagei Tefillah Eretz Yisrael im be-Tekufat ha-Genizah*, Magnes Press, Jerusalem 1988.

5.   **Abudraham, D. ben Y. ben D.:** *Sefer Abudraham Hashalem*, Usha Publishing, Jerusalem 1963.

6.   **Buber, S.:** *Midrash Tehilim: ha-Mechuneh Shocher Tov*, ha-Almanah v'ha-Achim Rom, Vilna 1891.
Braude, W.G.: *The Midrash on Psalms* (2 Vols), New Haven: Yale University Press, New Haven 1987.

7.   *Le Livre des Psaumes Hébreu-Français et Phonétique, Op. Cit.*
Azulai, H.Y.D.: *Sefer Tehillim Sha'arei Rachamim: im Segulot v'Tefilot ha'Chida, Op. Cit.*
Ronen, D.: *Tehilim Kavvanot ha-Lev, Op. Cit.*

8.   **Brauner, R.:** *Synopsis of Sefer Shimush Tehillim. Op. Cit.*

9.   *Ibid.*
Kimchi, D. ben Y.: *Sefer Tehillim, Op. Cit.*
Sefer Shimmush Tehillim, Op. Cit.
Seder Tefilot Tikun Ezra, Op. Cit.
Grünwald, M.: *Ueber den Einfluss der Psalmen auf die Katholische Liturgie, Op. Cit.*
Singer, I. & Adler, C.: *The Jewish Encyclopedia, Op. Cit.*
Refuah v'Chayim m'Yerushalayim im Shimush Tehilim, Op. Cit.
Rebiger, B.: *Sefer Shimmush Tehillim, Op. Cit.*
Landsberg, M.: *Sefer Tehillim im Peirush Rashi, Op. Cit.*
Hai ben Sherira Gaon & Varady, A.N.: *Shimush Tehillim* (*the Theurgical Use of Psalms*), *Op. Cit.*

10.   **Rebiger, B.:** *Ibid.*

11.   *Ibid.*

12.   *Ibid.*
Kimchi, D. ben Y.: *Sefer Tehillim, Op. Cit.*
Sefer Shimmush Tehillim, Op. Cit.
Seder Tefilot Tikun Ezra, Op. Cit.
Grünwald, M.: *Ueber den Einfluss der Psalmen auf die Katholische Liturgie, Op. Cit.*
Singer, I. & Adler, C.: *The Jewish Encyclopedia, Op. Cit.*
Refuah v'Chayim m'Yerushalayim im Shimush Tehilim, Op. Cit.
Brauner, R.: *Synopsis of Sefer Shimush Tehillim. Op. Cit.*
Landsberg, M.: *Sefer Tehillim im Peirush Rashi, Op. Cit.*
Hai ben Sherira Gaon & Varady, A.N.: *Shimush Tehillim* (*the Theurgical Use of Psalms*), *Op. Cit.*

13. *Ibid.*
14. **Zacutto, M.:** *Shorshei ha-Shemot, Op. Cit.*
15. *Ibid..*
    Swart, J.G.: *The Book of Sacred Names, Op. Cit.*
    —*The Book of Immediate Magic - Part 1, Op. Cit.*
16. **Kimchi, D. ben Y.:** *Sefer Tehillim, Op. Cit.*
    Sefer Shimmush Tehillim, Op. Cit.
    Seder Tefilot Tikun Ezra, Op. Cit.
    Grünwald, M.: *Ueber den Einfluss der Psalmen auf die Katholische Liturgie, Op. Cit.*
    Singer, I. & Adler, C.: *The Jewish Encyclopedia, Op. Cit.*
    Refuah v'Chayim m'Yerushalayim im Shimush Tehilim, Op. Cit.
    Brauner, R.: *Synopsis of Sefer Shimush Tehillim. Op. Cit.*
    Rebiger, B.: *Sefer Shimmush Tehillim, Op. Cit.*
    Landsberg, M.: *Sefer Tehillim im Peirush Rashi, Op. Cit.*
    Hai ben Sherira Gaon & Varady, A.N.: *Shimush Tehillim* (the *Theurgical Use of Psalms*), *Op. Cit.*
17. **Selig, G.:** *Sepher Schimmusch Tehillim, Op. Cit.*
    The Sixth and Seventh Books of Moses, Op. Cit.
    Peterson, J.H.: *The Sixth and Seventh Books of Moses, Op. Cit.*
18. *Ibid.*
19. **Kimchi, D. ben Y.:** *Sefer Tehillim, Op. Cit.*
    Sefer Shimmush Tehillim, Op. Cit.
    Seder Tefilot Tikun Ezra, Op. Cit.
    Grünwald, M.: *Ueber den Einfluss der Psalmen auf die Katholische Liturgie, Op. Cit.*
    Singer, I. & Adler, C.: *The Jewish Encyclopedia, Op. Cit.*
    Refuah v'Chayim m'Yerushalayim im Shimush Tehilim, Op. Cit.
    Brauner, R.: *Synopsis of Sefer Shimush Tehillim. Op. Cit.*
    Rebiger, B.: *Sefer Shimmush Tehillim, Op. Cit.*
    Landsberg, M.: *Sefer Tehillim im Peirush Rashi, Op. Cit.*
    Hai ben Sherira Gaon & Varady, A.N.: *Shimush Tehillim* (the *Theurgical Use of Psalms*), *Op. Cit.*
20. *Ibid.*
21. **Singer, I. & Adler, C.:** *The Jewish Encyclopedia, Op. Cit.*
    Brauner, R.: *Synopsis of Sefer Shimush Tehillim. Op. Cit.*
22. **Eliram (Amslam), S.:** *Sefer Segulot, Terufot u'Mazalot, Op. Cit.*
23. **Skinner, S. & Rankine, D.:** *A Collection of Magical Secrets, Op. Cit.*
24. **Zellmann-Rohrer, M.:** *Psalms Useful for Everything, Op. Cit.*
25. **Rankine, D. & Barron, P.H.:** *The Book of Gold, Op. Cit.*
    Marty, J. & MacParthy, F.: *Usage Mago-Théurgiques des Psaumes, Op. Cit.*

26. **Kayser, C.:** *Gebrauch von Psalmen zur Zauberei, Op. Cit.*
27. **Mathers, S.L. Macgregor:** *Key of Solomon the King, Op. Cit.*
28. *Ibid.*
29. *Ibid.*

Psalm 23

1. **Nulman, M.:** *The Encyclopedia of Jewish Prayer, Op. Cit.*
2. *Ibid.*
3. *Ibid.*
   Glazerson, M.: *Building Blocks of the Soul, Op. Cit.*
   Hirschfeld, B.: *Meriting a Good Parnasah: Deeds and Attitudes to Merit a Comfortable Livelihood, Compiled in a Practical Setting,* Torah Life Institute, Cleveland 2012.
4. **Lipshitz, S. ben Y.Y.:** *Segulot Yisrael, Op. Cit.*
   Eliram (Amslam), S.: *Sefer Segulot, Terufot u'Mazalot, Op. Cit.*
5. **Nulman, M.:** *The Encyclopedia of Jewish Prayer, Op. Cit.*
   Glazerson, M.: *Building Blocks of the Soul, Op. Cit.*
   Hirschfeld, B.: *Meriting a Good Parnasah, Op. Cit.*
6. **Nulman, M.:** *Ibid.*
   Rosenwald, D.J.: Sefer Tiferet ha-Shabat, Haifa 1968;
   Shapira, H.E. & Gold, Y.M.: *Darchei Chayim v'Shalom,* Hotza'at Emet, Brooklyn 2014.
7. **Nulman, M.:** *Ibid.*
8. *Ibid.*
   Toledano, H.; Toledano, Y; Amar, M. & Bentov, H.: *Sefer Pi Hachamim,* Orot Yahadut ha-Magreb, Lod 1999.
9. **Azulai, H.Y.D.:** *Sefer Tehillim Sha'arei Rachamim: im Segulot v'Tefilot ha'Chida, Op. Cit.*
   Trachtenberg, J.: *Jewish Magic and Superstition, Op. Cit.*
   Brauner, R.: *Synopsis of Sefer Shimush Tehillim. Op. Cit.*
   Ronen, D.: *Tehilim Kavvanot ha-Lev, Op. Cit.*
10. *Le Livre des Psaumes Hébreu-Français et Phonétique, Op. Cit.*
    Singer, I. & Adler, C.: *The Jewish Encyclopedia, Op. Cit.*
    Brauner, R.: *Synopsis of Sefer Shimush Tehillim. Op. Cit.*
11. **Kimchi, D. ben Y.:** *Sefer Tehillim, Op. Cit.*
    Refuah v'Chayim m'Yerushalayim im Shimush Tehilim, Op. Cit.
    Rebiger, B.: *Sefer Shimmush Tehillim, Op. Cit.*
    Landsberg, M.: *Sefer Tehillim im Peirush Rashi, Op. Cit.*
12. **Rebiger, B.:** *Ibid.*
13. *Ibid.*
    Kimchi, D. ben Y.: *Sefer Tehillim, Op. Cit.*
    Refuah v'Chayim m'Yerushalayim im Shimush Tehilim, Op. Cit.
    Landsberg, M.: *Sefer Tehillim im Peirush Rashi, Op. Cit.*
14. *Ibid.*
15. **Selig, G.:** *Sepher Schimmusch Tehillim, Op. Cit.*

The Sixth and Seventh Books of Moses, Op. Cit.
Peterson, J.H.: *The Sixth and Seventh Books of Moses, Op. Cit.*
16. *Ibid.*
17. *Ibid.*
18. **Rebiger, B.:** *Sefer Shimmush Tehillim, Op. Cit.*
19. *Ibid.*
20. **Schäfer, P. & Shaked, S.:** *Magische Texte aus der Kairoer Geniza*, Vol. 1, J.C.B. Mohr, Tübingen 1994.
Harari, Y.: *Jewish Magic before the Rise of Kabbalah, Op. Cit.*
Swartz, M.D.: *The Mechanics of Providence: The Workings of Ancient Jewish Magic and Mysticism*, Mohr Siebeck GmbH & Co. KG, Tübingen 2018.
Lesses, R.M.: *Ritual Practices to Gain Power: Angels, Incantations, and Revelation in Early Jewish Mysticism*, Trinity Press International, Harrisburg 1998.
21. *Ibid.*
22. **Swartz, M.D.:** *The Mechanics of Providence, Op. Cit.*
23. *Ibid.*
24. **Zacutto, M.:** *Shorshei ha-Shemot, Op. Cit.*
Swart, J.G.: *The Book of Sacred Names, Op. Cit.*
25. *Ibid.*
26. *Ibid.*
27. *Ibid.*
28. *Ibid.*
29. **Swart, J.G.:** *Ibid.*
30. *Ibid.*
Zacutto, M.: *Shorshei ha-Shemot, Op. Cit.*
31. *Ibid.*
32. *Ibid.*
33. *Ibid.*
34. *Ibid.*
35. **Veltri, G.:** *"Watermarks" in the MS Munich, Hebr. 95: Magical Recipes in Historical Context*, in **Shaked, S.:** *Officina Magica: Essays on the Practice of Magic in Antiquity*, Koninklijke Brill NV, Leiden 2005.
36. **Swart, J.G.:** *The Book of Seals & Amulets, Op. Cit.*
37. **Rankine, D. & Barron, P.H.:** *The Book of Gold, Op. Cit.*
Marty, J. & MacParthy, F.: *Usage Mago-Théurgiques des Psaumes, Op. Cit.*
38. *Ibid.*
39. **Skinner, S. & Rankine, D.:** *A Collection of Magical Secrets, Op. Cit.*
40. *Ibid.*

Psalm 24

1. **Nulman, M.:** *The Encyclopedia of Jewish Prayer, Op. Cit.*
   Magonet, J.: *A Rabbi Reads the Psalms, Op. Cit.*
2. **Nulman, M.:** *Ibid.*
3. *Ibid.*
4. **Margoliot, E.Z.:** *Sefer Mateh Efrayim,* Levin-Epshtein, Jerusalem 1964.
   Hirschfeld, B.: *Meriting a Good Parnasah, Op. Cit.*
5. *Ibid.*
   Lipshitz, S. ben Y.Y.: *Segulot Yisrael, Op. Cit.*
   Eliram (Amslam), S.: *Sefer Segulot, Terufot u'Mazalot, Op. Cit.*
   Nulman, M.: *The Encyclopedia of Jewish Prayer, Op. Cit.*
6. **Hirschfeld, B.:** *Meriting a Good Parnasah, Op. Cit.*
7. **Nulman, M.:** *The Encyclopedia of Jewish Prayer, Op. Cit.*
8. *Ibid.*
9. *Ibid.*
10. *Ibid.*
    Margoliot, E.Z.: *Sefer Mateh Efrayim, Op. Cit.*
    Hirschfeld, B.: *Meriting a Good Parnasah, Op. Cit.*
11. **Swart, J.G.:** *The Book of Sacred Names, Op. Cit.*
12. **Rebiger, B.:** *Sefer Shimmush Tehillim, Op. Cit.*
13. *Ibid.*
14. *Ibid.*
15. **Swart, J.G.:** *The Book of Sacred Names, Op. Cit.*
16. *Ibid.*
17. *Ibid.*
18. **Rebiger, B.:** *Sefer Shimmush Tehillim, Op. Cit.*
19. **Eliram (Amslam), S.:** *Sefer Segulot, Terufot u'Mazalot, Op. Cit.*
20. **Kimchi, D. ben Y.:** *Sefer Tehillim, Op. Cit.*
    Sefer Shimmush Tehillim, Op. Cit.
    Seder Tefilot Tikun Ezra, Op. Cit.
    Grünwald, M.: *Ueber den Einfluss der Psalmen auf die Katholische Liturgie, Op. Cit.*
    Refuah v'Chayim m'Yerushalayim im Shimush Tehilim, Op. Cit.
    Rebiger, B.: *Sefer Shimmush Tehillim, Op. Cit.*
    Landsberg, M.: *Sefer Tehillim im Peirush Rashi, Op. Cit.*
    Hai ben Sherira Gaon & Varady, A.N.: *Shimush Tehillim (the Theurgical Use of Psalms), Op. Cit.*
21. *Ibid.*
    Le Livre des Psaumes Hébreu-Français et Phonétique, Op. Cit.

Azulai, H.Y.D.: *Sefer Tehillim Sha'arei Rachamim: im Segulot v'Tefilot ha'Chida, Op. Cit.*
Ronen, D.: *Tehilim Kavvanot ha-Lev, Op. Cit.*
22. **Singer, I. & Adler, C.:** *The Jewish Encyclopedia, Op. Cit.*
23. **Selig, G.:** *Sepher Schimmusch Tehillim, Op. Cit.*
The Sixth and Seventh Books of Moses, Op. Cit.
Peterson, J.H.: *The Sixth and Seventh Books of Moses, Op. Cit.*
24. *Ibid.*
25. **Zacutto, M.:** *Shorshei ha-Shemot, Op. Cit.*
26. *Ibid.*
Swart, J.G.: *The Book of Sacred Names, Op. Cit.*
—*The Book of Immediate Magic - Part 1, Op. Cit.*
27. **Mathers, S.L. Macgregor:** *Key of Solomon the King, Op. Cit.*
28. **Zellmann-Rohrer, M.:** *Psalms Useful for Everything, Op. Cit.*
29. *Ibid.*
30. **Tselikas, A.:** *Spells and Exorcisms in Three Post-Byzantine Manuscripts, Op. Cit.*
Lecouteux, C.: *Dictionary of Ancient Magic Words and Spells from Abraxas to Zoar, Op. Cit.*
31. **Rankine, D. & Barron, P.H.:** *The Book of Gold, Op. Cit.*
Marty, J. & MacParthy, F.: *Usage Mago-Théurgiques des Psaumes, Op. Cit.*
32. **Mathers, S.L. Macgregor:** *Key of Solomon the King, Op. Cit.*

Psalm 25

1. **Kirkpatrick, A.L.:** *The Book of Psalms*, Vol. 1, C.J. Clay and Sons, London 1897.
2. **Elbogen, I.:** *Jewish Liturgy: A Comprehensive History*, transl. by Scheindlin, R.P., Jewish Publication Society, New York 1993.
Nulman, M.: *The Encyclopedia of Jewish Prayer, Op. Cit.*
3. **Nulman, M.:** *Ibid.*
Hoffman, L.A.: *My People's Prayer Book: Vol. 6, Op. Cit.*
4. **Swart, J.G.:** *The Book of Self Creation, Op. Cit.*
5. **Nulman, M.:** *The Encyclopedia of Jewish Prayer, Op. Cit.*
Hoffman, L.A.: *My People's Prayer Book: Vol. 6, Op. Cit.*
Eisenberg, R.L.: *The JPS Guide to Jewish Traditions, Op. Cit.*
6. **Nulman, M.:** *Ibid.*
7. **Kaplan, A.:** *Meditation and Kabbalah, Op. Cit.*
Jacobs, L: *The Book of Jewish Belief*, Jewish Publication Society, Philadelphia 2008.
8. **Lifshitz, B.:** *The Jewish Law Annual*, Vol. 16, Routledge,

London & New York 2006.

9. **Kaplan, A.**: *Meditation and The Bible, Op. Cit.*
10. *Ibid.*
11. **Singer, I. & Adler, C.**: *The Jewish Encyclopedia, Op. Cit.*
12. **Brauner, R.**: *Synopsis of Sefer Shimush Tehillim. Op. Cit.*
13. **Rosenberg, Y.Y.**: *Rafael ha-Malach, Op. Cit.*
14. *Le Livre des Psaumes Hébreu-Français et Phonétique, Op. Cit.*
15. **Azulai, H.Y.D.**: *Sefer Tehillim Sha'arei Rachamim: im Segulot v'Tefilot ha'Chida, Op. Cit.*
    Ronen, D.: *Tehilim Kavvanot ha-Lev, Op. Cit.*
16. **Kimchi, D. ben Y.**: *Sefer Tehillim, Op. Cit.*
    Sefer Shimmush Tehillim, Op. Cit.
    Seder Tefilot Tikun Ezra, Op. Cit.
    Grünwald, M.: *Ueber den Einfluss der Psalmen auf die Katholische Liturgie, Op. Cit.*
    Refuah v'Chayim m'Yerushalayim im Shimush Tehilim, Op. Cit.
    Rebiger, B.: *Sefer Shimmush Tehillim, Op. Cit.*
    Landsberg, M.: *Sefer Tehillim im Peirush Rashi, Op. Cit.*
    Hai ben Sherira Gaon & Varady, A.N.: *Shimush Tehillim (the Theurgical Use of Psalms), Op. Cit.*
17. **Rebiger, B.**: *Ibid.*
18. **Selig, G.**: *Sepher Schimmusch Tehillim, Op. Cit.*
    The Sixth and Seventh Books of Moses, Op. Cit.
    Peterson, J.H.: *The Sixth and Seventh Books of Moses, Op. Cit.*
19. **Zacutto, M.**: *Shorshei ha-Shemot, Op. Cit.*
20. **Rebiger, B.**: *Ibid.*
21. **Zacutto, M.**: *Shorshei ha-Shemot, Op. Cit.*
22. *Ibid.*
23. *Ibid.*
24. **Zellmann-Rohrer, M.**: *Psalms Useful for Everything, Op. Cit.*
25. *Ibid.*
26. **Rankine, D. & Barron, P.H.**: *The Book of Gold, Op. Cit.*
    Marty, J. & MacParthy, F.: *Usage Mago-Théurgiques des Psaumes, Op. Cit.*
27. **Skinner, S. & Rankine, D.**: *A Collection of Magical Secrets, Op. Cit.*
28. **Kayser, C.**: *Gebrauch von Psalmen zur Zauberei, Op. Cit.*

Psalm 26

1. **Goodman, P.**: *The Sukkot and Simhat Torah Anthology*, The Jewish Publication Society, Philadelphia 1988.
   Holm, J. & Bowker, J.: *Worship*, Pinter Publishers Ltd., London 1994.
2. **Nulman, M.**: *The Encyclopedia of Jewish Prayer, Op. Cit.*

3. *Le Livre des Psaumes Hébreu-Français et Phonétique, Op. Cit.*
   Azulai, H.Y.D.: *Sefer Tehillim Sha'arei Rachamim: im Segulot v'Tefilot ha'Chida, Op. Cit.*
   Ronen, D.: *Tehilim Kavvanot ha-Lev, Op. Cit.*
   Brauner, R.: *Synopsis of Sefer Shimush Tehillim. Op. Cit.*
4. **Rosenberg, Y.Y.:** *Rafael ha-Malach, Op. Cit.*
5. **Kimchi, D. ben Y.:** *Sefer Tehillim, Op. Cit.*
   Sefer Shimmush Tehillim, Op. Cit.
   Seder Tefilot Tikun Ezra, Op. Cit.
   Grünwald, M.: *Ueber den Einfluss der Psalmen auf die Katholische Liturgie, Op. Cit.*
   Refuah v'Chayim m'Yerushalayim im Shimush Tehilim, Op. Cit.
   Brauner, R.: *Synopsis of Sefer Shimush Tehillim. Op. Cit.*
   Rebiger, B.: *Sefer Shimmush Tehillim, Op. Cit.*
   Landsberg, M.: *Sefer Tehillim im Peirush Rashi, Op. Cit.*
   Hai ben Sherira Gaon & Varady, A.N.: *Shimush Tehillim (the Theurgical Use of Psalms), Op. Cit.*
6. **Singer, I. & Adler, C.:** *The Jewish Encyclopedia, Op. Cit.*
   Brauner, R.: *Synopsis of Sefer Shimush Tehillim. Op. Cit.*
7. **Chamui, A.:** *He'ach Nafsheinu,* Hotsa'at Backal, Jerusalem 1981.
   Eliram (Amslam), S.: *Sefer Segulot, Terufot u'Mazalot, Op. Cit.*
8. *Ibid.*
9. **Weisberg, C.:** *Expecting Miracles: Finding Meaning and Spirituality in Pregnancy through Judaism,* Urim Publications, Jerusalem 2004.
10. **Kimchi, D. ben Y.:** *Sefer Tehillim, Op. Cit.*
    Sefer Shimmush Tehillim, Op. Cit.
    Seder Tefilot Tikun Ezra, Op. Cit.
    Grünwald, M.: *Ueber den Einfluss der Psalmen auf die Katholische Liturgie, Op. Cit.*
    Refuah v'Chayim m'Yerushalayim im Shimush Tehilim, Op. Cit.
    Brauner, R.: *Synopsis of Sefer Shimush Tehillim. Op. Cit.*
    Rebiger, B.: *Sefer Shimmush Tehillim, Op. Cit.*
    Landsberg, M.: *Sefer Tehillim im Peirush Rashi, Op. Cit.*
    Hai ben Sherira Gaon & Varady, A.N.: *Shimush Tehillim (the Theurgical Use of Psalms), Op. Cit.*
11. **Rebiger, B.:** *Ibid.*
12. **Selig, G.:** *Sepher Schimmusch Tehillim, Op. Cit.*
    The Sixth and Seventh Books of Moses, Op. Cit.
    Peterson, J.H.: *The Sixth and Seventh Books of Moses, Op. Cit.*
13. **Kimchi, D. ben Y.:** *Sefer Tehillim, Op. Cit.*

Sefer Shimmush Tehillim, Op. Cit.
Seder Tefilot Tikun Ezra, Op. Cit.
Grünwald, M.: *Ueber den Einfluss der Psalmen auf die Katholische Liturgie, Op. Cit.*
Refuah v'Chayim m'Yerushalayim im Shimush Tehilim, Op. Cit.
Brauner, R.: *Synopsis of Sefer Shimush Tehillim. Op. Cit.*
Landsberg, M.: *Sefer Tehillim im Peirush Rashi, Op. Cit.*
Hai ben Sherira Gaon & Varady, A.N.: *Shimush Tehillim (the Theurgical Use of Psalms), Op. Cit.*

14. **Selig, G.:** *Sepher Schimmusch Tehillim, Op. Cit.*
The Sixth and Seventh Books of Moses, Op. Cit.
Peterson, J.H.: *The Sixth and Seventh Books of Moses, Op. Cit.*
15. **Rebiger, B.:** *Sefer Shimmush Tehillim, Op. Cit.*
16. **Rosenberg, Y.Y.:** *Rafael ha-Malach, Op. Cit.*
Davis, E. & Frenkel, D.A.: *Ha-Kami'a ha-Ivri, Op. Cit.*
Green, A.: *Judaic Artifacts, Op. Cit.*
17. **Zacutto, M.:** *Shorshei ha-Shemot, Op. Cit.*
Swart, J.G.: *The Book of Sacred Names, Op. Cit.*
—*The Book of Immediate Magic - Part 1, Op. Cit.*
18. **Zellmann-Rohrer, M.:** *Psalms Useful for Everything, Op. Cit.*
19. *Ibid.*
20. *Ibid.*
21. **Rankine, D. & Barron, P.H.:** *The Book of Gold, Op. Cit.*
Marty, J. & MacParthy, F.: *Usage Mago-Théurgiques des Psaumes, Op. Cit.*
22. *Ibid.*
23. **Skinner, S. & Rankine, D.:** *A Collection of Magical Secrets, Op. Cit.*

Psalm 27

1. **Nulman, M.:** *The Encyclopedia of Jewish Prayer, Op. Cit.*
Finkel, A.Y.: *The Essence of the Holy Days: Insights from the Jewish Sages*, J. J. Aronson. Northvale 1993.
Isaacs, R.H.: *Every Person's Guide to Sukkot, Shemini Atzeret, and Simchat Torah*, J. Aronson. Northvale 2000.
Isaacs, R.H.: *Questions Christians Ask the Rabbi*, KTAV Publishing House Inc., Jersey City 2006.
Robinson, G.: *Essential Judaism: Updated Edition: A Complete Guide to Beliefs, Customs, and Rituals*, Atria Paperback, New York 2016.
2. *Ibid.*
3. *Ibid.*
4. **Nulman, M.:** *Ibid.*

5.   *Ibid.*

6.   *Ibid.*

Finkel, A.Y.: *The Essence of the Holy Days: Insights from the Jewish Sages*, J. J. Aronson. Northvale 1993.

Isaacs, R.H.: *Every Person's Guide to Sukkot, Shemini Atzeret, and Simchat Torah*, J. Aronson. Northvale 2000.

Isaacs, R.H.: *Questions Christians Ask the Rabbi*, KTAV Publishing House Inc., Jersey City 2006.

Robinson, G.: *Essential Judaism: Updated Edition: A Complete Guide to Beliefs, Customs, and Rituals*, Atria Paperback, New York 2016.

7.   *Le Livre des Psaumes Hébreu-Français et Phonétique, Op. Cit.*

Azulai, H.Y.D.: *Sefer Tehillim Sha'arei Rachamim: im Segulot v'Tefilot ha'Chida, Op. Cit.*

Ronen, D.: *Tehilim Kavvanot ha-Lev, Op. Cit.*

Brauner, R.: *Synopsis of Sefer Shimush Tehillim. Op. Cit.*

Rebiger, B.: *Sefer Shimmush Tehillim, Op. Cit.*

8.   *Ibid.*

Kimchi, D. ben Y.: *Sefer Tehillim, Op. Cit.*

Sefer Shimmush Tehillim, Op. Cit.

Seder Tefilot Tikun Ezra, Op. Cit.

Grünwald, M.: *Ueber den Einfluss der Psalmen auf die Katholische Liturgie, Op. Cit.*

Refuah v'Chayim m'Yerushalayim im Shimush Tehilim, Op. Cit.

Brauner, R.: *Synopsis of Sefer Shimush Tehillim. Op. Cit.*

Landsberg, M.: *Sefer Tehillim im Peirush Rashi, Op. Cit.*

9.   **Rebiger, B.:** *Sefer Shimmush Tehillim, Op. Cit.*

10.   *Ibid.*

11.   *Ibid.*

Brauner, R.: *Synopsis of Sefer Shimush Tehillim. Op. Cit.*

Singer, I. & Adler, C.: *The Jewish Encyclopedia, Op. Cit.*

Hai ben Sherira Gaon & Varady, A.N.: *Shimush Tehillim (the Theurgical Use of Psalms), Op. Cit.*

12.   **Selig, G.:** *Sepher Schimmusch Tehillim, Op. Cit.*

The Sixth and Seventh Books of Moses, Op. Cit.

Peterson, J.H.: *The Sixth and Seventh Books of Moses, Op. Cit.*

13.   **Lipshitz, S. ben Y.Y.:** *Segulot Yisrael, Op. Cit.*

Eliram (Amslam), S.: *Sefer Segulot, Terufot u'Mazalot, Op. Cit.*

14.   **Davis, E. & Frenkel, D.A.:** *Ha-Kami'a ha-Ivri, Op. Cit.*

Green, A.: *Judaic Artifacts, Op. Cit.*

15.   **Zacutto, M.:** *Shorshei ha-Shemot, Op. Cit.*

Swart, J.G.: *The Book of Sacred Names, Op. Cit.*

16. **Zellmann-Rohrer, M.**: *Psalms Useful for Everything, Op. Cit.*
17. *Ibid.*
18. *Ibid.*
19. *Ibid.*
20. *Ibid.*
21. **Heim, R.**: *Incantamenta Magica Graeca Latina, Op. Cit.*
    Singer, I. & Adler, C.: *The Jewish Encyclopedia, Op. Cit.*
22. **Rankine, D. & Barron, P.H.**: *The Book of Gold, Op. Cit.*
    Marty, J. & MacParthy, F.: *Usage Mago-Théurgiques des Psaumes, Op. Cit.*
23. *Ibid.*
24. **Mathers, S.L. Macgregor**: *Key of Solomon the King, Op. Cit.*
25. *Ibid.*

Psalm 28

1. *Le Livre des Psaumes Hébreu-Français et Phonétique, Op. Cit.*
   Azulai, H.Y.D.: *Sefer Tehillim Sha'arei Rachamim: im Segulot v'Tefilot ha'Chida, Op. Cit.*
   Ronen, D.: *Tehilim Kavvanot ha-Lev, Op. Cit.*
   Brauner, R.: *Synopsis of Sefer Shimush Tehillim. Op. Cit.*
2. **Singer, I. & Adler, C.**: *The Jewish Encyclopedia, Op. Cit.*
3. **Kimchi, D. ben Y.**: *Sefer Tehillim, Op. Cit.*
   Sefer Shimmush Tehillim, Op. Cit.
   Seder Tefilot Tikun Ezra, Op. Cit.
   Grünwald, M.: *Ueber den Einfluss der Psalmen auf die Katholische Liturgie, Op. Cit.*
   Refuah v'Chayim m'Yerushalayim im Shimush Tehilim, Op. Cit.
   Brauner, R.: *Synopsis of Sefer Shimush Tehillim. Op. Cit.*
   Rebiger, B.: *Sefer Shimmush Tehillim, Op. Cit.*
   Landsberg, M.: *Sefer Tehillim im Peirush Rashi, Op. Cit.*
   Hai ben Sherira Gaon & Varady, A.N.: *Shimush Tehillim (the Theurgical Use of Psalms), Op. Cit.*
4. *Ibid.*
5. **Rebiger, B.**: *Ibid.*
6. *Ibid.*
   Kimchi, D. ben Y.: *Sefer Tehillim, Op. Cit.*
   Sefer Shimmush Tehillim, Op. Cit.
   Seder Tefilot Tikun Ezra, Op. Cit.
   Grünwald, M.: *Ueber den Einfluss der Psalmen auf die Katholische Liturgie, Op. Cit.*
   Refuah v'Chayim m'Yerushalayim im Shimush Tehilim, Op. Cit.
   Brauner, R.: *Synopsis of Sefer Shimush Tehillim. Op. Cit.*
   Landsberg, M.: *Sefer Tehillim im Peirush Rashi, Op. Cit.*
   Hai ben Sherira Gaon & Varady, A.N.: *Shimush Tehillim (the*

Theurgical Use of Psalms), *Op. Cit.*
7. **Selig, G.:** *Sepher Schimmusch Tehillim, Op. Cit.*
    The Sixth and Seventh Books of Moses, Op. Cit.
    Peterson, J.H.: *The Sixth and Seventh Books of Moses, Op. Cit.*
8. **Rebiger, B.:** *Sefer Shimmush Tehillim, Op. Cit.*
9. *Ibid.*
10. **Rankine, D. & Barron, P.H.:** *The Book of Gold, Op. Cit.*
    Marty, J. & MacParthy, F.: *Usage Mago-Théurgiques des Psaumes, Op. Cit.*
11. *Ibid.*
12. *Ibid.*
13. *Ibid.*
14. **Zellmann-Rohrer, M.:** *Psalms Useful for Everything, Op. Cit.*
15. *Ibid.*

Psalm 29

1. **Nulman, M.:** *The Encyclopedia of Jewish Prayer, Op. Cit.*
2. *Ibid.*
    Hoffman, L.A.: *My People's Prayer Book: Traditional Prayers, Modern Commentaries Vol. 8: Kabbalat Shabbat* (*Welcoming Shabbat in the Synagogue*), Jewish Lights Publishing, Woodstock 2005.
3. **Nulman, M.:** *Ibid.*
4. *Ibid.*
5. **Boeckler, A.M.:** *The Liturgical Understanding of Psalms in Judaism: Demonstrated with Samples from Psalms 90-106, with a Special Focus on Psalm 92, Mizmor shir leYom haShabbat*, in **Magonet, J.:** *European Judaism: A Journal for the New Europe* Vol. 48 No. 2, Berghahn Books, New York 2015.
6. *Ibid.*
7. *Ibid.*
    Hoffman, L.A.: *My People's Prayer Book—Vol. 8, Op. Cit.*
    Fine, L.: *Physician of the Soul, Healer of the Cosmos: Isaac Luria and His Kabbalistic Fellowship*, Stanford University Press, Stanford 2003.
8. **Nulman, M.:** *The Encyclopedia of Jewish Prayer, Op. Cit.*
9. *Ibid.*
10. **Jacobs, L.:** *The Jewish Mystics*, Schocken Books, New York 1977.
    Cohn-Sherbok, D.: *Kabbalah and Jewish Mysticism: An Introductory Anthology*, Oneworld Publications, London 2006.
    —with Cohn-Sherbok, L.: *Jewish & Christian Mysticism: An Introduction*, The Continuum Publishing Company, New York 1994.

11.   *Ibid.*

12.   **Hoffman, L.A.:** *My People's Prayer Book—Vol. 8, Op. Cit.*

13.   **Nulman, M.:** *The Encyclopedia of Jewish Prayer, Op. Cit.*

14.   **Zacutto, M.:** *Shorshei ha-Shemot, Op. Cit.*

15.   **Nulman, M.:** *The Encyclopedia of Jewish Prayer, Op. Cit.*
    Hoffman, L.A.: *My People's Prayer Book—Vol. 8, Op. Cit.*

16.   *Ibid.*

17.   *Ibid.*

18.   **Jacobs, L.:** *The Jewish Mystics, Op. Cit.*
    Cohn-Sherbok, D.: *Kabbalah and Jewish Mysticism, Op. Cit.*
    —with Cohn-Sherbok, L.: *Jewish & Christian Mysticism, Op. Cit.*

19.   **Nulman, M.:** *The Encyclopedia of Jewish Prayer, Op. Cit.*
    Hoffman, L.A.: *My People's Prayer Book—Vol. 8, Op. Cit.*

20.   **Hoffman, L.A.:** *Ibid.*

21.   *Ibid.*

22.   *Ibid.*
    Jacobs, L.: *The Jewish Mystics, Op. Cit.*
    Cohn-Sherbok, D.: *Kabbalah and Jewish Mysticism, Op. Cit.*
    —with Cohn-Sherbok, L.: *Jewish & Christian Mysticism, Op. Cit.*

23.   **Swart, J.G.:** *The Book of Sacred Names, Op. Cit.*
    —The Book of Seals & Amulets, Op. Cit.
    —The Book of Immediate Magic - Part 2, Op. Cit.

24.   **Hoffman, L.A.:** *My People's Prayer Book—Vol. 8, Op. Cit.*
    Jacobs, L.: *The Jewish Mystics, Op. Cit.*
    Cohn-Sherbok, D.: *Kabbalah and Jewish Mysticism, Op. Cit.*
    —with Cohn-Sherbok, L.: *Jewish & Christian Mysticism, Op. Cit.*

25.   **Hoffman, L.A.:** *Ibid.*

26.   **Jacobs, L.:** *The Jewish Mystics, Op. Cit.*
    Cohn-Sherbok, D.: *Kabbalah and Jewish Mysticism, Op. Cit.*
    —with Cohn-Sherbok, L.: *Jewish & Christian Mysticism, Op. Cit.*

27.   *Ibid.*

28.   **Hoffman, L.A.:** *My People's Prayer Book—Vol. 8, Op. Cit.*

29.   *Ibid.*

30.   **Swart, J.G.:** *The Book of Self Creation, Op. Cit.*
    —The Book of Sacred Names, Op. Cit.
    —The Book of Seals & Amulets, Op. Cit.
    —The Book of Immediate Magic - Part 1, Op. Cit.
    —The Book of Immediate Magic - Part 2, Op. Cit.

31.   **Freeman, D.L. & Abrams, J.Z.:** *Illness and Health in the Jewish Tradition: Writings from the Bible to Today,* The Jewish

Publication Society, Philadelphia 1999.

32. **Blau, L.:** *Das Altjüdische Zauberwesen,* Karl J. Trübner, Strassburg 1898.
Trachtenberg, J.: *Jewish Magic and Superstition, Op. Cit.*

33. *Le Livre des Psaumes Hébreu-Français et Phonétique, Op. Cit.*
Azulai, H.Y.D.: *Sefer Tehillim Sha'arei Rachamim: im Segulot v'Tefilot ha'Chida, Op. Cit.*
Singer, I. & Adler, C.: *The Jewish Encyclopedia, Op. Cit.*
Ronen, D.: *Tehilim Kavvanot ha-Lev, Op. Cit.*
Brauner, R.: *Synopsis of Sefer Shimush Tehillim. Op. Cit.*

34. **Kimchi, D. ben Y.:** *Sefer Tehillim, Op. Cit.*
Rebiger, B.: *Sefer Shimmush Tehillim, Op. Cit.*
Landsberg, M.: *Sefer Tehillim im Peirush Rashi, Op. Cit.*

35. *Ibid.*
Brauner, R.: *Synopsis of Sefer Shimush Tehillim. Op. Cit.*

36. **Rebiger, B.:** *Sefer Shimmush Tehillim, Op. Cit.*

37. *Ibid.*
Kimchi, D. ben Y.: *Sefer Tehillim, Op. Cit.*
Landsberg, M.: *Sefer Tehillim im Peirush Rashi, Op. Cit.*

38. *Ibid.*

39. **Selig, G.:** *Sepher Schimmusch Tehillim, Op. Cit.*
The Sixth and Seventh Books of Moses, Op. Cit.
Peterson, J.H.: *The Sixth and Seventh Books of Moses, Op. Cit.*

40. *Ibid.*

41. **Rebiger, B.:** *Sefer Shimmush Tehillim, Op. Cit.*

42. *Ibid.*

43. **Brauner, R.:** *Synopsis of Sefer Shimush Tehillim. Op. Cit.*

44. **Zacutto, M.:** *Shorshei ha-Shemot, Op. Cit.*
Swart, J.G.: *The Book of Sacred Names, Op. Cit.*
—*The Book of Immediate Magic - Part 1, Op. Cit.*

45. *Ibid.*

46. *Ibid.*

47. *Ibid.*

48. *Ibid.*

49. **Swart, J.G.:** *The Book of Immediate Magic - Part 1, Op. Cit.*

50. **Daiches, J.:** *Babylonian Oil Magic in the Talmud and in the Later Jewish Literature, Op. Cit.*

51. *Ibid.*

52. *Ibid.*

53. **Zellmann-Rohrer, M.:** *Psalms Useful for Everything, Op. Cit.*

54. *Ibid.*

55. *Ibid.*

56.   *Ibid.*
57.   **Kayser, C.:** *Gebrauch von Psalmen zur Zauberei, Op. Cit.*
58.   **Rankine, D. & Barron, P.H.:** *The Book of Gold, Op. Cit.*
     Marty, J. & MacParthy, F.: *Usage Mago-Théurgiques des Psaumes, Op. Cit.*
59.   *Ibid.*
60.   **Mathers, S.L. Macgregor:** *Key of Solomon the King, Op. Cit.*

Psalm 30

1.   **Nulman, M.:** *The Encyclopedia of Jewish Prayer, Op. Cit.*
     Baumol, A.: The Poetry of Prayer: Tehillim in Tefillah, Gefen Publishing House, Jerusalem & New York 2009.
2.   **Mindel, N.:** *My Prayer: A Commentary on the Daily Prayers,* Vol. 1, Merkos L'Inyonei Chinuch, Brooklyn 2000.
3.   *Ibid.*
4.   *Ibid.*
5.   **Chamui, A.S.H.:** *Yamlit Nafsho,* Josef Kohen, Jerusalem 1990.
6.   *Ibid.*
7.   **Mindel, N.:** *My Prayer, Op. Cit.*
     Nulman, M.: *The Encyclopedia of Jewish Prayer, Op. Cit.*
8.   **Chamui, A.S.H.:** *Yamlit Nafsho, Op. Cit.*
9.   **Mindel, N.:** *My Prayer, Op. Cit.*
     Nulman, M.: *The Encyclopedia of Jewish Prayer, Op. Cit.*
10.   *Ibid.*
11.   *Le Livre des Psaumes Hébreu-Français et Phonétique, Op. Cit.*
     Azulai, H.Y.D.: *Sefer Tehillim Sha'arei Rachamim: im Segulot v'Tefilot ha'Chida, Op. Cit.*
     Singer, I. & Adler, C.: *The Jewish Encyclopedia, Op. Cit.*
     Ronen, D.: *Tehilim Kavvanot ha-Lev, Op. Cit.*
     Brauner, R.: *Synopsis of Sefer Shimush Tehillim. Op. Cit.*
12.   **Kimchi, D. ben Y.:** *Sefer Tehillim, Op. Cit.*
     Sefer Shimmush Tehillim, Op. Cit.
     Seder Tefilot Tikun Ezra, Op. Cit.
     Rebiger, B.: *Sefer Shimmush Tehillim, Op. Cit.*
     Landsberg, M.: *Sefer Tehillim im Peirush Rashi, Op. Cit.*
     Hai ben Sherira Gaon & Varady, A.N.: *Shimush Tehillim (the Theurgical Use of Psalms), Op. Cit.*
     Selig, G.: *Sepher Schimmusch Tehillim, Op. Cit.*
     The Sixth and Seventh Books of Moses, Op. Cit.
     Peterson, J.H.: *The Sixth and Seventh Books of Moses, Op. Cit.*
13.   **Rebiger, B.:** *Ibid.*
14.   **Zacutto, M.:** *Shorshei ha-Shemot, Op. Cit.*
15.   *Ibid.*

16. *Ibid..*
17. **Rebiger, B.:** *Sefer Shimmush Tehillim, Op. Cit.*
18. *Ibid.*
19. *Ibid.*
20. **Zacutto, M.:** *Shorshei ha-Shemot, Op. Cit.*
21. *Ibid.*
22. **Davis, E. & Frenkel, D.A.:** *Ha-Kami'a ha-Ivri, Op. Cit.*
     Green, A.: *Judaic Artifacts, Op. Cit.*
23. *Ibid.*
24. **Zacutto, M.:** *Shorshei ha-Shemot, Op. Cit.*
     Swart, J.G.: *The Book of Sacred Names, Op. Cit.*
     —*The Book of Immediate Magic - Part 1, Op. Cit.*
25. **Rankine, D. & Barron, P.H.:** *The Book of Gold, Op. Cit.*
     Marty, J. & MacParthy, F.: *Usage Mago-Théurgiques des Psaumes, Op. Cit.*
26. **Skinner, S. & Rankine, D.:** *A Collection of Magical Secrets, Op. Cit.*
27. **Kayser, C.:** *Gebrauch von Psalmen zur Zauberei, Op. Cit.*
28. *Ibid.*
29. *Ibid.*
30. **Mathers, S.L. Macgregor:** *Key of Solomon the King, Op. Cit.*

Psalm 31

1. **Nulman, M.:** *The Encyclopedia of Jewish Prayer, Op. Cit.*
2. *Le Livre des Psaumes Hébreu-Français et Phonétique, Op. Cit.*
    Azulai, H.Y.D.: *Sefer Tehillim Sha'arei Rachamim: im Segulot v'Tefilot ha'Chida, Op. Cit.*
    Singer, I. & Adler, C.: *The Jewish Encyclopedia, Op. Cit.*
    Ronen, D.: *Tehilim Kavvanot ha-Lev, Op. Cit.*
    Brauner, R.: *Synopsis of Sefer Shimush Tehillim. Op. Cit.*
3. **Lipshitz, S. ben Y.Y.:** *Segulot Yisrael, Op. Cit.*
    Eliram (Amslam), S.: *Sefer Segulot, Terufot u'Mazalot, Op. Cit.*
4. **Kimchi, D. ben Y.:** *Sefer Tehillim, Op. Cit.*
    Seder Tefilot Tikun Ezra, Op. Cit.
    Refuah v'Chayim m'Yerushalayim im Shimush Tehilim, Op. Cit.
    Rebiger, B.: *Sefer Shimmush Tehillim, Op. Cit.*
    Landsberg, M.: *Sefer Tehillim im Peirush Rashi, Op. Cit.*
5. **Selig, G.:** *Sepher Schimmusch Tehillim, Op. Cit.*
    The Sixth and Seventh Books of Moses, Op. Cit.
    Peterson, J.H.: *The Sixth and Seventh Books of Moses, Op. Cit.*
6. **Zacutto, M.:** *Shorshei ha-Shemot, Op. Cit.*

7. *Ibid.*
8. *Ibid.*
9. *Ibid.*
10. **Rebiger, B.**: *Sefer Shimmush Tehillim, Op. Cit.*
11. **Davis, E. & Frenkel, D.A.**: *Ha-Kami'a ha-Ivri, Op. Cit.*
    Green, A.: *Judaic Artifacts, Op. Cit.*
12. *Ibid.*
13. *Ibid.*
14. *Ibid.*
15. **Zacutto, M.**: *Shorshei ha-Shemot, Op. Cit.*
16. **Zellmann-Rohrer, M.**: *Psalms Useful for Everything, Op. Cit.*
17. **Rankine, D. & Barron, P.H.**: *The Book of Gold, Op. Cit.*
    Marty, J. & MacParthy, F.: *Usage Mago-Théurgiques des Psaumes, Op. Cit.*
18. **Zellmann-Rohrer, M.**: *Psalms Useful for Everything, Op. Cit.*
19. **Mathers, S.L. Macgregor**: *Key of Solomon the King, Op. Cit.*

Psalm 32

1. **Nulman, M.**: *The Encyclopedia of Jewish Prayer, Op. Cit.*
2. *Ibid.*
3. *Ibid.*
4. *Le Livre des Psaumes Hébreu-Français et Phonétique, Op. Cit.*
   Azulai, H.Y.D.: *Sefer Tehillim Sha'arei Rachamim: im Segulot v'Tefilot ha'Chida, Op. Cit.*
   Ronen, D.: *Tehilim Kavvanot ha-Lev, Op. Cit.*
5. **Selig, G.**: *Sepher Schimmusch Tehillim, Op. Cit.*
   The Sixth and Seventh Books of Moses, Op. Cit.
   Peterson, J.H.: *The Sixth and Seventh Books of Moses, Op. Cit.*
6. **Kimchi, D. ben Y.**: *Sefer Tehillim, Op. Cit.*
   Seder Tefilot Tikun Ezra, Op. Cit.
   Grünwald, M.: *Ueber den Einfluss der Psalmen auf die Katholische Liturgie, Op. Cit.*
   Refuah v'Chayim m'Yerushalayim im Shimush Tehilim, Op. Cit.
   Brauner, R.: *Synopsis of Sefer Shimush Tehillim. Op. Cit.*
   Landsberg, M.: *Sefer Tehillim im Peirush Rashi, Op. Cit.*
   Hai ben Sherira Gaon & Varady, A.N.: *Shimush Tehillim (the Theurgical Use of Psalms), Op. Cit.*
7. **Rebiger, B.**: *Sefer Shimmush Tehillim, Op. Cit.*
8. *Ibid.*
9. *Ibid.*
10. **Rosenberg, Y.Y.**: *Rafael ha-Malach, Op. Cit.*
    Swart, J.G.: *The Book of Seals & Amulets, Op. Cit.*

11. *Ibid.*
12. *Ibid.*
13. **Zacutto, M.:** *Shorshei ha-Shemot, Op. Cit.*
14. *Ibid.*
15. *Ibid.*
16. *Ibid.*
17. *Ibid.*
18. *Ibid.*
19. **Singer, I. & Adler, C.:** *The Jewish Encyclopedia, Op. Cit.*
20. **Eliram (Amslam), S.:** *Sefer Segulot, Terufot u'Mazalot, Op. Cit.*
21. **Davis, E. & Frenkel, D.A.:** *Ha-Kami'a ha-Ivri, Op. Cit.*
    Green, A.: *Judaic Artifacts, Op. Cit.*
22. **Zacutto, M.:** *Shorshei ha-Shemot, Op. Cit.*
    Swart, J.G.: *The Book of Sacred Names, Op. Cit.*
23. *Ibid.*
24. *Ibid.*
25. *Ibid.*
26. *Ibid.*
27. **Zellmann-Rohrer, M.:** *Psalms Useful for Everything, Op. Cit.*
28. **Rankine, D. & Barron, P.H.:** *The Book of Gold, Op. Cit.*
    Marty, J. & MacParthy, F.: *Usage Mago-Théurgiques des Psaumes, Op. Cit.*
29. *Ibid.*
30. **Skinner, S. & Rankine, D.:** *A Collection of Magical Secrets, Op. Cit.*
31. **Kayser, C.:** *Gebrauch von Psalmen zur Zauberei, Op. Cit.*
32. **Mathers, S.L. Macgregor:** *Key of Solomon the King, Op. Cit.*

Psalm 33

1. **Mindel, N.:** *My Prayer, Op. Cit.*
   Nulman, M.: *The Encyclopedia of Jewish Prayer, Op. Cit.*
2. *Ibid.*
3. *Ibid.*
4. *Ibid.*
   Pirke Avot: Sayings of the Fathers, Behrman House Inc., Springfield 1945.
   Pirke d'Rabbi Eliezer: The Chapters of Rabbi Eliezer the Great, transl. Friendlander, G., Sepher Hermon Press, New York 1916.
5. *Ibid.*
6. **Swart, J.G.:** *The Book of Self Creation, Op. Cit.*
7. *Ibid.*
8. **Mindel, N.:** *My Prayer, Op. Cit.*

	Nulman, M.: *The Encyclopedia of Jewish Prayer, Op. Cit.*
9.	**Swart, J.G.**: *The Book of Self Creation, Op. Cit.*
10.	*Ibid.*
11.	*Le Livre des Psaumes Hébreu-Français et Phonétique, Op. Cit.*

Azulai, H.Y.D.: *Sefer Tehillim Sha'arei Rachamim: im Segulot v'Tefilot ha'Chida, Op. Cit.*

Ronen, D.: *Tehilim Kavvanot ha-Lev, Op. Cit.*

Harari, Y.: *Jewish Magic before the Rise of Kabbalah, Op. Cit.*

Brauner, R.: *Synopsis of Sefer Shimush Tehillim. Op. Cit.*

| | |
| 12. | **Kimchi, D. ben Y.**: *Sefer Tehillim, Op. Cit.* |

Sefer Shimmush Tehillim, Op. Cit.

Seder Tefilot Tikun Ezra, Op. Cit.

Grünwald, M.: *Ueber den Einfluss der Psalmen auf die Katholische Liturgie, Op. Cit.*

Refuah v'Chayim m'Yerushalayim im Shimush Tehilim, Op. Cit.

Rebiger, B.: *Sefer Shimmush Tehillim, Op. Cit.*

Landsberg, M.: *Sefer Tehillim im Peirush Rashi, Op. Cit.*

Hai ben Sherira Gaon & Varady, A.N.: *Shimush Tehillim (the Theurgical Use of Psalms), Op. Cit.*

Selig, G.: *Sepher Schimmusch Tehillim, Op. Cit.*

The Sixth and Seventh Books of Moses, Op. Cit.

Peterson, J.H.: *The Sixth and Seventh Books of Moses, Op. Cit.*

13.	*Ibid.*
14.	**Rebiger, B.**: *Sefer Shimmush Tehillim, Op. Cit.*
15.	*Ibid.*
16.	*Ibid.*
17.	**Zacutto, M.**: *Shorshei ha-Shemot, Op. Cit.*

Swart, J.G.: *The Book of Seals & Amulets, Op. Cit.*

18.	*Ibid.*
19.	*Ibid.*
20.	**Swart, J.G.**: *The Book of Sacred Names, Op. Cit.*

—The Book of Seals & Amulets, Op. Cit.

| 21. | **Zacutto, M.**: *Shorshei ha-Shemot, Op. Cit.* |
| 22. | **Davis, E. & Frenkel, D.A.**: *Ha-Kami'a ha-Ivri, Op. Cit.* |

Green, A.: *Judaic Artifacts, Op. Cit.*

23.	**Brauner, R.**: *Synopsis of Sefer Shimush Tehillim. Op. Cit.*
24.	**Singer, I. & Adler, C.**: *The Jewish Encyclopedia, Op. Cit.*
25.	**Kimchi, D. ben Y.**: *Sefer Tehillim, Op. Cit.*

Sefer Shimmush Tehillim, Op. Cit.

Seder Tefilot Tikun Ezra, Op. Cit.

Grünwald, M.: *Ueber den Einfluss der Psalmen auf die Katholische Liturgie, Op. Cit.*

Refuah v'Chayim m'Yerushalayim im Shimush Tehilim, Op. Cit.

Rebiger, B.: *Sefer Shimmush Tehillim, Op. Cit.*
Landsberg, M.: *Sefer Tehillim im Peirush Rashi, Op. Cit.*
Hai ben Sherira Gaon & Varady, A.N.: *Shimush Tehillim* (*the Theurgical Use of Psalms*), *Op. Cit.*
26. Selig, G.: *Sepher Schimmusch Tehillim, Op. Cit.*
     The Sixth and Seventh Books of Moses, Op. Cit.
     Peterson, J.H.: *The Sixth and Seventh Books of Moses, Op. Cit.*
27. Swart, J.G.: *The Book of Sacred Names, Op. Cit.*
28. *Ibid.*
29. *Ibid.*
30. *Ibid.*
31. Davis, E. & Frenkel, D.A.: *Ha-Kami'a ha-Ivri, Op. Cit.*
     Green, A.: *Judaic Artifacts, Op. Cit.*
32. Ochana, R.H.: *Sefer Mar'eh ha-Yeladim*, Yerid ha-Sefarim, Jerusalem 1990.
     Eliram (Amslam), S.: *Sefer Segulot, Terufot u'Mazalot, Op. Cit.*
33. Zacutto, M.: *Shorshei ha-Shemot, Op. Cit.*
     Swart, J.G.: *The Book of Sacred Names, Op. Cit.*
34. *Ibid.*
35. Rankine, D. & Barron, P.H.: *The Book of Gold, Op. Cit.*
     Marty, J. & MacParthy, F.: *Usage Mago-Théurgiques des Psaumes, Op. Cit.*
36. Kayser, C.: *Gebrauch von Psalmen zur Zauberei, Op. Cit.*

Psalm 34

1. Nulman, M.: *The Encyclopedia of Jewish Prayer, Op. Cit.*
2. *Ibid.*
3. *Ibid.*
4. *Ibid.*
5. *Ibid.*
6. *Ibid.*
7. *Ibid.*
8. Swart, J.G.: *The Book of Sacred Names, Op. Cit.*
     —*The Book of Immediate Magic - Part 1, Op. Cit.*
9. *Le Livre des Psaumes Hébreu-Français et Phonétique, Op. Cit.*
     Azulai, H.Y.D.: *Sefer Tehillim Sha'arei Rachamim: im Segulot v'Tefilot ha'Chida, Op. Cit.*
     Ronen, D.: *Tehilim Kavvanot ha-Lev, Op. Cit.*
     Brauner, R.: *Synopsis of Sefer Shimush Tehillim. Op. Cit.*
10. Rosenberg, Y.Y.: *Rafael ha-Malach, Op. Cit.*
11. Kimchi, D. ben Y.: *Sefer Tehillim, Op. Cit.*

Sefer Shimmush Tehillim, Op. Cit.
Seder Tefilot Tikun Ezra, Op. Cit.
Grünwald, M.: *Ueber den Einfluss der Psalmen auf die Katholische Liturgie, Op. Cit.*
Refuah v'Chayim m'Yerushalayim im Shimush Tehilim, Op. Cit.
Rebiger, B.: *Sefer Shimmush Tehillim, Op. Cit.*
Landsberg, M.: *Sefer Tehillim im Peirush Rashi, Op. Cit.*
Hai ben Sherira Gaon & Varady, A.N.: *Shimush Tehillim (the Theurgical Use of Psalms), Op. Cit.*

12. **Selig, G.:** *Sepher Schimmusch Tehillim, Op. Cit.*
The Sixth and Seventh Books of Moses, Op. Cit.
Peterson, J.H.: *The Sixth and Seventh Books of Moses, Op. Cit.*

13. **Kimchi, D. ben Y.:** *Sefer Tehillim, Op. Cit.*
Sefer Shimmush Tehillim, Op. Cit.
Seder Tefilot Tikun Ezra, Op. Cit.
Grünwald, M.: *Ueber den Einfluss der Psalmen auf die Katholische Liturgie, Op. Cit.*
Refuah v'Chayim m'Yerushalayim im Shimush Tehilim, Op. Cit.
Rebiger, B.: *Sefer Shimmush Tehillim, Op. Cit.*
Landsberg, M.: *Sefer Tehillim im Peirush Rashi, Op. Cit.*
Hai ben Sherira Gaon & Varady, A.N.: *Shimush Tehillim (the Theurgical Use of Psalms), Op. Cit.*

14. **Selig, G.:** *Sepher Schimmusch Tehillim, Op. Cit.*
The Sixth and Seventh Books of Moses, Op. Cit.
Peterson, J.H.: *The Sixth and Seventh Books of Moses, Op. Cit.*

15. **Rosenberg, Y.Y.:** *Rafael ha-Malach, Op. Cit.*

16. *Ibid.*
Singer, I. & Adler, C.: *The Jewish Encyclopedia, Op. Cit.*
Brauner, R.: *Synopsis of Sefer Shimush Tehillim. Op. Cit.*

17. **Kimchi, D. ben Y.:** *Sefer Tehillim, Op. Cit.*
Sefer Shimmush Tehillim, Op. Cit.
Seder Tefilot Tikun Ezra, Op. Cit.
Grünwald, M.: *Ueber den Einfluss der Psalmen auf die Katholische Liturgie, Op. Cit.*
Refuah v'Chayim m'Yerushalayim im Shimush Tehilim, Op. Cit.
Rebiger, B.: *Sefer Shimmush Tehillim, Op. Cit.*
Landsberg, M.: *Sefer Tehillim im Peirush Rashi, Op. Cit.*
Hai ben Sherira Gaon & Varady, A.N.: *Shimush Tehillim (the Theurgical Use of Psalms), Op. Cit.*
Selig, G.: *Sepher Schimmusch Tehillim, Op. Cit.*
The Sixth and Seventh Books of Moses, Op. Cit.
Peterson, J.H.: *The Sixth and Seventh Books of Moses, Op. Cit.*

18. **Harari, Y.:** *Jewish Magic before the Rise of Kabbalah, Op. Cit.*
19. *Ibid.*
20. **Rebiger, B.:** *Sefer Shimmush Tehillim, Op. Cit.*
21. *Ibid.*
22. **Harari, Y.:** *Jewish Magic before the Rise of Kabbalah, Op. Cit.*
23. **Zacutto, M.:** *Shorshei ha-Shemot, Op. Cit.*
24. *Ibid.*
    Davis, E. & Frenkel, D.A.: *Ha-Kami'a ha-Ivri, Op. Cit.*
    Green, A.: *Judaic Artifacts, Op. Cit.*
25. *Ibid.*
26. *Ibid.*
27. *Ibid.*
28. **Zacutto, M.:** *Shorshei ha-Shemot, Op. Cit.*
29. *Ibid.*
30. **Zacutto, M.:** *Shorshei ha-Shemot, Op. Cit.*
    Swart, J.G.: *The Book of Sacred Names, Op. Cit.*
    —*The Book of Immediate Magic - Part 1, Op. Cit.*
31. *Ibid.*
32. *Ibid.*
33. **Zellmann-Rohrer, M.:** *Psalms Useful for Everything, Op. Cit.*
34. *Ibid.*
35. **Rankine, D. & Barron, P.H.:** *The Book of Gold, Op. Cit.*
    Marty, J. & MacParthy, F.: *Usage Mago-Théurgiques des Psaumes, Op. Cit.*
36. **Skinner, S. & Rankine, D.:** *A Collection of Magical Secrets, Op. Cit.*
37. **Zellmann-Rohrer, M.:** *The Tradition of Greek and Latin Incantations and related Ritual Texts from Antiquity through the Medieval and Early Modern Periods, Doctoral Dissertation,* University of California, Berkeley Spring 2016.
38. **Vikan, G.:** *Art, Medicine and Magic in Early Byzantium,* in Dumbarton Oaks Papers Vol. 38: Symposium on Byzantine Medicine 1984, Dunbarton Oaks, Trustees for Harvard University.
39. **Lecouteux, C.:** *Dictionary of Ancient Magic Words and Spells from Abraxas to Zoar, Op. Cit.*
40. **Heim, R.:** *Incantamenta Magica Graeca Latina, Op. Cit.*
    Zellmann-Rohrer, M.: *The Tradition of Greek and Latin Incantations and related Ritual Texts from Antiquity through the Medieval and Early Modern Periods, Op. Cit.*
41. **Kayser, C.:** *Gebrauch von Psalmen zur Zauberei, Op. Cit.*
42. *Ibid.*

468

Psalm 35

1. **Singer, I. & Adler, C.:** *The Jewish Encyclopedia, Op. Cit.*
2. *Le Livre des Psaumes Hébreu-Français et Phonétique, Op. Cit.*
   Azulai, H.Y.D.: *Sefer Tehillim Sha'arei Rachamim: im Segulot v'Tefilot ha'Chida, Op. Cit.*
   Ronen, D.: *Tehilim Kavvanot ha-Lev, Op. Cit.*
3. **Kimchi, D. ben Y.:** *Sefer Tehillim, Op. Cit.*
   Sefer Shimmush Tehillim, Op. Cit.
   Seder Tefilot Tikun Ezra, Op. Cit.
   Grünwald, M.: *Ueber den Einfluss der Psalmen auf die Katholische Liturgie, Op. Cit.*
   Refuah v'Chayim m'Yerushalayim im Shimush Tehilim, Op. Cit.
   Rebiger, B.: *Sefer Shimmush Tehillim, Op. Cit.*
   Brauner, R.: *Synopsis of Sefer Shimush Tehillim. Op. Cit.*
   Landsberg, M.: *Sefer Tehillim im Peirush Rashi, Op. Cit.*
   Hai ben Sherira Gaon & Varady, A.N.: *Shimush Tehillim (the Theurgical Use of Psalms), Op. Cit.*
4. **Harari, Y.:** *Jewish Magic before the Rise of Kabbalah, Op. Cit.*
5. **Kimchi, D. ben Y.:** *Sefer Tehillim, Op. Cit.*
   Sefer Shimmush Tehillim, Op. Cit.
   Seder Tefilot Tikun Ezra, Op. Cit.
   Grünwald, M.: *Ueber den Einfluss der Psalmen auf die Katholische Liturgie, Op. Cit.*
   Refuah v'Chayim m'Yerushalayim im Shimush Tehilim, Op. Cit.
   Rebiger, B.: *Sefer Shimmush Tehillim, Op. Cit.*
   Brauner, R.: *Synopsis of Sefer Shimush Tehillim. Op. Cit.*
   Landsberg, M.: *Sefer Tehillim im Peirush Rashi, Op. Cit.*
   Hai ben Sherira Gaon & Varady, A.N.: *Shimush Tehillim (the Theurgical Use of Psalms), Op. Cit.*
6. **Selig, G.:** *Sepher Schimmusch Tehillim, Op. Cit.*
   The Sixth and Seventh Books of Moses, Op. Cit.
   Peterson, J.H.: *The Sixth and Seventh Books of Moses, Op. Cit.*
7. **Rosenberg, Y.Y.:** *Rafael ha-Malach, Op. Cit.*
8. **Weintraub, S.Y.:** *Healing Activities and P'sukim from Tehillim, Op. Cit.*
9. **Zacutto, M.:** *Shorshei ha-Shemot, Op. Cit.*
   Swart, J.G.: *The Book of Sacred Names, Op. Cit.*
   —*The Book of Immediate Magic - Part 1, Op. Cit.*
10. **Zellmann-Rohrer, M.:** *Psalms Useful for Everything, Op. Cit.*
11. **Skinner, S. & Rankine, D.:** *A Collection of Magical Secrets,*

Op. Cit.

12. **Kayser, C.:** *Gebrauch von Psalmen zur Zauberei, Op. Cit.*
13. **Zellmann-Rohrer, M.:** *Psalms Useful for Everything, Op. Cit.*
14. *Ibid.*
15. **Grünwald, M.:** *Ueber den Einfluss der Psalmen auf die Katholische Liturgie, Op. Cit.*
16. **Zellmann-Rohrer, M.:** *Psalms Useful for Everything, Op. Cit.*
17. **Rankine, D. & Barron, P.H.:** *The Book of Gold, Op. Cit.*
    Marty, J. & MacParthy, F.: *Usage Mago-Théurgiques des Psaumes, Op. Cit.*
18. *Ibid.*

Psalm 36

1. **Nulman, M.:** *The Encyclopedia of Jewish Prayer, Op. Cit.*
2. *Ibid.*
3. *Ibid.*
4. **Matt, D.C.:** *The Zohar*, Pritzker Edition Vol 5, *Op. Cit.*
5. *Ibid.*
6. *Ibid.*
7. *Ibid.*
8. *Ibid.*
9. *Ibid.*
10. *Ibid.*
11. *Le Livre des Psaumes Hébreu-Français et Phonétique, Op. Cit.*
    Azulai, H.Y.D.: *Sefer Tehillim Sha'arei Rachamim: im Segulot v'Tefilot ha'Chida, Op. Cit.*
    Ronen, D.: *Tehilim Kavvanot ha-Lev, Op. Cit.*
    Brauner, R.: *Synopsis of Sefer Shimush Tehillim. Op. Cit.*
12. **Kimchi, D. ben Y.:** *Sefer Tehillim, Op. Cit.*
    Singer, I. & Adler, C.: *The Jewish Encyclopedia, Op. Cit.*
    Refuah v'Chayim m'Yerushalayim im Shimush Tehilim, Op. Cit.
    Rebiger, B.: *Sefer Shimmush Tehillim, Op. Cit.*
    Brauner, R.: *Synopsis of Sefer Shimush Tehillim. Op. Cit.*
    Landsberg, M.: *Sefer Tehillim im Peirush Rashi, Op. Cit.*
13. **Selig, G.:** *Sepher Schimmusch Tehillim, Op. Cit.*
    The Sixth and Seventh Books of Moses, Op. Cit.
    Peterson, J.H.: *The Sixth and Seventh Books of Moses, Op. Cit.*
14. **Kimchi, D. ben Y.:** *Sefer Tehillim, Op. Cit.*
    Singer, I. & Adler, C.: *The Jewish Encyclopedia, Op. Cit.*
    Refuah v'Chayim m'Yerushalayim im Shimush Tehilim, Op. Cit.
    Rebiger, B.: *Sefer Shimmush Tehillim, Op. Cit.*
    Brauner, R.: *Synopsis of Sefer Shimush Tehillim. Op. Cit.*

Landsberg, M.: *Sefer Tehillim im Peirush Rashi, Op. Cit.*
ı5.   Selig, G.: *Sepher Schimmusch Tehillim, Op. Cit.*
The Sixth and Seventh Books of Moses, Op. Cit.
Peterson, J.H.: *The Sixth and Seventh Books of Moses, Op. Cit.*
16.   Rebiger, B.: *Sefer Shimmush Tehillim, Op. Cit.*
17.   Zacutto, M.: *Shorshei ha-Shemot, Op. Cit.*
18.   *Ibid.*
19.   *Ibid.*
20.   *Ibid.*
Swart, J.G.: *The Book of Sacred Names, Op. Cit.*
21.   Zellmann-Rohrer, M.: *Psalms Useful for Everything, Op. Cit.*
22.   Kayser, C.: *Gebrauch von Psalmen zur Zauberei, Op. Cit.*
23.   Thiers, J.B.: *Traité des Superstitions selon l'Ecriture sainte, les décrets des conciles et les sentiments des saints Pères et des théologiens,* Vol. 1, Antoine Dezallier, Paris 1697.
Lecouteux, C.: *Dictionary of Ancient Magic Words and Spells from Abraxas to Zoar, Op. Cit.*
24.   Kayser, C.: *Gebrauch von Psalmen zur Zauberei, Op. Cit.*
25.   Rankine, D. & Barron, P.H.: *The Book of Gold, Op. Cit.*
Marty, J. & MacParthy, F.: *Usage Mago-Théurgiques des Psaumes, Op. Cit.*
26.   Skinner, S. & Rankine, D.: *A Collection of Magical Secrets, Op. Cit.*

Psalm 37

1.   *Le Livre des Psaumes Hébreu-Français et Phonétique, Op. Cit.*
Azulai, H.Y.D.: *Sefer Tehillim Sha'arei Rachamim: im Segulot v'Tefilot ha'Chida, Op. Cit.*
Singer, I. & Adler, C.: *The Jewish Encyclopedia, Op. Cit.*
Ronen, D.: *Tehilim Kavvanot ha-Lev, Op. Cit.*
Brauner, R.: *Synopsis of Sefer Shimush Tehillim. Op. Cit.*
2.   Rebiger, B.: *Sefer Shimmush Tehillim, Op. Cit.*
Harari, Y.: *Jewish Magic before the Rise of Kabbalah, Op. Cit.*
3.   *Ibid.*
4.   *Ibid.*
Kimchi, D. ben Y.: *Sefer Tehillim, Op. Cit.*
Sefer Shimmush Tehillim, Op. Cit.
Seder Tefilot Tikun Ezra, Op. Cit.
Grünwald, M.: *Ueber den Einfluss der Psalmen auf die Katholische Liturgie, Op. Cit.*
Refuah v'Chayim m'Yerushalayim im Shimush Tehilim, Op. Cit.
Landsberg, M.: *Sefer Tehillim im Peirush Rashi, Op. Cit.*
Hai ben Sherira Gaon & Varady, A.N.: *Shimush Tehillim (the*

Theurgical Use of Psalms), *Op. Cit.*
Selig, G.: *Sepher Schimmusch Tehillim, Op. Cit.*
The Sixth and Seventh Books of Moses, Op. Cit.
Peterson, J.H.: *The Sixth and Seventh Books of Moses, Op. Cit.*

5.   **Kimchi, D. ben Y.:** *Ibid.*
Sefer Shimmush Tehillim, Ibid.
Seder Tefilot Tikun Ezra, Ibid.
Grünwald, M.: *Ibid.*
Refuah v'Chayim m'Yerushalayim im Shimush Tehilim, Ibid.
Rebiger, B.: *Ibid.*
Landsberg, M.: *Ibid.*
Hai ben Sherira Gaon & Varady, A.N.: *Ibid.*

6.   **Rebiger, B.:** *Sefer Shimmush Tehillim, Op. Cit.*

7.   **Zacutto, M.:** *Shorshei ha-Shemot, Op. Cit.*
Swart, J.G.: *The Book of Sacred Names, Op. Cit.*
—*The Book of Immediate Magic - Part 1, Op. Cit.*

8.   **Zellmann-Rohrer, M.:** *Psalms Useful for Everything, Op. Cit.*

9.   *Ibid.*

10.   **Rankine, D. & Barron, P.H.:** *The Book of Gold, Op. Cit.*
Marty, J. & MacParthy, F.: *Usage Mago-Théurgiques des Psaumes, Op. Cit.*

11.   **Mathers, S.L. Macgregor:** *Key of Solomon the King, Op. Cit.*

Psalm 38

1.   **Nulman, M.:** *The Encyclopedia of Jewish Prayer, Op. Cit.*

2.   *Le Livre des Psaumes Hébreu-Français et Phonétique, Op. Cit.*
Azulai, H.Y.D.: *Sefer Tehillim Sha'arei Rachamim: im Segulot v'Tefilot ha'Chida, Op. Cit.*
Ronen, D.: *Tehilim Kavvanot ha-Lev, Op. Cit.*
Brauner, R.: *Synopsis of Sefer Shimush Tehillim. Op. Cit.*
Hai ben Sherira Gaon & Varady, A.N.: *Ibid.*

3.   **Brauner, R.:** *Ibid.*
Singer, I. & Adler, C.: *The Jewish Encyclopedia, Op. Cit.*

4.   **Kimchi, D. ben Y.:** *Sefer Tehillim, Op. Cit.*
Sefer Shimmush Tehillim, Op. Cit.
Seder Tefilot Tikun Ezra, Op. Cit.
Grünwald, M.: *Ueber den Einfluss der Psalmen auf die Katholische Liturgie, Op. Cit.*
Rebiger, B.: *Sefer Shimmush Tehillim, Op. Cit.*
Hai ben Sherira Gaon & Varady, A.N.: *Shimush Tehillim (the Theurgical Use of Psalms), Op. Cit.*

5.   *Refuah v'Chayim m'Yerushalayim im Shimush Tehilim, Op. Cit.*

Landsberg, M.: *Sefer Tehillim im Peirush Rashi, Op. Cit.*

6.   *Ibid.*

Kimchi, D. ben Y.: *Sefer Tehillim, Op. Cit.*
Sefer Shimmush Tehillim, Op. Cit.
Seder Tefilot Tikun Ezra, Op. Cit.
Grünwald, M.: *Ueber den Einfluss der Psalmen auf die Katholische Liturgie, Op. Cit.*
Rebiger, B.: *Sefer Shimmush Tehillim, Op. Cit.*
Hai ben Sherira Gaon & Varady, A.N.: *Shimush Tehillim (the Theurgical Use of Psalms), Op. Cit.*

7.   *Ibid.*

8.   **Selig, G.:** *Sepher Schimmusch Tehillim, Op. Cit.*
The Sixth and Seventh Books of Moses, Op. Cit.
Peterson, J.H.: *The Sixth and Seventh Books of Moses, Op. Cit*

9.   *Ibid.*

10.   **Zacutto, M.:** *Shorshei ha-Shemot, Op. Cit.*

11.   **Rebiger, B.:** *Sefer Shimmush Tehillim, Op. Cit.*

12.   *Ibid.*

13.   **Davis, E. & Frenkel, D.A.:** *Ha-Kami'a ha-Ivri, Op. Cit.*
Green, A.: *Judaic Artifacts, Op. Cit.*

14.   *Ibid.*

15.   *Ibid.*

16.   **Zacutto, M.:** *Shorshei ha-Shemot, Op. Cit.*
Swart, J.G.: *The Book of Sacred Names, Op. Cit.*
—*The Book of Immediate Magic - Part 1, Op. Cit.*

17.   **Kayser, C.:** *Gebrauch von Psalmen zur Zauberei, Op. Cit.*

18.   **Rankine, D. & Barron, P.H.:** *The Book of Gold, Op. Cit.*
Marty, J. & MacParthy, F.: *Usage Mago-Théurgiques des Psaumes, Op. Cit.*

19.   *Ibid.*

20.   **Skinner, S. & Rankine, D.:** *A Collection of Magical Secrets, Op. Cit.*

Psalm 39

1.   *Le Livre des Psaumes Hébreu-Français et Phonétique, Op. Cit.*
Azulai, H.Y.D.: *Sefer Tehillim Sha'arei Rachamim: im Segulot v'Tefilot ha'Chida, Op. Cit.*
Ronen, D.: *Tehilim Kavvanot ha-Lev, Op. Cit.*

2.   **Brauner, R.:** *Synopsis of Sefer Shimush Tehillim. Op. Cit.*
Hai ben Sherira Gaon & Varady, A.N.: *Shimush Tehillim (the Theurgical Use of Psalms), Op. Cit.*

3.   *Ibid.*

Kimchi, D. ben Y.: *Sefer Tehillim, Op. Cit.*
Sefer Shimmush Tehillim, Op. Cit.
Seder Tefilot Tikun Ezra, Op. Cit.
Grünwald, M.: *Ueber den Einfluss der Psalmen auf die Katholische Liturgie, Op. Cit.*
Refuah v'Chayim m'Yerushalayim im Shimush Tehilim, Op. Cit.
Rebiger, B.: *Sefer Shimmush Tehillim, Op. Cit.*
Landsberg, M.: *Sefer Tehillim im Peirush Rashi, Op. Cit.*

4.   *Ibid.*
Selig, G.: *Sepher Schimmusch Tehillim, Op. Cit.*
The Sixth and Seventh Books of Moses, Op. Cit.
Peterson, J.H.: *The Sixth and Seventh Books of Moses, Op. Cit.*

5.   Rebiger, B.: *Sefer Shimmush Tehillim, Op. Cit.*
6.   Singer, I. & Adler, C.: *The Jewish Encyclopedia, Op. Cit.*
7.   Zacutto, M.: *Shorshei ha-Shemot, Op. Cit.*
8.   *Ibid.*
9.   *Ibid.*
Swart, J.G.: *The Book of Sacred Names, Op. Cit.*
10.   *Ibid.*
11.   Zellmann-Rohrer, M.: *Psalms Useful for Everything, Op. Cit.*
12.   Rankine, D. & Barron, P.H.: *The Book of Gold, Op. Cit.*
Marty, J. & MacParthy, F.: *Usage Mago-Théurgiques des Psaumes, Op. Cit.*

Psalm 40

1.   Kimchi, D. ben Y.: *Sefer Tehillim, Op. Cit.*
Azulai, H.Y.D.: *Sefer Tehillim Sha'arei Rachamim: im Segulot v'Tefilot ha'Chida, Op. Cit.*
Sefer Shimmush Tehillim, Op. Cit.
Seder Tefilot Tikun Ezra, Op. Cit.
Grünwald, M.: *Ueber den Einfluss der Psalmen auf die Katholische Liturgie, Op. Cit.*
Le Livre des Psaumes Hébreu-Français et Phonétique, Op. Cit.
Refuah v'Chayim m'Yerushalayim im Shimush Tehilim, Op. Cit.
Brauner, R.: *Synopsis of Sefer Shimush Tehillim. Op. Cit.*
Rebiger, B.: *Sefer Shimmush Tehillim, Op. Cit.*
Ronen, D.: *Tehilim Kavvanot ha-Lev, Op. Cit.*
Landsberg, M.: *Sefer Tehillim im Peirush Rashi, Op. Cit.*
Hai ben Sherira Gaon & Varady, A.N.: *Shimush Tehillim* (*the Theurgical Use of Psalms*), *Op. Cit.*
Selig, G.: *Sepher Schimmusch Tehillim, Op. Cit.*
The Sixth and Seventh Books of Moses, Op. Cit.

474

Peterson, J.H.: *The Sixth and Seventh Books of Moses, Op. Cit.*
2. Kimchi, D. ben Y.: *Ibid.*
Sefer Shimmush Tehillim, Ibid.
Seder Tefilot Tikun Ezra, Ibid.
Grünwald, M.: *Ibid.*
Refuah v'Chayim m'Yerushalayim im Shimush Tehilim, Ibid.
Rebiger, B.: *Ibid.*
Landsberg, M.: *Ibid.*
Hai ben Sherira Gaon & Varady, A.N.: *Ibid.*
3. Rebiger, B.: *Sefer Shimmush Tehillim, Op. Cit.*
4. Zacutto, M.: *Shorshei ha-Shemot, Op. Cit.*
Swart, J.G.: *The Book of Sacred Names, Op. Cit.*
5. Zellmann-Rohrer, M.: *Psalms Useful for Everything, Op. Cit.*
6. Kayser, C.: *Gebrauch von Psalmen zur Zauberei, Op. Cit.*
7. Rankine, D. & Barron, P.H.: *The Book of Gold, Op. Cit.*
Marty, J. & MacParthy, F.: *Usage Mago-Théurgiques des Psaumes, Op. Cit.*
8. Skinner, S. & Rankine, D.: *A Collection of Magical Secrets, Op. Cit.*

Psalm 41

1. *Le Livre des Psaumes Hébreu-Français et Phonétique, Op. Cit.*
Azulai, H.Y.D.: *Sefer Tehillim Sha'arei Rachamim: im Segulot v'Tefilot ha'Chida, Op. Cit.*
Singer, I. & Adler, C.: *The Jewish Encyclopedia, Op. Cit.*
Ronen, D.: *Tehilim Kavvanot ha-Lev, Op. Cit.*
2. Kimchi, D. ben Y.: *Sefer Tehillim, Op. Cit.*
Sefer Shimmush Tehillim, Op. Cit.
Seder Tefilot Tikun Ezra, Op. Cit.
Grünwald, M.: *Ueber den Einfluss der Psalmen auf die Katholische Liturgie, Op. Cit.*
Refuah v'Chayim m'Yerushalayim im Shimush Tehilim, Op. Cit.
Rebiger, B.: *Sefer Shimmush Tehillim, Op. Cit.*
Landsberg, M.: *Sefer Tehillim im Peirush Rashi, Op. Cit.*
Hai ben Sherira Gaon & Varady, A.N.: *Shimush Tehillim (the Theurgical Use of Psalms), Op. Cit.*
3. Selig, G.: *Sepher Schimmusch Tehillim, Op. Cit.*
The Sixth and Seventh Books of Moses, Op. Cit.
Peterson, J.H.: *The Sixth and Seventh Books of Moses, Op. Cit.*
4. Rebiger, B.: *Sefer Shimmush Tehillim, Op. Cit.*
5. Rosenberg, Y.Y.: *Rafael ha-Malach, Op. Cit.*
6. Davis, E. & Frenkel, D.A.: *Ha-Kami'a ha-Ivri, Op. Cit.*

Green, A.: *Judaic Artifacts, Op. Cit.*

7.   *Ibid.*
8.   *Ibid.*
9.   **Zacutto, M.:** *Shorshei ha-Shemot, Op. Cit.*
10.   *Ibid.*
11.   **Rosenberg, Y.Y.:** *Rafael ha-Malach, Op. Cit.*
       Davis, E. & Frenkel, D.A.: *Ha-Kami'a ha-Ivri, Op. Cit.*
       Green, A.: *Judaic Artifacts, Op. Cit.*
12.   **Zellmann-Rohrer, M.:** *Psalms Useful for Everything, Op. Cit.*
13.   *Ibid.*
14.   *Ibid.*
15.   **Rankine, D. & Barron, P.H.:** *The Book of Gold, Op. Cit.*
       Marty, J. & MacParthy, F.: *Usage Mago-Théurgiques des Psaumes, Op. Cit.*
16.   *Ibid.*
17.   *Ibid.*
18.   **Kayser, C.:** *Gebrauch von Psalmen zur Zauberei, Op. Cit.*
19.   **Skinner, S. & Rankine, D.:** *A Collection of Magical Secrets, Op. Cit.*
20.   *Ibid.*

Shadow Tree Series
Volume 1

THE BOOK OF
SELF CREATION

Jacobus G. Swart

'The Book of Self Creation' is a study guide for all who seek God within and who prefer to steer the course of their lives in a personal manner. The doctrines and techniques addressed in this book will aid practitioners in the expansion of personal consciousness and spiritual evolution. Combining the principles and teachings of Kabbalah and Ceremonial Magic, the book offers step by step instructions on the conscious creation of physical life circumstances, such being always in harmony with the mind-set of the practitioner.

'The Book of Self Creation is a rich and resourceful workbook
of practical kabbalah from the hands of a master kabbalist
who is both compassionate and insightful.'
Caitlin Matthews, author of Walkers Between the Worlds and
Sophia, Goddess of Wisdom.

The 'Shadow Tree Series' comprises a unique collection of Western Esoteric studies and practices which Jacobus Swart, spiritual successor to William G. Gray, has actuated and taught over a period of forty years. Regarding the author of this series, William Gray wrote 'It is well to bear in mind that Jacobus Swart is firstly and lastly a staunchly practicing member of the Western Inner Tradition and perforce writes from that specific angle alone. Moreover, he writes well, lucidly, and absolutely honestly.'

ISBN 978-0-620-42882-2   Paperback

Shadow Tree Series
Volume 2

THE BOOK OF
SACRED NAMES

Jacobus G. Swart

'The Book of Sacred Names' is a practical guide into the meditational and magical applications of ancient Hebrew Divine Names. Perpetuating the tenets of traditional Kabbalists who recognised the fundamental bond between 'Kabbalah' and 'Magic,' Jacobus Swart offers step by step instructions on the deliberate and conscious control of personal life circumstances, by means of the most cardinal components of Kabbalistic doctrines and techniques—Divine Names!

The material addressed in this tome derives from the extensive primary literature of '"Practical Kabbalah",' much of which is appearing in print for the first time in English translation.

The 'Shadow Tree Series' comprises a unique collection of Western Esoteric studies and practices which Jacobus Swart, spiritual successor to William G. Gray and co-founder of the Sangreal Sodality, has actuated and taught over a period of forty years. Having commenced his Kabbalah studies in Safed in the early 1970's, he later broadened his 'kabbalistic horizons' under the careful guidance of the famed English Kabbalist William G. Gray.

ISBN 978-0-620-50702-8   Paperback

also published by The Sangreal Sodality Press

Shadow Tree Series
Volume 3

THE BOOK OF SEALS & AMULETS

Jacobus G. Swart

Having introduced a 'nuts and bolts' insight into the inner workings of Ceremonial Magic and "Practical Kabbalah" in 'The Book of Self Creation' and 'The Book of Sacred Names,' Jacobus Swart unfolds further magical resources in "The Book of Seals & Amulets." This tome comprises a comprehensive investigation into the meaning and relevance of Celestial Alphabets, Magical Seals, Magic Squares, Divine and Angelic Names, etc., as well as their employment in Hebrew Amulets in order to benefit personal well-being in a most significant manner.

Continuing the standards set in the earlier volumes of this series, Jacobus Swart offers detailed instruction on the contents and construction of Hebrew Amulets. He again consulted the enormous array of relevant primary Hebrew literature, large sections of which are available to an English readership for the first time.

The 'Shadow Tree Series' comprises a unique collection of Western Esoteric studies and practices which Jacobus G. Swart, spiritual successor to William G. Gray and co-founder of the Sangreal Sodality, actuated and taught over a period of forty years. He commenced his Kabbalah odyssey in Safed in the early 1970's studying the doctrines of Lurianic Kabbalah. He also incorporated the teachings of his late mentor, the celebrated English Kabbalist William G. Gray, in his personal Kabbalistic worldview.

ISBN 978-0-620-59698-5   Paperback

also published by The Sangreal Sodality Press

Shadow Tree Series
Volume 4

THE BOOK OF
IMMEDIATE MAGIC - PART 1

Jacobus G. Swart

'The Book of Immediate Magic - Part One' perpetuates the fundamental tenets of "Self Creation" in which it is maintained that the 'Centre' establishes the 'Circumference,' and that personal reality is emanated in harmony with personal 'Will.' Hence this tome comprises an enhancement and expansion of the magical doctrines of Kabbalah Ma'asit ("Practical Kabbalah") addressed in the first three volumes of this "Shadow Tree Series" of Jewish Magical texts. Jacobus Swart claims that working "Immediate Magic" is neither impossible when we fully understand that consciousness is just one vast ocean, and that thoughts are the waves we make in it. It is all a matter of coordinating consciousness.

The 'Shadow Tree Series' comprises a unique collection of Western Esoteric studies and practices which Jacobus G. Swart, spiritual successor to William G. Gray and co-founder of the Sangreal Sodality, has actuated and taught over a period of forty years. He commenced his journey into the domain of Jewish Mysticism in the early 1970's investigating mainstream Kabbalah, later diversifying into the magical mysteries of Practical Kabbalah. He equally expanded his personal perspectives of the Western Magical Tradition under the careful tutelage of the celebrated English Kabbalist William G. Gray.

ISBN 978-0-620-69313-4   Paperback

also published by The Sangreal Sodality Press

Shadow Tree Series
Volume 4

THE BOOK OF
IMMEDIATE MAGIC - PART 2

Jacobus G. Swart

'The Book of Immediate Magic - Part One' perpetuates the fundamental tenets of "Self Creation" in which it is maintained that the 'Centre' establishes the 'Circumference,' and that personal reality is emanated in harmony with personal 'Will.' Hence this tome comprises an enhancement and expansion of the magical doctrines of Kabbalah Ma'asit ("Practical Kabbalah") addressed in the first three volumes of this "Shadow Tree Series" of Jewish Magical texts. Jacobus Swart claims that working "Immediate Magic" is neither impossible when we fully understand that consciousness is just one vast ocean, and that thoughts are the waves we make in it. It is all a matter of coordinating consciousness.

As in the case of all the previous volumes, the current text is dealing with the topic of the 'magical' in this Tradition. In this regard, Jacobus Swart again consulted an array of primary Hebrew literature, major portions of which are being made accessible in translation to an English readership.

The 'Shadow Tree Series' comprises a unique collection of Western Esoteric studies and practices which Jacobus G. Swart, spiritual successor to William G. Gray and co-founder of the Sangreal Sodality, has actuated and taught over a period of forty years. He commenced his journey into the domain of Jewish Mysticism in the early 1970's investigating mainstream Kabbalah, later diversifying into the magical mysteries of Practical Kabbalah. He equally expanded his personal perspectives of the Western Magical Tradition under the careful tutelage of the celebrated English Kabbalist William G. Gray.

ISBN 978-0-620-69313-4   Paperback

also published by The Sangreal Sodality Press

THE LADDER OF LIGHTS
(OR QABALAH RENOVATA)

William G. Gray

The Tree of Life works in relation to consciousness somewhat like a computer. Data is fed in, stored in associative banks, and then fed out on demand. The difference between the Tree and a computer, however, is that a computer can only produce various combinations of the information that has been programmed into it. The Tree, operating through the intelligent consciousness of living beings, whether embodied in this world or not, acts as a sort of Universal Exchange throughout the entire chain of consciousness sharing its scheme, and the extent of this is infinite and incalculable.

The Tree of Life is a means and not an end. It is not in itself an object for worship or some idol for superstitious reverence. It is a means, a method, a map and a mechanism for assisting the attainment of the single objective common to all creeds, systems, mysteries and religions—namely, the mystical union of humanity and divinity. With this end in view, this book is an aid to whoever desires to climb the Tree of Life.

'.....the most original commentary on basic Kabbalistic knowledge that I have read for God knows how many years.'
Israel Regardie

'.....beautifully presented and set in excellent marching order.....For one new to the subject, this is a fine text and an exceptionally lucid introduction to a veiled and meditative lore which is still being enlarged from year to year.'
Max Freedom Long (Huna Vistas)

ISBN 978-0-620-40303-0   Paperback

also published by The Sangreal Sodality Press

AN OUTLOOK ON OUR INNER WESTERN WAY

William G. Gray

'An Outlook on Our Inner Western Way' is a unique book. This is no dusty, quaint grimoire — it is a sane and simple method of true attainment for those who seek communion with their higher selves.

In this book, William Gray shows simply and lucidly, how to live the Western Inner Tradition. Tracing the cosmology of Western magic, he substantiates its vitality and urgency for our future.

William G. Gray is rated one of the most prolific — and controversial — occultists today. Blending keen insight, modern psychological models and an overall sense of practicality, his books have torn at the mouldy veils of so-called occult secrets, laying out a no-non sense foundation by which modern Western humanity may once again regain its precious magical soul.

ISBN 978-0-620-40306-1   Paperback

also published by The Sangreal Sodality Press

Sangreal Sodality Series
Volume 1

WESTERN INNER WORKINGS

William G. Gray

The 'Sangreal Sodality Series' is a home study course comprising the fundamental text books of the Sangreal Sodality, that revives the instrumentality inherent in our western Tradition. The series makes available to us, in our own cultural symbolism, a way to enlightenment that we can practice on a daily basis.

'Western Inner Workings' provides a practical framework for the western student's psycho-spiritual development. Each day includes a morning meditation, a mid-day invocation, evening exercises, and a sleep subject. Incorporating symbols that are 'close to home,' these rituals increase consciousness in comfortable increments.

ISBN 978-0-620-40304-7   Paperback

also published by The Sangreal Sodality Press

A BEGINNERS GUIDE TO LIVING KABBALAH

William G. Gray

This compendium comprises six Kabbalistic works by William G. Gray, some of which are appearing here in print for the first time. The texts included in this compilation are ranging from the simplest introduction to the Spheres and Paths of the Kabbalistic Tree of Life system, to related meditation techniques and associated ritual magical procedures, to an advanced system of what could be termed 'inter-dimensional spiritual communication.'

The title 'A Beginners Guide to Living Kabbalah' is perhaps somewhat misleading, as this compilation equally contains works of an advanced nature, and the ritual and meditation techniques addressed in this tome, pertain to both beginners as well as advanced practitioners of 'Practical Kabbalah.'

ISBN 978-0-620-42887-3   Paperback

also published by The Sangreal Sodality Press

LESSONS LEARNED FROM OCCULT LETTERS

William G. Gray

In this book William G. Gray, the renowned English Kabbalist and Ceremonial Magician, delineated some of the lessons he learned from the letters which passed between himself and Emil Napoleon Hauenstein, his Austrian mentor and friend, whom he affectionately called "E.N.H." Contrary to opinions expressed regarding Emil Napoleon Hauenstein's status as a "Magus," it should be noted that he was nothing of the kind. He classified himself a "mystic," and was a Martinist. Whilst he was an "Initiate" of the well-known French Occultist Papus (Gerard Encausse), he had a particularly poor opinion of ritual magic and never shared a single magical practice with William Gray.

On the other hand, E.N.H. addressed important psycho-spiritual occult principles and doctrines in his letters, and encouraged his young friend to acquire a greater understanding of what it means to be an "Occultist." William Gray gained a clear comprehension that "Goodness, Love, Truth, Kindness, and such Spiritual qualities in us that come direct from God must come first. Cleverness, intellectuality, and mental attributes can then be safely developed in the course of time." Since "Occultism is the study and practice of subjects and laws which are beyond the bounds and limitations of ordinary physical or even mental experience," Emil Napoleon Hauenstein directed his young protegé in unfolding a well-regulated "Self," who is in full control of all his personal faculties, whether these be physical, mental, emotional or spiritual. This is of particular importance in understanding, as William Gray noted, that "Occultism is not a pastime, it is a Power, a Purpose, a Progress, and a Path"—a Way of Life!

ISBN 978-0-620-79024-6   Paperback

Made in United States
North Haven, CT
04 October 2024

58336658R00305